THE TRAVELS OF MARCO POLO THE VENETIAN

THE TRAVELS
OF
MARCO POLO
THE VENETIAN

MARCO POLO & JOHN MASEFIELD

GYAN

Published by

GYAN

Gyan Publishing House
5, Ansari Road
Daryaganj, New Delhi-110002
Phone: 011-47034999, 9811692060
E-mail: books@gyanbooks.com

Distribution Network
gyanbooks.com
India, USA, Canada, UK, Australia, France

ISBN : 978-81-212-4161-8 (PB)
First Published, 1908

2nd Impression 2020

Printed at: Gyan Press, Delhi.

The book at your disposal is the edition of an old book originally published long back. The Text quality of this book may not be at par as compared to our other books but many readers approached us to reprint this important book so that it could satiate their hunger. We request all the readers of this book to help us to improve its quality by providing the necessary text of those pages which are not properly visible. Your valuable support in this case will be highly appreciated and acknowledged and our future readers will be benefitted immensely.

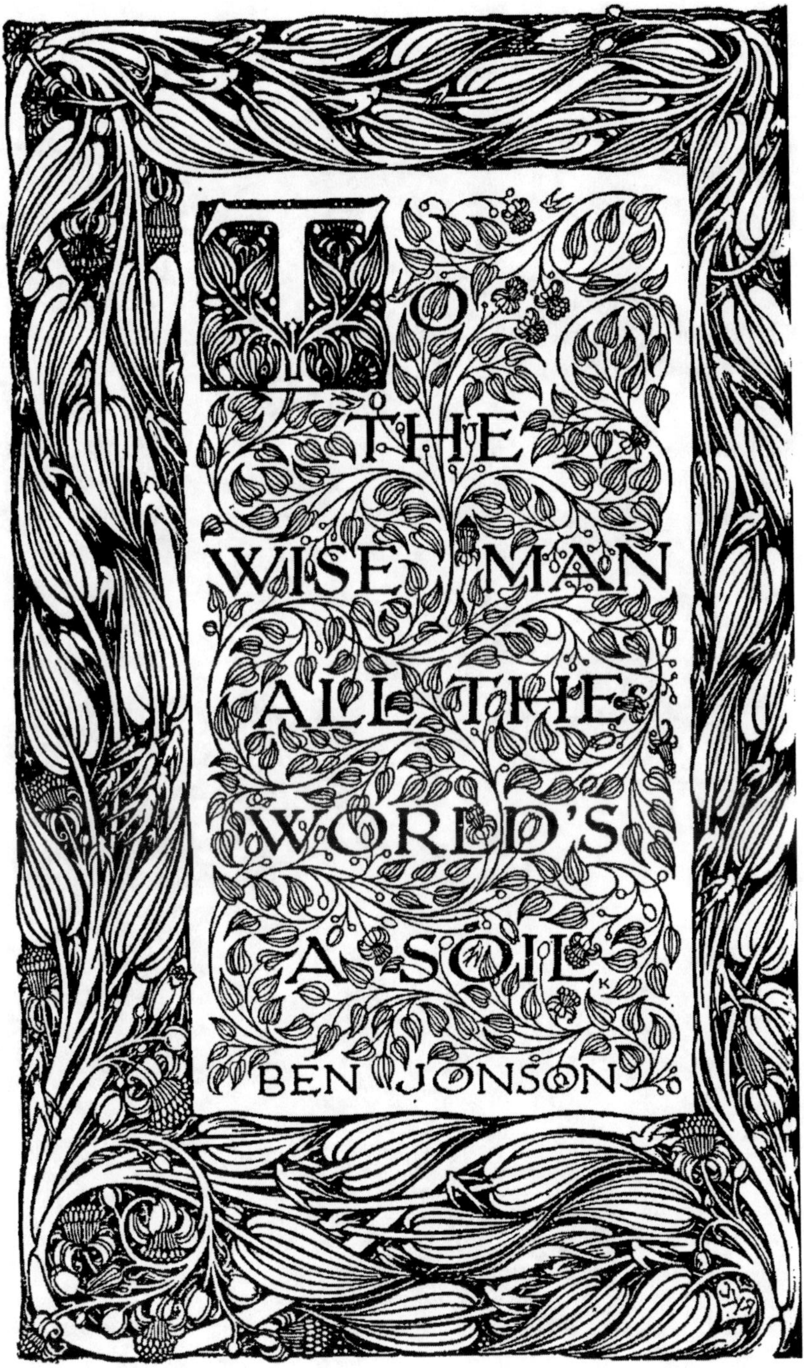
TO THE WISE MAN ALL THE WORLD'S A SOIL
BEN JONSON

The TRAVELS of MARCO POLO the VENETIAN

EVERYMAN I WILL GO WITH THEE & BE THY GUIDE

IN THY MOST NEED TO GO BY THY SIDE

LONDON: PUBLISHED
by J·M·DENT·&·SONS·LTD
AND IN NEW YORK
BY E·P·DUTTON & CO

INTRODUCTION

MARCO POLO, the subject of this memoir, was born at Venice in the year 1254. He was the son of Nicolo Polo, a Venetian of noble family, who was one of the partners in a trading house, engaged in business with Constantinople. In the year 1260, this Nicolo Polo, in company with his junior partner, his brother Maffeo, set out across the Euxine on a trading venture to the Crimea. They prospered in their business, but were unable to return to their base, owing to the breaking out of a Tartar war on the road by which they had come. As they could not go back, they went forward, crossing the desert to Bokhara, where they stayed for three years. At the end of the third year (the fifth of their journey) they were advised to visit the Great Khan Kublai, the "Kubla Khan" of Coleridge's poem. A party of the Great Khan's envoys were about to return to Cathay, and the two brothers therefore joined the party, travelling forward, "northward and northeastward," for a whole year, before they reached the Khan's Court in Cathay. The Khan received them kindly, and asked them many questions about life in Europe, especially about the emperors, the Pope, the Church, and "all that is done at Rome." He then sent them back to Europe on an embassy to the Pope, to ask His Holiness to send a hundred missionaries to convert the Cathaians to the Christian faith. He also asked for some of the holy oil from the lamp of the Holy Sepulchre. The return journey of the brothers (from Cathay to Acre) took three years. On their arrival at Acre the travellers discovered that the Pope was dead. They therefore decided to return home to Venice to wait until the new Pope should be elected. They arrived at Venice in 1269, to find that Nicolo's wife had died during her husband's absence. His son Marco, our traveller, was then fifteen years old. He had probably passed his childhood in the house of one of his uncles at Venice.

Nicolo and Maffeo Polo remained at Venice for a couple of years, waiting for a Pope to be elected, but as there seemed to be no prospect of this happening, they determined to return to the Great Khan, to tell him how their mission had failed. They therefore set out again (in 1271) and Marco, now seventeen years old, went with them. At Acre they obtained a letter from a Papal Legate, stating how it came about that the message had not been delivered. They had already obtained some of the holy oil, so that they were free to proceed. They had not gone very far upon their journey when they were recalled to Acre by the above-mentioned Syrian Legate, who had just heard that he had been elected Pope. The new Pope did not send a hundred missionaries, as Kublai had asked, but he appointed instead two preaching friars, who accompanied the Polos as far as Armenia, where rumours of war frightened them into returning. The Polos journeyed on for three years and a half, and arrived at the Khan's court (at Shangtu, not far from Pekin) in the middle of 1275. The Khan received them "honourably and graciously," making much of Marco, "who was then a young gallant." In a little while, when Marco had learned the speech and customs of the "Tartars," the Khan employed him in public business, sending him as a visiting administrator to several wild and distant provinces. Marco noted carefully the strange customs of these provinces, and delighted the Khan with his account of them. On one of these journeys Marco probably visited the southern states of India.

After some seventeen years of honourable service with Kublai, the three Venetians became eager to return to Venice. They were rich men, and Kublai was growing old, and they knew that Kublai's death "might deprive them of that public assistance by which alone they could expect to surmount the innumerable difficulties of so long a journey." But Kublai refused to allow them to leave the Court, and even "appeared hurt at the application." It chanced, however, that at this time, Arghun, Khan of Persia, had sent ambassadors to Kublai to obtain the hand of a maiden "from among the relatives of his deceased wife." The maiden, aged seventeen, and very beautiful, was about to accompany the ambassadors to Persia; but the ordinary overland routes to Persia were unsafe, owing to wars among the Tartars. It was necessary for her to travel to Persia by ship. The envoys begged Kublai that the three Venetians might come with them in the ships "as being persons well skilled in the practice of navigation." Kublai granted their request, though not very gladly. He fitted out a splendid squadron of ships, and despatched the three Venetians with the Persians, first granting them the golden tablet or safe-conduct, which would enable them to obtain supplies on the way. They sailed from a Chinese port about the beginning of 1292.

The voyage to Persia occupied about two years, during which time the expedition lost six hundred men. The Khan of Persia was dead when they arrived; so the beautiful maiden was handed over to his son, who received her kindly. He gave the Venetians safe-conduct through Persia; indeed he sent them forward with troops of horse, without which, in those troublous days, they could never have crossed the country. As they rode on their way they heard that the great Khan Kublai, their old master, had died. They arrived safely at Venice some time in the year 1295.

There are some curious tales of their arrival at home. It is said that they were not recognised by their relatives, and this is not strange, for they returned in shabby Tartar clothes, almost unable to speak their native tongue. It was not until they had ripped the seams of the shabby clothes, producing stores of jewels from the lining, that the relatives decided to acknowledge them. (This tale may be read as allegory by those who doubt its truth as history.) Marco Polo did not stay long among his relatives. Venice was at war with Genoa, and the Polo family, being rich, had been called upon to equip a galley, even before the travellers returned from Asia. Marco Polo sailed in command of this galley, in the fleet under Andrea Dandolo, which was defeated by the Genoese off Curzola on the 7th September 1296. Marco Polo was carried as a prisoner to Genoa, where he remained, in spite of efforts made to ransom him, for about three years, during which time he probably dictated his book in very bad French to one Rustician of Pisa, a fellow-prisoner. He returned to Venice during the year 1299, and probably married shortly afterwards.

Little is known of his life after his return from prison. We know that he was nicknamed " Il Milione " on account of his wonderful stories of Kublai's splendour; but as he was rich and famous the slighting nickname was probably partly a compliment. Colonel Yule, the great editor of Marco Polo, has discovered that he stood surety for a wine-smuggler, that he gave a copy of his book to a French noble, and that he sued a commission agent for the half profits on the sale of some musk. It was at one time thought that he was the Marco Polo who failed (in 1302) to have his water-pipe inspected by the town plumber. This sin has now been laid upon another man of the same name, who "was ignorant of the order on that subject." On the 9th of January, 1324, feeling himself to be growing daily feebler, he made his will, which is still preserved. He named as his trustees his wife Donata and his three daughters, to whom the bulk of his estate was left. He died soon after the execution of this will. He was buried in Venice without the door of the Church of San Lorenzo; but the exact site of the grave is unknown. No known authentic portrait of the man exists; but as in the case of Columbus, there are several fanciful portraits, of which the best dates from the seventeenth century.

Marco Polo's book was not received with faith by his contemporaries. Travellers who see marvellous things, even in our own day (the name of Bruce will occur to everyone) are seldom believed by those who, having stayed at home, have all the consequences of their virtue. When Marco Polo came back from the East, a misty, unknown country, full of splendour and terrors, he could not tell the whole truth. He had to leave his tale half told lest he should lack believers. His book was less popular in the later Middle Ages than the fictions and plagiarisms of Sir John Mandeville. Marco Polo tells of what he saw; the compiler of Mandeville, when he does not steal openly from Pliny, Friar Odoric, and others, tells of what an ignorant person might expect to see, and would, in any case, like to read about, since it is always blessed to be confirmed in an opinion, however ill-grounded it may be. How little Marco Polo was credited may be judged from the fact that the map of Asia was not modified by his discoveries till fifty years after his death.

His book is one of the great books of travel. Even now, after the lapse of six centuries, it remains the chief authority for parts of Central Asia, and of the vast Chinese Empire. Some of his wanderings are hard to follow; some of the places which he visited are hard to identify; but the labour of Colonel Yule has cleared up most of the difficulties, and confirmed most of the strange statements. To the geographer, to the historian, and to the student of Asiatic life, the book of Marco Polo will always be most valuable. To the general reader, the great charm of the book is its romance.

It is accounted a romantic thing to wander among strangers and to eat their bread by the camp-fires of the other half of the world. There is romance in doing thus, though the romance has been over-estimated by those whose sedentary lives have created in them a false taste for action. Marco Polo wandered among strangers; but it is open to anyone (with courage and the power of motion) to do the same. Wandering in itself is merely a form of self-indulgence. If it adds not to the stock of human knowledge, or if it gives not to others the imaginative possession of some part of the world, it is a pernicious habit. The acquisition of knowledge, the accumulation of fact, is noble only in those few who have that alchemy which transmutes such clay to heavenly eternal gold. It may be thought that many travellers have given their readers great imaginative possessions; but the imaginative possession is not measured in miles and parasangs, nor do the people of that country write accounts of birds and beasts. It is only the wonderful traveller who sees a wonder, and only five travellers in the world's history have seen wonders. The others have seen birds and beasts, rivers and wastes, the earth and the (local) fulness thereof. The five travellers are Herodotus, Gaspar, Melchior, Balthazar, and Marco Polo himself. The wonder of Marco Polo is this—that he created Asia for the European mind.

When Marco Polo went to the East, the whole of Central Asia, so full of splendour and magnificence, so noisy with nations and kings, was like a dream in men's minds. Europeans touched only the fringe of the East. At Acre, at Byzantium, at the busy cities on the Euxine, the merchants of Europe bartered with the stranger for silks, and jewels and precious balms, brought over the desert at great cost, in caravans from the unknown. The popular conception of the East was taken from the Bible, from the tales of old Crusaders, and from the books of the merchants. All that men knew of the East was that it was mysterious, and that our Lord was born there. Marco Polo, almost the first European to see the East, saw her in all her wonder, more fully than any man has seen her since. His picture of the East is the picture which we all make in our minds when we repeat to ourselves those two strange words, "the East," and give ourselves up to the image which that symbol evokes. It may be that the Western mind will turn to Marco Polo for a conception of Asia long after "Cathay" has become an American colony.

It is difficult to read Marco Polo as one reads historical facts. One reads him as one reads romance; as one would read, for instance, the "Eve of St. Mark," or the "Well at the World's End." The East of which he writes is the East of romance, not the East of the Anglo-Indian, with his Simla, his missions to Tibet, and Reuter telegrams. In the East of romance there grows "the tree of the sun, or dry tree" (by which Marco Polo passed), a sort of landmark or milestone, at the end of the great desert. The apples of the sun and moon grow upon that tree. Darius and Alexander fought in its shade. Those are the significant facts about the tree according to Marco Polo. We moderns, who care little for any tree so soon as we can murmur its Latin name, have lost wonder in losing faith.

The Middle Age, even as our own age is, was full of talk of the Earthly Paradise. It may be that we have progressed, in learning to talk of it as a social possibility, instead of as a geographical fact. We like to think that the old Venetians went eastward, on their famous journey, half believing that they would arrive there, just as Columbus (two centuries later) half expected to sight land "where the golden blossoms burn upon the trees forever." They did not find the Earthly Paradise; but they saw the splendours of Kublai, one of the mightiest of earthly kings. One feels the presence of Kublai all through the narrative, as the red wine, dropped into the water-cup, suffuses all, or as the string supports the jewels on a trinket. The imagination is only healthy when it broods upon the kingly and the saintly. In Kublai, the reader will find enough images of splendour to make glorious the temple of his mind. When we think of Marco Polo, it is of Kublai that we think; and, apart from the romantic wonder which surrounds him, he is a noble person, worth our contemplation. He is like a king in a romance. It was the task of a kingly nature to have created him as he appears in the book here. It makes us proud and reverent of the poetic gift, to reflect that this king, "the lord of lords," ruler of so many cities, so many gardens, so many fishpools, would be but a name, an image covered by the sands, had he not welcomed two dusty travellers, who came to him one morning from out of the unknown, after long wandering over the world. Perhaps when he bade them farewell the thought occurred to him (as it occurred to that other king in the poem) that he might come to be remembered "but by this one thing," when all his glories were fallén from him, and he lay silent, the gold mask upon his face, in the drowsy tomb, where the lamp, long kept alight, at last guttered, and died, and fell to dust.

JOHN MASEFIELD.

December 1907.

ITINERARY

THE elder Polos, when they left Constantinople in the year 1260, had not planned to go far beyond the northern borders of the Euxine. They first landed at Soldaia, in the Crimea, then an important trading city. From Soldaia they journeyed in a northerly and east-northeasterly direction to Sara, or Sarra, a vast city on the Volga, where King Cambuscan lived, and to Bolgara, or Bolghar, where they stayed for a year. Going south a short distance to Ucaca, another city on the Volga, they journeyed direct to the south-east, across the northern head of the Caspian, on the sixty days' march to Bokhara, where they stayed for three years. From Bokhara they went with the Great Khan's people northward to Otrar, and thence in a north-easterly direction to the Court of the Khan near Pekin. On their return journey, they arrived at the sea-coast at Layas, in Armenia. From Layas they went to Acre, and from Acre to Negropont in Roumania, and from Negropont to Venice, where they stayed for about two years.

On the second journey to the East, with the young Marco Polo, they sailed direct from Venice to Acre towards the end of the year 1271. They made a short journey southward to Jerusalem, for the holy oil, and then returned to Acre for letters from the Papal Legate. Leaving Acre, they got as far as Layas, in Armenia, before they were recalled by the newly elected Pope. On setting out again, they returned to Layas, at that time a great city, where spices and cloth of gold were sold, and from which merchants journeying to the East generally started. From Layas they pushed northward into Turcomania, past Casaria and Sivas, to Arzingan, where the people wove "good buckrams." Passing Mount Ararat, where Noah's Ark was supposed to rest, they heard stories of the Baku oil-fields. From here they went to the south-eastward, following the course of the Tigris to Bandas. From Bandas they seem to have made an unnecessary journey to the Persian Gulf. The book leads one to suppose that they travelled by way of Tauriz (in Persian Irak) Yezd, and Kerman, to the port of Ormuz, as though they intended to take ship there. They could, however, have progressed more swiftly had they followed the Tigris to Busrah, there taken ship upon the Gulf, and sailed by way of Keis or Kisi to Ormuz. After visiting Ormuz, they returned to Kerman by another road, and then pushed on, over the horrible salt desert of Kerman, through Khorassan to Balakshan. It is possible that their journey was broken at Balakshan, owing to the illness of Marco, who speaks of having at some time stayed nearly a year here to recover his health. On leaving Balakshan they proceeded through the high Pamirs to Kashgar, thence south-eastward by way of Khotan, not yet buried under the sands, to the Gobi desert. The Gobi desert, like all deserts, had a bad name as being "the abode of many evil spirits, which amuse travellers to their destruction." The Polos crossed the Gobi in the usual thirty days, halting each night by the brackish ponds which make the passage possible. After crossing the desert, they soon entered China. At Kan Chau, one of the first Chinese cities which they visited, they may have stayed for nearly a year, on account of "the state of their concerns," but this stay probably took place later, when they were in Kublai's service. They then crossed the province of Shen-si, into that of Shan-si, finally arriving at Kai-ping-fu, where Kublai had built his summer pleasure garden.

On the return journey, the Polos set sail from the port of Zaitum, in the province of Fo-Kien. They hugged the Chinese coast (in order to avoid the Pratas and Pracel Reefs) and crossed the Gulf of Tong King to Champa in the south-east of Cambodia. Leaving Champa, they may have made some stay at Borneo, but more probably they sailed direct to the island of Bintang, at the mouth of the Straits of Malacca, and to Sumatra, where the fleet was delayed for five months by the blowing of the contrary monsoon. The ships seem to have waited for the monsoon to change in a harbour on the north-east coast, in the kingdom of Sumatra. On getting a fair wind, they passed by the Nicobar and Andaman Islands, and then shaped a course for Ceylon. They put across to the coast of Coromandel, and may perhaps have coasted as far to the northward upon the Madras coast as Masulipatam. On the Bombay side, they would seem to have hugged the coast as far as they could, as far perhaps as Surat, in the

Gulf of Cambay; but it is just possible that the descriptions of these places were taken from the tales of pilots, and that his fleet put boldly out to avoid the coast pirates. Marco Polo tells us much about Aden, and about towns on the Arabian coasts; but the fleet probably never touched at them. All that is certainly known is that they arrived at Ormuz, in the Persian Gulf, and passed inland to Khorassan. On leaving Khorassan they journeyed overland, through Persia and Greater Armenia, until they came to Trebizonda on the Euxine Sea. Here they took ship, and sailed home to Venice, first touching at Constantinople and at Negropont. "And this was in the year 1295 of Christ's Incarnation."

J. M.

CONTENTS

BOOK I

Contents

Contents

Contents

BOOK II

BOOK III

Contents

THE TRAVELS OF MARCO POLO

BOOK I

PROLOGUE[1]

YE emperors, kings, dukes, marquises, earls, and knights, and all other people desirous of knowing the diversities of the races of mankind, as well as the diversities of kingdoms, provinces, and regions of all parts of the East, read through this book, and ye will find in it the greatest and most marvellous characteristics of the peoples especially of Armenia, Persia, India, and Tartary, as they are severally related in the present work by Marco Polo, a wise and learned citizen of Venice, who states distinctly what things he saw and what things he heard from others. For this book will be a truthful one. It must be known, then, that from the creation of Adam to the present day, no man, whether Pagan, or Saracen, or Christian, or other, of whatever progeny or generation he may have been, ever saw or inquired into so many and such great things as Marco Polo above mentioned. Who, wishing in his secret thoughts that the things he had seen and heard should be made public by the present work, for the benefit of those who could not see them with their own eyes, he himself being in the year of our Lord 1295[2] in prison at Genoa, caused the things which are contained in the present work to be written by master Rustigielo, a citizen of Pisa, who was with him in the same prison at Genoa; and he divided it into three parts.

[1] This prologue, omitted by Marsden, is here translated from the Latin text published by the French Geographical Society. It is found in the early French version published by the same society, and in some of the Italian manuscripts; but is only given in an abridged form in Boni's Italian text.

[2] The early French translation gives the date 1298, with which the Italian prologues seem to agree.

CHAPTER I

§ 1. It should be known to the reader that, at the time when Baldwin II. was emperor of Constantinople,[1] where a magistrate representing the doge of Venice then resided,[2] and in the year of our Lord 1250,[3] Nicolo Polo, the father of the said Marco, and Maffeo, the brother of Nicolo, respectable and well-

[1] Baldwin II. count of Flanders, and cousin of Louis IX. king of France, who reigned from 1237 to 1261, was the last of the Latin emperors of Constantinople.

[2] The passage which in Ramusio's text is, "dove all' hora soleva stare un podestà di Venetia, per nome di messer lo Dose," and upon which he has written a particular dissertation, has nothing corresponding to it in the Latin or French versions, or in the Italian text published by Boni. The city of Constantinople and the Greek provinces had been conquered, in 1204, by the joint arms of the French and the Venetians, the latter of whom were commanded by their doge, the illustrious Henry Dandolo, in person. Upon the division of the territory and the immense spoil that fell into their possession, a larger share (including the celebrated bronze horses of Lysippus) was assigned to the republic than to the emperor elected on the occasion, and the aged doge, who had himself declined the imperial title, but accepted that of Prince of Romania, maintained an independent jurisdiction over three parts out of eight of the city, with a separate tribunal of justice, and ended his days at the head of an army that besieged Adrianople. It is doubtful whether any of his successors in the high office of chief of the republic made the imperial city their place of residence. "The doge, a slave of state," says Gibbon, "was *seldom* permitted to depart from the helm of the republic; but his place was supplied by the bail, or regent, who exercised a supreme jurisdiction over the colony of Venetians." Such was the podestà, sometimes termed bailo, and sometimes despoto, whose cotemporary government is here spoken of, and whose political importance in the then degraded state of the empire was little inferior to that of Baldwin; whilst in the eyes of the Polo family, as Venetian citizens, it was probably much greater. The name of the person who exercised the functions at the time of their arrival, is said, in the Sorenzo manuscript, to have been Misier Ponte de Veniexia, and, in 1261, when the empire, or rather the city, was reconquered from the Latins, the podestà was Marco Gradenigo.

[3] There are strong grounds, Marsden says, for believing that this date of 1250, although found in all the editions, is incorrect. In the manuscript, of which there are copies in the British Museum and Berlin libraries, the commencement of the voyage is placed in 1252, and some of the events related in the sequel render it evident that the departure, at least, of our travellers from Constantinople, must have been some years later than the middle of the century, and probably not sooner than 1255. How long they were detained in that city is not stated; but, upon any calculation of the period of their arrival or departure, it is surprising that Grynæus, the editor of the Basle and Paris edition of 1532, and after him the learned Müller and Bergeron, should, notwithstanding the anachronism, introduce into their texts the date of 1269, which was eight years after the expulsion of the emperor Baldwin, and was, in fact, the year in which they returned to Syria from their first Tartarian journey.

informed men, embarked in a ship of their own, with a rich and varied cargo of merchandise, and reached Constantinople in safety. After mature deliberation on the subject of their proceedings, it was determined, as the measure most likely to improve their trading capital, that they should prosecute their voyage into the Euxine or Black Sea.[1] With this view they made purchases of many fine and costly jewels, and taking their departure from Constantinople, navigated that sea to a port named Soldaia,[2] from whence they travelled on horseback many days until they reached the court of a powerful chief of the Western Tartars, named Barka,[3] who dwelt in the cities of Bolgara and Assara,[4] and had the reputation of being one of the most liberal and civilized princes hitherto known amongst the tribes of Tartary. He expressed much satisfaction at the arrival of these travellers, and received them with marks of distinction. In return for which courtesy, when they had laid before him the jewels they brought with them, and perceived that their beauty pleased him, they presented them for his acceptance. The liberality of this conduct

[1] The prosperity, riches, and political importance of the state of Venice having arisen entirely from its commerce, the profession of a merchant was there held in the highest degree of estimation, and its nobles were amongst the most enterprising of its adventurers in foreign trade. To this illustrious state might have been applied the proud character drawn by Isaiah of ancient Tyre, which he describes as "the crowning city, whose merchants are princes, whose traffickers are the honourable of the earth."

[2] Soldaia was the name given in the middle ages to the place (the Tauro-Scythian port of the ancients) now called Sudak, situated near the southern extremity of the Crimea or Tauric Chersonesus. It is described in these words: "About the midst of the said province towards the south, as it were upon a sharp angle or point, standeth a city called Soldaia, directly against Synopolis. And there doe all the Turkie merchants, which traffique into the north countries, in their journey outward, arrive, and as they return homeward also from Russia, and the said northern regions, into Turkie."—Purchas, vol. iii. p. 2.

[3] This Tartar prince is usually named Bereké, the successor, and said to be the brother, of Batu, the son of Tushi, eldest son of Jengiz-khan; who inherited, as his portion of the dominions of his grandfather (although not in full sovereignty), the western countries of Kapchak or Kipchak, Allân, Russ, and Bulgar, and died in 1256.

[4] The Bolgar, Bulgar, or Bulghar, here spoken of, is the name of a town and an extensive district in Tartary, lying to the eastward of the Wolga, and now inhabited by the Bashkirs, sometimes distinguished from the Bulgaria on the Danube, by the appellation of the Greater Bulgaria. Assara is the city of Saraï (with the definitive article prefixed), situated on the eastern arm of the Wolga, or Achtuba. "The Astrachan mentioned by Balducci Pegoletti was not on the same spot where that town stands now, but the ancient Astrachan was demolished, together with Saray, by the emperor Timur, in the winter of 1395. The old town of Saray was pretty near the ancient Astrachan."—Forster.

on the part of the two brothers struck him with admiration; and being unwilling that they should surpass him in generosity, he not only directed double the value of the jewels to be paid to them, but made them in addition several rich presents.

The brothers having resided a year in the dominions of this prince, they became desirous of revisiting their native country, but were impeded by the sudden breaking out of a war between him and another chief, named Alaù, who ruled over the Eastern Tartars.[1] In a fierce and very sanguinary battle that ensued between their respective armies, Alaù was victorious, in consequence of which, the roads being rendered unsafe for travellers, the brothers could not attempt to return by the way they came; and it was recommended to them, as the only practicable mode of reaching Constantinople, to proceed in an easterly direction, by an unfrequented route, so as to skirt the limits of Barka's territories. Accordingly they made their way to a town named Oukaka,[2] situated on the confines of the kingdom of the Western Tartars. Leaving that place, and advancing still further, they crossed the Tigris,[3] one of the four rivers of Paradise, and came to a desert, the extent of which was seventeen days' journey, wherein they

[1] These Eastern Tartars, as they are relatively termed, but whose country extended no further to the east than the provinces of Persia and Khorasan, were so named to distinguish them from the Western (or more properly, North-Western) Tartars mentioned in the preceding note, who occupied the countries in the neighbourhood of the Wolga, and from thence to the confines, or beyond the confines, of Europe. Their chief, here named Ala-û or Hala-û, is the celebrated Hulagu, the son of Tuli or Tulwi, and equally with Batu, Mangu, and Kublaï (the latter of whom were his brothers), the grandson of Jengiz-khan. Being appointed by his elder brother Mangu, to command in the southern provinces of the empire, he left Kara-korum, a short time before the visit of Rubruquis to that Tartar capital, and in the year 1255 crossed the Jihun or Oxus, with a large army. In the following year, he destroyed the race or sect of the Ismaelians, called also Malahidet, of whom a particular account will be given hereafter, and then turned his arms against the city of Baghdâd, which he sacked in 1258; putting to death Mostasem Billah, the last of the Abbassite khalifs. Upon the death of Mangu, in 1259, Hulagu became effectively the sovereign of Persian and Babylonian Irak, together with Khorasan; yet he still continued to profess a nominal and respectful allegiance to his brother Kublaï, who was acknowledged as the head of the Moghul family, and reigned in China. His death took place in 1265, at Tauris or Tabriz, his capital.

[2] There can be little doubt of this being the Okak of Abulfeda; from hence the route of our travellers may be presumed to have lain towards the town of Jaik, on the river of that name, and afterwards, in a southeasterly direction, to the Sihun.

[3] The great river crossed by our travellers, and which from its magnitude they might think entitled to rank as one of the rivers of Paradise, was evidently the Sihun, otherwise named the Sirr.

found neither town, castle, nor any substantial building, but only Tartars with their herds, dwelling in tents on the plain.[1] Having passed this tract they arrived at length at a well-built city called Bokhara,[2] in a province of that name, belonging to the dominions of Persia, and the noblest city of that kingdom, but governed by a prince whose name was Barak.[3] Here, from inability to proceed further, they remained three years.

It happened while these brothers were in Bokhara, that a person of consequence and gifted with eminent talents made his appearance there. He was proceeding as ambassador from Alaù before mentioned, to the grand khan, supreme chief of all the Tartars, named Kublaï,[4] whose residence was at the extremity of the continent, in a direction between north-east and east.[5] Not having ever before had an opportunity,

[1] The desert here mentioned is that of Karak, in the vicinity of the Sihun or Sirr, which travellers from the north must unavoidably pass, in order to arrive at Bokhâra.

[2] This celebrated city, the name of which could not be easily mistaken, and has not been disguised by the transcribers, serves materially to establish the general direction of their course; for, having proceeded northwards from the Crimea, they could not have reached Bokhâra otherwise than by crossing the several rivers with discharge themselves into the upper or northern part of the Caspian.

[3] This appears to be the prince whom Pétis de la Croix names Berrac Can, and D'Herbelot Barak-khan, great-grandson of Jagataï, the second son of Jengiz-khan, who inherited Transoxiana, or the region now possessed by the Usbek Tartars. Barak is said, by the latter, to have attempted to wrest the kingdom of Khorasan from the dominion of Abaka the son of Hulagu; but this must be a mistake, as the death of Barak is placed by the generality of historians in 1260 (by D'Herbelot, unaccountably, in 1240), and that of Hulagu in 1265.

[4] Mangu appointed Kublaï his viceroy in China, and gave to Hulagu the government of such of the southern provinces of Asia as he could reduce to obedience. Returning himself to China in 1258, he died at the siege of Ho-cheu, in the province of Se-chuen, in the following year. Kublaï was at this time in the province of Hu-kuang, and persevered in his efforts to render himself master of Vu-chang-fu, its capital, until he was called away to suppress a revolt excited by his younger brother Artigbuga, whom Mangu had left as his lieutenant at Kara-korum. Contenting himself with exacting from the emperor of the Song, who ruled over Manji, or southern China, the payment of an annual tribute, he retreated to the northward, and in 1260 was proclaimed grand khan, at Shang-tu, which from that time became his summer residence. We are told, however, that he had hesitated for some time to assume the title, and did not declare his acquiescence until the arrival of an envoy sent by his brother Hulagu (by some supposed to have been the elder), who urged him to accept the empire. This envoy we may reasonably presume to have been the person who arrived at Bokhâra, in his way from Persia to Khataï, during the time that Nicolo and Maffeo Polo were detained in that city; and the period is thereby ascertained to have been about the year 1258.

[5] This vague designation of the place of residence of the grand khan must be understood as applying to Khataï, or northern China, from

although he wished it, of seeing any natives of Italy, he was gratified in a high degree at meeting and conversing with these brothers, who had now become proficients in the Tartar language; and after associating with them for several days, and finding their manners agreeable to him, he proposed to them that they should accompany him to the presence of the great khan, who would be pleased by their appearance at his court, which had not hitherto been visited by any person from their country; adding assurances that they would be honourably received, and recompensed with many gifts. Convinced as they were that their endeavours to return homeward would expose them to the most imminent risks, they agreed to this proposal, and recommending themselves to the protection of the Almighty, they set out on their journey in the suite of the ambassador, attended by several Christian servants whom they had brought with them from Venice. The course they took at first was between the north-east and north, and an entire year was consumed before they were enabled to reach the imperial residence, in consequence of the extraordinary delays occasioned by the snows and the swelling of the rivers, which obliged them to halt until the former had melted and the floods had subsided. Many things worthy of admiration were observed by them in the progress of their journey, but which are here omitted, as they will be described by Marco Polo, in the sequel of the book.

§ 2. Being introduced to the presence of the grand khan, Kublaï, the travellers were received by him with the condescension and affability that belonged to his character, and as they were the first Latins who had made their appearance in that country, they were entertained with feasts and honoured with other marks of distinction. Entering graciously into conversation with them, he made earnest inquiries on the subject of the western parts of the world, of the emperor of the Romans,[1] and of other Christian kings and princes. He wished to be informed of their relative consequence, the extent of their possessions, the manner in which justice was administered in their several kingdoms and principalities, how

which, or the adjoining district of Karchin, where Shang-tu was situated, he was rarely absent.

[1] By the emperor of the Romans is meant the emperor, whether Greek or Roman, who reigned at Constantinople. Those countries which now form the dominion of the Turks in Europe and Asia Minor, are vaguely designated, amongst the more Eastern people, by the name of Rûm, and their inhabitants by that of Rûmi.

they conducted themselves in warfare, and above all he questioned them particularly respecting the pope, the affairs of the church, and the religious worship and doctrine of the Christians. Being well instructed and discreet men, they gave appropriate answers upon all these points, and as they were perfectly acquainted with the Tartar (Moghul) language, they expressed themselves always in becoming terms; insomuch that the grand khan, holding them in high estimation, frequently commanded their attendance.

When he had obtained all the information that the two brothers communicated with so much good sense, he expressed himself well satisfied, and having formed in his mind the design of employing them as his ambassadors to the pope, after consulting with his ministers on the subject, he proposed to them, with many kind entreaties, that they should accompany one of his officers, named Khogatal, on a mission to the see of Rome. His object, he told them, was to make a request to his holiness that he would send to him a hundred men of learning, thoroughly acquainted with the principles of the Christian religion, as well as with the seven arts, and qualified to prove to the learned of his dominions by just and fair argument, that the faith professed by Christians is superior to, and founded upon more evident truth than, any other; that the gods of the Tartars and the idols worshipped in their houses were only evil spirits, and that they and the people of the East in general were under an error in reverencing them as divinities. He moreover signified his pleasure that upon their return they should bring with them, from Jerusalem, some of the holy oil from the lamp which is kept burning over the sepulchre of our Lord Jesus Christ, whom he professed to hold in veneration and to consider as the true God. [1] Having

[1] We may reasonably suspect (without entertaining any doubt of the embassy itself) that the expressions here put into the mouth of the emperor, both as they regard the worship of the Tartars and the divinity of Christ, have been heightened by the zeal of Christian transcribers. The circumstance of Kublai, who is known to have been of an active and inquisitive mind, requesting to be furnished with a number of missionaries from Europe, to instruct his ignorant Tartar subjects in religion, and more especially in the practice of useful arts, is no more than what has been frequently done since, by the princes of half-barbarous nations, amongst whom the doctrine of the Koran had not already taken root. With regard to the holy oil, we find its importance thus stated by Chardin: " Ce qu'il (le clergé Arménien) vend le plus cher, ce sont les saintes huiles, que les Grecs appellent *myrone*. La plûpart des chrétiens orientaux s'imaginent que c'est un baume physiquement salutaire contre toutes les maladies de l'ame. Le patriarche a seul le droit de la consacrer. Il la vend aux évêques et aux prêtres. Il y a quelques douze

heard these commands addressed to them by the grand khan they humbly prostrated themselves before him, declaring their willingness and instant readiness to perform, to the utmost of their ability, whatever might be the royal will. Upon which he caused letters, in the Tartarian language, to be written in his name to the pope of Rome, and these he delivered into their hands. He likewise gave orders that they should be furnished with a golden tablet displaying the imperial cipher,[1] according to the usage established by his majesty; in virtue of which the person bearing it, together with his whole suite, are safely conveyed and escorted from station to station by the governors of all places within the imperial dominions, and are entitled, during the time of their residing in any city, castle, town, or village, to a supply of provisions and everything necessary for their accommodation.

Being thus honourably commissioned they took their leave of the grand khan, and set out on their journey, but had not proceeded more than twenty days when the officer, named Khogatal, their companion, fell dangerously ill, in the city named Alau.[2] In this dilemma it was determined, upon consulting all who were present, and with the approbation of the man himself, that they should leave him behind. In the prosecution of their journey they derived essential benefit from being provided with the royal tablet, which procured them attention in every place through which they passed. Their expenses were defrayed, and escorts were furnished. But notwithstanding these advantages, so great were the natural difficulties they had to encounter, from the extreme cold, the snow, the ice, and the flooding of the rivers, that their progress was unavoidably tedious, and three years elapsed before they were enabled to reach a sea-port town in the lesser

ans que celui de Perse se mit en tête d'empêcher les ecclésiastiques Arméniens de tout l'orient, de se pourvoir des saintes huiles ailleurs que chez lui. Ceux de Turquie s'en fournissent depuis long-tems à Jerusalem, auprès du patriarche Arménien qui y réside, et qui est le chef de tous les Chrétiens Arméniens de l'empire Ottoman."—Voy. en Perse, tom. i. p. 170, 4to.

[1] Frequent mention is made in the Chinese writings of the tchikouei, or tablet of honour, delivered to great officers on their appointment; upon which their titles are set forth in gold letters, and which entitles them to considerable privileges in travelling. That which is here spoken of may be supposed to have been of nearly the same kind. In the vulgar European dialect of Canton, it is termed the emperor's grand chop, a word used to express " seal, mark, warrant, licence, or passport."

[2] The name of the place where Khogatal was left is omitted in Marsden, and in the French and some of the Italian texts.

Armenia, named Laiassus.[1] Departing from thence by sea, they arrived at Acre[2] in the month of April, 1269, and there learned, with extreme concern, that pope Clement the Fourth was recently dead.[3] A legate whom he had appointed, named M. Tebaldo de' Vesconti di Piacenza, was at this time resident in Acre,[4] and to him they gave an account of what they had in command from the grand khan of Tartary. He advised them by all means to wait the election of another pope, and when that should take place, to proceed with the object of their embassy. Approving of this counsel, they determined upon employing the interval in a visit to their families in Venice. They accordingly embarked at Acre in a ship bound to Negropont, and from thence went on to Venice, where Nicolo Polo found that his wife, whom he had left with child at his departure, was dead, after having been delivered of a son, who received the name of Marco, and was now of the age of nineteen years.[5] This is the Marco by whom the present work is com-

[1] We have given the name Laiassus from the Latin text, instead of Giazza, given in Marsden's text, which is an evident corruption. The place meant is a port on the northern side of the gulf of Scandaroon, or Issus, which in our modern maps and books of geography has the various appellations of Lajazzo, Aiazzo, Aiasso, L'Aïas, and Layassa.

[2] Acre, properly Akkâ, the ancient Ptolemaïs, a maritime city of Palestine, was taken from the Saracens, in 1110, by the Crusaders. In 1187 it fell into the hands of Saladin or Salah-eddîn; and in 1191 it was wrested from him by the Christian forces, under Philippe Auguste, king of France, and Richard Cœur de Lion, king of England. In 1265, and again in 1269 (about the period at which our travellers arrived there), it was unsuccessfully attacked by Bibars, sultan of Egypt. In 1291 it was finally conquered from the Christians, and in great part demolished, by Khalil, another Egyptian sultan, of the dynasty of Mameluk Baharites. In modern days, it suddenly arose from the obscurity in which it had lain for five centuries, and once more became celebrated for the determined and triumphant resistance there made, in 1798 and 1799, by Jezzar Pasha, assisted by a small British squadron and the gallantry of its distinguished commander, against the furious and sanguinary efforts of the invader of Egypt.

[3] Clement IV. died on the 29th of November, of the year 1268. The event was consequently a recent one when our travellers arrived at Acre in April, 1269. It may be observed that the date of their arrival is differently stated in the MSS., some reading 1260, the Latin text having 1270, and others 1272. Some MSS. specify the 30th of April as the day of their arrival.

[4] That Acre was the residence of a legate from the papal see about this period is proved by other records.

[5] The Basle, as well as the earlier Latin version, and the Italian epitomes, state the age of Marco, who was to become the historian of the family, to have been then only fifteen years. If this reading be correct, as probably it is, the father, who arrived at Acre in 1269, and may be presumed to have reached Venice in 1270, must have left home about the year 1255. (See Note [3], on p. 10.) The age of nineteen seems to have been assigned in order to make it consistent with the supposed departure in 1250

posed, and who will give therein a relation of all those matters of which he has been an eye-witness.

§ 3. In the meantime the election of a pope was retarded by so many obstacles, that they remained two years in Venice, continually expecting its accomplishment;[1] when at length, becoming apprehensive that the grand khan might be displeased at their delay, or might suppose it was not their intention to revisit his country, they judged it expedient to return to Acre; and on this occasion they took with them young Marco Polo. Under the sanction of the legate they made a visit to Jerusalem, and there provided themselves with some of the oil belonging to the lamp of the holy sepulchre, conformably to the directions of the grand khan. As soon as they were furnished with his letters addressed to that prince bearing testimony to the fidelity with which they had endeavoured to execute his commission, and explaining to him that the pope of the Christian church had not as yet been chosen, they proceeded to the before-mentioned port of Laiassus. Scarcely however had they taken their departure, when the legate received messengers from Italy, despatched by the college of cardinals, announcing his own elevation to the papal chair; and he thereupon assumed the name of Gregory the Tenth.[2] Considering that he was now in a situation that enabled him fully to satisfy the wishes of the Tartar sovereign, he hastened to transmit letters to the king of Armenia,[3] communicating to him the event of his election,

[1] A vacancy in the papal see, for a period of nearly three years, occurred on this occasion, in consequence of the cabals existing in the Sacred College; when, at length, it was determined to refer the choice of a pope to six of the cardinals, who elected Tebaldo of Piacenza, on the first day of September, 1271. In order to prevent the inconvenience and scandal of such delays for the future, the institution of the Conclave (upon a principle that resembles the impanelling of our English juries) was established.

[2] In the list of sovereign pontiffs we find him styled "B. Gregorius X. Placentinus." His election, as has been mentioned, took place on the 1st of September, 1271. He was then acting as legate in Syria; but, having early notice of the event, he was enabled to take his departure from thence so soon as the 18th November following, and landed at Brindisi, near Otranto, in January, 1272.

[3] At this time Leon, or Livon II., reigned in the lesser Armenia, the capital of which was Sis, and Aïas, or Aïazzo, its chief port. His father, whom we call Haiton, and the Arabian writers Hatem, had acted a conspicuous part in the late transactions, having accompanied Hulagu from the court of Mangu-khan to Persia, and assisted in his wars with the Mussulmans. In 1270 he had obtained the consent of Abaka the son of Hulagu, then his liege sovereign, for transferring the crown of Armenia, on account of his age and infirmities, to his son Leon. The principal actions of his life are recorded by his namesake, relation and cotem-

and requesting, in case the two ambassadors who were on their way to the court of the grand khan should not have already quitted his dominions, that he would give directions for their immediate return. These letters found them still in Armenia, and with great alacrity they obeyed the summons to repair once more to Acre; for which purpose the king furnished them with an armed galley; sending at the same time an ambassador from himself, to offer his congratulations to the sovereign pontiff.

Upon their arrival, his holiness received them in a distinguished manner, and immediately despatched them with letters papal, accompanied by two friars of the order of Preachers, who happened to be on the spot; men of letters and of science, as well as profound theologians. One of them was named Fra Nicolo da Vicenza, and the other, Fra Guielmo da Tripoli. To them he gave licence and authority to ordain priests, to consecrate bishops, and to grant absolution as fully as he could do in his own person. He also charged them with valuable presents, and among these, several handsome vases of crystal, to be delivered to the grand khan in his name, and along with his benediction. Having taken leave, they again steered their course to the port of Laiassus,[1] where they landed, and from thence proceeded into the country of Armenia. Here they received intelligence that the soldan of Babylonia, named Bundokdari, had invaded the Armenian territory with a numerous army, and had overrun and laid waste the country to a great extent.[2] Terrified at these accounts, and appre-

porary, who, having long distinguished himself as a soldier, became an ecclesiastic. His work was edited by Grynæus, at Basle and Paris, in 1532, under the title of "Haithonis Armeni de Tartaris liber," and again, by Andreas Müller, in 1671, under that of "Haithoni Armeni Historia Orientalis: quæ eadem et de Tartaris inscribitur." See also Abul-Pharajii Hist. pp. 328—357; and De Guignes, Hist. Gén. liv. xv. pp. 125—249.

[1] As it may be presumed that our travellers commenced their journey about the time of the sailing of Pope Gregory from Acre, the period is fixed by authority that will scarcely admit dispute, to the end of the year 1271, or beginning of 1272.

[2] This soldan was Bibars, surnamed Bundokdari, Mameluk sultan of Egypt (which is meant by Babylonia), who had conquered the greater part of Syria, and had already (in or about 1266) invaded Armenia, and plundered the towns of Sis and Aïs. In 1270 he made himself master of Antioch, slew or made captives of all the Christian inhabitants, and demolished its churches, the most magnificent and celebrated in the East. It must have been about the beginning of the year 1272 that our travellers entered Armenia; and, although it is not stated specifically that any irruption by the soldan took place at that time, it is evident that he had not ceased to harass the neighbouring country of Syria; and,

hensive for their lives, the two friars determined not to proceed further, and delivering over to the Venetians the letters and presents entrusted to them by the pope, they placed themselves under the protection of the master of the knights templars,[1] and with him returned directly to the coast. Nicolo, Maffeo, and Marco, however, undismayed by perils or difficulties (to which they had long been inured), passed the borders of Armenia, and prosecuted their journey. After crossing deserts of several days' march, and passing many dangerous defiles, they advanced so far, in a direction between north-east and north, that at length they gained information of the grand khan, who then had his residence in a large and magnificent city named Cle-men-fu.[2] Their whole journey to this place occupied no less than three years and a half; but, during the winter months, their progress had been inconsiderable.[3] The grand khan having notice of their approach whilst still remote, and being aware how much they must have suffered from fatigue, sent forward to meet them at the distance of forty days' journey, and gave orders to prepare in every place through which they were to pass, whatever might be requisite to their comfort. By these means, and through the blessing of God, they were conveyed in safety to the royal court.

notwithstanding the formidable combination just mentioned, we find him again, in 1276, invading the province of Rûm, immediately bordering on the lesser Armenia to the northward. The alarms must have been perpetual, and these alone may have been sufficient to deter the two theologians from proceeding with their more adventurous companions; who did not, however, meet with the enemy.

[1] It is well known that the knights of the hospital of St. John of Jerusalem, and the knights of the Temple, were two great monastic military orders that arose from the fanaticism of the crusades, and became the most regular and effective support of the Christian cause in Asia. It is not unlikely that a body of the latter may have been stationed in this part of Armenia (which we should term the pashalic of Marash), for its defence, and the ecclesiastics would naturally seek the protection of its commander, who may have been the master, but was more probably only a knight of the order.

[2] The ordinary residence of Kublaï at this period must have been Yen-king (near the spot where Peking now stands), whilst he was employed in laying the foundations of his new capital of Ta-tu, of which particular mention will be made in the sequel. The operations of war, or the regulations of newly-conquered provinces, might, however, occasion his visiting other cities; and our travellers may have found him in the western part of his dominions. "Il établit sa cour d'abord," says Du Halde, "à Tai-yuen-fou, capitale de la province de Chan-si, et ensuite il la transporta à Peking."—Descript. de la Chine, tom. i. p. 496.

[3] When the Teshu Lama of Tibet visited (in 1779-80) the late emperor of China, at Peking, his journey (although from what we consider a neighbouring country, and which has since been garrisoned by Chinese troops) occupied ten months, during four of which he was detained at one place by the snow.

§ 4. Upon their arrival they were honourably and graciously received by the grand khan, in a full assembly of his principal officers. When they drew nigh to his person, they paid their respects by prostrating themselves on the floor. He immediately commanded them to rise, and to relate to him the circumstances of their travels, with all that had taken place in their negotiation with his holiness the pope. To their narrative, which they gave in the regular order of events, and delivered in perspicuous language, he listened with attentive silence. The letters and the presents from pope Gregory were then laid before him, and, upon hearing the former read, he bestowed much commendation on the fidelity, the zeal, and the diligence of his ambassadors; and receiving with due reverence the oil from the holy sepulchre, he gave directions that it should be preserved with religious care. Upon his observing Marco Polo, and inquiring who he was, Nicolo made answer, "This is your servant, and my son;" upon which the grand khan replied, "He is welcome, and it pleases me much," and he caused him to be enrolled amongst his attendants of honour. And on account of their return he made a great feast and rejoicing; and as long as the said brothers and Marco remained in the court of the grand khan, they were honoured even above his own courtiers. Marco was held in high estimation and respect by all belonging to the court. He learnt in a short time and adopted the manners of the Tartars, and acquired a proficiency in four different languages, which he became qualified to read and write.[1] Finding him thus accomplished, his master was desirous of putting his talents for business to the proof, and sent him on an important concern of state to a city named Karazan,[2] situated at the distance of six

[1] Perhaps the Moghul or Mungal, Ighur, Manchu, and Chinese. The last will be thought the least probable; but no inference should be drawn from his orthography of Chinese names in European characters, and particularly in the corrupted state of the text. The Latin text says that Marco learnt "the Tartar and four other languages;" the French text says, "their language and four different characters" of writing.

[2] Having here the name merely, without any circumstance but that of its remoteness from the capital of China, we must presume it to be intended for a city of Khorasan; to which there is no objection but the probability of his having passed through that province when he first visited Tartary, and that it is not here spoken of as a place with which he had been previously acquainted. It was then (together with Persia) under the dominion of the second son of Hulagu, who succeeded his brother Abaka, and took the name of Ahmed Khan, upon his embracing the Mahometan religion. It would, perhaps, be taking a liberty with the orthography to suppose that the name might be intended for Khorasmia, the Kharism of modern geographers.

months' journey from the imperial residence; on which occasion he conducted himself with so much wisdom and prudence in the management of the affairs entrusted to him, that his services became highly acceptable. On his part, perceiving that the grand khan took a pleasure in hearing accounts of whatever was new to him respecting the customs and manners of people, and the peculiar circumstances of distant countries, he endeavoured, wherever he went, to obtain correct information on these subjects, and made notes of all he saw and heard, in order to gratify the curiosity of his master. In short, during seventeen years [1] that he continued in his service, he rendered himself so useful, that he was employed on confidential missions to every part of the empire and its dependencies; and sometimes also he travelled on his own private account, but always with the consent, and sanctioned by the authority, of the grand khan. Under such circumstances it was that Marco Polo had the opportunity of acquiring a knowledge, either by his own observation, or what he collected from others, of so many things, until his time unknown, respecting the eastern parts of the world, and which he diligently and regularly committed to writing, as in the sequel will appear. And by this means he obtained so much honour, that he provoked the jealousy of the other officers of the court.

§ 5. Our Venetians having now resided many years at the imperial court, and in that time having realized considerable wealth, in jewels of value and in gold, felt a strong desire to revisit their native country, and, however honoured and caressed by the sovereign, this sentiment was ever predominant in their minds. It became the more decidedly their object, when they reflected on the very advanced age of the grand khan, whose death, if it should happen previously to their departure, might deprive them of that public assistance by which alone they could expect to surmount the innumerable difficulties of so long a journey, and reach their homes in

[1] In Ramusio's text the period is said to be *ventisei anni*, "twenty-six years," and Purchas endeavours to explain in what sense this number should be understood; but I prefer, in this instance, the reading of the Latin version, which has "xvii annos," as more consistent with the fact. It is certain that the family did not leave Acre, on their return to China, before the end of 1271; and as there is reason to believe that they did not reach the emperor's court before 1273 or 1274, nor remain there beyond 1291, it follows that the period of Marco's service could not have exceeded seventeen years by more than a few months. Twenty-six years include the whole of the period elapsed since the first visit of his father and uncle in 1264 or 1265.

safety; which on the contrary, in his lifetime, and through his favour, they might reasonably hope to accomplish. Nicolo Polo accordingly took an opportunity one day, when he observed him to be more than usually cheerful, of throwing himself at his feet, and soliciting on behalf of himself and his family to be indulged with his majesty's gracious permission for their departure. But far from showing himself disposed to comply with the request, he appeared hurt at the application, and asked what motive they could have for wishing to expose themselves to all the inconveniences and hazards of a journey in which they might probably lose their lives. If gain, he said, was their object, he was ready to give them the double of whatever they possessed, and to gratify them with honours to the extent of their desires; but that, from the regard he bore to them, he must positively refuse their petition.

It happened, about this period, that a queen named Bolgana,[1] the wife of Arghun,[2] sovereign of India, died, and as her last request (which she likewise left in a testamentary writing) conjured her husband that no one might succeed to her place on his throne and in his affections, who was not a descendant of her own family, now settled under the dominion of the grand khan,[3]

[1] Although we do not find in the histories of this period that have come to our hands, any mention of the consort of Arghun-khan, yet the name that is here written Bolgana, and in the Latin of the Basle edition, as well as that of the British Museum manuscript, Balgana occurs, with little difference of orthography, amongst the females of the family. The daughter of Jagataï, son of Jengiz-khan and uncle of Hulagu, was named Bolghân-khâtûn, as appears from the "Rouzat alsafà" of Mirkhond. The Latin and French texts, and the Italian text in Boni's edition, call the queen Bolgara.

[2] Arghun-khan, the son of Abaka-khan, and grandson of Hulagu-il-khan, succeeded his uncle Ahmed-khan Nikodar on the throne of Persia, Khorasan, and other neighbouring countries, in 1284; and his first act, as we are informed by De Guignes (Liv. xvii. p. 265) was to send to the emperor Kublaï, as the head of the family and his liege sovereign, to demand the investiture of his estates. The death of his queen, here spoken of, must, from the circumstances mentioned in the sequel, have taken place about the year 1287, and he himself died in 1291. The name in all the versions of the work is uniformly written Argon, which approaches extremely near to the Persian orthography.

[3] The grand khan, at whose court the family of this queen is said to have resided in Kataia, was the grand-uncle of Arghun, her husband, and the queen herself was probably of the same royal Moghul family, from the common stock of Jengiz-khan. Her anxiety therefore was, that her husband should not degrade himself and her memory, by contracting a marriage with any person of less noble lineage than their own. Viewing the circumstances therefore in their proper light, it will be found that what might at first be thought a romantic story, of a king of India sending an embassy to an emperor of China, for the purpose of obtaining a wife, resolves itself into the simple and natural transaction, of one of the younger members of a great family applying to the head of the house

in the country of Kathay.[1] Desirous of complying with this solemn entreaty, Arghun deputed three of his nobles, discreet men, whose names were Ulatai, Apusca, and Goza,[2] attended by a numerous retinue, as his ambassadors to the grand khan, with a request that he might receive at his hands a maiden to wife, from among the relatives of his deceased queen. The application was taken in good part, and under the directions of his majesty, choice was made of a damsel aged seventeen, extremely handsome and accomplished, whose name was Kogatin,[3] and of whom the ambassadors, upon her being shown to them, highly approved. When everything was arranged for their departure, and a numerous suite of attendants appointed, to do honour to the future consort of king Arghun, they received from the grand khan a gracious dismissal, and set out on their return by the way they came. Having travelled for eight months, their further progress was

to be allowed to strengthen the connexion, by marrying from amongst those who were probably his cousins in the second degree; for we may presume that if this female had not been one of Kublaï's own immediate race, (a granddaughter, perhaps, as he was then advanced in years,) there would not have existed a necessity for making so formal a demand. In regard to the distance between Persia and China, which might be considered an objection to the probability of the fact, it is well known that amongst all the branches of this Moghul family, however remote from each other, a continual intercourse had, up to that period, been maintained, and Arghun himself had applied for and received his investiture from the same monarch. In the event, however, it proved that the difficulties attending the returning journey, over land, had become insuperable.

[1] The situation of Khataï, or Kataia, (or as it was usually called by the medieval writers, Cathay,) has been a subject of much discussion amongst the learned; but it cannot, I think, be doubted by those who consult the eastern geographers and historians rather than the Greek, that they apply the name to the northern provinces of what we call China, which were conquered by Jengiz-khan, and his son, Oktaï, not from a Chinese government, but from a race of eastern Tartars, called Niu-che and Kin, by whom they had been subdued about one hundred and twenty years before. Whether they confine it strictly to these provinces, or include some of the adjoining parts of Tartary, without-side the wall, it is not easy to determine, as their accounts of these regions are far from being precise; but the former I should judge to be the case.

[2] These names vary considerably in the different versions and editions, where they appear in the forms of Ulatai and Gulatay, Apusca, Apusta, and Ribusca, Goza, and Coyla; all of them, probably, much disfigured by transcribing from indistinct manuscripts. The Latin text calls them Oulata, Alpusca, and Cor. They are not, however, of any historical importance.

[3] One of the wives of Hulagu, and mother of Ahmed-khan Nikodar (the uncle of Arghun), was named Kutai-khatun, of which Kogatin, (otherwise written Gogatim and Koganyn) may perhaps be a corruption. The word khatun, which signifies "lady," is very frequently annexed to, or forms parts of proper names, borne by Persian and Tartar women of rank.

obstructed and the roads shut up against them, by fresh wars that had broken out amongst the Tartar princes.[1] Much against their inclinations, therefore, they were constrained to adopt the measure of returning to the court of the grand khan, to whom they stated the interruption they had met with.

About the time of their reappearance, Marco Polo happened to arrive from a voyage he had made, with a few vessels under his orders, to some parts of the East Indies,[2] and reported to the grand khan the intelligence he brought respecting the countries he had visited, with the circumstances of his own navigation, which, he said, was performed in those seas with the utmost safety. This latter observation having reached the ears of the three ambassadors, who were extremely anxious to return to their own country, from whence they had now been absent three years, they presently sought a conference with our Venetians, whom they found equally desirous of revisiting their home; and it was settled between them that the former, accompanied by their young queen, should obtain an audience of the grand khan, and represent to him with what convenience and security they might effect their return by sea, to the dominions of their master; whilst the voyage would be attended with less expense than the journey by land,[3] and be performed in a shorter time; according to the experience of Marco Polo, who had lately sailed in those parts. Should his majesty incline to give his consent to their adopting that mode of conveyance, they were then to urge him to suffer the three Europeans, as being persons well skilled in the practice of navigation, to accompany them until they should reach the

[1] These wars must have taken place about the year 1289, and probably in the country of Mawara'lnahr, or Transoxiana, amongst the descendants of Jagataï or Zagataï, whose history is particularly obscure; but there is reason to believe that they (or any of the Moghul princes) were seldom in a state of tranquillity. Troubles were also excited, nearer to China, by a younger brother of Kublaï, who attempted to dispute with him the right to the empire.

[2] What are here termed the East Indies must not be understood of the continent of India, but of some of the islands in the eastern archipelago, perhaps the Philippines, or possibly the coast of Tsiampa, or Champa, which, in another part of the work, our author speaks of having visited. The voyage here mentioned was subsequent to the grand and disastrous expedition which the active genuis of Kublaï led him to fit out against the kingdom of Japan. It should be observed that the Latin and French texts, and the Italian published by Boni, say nothing of the ships, but merely state that he was returning from an embassy to India.

[3] The suggestion of this economical motive may seem extraordinary, but attachment to money was one of the weak parts of Kublaï's character, and the practices he adopted, or connived at, for raising it, have been the subject of much reprehension.

territory of king Arghun. The grand khan upon receiving this application showed by his countenance that it was exceedingly displeasing to him, averse as he was to parting with the Venetians. Feeling nevertheless that he could not with propriety do otherwise than consent, he yielded to their entreaty. Had it not been that he found himself constrained by the importance and urgency of this peculiar case, they would never otherwise have obtained permission to withdraw themselves from his service. He sent for them, however, and addressed them with much kindness and condescension, assuring them of his regard, and requiring from them a promise that when they should have resided some time in Europe and with their own family, they would return to him once more. With this object in view he caused them to be furnished with the golden tablet (or royal *chop*), which contained his order for their having free and safe conduct through every part of his dominions, with the needful supplies for themselves and their attendants. He likewise gave them authority to act in the capacity of his ambassadors to the pope, the kings of France and Spain, and the other Christian princes.[1]

At the same time preparations were made for the equipment of fourteen ships, each having four masts, and capable of being navigated with nine sails,[2] the construction and rigging of which would admit of ample description; but, to avoid prolixity, it is for the present omitted. Among these vessels there were at least four or five that had crews of two hundred and fifty or two hundred and sixty men. On them were embarked the ambassadors, having the queen under their protection,

[1] In the Latin version it is said that he appointed ambassadors of his own to these monarchs to accompany the expedition; but as no allusion is afterwards made to such personages, although an obvious occasion (that of the mortality) presents itself, the Italian reading is considered as preferable.

[2] For the modern practice, in the northern part of China, and particularly on the Pe-ho, of rigging vessels intended to be employed in foreign voyages, with *four* masts, we have the authority of Barrow, who says: "It is impossible not to consider the notices given by this early traveller (Marco Polo) as curious, interesting, and valuable; and as far as they regard the empire of China, they bear internal evidence of their being generally correct. He sailed from China in a fleet consisting of fourteen ships, each carrying *four* masts, and having their holds partitioned into separate chambers. . . . We observed many hundreds of a larger description, that are employed in foreign voyages, all carrying *four* masts." —Travels in China, p. 45. In the Latin version the words are, "quarum quælibet habebat quatuor malos, et multæ ex illis ibant cum duodecim velis,"—"of which each had four masts, and many of them went with twelve sails." It is well known that now Chinese vessels do not carry any kind of topsail.

together with Nicolo, Maffeo, and Marco Polo, when they had first taken their leave of the grand khan, who presented them with many rubies and other handsome jewels of great value. He also gave directions that the ships should be furnished with stores and provisions for two years.[1]

§ 6. After a navigation of about three months, they arrived at an island which lay in a southerly direction, named Java,[2] where they saw various objects worthy of attention, of which notice shall be taken in the sequel of the work. Taking their departure from thence, they employed eighteen months in the Indian seas before they were enabled to reach the place of their destination in the territory of king Arghun;[3] and during this part of their voyage also they had an opportunity of observing many things, which shall, in like manner, be related hereafter. But here it may be proper to mention, that between the day of their sailing and that of their arrival, they lost by deaths, of the crews of the vessels and others who were embarked, about six hundred persons; and of the three ambassadors, only one, whose name was Goza, survived the voyage; whilst of all the ladies and female attendants one only died.[4]

Upon landing they were informed that king Arghun had died some time before,[5] and that the government of the country was then administered, on behalf of his son, who was still a youth, by a person of the name of Ki-akato.[6] From

[1] The sailing of this remarkable expedition from the Pe-ho, or river of Peking, we may infer, from circumstances mentioned in different parts of the work, to have taken place about the beginning of 1291, three years before the death of the emperor Kublaï, and four years previous to the arrival of the Polo family at Venice, in 1295.

[2] Some details of this part of the voyage are given in book iii. chap. x., where the island here called Java, is termed Java minor, and is evidently intended for Sumatra. It will appear that they wanted the change of the monsoon in a northern port of that island, near the western entrance of the straits of Malacca.

[3] The place where the expedition ultimately arrived is not directly mentioned in any part of the work; but there are strong grounds for inferring it to have been the celebrated port of Ormuz. With respect to the prince named Arghun-khan, see Note[2], on p. 23.

[4] This mortality is no greater than might be expected in vessels crowded with men unaccustomed to voyages of such duration, and who had passed several months at an anchorage in the straits of Malacca; and although it should have amounted to one-third of their whole number, the proportion would not have exceeded what was suffered by Lord Anson and other navigators of the seventeenth and eighteenth centuries.

[5] Arghun-khan, according to the authorities followed by De Guignes, died in the third month of the year 690 of the hejrah, answering to March in the year of our Lord 1291.

[6] The person here named Ki-akato, or Chiacato in the Italian orthography, and described as the ruler of the country in the name of the late

him they desired to receive instructions as to the manner in which they were to dispose of the princess, whom, by the orders of the late king, they had conducted thither. His answer was, that they ought to present the lady to Kasan,[1] the son of Arghun, who was then at a place on the borders of Persia, which has its denomination from the Arbor secco,[2] where an army of sixty thousand men was assembled for the purpose of guarding certain passes against the irruption of the enemy.[3] This they proceeded to carry into execution, and having effected it, they returned to the residence of Ki-akato, because the road they were afterwards to take lay in that direction.[4] Here, however, they reposed themselves for

king's son, was Kai-khatu, the second son of Abaka-khan, and consequently the brother of Arghun, upon whose death he is said to have seized the throne (although perhaps only as regent or protector), to the prejudice of his nephew, then a minor.

[1] The prince whose name is here written Kasan, or Casan, and by De Guignes Cazan, was Chazan-khan, the eldest son of Arghun. He did not succeed to the throne of Persia until the end of the year 1295, nearly five years after the death of his father, who had sent him to reside in Khorasan, under the tutelage of an atabeg, or governor, named Nuroz, by whose persuasion he afterwards embraced the Mussulman faith, and took the name of Mahmûd. It does not appear that he was molested in that province by his uncle Kai-khatu, and this recommendation, that the princess should be conveyed to him as the representative of his father, serves to show that they were not upon terms of actual hostility. It is further proved by the circumstance, that when, upon the murder of Kai-khatu, the government fell into the hands of Baidu (a grandson of Hulagu in a different line), and Ghazan marched with an army to Rey (Rages) to assert his hereditary claims, the first demand he made was, that the assassins of his uncle should be delivered up to him. After a doubtful struggle maintained during a period of eight months, the defection of his principal officers led to the destruction of the usurper, and Ghazan ascended the throne of Persia, about two years subsequently to the arrival of the princess, of whom nothing further is recorded.

[2] More circumstantial mention is made of this district, and of the tree from whence it is said to derive its appellation, in chap. xx. of this book.

[3] This is the important pass known to the ancients by the appellation of Portæ Caspiæ or Caspian Straits (to be distinguished from those of Derbend, as well as of Rudbar), and termed by Eastern geographers the Straits of Khowar, or Khawr, from a Persian word, signifying a valley between two mountains, or from a small town near the eastern entrance which bears the same name. "This remarkable chasm," says Rennell, "is now called the strait or passage of Khowar (Chora of the ancients), from a town or district in the neighbourhood. It is situated at the termination of the great Salt Desert, almost due north from Ispahan, and about fifty miles to the eastward of the ruins of Rey (or Rages). Alexander passed through it in his way from Rages towards Aria and Bactria. Della Valle and Herbert amongst the moderns, and Pliny amongst the ancients, have described it particularly. It is eight miles through, and generally forty yards in breadth."—Geographical System of Herodotus examined and explained, p. 174, note.

[4] From the preceding part of the narrative we might be led to suppose the residence of Kai-khatu to have been in one of the southern provinces

the space of nine months.[1] When they took their leave he furnished them with four golden tablets, each of them a cubit in length, five inches wide, and weighing three or four marks of gold.[2] Their inscription began with invoking the blessing of the Almighty upon the grand khan,[3] that his name might be held in reverence for many years, and denouncing the punishment of death and confiscation of goods to all who should refuse obedience to the mandate. It then proceeded to direct that the three ambassadors, as his representatives, should be treated throughout his dominions with due honour, that their expenses should be defrayed, and that they should be provided with the necessary escorts. All this was fully complied with, and from many places they were protected by bodies of two hundred horse; nor could this have been dispensed with as the government of Ki-akato was unpopular, and the people were disposed to commit insults and proceed to outrages, which they would not have dared to attempt under the rule of their proper sovereign.[4] In the course of their journey our

of Persia; but here, on the contrary, we find, that, conformably with the histories of the times, it lay in the route between the place where Ghazan was encamped, on the eastern side of the Caspian straits, and the country of Armenia, towards which our travellers were advancing. By D'Herbelot, De Guignes, and others, we are accordingly told that the capital of the princes of this dynasty was the city of Tauris or Tabriz, in Aderbijan, but that they frequently resided (especially in summer) at Hamadan, in Aljebal, in order to be nearer to the Syrian frontier.

[1] From what has been said in the preceding note, we may presume this place to have been Tabriz.

[2] The mark being eight ounces, the tablets must have been unnecessarily expensive and inconveniently ponderous. The other versions do not specify either weight or size, and some state them to be only *two additional* tablets.

[3] This shows that the sovereignty of the head of the family was still acknowledged by these branches, and Kai-khatu might have particular motives for courting its sanction. Ghazan is said to have been the first who renounced this slight species of vassalage, and probably did not send an ambassador to China to demand the investiture.

[4] In the conduct here described we have a proof of the general doubt entertained respecting his right to the throne, although the Moghul chiefs affected to consider it as dependent upon their election. The historians all agree in reprobating his habits as debauched and infamous, and these chiefs, indignant at being governed by a prince so corrupt, "equally hated by his subjects and despised by foreigners," resolved to remove him, and made an offer of the crown, not to Ghazan, whom they might think still too young, or too feeble in bodily frame, for their purpose, but to Baidu, a grandson of Hulagu, and cousin of the late king, who was then governor of Baghdad. A battle was fought, in which Kai-khatu, personally brave, found himself deserted by a principal officer who commanded a wing of his army, was defeated, and subsequently strangled. For a circumstantial detail of these transactions on the authority of Khondemir, see the Bibliothèque Orientale, under the article Baidu. See also the article Gangiatu, "que l'on trouve aussi

travellers received intelligence of the grand khan (Kublaï) having departed this life;[1] which entirely put an end to all prospect of their revisiting those regions. Pursuing, therefore, their intended route, they at length reached the city of Trebizond, from whence they proceeded to Constantinople, then to Negropont,[2] and finally to Venice, at which place, in the enjoyment of health and abundant riches, they safely arrived in the year 1295. On this occasion they offered up their thanks to God, who had now been pleased to relieve them from such great fatigues, after having preserved them from innumerable perils. The foregoing narrative may be considered as a preliminary chapter, the object of which is to make the reader acquainted with the opportunities Marco Polo had of acquiring a knowledge of the things he describes, during a residence of so many years in the eastern parts of the world.

CHAPTER II

OF ARMENIA MINOR—OF THE PORT OF LAIASSUS—AND OF THE BOUNDARIES OF THE PROVINCE.

In commencing the description of the countries which Marco Polo visited in Asia, and of things worthy of notice which he

nommé Caictu, et Caicatu." "Khondemir remarque que le véritable nom de ce prince stoit Aicatu, ou Gaicatu." We should learn from hence to hesitate before we condemn the orthography of our author, whose mode of writing this uncouth name differs so little, if at all, from some of these high authorities. It is a circumstance extremely remarkable, that one of the principal motives assigned for the revolt of the Moghul chiefs against this prince, was his having attempted to establish in his dominions a system of *paper-money*, like that of China.—De Guignes, Hist. des Huns, Liv. xvii. p. 267.

[1] Kublaï, whose name the Chinese pronounce Hupili or Hupilé, whilst in their annals they bestow on him that of Chi-tsu, was proclaimed grand khan in the year 1260, became emperor of China upon the destruction of the dynasty of the Song, who reigned in Manji or the provinces south of the great river Kiang, in 1280, and died in the beginning of 1294, at the age of eighty years. It is not surprising that the news of an event so important to all the tribes of Moghuls or Tartars should have found its way to the court of Persia, and consequently to our travellers, with extraordinary expedition.

[2] Their most direct route from Tabriz would have lain through Bedlis in Kurdistan to Aleppo, but at this time the sultans of Egypt, with whom the kings of Persia were continually at war, had possession of all the seaports of Syria, and would pay little respect to their passports. By the way of Georgia to Trebisond, on the Euxine, their land-journey was shorter and more secure, and when at that place they were under the protection of the Christian prince, whose family reigned in the small independent kingdom of Trebisond, from 1204 to 1462.

observed therein, it is proper to mention that we are to distinguish two Armenias, the Lesser and the Greater.[1] The king of the Lesser Armenia dwells in a city called Sebastoz,[2] and rules his dominions with strict regard to justice. The towns, fortified places, and castles are numerous. There is abundance of all necessaries of life, as well as of those things which contribute to its comfort. Game, both of beasts and birds, is in plenty. It must be said, however, that the air of the country is not remarkably healthy. In former times its gentry were esteemed expert and brave soldiers; but at the present day they are great drinkers, pusillanimous, and worthless. On the sea-coast there is a city named Laiassus,[3] a place of considerable traffic. Its port is frequented by merchants from Venice, Genoa, and many other places, who trade in spiceries and drugs of different sorts, manufactures of silk and of wool, and other rich commodities. Those persons who design to

[1] This distinction of the Armenias into the Greater and the Lesser, is conformable to what we find in Ptolemy and the geographers of the middle ages; although other divisions have taken place since that part of Asia has been subject to the Ottoman empire. The Lesser Armenia is defined by Büsching as comprehending that part of Cappadocia and Cilicia which lies along the western side of the Greater Armenia, and also on the western side of the Euphrates. That in the days of Haiton it extended south of Taurus, and included Cilicia (campestris), which was not the case in more ancient times, we have the unexceptionable authority of that historian.

[2] As it appears from the passage quoted in the preceding note, as well as from other authorities, that Sîs was the capital of the Lesser Armenia during the reigns of the Leons and Haitons, we are led to suppose the Sebastoz here mentioned to have been the ancient name of that city, or of one that stood on the same site. It is obvious, indeed, from the geography of Ptolemy, that there were many places in Asia Minor that bore the names of Sebastia, Sebaste, and Sebastopolis (besides one in Syria), and in his enumeration of the towns of Cilicia, we find a Sebaste, to which, in the Latin translation, published at Venice in 1562, the epithet of "augusta" is annexed. Upon the foundations of this, Leon I. (from whom the country is called by the Arabians, Belan Leon, as well as Belad Sîs), may have built the modern city, and the Greek name may have been still prevalent. We are told, however, that the city which preceded Sîs, as the capital of Armenia Minor, was named Messis, Massis, or Massissa, the ancient Mopsuestia, and it must be confessed that if authority was not in opposition to conjecture, the sound of these names might lead us to suppose that the modern name was only an abbreviation of Mes-sis, and Sebastoz a substitution for Mopsueste. In a subsequent part of the chapter the city of Sevasta or Sevaste, the modern Siwas or Sivas, is spoken of under circumstances that appear to distinguish it entirely from the Armenian capital; having been recently conquered by the Moghuls from the Seljuk princes.

[3] Lajazzo, or Aîas, is situated in a low, morassy country, formed by the alluvion of the two rivers Sihon and Jihon (of Cilicia), and (as observed to me by Major Rennell) at the present mouth of the latter. Its trade has been transferred to Alexandretta or Scanderoon, on the opposite or Syrian side of the gulf.

travel into the interior of the Levant,[1] usually proceed in the first instance to this port of Laiassus. The boundaries of the Lesser Armenia are, on the south, the Land of Promise, now occupied by the Saracens;[2] on the north, Karamania, inhabited by Turkomans; towards the north-east lie the cities of Kaisariah, Sevasta,[3] and many others subject to the Tartars; and on the western side it is bounded by the sea, which extends to the shores of Christendom.

CHAPTER III

OF THE PROVINCE CALLED TURKOMANIA, WHERE ARE THE CITIES OF KOGNI, KAISARIAH, AND SEVASTA, AND OF ITS COMMERCE.

THE inhabitants of Turkomania[4] may be distinguished into three classes. The Turkomans, who reverence Mahomet and follow his law, are a rude people, and dull of intellect. They

[1] Levant is a translation of the word Anatolia or Anadoli, from the Greek ἀνατολὴ "ortus, oriens," signifying the country that lies *eastward* from Greece. As the name of a region therefore it should be equivalent to Natolia, in its more extensive acceptation; and it is evident that our author employs it to denote Asia Minor. Smyrna is at present esteemed the principal port in the Levant, and the term seems to be now confined to the sea-coast, and to mercantile usage.

[2] For the Land of Promise, or Palestine, which extends no further to the north than Tyre, is here to be understood Syria, or that part of itcalled Cœlo-Syria, which borders on Cilicia or the southern part of Armenia Minor. As the more general denomination of Syria includes Palestine, and the latter name was, in the time of the Crusades, more familiar to Europeans than the former, it is not surprising that they should sometimes be confounded. The Saracens here spoken of were the subjects of the Mameluk sultans or soldans of Egypt, who recoverd from the Christian powers in Syria, what the princes of the family of Saladin, or of the Ayubite dynasty, had lost. In other parts of the work the term is employed indiscriminately with that of Mahometan.

[3] The Turkomans of Karamania were a race of Tartars settled in Asia Minor, under the government of the Seljuk princes, of whom an account will be found in the following note. Kaisariah or Cæsarea, and Sevasta or Sebaste, the Sebastopolis Cappadociæ of Ptolemy and Siwas or Sivas of the present day, were cities belonging to the same dynasty, that had been conquered by the Moghuls in the year 1242.

[4] By Turkomania we are to understand, generally, the possessions of the great Seljuk dynasty in Asia Minor, extending from Cilicia and Pamphylia, in the south, to the shores of the Euxine sea, and from Pisidia and Mysia, in the west, to the borders of Armenia Minor; including the greater part of Phrygia and Cappadocia, together with Pontus, and particularly the modern provinces of Karamania and Rumiyah, or

dwell amongst the mountains and in places difficult of access, where their object is to find good pasture for their cattle, as they live entirely upon animal food. There is here an excellent breed of horses which has the appellation of Turki, and fine mules which are sold at high prices.[1] The other classes are Greeks and Armenians, who reside in the cities and fortified places, and gain their living by commerce and manufacture. The best and handsomest carpets in the world are wrought here, and also silks of crimson and other rich colours.[2] Amongst its cities are those of Kogni, Kaisariah, and Sevasta, in which last Saint Blaise obtained the glorious crown of martyrdom.[3] They are all subject to the great khan, emperor of the Oriental Tartars, who appoints governors to them.[4] We shall now speak of the Greater Armenia.

the country of Rûm. Of the former of these, the capital was Iconium, corrupted by the oriental writers to Kuniyah, and by those of the Crusades to Kogni; of the latter, Sebaste or Sebastopolis, corrupted to Siwas or Sivas. The chief from whom the dynasty of Seljuks derived its appellation, was by birth a Turkoman, of Turkistan, on the north-eastern side of the river Sihon or Jaxartes, but in the service of a prince of Khozar, on the Wolga, from which he fled and pursued his fortune in Transoxiana; as did some of his family in Khorasan. Having acquired great celebrity, they were at length enabled, by the means of numerous tribes of Turkomans who joined their standard, to establish a sovereignty, or, in point of extent, an empire, the principal seat of which was in Persia. Another branch, about the year 1080, wrested the fine provinces of Asia Minor from the Greek emperors, and formed the kingdom of which we are now speaking. Through its territory the Christian princes repeatedly forced their way in their progress to the Holy Land, and it is computed by historians that not fewer than six hundred thousand men perished in this preliminary warfare. At length the power of the Seljuks yielded to the overwhelming influence of the house of Jengiz-khan, and in our author's time they were reduced to insignificance; but from their ruins sprang the empire of the Ottomans, the founder of which had been in the service of one of the last sultans of Iconium.

1 The pastoral habits of the Turkoman Tartars are preserved to this day, even in Asia Minor, and the distinction of their tribes subsists also. The Turki breed of horses is esteemed throughout the East, for spirit and hardiness.

2 "Et ibi fiunt soriani et tapeti pulchriores de mundo et pulchrioris coloris," are the words of the Latin text.

3 "Blaise, bishop of Sebasta, in Cappadocia, in the second and third centuries," says the Biographical Dictionary, "suffered death under Diocletian, by decapitation, after being whipped and having his flesh torn with iron combs. . . . It is difficult to say how the invention (of wool combing) came to be attributed to him; but it had probably no better origin than the circumstance of his being tortured with the instruments used in the combing of wool."

4 It is the family of Hulagu, and the tribes who followed his standard from the north, whom our author always designates by the name of Oriental Tartars, to distinguish them from the descendants of Batu, who settled near the Wolga, on the north-western side of the Caspian, and extended their conquests towards Europe; whilst the former entered Persia from the Eastern quarter, by the way of Transoxiana and Khorasan.

CHAPTER IV

OF ARMENIA MAJOR, IN WHICH ARE THE CITIES OF ARZINGAN, ARGIRON, AND DARZIZ—OF THE CASTLE OF PAIPURTH—OF THE MOUNTAIN WHERE THE ARK OF NOAH RESTED—OF THE BOUNDARIES OF THE PROVINCE—AND OF A REMARKABLE FOUNTAIN OF OIL.

ARMENIA Major is an extensive province, at the entrance of which is a city named Arzingan,[1] where there is a manufacture of very fine cotton cloth called bombazines,[2] as well as of many other curious fabrics, which it would be tedious to enumerate. It possesses the handsomest and most excellent baths of warm water, issuing from the earth, that are anywhere to be found.[3] Its inhabitants are for the most part

[1] Arzengân, or, as written by the Arabians, who have not the Persian g, Arzenjân, is a city near the frontier of Rumiyah, but just within the limits of Armenia Major. "Cette ville," says D'Herbelot, "appartient plutôt à l'Arménie, et fut prise par les Mogols ou Tartares l'an 640 de l'Hégire, de J. C. 1242, après la défaite de Kaikhosrou, fils d'Aladin le Selgiucide, aussi bien que les villes de Sébaste et de Césarée." By an oriental geographer it is said to be, "Oppidum celeberrimum, elegans, amœnum, copiosum bonis rebus, incolisque: pertinens ad Armeniam: inter Rumæas provincias et Chalatam situm, haud procul Arzerroumo: esseque incolas ejus maixmam partem Armenios." Alberti Schultens Index Geographicus in Vitam Saladini. Josaphat Barbaro, a Venetian, who travelled into Persia, in the fifteenth century, speaks of Arsengan as a place that had formerly been of consequence, but was then mostly in ruins.

[2] The name of a species of cloth which I have here translated "bombazine," is in the Italian of Ramusio, "bochassini di bambagio," and in the Latin versions "buchiranus, buchyramis, and bucaramus." Its substance or texture is not clearly explained in our dictionaries. That of Cotgrave, printed in 1611, defines "boccasin," to be "a kind of fine buckeram, that hath a resemblance of taffata, and is much used for lining; also the stuffe callimanco." But this, it is evident, cannot apply to a manufacture of bombagio or cotton; and the Vocabolario della Crusca, as well as the Glossary of Du Cange, speak of "bucherame bianchissima," and "bucherame bambagino," and both of them quote our author for the use of the word. All the examples convey the idea of fine, white, and soft cotton cloth; the reverse of what is now called buckram. The early Latin text speaks of boccorame and bambace as two distinct things.

[3] Natural warm baths are found in many parts of Asia Minor, and particularly near Ancyra, the modern Angora or Anguri, which are still much frequented. Their situation is denoted by the word Thermæ, in Rennell's map explanatory of the Retreat of the Ten thousand. They are also spoken of at Teflis in Georgia; but of their existence at Arzengan I have not been able to find notice in the works of the Eastern geographers.

native Armenians, but under the dominion of the Tartars. In this province there are many cities, but Arzingan is the principal, and the seat of an archbishop; and the next in consequence are Argiron [1] and Darziz.[2] It is very extensive, and, in the summer season, the station of a part of the army of the Eastern Tartars, on account of the good pasture it affords for their cattle; but on the approach of winter they are obliged to change their quarters, the fall of snow being so very deep that the horses could not find subsistence, and for the sake of warmth and fodder they proceed to the southward. Within a castle named Paipurth,[3] which you meet with in going from Trebisond to Tauris, there is a rich mine of silver.[4] In the central part of Armenia stands an exceedingly large and high mountain, upon which, it is said, the ark of Noah rested, and for this reason it is termed the mountain of the ark.[5] The

[1] Argiron, or, in the Latin versions, Argyron, is a corruption of Arzerrûm, Erzerûm, or Arzen er-rûm, a distinctive name given to a city called Arzen, as being the last strong place, in that direction, belonging to the Greek empire. "Arzerrûm," says Abulfeda, "est extremus finis regionum Rumæorum ab oriente. In ejus orientali et septentrionali latere est fons Euphratis."

[2] Darziz, which in the Basle edition is Darzirim, in the older Latin, Arziu, and in the Italian epitomes, Arciri and Arziri, is the town now called Arjîs, situated on the border of the Lake Van, anciently named Arsissa palus. "Argish," says Macdonald Kinneir, "is a town containing six thousand inhabitants, situated on the north-west side of the lake, three days' journey from Van. There are four islands in the lake, on one of which is an Armenian monastery, and three hundred priests." Memoir of the Persian Empire, pp. 328, 329. These places, it may be observed, lay in our author's returning route, from Tauris to Trebisond.

[3] Paipurth, the Baiburt of D'Anville's and Rennell's maps, is situated among the mountains, in a northerly direction from Arzerrûm. As the word *purt* signifies a castle in the Armenian language, and as the Arabian geographers, from not having the letter *p* in their alphabet, are obliged to substitute the *b*, it is probable that the former is the more genuine orthography. This castle is particularly noted by Josaphat Barbaro, who says, "Partendo d'essa (Trabisonda) per andar à Thauris . . . il primo luogo notabile che si trova, è uno castello in piano in una valle d' ognitorno circondata da monti, nominato Baiburth, castel forte e murato. . . . Cinque giornate piu in la, si trova Arsengan. . . . Poi si ritrova un castello nominato Carpurth."—Viaggio in Persia, p. 48, ed. 1545, 12mo.

[4] Although this particular mine may have been exhausted, silver mines are known to exist in this part of Armenia.

[5] The mountain of Armenia (the Ararat of Scripture) upon which the ark is believed by the Christians of that country to have rested, stands not far from the city of Erivan or Irwân. The Mahometans, however, assign to it a different situation. "L'opinion commune des Orientaux," says D'Herbelot, "est que l'arche de Noë s'arrêta sur la montagne de Gioudi, qui est une des croupes du mont Taurus ou Gordiæus en Arménie, et cette tradition est autorisé en ce pays-là par plusieurs histoires qui approchent fort de la fable." "Joudi," says Ibn Haukal, "is a mountain near Nisibin. It is said that the ark of Noah (to whom

circuit of its base cannot be compassed in less than two days The ascent is impracticable on account of the snow towards the summit, which never melts, but goes on increasing by each successive fall. In the lower region, however, near the plain, the melting of the snow fertilizes the ground, and occasions such an abundant vegetation, that all the cattle which collect there in summer from the neighbouring country, meet with a never-failing supply.[1] Bordering upon Armenia, to the south-west, are the districts of Mosul and Maredin, which shall be described hereafter, and many others too numerous to particularize. To the north lies Zorzania, near the confines of which there is a fountain of oil which discharges so great a quantity as to furnish loading for many camels.[2] The use made of it is not for the purpose of food, but as an unguent for the cure of cutaneous distempers in men and cattle, as well as other complaints; and it is also good for burning. In the neighbouring country no other is used in their lamps, and people come from distant parts to procure it.

be peace,) rested on the summit of this mountain." Ouseley's translation, p. 60. Major Rennell observes, that Jeudi is the part of the Carduchian mountains opposite to the Jezirat ibn Omar, and that the dervishes keep a light burning there, in honour of Noah and his ark.

[1] This fertility of the country in the vicinity of the mountains, is noticed by Moses Chorenensis, who says, " Habet autem Araratia montes camposque, atque omnem fœcunditatem."—Geographia, p. 361.

[2] Springs of petroleum or earth (properly, rock) oil, are found in many parts of the world. The spring or fountain here spoken of is that of Baku in Shirvan, on the border of the Caspian. " Near to this place," says John Cartwright, in what are termed the Preacher's Travels, " is a very strange and wonderful fountain under ground, out of which there springeth and issueth a marvellous quantity of black oyl, which serveth all parts of Persia to burn in their houses; and they usually carry it all over the country upon kine and asses, whereof you shall oftentimes meet three or four hundred in company."—Oxford Coll. of Voyages, vol. i. (vii.) p. 731. Strahlenberg speaks of this as a spring of white naphtha, which he distinguishes from the black sort of bitumen; but the most satisfactory account of both white and black naphtha in this district is given by Kæmpfer, in his Amœnitates Exoticæ, p. 274—281.

CHAPTER V

OF THE PROVINCE OF ZORZANIA AND ITS BOUNDARIES—OF THE PASS WHERE ALEXANDER THE GREAT CONSTRUCTED THE GATE OF IRON—AND OF THE MIRACULOUS CIRCUMSTANCES ATTENDING A FOUNTAIN AT TEFLIS.

IN Zorzania[1] the king is usually styled David Melik, which in our language signifies David the king.[2] One part of the country is subject to the Tartars, and the other part, in consequence of the strength of its fortresses, has remained in the possession of its native princes. It is situated between two seas, of which that on the northern (western) side is called the Greater sea (Euxine), and the other, on the eastern side, is called the sea of Abakù (Caspian).[3] This latter is in circuit two thousand eight hundred miles, and partakes of the nature of a lake, not communicating with any other sea. It has several islands, with handsome towns and castles, some of which are inhabited by people who fled before the grand Tartar, when he laid waste the kingdom or province of Persia,[4] and took shelter in these islands or in the fastnesses of the mountains, where they hoped to find security. Some of the islands are uncultivated. This sea produces abundance of fish, particularly sturgeon and salmon at the mouths of the rivers,

[1] By Zorzania is meant the kingdom of Georgia, bordering on Armenia, and of which Teflis was the capital. The substitution of the *z* for the soft *g*, belonged to the old Venetian dialect, in which the original of our author's work is understood to have been written, and the orthography has been preserved in some of the Latin, as well as in the vulgar Italian versions. The early Latin text reads Georgia.

[2] The name of David or Davit frequently occurs in the list of kings who have reigned in Georgia, and their predilection for it is traced to a very remote source. It is not surprising, therefore, that a traveller should suppose the names of the Georgian kings to have been, invariably, David. The title of Melik shows that our author's information was derived from Arabs or Moghuls, who would naturally substitute it for the native title of Meppe.

[3] The Caspian, which is generally termed by oriental writers the sea of Khozar, was also called by the Persians the sea of Baku, and by this name (Mar di Bachau) it appears in the maps to an edition of Ptolemy, printed at Venice in 1562. It derives the appellation from the celebrated city and port of Baku, on its south-western coast.

[4] This refers to the conquest and devastation of Persia by the armies of Jengiz-khan, about the year 1221. The islands, to which it is not improbable a number of the wretched inhabitants fled for security, are at present uninhabited, or frequented only by fishermen.

as well as others of a large sort.[1] The general wood of the country is the box-tree.[2] I was told that in ancient times the kings of the country were born with the mark of an eagle on the right shoulder.[3] The people are well made, bold sailors, expert archers, and fair combatants in battle. They are Christians, observing the ritual of the Greek Church, and wear their hair short, in the manner of the Western clergy. This is the province into which, when Alexander the Great attempted to advance northwards, he was unable to penetrate, by reason of the narrowness and difficulty of a certain pass, which on one side is washed by the sea, and is confined on the other by high mountains and woods, for the length of four miles; so that a very few men were capable of defending it against the whole world. Disappointed in this attempt, Alexander caused a great wall to be constructed at the entrance of the pass, and fortified it with towers, in order to restrain those who dwelt beyond it from giving him molestation. From its uncommon strength the pass obtained the name of the Gate of Iron,[4] and Alexander is commonly said to have enclosed the

[1] The fishery of the Caspian, especially about the mouths of the Wolga, has at all periods been important. "Among the great variety of fish with which this river abounds," says P. H. Bruce, "the sturgeon is none of the least considerable, whose eggs afford what the Russians call ikari, and we caviar: the beluga, or white fish, deserves also to be mentioned; they are from five to six yards long, and thick in proportion. Besides these it yields also the osotrin, another very large fish, very fat and delicious: this river also abounds with salmon, sterlitz, a most delicious fish, and innumerable other sorts too tedious to mention."—Memoirs, p. 236. Strahlenberg also notices the beluja as "the largest eatable river-fish in the world, having seen one fifty-six feet in length, and eighteen in girth."—P. 337.

[2] By modern travellers the box-tree is merely enumerated amongst the vegetable productions of the country, without any notice of its prevalence; but by Ambrogio Cantareno, who travelled in the fifteenth century, it is more particularly distinguished. "Era in detta pianura," he says, in speaking of Mingrelia, "di molti arbori in modo di bussi, ma molto maggiori."—P. 65, 12mo.

[3] By this pretended tradition it may be understood that they were, or affected to be thought, a branch of the imperial family of Constantinople, who bore the Roman eagle amongst their insignia.

[4] This is the celebrated pass between the foot of Mount Caucasus and the Caspian sea, where stands the small but strong city of Derbend, called by the Arabs, Bab-al-abuab, or the "Gate of gates," by the Turks, Demir-capi, or the "Gate of iron," and by the Persians, Derbend, or the "Barrier," between Georgia and the Persian province of Shirvan. "The natives in general are of opinion," says P. H. Bruce, "that the city of Derbent was built by Alexander the Great, and that the long wall that reached to the Euxine, was built by his order, to prevent the incursions of the Scythians into Persia."—Memoirs, p. 284. The wall is said to have been repaired by Yezdegerd II. of the Sassanian dynasty, who reigned about the middle of the fifth century, and again by Nushirvan, of the same family, who died in 579.

Tartars between two mountains. It is not correct, however, to call the people Tartars, which in those days they were not, but of a race named Cumani,[1] with a mixture of other nations. In this province there are many towns and castles; the necessaries of life are in abundance; the country produces a great quantity of silk, and a manufacture is carried on of silk interwoven with gold.[2] Here are found vultures of a large size, of a species named *avigi*.[3] The inhabitants in general gain their livelihood by trade and manual labour. The mountainous nature of the country, with its narrow and strong defiles, have prevented the Tartars from effecting the entire conquest of it. At a convent of monks dedicated to Saint Lunardo, the following miraculous circumstances are said to take place. In a salt-water lake, four days' journey in circuit, upon the border of which the church is situated, the fish never make their appearance until the first day of Lent, and from that time to Easter-eve they are found in vast abundance; but on Easter-day they are no longer to be seen, nor during the remainder of the year. It is called the lake of Geluchalat.[4] Into the before-

[1] The notices we have, respecting the people named Comani or Comanians, are in general obscure and vague. It appears, however, that in the thirteenth century they were the inhabitants of the countries lying on the north-western side of the Caspian, and extending from the Wolga towards the Euxine, who were afterwards subdued and supplanted by the Kapchak Tartars. "The Comans," says Gibbon, "were a Tartar or Turkman horde which encamped in the XIth and XIIth centuries on the verge of Moldavia. The greater part were pagans, but some were Mahometans, and the whole horde was converted to Christianity (A.D. 1370) by Lewis, king of Hungary."

[2] Some of the provinces of Georgia, as well as of Armenia and the adjoining parts of Persia, have in all ages been famous for the culture of the silk-worm and commerce in silk.

[3] I know not what species of vulture is here meant, nor can we be certain of the correctness of the orthography of the word *avigi*. That the country is noted for birds of this class, appears from the writings of several travellers. When Chardin arrived in Mingrelia he found it necessary to deceive the Turks by giving out that he was a merchant, whose object in visiting the country was to procure birds of prey for the European market.

[4] Within the proper boundaries of Georgia I am unable to identify this large salt-water lake of Gelu-chalat. Upon an island in that near Erivan, which D'Anville names Gheuk-sha ou Eau bleu, stands a very ancient monastery, which Chardin tells us was founded six hundred years before his time, or in the eleventh century, and must therefore have existed in our author's days; but on the other hand, its waters are described as being fresh and sweet, and it is separated from Georgia by a ridge of mountains. There is more reason for supposing it to be the lake now called Van or Wan, and formerly Arjish, although this lies still further within the boundary of Armenia. In its neighbourhood was situated a town of some celebrity, named Khalât and Akhlât. Its circumference is described by Abulfeda as being of four days' journey, and he says it is noted for a peculiar species of fish called tharnag, said to resemble the herring.

mentioned sea of Abakù, which is encompassed with mountains, the great rivers Herdil,[1] Geihon, Kur, and Araz, with many others, disembogue. The Genoese merchants have recently begun to navigate it, and they bring from thence the kind of silk called *ghellie.*[2] In this province there is a handsome city named Teflis,[3] around which are suburbs and many fortified posts. It is inhabited by Armenian and Georgian Christians, as well as by some Mahometans and Jews;[4] but these last are in no great numbers. Manufactures of silks and of many other articles are carried on there. Its inhabitants are subjects of the great king of the Tartars.[5] Although we speak only of a few of the principal cities in each province, it is to be understood that there are many others, which it is unnecessary to particularise, unless they happened to contain something remarkable; but should the occasion present itself, these will be hereafter described. Having spoken of the countries bordering on Armenia to the north, we shall now mention those which lie to the south and to the east.

[1] By the Arabians and Turks the name of Etol is given to the Wolga, and it is here corrupted to Herdil. This river, according to Ibn Haukal, comes from the countries of Rûss and Bulgar, and at the season when its waters are collected, it is said to be greater than the river Jihun, rushing into the sea with such a body that it seems to conquer the waters of the Caspian. See Ouseley's translation, pp. 185—187. The names of Jihon or Oxus, Kur or Cyrus, and Araz or Araxes, do not require any particular remark.

[2] The province of Ghilan (called also al-Ghil), on the Caspian, being famous for its trade in silk, we can scarcely doubt that this word *ghellie* or *ghilli* was a name given to the article on that account; as florentine, a species of silk, has (or may be presumed to have) its appellation from Florence. The red silk of Ghilan is mentioned by Niebuhr; and Elphinstone, speaking of the trade of Caubul with Persia, says, "The imports are raw silk of Gheelaun and Resht, silken stuffs made at Yezd and Kashaun."—P. 295.

[3] For a particular account of the city of Teflis, the capital of Georgia see Chardin, p. 220, fo. with the Plate. Our author's route from Tabriz to Trebisond did not carry him to this city, and there is reason to conclude that what little he says of it is from the report of others.

[4] In Chardin's time this city contained fourteen churches, of which six belonged to the Georgian, and eight to the Armenian Christians. Being then subject to the Persian government, frequent attempts were made by the Mahometans to erect mosques, but without success; the populace never failing to demolish the work.

[5] By the king of the (Moghul) Tartars must here be understood the descendant of Hulagu, who ruled over Persia and the neighbouring countries; not the grand khan.

CHAPTER VI

OF THE PROVINCE OF MOSUL AND ITS DIFFERENT INHABITANTS—OF THE PEOPLE NAMED KURDS—AND OF THE TRADE OF THIS COUNTRY.

MOSUL is a large province[1] inhabited by various descriptions of people, one class of whom pay reverence to Mahomet, and are called Arabians.[2] The others profess the Christian faith, but not according to the canons of the church, which they depart from in many instances, and are denominated Nestorians, Jacobites, and Armenians. They have a patriarch whom they call Jacolit,[3] and by him archbishops, bishops, and abbots are consecrated and sent to all parts of India, to Cairo, to Baldach (Baghdad), and to all places inhabited by Christains; in the same manner as by the pope of the Romish church. All those cloths of gold and of silk which we call muslins[4] are of

[1] The city of Mosul, or according to the Arabic pronunciation, Mausil, formerly the capital of Mesopotamia and now of the Turkish pashalik bearing its own name, stands upon the right or western bank of the Tigris, opposite to the site of the ancient Nineveh, with which it is connected by a bridge of boats. It is described by Abulfeda and all the oriental geographers as one of the most distinguished cities under the Mahometan government. Although our author terms it a province, he may be thought to describe it rather as a city; but the district itself is called by the Arabians Diyar Mausil as well as Diyar al-Jezirah.

[2] The bulk of the population is at this day Arabian, and that language is the general medium of communication amongst the inhabitants, whatever their national origin or religion may be.

[3] This word, in some editions written Jacolich, presents a striking example of the degree of corruption our author's text has unfortunately experienced, being no other than the title of Catholicos, by which the patriarchs of the Greek church in Georgia and Armenia are distinguished. The extent of their jurisdiction I am unable to ascertain, but suppose it embraces all the communities of the same sect, wherever situated. The Catholicos or Patriarch of Georgia, who was at the same time brother to the Mahometan prince of the country, is mentioned by Chardin.

[4] The origin of the word "muslin," in French, "mousseline," and in Italian (from whence the others are borrowed), "mussolo e mussolino, sorta di tela bambagina, cosi detta dal nome del paese dove per lo più si fabbrica," is here satisfactorily pointed out; but our author, if his editors have not misrepresented his meaning, includes under that denomination articles of a nature very different from that to which we apply the name. It is not, however, improbable that the city of Mosul, being at this time one of the greatest entrepôts of eastern commerce, and also itself a place of considerable manufacture, may have given the appellation to various productions of the loom conveyed from thence to the Mediterranean, although in later days the word *mussolino* has been exclusively applied to the well-known Indian fabric or its imitations. When Ives, in the account of his journey, tells us that "this city's manufacture is mussolen

the manufacture of Mosul, and all the great merchants termed Mossulini, who convey spices and drugs, in large quantities, from one country to another, are from this province. In the mountainous parts there is a race of people named Kurds, some of whom are Christians of the Nestorian and Jacobite sects, and others Mahometans. They are all an unprincipled people, whose occupation it is to rob the merchants.[1] In the vicinity of this province there are places named Mus and Maredin,[2] where cotton is produced in great abundance, of which they prepare the cloths called boccasini, and many other fabrics. The inhabitants are manufacturers and traders, and are all subjects of the king of the Tartars. We shall now speak of the city of Baldach.

CHAPTER VII

OF THE GREAT CITY OF BALDACH OR BAGADET, ANCIENTLY CALLED BABYLON—OF THE NAVIGATION FROM THENCE TO BALSARA, SITUATED IN WHAT IS TERMED THE SEA OF INDIA, BUT PROPERLY THE PERSIAN GULF—AND OF THE VARIOUS SCIENCES STUDIED IN THAT CITY.

BALDACH is a large city, heretofore the residence of the khalif[3] or pontiff of all the Saracens, as the pope is of all Christians.

(a cotton cloth), which they make very strong and pretty fine, and sell for the European and other markets," it is evident that he does not describe a cloth of the delicate or flimsy texture that we call muslin, but rather the kind that with us has acquired the name of calico, from the city of Calicut in the East Indies.

[1] Kurdistan, which formed the northern part of the ancient Assyria, is a mountainous region to the eastward of the Tigris, and immediately at the back of Mosul, Nisibin, and Maredin. The inhabitants for the most part speak a corrupt dialect of Persian, but in their habits and manners resemble the Bedouin Arabs, and like them make a practice of robbing the caravans when not adequately protected. Cartwright terms them "a most thievish people;" and the accounts of all subsequent travellers agree in describing them as systematical plunderers: a state of society that results from their local situation, being that of a mountainous tract which must necessarily be traversed in passing from one rich country to another. The principal articles of commerce in this country appear to be gall-nuts, cotton, and a species of silk called *kas* or *kès*, described by Niebuhr as growing on trees.—Voyage, tom. ii. p. 268.

[2] For an account of Maredin, a city of Mesopotamia, in the district of Diyar-Rabiah, see the Voyage par Niebuhr. He speaks of its manufactures of flax and cotton. Mush is a town on the borders of Kurdistan and Armenia, between Bedlis and the Euphrates in the upper part of its course.

[3] The city of Baghdâd was built by Abu Jâfar al-Mansur, second khalif

A great river flows through the midst of it,[1] by means of which the merchants transport their goods to and from the sea of India; the distance being computed at seventeen days' navigation, in consequence of the windings of its course. Those who undertake the voyage, after leaving the river, touch at a place named Kisi,[2] from whence they proceed to sea: but previously to their reaching this anchorage they pass a city named Balsara,[3] in the vicinity of which are groves of palm-trees producing the best dates in the world. In Baldach there is a manufacture of silks wrought with gold, and also of damasks, as well as of velvets ornamented with the figures of birds and beasts.[4] Almost all the pearls brought to Europe from India have undergone the process of boring, at this place. The Mahometan law is here regularly studied, as are also magic, physics, astronomy, geomancy, and physiognomy. It is the noblest and most extensive city to be found in this part of the world.

of the Abbassite dynasty, about the year 765, and continued to be the residence of his successors until the death of the last khalif of that race, in the year 1258, when it fell under the dominion of the Moghuls.

[1] This river is the Tigris, named Dijleh by the Arabs, which falls into the Euphrates, when their united streams acquire the appellation of Shat-al-arab, and discharge themselves into the Persian Gulf. The modern city of Baghdad stands on the eastern bank, and is connected with the suburb on the western side of the river by a bridge of boats; but on that side there are also found the ruins of buildings that belonged to the ancient city or seat of the khalifs; and our author is therefore correct in describing it as divided by the river in his time. Abulfeda speaks of it as occupying both banks of the Tigris.

[2] Kisi, or Chisi in the Italian orthography, is a small island on the eastern side of the Gulf of Persia, named Kîs or Kês, to which the trade of Siraf, a port on the neighbouring continent, much celebrated by eastern geographers, was transferred; in consequence, as it may be presumed, of wars in that quarter, and of injuries sustained by the merchants. The exact situation of the latter is not now pointed out by any remains.

[3] Balsara, more commonly written Balsora, but properly Basrah, is a city of great commercial importance, situated on the south-west side of the Shat-al-arab, about half-way between the point where the Euphrates and Tigris unite their streams, and the Persian Gulf. It lies, consequently, in the way (as our author remarks) of those who navigate from Baghdad to the island of Kîs.

[4] It may be suspected that instead of "velluti" (velvets), we should here read "tappeti" (carpets), for the manufacture of which Persia has always been celebrated. With respect to the figures of animals, the Mahometans of the Shiah sect have never been strict, as those of the Sunni are known to be, in prohibiting the representation of them in their ornamental works.

CHAPTER VIII

CONCERNING THE CAPTURE AND DEATH OF THE KHALIF OF BALDACH, AND THE MIRACULOUS REMOVAL OF A MOUNTAIN.

THE above-mentioned khalif, who is understood to have amassed greater treasures than had ever been possessed by any other sovereign, perished miserably under the following circumstances.[1] At the period when the Tartar princes began to extend their dominion, there were amongst them four brothers, of whom the eldest, named Mangu, reigned in the royal seat of the family. Having subdued the country of Cathay, and other districts in that quarter, they were not satisfied, but coveting further territory, they conceived the idea of universal empire, and proposed that they should divide the world amongst them. With this object in view, it was agreed that one of them should proceed to the east, that another should make conquests in the south, and that the other two should direct their operations against the remaining quarters. The southern portion fell to the lot of Ulaù, who assembled a vast army, and having subdued the provinces through which his route lay, proceeded in the year 1255 to the attack of this city of Baldach.[2] Being aware, however, of its great strength and the prodigious number of its inhabitants, he trusted rather to stratagem than to force for its reduction, and in order to deceive the enemy with regard to the number of his troops, which consisted of a hundred thousand horse, besides foot soldiers, he posted one division of his army on the one side, another division on the other side of the approach to the city, in such a manner as to be concealed by a

[1] Mostasem Billah, the last of the Abbassite khalifs of Baghdad, began to reign in 1242, and was put to death in 1258. His character was that of a weak, indolent, voluptuous, and at the same time avaricious prince, who neglected the duties of his government, and committed them to the hands of a wicked minister, by whom he was at length betrayed to his mortal enemy.

[2] This date is given in the early Latin text. Marsden has 1250; but he observes that according to the most accurate oriental historians, it was not until the year 1255 that Hulagu (whom Haiton calls Haolanus or Haolo, P. Gaubil Holayou, and our author Ula-u) crossed the Oxus. In 1256 he required Mostasem to assist him in the reduction of the Ismaelians, and in 1258 obtained possession of Baghdad. P. Gaubil, upon the authority of the Chinese annals, places this event in 1257.

wood, and placing himself at the head of the third, advanced boldly to within a short distance of the gate. The khalif made light of a force apparently so inconsiderable, and confident in the efficacy of the usual Mahometan ejaculation, thought of nothing less than its entire destruction, and for that purpose marched out of the city with his guards; but as soon as Ulaù perceived his approach, he feigned to retreat before him, until by this means he had drawn him beyond the wood where the other divisions were posted. By the closing of these from both sides, the army of the khalif was surrounded and broken, himself was made prisoner, and the city surrendered to the conquerer. Upon entering it, Ulaù discovered, to his great astonishment, a tower filled with gold. He called the khalif before him, and after reproaching him with his avarice, that prevented him from employing his treasures in the formation of an army for the defence of his capital against the powerful invasion with which it had long been threatened, gave orders for his being shut up in this same tower, without sustenance; and there, in the midst of his wealth, be soon finished a miserable existence.

I judge that our Lord Jesus Christ herein thought proper to avenge the wrongs of his faithful Christians, so abhorred by this khalif. From the time of his accession in 1225, his daily thoughts were employed on the means of converting to his religion those who resided within his dominions, or, upon their refusal, in forming pretences for putting them to death. Consulting with his learned men for this purpose, they discovered a passage in the Gospel where it is said: "If ye have faith as a grain of mustard seed, ye shall say unto this mountain, Remove hence to yonder place, and it shall remove," (upon prayer to that effect addressed to the Divine Majesty); and being rejoiced at the discovery, persuaded as he was that the thing was utterly impossible, he gave orders for assembling all the Nestorian and Jacobite Christians who dwelt in Baghdad, and who were very numerous. To these the question was propounded, whether they believed all that is asserted in the text of their Gospel to be true, or not. They made answer that it was true. "Then," said the khalif, "if it be true, let us see which of you will give the proof of his faith; for certainly if there is not to be found one amongst you who possesses even so small a portion of faith in his Lord, as to be equal to a grain of mustard, I shall be justified in regarding you, henceforth, as a wicked, reprobate, and faithless people. I allow you therefore ten days, before the expiration of which you must either, through the power of Him whom you worship, remove the mountain now before you, or embrace the law of our prophet; in either of which cases you will be safe; but otherwise you must all expect to suffer the most cruel deaths." The Christians, acquainted as they were with his merciless disposition, as well as his eagerness to despoil them of their property, upon hearing these words, trembled for their lives; but nevertheless, having confidence in their Redeemer, that He would deliver them from their peril, they held an assembly and deliberated on the course they ought to take. None other presented itself than that of imploring the Divine Being to grant them the aid of his mercy. To obtain this, every individual, great and small, prostrated himself night and day upon the earth, shedding tears profusely, and attending to no other occupation than that of prayer to the Lord. When they had thus persevered during eight days, a divine revelation came at length, in a dream, to a bishop of exemplary life, directing him to proceed in search of a certain shoemaker (whose name is not known) having only one eye, whom he should summon to the mountain, as a person capable of effecting its removal, through the divine grace. Having found the shoemaker and made him acquainted with the revelation, he replied that he did not feel himself worthy of the undertaking, his merits not being such as to entitle him to the reward of such abundant grace. Importuned, however, by the poor terrified Christians, he at length assented. It should be understood that he was a man of strict morals and pious conversation, having his mind pure and faithful to his God, regularly attending the celebration of the mass and other divine offices, fervent in works of charity, and rigid in the observance of fasts. It once happened to him, that a handsome young woman who came to his shop in order to be fitted with a pair of slippers, in presenting her foot, accidentally exposed a part of her leg, the beauty of which excited in him a momentary concupiscence; but recollecting himself, he presently dismissed her, and calling to mind the words of the Gospel, where it is said, "If thine eye offend thee, pluck it out and cast it from thee; for it is better to enter the kingdom of God with one eye, than having two eyes, to be cast into hell fire," he immediately, with an instrument of his trade, scooped out his right eye; evincing by that act, beyond all doubt, the excellence of his faith.

The appointed day being arrived, divine service was performed at an early hour, and a solemn procession was made to the plain where the mountain stood, the holy cross being borne in front. The khalif likewise, in the conviction of its proving a vain ceremony on the part of the Christians, chose to be present, accompanied by a number of his guards, for the purposing of destroying them in the event of failure. Here the pious artisan, kneeling before the cross, and lifting up his hands to heaven, humbly besought his Creator that he would compassionately look down upon earth, and for the glory and excellence of his name, as well as for the support and confirmation of the Christian faith, would lend assistance to his people in the accomplishment of the task imposed upon them, and thus manifest his power to the revilers of his law. Having concluded his prayer, he cried with a loud voice: "In the name of the Father, Son, and Holy Ghost, I command thee, O mountain, to remove thyself!" Upon these words being uttered, the mountain moved, and the earth at the same time trembled in a wonderful and alarming manner. The khalif and all those by whom he was surrounded, were struck with terror, and remained in a state of stupefaction. Many of the latter became Christians, and even the khalif secretly embraced Christianity, always wearing a cross concealed under his garment, which after his death was found upon him; and on this account it was that they did not entomb him in the shrine of his predecessors. In commemoration of this singular grace bestowed upon them by God, all the Christians, Nestorians, and Jacobites, from that time forth have continued to celebrate in a solemn manner the return of the day on which the miracle took place; keeping a fast also on the vigil.[1]

CHAPTER IX

OF THE NOBLE CITY OF TAURIS, IN IRAK, AND OF ITS COMMERCIAL AND OTHER INHABITANTS.

TAURIS is a large and very noble city belonging to the province of Irak, which contains many other cities and fortified

[1] The pretended miracle is here more minutely detailed than in other versions, and the Latin text states it to have taken place at Tauris, and not at Baghdad, although that would have been inconsistent with the presence of the khalif. [The early Latin text says it occurred in 1275, "inter Baldach et Mesul;" and the French text agrees with it.]

places, but this is the most eminent and most populous.[1] The inhabitants support themselves principally by commerce and manufactures, which latter consist of various kinds of silk, some of them interwoven with gold, and of high price. It is so advantageously situated for trade, that merchants from India, from Baldach, Mosul, Cremessor,[2] as well as from different parts of Europe, resort thither to purchase and to sell a number of articles. Precious stones and pearls in abundance may be procured at this place.[3] The merchants concerned in foreign commerce acquire considerable wealth, but the inhabitants in general are poor. They consist of a mixture of various nations and sects, Nestorians, Armenians, Jacobites, Georgians, Persians, and the followers of Mahomet, who form the bulk of the population, and are those properly called Taurisians.[4] Each description of people have their peculiar language. The city is surrounded with delightful gardens, producing the finest fruits.[5] The Mahometan inhabitants are treacherous and unprincipled. According to their doctrine, whatever is stolen or plundered from others of a different faith, is properly taken, and the theft is no crime; whilst those who suffer death or injury by the hands of Christians, are considered as martyrs. If, therefore, they were not pro-

[1] The city of Tauris, by the Persians and other orientals named Tabriz, is situated in the province of Aderbijan, which borders on that of Al-Jebal, or the Persian Irak, and formed with it the ancient kingdom of Media. It has been, at all periods, a place of great importance. Upon the conquest of Persia by the Moghuls, about the year 1255, it became the principal residence of Hulagu and his descendants, until the founding of Sultaniyah, in the beginning of the fourteenth century.

[2] Cremessor, otherwise written Cremosor, Cormosa, Cremos, and Cormos, is no other than the famous city of Ormuz or Hormuz, by the ancients called Harmuza, at the entrance of the Persian Gulf; of which there will be occasion to speak more particularly hereafter. Baldach, we have already seen, is the city of Baghdad.

[3] Chardin mentions a particular bazaar ("le plus beau de tous") for the sale of jewels, and other articles of extraordinary value. The pearls, both from the fisheries of Ceylon, and from Bahrein in the Gulf of Persia, appear to have been conveyed in the first instance to Baghdad, where they were polished and bored, and from thence to the other markets of Asia and Europe, and particularly to Constantinople.

[4] These Persians, as distinguished from the Mahometans, must have been the original inhabitants of Farsistan, who retained the ancient religion of Zerdusht, or Zoroaster, the characteristic of which was the worship of fire, and whom (in their modern state of expatriation) we term Parsis. They constitute at this time the most wealthy, as well as the most ingenious class of native inhabitants, living under the English protection at Bombay.

[5] Abulfeda praises its gardens; and the abundance and variety of its fruits are noticed by Chardin.

hibited and restrained by the powers who now govern them,[1] they would commit many outrages. These principles are common to all the Saracens. When they are at the point of death, their priest attends upon them, and asks whether they believe that Mahomet was the true apostle of God. If their answer be that they do believe, their salvation is assured to them; and in consequence of this facility of absolution, which gives free scope to the perpetration of everything flagitious, they have succeeded in converting to their faith a great proportion of the Tartars, who consider it as relieving them from restraint in the commission of crimes. From Tauris to Persia is twelve days' journey.[2]

CHAPTER X

OF THE MONASTERY OF SAINT BARSAMO, IN THE NEIGHBOURHOOD OF TAURIS.

Not far from Tauris is a monastery that takes its name from the holy saint Barsamo,[3] and is eminent for devotion. There is here an abbot and many monks, who resemble the order of Carmelites in the fashion of their dress. That they may not lead a life of idleness, they employ themselves continually in the weaving of woollen girdles, which they place upon the altar of their saint during the celebration of divine service, and when they make the circuit of the provinces, soliciting alms (in the same manner as do the brethren of the order of the Holy Ghost), they present these girdles to their friends and to persons of distinction; being esteemed good for rheumatic pains, on which account they are devoutly sought for by all ranks.

[1] That is, by their new lords, the Moghul Tartars.

[2] This must be understood of Persia Proper, Fars or Farsistan, of which Persepolis was the ancient capital, as Shiraz is the modern; but he probably means the distance from Tauris to Kasbin, which he speaks of in the next chapter as the first city upon entering Persia.

[3] This saint is no doubt St. Barsimæus, bishop of Edessa in the second century.

CHAPTER XI

OF THE PROVINCE OF PERSIA.

PERSIA was anciently a large and noble province, but it is now a great part destroyed by the Tartars. In Persia there is a city which is called Saba, from whence were the three magi who came to adore Christ in Bethlehem; and the three are buried in that city in a fair sepulchre, and they are all three entire with their beards and hair. One was called Baldasar, the second Gaspar, and the third Melchior. Marco inquired often in that city concerning the three magi, and nobody could tell him anything about them, except that the three magi were buried there in ancient times. After three days' journey you come to a castle which is called Palasata, which means the castle of the fire-worshippers; and it is true that the inhabitants of that castle worship fire, and this is given as the reason. The men of that castle say, that anciently three kings of that country went to adore a certain king who was newly born, and carried with them three offerings, namely, gold, frankincense, and myrrh: gold, that they might know if he were an earthly king; frankincense, that they might know if he were God; and myrrh, that they might know if he were a mortal man. When these magi were presented to Christ, the youngest of the three adored him first, and it appeared to him that Christ was of his stature and age. The middle one came next, and then the eldest, and to each he seemed to be of their own stature and age. Having compared their observations together, they agreed to go all to worship at once, and then he appeared to them all of his true age. When they went away, the infant gave them a closed box, which they carried with them for several days, and then becoming curious to see what he had given them, they opened the box and found in it a stone, which was intended for a sign that they should remain as firm as a stone in the faith they had received from him. When, however, they saw the stone, they marvelled, and thinking themselves deluded, they threw the stone into a certain pit, and instantly fire burst forth in the pit. When they saw this, they repented bitterly of what they had done, and taking some of the fire with them they carried it home. And having placed it in one of their churches, they keep it continually burning, and adore that fire as a god, and make all their sacrifices with it; and if it happen to be extinguished, they go for more to the original fire in the pit where they threw the stone, which is never extinguished, and they take of none other fire. And therefore the people of that country worship fire. Marco was told all this by the people of the country; and it is true that one of those kings was of Saba, and the second was of Dyava, and the third was of the castle.[1] Now we will treat of the people of Persia and of their customs.

CHAPTER XII

OF THE NAMES OF THE EIGHT KINGDOMS THAT CONSTITUTE THE PROVINCE OF PERSIA, AND OF THE BREED OF HORSES AND OF ASSES FOUND THEREIN.

In Persia, which is a large province, there are eight kingdoms,[2] the names of which are as follows:—The first which you meet with upon entering the country is Kasibin;[3] the second,

[1] This story of the magi is no doubt of Eastern origin, as it does not coincide with the Western legends. In other manuscripts the name is written Kalasata-perinsta. The idea of a well ignited by celestial fire is obviously founded on the existence of burning wells or caverns in various parts of Asia, particularly at Baku, near the Caspian, and on the coast of Karamania, seen by Capt. Beaufort; but to the Persian scholar the name of the place will present the strongest criterion of veracity, as he must perceive that the words Kala sata-perinsta are intended for Kalàt perestân, or perhaps Kalah âtish perestân, literally, the "Castle of the fire-worshippers." The name of Saba, which is certainly not to be discovered among the towns of Persia, may be thought to have a reference to the doctrines of Sabaïsm, so nearly connected with those of the Guebers.

[2] In the ordinary use of these terms, a kingdom is understood to consist of provinces; but upon the partition of the immense empire inherited by the descendants of Jengiz-khan, the province assigned (as a fief) to each of his sons or grandsons comprehend what were, before his conquests, independent kingdoms.

[3] Upon entering Persian Irak from the side of Tauris, the first great city (Sultaniyah not being then built) is Kasbin, or more properly Kazvin, which has at different periods of its history been a royal residence. In the enumeration of these eight kingdoms, our author sometimes gives the name of the capital, as in this instance, and sometimes that of the province or district, as in those which immediately follow. He seems to have written down or dictated the names as they occurred to his recollection, without system, and with little regard to arrangement.

lying towards the south (west), is Kurdistan;[1] the third is Lor;[2] towards the north, the fourth is Suolistan;[3] the fifth, Spaan;[4] the sixth, Siras;[5] the seventh, Soncara;[6] the eighth, Timocain,[7] which is at the extremity of Persia. All these kingdoms lie to the south, excepting Timocain, and this is to

[1] We should not have expected to find Kurdistan, which belonged to the ancient Assyria, stated as one of the component parts of Persia, although many parts of it have at times been brought under subjection to that monarchy; nor, if included, can it be said to lie to the south. It may, indeed, be conjectured that Khuristan (often written Khuzistan), the ancient Susiana, situated at the head of the Persian gulf, and consequently south from Kazvin, and not Kurdistan, which lies to the west, is the district intended. "Churestan, ait Ol Muschtarek, etiam Chuzestan appellatur. Est ampla provincia, multas urbes tenens, inter Al Basram et Persiam."—Abulfedæ Geographia.

[2] If the former place be meant for Khuristan, Lôr or Lûr may with propriety be said to lie to the north of it, although with respect to Kazvin, and Persia in general, it is a southern province. "Il ne faut pas confondre," says D'Herbelot, "le pays de Lor avec celui de Lar ou Laristan, qui s'étend le long du gulfe Persique. Celui de Lor ou Lour est montagneux, et dépendoit autrefois de la province nommée Kouzistan, qui est l'ancienne Susiane."—Biblioth. Orient.

[3] Of Suolistan it would be difficult to form any conjecture; but finding the name, in other versions, written Cielstam, Ciliestam, and in the early Italian epitome, Ciestan, I have little doubt of its being intended for Sejestan, also written Siyestan, a province which lies in the eastern quarter of Persia.

[4] The city of Spaan, Spahan, or Ispahan, by the Arabians called Isfahan, situated in the southern part of Persian Irak, is well known as the magnificent capital of the kings of the Sefi family, which, especially during the reign of Shah Abbas II., exceeded in splendour, as well as extent, most Asiatic cities. It fell under the dominion of the Moghuls in 1221, and was taken, plundered, and nearly destroyed by Tamerlane in 1387.

[5] Shiraz, the capital of Fars or Persia proper, and, at some periods, of the Persian empire, is also too well known, by the description of travellers, to render it necessary to say more here than that it ranks next to Ispahan amongst the royal cities.

[6] This much corrupted name, which is Soncara in Ramusio's text, Socham in that of the Basle edition, Sontara in the earlier Latin, Concara in the B. M., and Soncara (according to Müller) in the Berlin manuscript, Corcata in the Italian epitomes, and Corchara in the old English version, is the Korkan or Gurkan of eastern geographers, and evidently connected with the Hyrcania of the ancients. Its situation is at the south-eastern extremity of the Caspian, north of the Damaghan range and of the province of Kumis or Comisene.

[7] However distant the resemblance of the names may be thought, Timocain (which in the Basle edition is Tymochaim, and in the older Latin, Thymachaym) is undoubtedly intended for Damaghân, the capital of the small province of Kumis, in the north-eastern quarter of Persia. By Josaphat Barbaro, the Venetian ambassador to that court, it is called Tremigan; and by our countryman, Thomas Herbert, Diurgument: but this, we find, was not his own corruption; for in one of the letters of Pietro della Valle, he complains of this abuse and uncertainty in the names of places: "Come per essempio, quel Diargument, che l'Epitome Geografica dice esser nome moderno dell' Hircania."

the north, near the place called Arbor Secco.[1] The country is distinguished for its excellent breed of horses, many of which are carried for sale to India, and bring high prices, not less in general than two hundred livres tournois.[2] It produces also the largest and handsomest breed of asses in the world, which sell (on the spot) at higher prices than the horses, because they are more easily fed, are capable of carrying heavier burthens, and travel further in the day than either horses or mules, which cannot support an equal degree of fatigue. The merchants, therefore, who in travelling from one province to another are obliged to pass extensive deserts and tracts of sand, where no kind of herbage is to be met with, and where, on account of the distance between the wells or other watering places, it is necessary to make long journeys in the course of the day, are desirous of providing themselves with asses in preference, as they get sooner over the ground and require a smaller allowance of food. Camels also are employed here, and these in like manner carry great weights and are maintained at little cost, but they are not so swift as the asses. The traders of these parts convey the horses to Kisi,[3] to Ormus, and to other places on the coast of the Indian sea, where they are purchased by those who carry them to India. In consequence, however, of the greater heat of that country, they do not last many years, being natives of a temperate climate. In some of these districts, the people are savage and bloodthirsty, making a common practice of wounding and murdering each other. They would not refrain from doing injury to the merchants and travellers, were they not in terror of the eastern Tartars,[4] who cause them to be severely punished. A regulation is also established, that in all roads where danger is apprehended, the inhabitants shall be obliged,

[1] The district to which the appellation of Arbor Secco was given has already been adverted to, and will be found more particularly mentioned in a subsequent chapter.

[2] The excellence of the Persian horses, for which they may perhaps be indebted to the mixture of the Arabian and the Turki breed, is well known. A detailed account of their qualities is given by Chardin (tom. ii. chap. viii. p. 25, 4to); and also by Malcolm (Hist. of Persia, vol. ii. p. 516). As the livre tournois, in the fourteenth century, was at the proportionate value of twenty-five to one livre of the present times, it follows that the price at which the Persian horse sold in India was from fifteen hundred to two thousand rupees.

[3] Kisi or Chisi has been shown (p. 43, note,) to be the island of Kîs or Kês, to which the trade of Siraf, in the Persian gulf, was removed. Of the celebrated port of Ormuz, there will be occasion to speak hereafter.

[4] By "the eastern Tartars" are meant the Moghul Tartars, who entered Persia from the eastern side of the Caspian.

upon the requisition of the merchants, to provide active and trusty conductors for their guidance and security, between one district and another; who are to be paid at the rate of two or three groats [1] for each loaded beast, according to the distance. They are all followers of the Mahometan religion. In the cities, however, there are merchants and numerous artisans, who manufacture a variety of stuffs of silk and gold.[2] Cotton grows abundantly in this country, as do wheat, barley,[3] millet, and several other sorts of grain; together with grapes and every species of fruit. Should any one assert that the Saracens do not drink wine, being forbidden by their law, it may be answered that they quiet their consciences on this point by persuading themselves that if they take the precaution of boiling it over the fire, by which it is partly consumed and becomes sweet, they may drink it without infringing the commandment; for having changed its taste, they change its name, and no longer call it wine, although it is such in fact.[4]

[1] The Italian grossi, or groats, were a small silver coin, which have differed in weight and value at different periods.

[2] "Je ne parlerai point," says Chardin, "d'une infinité de sortes d'étoffes de soye pure, ni des étoffes de soye avec du coton. . . . Je ne parlerai que de leurs brocards. Ils appellent le brocard Zerbafe, c'est-à-dire, tissure d'or. . . . Il ne se fait point d'étoffe si chère par tout le monde." (tom. ii. p. 86, 4to.) Pottinger, speaking of the manufactures of Kashan, says: "Its staples are copper-ware, carpets, and coloured and flowered silks, which latter are exquisitely beautiful. I purchased some of them made in scarfs, in imitation of the richest Kashmeer shawls."—Travels in Beloochistan, p. 244.

[3] Wheat grows in the northern provinces of Persia, and also in the southern, although less commonly. "Barley," says Malcolm, "is often sold in Persia at one farthing per pound, and wheat is not on the average more than a third of the price dearer than barley."—Hist. of Persia, vol. ii. p. 519.

[4] The practice of boiling wine is known to be common amongst the eastern people, but whether the motive for it here assigned be the true one, or whether we should not rather conclude that they prefer the taste, may be doubted. The Persians have always been less strict than the other more orthodox Mahometans, in regard to indulgence in wine; and Pietro della Valle mentions two ordinances of Shah Abbas; the one forbidding the use of it, which shows that the religious precept had failed of its effect; and a second annulling the prohibition, upon his finding that the people, and especially the soldiers, had substituted for wine a liquid preparation of opium, by which their health was injured.

CHAPTER XIII

OF THE CITY OF YASDI AND ITS MANUFACTURES, AND OF THE ANIMALS FOUND IN THE COUNTRY BETWEEN THAT PLACE AND KIERMAN.

YASDI is a considerable city on the confines of Persia, where there is much traffic.[1] A species of cloth of silk and gold manufactured there is known by the appellation of Yasdi, and is carried from thence by the merchants to all parts of the world.[2] Its inhabitants are of the Mahometan religion. Those who travel from that city, employ eight days in passing over a plain, in the course of which they meet with only three places that afford accommodation.[3] The road lies through extensive groves of the date-bearing palm, in which there is abundance of game, as well beasts as partridges and quails; and those travellers who are fond of the amusements of the chase, may here enjoy excellent sport. Wild asses [4] are likewise to be met with, very numerous and handsome. At the end of eight days you arrive at a kingdom named Kierman.[5]

[1] Yezd is the most eastern city of the province of Fars or Persia Proper. Captain Christie, by whom it was visited in 1810, describes it as "a very large and populous city, situated on the edge of a sandy desert, contiguous to a range of mountains running east and west." "It is celebrated," he observes, "by all merchants, for the protection afforded to speculators, and the security of its inhabitants and their property. It is the grand mart between Hindoostan, Khorasan, Bagdad, and Persia, and is said to be a place of greater trade than any other in the latter empire."—Trav. in Beloochistan, App. p. 421.

[2] D'Herbelot observes that "les étoffes de soye qu'on y travaille, et que l'on appelle en Turc et en Persan comasche Yezdi, la rendent fort marchande." In the Memoirs of Abdulkurrim, also, we read of a donation made to an ambassador, by Nadir Shah, consisting of twenty-five pieces of Yezdy brocade.

[3] This is usually named the Desert of Kirman.

[4] We read of wild asses delivered as presents, and consequently as curiosities, to Shah Abbas, and other kings of Persia. Rennell observes that "the wild asses remarked by Xenophon for their swiftness, bear much the same character at present. Texeira in 1606 saw herds of them in the Arabian desert, immediately opposite to the desert of Mesopotamia, where Xenophon saw them."—Illustrations, p. 100.

[5] The distance between Yezd and the capital of Kirman is about one hundred and sixty geographical miles, which would be at the rate of twenty miles per day. But the average travelling rate of a light caravan, as deduced by Major Rennell, is only fifteen to fifteen and a half, with camels, or seventeen to eighteen with mules; when on long journeys. It may, indeed, be understood that the desert alone, exclusive of some portion of cultivated country, employed eight days. Some of the manuscripts have seven days.

CHAPTER XIV

OF THE KINGDOM OF KIERMAN, BY THE ANCIENTS NAMED KARMANIA—OF ITS FOSSIL AND MINERAL PRODUCTIONS—ITS MANUFACTURES—ITS FALCONS—AND OF A GREAT DESCENT OBSERVED UPON PASSING OUT OF THAT COUNTRY.

KIERMAN is a kingdom on the eastern confines of Persia,[1] which was formerly governed by its own monarchs, in hereditary succession; but since the Tartars have brought it under their dominion, they appoint governors to it at their pleasure. In the mountains of this country are found the precious stones that we call turquoises.[2] There are also veins of steel[3] and of antimony[4] in large quantities. They manufacture here in great perfection all the articles necessary for

[1] Kirmân is a province of Persia, situated at the south-eastern extremity of that kingdom. Its capital city appears to be most usually called by the same name, but is also known by that of Sirgan, as the word is pronounced by the Persians, or Sirjan, as pronounced by the Arabs. "The city of Kirman," says Pottinger, "is situated on the western side of a capacious plain, so close to the mountains, that two of them, on which there are ancient decayed forts, completely command it. It was once the most flourishing in Persia, and in size was second to none, except the capital, Isfahan. . . . No city in the East has been more subject to reverses of fortune, or oftener the scene of the most destructive wars, both foreign and domestic, than Kirman."—P. 222. It would seem that our author did not consider Kirman as being, in his time, an integral part of Persia, from his not including it amongst the eight provinces or kingdoms which he enumerates; and in this light also it was held by Edrisi, who wrote in the twelfth century, and says, "Et verò terra Karman interjacet terræ Persia et terræ Mecran."—P. 129.

[2] "La plus riche mine de Perse," says Chardin, "est celle des turquoises. On en a en deux endroits, à Nichapour en Carasson, et dans une montagne qui est entre l'Hyrcanie et la Parthide, à quatre journées de la Mer Caspienne, nommée Phirous-cou."—Tom. ii. p. 24, 4to. "In these mountains," says Malcolm, speaking of Nishapore, "the Ferouzah or turquoise stone is found."—Hist. of Persia, vol. ii. p. 220, note.

[3] "Les mines de fer," says Chardin, "sont dans l'Hyrcanie, dans la Médie septentrionale, au païs des Parthes, et dans la Bactriane. Les mines d'acier se trouvent dans les mêmes païs, et y produisent beaucoup."—P. 23. He then proceeds to describe its particular qualities, and to compare it with the steel of India.

[4] The word "andanico" of Ramusio's text, or "andanicum" of the Basle edition, is not to be found in any dictionary, nor have preceding translators attempted to render it by any corresponding term, but have let the word stand as they found it in their copy. I should not, from any resemblance of sound, have hazarded the conjecture of its being intended for "antimonio;" but learning from the travels of Chardin that antimony is the produce of countries on the eastern side of Persia, of which our author here speaks, I consider the probability of such a corruption as having some weight.

warlike equipment, such as saddles, bridles, spurs, swords, bows, quivers, and every kind of arms in use amongst these people. The women and young persons work with the needle, in embroideries of silk and gold, in a variety of colours and patterns, representing birds and beasts, with other ornamental devices.[1] These are designed for the curtains, coverlets, and cushions of the sleeping places of the rich; and the work is executed with so much taste and skill as to be an object of admiration. In the mountainous parts are bred the best falcons that anywhere take wing. They are smaller than the peregrine falcon; reddish about the breast, belly, and under the tail; and their flight is so swift that no bird can escape them. Upon leaving Kierman, you travel for seven days along a plain, by a pleasant road, and rendered still more delightful by the abundance of partridges and other game.[2] You also meet frequently with towns and castles, as well as scattered habitations; until at length you arrive at a mountain whence there is a considerable descent, which occupies two days. Fruit trees are found there in great numbers; the district having formerly been peopled, though at present without inhabitants, except herdsmen alone, who are seen attending the pasturing of their cattle. In that part of the country which you pass before you reach the descent, the cold is so severe that a man can with difficulty defend himself against it by wearing many garments and pelisses.[3]

[1] "I learn," says Pottinger, "from a manuscript history of the conquest of Mukran, in the ninetieth year of the hijree, that Kirman was then a very extensive city, full of riches, and celebrated for the excellence of the shawls and arms made in it."—P. 222. "The trade of Kirman, though still considerable, has never revived in a manner to be compared to what it was previous to its last depopulation. . . . Its manufactures of shawls, matchlocks, and *numuds* or felts, are celebrated all over Asia, and are said to afford employment to upwards of one-third of the inhabitants, whether male or female."—P. 225.

[2] "Les perdrix de Perse," says Chardin, "sont, comme je crois, les pluns grosses perdrix du monde et du goût le plus excellent."—P. 30.

[3] The road from the city of Kirman towards the Persian Gulf, here described, probably lay through the town of Bam or Bumm, which stands near the boundary line between what are considered as the cold and the warm regions of Kirman. "The province of Nurmansheer," says Pottinger, "extends from the waste dividing it from Beloochistan to the city of Bumm. . . . Its boundary to the westward is the province of Kirman, of which, I believe, it is now deemed a component district; to the eastward it has the desert, as already mentioned; and, north and south, two ranges of mountains, the last of which are by much the highest, and I imagine, at all seasons, crowned with snow, as they were when I saw them, at which period it was exceedingly hot in the plain beneath."—P. 199. These appear to be the mountains of Maren, which, says Ibn Haukal, "belong to the cold region of Kirman; snow falls on them."—P. 141.

CHAPTER XV

OF THE CITY OF KAMANDU, AND DISTRICT OF REOBARLE—OF CERTAIN BIRDS FOUND THERE—OF A PECULIAR KIND OF OXEN—AND OF THE KARAUNAS, A TRIBE OF ROBBERS.

At the end of the descent of this mountain, you arrive at a plain that extends, in a southern direction, to the distance of five days' journey; at the commencement of which there is a town named Kamandu,[1] formerly a very large place and of much consequence, but not so at this day, having been repeatedly laid waste by the Tartars. The neighbouring district is called Reobarle.[2] The temperature of the plain is very warm. It produces wheat, rice, and other grains. On that part of it which lies nearest to the hills, dates, pomegranates, quinces, and a variety of other fruits, grow, amongst which is one called Adam's apple,[3] not known in our cool climate. Turtle-doves are found here in vast numbers, occasioned by the plenty of small fruits which supply them with food, and their not been eaten by the Mahometans, who hold them in abomination.[4] There are likewise many pheasants and francolins, which latter do not resemble those of other coun-

[1] The geography of the country lying between the capital of the province of Kirman and the Persian Gulf is very imperfectly known; and even Pottinger's map, the most modern we possess, exhibits but one solitary name in that tract, although the chains of hills are there laid down with an appearance of precision. It is difficult therefore to ascertain the place intended by Kamandu (in the B. M. and Berlin manuscripts, Camandi, and in the Italian epitomes, Edgamad), even if there were grounds to believe that this town, which had lost its consequence before our author's time, is still in existence. It may perhaps be the Memaun of D'Anville's map, which is called Mahân by Ibn Haukal, or else the Koumin of the latter: but these are offered as mere conjectures.

[2] Reobarle is obviously meant for Rud-bâr, a descriptive term applied, in numerous instances, to towns or districts in Persia and the neighbouring countries. It signifies " a river in a valley, the channel of a torrent, and also a place where many streams run; " and the district here spoken of as answering that description, would seem from the circumstances to have occupied the banks of the river which in D'Anville's and Malcolm's maps bears the name of Div Rud, and must be crossed in the way from Kirman or Ormuz.

[3] *Pomus Adami* is a name that has been given to the fruit called pumplenose, shaddock, or *citrus decumanus* of Linnæus; but here it may probably be intended for the orange itself, or *pomum aurantium*, named by the Arabians and Persians *naranj*.

[4] This objection to the flesh of doves, as food, may have been a local prejudice; for it does not appear that they are generally regarded as an unclean meat by a Mahometan.

tries, their colour being a mixture of white and black with red legs and beak.[1] Among the cattle also there are some of an uncommon kind, particularly a species of large white oxen, with short, smooth coats (the effect of a hot climate), horns short, thick, and obtuse, and having between the shoulders a gibbous rising or hump, about the height of two palms.[2] They are beautiful animals, and being very strong are made to carry great weights. Whilst loading, they are accustomed to kneel down like the camel, and then to rise up with the burthen. We find here also sheep that are equal to the ass in size, with long and thick tails, weighing thirty pounds and upwards, which are fat and excellent to eat.[3] In this province there are many towns encompassed with lofty and thick walls of earth,[4] for the purpose of defending the inhabitants against

[1] The *tetrao francolinus*, or francoline partridge of the Levant, has red legs and beak, as here described. Dr. Russell calls it *francolinus olinæ*, "known to the French by the name of gelinot (gélinotte)." The flesh, he says, is delicious, but the bird is not to be met with at less than a day's journey from the city.—(Nat. Hist. of Aleppo.)

[2] This species of ox, commonly employed at Surat and other places on the western coast of India, in drawing the carriages called hakkries, was probably introduced from thence to the eastern provinces of Persia. It has been described by many writers, and among others by Niebuhr. See Voyage en Arabie, etc. tom. ii. p. 52. tab. xii.

[3] This extraordinary breed of sheep (*ovis laticaudata*) is a native of various parts of Asia and Africa, and has been often described. In the Natural History of Aleppo, the following circumstantial account of it is given, with a plate:—"They have two sorts of sheep," says Russell, "in the neighbourhood of Aleppo: the one called Beduin sheep, which differ in no respect from the larger kinds of sheep in Britain, except that their tails are somewhat longer and thicker: the others are those often mentioned by travellers on account of their extraordinary tails; and this species is by much the most numerous. This tail is very broad and large, terminating in a small appendage that turns back upon it. It is of a substance between fat and marrow, and is not eaten separately, but mixed with the lean meat in many of their dishes, and also often used instead of butter. A common sheep of this sort, without the head, feet, skin and entrails, weighs about twelve or fourteen Aleppo rotoloes (of five pounds), of which the tail is usually three rotoloes or upwards; but such as are of the largest breed and have been fattened, will sometimes weigh above thirty rotoloes, and the tails of these, ten (or fifty pounds); a thing to some scarce credible. These very large sheep being, about Aleppo, kept up in yards, are in no danger of injuring their tails; but in some other places, where they feed in the fields, the shepherds are obliged to fix a piece of thin board to the under part of the tail, to prevent its being torn by bushes, thistles, etc.; and some have small wheels, to facilitate the dragging of this board after them; whence, with a little exaggeration, the story of having carts to carry their tails."—P. 51. Chardin's account of "les moutons à grosse queüe," of Persia, whose tails, he says, weigh thirty pounds, corresponds exactly with the above.

[4] Frequent mention is made by Hamilton of these mud entrenchments. "The Ballowches," he says, "appeared near the town of Gombroon, on a swift march towards it, which scared the (Persian) governor

the incursions of the Karaunas, who scour the country and plunder every thing within their reach.[1] In order that the reader may understand what people these are, it is necessary to mention that there was a prince named Nugodar, the nephew of Zagataï, who was brother of the Grand Khan (Oktaï), and reigned in Turkestan.[2] This Nugodar, whilst living at Zagataï's court, became ambitious of being himself a sovereign, and having heard that in India there was a province called Malabar,[3] governed at that time by a king named

so much, that, although there was an high mud wall between him and them, he got on horseback and fled. . . . The Ballowches came first to the west quarter of the town, where our factory stands, and soon made passages through the mud walls."—New Account of the East Indies, vol. i. p. 108. "The village of Bunpoor," says Pottinger, "is small and ill-built: it has been at one time surrounded by a low mud wall, with small bastions at intervals; but the whole is now gone to decay."—Travels in Beloochistan and Sinde, p. 176.

[1] The early Latin text calls them "Scarani et Malandrini." The Karaunas we may presume to be the inhabitants of Makrân, a tract of country extending from the vicinity of the Indus towards the Persian Gulf, and which takes its name from the word *karána*, signifying a "shore, coast, or border." They appear to differ little from the neighbouring people of Balûchistan, if they be not in fact the same race; and what our author states of them is a faithful picture of the predatory habits ascribed to the latter. "The Boloujes," says Ibn Haukal, "are in the desert of Mount Kefes, and Kefes in the Parsi language is Kouje; and they call these two people Koujes and Boloujes. The Boloujes are people who dwell in the desert; they infest the roads, and have not respect for any person."—P. 140. Of the habits of this people we have the most particular account in the journal of Lieut. Pottinger, who says, "The Nharooés are the most savage and predatory class of Belooches; and whilst they deem private theft dishonourable and disgraceful in the extreme, they contemplate the plunder and devastation of a country with such opposite sentiments, that they consider it an exploit deserving of the highest commendation; and steeled by that feeling, they will individually recount the assistance they have rendered on such occasions, the numbers of men, women, and children they have made captives and carried away or murdered, the villages they have burned and plundered, and the flocks they have slaughtered when unable to drive them off." —P. 58. "We are now in Mukran," said a native of Beloochistan to the same traveller, "where every individual is a robber by caste, and where they do not hesitate to plunder brothers and neighbours."—P. 139.

[2] Nikodar Oghlan was the son of Hulagu, and grand nephew of Jagataï; he succeeded his brother Abaka in the throne of Persia, by the name of Ahmed Khan, and was the first of his family who made public profession of Mahometanism. If the Nikodar, who pushed his fortune, as we are here told, on the side of India, did actually visit the court of Jagataï, who died in 1240, he must have belonged to the preceding generation, as it was not until 1282 that Ahmed Khan Nikodar became the sovereign of Persia, and forty-two years is an interval too great to admit of our supposing him to have been the eastern adventurer. There may have been an earlier Nikodar amongst the numerous grandsons of Jengiz-khan, and in fact the consistency of the story requires that the event should have taken place long before our author's time.

[3] I must here be indulged in a conjecture, which, however bold it may seem, will be justified by the sequel: that instead of Malabar or Malawar

As-idin Sultan,[1] which had not yet been brought under the dominion of the Tartars, he secretly collected a body of about ten thousand men, the most profligate and desperate he could find, and separating himself from his uncle without giving him any intimation of his designs, proceeded through Balashan[2] to the kingdom of Kesmur,[3] where he lost many of his people and cattle, from the difficulty and badness of the roads, and at length entered the province of Malabar.[4] Coming thus upon As-idin by surprise, he took from him by force a city called Dely, as well as many others in its vicinity, and there began to reign.[5] The Tartars whom he carried thither, and who were men of a light complexion, mixing with the dark Indian women, produced the race to whom the appellation of Karaunas is given, signifying, in the language of the country, a mixed breed;[6] and these are the people who have since been

(as it is often written) the word should be, and was in the original, Lahawar, or, as commonly pronounced, Lahore; for through this province, and certainly not through Malabar, this adventurer must necessarily have passed in his way to Delhi.

[1] Azz-eddin, Ghiyas-eddin, and Moazz-eddin, with the addition of Sultân, were common titles of the Patan sovereigns of Delhi, as well as of the princes who governed the provinces of their empire.

[2] Badakhshan, near the sources of the Oxus, lies on that side of Jagataï's country which is nearest to the heads of the Indus and Ganges, and consequently in the line of march towards Delhi.

[3] Kesmur can be no other than Kashmir, which lies in the direction from Badakhshan towards Lahore, Sirhind, and the capital. The more common route is by Kabul, but the object of this petty invader was, to keep amongst the mountains, and thereby conceal his intentions.

[4] Here it becomes perfectly obvious, that the country into which he penetrated upon leaving Kashmir was the Panjâb, of which Lahawar or Lahore is the principal city.

[5] We do not read in any native historian, of this conquest of Delhi by the Moghul Tartars, antecedent to the invasion by Tamerlane. But we learn from the History of Hindustan, as translated by Dow from the text of Ferishta, that Moazz-eddin Byram Shah, king of Delhi, whose reign began in 1239 and ended in 1242, was involved in troubles with his vizir and principal omrahs, by whom a mutiny was excited amongst his troops. At this crisis, "news arrived that the Moghuls of the great Zingis had invested Lahore; that Malek, the viceroy of that place, finding his troops mutinous, had been obliged to flee in the night, and was actually on his way to Delhi; and that Lahore was plundered by the enemy, and the miserable inhabitants carried away prisoners." "The vizir, in the meantime, advanced with the army to the capital, which he besieged for three months and a half. Rebellion spreading at last among the citizens, the place was taken in the year 1241. Byram was thrown into prison, where, in a few days, he came to a tragical end. The Moghuls after plundering the provinces on the banks of the five branches of the Indus, returned to Ghizni." Thus we perceive that at the very period in question, which was a little before or after the death of Jagataï in 1240, an army of Moghuls did advance into provinces subject to the king of Delhi, and plundered his frontier cities.

[6] One of the meanings of the Sanskrit word karana is, "a person of a mixed breed."

in the practice of committing depredations, not only in the country of Reobarle, but in every other to which they have access. In India they acquired the knowledge of magical and diabolical arts, by means of which they are enabled to produce darkness, obscuring the light of day to such a degree, that persons are invisible to each other, unless within a very small distance.[1] Whenever they go on their predatory excursions, they put this art in practice, and their approach is consequently not perceived. Most frequently this district is the scene of their operations; because when the merchants from various parts assemble at Ormus, and wait for those who are on their way from India, they send, in the winter season, their horses and mules, which are out of condition from the length of their journey, to the plain of Reobarle, where they find abundance of pasture and become fat. The Karaunas, aware that this will take place, seize the opportunity of effecting a general pillage, and make slaves of the people who attend the cattle, if they have not the means of ramsom. Marco Polo himself[2] was once enveloped in a factitious obscurity of this kind, but escaped from it to the castle of Konsalmi.[3] Many of his companions, however, were taken and sold, and others were put to death. These people have a king named Corobar.

[1] The belief in such supernatural agency was the common weakness of the darker ages. Although the appearance and effects are materially different, it may be suspected that there is some connexion between this story of mists produced by enchantment, and the optical deception noticed by Elphinstone, in his journey across what may be considered as an extension of the same desert, notwithstanding the separation of its parts by the country through which the Indus takes its course. "Towards evening," he says, "many persons were astonished with the appearance of a long lake, enclosing several little islands. . . . It was, however, only one of those illusions which the French call mirage, and the Persians sirraub. I had imagined this phenomenon to be occasioned by a thin vapour (or something resembling a vapour), which is seen over the ground in the hot weather in India, but this appearance was entirely different, and, on looking along the ground, no vapour whatever could be perceived. . . . I shall not attempt to account for this appearance, but shall merely remark, that it seems only to be found in level, smooth, and dry places."—Account of Caubul, p. 16.

[2] The story may amount to nothing more than that these robbers, having their haunts in the neighbourhood of mountains, availed themselves of the opportunity of thick mists, to make their attacks on the caravans with the more security; whilst their knowledge of the country enabled them to occupy those narrow defiles through which the travellers must unavoidably pass.

[3] This castle of Konsalmi, or, according to another reading, Kanosalim, is not now to be discovered in our maps, but it may be remarked that the Persian words Khanah al-salam signify, "the house of safety, or peace." "A small but neat tower," says Elphinstone, "was seen in this march (through the desert), and we were told it was a place of refuge for travellers, against the predatory hordes who infest the route of caravans."—P. 17.

CHAPTER XVI

OF THE CITY OF ORMUS, SITUATED ON AN ISLAND NOT FAR FROM THE MAIN, IN THE SEA OF INDIA—OF ITS COMMERCIAL IMPORTANCE—AND OF THE HOT WIND THAT BLOWS THERE.

At the extremity of the plain before mentioned as extending in a southern direction to the distance of five days' journey, there is a descent for about twenty miles, by a road that is extremely dangerous, from the multitude of robbers, by whom travellers are continually assaulted and plundered.[1] This declivity conducts you to another plain, very beautiful in its appearance, two days' journey in extent, which is called the plain of Ormus. Here you cross a number of fine streams, and see a country covered with date-palms, amongst which are found the francoline partridge, birds of the parrot kind, and a variety of others unknown to our climate. At length you reach the border of the ocean, where, upon an island, at no great distance from the shore, stands a city named Ormus,[2]

[1] "In the mountains near Hormuz, it is said, there is much cultivated land, and cattle, and many strong places. On every mountain there is a chief, and they have an allowance from the sultan or sovereign; yet they infest the roads of Kirman, and as far as the borders of Fars and Sejestan. They commit their robberies on foot; and it is said that their race is of Arabian origin, and that they have accumulated vast wealth." —Sir W. Ouseley's transl. of Ibn Haukal, p. 140.

[2] The original city of Ormuz, or Hormûz, was situated on the eastern shore of the Gulf of Persia, in the province of Mogostan, and kingdom of Kirman. Ibn Haukal, about the latter part of the tenth century, speaks evidently of this city, on the main, when he says: "Hormuz is the emporium of the merchants in Kirman, and their chief sea-port: it has mosques and market-places, and the merchants reside in the suburbs." —P. 142. It was destroyed by one of the princes who reigned in Kirman, of the Seljuk dynasty, according to some accounts, or the Moghul, according to others. The exact period is not satisfactorily ascertained. On this occasion, the inhabitants removed, with their most valuable effects, to the neighbouring island of Jerun, about thirteen geographical miles from the former situation, where the foundation of the new city of Hormuz, or Ormuz, destined to acquire still greater celebrity than the former, was laid,—although under the disadvantages of wanting water, and of a soil impregnated with salt and sulphur. Abulfeda, who wrote in the early part of the fourteenth century, and was a contemporary of our author, describes the insular city. This island was taken from the native princes, in 1507, by the Portuguese, under the famous Alfonso Albuquerque. "In their hands," says Robertson, "Ormuz soon became the great mart from which the Persian empire, and all the provinces of Asia to the west of it, were supplied with the productions of India; and a city which they built on that barren island, destitute of water, was rendered one of the chief seats of opulence, splendour, and

whose port is frequented by traders from all parts of India, who bring spices and drugs, precious stones, pearls, gold tissues, elephants' teeth, and various other articles of merchandize. These they dispose of to a different set of traders, by whom they are dispersed throughout the world. This city, indeed, is eminently commercial, has towns and castles dependent upon it, and is esteemed the principal place in the kingdom of Kierman.[1] Its ruler is named Rukmedin Achomak,[2] who governs with absolute authority, but at the same time acknowledges the king of Kierman[3] as his liege

luxury in the eastern world."—Historical Disquisition, p. 140. From them it was wrested, in 1622, by Shah Abbas, with the assistance of an English squadron. Its fortifications, and other public structures, were razed by that conqueror; and its commerce was transferred to a place on the neighbouring coast, called Gambrûn, to which he gave the name of Bandar Abbassi. But in the meantime the discovery of the passage from Europe by the Cape of Good Hope operated to divert the general trade into a new channel, and that which was carried on by the medium of ports in the Gulf of Persia rapidly declined. In the year 1765, when Niebuhr visited these parts, the island on which Hormuz stood was possessed by a person who had been in the naval service of Nadir Shah, and the place was become quite insignificant.

[1] By this must be meant, that Hormuz exceeded the other cities in opulence, and perhaps in population; but Sirgan or Sirjan, also called Kirman, was the capital of what we term the province of that name, and there the sovereign resided.

[2] In the list of sultans of Hormuz furnished by Texeira in his translation of the annals of Turan-shah, we find one named Rukn-eddin Mahmud, who, although the dates are very imperfect, may be supposed to have reigned about the period of our author's visit to the Gulf of Persia, and to be the prince here called Rukmedin Achomak. The latter name is evidently intended for Achmet, in which mode that of Ahmed has been commonly though improperly written; and it is well known that oriental writers themselves frequently commit errors by confounding the three names of Ahmed, Muhammed, and Mahmud.

[3] No record of the kings of Kirman can be traced to a later date than the year 1187, when Malik Dinar, of the race of Ali (a Seyed), expelled the last of the Seljuk princes, and established himself on the throne; but under Hulagu and his successors, who conquered Persia in the following century, and formed a Moghul dynasty, it must have become again a province or fief of that empire, governed (as it is at the present day) by a branch of the reigning family. De Barros (Decade ii. liv. ii. cap. 2) informs us that a king or chief of Hormuz (in the district of Mogostan, on the main,) obtained from his neighbour, the Malek of Kâez, a cession of the island of Jerun, lying near his part of the coast, and established there a naval force, for the purpose of commanding the straits; that in the event of a war, provoked by this assumption of power, he became master of the island of Kâez also; that the king of Persia (or, rather, the ruler of Kirman), to whom the Malek had been used to pay tribute, marched an army into Mogostan, and compelled the king of Hormuz to abandon his city on the continent, and to take refuge in the island of Jerun, where he founded the new city of Hormuz; that upon his consenting to acknowledge vassalage and pay tribute (a share of the tolls on shipping) to the Persian king, he was suffered to remain in possession of both islands; and that in his new establishment he afterwards reigned thirty years.—The

lord. When any foreign merchant happens to die within his jurisdiction, he confiscates the property, and deposits the amount in his treasury.[1] During the summer season, the inhabitants do not remain in the city, on account of the excessive heat, which renders the air unwholesome, but retire to their gardens along the shore or on the banks of the river, where with a kind of ozier-work they construct huts over the water. These they enclose with stakes, driven in the water on the one side, and on the other upon the shore, making a covering of leaves to shelter them from the sun. Here they reside during the period in which there blows, every day, from about the hour of nine until noon, a land-wind so intensely hot as to impede respiration, and to occasion death by suffocating the person exposed to it. None can escape from its effects who are overtaken by it on the sandy plain.[2] As soon as the approach of this wind is perceived by the inhabitants, they immerge themselves to the chin in water, and continue in that situation until it ceases to blow.[3] In proof

circumstances thus stated by De Barros agree in the material parts with what our author relates at this place, and more particularly in book iii. chap. xliii.; but the Portuguese historian refers all the transactions to the single reign of Gordun-shah, who, he says, obtained the cession of Jerun in 1273, and who, according to Texeira's list, where he is named Azz-eddin Gordan-shah, died in 1318. There is reason, however, to believe that he gives an unfounded extension to this reign, and that the earlier events spoken of belonged to those of Seif-eddin and Rukn-eddin, who were probably the father and grandfather of that prince.

[1] This odious right is known to have been exercised in Europe, in very modern times, under the name of "droit d'aubaine."

[2] The hot wind known in Italy by the name of Il Sirocco, and in Africa by that of Harmatan, has been often described by travellers. In the deserts of the south of Persia its effects are perhaps most violent. "The winds in this desert," says Pottinger, "are often so scorching (during the hot months from June to September) as to kill anything, either animal or vegetable, that may be exposed to them, and the route by which I travelled is then deemed impassable. This wind is distinguished everywhere in Beloochistan, by the different names of Julot or Julo (the flame), and Badé sumoom (the pestilential wind). So powerfully searching is its nature, that it has been known to kill camels, or other hardy animals; and its effects on the human frame were related to me, by those who had been eye-witnesses of them, as the most dreadful that can be imagined: the muscles of the unhappy sufferer become rigid and contracted; the skin shrivels; an agonizing sensation, as if the flesh was on fire, pervades the whole frame, and in the last stage it cracks into deep gashes, producing hemorrhage, that quickly ends this misery."—P. 136.

[3] For this practice of immersion we have the testimony of Pietro della Valle, who was in the Gulf of Persia during the siege of Hormuz, and visited the island immediately after its falling into the hands of the Persians. "Hormuz," he writes in his letter of the 18th January, 1623, "comunemente si stima la piu calda terra del mondo. . . . E mi dicono, che in certo tempo dell' anno, le genti di Hormuz non potrebbero vivere, se non vi stessero qualche hora del giorno immersi fin' alla gola

of the extraordinary degree of this heat, Marco Polo says that he happened to be in these parts when the following circumstance occurred. The ruler of Ormus having neglected to pay his tribute to the king of Kierman, the latter took the resolution of enforcing it at the season when the principal inhabitants reside out of the city, upon the main land, and for this purpose despatched a body of troops, consisting of sixteen hundred horse and five thousand foot, through the country of Reobarle, in order to seize them by surprise. In consequence, however, of their being misled by the guides, they failed to arrive at the place intended before the approach of night, and halted to take repose in a grove not far distant from Ormus; but upon recommencing their march in the morning, they were assailed by this hot wind, and were all suffocated; not one escaping to carry the fatal intelligence to his master. When the people of Ormus became acquainted with the event, and proceeded to bury the carcases, in order that their stench might not infect the air, they found them so baked by the intenseness of the heat, that the limbs, upon being handled, separated from the trunks, and it became necessary to dig the graves close to the spot where the bodies lay.[1]

nell' acqua, che, a questo fine, in tutte le case, tengono in alcune vasche, fatte a posta." Although additional testimony be not wanting, I shall give that of Schillinger, an intelligent Swabian traveller, who visited these countries in the year 1700, and furnishes a good description of Hormuz and Gambrûn. "Wann die grosse Hitze einfallet," he says, "legen sich die Innwohner den gantzen Tag durch in darzu bequemte Wasser-tröge, oder stehen in mit wasser angefüllten Fassern biss an hals, umb also zu ruhen, und sich der unleydentlichen Hitze zu erwehren." —Persianische Reis, p. 279.

[1] With regard to the state of the bodies, however extraordinary the circumstances may appear, they are fully corroborated by Chardin, who, speaking further of this wind, says, "Son effet le plus surprenant n'est pas même la mort qu'il cause; c'est que les corps qui en meurent sont comme dissous, sans perdre pourtant leur figure, ni même leur couleur, en sorte qu'on diroit qu'ils ne sont qu'endormis, quoiqu'ils soient morts, et que si on les prend quelque part, la pièce demeure à la main." He then proceeds to adduce some recent facts in proof of his assertion.—Tom. ii. p. 9, 4to.

CHAPTER XVII

OF THE SHIPPING EMPLOYED AT ORMUS—OF THE SEASON IN WHICH THE FRUITS ARE PRODUCED—AND OF THE MANNER OF LIVING AND CUSTOMS OF THE INHABITANTS.

The vessels built at Ormus are of the worst kind, and dangerous for navigation, exposing the merchants and others who make use of them to great hazards. Their defects proceed from the circumstance of nails not being employed in the construction; the wood being of too hard a quality, and liable to split or to crack like earthenware. When an attempt is made to drive a nail, it rebounds, and is frequently broken. The planks are bored, as carefully as possible, with an iron auger, near the extremities; and wooden pins or trenails being driven into them, they are in this manner fastened (to the stem and stern). After this they are bound, or rather sewed together, with a kind of rope-yarn stripped from the husk of the Indian (cocoa) nuts, which are of a large size, and covered with a fibrous stuff like horse-hair. This being steeped in water until the softer parts putrefy, the threads or strings remain clean, and of these they make twine for sewing the planks, which lasts long under water.[1] Pitch is not used for preserving the bottoms of vessels, but they are smeared with an oil made from the fat of fish, and then caulked with oakum. The vessel has no more than one mast, one helm,

[1] We know little of the shipping employed in the Gulf of Persia before the conquest of Hormuz by the Portuguese; and since that period the influence and example of these and other Europeans have much changed the system of Persian and Indian navigation; yet the account given by our author corresponds in every essential particular with the kind of vessel described by Niebuhr. Such also are the boats employed at the present day on the coast of Coromandel, called *chelingues* by the French, and *masulah boats* by the English, which are thus described by Le Gentil: "Les bateaux dans lesquels se passent ces barres, se nomment chelingues; ils sont faits exprès; ce sont des planches mises l'une au-dessus de l'autre, et cousues l'une à l'autre, avec du fil fait de l'écorce intérieur du cocotier (de la noix du coco); les coûtures sont calfatées avec de l'étoupe faite de la même écorce, et enfoncée sans beaucoup de façons avec un mauvais couteau. Le fond de ces bateaux est plat et formé comme les bords; ces bateaux ne sont guère plus longs que larges, et il n'entre pas un seul clou dans leur construction." (Voyage, tom. i. p. 540.) This twine, manufactured from the fibrous husk of the cocoa-nut (not from the bark of the tree, as M. Le Gentil supposed), is well known in India by the name of *coire*, and is worked into ropes for running-rigging aud cables.

and one deck.[1] When she has taken in her lading it is covered over with hides, and upon these hides they place the horses which they carry to India. They have no iron anchors, but in their stead employ another kind of ground-tackle;[2] the consequence of which is, that in bad weather, (and these seas are very tempestuous,) they are frequently driven on shore and lost.

The inhabitants of the place are of a dark colour, and are Mahometans. They sow their wheat, rice, and other grain in the month of November, and reap their harvest in March.[3] The fruits also they gather in that month, with the exception of the dates, which are collected in May. Of these, with other ingredients, they make a good kind of wine.[4] When it is drunk, however, by persons not accustomed to the beverage, it occasions an immediate flux; but upon their recovering from its first effects, it proves beneficial to them, and contributes to render them fat. The food of the natives is different from ours; for were they to eat wheaten bread and flesh meat their health would be injured. They live chiefly upon dates and salted fish, such as the thunnus, cepole (*cepola tania*), and others which from experience they know to be wholesome. Excepting in marshy places, the soil of this country is not covered with grass, in consequence of the extreme heat, which burns up everything. Upon the death of men of rank, their wives loudly bewail them, once in the course of each day, during four successive weeks; and there are also

[1] It is to be observed that the numerous praws which cover the seas of the further East, are steered, in general, with two helms or kamûdis; and that such vessels had recently been under the notice of our author in his passage to the straits of Malacca.

[2] Neither are the vessels of the Malays commonly provided with iron anchors; which I presume to be what is meant by "ferri di sorzer," although the term is not to be met with either in the general or the marine dictionaries. Their anchors are formed of strong and heavy wood, have only one arm or fluke, and are sunk by means of heavy stones attached to them.

[3] We might not expect to read of wheat being cultivated in so hot a climate, but the fact is well ascertained.

[4] What has usually been termed palm-wine, or toddy, is a liquor extracted from trees of the class of palms, by cutting off the shoot for fructification, and applying to the wounded part a vessel into which the liquor distils; but we read also of an inebriating liquor prepared from ripe dates, by steeping them in warm water, until they undergo vinous fermentation. Pottinger, speaking of the people of Mukran (adjoining to the province of Kirman), says: "They likewise drink great quantities of an intoxicating beverage, made from the fermented dates, which must be exceedingly pernicious in its effects." (P. 306.) In the Anabasis of Xenophon, this liquor is spoken of as having been met with by the Greeks in the villages of Babylonia.

people to be found here who make such lamentations a profession, and are paid for uttering them over the corpses of persons to whom they are not related.[1]

CHAPTER XVIII

OF THE COUNTRY TRAVELLED OVER UPON LEAVING ORMUS, AND RETURNING TO KIERMAN BY A DIFFERENT ROUTE; AND OF A BITTERNESS IN THE BREAD OCCASIONED BY THE QUALITY OF THE WATER.

HAVING spoken of Ormus, I shall for the present defer treating of India, intending to make it the subject of a separate Book, and now return to Kierman in a northerly direction. Leaving Ormus, therefore, and taking a different road to that place, you enter upon a beautiful plain, producing in abundance every article of food; and birds are numerous, especially partridges: but the bread, which is made from wheat grown in the country, cannot be eaten by those who have not learned to accommodate their palates to it, having a bitter taste derived from the quality of the waters, which are all bitter and salsuginous. On every side you perceive warm, sanative streams, applicable to the cure of cutaneous and other bodily complaints. Dates and other fruits are in great plenty.

CHAPTER XIX

OF THE DESERT COUNTRY BETWEEN KIERMAN AND KOBIAM, AND OF THE BITTER QUALITY OF THE WATER.

UPON leaving Kierman and travelling three days, you reach the borders of a desert extending to the distance of seven

[1] These excessive lamentations, so common in the East, and not unknown in some parts of Europe, as well as the practice of hiring professional mourners, have been often described by travellers. "Les femmes sur tout," says Chardin, "s'emportent aux excès de fureur et de désolation les plus outrez, qu'elles entremêlent de longues complaintes, de récits tendres et touchans, et de doulloureuses apostrophes au cadavre insensible." (Tom. ii. p. 385.) "It is usual," says Fryer, "to hire people to lament; and the widow, once a moon, goes to the grave with her acquaintance to repeat the doleful dirge." (Account of East India and Persia, p. 94.) It may be observed, that in the early Latin and other early texts the time of mourning is stated to be four years instead of four weeks.

days' journey, at the end of which you arrive at Kobiam.[1] During the first three days (of these seven) but little water is to be met with, and that little is impregnated with salt, green as grass, and so nauseous that none can use it as drink. Should even a drop of it be swallowed, frequent calls of nature will be occasioned; and the effect is the same from eating a grain of the salt made from this water.[2] In consequence of this, persons who travel over the desert are obliged to carry a provision of water along with them. The cattle, however, are compelled by thirst to drink such as they find, and a flux immediately ensues. In the course of these three days not one habitation is to be seen. The whole is arid and desolate. Cattle are not found there, because there is no subsistence for them.[3] On the fourth day you come to a river of fresh water, but which has its channel for the most part under ground. In some parts however there are abrupt openings, caused by the force of the current, through which the stream

[1] Kobiam (Gobiam in the early Latin text, Kobinam in others) is the Kabis of D'Anville, the Chabis of Edrisi, the Khebis, Khebeis, and Khubeis of Ibn Haukal, and the Khubees of Pottinger. "Khebeis," says Ibn Haukal, "is a town on the borders of this desert, with running water and date-trees. From that to Durak is one merhileh; and during this stage, as far as the eye can reach, everything wears the appearance of ruin and desolation; for there is not any kind of water." (Ouseley's translation, p. 199.) "It formerly flourished," says Pottinger, "and was the residence of a Beglerbeg on the part of the chief of Seistan, but now is a miserable decayed place, and the inhabitants are notorious robbers and outcasts, who subsist by infesting the highways of Khorasan and Persia, and plundering karawans."—P. 229.

[2] The salt springs and plains incrusted with salt, which Pottinger met with in Kirman and the adjacent countries, are thus spoken of: "We crossed a river of liquid salt, so deep as to take my horse to the knees; the surface of the plain for several hundred yards on each side was entirely hid by a thick incrustation of white salt, resembling a fall of frozen snow, that crackled under the horse's hoofs." (P. 237.) "The whole of these mountains (of Kohistan) abound with mineral productions: in several places there are brooks of liquid salt, and pools of water covered with a scum similar to the naphtha, or bitumen, found near the Caspian sea." (P. 312.) "On the high road from Kelat to Kutch Gundava there is a range of hills, from which a species of salt, perfectly red in its colour, is extracted, that possesses very great aperient qualities. Sulphur and alum are to be had at the same place." (P. 323.) It would seem from its effects that the salt of these deserts contains sulphate of magnesia, and the green colour noticed by our author may proceed from a mixture of sulphate of iron.

[3] "On the east," says Ibn Haukal, "the desert of Khorasan partly borders the province of Makran and partly Seistan; to the south it has Kirman and Fars, and part of the borders of Isfahan. . . . This desert is almost totally uninhabited and waste. . . . It is the haunt of robbers and thieves, and without a guide it is very difficult to find the way through it, and one can only go by the well-known paths."—Pp. 192—194.

becomes visible for a short space, and water is to be had in abundance. Here the wearied traveller stops to refresh himself and his cattle after the fatigues of the preceding journey.[1] The circumstances of the latter three days resemble those of the former, and conduct him at length to the town of Kobiam.

CHAPTER XX

OF THE TOWN OF KOBIAM, AND ITS MANUFACTURES.

KOBIAM is a large town, the inhabitants of which observe the law of Mahomet. They have plenty of iron, *accarum*, and *andanicum*. Here they make mirrors of highly polished steel, of a large size and very handsome. Much antimony or zinc is found in the country, and they procure tutty which makes an excellent collyrium, together with spodium, by the following process. They take the crude ore from a vein that is known to yield such as is fit for the purpose, and put it into a heated furnace. Over the furnace they place an iron grating formed of small bars set close together. The smoke or vapour ascending from the ore in burning attaches itself to the bars, and as it cools becomes hard. This is the tutty; whilst the gross and heavy part, which does not ascend, but remains as a cinder in the furnace, becomes the spodium.[2]

[1] This place of refreshment may perhaps be Shûr, which Ibn Haukal terms a stream of water in the desert, on the road which begins from the Kirman side. In another place he says it is one day's journey from Durak, (mentioned in note[1], p. 70,) and describes it as a broad water-course of rain-water. No notice, however, is there taken of its passing under ground; and the identity, therefore, is not to be insisted upon; but the subterraneous passage of rivers is not very uncommon.

[2] In Note[4], p. 56, a reason was assigned for supposing that by the word *andanico* was meant antimony, which is stated by Chardin and others to be found in the quarter of Persia here spoken of; but from the process of making tutty and spodium so particularly described in this place, we should be led to infer that lapis calaminaris, or zinc, is the mineral to which our author gives that name, or rather, the name of which andanico is the corruption. How far the qualities of antimony and of zinc may render them liable to be mistaken for each other, I do not pretend to judge, but upon this point there seems to exist a degree of uncertainty that may excuse our author, if he supposed that the former, instead of the latter, was employed in the manufacture of tutia or tutty. "The argillaceous earth," says Bontius, "of which tutty is made, is found in great quantities in the province of Persia called Kirmon, as I have often been told by Persian and Armenian merchants." (Account of Diseases,

CHAPTER XXI

OF THE JOURNEY FROM KOBIAM TO THE PROVINCE OF TIMOCHAIN ON THE NORTHERN CONFINES OF PERSIA—AND OF A PARTICULAR SPECIES OF TREE.

LEAVING Kobiam you proceed over a desert of eight days' journey exposed to great drought; neither fruits nor any kind of trees are met with, and what water is found has a bitter taste. Travellers are therefore obliged to carry with them so much as may be necessary for their sustenance. Their cattle are constrained by thirst to drink such as the desert affords, which their owners endeavour to render palatable to them by mixing it with flour. At the end of eight days you reach the province of Timochain, situated towards the north, on the borders of Persia, in which are many towns and strong places.[1] There is here an extensive plain remarkable for the production of a species of tree called the tree of the sun, and by Christians *arbor secco*, the dry or fruitless tree. Its nature and qualities are these:—It is lofty, with a large stem, having its leaves green on the upper surface, but white or glaucous on the under. It produces husks or capsules

Natural Hist. etc. of the East Indies, chap. xiii. p. 180.) Pottinger, in the journal of his travels through Beloochistan towards Kirman, speaks of a caravansery "called Soormu-sing, or the stone of antimony, a name which it derives from the vast quantities of that mineral to be collected in the vicinity." (P. 38.) That the collyrium so much in use amongst the eastern people, called *surmeh* by the Persians, and *anjan* or *unjun* by the natives of Hindustan, has tutty for its basis, will not, I suppose, be disputed: but in the Persian and Hindustani dictionaries it will be found that surmeh and unjan are likewise the terms for antimony. Whatever may be the proper application of the names, he is at least substantially correct in the fact that tutty, employed as a collyrium or ophthalmic unguent, is prepared from a mineral substance found in the province of Kirman.

[1] It has already been shown that the Timocain or Timochain of our text is no other than Damaghân, a place of considerable importance on the north-eastern confines of Persia, having the ancient Hyrcania, from which it is separated by a chain of mountains, to the north, the province of Khorasan to the east, and the small province of Kumis, of which it is the capital, together with the salt-desert, to the south. In this neighbourhood it was that Ghazan the son of Arghun, heir to the throne of Persia, then occupied by his uncle, was stationed with an army to guard the important pass of Khowar or the Caspian Straits, at the period of the arrival of the Polo family from China; and thither they were directed to proceed, in order to deliver into his hands their precious charge, a princess of the house of Kublaï.

like those in which the chestnut is enclosed, but these contain no fruit. The wood is solid and strong, and of a yellow colour resembling the box.[1] There is no other species of tree near it for the space of a hundred miles, excepting in one quarter, where trees are found within the distance of about ten miles. It is reported by the inhabitants of this district that a battle was fought there between Alexander, king of Macedonia, and Darius.[2] The towns are well supplied with every necessary and convenience of life, the climate being temperate and not subject to extremes either of heat or cold.[3] The people are of the Mahometan religion. They are in general a handsome race, especially the women, who, in my opinion, are the most beautiful in the world.

CHAPTER XXII

OF THE OLD MAN OF THE MOUNTAIN—OF HIS PALACE AND GARDENS—OF HIS CAPTURE AND HIS DEATH.

HAVING spoken of this country, mention shall now be made of the old man of the mountain.[4] The district in which his

[1] This tree, to which the name of *arbor secco* was applied, would seem to be a species of fagus, and to partake of the character of the chestnut. But from various passages of later writers, we shall be justified in considering it was intended for a variety of the platanus, or plane-tree. The epithet of *secco* seems to imply nothing more than this: that when the form of the husk promises an edible nut, the stranger who gathers it is disappointed on finding no perceptible contents, or only a dry and tasteless seed.

[2] The last battle fought between Alexander and Darius was at Arbela (Arbîl), in Kurdistan, not far from the Tigris, but in the subsequent operations, the vanquished king of Persia was pursued from Ecbatana (Hamadan), through the Caspian Straits or pass of Khowar, which Alexander's troops penetrated without opposition, into the province of Comisene (Kumis), of which Hecatompylos (supposed to be Damaghân) was the capital; nor did the pursuit cease until the unfortunate monarch was murdered by his own subjects not far from the latter city. Alexander himself advanced by a nearer way, but across a desert entirely destitute of water. Traditions respecting the Macedonian conqueror abound in this part of the country.

[3] The mildness of the climate, and at the same time its extreme unhealthiness, along the southern shore of the Caspian, is noticed by Olearius, Chardin, and other travellers; but the district about Damaghân, here spoken of, is separated by a chain of mountains from the swampy tract between Asterabad and Ferhabad (the places chiefly visited by Europeans during the reign of Shah Abbas, who frequently held his court in them), and occupies a much more elevated region.

[4] The appellation so well known in the histories of the crusades, of "Old man of the mountain," is an injudicious version of the Arabic title

residence lay obtained the name of Mulehet, signifying in the language of the Saracens, the place of heretics, and his people that of Mulehetites,[1] or holders of heretical tenets; as we apply the term of Patharini to certain heretics amongst Christians.[2] The following account of this chief, Marco Polo testifies to having heard from sundry persons. He was named Alo-eddin,[3] and his religion was that of Mahomet. In a beautiful valley enclosed between two lofty mountains, he had formed a luxurious garden, stored with every delicious

Sheikh al Jebal, signifying " chief of the mountainous region." But as the word *sheikh*, like *signor*, and some other European terms, bears the meaning of " elder," as well as of " lord or chief," a choice of interpretations was offered, and the less appropriate adopted. The places where this personage, who was the head of a religious or fanatical sect, exercised the rights of sovereignty, were the castles of Alamût, Lamsir, Kirdkuh, and Maimun-diz, and the district of Rudbar; all situated within the limits of that province which the Persians name Kuhestan, and the Arabians Al-jebal. " La position d'Alamout," says De Sacy, in his Mémoire sur la Dynastie des Assassins et sur l'Origine de leur Nom, "située au milieu d'un pays de montagnes, fit appeler le prince qui y régnoit *scheikh-aldjebal*, c'est-à-dire, le *scheikh* ou prince des montagnes, et l'équivoque du mot *scheikh*, qui signifie également *vieillard* et *prince*, a donné lieu aux historiens des croisades et au célèbre voyageur Marc Pol, de le nommer le Vieux de la montagne."

[1] This correct application of the Arabic term, Mulehet or Mulehed, is one of the many unquestionable proofs of the genuineness of our author's relation, and would be sufficient to remove the doubts of any learned and candid inquirers on the subject of his acquaintance with oriental matters. Under the article Melahedah, in the Bibliothèque Orientale of D'Herbelot, we read: " C'est le pluriel de Melhed, qui signifie un impie, un homme sans religion. Melahedah Kûhestan: Les Impies de la Montagne. C'est ainsi que sont appellés les Ismaëlians qui ont régné dans l'Iran, et particulièrement dans la partie montueuse de la Perse." This opprobrious epithet was bestowed by the orthodox Mussulmans upon the fanatic sect of Ismaelians, Batenians, or, as they style themselves, Refik, or Friends, who, under the influence of an adventurer named Hasan ben Sabbah, began to flourish in Persia about the year 1090, during the reign of Malik Shah Jelal-eddin, third sovereign of the Seljukian dynasty. With respect to the two grand divisions of the Mussulman political faith, they professed themselves to belong to the Shiahs or Rafedhi (as they are termed by their adversaries), who maintain the legitimate right to the khalifat in the descendants of Ali. Their particular tenets appear to have been connected with those of the more ancient Karmats and modern Wahabis.

[2] The Paterini are more generally known by the name of Waldenses, Albigenses, and amongst the French writers by that of Patalins or Patelins.

[3] Ala-eddin, the Ismaelian prince, was killed, after a long reign, about the end of the year 1255, and was succeeded by Rukn-eddin ben Ala-eddin, who reigned only one year before the destruction of his power under the circumstances our author proceeds to relate. He is correct therefore in attributing the actions which roused the indignation of the world to the former; but he does not appear to have been aware that it was the son against whom the attack of the Moghuls was directed, although the expedition must have been undertaken against Ala-eddin, the father.

fruit and every fragrant shrub that could be procured. Palaces of various sizes and forms were erected in different parts of the grounds, ornamented with works in gold, with paintings, and with furniture of rich silks. By means of small conduits contrived in these buildings, streams of wine, milk, honey, and some of pure water, were seen to flow in every direction. The inhabitants of these palaces were elegant and beautiful damsels, accomplished in the arts of singing, playing upon all sorts of musical instruments, dancing, and especially those of dalliance and amorous allurement. Clothed in rich dresses they were seen continually sporting and amusing themselves in the garden and pavilions, their female guardians being confined within doors and never suffered to appear. The object which the chief had in view in forming a garden of this fascinating kind, was this: that Mahomet having promised to those who should obey his will the enjoyments of Paradise, where every species of sensual gratification should be found, in the society of beautiful nymphs, he was desirous of its being understood by his followers that he also was a prophet and the compeer of Mahomet, and had the power of admitting to Paradise such as he should choose to favour. In order that none without his licence might find their way into this delicious valley, he caused a strong and inexpugnable castle to be erected at the opening of it, through which the entry was by a secret passage. At his court, likewise, this chief entertained a number of youths, from the age of twelve to twenty years, selected from the inhabitants of the surrounding mountains, who showed a disposition for martial exercises, and appeared to possess the quality of daring courage. To them he was in the daily practice of discoursing on the subject of the paradise announced by the prophet, and of his own power of granting admission; and at certain times he caused opium to be administered to ten or a dozen of the youths; and when half dead with sleep he had them conveyed to the several apartments of the palaces in the garden. Upon awakening from the state of lethargy, their senses were struck with all the delightful objects that have been described, and each perceived himself surrounded by lovely damsels, singing, playing, and attracting his regards by the most fascinating caresses, serving him also with delicate viands and exquisite wines; until intoxicated with excess of enjoyment amidst actual rivulets of milk and wine, he believed himself assuredly in Paradise, and felt an unwillingness to relinquish its delights.

When four or five days had thus been passed, they were thrown once more into a state of somnolency, and carried out of the garden. Upon their being introduced to his presence, and questioned by him as to where they had been, their answer was, "In Paradise, through the favour of your highness:" and then before the whole court, who listened to them with eager curiosity and astonishment, they gave a circumstantial account of the scenes to which they had been witnesses. The chief thereupon addressing them, said: "We have the assurances of our prophet that he who defends his lord shall inherit Paradise, and if you show yourselves devoted to the obedience of my orders, that happy lot awaits you." Animated to enthusiasm by words of this nature, all deemed themselves happy to receive the commands of their master, and were forward to die in his service.[1] The consequence of this system was, that when any of the neighbouring princes, or others, gave umbrage to this chief, they were put to death by these his disciplined assassins; none of whom felt terror at the risk of losing their own lives, which they held in little estimation, provided they could execute their master's will. On this account his tyranny became the subject of dread in all the surrounding countries. He had also constituted two deputies or representatives of himself, of whom one had his residence in the vicinity of Damascus, and the other in Kurdistan;[2] and these pursued the plan he had established for training their young dependants. Thus there was no person, however powerful, who, having become exposed to the enmity of the old man of the mountain, could escape assassination. His territory being situated within the dominions of Ulaù (Hulagu), the brother of the grand khan (Mangu), that prince had information of his atrocious practices, as above related, as well as of his employing people to rob travellers in their

[1] This story was the current belief of the people of Asia, who seem to have thought it necessary to assign extraordinary causes for an effect so surprising as that of the implicit devotion of these religious enthusiasts to the arbitrary will of their master. The name of Assassins, given to these people by other writers, is not found in Marco Polo.

[2] I cannot discover any traces of an establishment of Ismaelians, under a regular chief, in Kurdistan, although *daïs* or missionaries of the sect were frequently employed there; but of the existence of the subordinate government in Syria here mentioned we have ample testimony. (See De Sacy, Mémoire, p. 6, and De Guignes, Hist. gén. des Huns, liv. vi. p. 342.) I am the more particular in citing these authorities, to prove, in confirmation of what Marco Polo asserts, that the Persian was the original government, although the Syrian branch became better known in Europe, and to its sheikhs the title of "old man of the mountain" seems to have been generally if not exclusively applied.

passage through his country, and in the year 1262 sent one of his armies to besiege this chief in his castle. It proved, however, so capable of defence, that for three years no impression could be made upon it; until at length he was forced to surrender from the want of provisions, and being made prisoner was put to death. His castle was dismantled, and his garden of Paradise destroyed.[1] And from that time there has been no old man of the mountain.

CHAPTER XXIII

OF A FERTILE PLAIN OF SIX DAYS' JOURNEY, SUCCEEDED BY A DESERT OF EIGHT, TO BE PASSED IN THE WAY TO THE CITY OF SAPURGAN—OF THE EXCELLENT MELONS PRODUCED THERE—AND OF THE CITY OF BALACH.

LEAVING this castle, the road leads over a spacious plain, and then through a country diversified with hill and dale, where there is herbage and pasture, as well as fruits in great abundance, by which the army of Ulaù was enabled to remain so long upon the ground. This country extends to the distance of full six days' journey. It contains many cities and fortified places,[2] and the inhabitants are of the Mahometan

[1] The circumstances attending the destruction of this sect, which, as we have seen in the preceding notes, had erected itself into an independent sovereignty, are noticed by Abu'lfaraj, Hist. Dynast. p. 330, as well as by others amongst the Oriental writers, who record the actions of the descendants of Jengiz-khan, but by none with so much historical detail as by Mirkhond, whose account of the dynasty of the Ismaëlians of Persia was translated and published at Paris, together with the original text, by M. Jourdain. With regard to the date of 1262, which our author assigns to the commencement of these operations, there must be a mistake of about six years, as all the historians agree that Hulagu's expedition against the Mulhedites was prior to that against Baghdad, and the latter is known with sufficient certainty to have fallen in the year 1258. We have, at the same time, the circumstantial authority of Mirkhond for the reduction of the castles of the former in the years 1256 and 1257. This and similar inaccuracies of Marco Polo may be excused on the ground that the events having happened many years before the commencement of his travels, he must have depended upon the information of others for their dates, which may have been expressed according to modes of reckoning that required a calculation to reduce them to the Christian era.

[2] From Damaghân his course was nearly east, or in the direction of Balkh, and seems to have lain through Jan-Jerm and Nishapûr towards Meru-ar-rud; but the number of days' journeys is evidently too small, unless we can suppose him to have travelled at double the rate of the ordinary caravans, or full forty miles per day; which is less probable than that an omission of some stages has been made in the narrative.

religion. A desert then commences, extending forty or fifty miles,[1] where there is no water; and it is necessary that the traveller should make provision of this article at his outset. As the cattle find no drink until this desert is passed, the greatest expedition is necessary, that they may reach a watering place. At the end of the sixth day's journey,[2] he arrives at a town named Sapurgan,[3] which is plentifully supplied with every kind of provision, and is particularly celebrated for producing the best melons in the world. These are preserved in the following manner. They are cut spirally, in thin slices, as the pumpkin with us, and after they have been dried in the sun, are sent, in large quantities, for sale, to the neighbouring countries; where they are eagerly sought for, being sweet as honey.[4] Game is also in plenty there, both of beasts and birds.

Leaving this place, we shall now speak of another named Balach; a large and magnificent city.[5] It was formerly still more considerable, but has sustained much injury from the Tartars, who in their frequent attacks have partly demolished its buildings. It contained many palaces constructed of marble, and spacious squares, still visible, although in a ruinous state.[6] It was in this city, according to the report of

[1] The country of Khorasan, through which the route, whether from Alamut or from Damaghân to the place next mentioned must have lain, is said to be in general level, intersected with sandy deserts and irregular ridges of lofty mountains.

[2] It is quite necessary to the sense that this should mean six days' journey from the eastern side of the desert just mentioned.

[3] Of the identity of this place, which at first might seem to be intended for Nishapur, there can be no doubt. "Cheburgan, ville de Corassane, près du Gihon et de Balc," says Pétis de la Croix, the translator of Sherefeddin, "a 100 degrés de long. et 36° 45′ de latitude." In the tables of Nassir-eddin, from which the above situation is taken, it is named Ashburkan; in D'Anville's map, Ashburgan; in Strathlenberg's, Chaburga; in Macdonald Kinneir's, Subbergan; and in Elphinstone's, Shibbergaun. By the last writer it is spoken of as a dependency of the government of Balkh.

[4] The province of Khorasan is celebrated by all the eastern writers for the excellence of its fruits, and the importance here given to its melons is fully supported by the authority of Chardin. (Tom. ii. p. 19, 4to.) On the subject of the "melon du Khorasan," see also Relation de l'Egypte, notes, p. 126.

[5] Balach or Balkh, the "Bactra regia" of Ptolemy, which gave name to the province of Bactriana, of which it was the capital, is situated towards the heads of the Oxus, in the north-eastern extremity of Khorasan. It is one of the four royal cities of that province, and has been the seat of government perhaps more frequently even than Nishapur, Herat, or Meru-shahjan.

[6] Jengiz-khan, who took this city by assault in 1221, from the Khorazmians, caused all the inhabitants to be massacred (as we are told by his historian, Abu'lghazi) and the walls to be razed to their foundation. In 1369 it was taken from the descendants of that conqueror by Tamerlane,

the inhabitants, that Alexander took to wife the daughter of king Darius.[1] The Mahometan religion prevails here also.[2] The dominion of the lord of the Eastern Tartars extends to this place; and to it the limits of the Persian empire extend, in a north-eastern direction.[3] Upon leaving Balach and holding the same course for two days, you traverse a country that is destitute of every sign of habitation, the people having all fled to strong places in the mountains, in order to secure themselves against the predatory attacks of lawless marauders, by whom these districts are overrun. Here are extensive waters, and game of various kinds. Lions are also found in these parts,[4] very large and numerous. Provisions, however, are scarce in the hilly tract passed during these two days, and the traveller must carry with him food sufficient both for himself and his cattle.

whose family possessed it until they were obliged to give place to the Uzbek Tartars, between whom and the Persians it was subsequently the subject of perpetual contention. "All the Asiatics," Elphinstone observes, "are impressed with an idea of its being the oldest city in the world. . . . This ancient metropolis is now reduced to insignificance. Its ruins still cover a great extent, and are surrounded with a wall, but only one corner is inhabitated." (P. 464.) The houses are described by Macdonald Kinneir as being of brick, and the palace of the khan, an extensive building, nearly all of marble, brought from quarries in the neighbouring mountains.

[1] The Persian marriages of Alexander with Barsine or Statira, the daughter of Darius, and with Parisatis, the daughter of Ochus, are generally understood to have taken place at Susa.

[2] Abu'lghazi informs us that at the time of the destruction of Balkh by Jengiz-khan, it contained no fewer than 12,000 mosques; which, although an exaggeration, shows at least the prevalence of Islamism in that city.

[3] Khorasan being so frequently subject to Persian dominion, and particularly under the descendants of Hulagu, who possessed it at the time our author travelled there, it was natural for him to consider it as an integral part of the Persian empire. Balkh is correctly stated as lying on the north-eastern frontier. The Latin says, "usque ad istam terram durat dominium domini de Levante."

[4] Chardin enumerates lions amongst the wild animals of Persia, and especially in the frontier provinces. "Partout où il y a des bois," he says, "comme en Hircanie et en Curdistan, il y a beaucoup de bêtes sauvages, des lions, des ours, des tigres, des leopards, des porc-epy, et des sangliers."—Tom. ii. p. 29, 4to.

CHAPTER XXIV

OF THE CASTLE NAMED THAIKAN—OF THE MANNERS OF THE INHABITANTS—AND OF SALT-HILLS.

At the end of these two days' journey you reach a castle named Thaikan, where a great market for corn is held, it being situated in a fine and fruitful country. The hills that lie to the south of it are large and lofty.[1] They all consist of white salt, extremely hard, with which the people, to the distance of thirty days' journey round, come to provide themselves, for it is esteemed the purest that is found in the world; but it is at the same time so hard that it cannot be detached otherwise than with iron instruments.[2] The quantity is so great that all the countries of the earth might be supplied from thence. Other hills produce almonds and pistachio nuts,[3] in which articles the natives carry on a considerable trade. Leaving Thaikan

[1] This account of Thaikan or Taikân (written Caycam in the manuscripts, and Taitham in the Italian epitomes), which is situated amongst the sources of the Oxus, will be found remarkably correct. "Of Tokharestan," says Ibn Haukal, "the largest city (town) is Taikân, situated on a plain in the vicinity of mountains. It is watered by a considerable river, and has many orchards and gardens." (P. 224.) "From Taikân to Badakshan is seven days' journey." (P. 230.) See also Abulfeda. These authors clearly distinguish it from a place named Talkan, lying south-west of Balkh, near Meru-er-rûd, and situated on a steep rock; but Edrisi gives to the former the name of Talkan, and has been followed by modern geographers, and particularly by D'Anville, in whose map both places are written with the same letters. "Their course," says Lieut. Macartney, speaking of the streams of the Oxus, near whose junction Talikan (or Taikân) stands, "is through a mountainous country, but containing many excessively rich and fertile valleys, producing all kinds of fruit in the greatest abundance."—Elphinstone's Account of Caubul, Appendix, p. 650.

[2] This kind of hard fossil salt is found in several parts, and is thus described by Chardin: "Dans la Médie et à Ispahan le sel se tire des mines, et on le transporte par gros quartiers, comme la pierre de taille. Il est si dure en des endroits, comme dans la Caramanie déserte (Kirmân) qu'on en employe les pierres dans la construction des maisons des pauvres gens." (Tom. ii. p. 23.) "The road beyond," says Elphinstone, speaking of a place in the country of the Afghâns, "was cut out of solid salt, at the foot of cliffs of that mineral, in some places more than one hundred feet high above the river. The salt is hard, clear, and almost pure."—Account of Caubul, p. 37.

[3] Both almonds and pistachio nuts are enumerated by Chardin amongst the productions of the northern and eastern parts of Persia. "Il croît des pistaches à Casbin et aux environs. . . . Ils ont de plus les amandes, les noisettes, etc. Le plus grand transport de fruits se fait de Yesde."—Tom. ii. p. 21.

and travelling three days, still in a north-east direction, you pass through a well inhabited country, very beautiful, and abounding in fruit, corn, and vines. The people are Mahometans, and are blood-thirsty and treacherous. They are given also to debauchery, and to excess in drink, to which the excellence of their sweet wine encourages them.[1] On their heads they wear nothing but a cord, about ten spans in length, with which they bind them round. They are keen sportsmen, and take many wild animals, wearing no other clothing than the skins of the beasts they kill, of which materials their shoes also are made. They are all taught to prepare the skins.

CHAPTER XXV

OF THE TOWN OF SCASSEM, AND OF THE PORCUPINES FOUND THERE.

DURING a journey of three days there are cities and many castles, and at the end of that distance you reach a town named Scassem,[2] governed by a chief whose title is equivalent to

[1] This country has since been overrun by a different race of people. "The Uzbeks," says Elphinstone, "first crossed the Jaxartes about the beginning of the sixteenth century, and pouring on the possessions of the descendants of Tamerlane," who were themselves invaders, "soon drove them from Bokhaura, Khoarizm, and Ferghauna, and spread terror and dismay to the remotest parts of their extended empire. They now possess besides Bulkh (Balkh), the kingdoms of Khoarizm (or Orgunge), Bokhaura and Ferghauna, and perhaps some other little countries on this side of Beloot Taugh. I am told that they are to be found beyond Beloot Taugh, and as far east as Khoten at least; but of this I cannot speak with confidence. They belong to that great division of the human race which is known in Asia by the name of Toork, and which, with the Moghuls and Manshoors, compose what we call the Tartar nation. Each of these divisions has its separate language, and that of the Toorks is widely diffused throughout the west of Asia."—Account of Caubul, p. 465.

[2] This name, which in the Latin texts as well as in that of Ramusio is Scassem, and in the Italian epitomes Echasem, is evidently the Keshem of D'Anville's map, and the Kishm-abad of Elphinstone's, situated near the Ghori river which falls into the Oxus, and somewhat to the eastward of the meridian of Kabul or Caubul. Ibn Haukal, who describes it immediately after speaking of Taikân, and before he enters upon Badakhshan, names it Khesh, and says it is "the largest town in this mountainous country." J. R. Forster (Voyages in the North, p. 125) supposes Scassem to be Al-shash, on the river Sirr or Jaxartes, but against all probability, considering its vast distance from the last mentioned place; whilst Keshem or Kishm is not only in the vicinity, but in the direct route to that which is next described.

that of our barons or counts; and amongst the mountains he possesses other towns and strong places. Through the midst of this town runs a river of tolerable size. Here are found porcupines, which roll themselves up when the hunters set their dogs at them, and with great fury shoot out the quills or spines with which their skins are furnished, wounding both men and dogs. The people of this country have their peculiar language. The herdsmen who attend the cattle have their habitations amongst the hills, in caverns they form for themselves; nor is this a difficult operation, the hills consisting, not of stone, but only of clay. Upon departing from this place you travel for three days without seeing any kind of building, or meeting with any of the necessaries required by a traveller, excepting water; but for the horses there is sufficient pasture. You are therefore obliged to carry with you every article for which there may be occasion on the road. At the end of the third day you arrive at the province of Balashan.[1]

CHAPTER XXVI

OF THE PROVINCE OF BALASHAN—OF THE PRECIOUS STONES FOUND THERE AND WHICH BECOME THE PROPERTY OF THE KING—OF THE HORSES AND THE FALCONS OF THE COUNTRY—OF THE SALUBRIOUS AIR OF THE MOUNTAINS—AND OF THE DRESS WITH WHICH THE WOMEN ADORN THEIR PERSONS.

In the province of Balashan, the people are Mahometans, and have their peculiar language. It is an extensive kingdom, being in length full twelve days' journey, and is governed by princes in hereditary succession, who are all descended from Alexander, by the daughter of Darius, king of the Persians.

[1] This place is unquestionably Badakhshân, as the name is correctly written by Ibn Haukal and other geographers, although often pronounced Balakhshân. By D'Herbelot its situation is thus described: "Badakschian et Balakhschian, pays qui fait une partie de la province de Thokharestan, et qui s'étend vers la tête du fleuve Gihon ou Oxus, par lequel il est borné du côté du levant et du septentrion." "Budukhshaun," says Elphinstone, in his Account of Caubul, "though an extensive country, seems to be but one great valley running up from the province of Bulkh (Balkh) to Beloot Taugh, between the islands connected with the Pamere and the range of Hindoo Koosh."—P. 628.

All these have borne the title in the Saracenic tongue of Zulkarnen, being equivalent to Alexander.[1] In this country are found the precious stones called balass rubies, of fine quality and great value, so called from the name of the province.[2] They are imbedded in the high mountains, but are searched for only in one, named Sikinan.[3] In this the king causes mines to be worked, in the same manner as for gold or silver; and through this channel alone they are obtained; no person daring under pain of death, to make an excavation for the purpose, unless as a special favour he obtains his majesty's

[1] Abu'lfazl, speaking of the districts of Sewad and Bijore, which he describes as consisting of hills and wilds, and inhabited by the tribe of Yousef Zy, proceeds to say: " In the time of Mirza Ulugh Beg (1450), the tribe of Sultan, who assert themselves to be the descendants of the daughter of Sultan Secunder Zulkernain, came from Cabul, and possessed themselves of this country. They say that Secunder left treasure in Cabul under the care of some of his relations; and some of their descendants, who carry their genealogical table in their hands, now dwell in the mountainous parts." (Ayin Akbari, vol. ii. p. 195.) This filiation is also noticed by Lieut. Macartney, who says in his Memoir: " The king of Derwauz (near the sources of the Oxus) claims his descent from Alexander the Great, and his pretensions are admitted by all his neighbours." (Account of Caubul, App. p. 628.) It is almost unnecessary to observe that the word *zul'-karnein* signifies " having horns," and that it was given by the orientals to Alexander, whom they name Sekunder, from the appearance of his head on the Greek coins, which long circulated, and were afterwards initated, in Persia.

[2] Every writer who has treated of this country, mentions its two productions, the balass ruby (classed by the orientals as a species of hyacinth) and the lapis lazuli. " Badakhshan," says Ibn Haukal, " produces the ruby (*ladl*), and lapis lazuli (*lajaward*). The mines are in the mountains." (P. 225.) " C'est dans ses montagnes," says D'Herbelot, " que se trouve la mine des rubis que les orientaux appellent Badakhschiani et Balakhschiani, et que nous nommons rubis balays." " The part of Beloot Taugh within Budukhshaun," says Elphinstone, " produces iron, salt, and sulphur, as well as abundance of lapis lazuli; but the celebrated mines of rubies, which occasion Budukhshaun to be so often alluded to by the Persian poets, are situated in the lower hills near the Oxus. They are not now wrought."—P. 629.

[3] It may be thought a vain attempt to find corresponding authority for the name of the particular mountain from whence these stones were procured; but one which strongly resembles that of Sikinan presents itself as belonging to a district in the vicinity of the places of which we have been speaking. " The river Jihun (or Oxus)," says Ibn Haukal, " rises within the territories of Badakhshan, and receives the waters of many other streams. . . . The Wekhshab comes out of Turkestan into the land of Wekhsh, near a mountain where there is a bridge between Khotlan and the borders of Weish-kird (the Vash-gherd of D'Anville). . . . Near Wekhsh there are some districts (of Mawaralnahr), such as Dekhan and Sekineh: these two belong to the infidels. . . . There are mines of gold and silver in Wekhshab." (P. 239.) By " infidels " are probably here meant the race of people named Káfirs, whose country and peculiarities are described in the Appendix to Elphinstone's Account of Caubul, under the head of Caufiristaun, p. 617; and whom some suppose to be the descendants of the Greeks of Bactriana.

licence. Occasionally the king gives them as presents to strangers who pass through his dominions, as they are not procurable by purchase from others, and cannot be exported without his permission. His object in these restrictions is, that the rubies of his country, with which he thinks his credit connected, should preserve their estimation and maintain their high price; for if they could be dug for indiscriminately, and every one could purchase and carry them out of the kingdom, so great is their abundance, that they would soon be of little value. Some he sends as complimentary gifts to other kings and princes; some he delivers as tribute (to his superior lord); and some also he exchanges for gold and silver. These he allows to be exported. There are mountains likewise in which are found veins of lapis lazuli, the stone which yields the azure colour (ultramarine),[1] here the finest in the world. The mines of silver, copper, and lead, are likewise very productive. It is a cold country. The horses bred here are of a superior quality, and have great speed. Their hoofs are so hard that they do not require shoeing.[2] The natives are in the practice of galloping them on declivities where other cattle could not or would not venture to run. They asserted that not long since there were still found in this province horses of the breed of Alexander's celebrated Bucephalus, which were all foaled with a particular mark in the forehead. The whole of the breed was in the possession of one of the king's uncles, who, upon his refusal to yield them to his nephew, was put to death; whereupon his widow, exasperated at the murder, caused them all to be destroyed; and thus the race was lost to the world. In the mountains there are falcons of the species called saker (*falco sacer*), which are excellent birds, and of strong flight; as well as of that called laner, (*falco lanarius*). There are also goshawks of a perfect kind (*falco astur*, or *palumbarius*), and sparrow hawks (*falco nisus*). The people of the country are expert at the chase both of beasts and birds. Good wheat is grown there, and a species of barley without

[1] Speaking of Badakhshan, Abulfeda says: "Inde effertur ol lazurd et ol bellaur, seu lapis lazuli et beryllus." (Geogr. p. 352.) See also a passage to the same effect, from Ibn Haukal, in note [3], p. 83.

[2] Elphinstone observes that "by far the best breeding country (for horses) in the Caubul dominions is Bulkh (Balkh), and it is from that province (bordering on Badakhshan) and the Toorkmun country lower down the Oxus, that the bulk of those exported are brought." (P. 296.) The practice of shoeing horses seems to be unnecessary where the country is not stony nor particularly hard. In Sumatra they are never shodden, nor in Java, excepting in some instances for the paved streets of Batavia.

the husk.[1] There is no oil of olives, but they express it from certain nuts, and from the grain called sesame,[2] which resembles the seed of flax, excepting that it is light-coloured; and the oil this yields is better, and has more flavour than any other. It is used by the Tartars and other inhabitants of these parts.

In this kingdom there are many narrow defiles, and strong situations, which diminish the apprehension of any foreign power entering it with a hostile intention. The men are good archers and excellent sportsmen; generally clothing themselves with the skins of wild animals; other materials for the purpose being scarce. The mountains afford pasture for an innumerable quantity of sheep, which ramble about in flocks of four, five, and six hundred, all wild; and although many are taken and killed, there does not appear to be any diminution.[3] These mountains are exceedingly lofty, insomuch that it employs a man from morning till night to ascend to the top of them. Between them there are wide plains clothed with grass and with trees, and large streams of the purest water precipitating themselves through the fissures of the rocks. In these streams are trout and many other delicate sorts of fish. On the summits of the mountains the air is so pure and so salubrious, that when those who dwell in the towns, and in the plains and valleys below, find themselves attacked with fevers or other inflammatory complaints, they immediately remove thither, and remaining for three or four days in that situation, recover their health. Marco Polo affirms that he had experience in his own person of its excellent effects; for having been confined by sickness, in this country, for nearly a year,[4] he was advised to change the air by ascending the hills; when he presently became convalescent. A peculiar fashion of dress prevails amongst the women of the superior

[1] The barley here described is the kind known by the appellations of *hordeum nudum*, *hordeum glabrum*, and *hordeum vulgare seminibus decorticatis*. Our author's expression of *senza scorza* is exactly therefore the specific name given to it by Linnæus.

[2] In India oil is chiefly procured from this grain, the *sesamum orientale*. Both walnuts and hazel nuts, from which oil may be extracted, are found in the northern parts of Persia.

[3] "Les provinces de Perse les plus abondantes en bétail," says Chardin, "sont la Bactriane, etc. J'y ai vû des troupeaux de moutons qui couvroient quatre à cinq lieues de païs." Tom. ii. p. 29, 4to.

[4] The residence in Badakhshan to which our author here adverts, must have taken place at the period when he was sent on a mission by the emperor Kublaï to the province of Khorasan or of Khorasmia, of which mention is made in the latter part of the first chapter.

class, who wear below their waists, in the manner of drawers, a kind of garment, in the making of which they employ, according to their means, an hundred, eighty, or sixty ells of fine cotton cloth; which they also gather or plait, in order to increase the apparent size of their hips; those being accounted the most handsome who are the most bulky in that part.[1]

CHAPTER XXVII

OF THE PROVINCE OF BASCIA LYING SOUTH OF THE FORMER—OF THE GOLDEN ORNAMENTS WORN BY THE INHABITANTS IN THEIR EARS—AND OF THEIR MANNERS.

LEAVING Balashan and travelling in a southerly direction for ten days, you reach the province of Bacià,[2] the people of which have a peculiar language. They worship idols; are of a dark complexion, and of evil disposition; and are skilled in the art of magic, and the invocation of demons, a study to which they continually apply themselves. They wear in their ears pendent rings of gold and silver, adorned with pearls and precious stones.[3] The climate of the province is

[1] In describing the dress worn by the Belooche women, Pottinger says: "Their trowsers are preposterously wide, and made of silk, or a fabrication of that and cotton mixed."—Travels in Beloochistan and Sinde, p. 65.

[2] From the southerly, or rather south-easterly, situation of this place with respect to the province of Badakhshan, its distance of about two hundred miles, and other circumstances, I should infer that by Bascia (in the epitomes Bassia) is meant Paishore or Peshawer, a city not far from the principal confluence of the rivers that form the Sind or Indus. It is described by Forster as large and populous, and in consequence of its well chosen position an important mart, the residence of wealthy merchants. He says, indeed, that it was founded by Akbar, whose reign began in 1556; but although that enlightened monarch might have improved Paishore, and did actually found Attok, lower down on the river, there is evidence in his own Institutes that the former was in existence before his time. It is there said: "Bekram, commonly called Paishore, enjoys a delightful spring season. Here is a temple called Gorekehtery, a place of religious resort, particularly for jowgies." (Ayin Akbari, vol. ii. p. 205.) This is not the description of a city of recent date; nor if built by his master, would Abu'lfazl have mentioned it in such slight terms. It is probable upon the whole that Forster applied to Paishore what he had been told of Attok.

[3] It is evident that the people here described, if not actually Indians, are nearly allied to them. "The houses, food, and habits of life of the tribes of Peshawer," says Elphinstone, "resemble those of the Eusofzyes. The dress has also some resemblance, being a mixture of that of the Indians with that of the Afghauns."—P. 359.

in some parts extremely hot.[1] The food of the inhabitants is meat and rice.[2]

CHAPTER XXVIII

OF THE PROVINCE OF KESMUR SITUATED TOWARDS THE SOUTH-EAST—OF ITS INHABITANTS WHO ARE SKILLED IN MAGIC—OF THEIR COMMUNICATION WITH THE INDIAN SEA—AND OF A CLASS OF HERMITS, THEIR MODE OF LIFE, AND EXTRAORDINARY ABSTINENCE.

Kesmur is a province distant from Bascià seven days' journey.[3] Its inhabitants also have their peculiar language.[4] They are adepts beyond all others in the art of magic; insomuch that they can compel their idols, although by nature dumb and deaf, to speak; they can likewise obscure the day, and perform many other miracles. They are pre-eminent amongst the

[1] "The heat of Peshour," says Forster, "seemed to me more intense than that of any other country I have visited in the upper parts of India. . . . The atmosphere in the summer solstice becomes almost inflammable." (Vol. ii. p. 50.) "Peshawer," says Elphinstone, "is situated in a low plain, surrounded on all sides except the east with hills. The air is consequently much confined, and the heat greatly increased. In the summer of 1809 . . . the thermometer was for several days at 112° and 113°, in a large tent artificially cooled."—P. 132.

[2] "The markets," Forster adds, "are abundantly supplied with provisions of an excellent kind, particularly the mutton, which is the flesh of the large-tailed sheep."—P. 50.

[3] Kesmur or Chesmur (Chesimur in the Latin versions and Cassimur in the Italian epitomes) is undoubtedly intended for Kashmir. The distance, indeed, from Paishore or Peshawer, as it cannot be less than two hundred miles, and in a mountainous country, should be more than seven days' journey; but we must not look for strict accuracy in this respect; and our own maps differ considerably in the relative position of the two places. For circumstantial accounts of this interesting country, the reader may consult the Ayin Akbari, Bernier's and Forster's Travels, Rennell's Memoir of a Map of Hindoostan, and Elphinstone's Account of Caubul. In the ages in which our author wrote its population appears to have been chiefly Hindu; as in more ancient times it was esteemed one of the principal seats of that religion and of Sanskrit literature. The wealth derived from its celebrated manufacture, and its idolatrous sanctity, tempted the avarice, and roused the fanatic zeal of the Mahometans, by whom it was invaded at an early period; but as it did not fall under the dominion of Jengiz-khan or his immediate successors, it is here spoken of as an independent kingdom.

[4] "The language of Kashmir," says Forster, "evidently springs from the Sanskrit stock, and resembles in sound that of the Mahrattas." (P. 22.) "The Cashmerians," says Elphinstone, "are a distinct nation of the Hindoo stock, and differ in language and manners from all their neighbours."—P. 506.

idolatrous nations, and from them the idols, worshipped in other parts, proceed.[1] From this country there is a communication by water with the Indian Sea.[2] The natives are of a dark complexion, but by no means black; and the women, although dark, are very comely. Their food is flesh,[3] with rice and other grains; yet they are in general of a spare habit. The climate is moderately warm.[4] In this province, besides the capital, there are many other towns and strong places. There are also woods, desert tracts, and difficult passes in the mountains, which give security to the inhabitants against invasion.[5] Their king is not tributary to any power. They have amongst them a particular class of devotees, who live in communities, observe strict abstinence in regard to eating, drinking, and the intercourse of the sexes, and refrain from every kind of sensual indulgence, in order that they may not give offence to the idols whom they worship. These persons live to a considerable age. They have several monas-

[1] This is consistent with what we are told in the Ayin Akbari, that "the Hindoos regard all Cashmeer as holy land, where forty-five places are dedicated to Mahadeo, sixty-four to Bishen, three to Brahma, and twenty-two to Durga (the goddess of mountains)." (Vol. ii. p. 156.) It is therefore by no means improbable that the Brahmins of this remote and sacred country may have supplied southern India with many of those images of their deities in stone and copper with which the temples abound: for idols of home manufacture, we may presume, have less honour in their own country than those imported from distant places of holy repute.

[2] "Most of the trade of the country," says the Ayin Akbari, "is carried on by water." The river Jeilum or Behut, which flows through the valley of Kashmír, and is there navigable, falls into the Indus, after uniting its waters with those of the Chenâb and the Râvi, not far from the city of Multân: but as its course, after leaving that valley, is through a mountainous country, the navigation must be interrupted in some places.

[3] If the population of Kashmir was at that time Hindu, as we have every reason to suppose, although it had been occasionally subdued by Mahometans, it may be thought difficult to reconcile to the customs of those people what is here said of their food consisting in part of flesh; but in fact, the Hindu castes are not practically so strict in regard to meats, as the precepts of their religion would lead us to believe. Add to this, that the Kashmirians being noted at all periods for their light and dissolute character, it is not among them (however holy their land) that we are to look for a strict observance of the Vêdas.

[4] The temperateness of its climate has always been a subject of panegyric, and was the occasion of its being the summer residence of the Moghul emperors of Hindustan. "The whole of this *soobah*," says the Ayin Akbari, "represents a garden in perpetual spring."—Vol. ii. p. 152.

[5] The valley of Kashmír, embosomed within the Hindu-koh of Indian Caucasus, is nearly surrounded by lofty mountains, and is consequently difficult of access to an army; but yet, from the unwarlike character of the natives, it has been exposed to frequent invasions. "The fortifications with which nature has furnished it," Abu'lfazl adds, "are of an astonishing height."

teries, in which certain superiors exercise the functions of our abbots, and by the mass of the people they are held in great reverence.[1] The natives of this country do not deprive any creature of life, nor shed blood, and if they are inclined to eat flesh-meat, it is necessary that the Mahometans who reside amongst them should slay the animal.[2] The article of coral carried thither from Europe is sold at a higher price than in any other part of the world.

If I were to proceed in the same direction, it would lead me to India; but I have judged it proper to reserve the description of that country for a third book; and shall therefore return to Balashan, intending to pursue from thence the straight road to Cathay, and to describe, as has been done from the commencement of the work, not only the countries through which the route immediately lies, but also those in its vicinity, to the right and left.[3]

[1] These monks appear to resemble the talapoins of Ava and Siam, and gylongs of Tibet, who reside in communities, under the discipline of a superior, termed a *sankra* in the former countries, and a *lama* in the latter. Like them also they were evidently Buddhists; and although that proscribed sect may have since disappeared from Kashmîr, as from most of the other provinces of Hindustan, Abu'lfazl, who wrote in the sixteenth century, notices some remains of them in his days. "The third time," he says, "that the author followed the imperial stirrup to the delightful territory of Kashmir, he met with some old men of this religion." (Vol. iii. p. 158.) In another place he tells us that "the most respectable people of this country are the *rishis*, who although they do not suffer themselves to be fettered with traditions (stories of the Puranas), are doubtless true worshippers of God. They revile not any other sect, and ask nothing of any one; they plant the roads with fruit trees to furnish the traveller with refreshment; they abstain from flesh; and have no intercourse with the other sex. There are near two thousand of this sect in Kashmir."—Vol. ii. p. 155.

[2] Abu'lfazl, speaking of the priests of the religion of Buddha in Kashmîr, observes, that although they will not kill an animal, they do not refuse any kind of food that is offered to them; and whatever dies of itself they consider to be killed by God, and therefore eat it. (Vol. iii. p. 158.) Amongst the Hindus many castes are allowed to eat of certain kinds of animal food, who yet are restrained from shedding blood.

[3] Our author here gives a consistent and intelligible account of the plan he pursues in his description of the several countries that came within the scope of his observation or knowledge; and it is only to be regretted that he has not drawn a clearer line of distinction between those places which he actually saw himself, and those respecting which he collected information from others. I am inclined to believe that he did not visit the Panjab (or country embraced by the streams which form the Indus), and that what he relates of Peshawer and Kashmîr was furnished to him during his long residence of Badakhshan, by persons who frequented those places for the purposes of trade.

CHAPTER XXIX

OF THE PROVINCE OF VOKHAN—OF AN ASCENT FOR THREE DAYS, LEADING TO THE SUMMIT OF A HIGH MOUNTAIN—OF A PECULIAR BREED OF SHEEP FOUND THERE—OF THE EFFECT OF THE GREAT ELEVATION UPON FIRES—AND OF THE SAVAGE LIFE OF THE INHABITANTS.

LEAVING the province of Balashan, and travelling in a direction between north-east and east, you pass many castles and habitations on the banks of the river, belonging to the brother of the king of that place, and after three days' journey, reach a province named Vokhan; which itself extends in length and width to the distance of three days' journey.[1] The people are Mahometans, have a distinct language, are civilised in their manners, and accounted valiant in war. Their chief holds his territory as a fief dependent upon Bala-

[1] After having traced our author's line of description through countries where the writings of other travellers enabled us to recognise his steps, if we should now find ourselves in a region of greater uncertainty, the change is not to be attributed so much to any additional obscurity on his part, as to the want of corresponding information on ours, this tract being very imperfectly known to us. With respect, however, to the name and situation of Vokhan (the orthography of which differs little in the several versions), we are not entirely without lights, both ancient and modern. It is identified, in the first instance, by its connexion with a place named Weishgerd or Weishkird; concerning which Ibn Haukal says: "The river Wekhshab comes out of Turkestan, into the land of Wekhsh, near a mountain where there is a bridge between Khotlan and the borders of Weishkird. From that it runs towards Balkh, and falls into the Jihoon at Termed." (P. 239.) In the following passage from the work of Edrisi, we find the Vokhan of our text brought into contact with the places here mentioned: "De regionibus finitimis Vachas (Wekhsh or Wakhsh) et Gil, sunt Vachan (Vokhan) et Sacqita (Sakftah), in terra Torc. Inter Vachan et Tobbat intercedit iter octodecim dierum. In Vachan extant fodines argenti." (P. 141.) Weishgerd here appears to be the country intermediate between Badakhshan and Vokhan, which our author tells us was governed by a brother of the king of the former. What Edrisi states respecting this valley, as well as our author's account of it, are fully justified by the Memoir explaining the map prefixed to the Account of Caubul, where Lieut. Macartney, speaking of the river Ammu or Oxus, says: "This river . . . has its source from the high lands of Pamer. It issues from a narrow valley, two or three hundred yards broad, in Wukhan, the southern boundary of Pamer. This valley is inclosed on three sides by the high snowy mountain called Pooshtikhur, to the south, east, and west. The stream is seen coming from under the ice." (Appendix, p. 646.) The mere verification of the name and position of a district so secluded must be allowed to furnish an unexceptionable test of the genuineness of our traveller's relation.

shan. They practise various modes of taking wild animals. Upon leaving this country, and proceeding for three days, still in an east-north-east course, ascending mountain after mountain, you at length arrive at a point of the road, where you might suppose the surrounding summits to be the highest lands in the world. Here, between two ranges, you perceive a large lake, from which flows a handsome river, that pursues its course along an extensive plain, covered with the richest verdure. Such indeed is its quality that the leanest cattle turned upon it would become fat in the course of ten days. In this plain there are wild animals in great numbers, particularly sheep of a large size, having horns, three, four, and even six palms in length. Of these the shepherds form ladles and vessels for holding their victuals; and with the same materials they construct fences for enclosing their cattle, and securing them against the wolves, with which, they say, the country is infested, and which likewise destroy many of these wild sheep or goats.[1] Their horns and bones being found in large quantities, heaps are made of them at the sides of the road, for the purpose of guiding travellers at the season when it is covered with snow. For twelve days the course is along this elevated plain, which is named Pamer;[2] and as during all that time you do not meet with any habitations, it is necessary to make provision at the outset accordingly. So great is the height of the mountains, that no birds are to be seen near their summits; and however extraordinary it may be thought, it was affirmed, that from the keenness of the air, fires when lighted do not give the same heat as in lower situations, nor produce the same effect in dressing victuals.

After having performed this journey of twelve days, you have still forty days to travel in the same direction, over mountains, and through valleys, in perpetual succession, pass-

[1] From the length of the horns of these animals, and the uses to which they were applied, we might suppose them to be a species of ibex or mountain goat; and although called *montoni* in the first instance, they are afterwards spoken of as *becchi* or boucs. In Elphinstone's Account of Caubul, this conjecture is justified, where he says: "Goats are common in all the mountainous parts of the country, and are by no means scarce in the plains. Some breeds have remarkably long and curiously twisted horns." (P. 144.) J. Rh. Forster observes that these animals are termed *mouflons* and *muffioni*, by the French and Italian writers.

[2] We find the elevated plain of Pamer, Pamire, or Pamir, in all the maps of Persia and the neighbouring countries. In that which accompanies Macdonald Kinneir's Geographical Memoir, it occupies a place corresponding to the bearings we should infer from our author's description.

ing many rivers and desert tracts, without seeing any habitations or the appearance of verdure. Every article of provision must therefore be carried along with you. This region is called Beloro.[1] Even amidst the highest of these mountains, there live a tribe of savage, ill-disposed, and idolatrous people, who subsist upon the animals they can destroy, and clothe themselves with the skins.

CHAPTER XXX

OF THE CITY OF KASHCAR, AND OF THE COMMERCE OF ITS INHABITANTS.

At length you reach a place called Kashcar, which, it is said, was formerly an independent kingdom, but it is now subject to the dominion of the grand khan.[2] Its inhabitants are of the Mahometan religion. The province is extensive, and contains many towns and castles, of which Kashcar is the largest and most important.[3] The language of the people is peculiar to themselves. They subsist by commerce and

[1] This alpine region, named by eastern geographers Belûr or Belôr, is laid down in Strahlenberg's map, from whence, apparently, it has been transferred to those of D'Anville; but its position relatively to Pamîr and Badakhshan will be found still more conformable to our author's account, in the recent constructions of Macdonald Kinneir and Macartney. With respect to the nature of the country, it is spoken of by Elphinstone, in terms little differing from those employed in the text. "Izzut-Hoollah," he says, "gives a frightful picture of the cold and desolation of this elevated tract, which extends for three marches on the highest part of the country between Yarkund and Ley (or Ladauk)."—Note, p. 113.

[2] Kashgar, or Kashghar, is a well-known city and emporium for the trade carried on between Tartary, India, and China. It is situated in that part of Turkistan which Europeans term the Lesser Bucharia, and was formerly the capital of a kingdom of the same name. It was amongst the places overrun by the irresistible arms of Jengiz-khan, and upon the division of his empire, was included in the patrimony of his son Jagataï. About a century after our author's time, it was conquered by Tamerlane; and, in 1683, by the Kontaish, or great khan of the Kalmucks, from whom the eastern part of the Lesser Bucharia was wrested, in 1718, by the Chinese.

[3] "Al Bergendi dit," says D'Herbelot, "qu'elle est fort grande, et qu'elle passe pour la capitale de tout le pays; que ses habitans sont Mussulmans, et que beaucoup de scavans-hommes en sont sortis." Macdonald Kinneir's Itineraries speak of it as being situated on a well-cultivated plain, near a fine river, but not navigable, on the southern side of a range of mountains called Teeruck Duan.

manufacture, particularly works of cotton. They have handsome gardens, orchards, and vineyards. Abundance of cotton is produced there, as well as flax and hemp. Merchants from this country travel to all parts of the world; but in truth they are a covetous, sordid race,[1] eating badly and drinking worse. Besides the Mahometans there are amongst the inhabitants several Nestorian Christians, who are permitted to live under their own laws, and to have their churches. The extent of the province is five days' journey.

CHAPTER XXXI

OF THE CITY OF SAMARCAN, AND OF THE MIRACULOUS COLUMN IN THE CHURCH OF ST. JOHN THE BAPTIST.

SAMARCAN is a noble city, adorned with beautiful gardens, and surrounded by a plain, in which are produced all the fruits that man can desire.[2] The inhabitants, who are partly Christians and partly Mahometans, are subject to the dominion of a nephew of the grand khan, with whom, however, he is not upon amicable terms, but on the contrary there is perpetual strife and frequent wars between them.[3] This city lies

[1] The people of Bucharia, in the central parts of Asia, appear to resemble, in their commercial habits and parsimony, the Armenians who frequent the principal cities of India, and whom Forster, in his Travels, describes as being industrious, servile, and dishonest; pursuing the different roads of traffic with unremitting ardour, and invariably measuring their pleasures by the mere extent of their wealth.—Vol. ii. p. 117.

[2] It is obvious here, that in order to introduce the description of a place so important as Samarkand, which our author had probably visited in one of his official journeys, he departs from the course he was pursuing towards Kataia, and makes what may be considered as an excursion into the Greater Bucharia, or Transoxiana. This celebrated city was taken from the Persians by the khalif Walid in the year 704, and from the sultan of Khaurizm in 1220, by Jengiz-khan, who gave it up to pillage and destroyed many of its buildings. From this, however, it might have recovered in the course of fifty or sixty years that intervened before the period of which we are speaking. By Timur or Tamerlane it was restored to all its ancient splendour, about the year 1370, and became the capital of his vast dominions; but falling subsequently into the hands of the Uzbek Tartars, with whom it remained at the close of the last century, its consequence had much declined.

[3] Kashgar being the place last mentioned, it might be presumed that he speaks of the bearing of Samarkand from thence, but as the actual direction, instead of being north-west (*maestro*), is nearly west-south-west, we are justified in looking rather to Badakhshan, where he had

in the direction of north-west. A miracle is said to have taken place there, under the following circumstances. Not long ago, a prince named Zagatai, who was own brother to the (then reigning) grand khan, became a convert to Christianity; greatly to the delight of the Christian inhabitants of the place, who under the favour and protection of the prince, proceeded to build a church, and dedicated it to St. John the Baptist. It was so constructed that all the weight of the roof (being circular) should rest upon a column in the centre, and beneath this, as a base, they fixed a square stone, which, with the permission of the prince, they had taken from a temple belonging to the Mahometans, who dared not to prevent them from so doing. But upon the death of Zagatai, his son who succeeded him showing no disposition to become a Christian, the Mussulmans had influence enough to obtain from him an order that their opponents should restore to them the stone they had appropriated; and although the latter offered to pay them a compensation in money, they refused to listen to the proposal, because they hoped that its removal would occasion the church to tumble down. In this difficulty the afflicted Christians had no other resource than with tears and humility to recommend themselves to the protection of the glorious St. John the Baptist. When the day arrived on which they were to make restitution of the stone, it came to pass that through the intercession of the Saint, the pillar raised itself from its base to the height of three palms, in order to facilitate the removal of the stone; and in that situation, without any kind of support, it remains to the present day.[1] Enough being said of this, we shall now proceed to the province of Karkan.

long resided, and from whence he professes to begin his account of the route to Kataia. The latitude of Samarkand, as taken with the famous mural quadrant of Ulug Beig, the grandson of Tamerlane, is 39° 37′ N., and its longitude, as estimated by Major Rennell, is about 64° 15′ E. of Greenwich, or 7½° W. of Kashgar. By D'Anville they are placed several degrees further to the eastward.

[1] This is one of the stories, in the way of episode, that have tended to bring our author's work into disrepute. Zagataï was in fact, as he says, the brother of Oktaï, who succeeded his father as grand khan of the Moghuls; but we have no authority for his having embraced Christianity, although the Christians experienced much indulgence under Jengiz-khan and his immediate successors, and Mangu, his grandson, the nephew of Zagataï, is said by Rubruquis and Haiton to have been baptized. The text from which Marsden translated states that the circumstance referred to occurred a hundred and twenty-five years before this book was written, upon which he observes that, doubtful or improbable as the circumstance of Zagataï's conversion may be, the difficulty it occasions would be more easily surmounted than that of the anachronism; for as he began to reign about the year 1227, and died in 1240, the time elapsed at the

CHAPTER XXXII

OF THE PROVINCE OF KARKAN, THE INHABITANTS OF WHICH ARE TROUBLED WITH SWOLLEN LEGS AND WITH GOITRES.

DEPARTING from thence you enter the province of Karkan,[1] which continues to the distance of five days' journey. Its inhabitants, for the most part Mahometans, with some Nestorian Christians, are subjects of the grand khan. Provisions are here in abundance, as is also cotton. The people are expert artisans. They are in general afflicted with swellings in the legs, and tumours in the throat, occasioned by the quality of the water they drink.[2] In this country there is not anything further that is worthy of observation.

period when Marco Polo's Travels were written could not be more than about seventy years, even if the event took place at the commencement of his reign; whereas the space of 125 years, as stated in the text, would carry it back to 1173, when his father was only nine years of age, and the family obscure. This species of absurd error I can neither account for nor palliate, otherwise than by supposing that the date, which does not appear in the Latin versions or Italian epitomes, has been an interpolation in one of the manuscripts followed by Ramusio. [All the early manuscripts agree in the phrase translated in the present edition—non è gran tempo che—non est magnum tempus quod—il fu voir qu'il ne a encore granment de tens que.]

[1] The visit to Samarkand being excursive, or out of the line of his present route, our author leads us back to a place in the Lesser Bucharia which at that time belonged to the kingdom of Kashgar, noticed in the preceding chapter. Carchan, or Karkan, was intended for the district, or rather its chief town, which is most generally known by the name of Yerken; although its orthography has been exposed to as much variation amongst the writers of latter times, as in the copies of our author's work. By the Portuguese missionary Benjamin Goez the word is written Hiarchan; by Du Halde, Yarkian; by Strahlenberg, in his map, Jerken, Hyarchan, or Gurkan; by D'Anville, Jĕrken; by De Guignes, Yerken; and by our modern travellers from the side of Hindustan, Yarkund. "It appears," says Lieut. Macartney, "that after five days' journey north-east of Cashmeer, an evident ascent commences, which is very great for three or four days' journey, after which it is less on to Leh (or Ladâk). The ascent continues even on to the great ridge which separates Tibet from Yarkund."—Account of Caubul, p. 646. Appendix.

[2] The permanent œdematous swelling of the leg to a monstrous size is a disorder well known in several parts of the East, and vulgarly termed in India the "Cochin leg." For an account of this species of *elephantiasis*, see Cordiner's Description of Ceylon, vol. i. p. 182. Respecting the cause of those glandulous tumours at the throat called *goitres*, much has been written by travellers and medical persons, who in general attribute it to the quality of the water, although the notion of its proceding from snow-water has been exploded. I have elsewhere ventured to express

CHAPTER XXXIII

OF THE CITY OF KOTAN, WHICH IS ABUNDANTLY SUPPLIED WITH ALL THE NECESSARIES OF LIFE.

FOLLOWING a course between north-east and east, you next come to the province of Kotan,[1] the extent of which is eight days' journey. It is under the dominion of the grand khan, and the people are Mahometans. It contains many cities and fortified places, but the principal city, and which gives its name to the province, is Kotan. Everything necessary for human life is here in the greatest plenty. It yields likewise cotton, flax, hemp, grain, wine, and other articles. The inhabitants cultivate farms and vineyards, and have numerous gardens.[2] They support themselves also by trade and manufactures, but they are not good soldiers. We shall now speak of a province named Peyn.

an opinion that these affections of the glands of the throat are occasioned by the dense mists which settle in the valleys between high mountains, and are not dispersed until a late hour of the day. (Hist. of Sumatra, 3d edit., p. 48.) See an ingenious paper on this subject by Dr. Reeves, published in the Phil. Trans. for the year 1808, vol. xcviii. p. 111.

[1] The name of Kotan is indubitably Khoten (the Yu-tien and Ho-tien of the Chinese, who soften the Tartar pronunciation), a place familiar to us, by name at least, as that from whence a great part of Asia is supplied with musk, which the natives rank amongst the most exquisite perfumes, and the Persian poets never cease to extol. Beyond this circumstance our information concerning it is very imperfect. "Khoten," says Malcolm, "was formerly of some importance, and its chiefs are often mentioned. It was conquered, with Kashgar, Yarkund, and other provinces in the same quarter, by the Chinese, in 1757, and now forms part of that great empire. A respectable inhabitant of Tartary, who visited the town of Khoten about twenty years ago, describes it as in a flourishing state, though inferior in size to the city of Yarkund, from which it is distant about 140 miles. Khoten is still, according to this traveller's account, celebrated for its musk."—Hist. of Persia, vol. i. p. 324, note.

[2] Although we do not meet with direct authority for the cultivation of the vine at Khoten, there can be little doubt of the fact, as we read of vineyards at Hami, or Khamil, to the eastward, as well as at Kashgar, to the northward of this place, and within the same canton or district.

CHAPTER XXXIV

OF THE PROVINCE OF PEYN—OF THE CHALCEDONIES AND JASPER FOUND IN ITS RIVER—AND OF A PECULIAR CUSTOM WITH REGARD TO MARRIAGES.

PEYN is a province of five days' journey in extent, in the direction of east-north-east.[1] It is under the dominion of the grand khan, and contains many cities and strong places, the principal one of which is likewise named Peyn. Through this flows a river, and in its bed are found many of those stones called chalcedonies and jasper.[2] All kinds of provision are obtained here. Cotton also is produced in the country. The inhabitants live by manufacture and trade. They have this custom, that if a married man goes to a distance from home to be absent twenty days, his wife has a right, if she is inclined, to take another husband; and the men, on the same principle, marry wherever they happen to reside. All the before-mentioned provinces, that is to say, Kashcar, Kotan, Peyn, and as far as the desert of Lop, are within the limits of Turkistan.[3] Next follows the province of Charchan.

[1] Our author's course of description now leads us to places situated on the eastern side of Khoten, and in the neighbourhood of the great sandy desert, where we are left without any guidance excepting the scanty notices with which he has furnished us. The situation assigned by D'Anville to Peyn or Pe-yn (which in the epitomes is Poim or Poin), being seven degrees of longitude from Khoten, seems to be too far to the eastward, and to approach too nearly to the frontier of China. In this opinion, which applies equally to the intermediate places which are the subject of the following chapters, I am warranted by that of Major Rennell, who says: "I think that our maps are in a great error with respect to the positions of the countries lying between Bucharia and China; all of which, in my idea, have been made to recede too much from Bucharia towards China."—Memoir of a Map of Hindustan, p. 191.

[2] The jasper, or a hard kind of stone resembling jasper, is noticed by several writers as the production of this part of Tartary; and Goez speaks of its being procured from the bed of the river at Khoten, which may probably be the same stream that afterwards runs to Peyn.

[3] The eastern limits of Turkistan, or Turquestan, are not well defined; but it may be considered generally as extending throughout that tract of Central Asia in which dialects of the Turki or Turko-Tartarian language are spoken; and as the Bukhar or Bucharian, although much mixed with Persian words, is one of these dialects, it follows that our author is warranted in considering places that belong to what Europeans term the Lesser Bucharia, and Eastern writers the kingdom of Kashgar, as forming a part of Turkistan, which consequently reaches to the borders of the great desert of Kobi. For the convenience of geography, it is distinguished into Chinese and Independent Turkistan, separated from each

CHAPTER XXXV

OF THE PROVINCE OF CHARCHAN—OF THE KINDS OF STONE FOUND IN ITS RIVERS—AND OF THE NECESSITY THE INHABITANTS ARE UNDER, OF FLYING TO THE DESERT ON THE APPROACH OF THE ARMIES OF THE TARTARS.

CHARCHAN is also a province of Turkistan, lying in an east-north-east direction (from Peyn). In former times it was flourishing and productive, but has been laid waste by the Tartars. The people are Mahometans. Its chief city is likewise named Charchan.[1] Through this province run several large streams, in which also are found chalcedonies and jaspers, which are carried for sale to Cathay,[2] and such is their abundance that they form a considerable article of commerce. The country from Peyn to this district, as well as throughout its whole extent, is an entire sand,[3] in which the water is for the most part bitter and unpalatable, although in particular places it is sweet and good. When an army of Tartars passes through these places, if they are enemies the inhabitants are plundered of their goods, and if friends their cattle are killed and devoured. For this reason, when they are aware of the approach of any body of troops, they flee, with their families and cattle, into the sandy desert, to the distance of two days' journey, towards some spot where they can find fresh water,

other by the great mountainous range of Belur-tag and Mush-tag or Imaus. Elphinstone refers to this division when he says: "Those (caravans from the side of India) which go to Chinese Toorkistaun, set off from Cashmeer and Peshawer: Caubul is the great mart of Independent Toorkistaun." (Account of Caubul, p. 293.) [The words of the early Latin version are, "Sunt de magna Turchia."]

[1] Charchan (in Ramusio, Ciarcian; in the Basle edition and older Latin, Ciartiam; and in the Italian epitome, Ciarchian) appears to correspond with the Schachan of Strahlenberg's map, although its situation seems to be rather that of Karashai. De Guignes speaks of a district named Chen-chen, to the south of Hami, and near the lake of Lop, which can be no other than this. See Hist. gén. des Huns, tom. i. part. ii. p. 11.

[2] The name of the place to which these jaspers are said to be carried is in Ramusio's text Ouchah or Oukah, but evidently by mistake. In the Basle edition the words are, "quos negotiatores deferunt ad provinciam Cathai," and in the manuscripts it is Catay: which is known to be the fact.

[3] In the Italian epitomes it is here said, rather more precisely: "Questa provincia e tutta piena de sabion per la mazor parte; e da Cata (Kataia) infino a Poin (Peyn) e molto sabion."

and are by that means enabled to subsist. From the same apprehension, when they collect their harvest, they deposit the grain in caverns amongst the sands; taking monthly from the store so much as may be wanted for their consumption; nor can any persons besides themselves know the places to which they resort for this purpose, because the tracks of their feet are presently effaced by the wind. Upon leaving Charchan the road lies for five days over sands, where the water is generally, but not in all places, bad. Nothing else occurs here that is worthy of remark. At the end of these five days you arrive at the city of Lop, on the borders of the great desert.

CHAPTER XXXVI

OF THE TOWN OF LOP—OF THE DESERT IN ITS VICINITY—AND OF THE STRANGE NOISES HEARD BY THOSE WHO PASS OVER THE LATTER.

THE town of Lop is situated towards the north-east, near the commencement of the great desert, which is called the Desert of Lop.[1] It belongs to the dominions of the grand khan, and its inhabitants are of the Mahometan religion. Travellers who intend to cross the desert usually halt for a considerable time at this place, as well to repose from their fatigues as to make the necessary preparations for their further journey. For this purpose they load a number of stout asses and camels with provisions and with their merchandise. Should the former be consumed before they have completed the passage, they kill

[1] The lake of Lop appears in the Jesuits' and D'Anville's maps. In the latter we find also a town named "Tantabée ou Tankabash, résidence de l'ancien khan de Tagazgaz, ville de Lop dans Marc-Paul;" but his authority for this supposition does not appear. "Ces deux villes dont je viens de parler," says De Guignes, speaking of Ciatiam (or Charchan) and Lop, "paroissent être les mêmes que celles de Kantcheou et de Hankiun-tcheou, que les envoyés Chinois trouvèrent dans leur route de Cha-tcheou à Khoten, mais il me paroît impossible d'en assigner la véritable position." (P. 17.) Instead of the name of Lop, which this desert bears in Ramusio's as well as in most of the other versions, the word in the early Italian epitomes is Job; and this variation of orthography gives rise to the conjecture that it may have been intended for Kobi, which is said to be the original Tartar name. "Tout cet espace," says Du Halde, "n'est qu'un terrain sec et sablonneux, le plus stérile qui qui soit dans toute la Tartarie. C'est ce que les Chinois appellent ordinairement Chamo (Shamo), quelquefois Kan-hai, comme qui diroit *mer* de sable. Les Tartares le nomment Cobi."—Tom. iv. p. 26.

and eat the cattle of both kinds; but camels are commonly here employed in preference to asses, because they carry heavy burthens and are fed with a small quantity of provender. The stock of provisions should be laid in for a month, that time being required for crossing the desert in the narrowest part. To travel it in the direction of its length would prove a vain attempt, as little less than a year must be consumed, and to convey stores for such a period would be found impracticable.[1] During these thirty days the journey is invariably over either sandy plains or barren mountains; but at the end of each day's march you stop at a place where water is procurable; not indeed in sufficient quantity for large numbers, but enough to supply a hundred persons, together wth their beasts of burthen. At three or four of these halting-places the water is salt and bitter, but at the others, amounting to about twenty, it is sweet and good. In this tract neither beasts nor birds are met with, because there is no kind of food for them.[2]

It is asserted as a well-known fact that this desert is the abode of many evil spirits, which amuse travellers to their destruction with most extraordinary illusions. If, during the day-time, any persons remain behind on the road, either when overtaken by sleep or detained by their natural occasions, until the caravan has passed a hill and is no longer in sight, they unexpectedly hear themselves called to by their names, and in a tone of voice to which they are accustomed. Supposing the call to proceed from their companions, they are led away by it

[1] In the Jesuits' map prefixed to Du Halde's "Description de la Chine," the desert is made to extend, with a partial interruption, from the meridian of Peking, westward to the thirty-fifth degree of longitude reckoned from that city. The impracticability, therefore, of travelling over it in that direction, as observed by our author, is evident.

[2] The general conformity of this description, as it regards the dreary aspect of the country and the nature of the halting places, with the account given by that excellent traveller John Bell of Antermony, who crossed another part of the same desert, in his route from Selinginsky to Peking, will be found very striking; and it is remarkable that the number of days employed was in the one case thirty, and in the other twenty-eight. The most material difference between them is, that Bell, during several days of his journey, met with sheep, and afterwards herds of antelopes, as well as a flock of plovers, whereas our author saw neither beasts nor birds in his passage. But it is not improbable that the desert may be more barren and inhospitable towards its western extremity; and it is at the same time reasonable to suppose that the line of road taken by the Chinese government for their communication with the Russian dominions, should be through that part where there was the best chance of finding the means of subsistence. It is also possible that some changes may have taken place in the course of four hundred and fifty years, and that a breed of sheep may have been carried to those spots which exhibited symptoms of vegetation.

from the direct road, and not knowing in what·direction to advance, are left to perish. In the night-time they are persuaded they hear the march of a large cavalcade on one side or the other of the road, and concluding the noise to be that of the footsteps of their party, they direct theirs to the quarter from whence it seems to proceed; but upon the breaking of day, find they have been misled and drawn into a situation of danger. Sometimes likewise during the day these spirits assume the appearance of their travelling companions, who address them by name and endeavour to conduct them out of the proper road. It is said also that some persons, in their course across the desert, have seen what appeared to them to be a body of armed men advancing towards them, and apprehensive of being attacked and plundered have taken to flight. Losing by this means the right path, and ignorant of the direction they should take to regain it, they have perished miserably of hunger. Marvellous indeed and almost passing belief are the stories related of these spirits of the desert, which are said at times to fill the air with the sounds of all kinds of musical instruments, and also of drums and the clash of arms; obliging the travellers to close their line of march and to proceed in more compact order.[1] They find it necessary also to take the precaution before they repose for the night, to fix an advanced signal, pointing out the course they are afterwards to hold, as well as to attach a bell to each of the beasts of burthen for the purpose of their being more easily kept from straggling. Such are the excessive troubles and dangers that must unavoidably be encountered in the passage of this desert.

CHAPTER XXXVII

OF THE PROVINCE OF TANGUTH—OF THE CITY OF SACHION—OF THE CUSTOM OBSERVED THERE UPON THE BIRTH OF A MALE CHILD—AND OF THE CEREMONY OF BURNING THE BODIES OF THE DEAD

WHEN the journey of thirty days across the desert has been completed, you arrive at a city called Sachion,[2] which belongs

[1] We find in the works of the Chinese geographers that these idle stories are the subject of general belief in the part of Tartary here described.

[2] Having crossed a narrow part of the great desert, in a direction from the towns of the kingdom of Kashgar towards the nearest point of China,

to the grand khan. The province is named Tanguth.[1] The people are worshippers of idols.[2] There are Turkomans among them, with a few Nestorian Christians and Mahometans.

our author's course naturally leads him to a place named Cha-tcheou, according to the French, or Sha-cheu according to our orthography. "A l'est du lac de Lop," says De Guignes, "on trouve une ville que M. Paul appelle Sachion, la Cha-tcheou ou *ville de sable* des Chinois." (P. 12.) The corruption of this name from Sha-cheu to Sachion will appear to have arisen chiefly from the difficulty of distinguishing the *u* from *n* in manuscripts; and it will be found that a great proportion of the Chinese names for towns, in the subsequent parts of the work, are affected by the same error. The place is situated about four degrees to the westward of So-cheu (an important garrison at the western extremity of the province of Shen-si), and commands the entrance of a famous pass or gorge of the mountains, named Yang-kuan. In the history of Jengiz-khan by Pétis de la Croix it is observed, that his occupation of this strong post was of the greatest advantage to his subsequent operations against the southern provinces of China. (P. 481.) It may appear an objection to this identifying of Sachion with Sha-cheu, which lies in the direct way to, and not very distant from the Chinese province of Shen-si, that in the next chapter he proceeds to speak of a place not intermediate, but on the contrary still further from the borders, and in a different direction. But it must be recollected that our author's work is not a simple itinerary, and that he professes to describe parts not in the line of his original journey, but which he might have visited subsequently whilst in the service of the emperor. Here, too, we may remark that he does not give any estimation of distance, as if the route were continuous, but breaks off in order to speak of other places, "at the head of the desert."

[1] It is not unusual to consider the names of Tangut and Tibet, both of which have been adopted by the Persians from the Moghuls, as synonymous; but the former applies to a larger portion of Tartary, bordering upon the western provinces of China, and including Tibet in its southern division, whilst its northern contains the districts of which our author now proceeds to speak. According to Du Halde's definition, however, it does not extend quite so far northward as the situation assigned to Cha-tcheou in the Jesuits' map.

[2] The inhabitants of the countries on the western side of the desert of Lop or Kobi were described by our author as being chiefly Mahometans; but upon crossing that tract and entering the province of Tangut, or Sifan, as it is termed by the Chinese, he properly speaks of the people as idolaters. By idolatry is here meant the religion generally known as that of the grand lama, or spiritual sovereign, whom his followers believe to be immortal, by means of successive regeneration of the same individual in different bodies, but do not worship, as has been supposed. Their adoration is paid to a number of images of deities, but principally to one, which is often of a colossal size, and is named by them Shakia-muni. This is the Buddha of the Hindu mythology, whose doctrines are more extensively disseminated throughout the east than even those of Mahomet. In Ava and Pegu the same idol is worshipped by the name of Gautama (equally with Shakia an epithet or attribute of Buddha), in Siam by that of Samana-kodom, in Cochin-China and Tonkin by that of But and Thika-mauni, in Japan by that of Shaka and Amida Buth, and in China, where the same system prevails amongst the bulk of the population, by that of Fo or Fuh. Many of the other objects of worship appear to belong to the Brahmanic mythology, and some are of a local character. It is evident at the same time that with respect to forms and ceremonies, of which there will be occasion to say more hereafter, many of them have been adopted from the Nestorian Christians.

Those who are idolaters have a language distinct from the others.[1] This city lies towards the east-north-east. They are not a commercial, but an agricultural people, having much wheat. There are in this country a number of monasteries and abbeys, which are filled with idols of various descriptions.[2] To these, which they regard with the profoundest reverence, they also offer sacrifices; and upon the birth of a son, they recommend him to the protection of some one of their idols. In honour of this deity the father rears a sheep in his house until the expiration of a year, when, upon the day of the idol's peculiar festival, they conduct their son, together with the sheep, into its presence, and there sacrifice the animal. The flesh they seethe, and then they carry it and lay it before the idol, and stand there until they have finished a long prayer, the subject of which is to entreat the idol to preserve the health of their child;[3] and they believe that during this interval it has sucked in all the savoury juices of the meat. The remaining substance they then carry home, and, assembling all their relations and friends, eat it with much devout festivity. They collect the bones, and preserve them in handsome urns. The priests of the idol have for their portion

[1] This we term the language of Tibet, which is monosyllabic in its principle, like the Chinese, but in every other respect differs from it. The written character bears more commonly the appellation of Tangut or Tangutian, and in its alphabetic arrangement acknowledges a *nagri* or Sanskrit origin.

[2] Of the numerous and capacious buildings erected in a country where every fourth male of a family is devoted to the monastic life, we find frequent mention in the writings of travellers, and particularly in the accounts of Bogle's mission in 1774, and Turner's in 1783, to the court of the southern grand lama. The plates annexed to the latter will furnish the curious reader with a perfect idea of the exterior appearance of these monasteries, some of which contain from two to three thousand *gylongs* or monks. An engraving of the same subject appears also amongst the plates connected with Lord Macartney's Embassy to China: various circumstances relative to the interior of the establishments will be found in Turner's pleasing narrative, and a general description, with a ground plan, in the Alphabetum Tibetanum of Georgi, p. 407. In the Mém. conc. les Chinois, tom. xiv., we find an elaborate account of the great *miao* or abbey of Putala, at Lhassa, which has "367 pieds quatre pouces de hauteur."

[3] The ceremony here described, in which the sacrifice of the sheep appears to be intended as a ransom for the child, who, at his birth, may have been devoted rather than recommended to the guardian deity, is consistent with what is remarked by the younger De Guignes, of a practice amongst the neighbours of this people. "Comme les Chinois," says this traveller, "implorent les génies dans toutes les circonstances de la vie, il n'est pas surprenant qu'ils les invoquent pour en obtenir la conservation de leurs enfans. Lorsqu'ils craignent de les perdre, ils les consacrent à quelque dieu." (Voyages à Peking, etc., tom. ii. p. 359.) A similar custom is said to exist in Bengal.

the head, the feet, the intestines, and the skin, together with some parts of the flesh. In respect to the dead, likewise, these idolaters have particular ceremonies. Upon the decease of a person of rank, whose body it is intended to burn,[1] the relations call together the astrologers, and make them acquainted with the year, the day, and the hour in which he was born; whereupon these proceed to examine the horoscope, and having ascertained the constellation or sign, and the planet therein presiding, declare the day on which the funeral ceremony shall take place. If it should happen that the same planet be not then in the ascendant, they order the body to be kept a week or more, and sometimes even for the space of six months, before they allow the ceremony to be performed. In the hope of a propitious aspect, and dreading the effects of a contrary influence, the relations do not presume to burn the corpse until the astrologers have fixed the proper time.[2] It being necessary on this account that, in many cases, the body should remain long in the house, in order to guard against the consequences of putrefaction, they prepare a coffin made of boards a palm in thickness, well fitted together and painted, in which they deposit the corpse, and along with it a quantity of sweet-scented gums, camphor, and other drugs; the joints or seams they smear with a mixture of pitch and lime, and the whole is then covered with silk. During this period the table is spread every day with bread, wine, and other provisions, which remain so long as is necessary for a convenient meal, as well as for the spirit of the deceased, which they suppose to be present on the occasion, to satisfy itself with the fumes of the victuals. Sometimes the astrologers signify to the relations that the body must not be conveyed from the house through the principal door, in consequence of their having discovered from the aspect of the heavens, or otherwise, that such a course would be unlucky, and it must therefore be taken out from a different side of the house.[3] In

[1] It is only on the bodies of personages of the highest rank that the honours of the funeral pile are bestowed; those of the inferior orders being exposed in unfrequented places, and sometimes on the tops of mountains, to be devoured by birds and other wild animals.

[2] The implicit deference paid to the skill of astrologers in determining the days and hours proper for the performance of all acts, public and domestic, solemn or trivial, is general throughout the East.

[3] This custom is found to prevail also amongst the Chinese with whom the inhabitants of a country so near to the borders of the empire, as that which our author is now describing, must have much in common. "C'est parmi eux," adds Du Halde, "un usage de faire de nouvelles ouvertures à leurs maisons, quand on doit transporter le corps de leurs parens

some instances, indeed, they oblige them to break through the wall that happens to stand opposite to the propitious and beneficent planet, and to convey the corpse through that aperture; persuading them that if they should refuse to do so, the spirit of the defunct would be incensed against the family and cause them some injury. Accordingly, when any misfortune befalls a house, or any person belonging to it meets with an accident or loss, or with an untimely death, the astrologers do not fail to attribute the event to a funeral not having taken place during the ascendency of the planet under which the deceased relative was born, but, on the contrary, when it was exposed to a malign influence, or to its not having been conducted through the proper door. As the ceremony of burning the body must be performed without the city, they erect from space to space in the road by which the procession is to pass, small wooden buildings, with a portico which they cover with silk; and under these, as it arrives at each, the body is set down. They place before it meats and liquors, and this is repeated until they reach the appointed spot, believing, as they do, that the spirit is thereby refreshed and acquires energy to attend the funeral pile. Another ceremony also is practised on these occasions. They provide a number of pieces of paper, made of the bark of a certain tree, upon which are painted the figures of men, women, horses, camels, pieces of money, and dresses, and these they burn along with the corpse, under the persuasion that in the next world the deceased will enjoy the services and use of the domestics, cattle, and all the articles depicted on the paper.[1] During the whole of these proceedings, all the musical instruments belonging to the place are sounded with an incessant din.[2] Having now spoken of this city, others lying towards the north-west, near the head of the desert, shall next be mentioned.

décédez au lieu de leur sépulture, et de les refermer aussitôt, afin de s'épargner la douleur que leur causeroit le fréquent souvenir du défunt, qui se renouvelleroit toutes les fois qu'ils passeroient par la même porte où est passé le cercüeil." (P. 128.) Nor is the prejudice here described confined to the eastern parts of the world; for in a town or village of North Holland (as I was informed on the spot) a corpse is never carried out through the front or principal door, but from the rear of the house.

[1] Could we suppose the missionaries to have derived their knowledge of the customs of these people from the writings of our author, the parallel could not be more complete than it will be found in various passages of Du Halde.

[2] All accounts of the ceremonies of these people notice the loud clangour of their music.

CHAPTER XXXVIII

OF THE DISTRICT OF KAMUL, AND OF SOME PECULIAR CUSTOMS RESPECTING THE ENTERTAINMENT OF STRANGERS

KAMUL is a district situated within the great province of Tanguth, subject to the grand khan, and contains many towns and castles, of which the principal city is also named Kamul.[1] This district lies in the intermediate space between two deserts; that is to say, the great desert already described, and another of smaller extent, being only about three days' journey across.[2] The inhabitants are worshippers of idols, and have their peculiar language.[3] They subsist on the fruits of the earth, which they possess in abundance, and are enabled to supply the wants of travellers.[4] The men are addicted to pleasure, and attend to little else than playing upon instruments, singing,

[1] Kamul, which the Tartars are said to pronounce Khamil, or Hamil with a strong aspiration, is the Hami of the Jesuits' map, softened in the Chinese pronunciation, as the title of *khan* is changed to *han*. In the narrative of B. Goez it is stated, that after leaving a place named Cialis (the Juldus of Strahlenberg's map), and passing another named Puciàn, also belonging to the kingdom of Cascàr, they reached Turphan and remained there a month. "Après ils parvindrent à Aramuth, et puis à Camul, place garnie de bonnes deffences. Ilz reposèrent icy avec leurs chevaux un autre mois. . . . Estans partis de Camul ilz arrivèrent dans neuf jours à ces murs septentrionaux du royaume de la Chine, en un lieu nommé Chiaicuon (Kia-yu-kuan). . . . Aians donc enfin esté reçus dans l'enclos de ces murailles, ilz arrivèrent en un jour en la ville de Socieu (So-cheu)." (Histoire de l'Expédition Chrestienne, par Trigault, pp. 482—485.) The distance, however, from Hami to So-cheu, the most western town of China, being by the maps about 280 miles, would render it a journey, for a caravan, of more than ten days.

[2] This account of the position of Kamul will be found to correspond exactly to that of Hami, which together with Turfan occupies a tract of cultivable land that seems nearly to divide the great desert of Kobi into two parts. See the Jesuits' maps accompanying Du Halde's "Description de la Chine."

[3] At the period of Shah Rokh's embassy, which was about a century and a half later than our author's visit to this place, it was under a Mahometan government.

[4] "Le pays," says Gerbillon, "est fort chaud en été; il y croît quantité de bons fruits." (P. 54.) The Abbé Grosier observes that "the country of Hami, though surrounded by deserts, is accounted one of the most delightful in the world. The soil produces abundance of grain, fruits, leguminous plants, and pasture of every kind. The rice which grows here is particularly esteemed in China. . . . There is no fruit more delicate or more in request than the melons of Hami, which are carried to Peking for the emperor's table . . . but the most useful and most esteemed production of the country is its dried raisins."—General Description of China, vol. i. p. 333.

dancing, reading, writing, according to the practice of the country, and the pursuit, in short, of every kind of amusement.[1] When strangers arrive, and desire to have lodging and accommodation at their houses, it affords them the highest gratification. They give positive orders to their wives, daughters, sisters, and other female relations, to indulge their guests in every wish, whilst they themselves leave their homes, and retire into the city, and the stranger lives in the house with the females as if they were his own wives, and they send whatever necessaries may be wanted; but for which, it is to be understood, they expect payment: nor do they return to their houses so long as the strangers remain in them. This abandonment of the females of their family to accidental guests, who assume the same privileges and meet with the same indulgences as if they were their own wives, is regarded by these people as doing them honour and adding to their reputation; considering the hospitable reception of strangers, who (after the perils and fatigues of a long journey) stand in need of relaxation, as an action agreeable to their deities, calculated to draw down the blessing of increase upon their families, to augment their substance, and to procure them safety from all dangers, as well as a successful issue to all their undertakings. The women are in truth very handsome, very sensual, and fully disposed to conform in this respect to the injunction of their husbands. It happened at the time when Mangu Khan held his court in this province, that the above scandalous custom coming to his knowledge, he issued an edict strictly commanding the people of Kamul to relinquish a practice so disgraceful to them, and forbidding individuals to furnish lodging to strangers, who should be obliged to accommodate themselves at a house of public resort or *caravanserai*. In grief and sadness the inhabitants obeyed for about three years the command of their master; but finding at length that the earth ceased to yield the accustomed fruits, and that many unfortunate events occurred in their families, they resolved to despatch a deputa-

[1] "Leurs divertissemens," says P. Amiot, speaking of the inhabitants of this part of the country, "consistent en chants et en danses. Ils se mettent par bandes de cinq ou six hommes et femmes pêle-mêle, se prennent par la main, et tournent ensemble, en faisant de tems en tems quelques sauts." (Mém. concern. les Chinois, tom. xiv. p. 152.) We should not have expected to find reading and writing classed amongst light and effeminate occupations; but allowance must be made for the prejudices of a person educated in a Tartar court. A detailed account of the manner and instruments of writing amongst these people will be found in the Alphabetum Tibetanum, pp. 561—567.

tion to the grand khan, in their names, to beseech him that he should be pleased to suffer them to resume the observance of a custom that had been solemnly handed down to them by their fathers, from their ancestors in the remotest times; and especially as since they had failed in the exercise of these offices of hospitality and gratification to strangers, the interest of their families had gone progressively to ruin. The grand khan, having listened to this application, replied:—"Since you appear so anxious to persist in your own shame and ignominy, let it be granted as you desire. Go, live according to your base customs and manners, and let your wives continue to receive the beggarly wages of their prostitution." With this answer the deputies returned home, to the great delight of all the people, who, to the present day, observe their ancient practice.[1]

CHAPTER XXXIX

OF THE CITY OF CHINCHITALAS

NEXT to the district of Kamul follows that of Chinchitalas, which in its northern part borders on the desert, and is in length sixteen days' journey.[2] It is subject to the grand khan,

[1] In Elphinstone's account of Caubul he gives a description of manners prevailing in the tribes that inhabit the eastern part of the Paropamisan mountains, so nearly similar to what our author mentions, that I am gratified by the occasion of verifying his statement by authority so respectable. "The women," he says, "are often handsome. . . . It is universally agreed that they are by no means remarkable for chastity; but I have heard different accounts of their libertinism. In the north-east, which is the most civilized part of the country, the women would prostitute themselves for money, while their husbands were out of the way. . . . In other parts of the country there prevails a custom called Kooroo Bistaun, by which the husband lends his wife to the embraces of his guests. This," he adds in a note, "is Moghul: one of the laws of the Yasa forbids adultery. The inhabitants of Caiader applied for, and received an exemption, on account of their old usage of lending their wives to their guests."—P. 483.

[2] Mention is made in L'Hist. générale des Huns of a place named Chen-chen, which has been supposed to be the Chinchitalas of our author. *Tala*, it should be observed, signifies in the Moghul-Tartar language, "a plain," and *talai* or *dalai*, "a sea or extensive lake:" *talas* may therefore be considered as an appellative, distinct from the proper name. "Ce pays," says De Guignes, "qui dans les historiens Chinois porte les deux noms de Leou-lan et de Chen-chen, est situé au midi de Hami. Il formoit anciennement un petit royaune dont la capitale étoit Kan-ni-tching voisine du lac de Lop. Tout ce pays est stérile, plein de sables, et l'on

and contains cities and several strong places. Its inhabitants consist of three religious sects. A few of them confess Christ, according to the Nestorian doctrine; others are followers of Mahomet; and a third class worship idols. There is in this district a mountain where the mines produce steel, and also zinc or antimony.[1] A substance is likewise found of the nature of the salamander, for when woven into cloth, and thrown into the fire, it remains incombustible.[2] The following mode of preparing it I learned from one of my travelling companions, named Curficar, a very intelligent Turkoman, who had the direction of the mining operations of the province for three years. The fossil substance procured from the mountain consists of fibres not unlike those of wool. This, after being exposed to the sun to dry, is pounded in a brass mortar, and is then washed until all the earthy particles are separated. The fibres thus cleansed and detached from each other, they then spin into thread and weave into cloth. In order to render the texture white, they put it into the fire, and suffer it to remain there about an hour, when they draw it out uninjured by the flame, and become white as snow. By the same process they afterwards cleanse it, when it happens to contract spots, no other abstergent lotion than an igneous one being ever applied to it.[3] Of the salamander under the form of a serpent, sup-

y rencontre peu de bonnes terres. On y comptoit environ quinze cents familles. Ces peuples cherchent les pâturages où ils nourissent des ânes, des chevaux et des chameaux. Ils tirent des pays voisins leurs denrées: ils ont les mêmes mœurs que les peuples du Tibet qui sont leurs voisins au sud-est. . . . Je pense que c'est dans ce canton qu'il faut placer la province que M. Paul appelle Chin-chin-talas, voisine du grand désert, et où il y avoit des Nestoriens, des Mahometans, et des idolatres.'" (Tom. i. pt. ii. p. xi.) It may, however, be doubted whether Chinchitalas is not the Cialis or Chialis of B. Goez, which he describes as a place dependent upon the king of Kashgar, and not far distant from Turfan and Kamul.

[1] Respecting this mineral, which in the Latin is *andanicum* or *audanicum*, and in the Italian of the epitomes, *andranico* and *andronico*, see notes on pp. 56 and 71.

[2] There can be no doubt that what the texts here call salamander was really the asbestos. [The passage in the early Latin text is, " Et in ista montana est una alia vena unde fit salamandra. Salamandra autem non est bestia sicut dicitur quæ vivat in igne, sed dicam vobis quomodo fit salamandra.]

[3] The asbestos is described as " a fossile stone that may be split into threads or filaments, from one to ten inches in length, very fine, brittle, yet somewhat tractable, silky, and of a greyish colour. It is indissoluble in water, and endued with the wonderful property of remaining unconsumed in the fire." " L'asbeste a eu autrefois," says M. Brongniart, " des usages assez remarquables. Les anciens, qui brûloient les corps, l'ont employé comme drap incombustible pour conserver les cendres des corps sans mélange. Lorsque les filamens de cette pierre sont assez

posed to exist in fire, I could never discover any traces in the eastern regions. It is said that they preserve at Rome a napkin woven from this material, in which was wrapped the *sudarium* of our Lord, sent as a gift from one of the Tartar princes to the Roman Pontiff.

CHAPTER XI

OF THE DISTRICT OF SUCCUIR, WHERE THE RHUBARB IS PRODUCED, AND FROM WHENCE IT IS CARRIED TO ALL PARTS OF THE WORLD

UPON leaving the district last mentioned, and proceeding for ten days in the direction of east-north-east, through a country where there are few habitations, and little of any kind worthy of remark, you arrive at a district named Succuir, in which are many towns and castles, the principal one being likewise named Succuir.[1] The inhabitants are in general idolaters, with some Christians.[2] They are subject to the dominion of

longs, assez doux, et assez flexibles, on parvient à les filer, sur-tout si on les mêle avec du lin. On peut en tisser une toile qui a une solidité et une flexibilité convenable, lors même qu'elle a été privée, par le moyen du feu, du fil végétal qu'elle contenoit. Lorsque cette toile est salie, le feu lui rend son premier éclat."—Traité élémentaire de Minéralogie, tom. i. p. 482.

[1] This appears, from all the circumstances mentioned, to be intended for So-cheu, a fortified town in the extreme western part of the province of Shen-si, or frontier of China in that quarter. Formerly, however, it did not belong to the empire, but to an independent Tartar nation. "Les places les plus occidentales de la province de Chensi," says De Guignes, "ayant fait partie de la Tartarie, nous croyons devoir les nommer ici d'autant plus que ce que nous en diront pourra servir à éclaircir M. Paul. . . . Sous le règne des Soui, on appella tout ce pays So-tcheou. . . . Il passa ensuite sous la domination des peuples du Toufan, et quelque tems après, les Chinois le reprirent; il fait aujourd'hui partie du Chensi." (Tom. i. pt. ii. p. ix.) The first notice we have of this place, after the time of our author, is by Shah Rokh's ambassadors, in 1420. "Sekgiou (which De Guignes, perhaps from a different translation, writes Sokjou) est une ville grande et forte, en forme de quarré parfait. . . . cette ville est donc la première de Khataï, éloignée de quatre-vingt-dix-neuf journées de la ville de Kan-Balik, qui est le lieu de la résidence de l'empereur, par un païs très-peuplé, car chaque journée on loge dans un gros bourg." Relations de Thevenot, tom. ii.

[2] During the long interval of three centuries that had elapsed between our author's time and that of Benedict Goez, an entire change appears to have taken place with respect to the Christian population, which he no longer found to exist; an effect that was produced by the ascendancy of the Mahometans in that quarter.

the grand khan. The extensive province, which contains these and the two districts which shall be next mentioned, is called Tanguth, and throughout all the mountainous parts of it the most excellent kind of rhubarb is produced, in large quantities, and the merchants who procure loadings of it on the spot convey it to all parts of the world.[1] It is a fact that when they take that road, they cannot venture amongst the mountains with any beasts of burthen excepting those accustomed to the country, on account of a poisonous plant growing there, which, if eaten by them, has the effect of causing the hoofs of the animal to drop off; but those of the country, being aware of its dangerous quality, take care to avoid it. The people of Succuir depend for subsistence upon the fruits of the earth and the flesh of their cattle, and do not engage in trade. The district is perfectly healthy, and the complexion of the natives is brown.

CHAPTER XLI

OF THE CITY OF KAMPION, THE PRINCIPAL ONE OF THE PROVINCE OF TANGUTH—OF THE NATURE OF THEIR IDOLS, AND OF THE MODE OF LIFE OF THOSE AMONGST THE IDOLATERS WHO ARE DEVOTED TO THE SERVICES OF RELIGION—OF THE ALMANAC THEY MAKE USE OF—AND THE CUSTOMS OF THE OTHER INHABITANTS WITH REGARD TO MARRIAGE

KAMPION, the chief city of the province of Tanguth,[2] is large and magnificent, and has jurisdiction over all the province.[3]

[1] The abundant growth of rhubarb in the mountainous region that forms the western boundary of China, is noticed by all the writers who have treated of these provinces. In the writings of Professor Pallas will be found a particular account of the trade in this article, which the Russians at Kiakta procure from the country of which we are speaking, through the agency of merchants from Bucharia residing on the spot.

[2] If it be admitted that Succuir is intended for So-cheu, it will follow that Kam-pion, or as it appears in other versions, Kan-pion, Kam-pition, and Kam-picion, is the city of Kan-cheu, the Kam-giou of the Persian ambassadors, the Kam-chick of Johnson, and Kan-ceu of Goez. Johnson mentions its being at the distance of five stages from the former.

[3] The relative importance of Kan-cheu, with respect to So-cheu and other towns in that part of Shen-si, has continued the same at all periods. Shah Rokh's ambassadors observe, that the governor who resided there was superior to all the other governors of bordering places; and Goez says, "En l'une de ces villes de la province de Scensi nommée Kanceù, demeure le viceroy avec les autres principaux magistratz."—P. 486.

The bulk of the people worship idols, but there are some who follow the religion of Mahomet, and some Christians. The latter have three large and handsome churches in the city.[1] The idolaters have many religious houses, or monasteries and abbeys, built after the manner of the country, and in these a multitude of idols, some of which are of wood, some of stone, and some of clay, are covered with gilding. They are carved in a masterly style. Among these are some of very large size, and others are small.[2] The former are full ten paces in length, and lie in a recumbent posture; the small figures stand behind them, and have the appearance of disciples in the act of reverential salutation.[3] Both great and small are held in extreme veneration. Those persons amongst the idolaters who are devoted to the services of religion lead more correct lives, according to their ideas of morality, than the other classes, abstaining from the indulgence of carnal and sensual appetites.[4]

[1] The disappearance in the course of three centuries, or even in a much shorter period, of these churches, which were probably built of wood, is no argument against their having existed in our author's time. It was not until the end of the sixteenth century that the Jesuits obtained a footing in China, and began to investigate the subject of an earlier dissemination of Christianity in that part of the world. During this interval an entire revolution had taken place in the Chinese government, and the Yuen or Moghul-Tartar family, distinguished for its tolerance or indifference in matters of religion, had been succeeded by the native dynasty of the Ming, whose princes were influenced by a different policy, and proscribed the lamas, as well as the Christian priests, to whom their predecessors were thought to have been too much attached. About this period also the Mahometans, becoming numerous at Kashgar and other places on the borders of the desert, were active and apparently successful in their endeavours to exterminate their rivals. A strong picture is drawn by Goez, of the intolerant insolence of these bigots, in the towns through which his route lay, from Hindustan, by the way of Lahore and Cabul, to China.

[2] In all countries where the religion of Buddha prevails, it appears to be an object of religious zeal to erect images representing him of an enormous magnitude, and not unfrequently to cover them with gilding. This we find to be the practice in Japan, Siam, and Ava, as well as in Tartary and China. Shaka-muni is one of the Hindu names of Buddha. P. Gerbillon, who accompanied the emperor of China into Tartary, speaks also of such gigantic images, one of which being measured with a quadrant, was found to be fifty-seven Chinese feet in height.

[3] Although the images of Buddha are usually represented sitting, with the legs crossed, some of these monstrous statues are in a recumbent posture, and surrounded with figures in an attitude of prayer or salutation. The ambassadors who visited this city of Kan-cheu in 1420, mention idols of the same extraordinary kind, and in a striking manner confirm the authenticity of our author's account. "In every complete temple," says Cordiner in his Description of Ceylon, "one colossal image of Buddha is represented in a sleeping posture, and a great many others of the same, sitting and standing, not larger than the life."—Vol. i. p. 150.

[4] "Their sole occupation," says Turner, speaking of the religious orders of Tibet. "lies in performing the duties of their faith. They are

The unlicensed intercourse of the sexes is not in general considered by these people as a serious offence; and their maxim is, that if the advances are made by the female, the connexion does not constitute an offence, but it is held to be such when the proposal comes from the man. They employ an almanac, in many respects like our own, according to the rules of which, during five, four, or three days in the month, they do not shed blood, nor eat flesh or fowl; as is our usage in regard to Friday, the Sabbath, and the vigils of the saints.[1] The laity take to themselves as many as thirty wives, some more, some fewer, according to their ability to maintain them; for they do not receive any dowry with them, but, on the contrary, settle dowers upon their wives, in cattle, slaves, and money.[2] The wife who is first married always maintains the superior rank in the family; but if the husband observes that any one amongst them does not conduct herself well to the rest, or if

exempt from labour; enjoined sobriety and temperance, and interdicted all intercourse with the other sex." (P. 170.) According to Morrison's Chinese Dictionary, the priests of the sect of Fuh or Fo (who are denominated Ho-shang, Sang, and Shamun,) "receive the five precepts: Not to kill living creatures; not to steal, or rob; not to practise lewdness; not to say what is untrue; not to drink wine."—P. 157.

[1] "The same superstition," says Turner, "that influences their view of the affairs of the world, pervades equally their general calculations. On this principle it is, that they frame their common calendar of time. I have one now in my possession; and as far as I can understand it from what has been explained to me, a recapitulation of lucky and unlucky times constitutes the chief merit of the work."—P. 320.

[2] Nothing has hitherto occurred in the course of the work, in which the direct assertion of our author is so much at variance with modern information, as this of the prevalence of the custom of polygamy amongst the people of Tangut. Bogle expressly tells us, that in the sense in which we commonly receive the word, polygamy is not in use in Tibet; but that it exists in a manner still more repugnant to European ideas, in the plurality of husbands; and that it is usual for the brothers in the family to have a wife in common. (Phil. Trans. vol. lxvii. p. 477, and Craufurd's Sketches, vol. ii. p. 177.) This is confirmed by Turner, who says: "The number of husbands is not, as far as I could learn, defined or restricted within any limits; it sometimes happens that in a small family there is but one female; and the number may seldom perhaps exceed that, which a native of rank, during my residence at Teshoo Loomboo, pointed out to me in a family resident in the neighbourhood, in which five brothers were then living together very happily, with one female, under the same connubial compact. Nor is this sort of league confined to the lower ranks of people alone." (P. 349.) To these authorities we can only oppose the qualified observation of M. Pallas, who tells us that polygamy, though forbidden by their religion, is not uncommon amongst the great. (Neue Nordische Beyträge, b. i. p. 204.) The distance, however, between Lhasa and Khan-cheu is so considerable (about ten degrees of latitude and eight of longitude) that although the inhabitants of each, as well as of the greater part of Tartary, follow the same religious worship, there may yet exist essential differences in their domestic manners.

she becomes otherwise disagreeable to him, he can send her away. They take to their beds those who are nearly related to them by blood, and even espouse their mothers-in-law. Many other mortal sins are regarded by them with indifference, and they live in this respect like the beasts of the field. In this city Marco Polo remained, along with his father and uncle, about the space of one year, which the state of their concerns rendered necessary.[1]

CHAPTER XLII

OF THE CITY OF EZINA—OF THE KINDS OF CATTLE AND BIRDS FOUND THERE—AND OF A DESERT EXTENDING FORTY DAYS' JOURNEY TOWARDS THE NORTH

LEAVING this city of Kampion, and travelling for twelve days in a northerly direction, you come to a city named Ezina,[2] at the commencement of the sandy desert, and within the province of Tanguth. The inhabitants are idolaters. They have camels, and much cattle of various sorts. Here you find lanner-falcons and many excellent sakers. The fruits of the soil and the flesh of the cattle supply the wants of the people,

[1] It is remarkable that Goez, who, although a missionary, travelled in the character of an Armenian merchant, was in like manner detained upwards of a year at the neighbouring town of So-cheu. The regulations of police appear to have required then, as they do at this day, that permission should be received from Peking before strangers are suffered to advance into the country.

[2] Having reached the borders of northern China, and spoken of two places that are within the line of what is termed the Great Wall, (but which will hereafter be shown to have consisted on this side of a mound of earth only, and not to have been the stupendous work of masonry it is described on the northern frontier,) our author ceases to pursue a direct route, and proceeds to the account of places lying to the north and south, some of them in the vicinity, and others in distant parts of Tartary, according to the information he had acquired of them on various occasions. Nor does he in the sequel furnish any distinct idea of the line he took upon entering China, in company with his father and uncle, on their journey to the emperor's court; although from what occurs in chap. lii. there is reason to believe that he went from Kan-cheu to Si-ning (by Professor Pallas called Selin), and there fell into the great road from Tibet to Peking. His description now takes a northerly course to a place named Ezina, which stood on a small river which flows by Kan-cheu towards the great desert of Kobi, which he had already crossed in a more western and narrower part. This town is known to us from the operations of Jengiz-khan, who took possession of it when he invaded Tangut in 1224 according to Pétis de la Croix, or 1226 according to De Guignes, and made it for some time the head-quarters of his army.

and they do not concern themselves with trade. Travellers passing through this city lay in a store of provisions for forty days, because, upon their leaving it to proceed northwards, that space of time is employed in traversing a desert, where there is not any appearance of dwelling, nor are there any inhabitants excepting a few during the summer, among the mountains and in some of the valleys. In these situations, frequented by wild asses and other animals equally wild,[1] they find water and woods of pine-trees. Having passed this desert, you arrive at a city on the northern side of it, named Karakoran. All the districts and cities previously mentioned, that is to say, Sakion, Kamul, Chinchitalas, Succuir, Kampion, and Ezina, belong to the great province of Tanguth.

CHAPTER XLIII

OF THE CITY OF KARAKORAN, THE FIRST IN WHICH THE TARTARS FIXED THEIR RESIDENCE

The city of Karakoran[2] is about three miles in circuit, and is the first place in which the Tartars established their residence in remote times. It is surrounded with a strong rampart of earth, there not being any good supply of stone in that part of the country. On the outside of the rampart, but near to it, stands a castle of great size, in which is a handsome palace occupied by the governor of the place.

[1] The wild ass here mentioned is probably that animal which the missionaries, rather unaccountably, call the wild mule, and describe as an inhabitant of this desert region. The wild ass or onager is the *equus asinus* of Linn., and the animal denominated the wild mule is the *equus hemionus*.

[2] The name of this city is properly written Kara-korum, but often Kara-kûm (signifying black sand). By the Chinese it is called Holin, which answers to Korin in Tartar pronunciation. It was built, or rather rebuilt, by Oktaï-khan, the son and successor of Jengiz-khan, about the year 1235; whose nephew, Mangu-khan, made it his principal residence. No traces of it have been in existence for some centuries, but its position is noted in the tables of Ulig-beig, and also in the Jesuits' and D'Anville's maps. It was visited in the year 1254 by William de Rubruquis, a friar minor, who together with some other ecclesiastics was sent by Louis IX. of France on a general mission to the Tartar princes. The account he gives of it conveys no high idea of its importance as a city, nor does his description of the court, of the state of civilization to which these conquerors had attained: but his whole narrative exhibits the illiberal prejudices of a vulgar mind.

CHAPTER XLIV

OF THE ORIGIN OF THE KINGDOM OF THE TARTARS—OF THE QUARTER FROM WHENCE THEY CAME—AND OF THEIR FORMER SUBJECTION TO UN-KHAN, A PRINCE OF THE NORTH, CALLED ALSO PRESTER JOHN

THE circumstances under which these Tartars first began to exercise dominion shall now be related. They dwelt in the northern countries of Jorza and Bargu,[1] but without fixed habitations, that is, without towns or fortified places; where there were extensive plains, good pasture, large rivers, and plenty of water. They had no sovereign of their own, and were tributary to a powerful prince, who (as I have been informed) was named in their language, Un-khan,[2] by some thought to

[1] What may be considered as the proper, although perhaps not the most ancient country of the Moghuls, as they are called by the Persians, or Mungals as the name is pronounced in the northern parts of Asia, including Kalmuks or Eleuts, Burats, and Kalkas, appears to be that tract which lies between the upper streams of the Amur river on the east, and those of the Yanisei and Irtish rivers, together with the Altaï range of mountains on the west; having on the north the Baikal lake, and on the south the great desert, which separates it from the country of Tangut, and the kingdom of China; including within these boundaries the Selinga river, near to which, in the former part of the last century, was the *urga* (station or encampment) of the Tush-du-khan or modern prince of the Mungals. The exact situation of the plains of Giorza, Jorza, or Jorja, and Bargu cannot be determined. In Strahlenberg's map there is a district adjoining to the south shore of Baikal, named "Campus Bargu;" but circumstances would lead us to suppose the places here spoken of to lie further to the north, and in D'Anville's map the name of Bargu appears on the north-east side of that lake. According to Klaproth the name by which the Manchou people (whom he considers to be the same race with the Tungusi) are known to the Tartars, is Chur-chur or Jurjur, by Abu'l-ghazi written Jurjît. These seem to be the Jorza tribes of our author; and the island of Zorza (to which criminals were banished) mentioned in book iii. chap. 2, may be that which lies off the mouth of the Sagalien-ula or river Amûr.

[2] This celebrated prince, whom our author names Umcan, or, with an allowable correction of the orthography of his language, Un-khan, and whom the historian Abu'lfaraj names Ung-khan, was chief of the tribe of Kera-it or Kerrît, and reigned in Kara-korum, which was afterwards rebuilt by Oktai and became his capital, as well as that of Mangu-khan his successor. He appears to have been the most powerful of the chiefs in that part of Tartary, and in the histories of his time is often termed the grand khan. By P. Gaubil, however, and those who follow the Chinese authorities, he is considered as a vassal of the Niu-tche Tartar emperor, Altun-khan, of the dynasty of Kin, who, besides his kingdoms of Leao-tung and Korea, ruled over the northern part of China, or Kataia. They further assert that his appellation of Ouang-han, as they write it, is no other than the Chinese title of Ouang or Vang (*regulus*), bestowed upon him by the sovereign for distinguished services, prefixed to his native

have the same signification as Prester John in ours.[1] To him these Tartars paid yearly the tenth part of (the increase of) their cattle. In process of time the tribe multiplied so exceedingly that Un-khan, that is to say, Prester John, becoming apprehensive of their strength, conceived the plan of separating them into different bodies, who should take up their abode in distinct tracts of country. With this view also, whenever the occasion presented itself, such as a rebellion in any of the provinces subject to him, he drafted three or four in the hundred of these people, to be employed on the service of quelling it; and thus their power was gradually diminished. He in like manner despatched them upon other expeditions, and sent among them some of his principal officers to see that his intentions were carried into effect. At length the Tartars, becoming sensible of the slavery to which he attempted to reduce them, resolved to maintain a strict union amongst themselves, and seeing that nothing short of their final ruin was in contemplation, they adopted the measure of removing from the places which they then inhabited, and proceeded in a northerly direction across a wide desert, until they felt assured that the distance afforded them security, when they refused any longer to pay to Un-khan the accustomed tribute.[2]

title of khan, his original name having been Toghrul. According to J. R. Forster, following the authority of Fischer's Hist. of Siberia, "he reigned over the Karaites, a tribe residing near the river Kallassui (Karasibi), which discharges itself into the Abakan, and afterwards into the Jenisea; and here at this very day live the Kirgises, who have a tribe among them which they call Karaites."—Voyages, etc. p. 141.

1 Whatever absurdity and ridicule may be thought to attach to this extraordinary appellation of Prester or Presbyter John, as applied to a Tartar prince, it is not to be placed to the account of our author, who only repeats, and in terms of particular caution, what had already been current throughout Europe and amongst the Christians of Syria and Egypt, respecting this imaginary sacerdotal character, but real personage. Nothing is here asserted on his own knowledge; the transactions were understood to have taken place nearly a century before the time when he wrote, and in speaking of them he employs the guarded expression, "*come intesi.*" [The best information on the subject of Prester John will be found in the Introduction to the "Relation des Mongols ou Tartares; par le frère Jean du Plan de Carpin," by M. D'Avezac.]

2 This assertion of independence is attributed by the Persian and Arabian historians to the enterprising character and military talents of Temujin (afterwards Jengiz-khan), who, when he had passed eighteen years in the service of Ung-khan, became the object of his jealousy, and was compelled to a precipitate flight in order to save his life. The successful issue of some partial engagements that ensued having increased considerably the number of those who were attached to him, he retired, with his little army, to the country of the Mungals, of which he was a native. Being received with open arms, he concerted with them his schemes of vengeance against his enemies.

CHAPTER XLV

CONCERNING CHINGIS-KHAN, FIRST EMPEROR OF THE TARTARS, AND HIS WARFARE WITH UN-KHAN, WHOM HE OVERTHREW, AND OF WHOSE KINGDOM HE POSSESSED HIMSELF

SOME time after the migration of the Tartars to this place, and about the year of our Lord 1162,[1] they proceeded to elect for their king a man who was named Chingis-khan, one of approved integrity, great wisdom, commanding eloquence, and eminent for his valour. He began his reign with so much justice and moderation, that he was beloved and revered as their deity rather than their sovereign; and the fame of his great and good qualities spreading over that part of the world, all the Tartars, however dispersed, placed themselves under his command. Finding himself thus at the head of so many brave men, he became ambitious of emerging from the deserts and wildernesses by which he was surrounded, and gave them orders to equip themselves with bows and such other weapons as they were expert at using, from the habits of their pastoral life. He then proceeded to render himself master of cities and provinces; and such was the effect produced by his character for justice and other virtues, that wherever he went, he found the people disposed to submit to him, and to esteem themselves happy when admitted to his protection and favour. In this manner he acquired the possession of about nine provinces. Nor is his success surprising, when we consider that at this period each town and district was either governed by the people themselves, or had its petty king or lord; and as there existed amongst them no general confederacy, it was impossible for them to resist, separately, so formidable a power. Upon the subjugation of these places, he appointed governors to them, who were so exemplary in their conduct that the inhabitants did not suffer, either in their persons or

[1] Our author appears in this instance to have mistaken the year of Jengiz-khan's birth (though some place it in 1155) for that of his elevation to the throne. It was not until the year 1201 that he is stated to have acquired the command of the Mungal armies, nor until 1202 according to the authorities followed by Pétis de la Croix, or 1206 according to De Guignes, that he was declared grand khan or emperor. About the same period it was that he changed his original name of Temujîn for that by which he was afterwards known. The Latin and other texts give this date as 1187.

their properties; and he likewise adopted the policy of taking along with him, into other provinces, the principal people, on whom he bestowed allowances and gratuities.[1] Seeing how prosperously his enterprises succeeded, he resolved upon attempting still greater things. With this view he sent ambassadors to Prester John, charged with a specious message, which he knew at the same time would not be listened to by that prince, demanding his daughter in marriage.[2] Upon receiving the application, the monarch indignantly exclaimed: "Whence arises this presumption in Chingis-khan, who, knowing himself to be my servant, dares to ask for the hand of my child? Depart instantly," he said, "and let him know from me, that upon the repetition of such a demand, I shall put him to an ignominious death." Enraged at this reply, Chingis-khan collected a very large army, at the head of which he entered the territory of Prester John, and encamping on a great plain called Tenduk, sent a message desiring him to defend himself. The latter advanced likewise to the plain with a vast army, and took his position at the distance of about ten miles from the other.[3] In this conjuncture Chingis-khan commanded his astrologers and magicians to declare to him which of the two armies, in the approaching conflict, should obtain the victory. Upon this they took a green reed, and dividing it lengthways into two parts, they wrote upon one the name of their master, and upon the other the name of Un-khan. They then placed them on the ground, at some distance from each other, and gave notice to the king that during the time of

[1] It was at the court of the grandson of Jengiz-khan that our author acquired an idea much too favourable of the virtues, although not perhaps of the military talents, of this extraordinary man, who should be regarded as one of those scourges of mankind, which, like plague, pestilence, or famine, is sent from time to time to visit and desolate the world.

[2] According to the writers whom Pétis de la Croix has followed, Temujin had been already married to the daughter of Ung-khan, when the intrigues of his rivals drove him from the court of his father-in-law, to whom he had rendered the most important military services.

[3] The name of this plain, which in the older Latin as well as in Ramusio's text is Tenduch, and in the Basle edition Tanduc, is Tangut in the Italian epitomes. This last may probably be a mistake, and certainly this place is not to be confounded with the Tangut already spoken of as connected with Tibet; but there is much reason to suppose that our author meant the country of the Tungusi (a name that bears no slight resemblance to Tangut), which is about the sources of the Amur, and in the vicinity of the Baikal lake. According to De Guignes and P. Gaubil, the meeting of the armies took place between the rivers Toula and Kerlon, where other great Tartar battles have since been fought, in consequence, as may be presumed, of the local circumstances being suited to the operations of large bodies of cavalry.

their pronouncing their incantations, the two pieces of reed, through the power of their idols, would advance towards each other, and that the victory would fall to the lot of that monarch whose piece should be seen to mount upon the other. The whole army was assembled to be spectators of this ceremony, and whilst the astrologers were employed in reading their books of necromancy, they perceived the two pieces begin to move and to approach, and after some small interval of time, that inscribed with the name of Chingis-khan to place itself upon the top of its adversary.[1] Upon witnessing this, the king and his band of Tartars marched with exultation to the attack of the army of Un-khan, broke through its ranks and entirely routed it. Un-khan himself was killed, his kingdom fell to the conqueror, and Chingis-khan espoused his daughter. After this battle he continued during six years to render himself master of additional kingdoms and cities; until at length, in the siege of a castle named Thaigin,[2] he was struck by an arrow in the knee, and dying of the wound, was buried in the mountain of Altaï.

CHAPTER XLVI

OF SIX SUCCESSIVE EMPERORS OF THE TARTARS, AND OF THE CEREMONIES THAT TAKE PLACE WHEN THEY ARE CARRIED FOR INTERMENT TO THE MOUNTAIN OF ALTAI

To Chingis-khan succeeded Cyhn-khan; the third was Bathyn-khan, the fourth Esu-khan, the fifth Mongù-khan, the sixth Kublai-khan,[3] who became greater and more powerful than all

[1] The mode of divination by what the French term *boguettes* is common in the East. Pétis de la Croix upon introducing into his text this story of "la canne verte," from our author's work, observes in a note: "Cette opération des cannes a été en usage chez les Tartares, et l'est encore à présent chez les Africains, chez les Turcs et autres nations Mahométanes."—P. 65.

[2] The accident here said to have befallen Jengiz-khan is not mentioned by any of the historians; nor does it appear what place is intended by the name of Thaigin. He is said, on the contrary, to have died of sickness (in 1226), shortly after the reduction of the city of Lin-tao, in the province of Shen-si, from whence he had retired, on account of the bad quality of the air where his army was encamped, to a mountain named Leou-pan. It is not, however, to be concluded that our author is therefore wrong, or that Jengiz did not receive a wound, which in an unwholesome climate might have occasioned or accelerated his death.

[3] This account of the successors of Jengiz-khan being so much less accurate than might be expected from one who was many years in the

the others, inasmuch as he inherited what his predecessors possessed, and afterwards, during a reign of nearly sixty

service of his grandson, it is not unreasonable to presume that some of the barbarous names of these princes may have been omitted and others disfigured by the early transcribers. We are the more warranted in this supposition, because in the different versions we find the names to vary considerably; and instead of the Chyn, Bathyn, and Esu of Ramusio's edition, we have in one text Cui, Barchim, and Allaù, and in another, Carce, Saim, and Rocon. In the name of Mongu, or Mangu, only they are all nearly agreed. As the most effectual way of detecting, and in some instances of reconciling the inaccuracies, I shall state the filiation according to the authority of historians, and compare with it the confused lists attributed to our author.

Jengiz-khan, who died about the end of the year 1226, had four sons, whose names were Juji, Jagataï, Oktaï, and Tuli; of these Juji, the eldest, who in other dialects is called Tushi and Dushi, died during the lifetime of Jengiz, leaving a son named Batu, called also, by the Mahometan writers, Saien-khan and Sagin-khan. He inherited, in right of his father, that portion of the empire which included Kapchak and other countries in the neighbourhood of the Wolga and the Don; and his conquests on the side of Russia, Poland, and Hungary, rendered him the terror of Europe. He did not succeed to the dignity of grand khan, or head of the family, and died in 1256. This was evidently the Bathyn of one version of our text, and the Saim of another; but the Barchim of a third seems rather to be intended for Barkah, his brother and successor. Jagataï, or Zagataï, had for his portion of his father's dominions the country beyond the Oxus, Turkistan, or, as it has since been termed, the country of the Uzbek Tartars. He died in 1240, and also without having succeeded to the imperial dignity. His name, although elsewhere mentioned by our author, is here omitted, as would on that account have been proper, if the name of Batu had not been introduced. Oktaï, or Ugdaï, the third son, was declared by Jengiz his successor as grand khan, or supreme head of the dynasty, with the new title of kaan. His particular share of the empire was the original country of the Moghuls or Mungals, with its dependencies, and the kingdom of the Niu-tché Tartars, including so much of Northern China as was then conquered. The total omission of his name, who was one of the most distinguished of the family, and particularly in the wars of the last-mentioned country, not more than thirty-five years before the arrival of our author, is quite extraordinary, if to be imputed to ignorance or want of recollection on his part. Oktaï died in 1241, and was succeeded in the imperial station (after a female regency of five years) by his son Kaiuk, or Gaiuk, who reigned only one year, and died in 1248. By Plano Carpini, a friar minor, (who was sent by Pope Innocent IV. to the court of Batu, whom he terms the Duke Baatu or Bathy, and by him to Gaiuk, his sovereign, then newly elected,) he is named Cuyne, by the Chinese Key-yeu, and by our author Chyn or Cui, according to different readings. The fourth son of Jengiz, whose name was Tuli or Tuluï, died in 1232, during the reign of his brother Oktaï, leaving four sons, named Mangu, Kublaï, Hulagu, and Artigbuga, besides others of less historical fame. Of these, Mangu or Mongu was chosen, in 1251, to succeed his cousin Gaiuk as grand khan, and chiefly through the influence of Batu, who had a superior claim, as the son of the eldest brother, but seems not to have affected that dignity. One of the first acts of Mangu was to send Hulagu (from Kara-korum, his capital) with a powerful army that enabled him to subdue the countries of Khorasan, Persia, Chaldea, and a great part of Syria. He founded the great dynasty of the Moghuls of Persia, which after a few generations threw off its dependence, more nominal than real, upon the years,[1] acquired, it may be said, the remainder of the world. The title of khan or kaan, is equivalent to emperor in our language. It has been an invariable custom, that all the grand khans, and chiefs of the race of Chingis-khan, should be carried for interment to a certain lofty mountain named Altaï, and in whatever place they may happen to die, although it should be at the distance of a hundred days' journey, they are nevertheless conveyed thither. It is likewise the custom, during the progress of removing the bodies of these princes, for those who form the escort to sacrifice such persons as they chance to meet on the road, saying to them, "Depart for the next world, and there attend upon your deceased master," being impressed with the belief that all whom they thus slay do actually become his servants in the next life. They do the same also with respect to horses, killing the best of the stud, in order that he may have the use of them. When the corpse of Mongù was transported to this mountain, the horsemen who accompanied it, having this blind and horrible persuasion, slew upwards of twenty thousand persons who fell in their way.[2]

head of the empire. The name of Hulagu, which in other parts of the work is softened to Alaù, seems to be that which is here still further corrupted to Esu, by the mistake of a letter, for Elu. In the Latin version of the same passage it is Allaù. Mangu died in 1259 (or 1256), in the province of Se-chuen in China, whilst engaged in the prosecution of the war in that country. Respecting *his* name there is no ambiguity. Kublaï, who was upon the spot, assumed the command of the army, and was soon after chosen grand khan, although with much opposition on the part of his brother Artigbuga, who was strongly supported, and ventured to set up the imperial standard at Kara-korum. Kublaï proceeded, in 1268, to subdue the kingdom of Manji, or Southern China, at that time ruled by the dynasty of Song, whose capital, named Hong-cheu, was taken in 1276, and the whole was annexed to his empire in 1280; from which year his reign, as emperor of China, is made to commence in the Chinese annals, where he appears by the title of Yuen-chitsu. His death is placed in the beginning of 1294, being then in the eightieth year of his age. He was the fifth grand khan of this family, and after his decease the descendants of their common ancestor, who ruled the provinces in the west and south, no longer acknowledged a paramount sovereign.

[1] As Kublaï was elected grand khan in 1260, and died in 1294, his reign was strictly about thirty-four years; but having been appointed viceroy to his brother Mangu, in China, so early as 1251, it may be considered as having lasted forty-three; and he was probably employed there in the command of armies at a period still earlier. The assertion, however, of his having reigned sixty years cannot be justified, and must have originated in a mistake or transposition of figures, which should perhaps have been XL instead of LX.

[2] The existence of such an atrocious custom amongst the Monghul Tartars has been questioned. But the Chinese annals are not without instances of the practice of immolation at funerals; and we find that, so late as the year 1661, the Tartar emperor Shun-chi commanded a human sacrifice upon the death of a favourite mistress. "Voluit tamen," says

CHAPTER XLVII

OF THE WANDERING LIFE OF THE TARTARS—OF THEIR DOMESTIC MANNERS, THEIR FOOD, AND THE VIRTUE AND USEFUL QUALITIES OF THEIR WOMEN

Now that I have begun speaking of the Tartars, I will tell you more about them. The Tartars never remain fixed, but as the winter approaches remove to the plains of a warmer region, in order to find sufficient pasture for their cattle; and in summer they frequent cold situations in the mountains, where there is water and verdure, and their cattle are free from the annoyance of horse-flies and other biting insects. During two or three months they progressively ascend higher ground, and seek fresh pasture, the grass not being adequate in any one place to feed the multitudes of which their herds and flocks consist.[1] Their huts or tents are formed of rods covered with felt, and

P. Couplet, "triginta hominum spontanea morte placari manes concubinæ, ritu apud Sinas execrando, quem barbarum *morem* successor deinde sustulit." (Tab. Chronologica Monarchiæ Sinicæ, p. 100.) In the account of the conquest of China by the Mantchou Tartars, written by the Jesuit Martinius, we are told that the Mantchou king Tien-ming, invading China to avenge the murder of his father, swore that, in allusion to the customs of the Tartars, he would celebrate the funeral of the murdered king by the slaughter of two hundred thousand Chinese. This supports Marco Polo's story in a remarkable manner. The number stated to have been sacrificed by those who accompanied the body of Mangu-khan varies considerably in the different versions, and in the epitomes is made to amount to 300,000. Marsden's text states it at 10,000, but the authority of the early manuscripts seems to be in favour of the number given in our text.

[1] This periodical migration of the Tartar tribes is matter of so much notoriety, that our author's account of it scarcely needs to be corroborated by authorities; but the following passage from Du Halde will be found circumstantially applicable: "Tous les Mongous vivent aussi de la même manière, errans çà et là avec leurs troupeaux, et demeurans campez dans les lieux où ils sont commodément, et où ils trouvent le meilleur fourage. En été ils sè placent ordinairement dans des lieux découverts prés de quelque rivière ou de quelque étang, et s'il n'y en a point, aux environs de quelque puits: en hyver ils cherchent les montagnes et les collines, ou du moins ils s'établissent derrière quelque hauteur, où ils soient à couvert du vent de Nord, qui est en ce pays-là extrêmement froid; la niege supplée à l'eau qui leur manque. Chaque souverain demeure dans son pays, sans qu'il soit permis ni à lui, ni à ses sujets, d'aller dans les terres des autres; mais dans l'étendue des terres qui leur appartiennent ils campent où ils voulent." (Tom. iv. p. 38.) "The summer station," says Elphinstone, "is called *eilauk*, and the winter station *kishlauk*, two words which both the Afghauns and Persians have borrowed from the Tartars."—Account of Caubul, p. 390.

being exactly round, and nicely put together, they can gather them into one bundle, and make them up as packages, which they carry along with them in their migrations, upon a sort of car with four wheels.[1] When they have occasion to set them up again, they always make the entrance front to the south.[2] Besides these cars they have a superior kind of vehicle upon two wheels, covered likewise with black felt, and so effectually as to protect those within it from wet, during a whole day of rain. These are drawn by oxen and camels, and serve to convey their wives and children, their utensils, and such provisions as they require.[3] The women it is who attend to their trading concerns, who buy and sell, and provide everything necessary for their husbands and their families;[4] the time of the men being entirely devoted to hunting and hawking, and matters that relate to the military life. They have the best falcons in the world, and also the best dogs. They subsist entirely

[1] The tents are thus described by Bell, as he saw them among the Kalmuks, encamped near the Wolga: "The Tartars had their tents pitched along the river side. These are of a conical figure; there are several long poles erected inclining to each other, which are fixed at the top into something like a hoop, that forms the circumference of an aperture for letting out the smoke or admitting the light: across the poles are laid some small rods, from four to six feet long, and fastened to them by thongs. This frame is covered with pieces of felt, made of coarse wool and hair. These tents afford better shelter than any other kind, and are so contrived as to be set up, taken down, folded, and packed up, with great ease and quickness, and so light that a camel may carry five or six of them." (Tom. i. p. 29.) See also Du Halde.

[2] "When they take downe their dwelling houses (from off their carts), they turn the doores always to the south." (Purchas, Journal of Rubruquis, vol. iii. p. 3.) This opening of the door-way to the south appears to be the universal practice in Tartary, as well with fixed as with moveable houses, in order to guard as much as possible against the rude effects of the northerly wind. It will be seen hereafter that the same custom subsists in the northern provinces of China.

[3] "They make certayne four-square baskets of small slender wickers as bigge as great chests; and afterward, from one side to another, they frame an hollow lidde or cover of such like wickers, and make a doore in the fore-side thereof. And then they cover the said chest or little house with black felt, rubbed over with tallow or sheep's milk to keep the rain from soaking through, which they deck likewise with painting or with feathers. And in such chests they put their whole household-stuffe and treasure. Also the same chests they do strongly binde upon other carts, which are drawne with camels."—Purchas, vol. iii. p. 3.

[4] This custom of the men committing to the females the management of their trading concerns, is authenticated by P. Gerbillon, who accompanied the emperor Kanghi in his expeditions. (Du Halde, tom. iv. p. 115.) Elphinstone, also, speaking of a tribe in the Afghân country, called Hazoureh, and whom he considers as the remnant of a Tartar army left there, remarks that "the wife manages the house, takes care of the property, does her share of the honours, and is very much consulted in all her husband's measures."—Account of Caubul, p. 483.

upon flesh and milk, eating the produce of their sport, and a certain small animal, not unlike a rabbit, called by our people Pharaoh's mice, which, during the summer season are found in great abundance in the plains.[1] But they likewise eat flesh of every description, horses, camels, and even dogs, provided they are fat. They drink mares' milk, which they prepare in such a manner that it has the qualities and flavour of white wine. They term it in their language *kemurs.*[2] Their women are not excelled in the world for chastity and decency of conduct, nor for love and duty to their husbands. Infidelity to the marriage bed is regarded by them as a vice not merely dishonourable, but of the most infamous nature;[3] whilst on the other hand it is admirable to observe the loyalty of the husbands towards their wives, amongst whom, although there are perhaps ten or twenty, there prevails a degree of quiet and union that is highly laudable. No offensive language is ever heard, their attention being fully occupied with their traffic (as already mentioned) and their several domestic employments, such as the provision of necessary food for the family,

[1] "On these hills (near the Selinga river) are a great number of animals called marmots, of a brownish colour, having feet like a badger, and nearly of the same size. They make deep burrows on the declivities of the hills; and it is said that in winter they continue in these holes, for a certain time, even without food. At this season, however, they sit or lie near their burrows, keeping a strict watch, and at the approach of danger rear themselves on their hind feet, giving a loud whistle, and then drop into their holes in a moment." (Bell's Travels, vol. i. p. 311.) The description given of the animal by Du Halde accords best with our author's account: "Cet animal (aussi petit qu'une hermine) est une espèce de rat de terre, fort commun dans certains quartiers des Kalkas. Les *tael-pi* se tiennent sous la terre, où ils creusent une suite d'autant de petites tanières qu'il y a de mâles dans leur troupe: un d'eux est toujours au dehors, qui fait le guet, mais qui fuit dès qu'il apperçoit quelqu'un, et se précipite en terre aussitôt qu'on s'approche de lui. . . . On en prend à la fois un très-grand nombre."—Tom. iv. p. 30.

[2] The word here written *chemurs* or *kemurs,* and in the Latin edition *chuinis* and *chemius,* is that which by other travellers is called *kimmis* or *kimmuz,* and (vulgarly) *cosmos.* It is a preparation of mares' milk, put into a state of fermentation by heat, beaten in a large skin bag (for the purpose, as it would seem, of separating the butter), and by such process rendered intoxicating to a certain degree. It will in this state bear keeping for several months, and is the favourite drink of all the tribes of Tartars. "The national beverage" of the Uzbeks, Elphinstone observes, "is *kimmiz,* an intoxicating liquor, well known to be prepared from mares' milk." (P. 470.) This (distilled) spirit, although produced from the same materials, must be distinguished from the *kimmuz,* with which, however, it is confounded by some writers. Rubruquis furnishes a circumstantial account of these preparations of milk in all their stages.

[3] "It must be observed," says Bell, "to the honour of their women, that they are very honest and sincere, and few of them lewd: adultery is a crime scarce ever heard of."—Vol. i. p. 31.

the management of the servants, and the care of the children, which are amongst them a common concern. And the more praiseworthy are the virtues of modesty and chastity in the wives, because the men are allowed the indulgence of taking as many as they choose.[1] Their expense to the husband is not great, and on the other hand the benefit he derives from their trading, and from the occupations in which they are constantly engaged, is considerable; on which account it is, that when he receives a young woman in marriage, he pays a dower to her parent.[2] The wife who is the first espoused has the privilege of superior attention, and is held to be the most legitimate, which extends also to the children borne by her. In consequence of this unlimited number of wives, the offspring is more numerous than amongst any other people. Upon the death of the father, the son may take to himself the wives he leaves behind, with the exception of his own mother. They cannot take their sisters to wife, but upon the death of their brothers they can marry their sisters-in-law.[3] Every marriage is solemnized with great ceremony.

CHAPTER XLVIII

OF THE CELESTIAL AND TERRESTRIAL DEITIES OF THE TARTARS, AND OF THEIR MODES OF WORSHIP—OF THEIR DRESS, ARMS, COURAGE IN BATTLE, PATIENCE UNDER PRIVATIONS, AND OBEDIENCE TO THEIR LEADERS

THE doctrine and faith of the Tartars are these: They believe in a deity whose nature is sublime and heavenly. To him

[1] "Quoique la polygamie," says P. Gerbillon, "ne soit plus défendue parmi eux, ils n'ont ordinairement qu'une femme." (Du Halde, tom. iv. p. 39.) The practice is described by other writers as more general; but in one tribe it may be more prevalent than in others.

[2] "Ils ne donnent point de douaire à leurs femmes," says Thevenot, "mais les maris font des présens à leur père et à leur frère sans lesquels ils ne trouveroient point de femmes." (Relation des Tartares, tom. i. p. 19.) "As touching marriages," says Rubruquis, "no man can have a wife till he hath bought her."—Purchas, vol. iii. p. 7.

[3] "Il n'y a que cette différence," adds the translator of Abu'lghazi, "entre les Tartares Mahometans et les autres, que les premiers observent quelques degrés de parenté dans lesquels il leur est défendu de se marier, au lieu que les Callmoucks et Moungales, à l'exception de leurs meres naturelles, n'observent aucune proximité du sang dans leurs mariages." (P. 36, note.) "The sonne," says Rubruquis, "marrieth sometimes all his father's wives except his owne mother."—Purchas, vol. iii. p. 7.

they burn incense in censers, and offer up prayers for the enjoyment of intellectual and bodily health.[1] They worship another likewise, named Natigay, whose image, covered with felt or other cloth, every individual preserves in his house. To this deity they associate a wife and children, placing the former on his left side, and the latter before him, in a posture of reverential salutation. Him they consider as the divinity who presides over their terrestrial concerns, protects their children, and guards their cattle and their grain.[2] They show him great respect, and at their meals they never omit to take a fat morsel of the flesh, and with it to grease the mouth of the idol, and at the same time the mouths of its wife and children. They then throw out of the door some of the liquor in which the meat has been dressed, as an offering to the other spirits.[3] This being done, they consider that their deity and his family have had their proper share, and proceed to eat and drink without further ceremony. The rich amongst

[1] "The religion of the Buraty," says Bell, "seems to be the same with that of the Kalmucks, which is downright paganism of the grossest kind. They talk, indeed, of an almighty and good Being, who created all things, whom they call Burchun; but seem bewildered in obscure and fabulous notions concerning his nature and government. They have two high priests, to whom they pay great respect; one is called Delay-lama, the other Kutukhtu." (Bell's Travels, vol. i. p. 248.) "The Mongalls believe in and worship one almighty Creator of all things. They hold that the Kutukhtu is God's vicegerent on earth, and that there will be a future state of rewards and punishments." (P. 281.) "I am informed that the religion of the Tonguts is the same with that of the Mongalls; that they hold the same opinions with respect to the transmigration of the Delay-lama as the Mongalls do about the Kutukhtu, and that he is elected in the same manner." (P. 283.) The hierarchy of which the Dalai or Grand Lama is generally considered as the head, was not established until so late as about the year 1426, according to Gaubil; but the lamas simply, as priests of Shakia-muni, appear to have existed from a remote period, and the shamuns, in the northern parts of Tartary, to be lamas in a ruder state of society. The Kutukhtus stand in the same relation to the Grand Lama as the cardinals, or perhaps more nearly the cardinal-legates, to the pope.

[2] This Tartar idol, whose name is written Natagai in the Latin editions, and Nachigai in the Italian epitomes, is the Itoga of Plan de Carpin; by whom the superstitious practices of these people are described in the following manner: "Ils s'adonnent fort aux prédictions, augures, vol des oiseaux, sorcelleries, et enchantemens. Lorsque le diable leur fait quelque réponse, ils croient que cela vient de Dieu même, et le nomment Itoga."—Bergeron, p. 32.

[3] "Then goeth a servant out of the house," says Rubruquis, "with a cup full of drinke, sprinkling it thrice towards the south, etc. . . . When the master holdeth a cup in his hand to drinke, before he tasteth thereof, he poureth his part upon the ground." (Purchas, vol. iii. p. 4.) [The words in the early Latin text of our author are, "Postea accipiunt de brodio et projiciunt super eum per ostium domus suæ cameræ ubi stat ille deus eorum."]

these people dress in cloth of gold and silks, with skins of the sable, the ermine, and other animals. All their accoutrements are of an expensive kind. Their arms are bows, iron maces, and in some instances, spears; but the first is the weapon at which they are the most expert, being accustomed, from children, to employ it in their sports.[1] They wear defensive armour made of the thick hides of buffaloes and other beasts, dried by the fire, and thus rendered extremely hard and strong. They are brave in battle, almost to desperation, setting little value upon their lives, and exposing themselves without hesitation to all manner of danger. Their disposition is cruel. They are capable of supporting every kind of privation, and when there is a necessity for it, can live for a month on the milk of their mares, and upon such wild animals as they may chance to catch. Their horses are fed upon grass alone, and do not require barley or other grain. The men are habituated to remain on horseback during two days and two nights, without dismounting; sleeping in that situation whilst their horses graze. No people upon earth can surpass them in fortitude under difficulties, nor show greater patience under wants of every kind. They are prefectly obedient to their chiefs, and are maintained at small expense. From these qualities, so essential to the formation of soldiers, it is, that they are fitted to subdue the world, as in fact they have done in regard to a considerable portion of it.

CHAPTER XLIX

OF THE TARTAR ARMIES, AND THE MANNER IN WHICH THEY ARE CONSTITUTED—OF THEIR ORDER OF MARCHING—OF THEIR PROVISIONS—AND OF THEIR MODE OF ATTACKING THE ENEMY

WHEN one of the great Tartar chiefs proceeds on an expedition, he puts himself at the head of an army of an hundred thousand horse, and organises them in the following manner. He appoints an officer to the command of every ten men, and others to command an hundred, a thousand, and ten thousand men, respectively. Thus ten of the officers commanding ten

[1] "They are armed," says Bell, "with bows and arrows, a sabre and lance, which they manage with great dexterity, acquired by constant practice from their infancy."—Vol. i. p. 30.

men take their orders from him who commands a hundred; of these, each ten, from him who commands a thousand; and each ten of these latter, from him who commands ten thousand. By this arrangement each officer has only to attend to the management of ten men or ten bodies of men; and when the commander of these hundred thousand men has occasion to make a detachment for any particular service, he issues his orders to the commanders of ten thousand to furnish him with a thousand men each; and these, in like manner, to the commanders of a thousand, who give their orders to those commanding a hundred, until the order reaches those commanding ten, by whom the number required is immediately supplied to their superior officers. A hundred men are in this manner delivered to every officer commanding a thousand, and a thousand men to every officer commanding ten thousand.[1] The drafting takes place without delay, and all are implicitly obedient to their respective superiors. Every company of a hundred men is denominated a *tuc*, and ten of these constitute a *toman*.[2] When the army proceeds on service, a body of men is sent two days' march in advance, and parties are stationed upon each flank and in the rear, in order to prevent its being attacked by surprise. When the service is distant, they carry but little with them, and that, chiefly what is requisite for their encampment, and utensils for cooking. They subsist for the most part upon milk, as has been said. Each man has, on an average, eighteen horses and mares, and when that which they ride is fatigued, they change it for another. They are provided with small tents made of felt, under which they shelter themselves against rain. Should circumstances render it necessary, in the execution of a duty that requires despatch, they can march for ten days together without dressing victuals, during which time they subsist upon the blood drawn from their horses, each man opening a vein, and drinking from his own cattle.[3] They make provision also

[1] The correctness of our author's account of the constitution of the Mungal armies will appear from comparing it with the detailed account in the French translation of Abu'lghazi's History of the Tartars.

[2] *Toman* is the usual Persian term for a body of 10,000 men. The word *tuc*, as signifying "a hundred," is not to be found in the dictionaries. It may, perhaps, be an orthographical corruption of *duz*, *sus*, *yuz*, by which that number is expressed in the dialects of different Tartar tribes.

[3] The Scythian or Sarmatian practice of drawing blood from horses, as an article of sustenance or luxurious indulgence, and also that of preserving milk for use, in a concrete form, were well known to the ancients.

of milk, thickened and dried to the state of a hard paste (or curd), which is prepared in the following manner. They boil the milk, and skimming off the rich or creamy part as it rises to the top, put it into a separate vessel as butter; for so long as that remains in the milk, it will not become hard. The latter is then exposed to the sun until it dries. Upon going on service they carry with them about ten pounds for each man, and of this, half a pound is put, every morning, into a leathern bottle, or small *outre*, with as much water as is thought necessary. By their motion in riding the contents are violently shaken, and a thin porridge is produced, upon which they make their dinner.[1] When these Tartars come to engage in battle, they never mix with the enemy, but keep hovering about him, discharging their arrows first from one side and then from the other, occasionally pretending to fly, and during their flight shooting arrows backwards at their pursuers, killing men and horses, as if they were combating face to face. In this sort of warfare the adversary imagines he has gained a victory, when in fact he has lost the battle; for the Tartars, observing the mischief they have done him, wheel about, and renewing the fight, overpower his remaining troops, and make them prisoners in spite of their utmost exertions. Their horses are so well broken-in to quick changes of movement, that upon the signal given, they instantly turn in every direction; and by these rapid manœuvres many victories have been obtained. All that has been here related is spoken of the original manners of the Tartar chiefs; but at the present day they are much corrupted.[2] Those who dwell at Ukaka, forsaking their own laws, have adopted the customs of the people who worship

[1] "On long marches," says Bell, "all their provisions consist of cheese, or rather dried curd, made up into little balls, which they drink when pounded and mixed with water." (Vol. i. p. 34.) "We were presented," says Turner, "with a profusion of fresh, rich milk, and a preparation called, in the language of India, *dhy*, which is milk acidulated by means of buttermilk boiled in it, and kept till it is slightly coagulated. The *kummus* of the Tartars is mares' milk, prepared by the same process: this is sometimes dried in masses till it resembles chalk; and is used to give a relish to the water they drink, by solution with it. I have been told that the operation of *drying* it is sometimes performed by tying the *dhy* tight in bags of cloth, and suspending it under the horses' bellies."—Embassy to Tibet, p. 195.

[2] By the corruption of manners he may be supposed to allude to the effects produced by the conquest of China, which gave to these rude and hardy people a taste for the enjoyment of ease and luxuries. So enervated did the Mungals become, before the expiration of a century, that they were ignominiously driven back to their deserts by an insurrection of the Chinese population.

idols, and those who inhabit the eastern provinces have adopted the manners of the Saracens.[1]

CHAPTER L

OF THE RULES OF JUSTICE OBSERVED BY THESE PEOPLE—AND OF AN IMAGINARY KIND OF MARRIAGE CONTRACTED BETWEEN THE DECEASED CHILDREN OF DIFFERENT FAMILIES

JUSTICE is administered by them in the following manner. When a person is convicted of a robbery not meriting the punishment of death, he is condemned to receive a certain number of strokes with a cane,—seven, seventeen, twenty-seven, thirty-seven, forty-seven, or as far as one hundred and seven, according to the value of the article stolen and circumstances of the theft; and many die under this chastisement.[2] When for stealing a horse or other article that subjects the offender to capital punishment, he is condemned to suffer death, the sentence is executed by cutting his body in two with a sword.[3] But if the thief has the means of paying nine times the value of the property stolen, he escapes all further punishment. It is usual for every chief of a tribe or other person possessing large cattle, such as horses, mares, camels, oxen, or cows, to distinguish them by his mark, and then to suffer them to graze at large, in any part of the plains or mountains, without employing herdsmen to look after them; and if any of them should happen to mix with the cattle of other proprietors, they are restored to the person whose mark they bear. Sheep and goats, on the contrary, have people to attend them. Their cattle of every kind are well-sized, fat, and exceedingly handsome.[4]

[1] As the situation of Ukaha, or Ouchacha, is here placed in opposition to that of the eastern provinces, we may presume it to be Okak, or Okaka, of Abulfeda, on the banks of the Etel or Wolga, not far from Sarai, which was visited by the father and uncle of our author, in their first journey. The relative term *eastern* is not, however, intended to apply to those provinces which we, in respect to China, call Eastern Tartary, but to the country lying eastward of the Caspian.

[2] To this punishment, which is known to be common in China, the Portuguese have given the name of *bastanado* (from *bastano*, a staff or cane).

[3] In China, where the criminal law of the Tartars may be supposed to have had much influence, the punishments of decapitation and of cutting the bodies into many pieces, are in use for certain great offences.

[4] "Their horned cattle," says Bell, "are very large. Their sheep have broad tails, and their mutton is excellent. They have also great abundance of goats."—Vol. i. p. 246.

When one man has had a son, and another man a daughter, although both may have been dead for some years, they have a practice of contracting a marriage between their deceased children, and of bestowing the girl upon the youth. They at the same time paint upon pieces of paper human figures to represent attendants with horses and other animals, dresses of all kinds, money, and every article of furniture; and all these, together with the marriage contract, which is regularly drawn up, they commit to the flames, in order that through the medium of the smoke (as they believe) these things may be conveyed to their children in the other world, and that they may become husband and wife in due form. After this ceremony, the fathers and mothers consider themselves as mutually related, in the same manner as if a real connexion had taken place between their living children.[1] Having thus given an account of the manners and customs of the Tartars, although not yet of the brilliant acts and enterprises of their grand khan, who is lord of all the Tartars, we shall now return to our former subject, that is, to the extensive plain which we were traversing when we stopped to relate the history of this people.

[1] This custom, however extraordinary, is of the same character as many of the grave absurdities to be found in the Chinese institutions. We are told by P. Navarette that it exists in one of the northern provinces, bordering on the country of the Mungals, and where of course we may look for a similarity of practices. "In the province of Shan-si," he says, "they have a ridiculous custom, which is, to marry dead folks. F. Michael Trigaucius, a Jesuit, who lived several years in that province, told it us whilst we were confined. It falls out that one man's son and another's daughter die. Whilst the coffins are in the house (and they use to keep them two or three years or longer) the parents agree to marry them; they send the usual presents as if they were alive, with much ceremony and music. After this they put together the two coffins, keep the wedding dinner before them, and lastly they lay them together in one tomb. The parents from this time are looked upon not only as friends but relations, as they would have been had their children been married living." (Churchill's Collect. vol. i. p. 69.) "This," says Malcolm, "is said to be still an usage in Tartary. They throw the contract in the fire, and conceive the smoke ascends to the departed children, who marry in the other world. Pétit de la Croix, in his life of Chenghiz, mentions this fact; and I find it stated in a Persian manuscript written by a man of learning and information."—Hist. of Persia. vol. i. p. 413, note.

CHAPTER LI

OF THE PLAIN OF BARGU NEAR KARA-KORAN—OF THE CUSTOMS OF ITS INHABITANTS—OF THE OCEAN, AT THE DISTANCE OF FORTY DAYS' JOURNEY FROM THENCE—OF THE FALCONS PRODUCED IN THE COUNTRY ON ITS BORDERS—AND OF THE BEARINGS OF THE NORTHERN CONSTELLATION TO AN OBSERVER IN THOSE PARTS

UPON leaving Kara-koran and the mountains of Altaï, the burial-place, as has been said, of the imperial Tartar family, you proceed, in a northern direction, through a country termed the plain of Bargu, extending to the distance of about forty days' journey.[1] The people who dwell there are called Mekriti,[2] a rude tribe, who live upon the flesh of animals, the largest of which are of the nature of stags; and these they also make use of for the purposes of travelling.[3] They feed

[1] The name of Bargu appears in Strahlenberg's map of Tartary, near the south-western part of the lake or sea of Baikal, and in D'Anville's on the north-east side, but by our author it is applied to the country extending from thence, many days' journey towards the Frozen Ocean, and seems to correspond to what we term Siberia. This misapplication (as he considers it) is noticed by Strahlenberg, who observes, that " the name of Bargu is to be found in the old map of Great Tartary, though in a very wrong place, viz. towards the Mare Glaciale." (Note 8, p. 14.) It may have happened, however, that in the course of four centuries one vague appellation may have superseded another; and I believe it will not be contended that Siberia is the indigenous name of the region on which it has been bestowed.

[2] Of this tribe of Mekriti, which in the epitomes is Mecriit, but in the Latin edition Meditæ (Mecaci in the early Latin), frequent mention is made in the Tartar histories, by the name of Merkit and Markät, whose country was amongst the first of the conquests made by Jengiz-khan, being in his immediate vicinity. Its situation is not pointed out with any degree of precision, but that it is far northwards may be inferred from a passage in L'Histoire générale des Huns, where, speaking of the defeat of the Naimans and dispersion of their princes, it is said: " Tous prirent la fuite, et se retirèrent vers la rivière d'Irtisch, où ils s'établirent, et y formèrent un puissant parti qui étoit soutenu par Toctabegh, khan des Merkites." (Liv. xv. p. 23.) " Ceux de la tribu des Markäts," says Abu'lghazi, " avoient du temps de Zingis-Chan un chan appellé Tochtabegi, qui estoit tousjours aux prises avec Zingis-Chan." (Hist. généal. p. 130.) This was probably the most northern tribe with whose name our author was acquainted, and although he now proceeds to speak (in very general terms) of those extensive regions which lie between the rivers Oby and Lena, it may be presumed that he knew nothing of them but from the report of others; nor does he attempt to make it understood that he had visited them in person.

[3] This is the well-known rein-deer, a large and beautiful species of cervus, in size equal to the elk, and in shape not unlike our red deer.

likewise upon the birds that frequent their numerous lakes and marshes, as well as upon fish. It is at the moulting season, or during summer, that the birds seek these waters, and being then, from want of their feathers, incapable of flight, they are taken by the natives without difficulty. This plain borders on the ocean at its northern extremity. The customs and manners of the people resemble those of the Tartars that have been described, and they are subjects of the grand khan. They have neither corn nor wine; and although in summer they derive subsistence from the chase, yet in winter the cold is so excessive that neither birds nor beasts can remain there.[1] Upon travelling forty days, as it is said, you reach the (northern) ocean.[2] Near to this is a mountain, in which, as well as in the neighbouring plain, vultures and peregrine falcons have their nests. Neither men nor cattle are found there, and of birds there is only a species called bargelak, and the falcons to which they serve for food. The former are about the size of a partridge, with tails like the swallow, claws like those of the parrot kind, and are swift of flight. When the grand khan is desirous of having a brood of peregrine falcons, he sends to procure them at this place; and in an island lying off the coast, gerfalcons are found in such numbers that his majesty may be supplied with as many of them as he pleases.[3] It must not be supposed that the gerfalcons sent from Europe for the use of the Tartars are conveyed to the court of the grand khan. They go only to some of the Tartar or other chiefs of the Levant, bordering on the countries of the Comanians and Armenians. This island is situated so far to the north that the polar constellation appears to be behind you, and to have in part a southerly bearing.[4]

[1] The description of these people and their country corresponds with what we read of many of the savage tribes that wander over those inhospitable deserts through which the great northern rivers flow.

[2] This distance of forty days' journey must be understood to commence from the plain or steppe of Bargu. He speaks of it in a qualified manner, and not as of a tract that he had himself visited.

[3] "In the province of Dauria," says Strahlenberg, "and near the river Amour (the Saghalien oula of the Jesuits) there are a great many milk-white falcons, which are sent in great numbers to China." (P. 361.) "I could not but admire," says Bell, "the beauty of these fine birds. . . . They are brought from Siberia, or places to the north of the river Amoor." (Travels, vol. ii. p. 79.) Among the presents sent by the Czar Ivan Basiliewitz, by his ambassador, to Queen Mary, in 1556 (as mentioned by Hakluyt), was "a large and fair white *jerfawcon*, for the wild swan, crane, goose, and other great fowls."

[4] The Italian words, "la stella tramontana," which in the text is translated "the polar constellation," should perhaps be, in strictness,

Having thus spoken of the regions in the vicinity of the northern ocean, we shall now describe the provinces lying nearer to the residence of the grand khan, and shall return to that of Kampion, of which mention has already been made.

CHAPTER LII

OF THE KINGDOM OF ERGINUL, ADJOINING TO THAT OF KAMPION, AND OF THE CITY OF SINGUI—OF A SPECIES OF OXEN COVERED WITH EXTREMELY FINE HAIR—OF THE FORM OF THE ANIMAL THAT YIELDS THE MUSK, AND THE MODE OF TAKING IT—AND OF THE CUSTOMS OF THE INHABITANTS OF THAT COUNTRY, AND THE BEAUTY OF THE WOMEN

UPON leaving Kampion, and proceeding five days' journey towards the east, in the course of which travellers are frequently terrified in the night-time by the voices of spirits, they reach a kingdom named Erginul,[1] subject to the grand khan, and included in the province of Tangut. Within the limits of this kingdom are several principalities, the inhabitants of which are, in general, idolaters, with some few Nestorian Christians and worshippers of Mahomet. Amongst many cities and strong places the principal one is Erginul. Proceeding from thence in a south-eastern direction, the road takes you to Cathay, and in that route you find a city called Singui,[2] in a district of the same name, where are many towns

the " polar star." We must presume his meaning to have been that the conspicuous stars in the tail of the lesser bear, or perhaps what are called the pointers of the greater, appeared to the south of a person situated at the extreme part of the northern continent. In Fra Mauro's map we find the words: " Qui la Tramontana roman in mezzodi."

[1] By the corrupted name of Erginul or Ergi-nur, is meant (as may be conjectured from the circumstances) that district of Tangut which is called by the Tartars Kokonor, and by the Chinese, Hohonor or Hohonol, and is by some considered as Tangut Proper. The distance of its lake from the city of Kampion or Kan-cheu is about one hundred and forty miles, in a direction nearly south, which could scarcely be travelled in five days, through a mountainous tract; but the situation of its principal town may have been much nearer to that place, and perhaps to the eastward of its meridian, on the banks of the Olanmuren. In the Basle edition the name is written Erigimul, in the older Latin, Ergimul, and in the Italian epitomes, Ergiuul; but none of them, apparently, more correct than the Ergi-nul of Ramusio; the latter part of which seems to be the word *nûr* or *nôr*, signifying a lake.

[2] Singui (as the name appears in the texts of Ramusio, of the Basle edition, and of the older Latin, but in the manuscripts, Signi and Sigui,

and castles, in like manner belonging to Tangut, and under the dominion of the grand khan.[1] The population of this country consists chiefly of idolaters; but there are also some Mahometans and Christians. Here are found many wild cattle that, in point of size, may be compared to elephants. Their colour is a mixture of white and black, and they are very beautiful to the sight. The hair upon every part of their bodies lies down smooth, excepting upon the shoulder, where it stands up to the height of about three palms. This hair, or rather wool, is white, and more soft and delicate than silk.[2] Marco Polo carried some of it to Venice, as a singular curiosity, and such it was esteemed by all who saw it. Many of these cattle taken wild have become domesticated, and the breed produced between them and the common cow are noble animals, and better qualified to undergo fatigue than any other kind. They are accustomed to carry heavier burthens and to perform twice the labour in husbandry that could be derived

and in the epitomes, Sirigai) has been supposed by some to mean the city of Si-gnan-fu, the capital of the province of Shen-si. But the latter is situated near the eastern border of the province, and in the heart of China; whereas it is Tangut that our author is still describing; and although the western extremity of Shen-si formerly belonged to the Sifan or Tufan (people of Tangut), such was not the case with respect to the interior part of the province. Singui or Signi, on the contrary, was, I have no doubt, intended for the celebrated mart of Si-ning (the Selin of Pallas), on the western verge of Shen-si, and distant only a few days' journey, in a south-eastern direction, from Hohonor. It has been at all periods, and is at this day, the great halting-place for travellers between Tibet and Peking, and therefore properly said to lie in the road to Cathay.

[1] These numerous castles or forts are likewise noticed by Du Halde, who describes the western part of Shen-si as consisting of two great valleys, diverging from a point, and advancing, the one in a northern, the other in a western direction, into the country of the Sifan. This tract formed no original part of the empire, but was a conquered district, taken from Tangut (to which our author considers it as belonging in his time) and annexed to Shen-si.

[2] This fine species of *bos* is particularly described by Turner, as well in his Embassy to Tibet, as in the Asiatic Researches, vol. iv., by the name of the *yak* of Tartary, or bushy-tailed bull of Tibet. "Over the shoulders," he observes, "rises a thick muscle, covered with a profusion of soft hair, which in general is longer and more copious than that along the ridge of the back to the setting on of the tail. The tail is composed of a prodigious quantity of long flowing, glossy hair. . . . The shoulders, rump, and upper part of the body are clothed with a sort of soft, thick wool; but the inferior parts with straight, pendent hair, that descends below the knee. . . . There is a great variety of colours amongst them, but black or white are the most prevalent." (Embassy, p. 186.) With respect to its height, which our author has magnified, it is said by Turner to be about that of the English bull; but, from the profuse quantity of hair with which it is covered, it seems to be "of great bulk." It is distinguished by the name of *bos grunniens*.

from the ordinary sort, being both active and powerful.[1] In this country it is that the finest and most valuable musk is procured.[2] The animal which yields it is not larger than the female goat, but in form resembles the antelope. It is called in the Tartar language, *gudderi*. Its coat is like that of the larger kind of deer: its feet and tail are those of the antelope, but it has not the horns. It is provided with four projecting teeth or tusks, three inches in length, two in the upper jaw pointing downwards, and two in the lower jaw pointing upwards; small in proportion to their length, and white as ivory. Upon the whole it is a handsome creature. The musk is obtained in the following manner. At the time when the moon is at the full, a bag or imposthume of coagulated blood forms itself about the umbilical region, and those whose occupation it is to take the animal avail themselves of the moonlight for that purpose, when they cut off the membrane, and afterwards dry it, with its contents, in the sun.[3] It

[1] "They (the *yaks*, Turner adds) are a very valuable property to the tribes of itinerant Tartars called Dukba, who live in tents, and tend them from place to place; they at the same time afford their herdsmen an easy mode of conveyance, a good covering, and wholesome subsistence. They are never employed in agriculture," (it is obvious that this may not be the case in every district,) "but are extremely useful as beasts of burden; for they are strong, sure-footed, and carry a great weight." (P. 187.) These qualities are strongly exemplified in Moorcroft's Journey to Lake Mánasaróvera.—Asiat. Res. vol. xii.

[2] It is generally asserted that the musk of Tibet, or of the part of Tartary bordering upon the north-west of China, is superior to that procured in the Chinese provinces.

[3] From Turner we have a particular, although unscientific, account of what is usually termed the musk deer, which in the language of Tibet he says, is called *la*, and the vascular covering of the musk, *latcha*. After speaking of the long-haired cattle, he proceeds in the next place (as does our author) to say: "The musk-deer too, which produce a valuable article of revenue, are in great abundance in the vicinity of these mountains. This animal is observed to delight in the most intense cold, and is always found in places bordering on snow. Two long curved tusks, proceeding from the upper jaw, and directed downwards, seem intended principally to serve him for the purpose of digging roots, which are said to be his usual food; yet it is possible they may also be weapons of offence. . . . They are about the height of a moderately-sized hog, which they resemble much in the figure of the body; but they are still more like the hog-deer, so termed in Bengal, from the same similitude. They have a small head, a thick and round hind quarter, no scut, and extremely delicate limbs. The greatest singularity in this animal, is the sort of hair with which it is covered, which is prodigiously copious, and grows erect all over the body, between two and three inches long, lying smooth only where it is short, on the head, legs, and ears. . . . The colour, at the base, is white, in the middle black, and brown at the points. The musk is a secretion formed in a little bag or tumour, resembling a wen, situated at the navel; and is found only in the male." (Embassy to Tibet, p. 200.) In a work published at Calcutta in 1798, called the "Oriental Miscellany," (vol. i. p. 129,) there is a scientific description

proves the finest musk that is known. Great numbers are caught, and the flesh is esteemed good to eat.[1] Marco Polo brought with him to Venice the head and the feet of one of them dried. The inhabitants of this country employ themselves in trade and manufactures. They have grain in abundance. The extent of the province is twenty-five [2] days' journey. Pheasants are found in it that are twice the size of ours, but something smaller than the peacock. The tail feathers are eight or ten palms in length.[3] There are other pheasants also, in size and appearance like our own, as well as a great variety of other birds, some of which have beautiful plumage. The inhabitants are idolaters.[4] In person they are inclined to corpulency, and their noses are small. Their hair is black, and they have scarcely any beard, or only a few scattered hairs on the chin.[5] The women of the superior class are in like manner free from superfluous hairs; their skins are fair, and they are well formed; but in their manners they are dissolute. The men are much devoted to female society; and, according to their laws and customs, they may have as many wives as they please, provided they are able to maintain them. If a young woman, although poor, be handsome, the rich are induced to take her to wife, and in order to obtain her, make valuable presents to her parents and relations, beauty alone being the quality held in estimation. We shall now take our leave of this district, and proceed to speak of another, situated further to the eastward.

of the "Thibet Musk," by Dr. Fleming, with a plate from an accurate drawing of the animal, made by Mr. Home. See also an engraving of the head, in Kirkpatrick's Account of Nepaul.

[1] The circumstance of the flesh serving for food is noticed by several modern writers.

[2] [The early Latin text reads fifteen.]

[3] This is probably the argus-pheasant (*phasianus argus*), which, although a native of Sumatra, is said to be also found in the northern part of China.

[4] The religion of the lamas, which is idolatrous, prevails in the neighbourhood of Si-ning, as well as in all the countries bordering on the provinces of Shen-si and Se-chuen, to the westward.

[5] [The early Latin text reads, "non habent barbam nisi in mento."]

CHAPTER LIII

OF THE PROVINCE OF EGRIGAIA, AND OF THE CITY OF KALACHA —OF THE MANNERS OF ITS INHABITANTS—AND OF THE CAMELOTS MANUFACTURED THERE

DEPARTING from Erginul, and proceeding easterly for eight days, you come to a country named Egrigaia, still belonging to the great province of Tangut, and subject to the grand khan, in which there are many cities and castles, the principal one of which is called Kalacha.[1] The inhabitants are in general idolaters; but there are three churches of Nestorian Christians. In this city they manufacture beautiful camelots, the finest known in the world, of the hair of camels and likewise of white wool.[2] These are of a beautiful white. They are purchased by the merchants in considerable quantities, and carried to many other countries, especially to Cathay. Leaving this province, we shall now speak of another situated towards the (north-) east, named Tenduk, and shall thus enter upon the territory of Prester John.

[1] Neither the names of Egrigaya, Eggaya, Egygaia, or Egregia, nor those of Kalacha, Calacia, Colatia, or Calatia, appear in any map that can be cited as authority. The former, however, has some resemblance to Uguria, Iguria, or the country of the Eighurs; and the latter to the name of the town called by Rubruquis, Cailac, and by B. Goez, Cialis; the supposed situation of which will be found in the map prefixed to Sherefeddin's History of Timur Bec, translated by Pétis de la Croix, at some distance to the westward of Turfan, by the name of Yulduz or Cialis. "We found one great citie there," says Rubruquis, "wherein was a mart, and great store of merchants frequenting it. . . . All this country was wont to be called Organum; and the people thereof had their proper language, and their peculiar kind of writing.". . . . "The first sort of these idolaters are called Jugures, whose land bordereth upon the foresaid land of Organum, within the said mountains eastward. . . . The citizens of the foresaid citie of Cailac had three idol-temples, and I entered into two of them, to behold their foolish superstitions."—Purchas, vol. iii. p. 20.

[2] It has been doubted (since the material used in the manufacture of shawls is known to be wool of a particular breed of sheep) whether the hair of camels is actually woven into cloth of any kind; but we learn from Elphinstone, that "oormuk, a fine cloth made of camels' wool, a quantity of cotton, and some lambs' skins are imported (into Caubul) from the Bokhara country."—P. 295.

CHAPTER LIV

OF THE PROVINCE OF TENDUK, GOVERNED BY PRINCES OF THE RACE OF PRESTER JOHN, AND CHIEFLY INHABITED BY CHRISTIANS—OF THE ORDINATION OF THEIR PRIESTS—AND OF A TRIBE OF PEOPLE CALLED ARGON, THE MOST PERSONABLE AND THE BEST INFORMED OF ANY IN THESE COUNTRIES

TENDUK,[1] belonging to the territory of Prester John,[2] is an eastern province, in which there are many cities and castles, subject to the rule of the grand khan; all the princes of that family having remained dependent, since Chingis, the first emperor, subdued the country. The capital is likewise named Tenduk. The king now reigning is a descendant of Prester John, and is still Prester John, and named George. He is both a Christian and a priest; the greater part of the inhabitants being also Christians. This king George holds his country as a fief of the grand khan; not, indeed, the entire possessions of the original Prester John, but a certain portion of them; and the khan always bestows upon him, as well as upon the other princes of his house, his daughters, and other females of the royal family, in marriage. In this province, the stone of which the azure colour is made is found in abundance, and of fine quality. Here likewise they manufacture stuffs of camels' hair. The people gain their subsistence by agriculture, trade, and mechanical labours. Although subject to the dominion of the grand khan, the king being a

[1] The plain of Tenduk has already been mentioned (p. 119, note [3]) as the scene of a famous battle, in which the army of Ung-khan was defeated and destroyed by Jengiz-khan; and although the name is not to be found in the Jesuits' map, its situation is nearly identified by P. Gaubil's informing us that the battle was fought in the space between the rivers Tula and Kerlon, whose sources approximate about the forty-eighth or forty-ninth degree of latitude. It was also in this tract, on the northern border of the desert, that the Kaldan or chief of the Eluts was defeated by the forces of the emperor Kang-hi, in the year 1696. I am strongly inclined to believe that the name of Tenduk, which Pétis de la Croix has confounded with Tangut, is no other than Tungus; as we find in the maps, the tribes of the Tungusi inhabiting this region, and particularly between the Amur river and Baikal lake. Adelung, indeed, remarks that in their language the names of the domesticated animals are the same as in that of the Mungals, from whom they received them; which is a proof of their ancient proximity and intercourse.

[2] See Appendix I.

Christian, as has been said, the government of the country is in the hands of Christians. Amongst the inhabitants, however, there are both worshippers of idols and followers of the law of Mahomet.[1] There is likewise a class of people known by the appellation of Argon,[2] because they are produced from a mixture of two races, namely, those natives of Tenduk who are idolaters, and the Mahometans. The men of this country are fairer complexioned and better looking than those in the other countries of which we have been speaking, and also better instructed, and more skilful traders.

CHAPTER LV

OF THE SEAT OF GOVERNMENT OF THE PRINCES OF THE FAMILY OF PRESTER JOHN, CALLED GOG AND MAGOG—OF THE MANNERS OF ITS INHABITANTS—OF THEIR MANUFACTURE OF SILK—AND OF THE MINES OF SILVER WORKED THERE

In this province (of Tenduk) was the principal seat of government of the sovereigns styled Prester John, when they ruled over the Tartars of this and the neighbouring countries, and which their successors occupy to the present hour. George, above-mentioned, is the fourth in descent from Prester John, of whose family he is regarded as the head. There are two regions in which they exercise dominion. These in our part of the world are named Gog and Magog, but by the natives Ung and Mongul; in each of which there is a distinct race of

[1] Under the dynasty of the Seljuks of Persia, which commenced in the eleventh century, the Mahometans established themselves in considerable numbers at Kashgar, and from thence gradually spread over Tartary in their character of merchants. During the reigns of the Moghul or Mungal emperors of China, they appeared in a higher capacity, frequently commanding armies and presiding at tribunals. Renaudot labours to prove that their earliest connexion with that country was by sea; which may have been the case with respect to the Arabs, although not to the Mahometans of Persia and Khorasan.

[2] This name of Argon appears to be the Orgon of the Jesuits and Archon of Bell's map. The river so called runs through the part of Tartary here described, and being joined by the Tula, their united streams fall into the Selinga. On the north-western bank of the Orgon we find, in modern times, the *urga*, or station of the grand lama of the Mungals. In nearly the same latitude, but more towards the east by several degrees, appears also another and more considerable river, named in the Jesuits' map Ergoné, or Argun, forming the boundary between the dominions of China and Russia in that quarter; near to which is a town or city called Argun-skoi.

people. In Ung they are Gog, and in Mongul they are Tartars.[1] Travelling seven days through this province, in an easterly direction, towards Cathay, you pass many towns inhabited by idolaters, as well as by Mahometans and Nestorian Christians.[2] They gain their living by trade and manufactures, weaving, fine-gold tissues, ornamented with mother-of-pearl, named *nascici*, and silks of different textures and colours, not unlike those of Europe; together with a variety of woollen cloths. These people are all subjects of the grand khan. One of the towns, named Sindichin, is celebrated for the manufacture of all kinds of arms, and every article necessary for the equipment of troops. In the mountainous part of the province there is a place called Idifa, in which is a rich mine of silver, from whence large quantities of that metal are obtained.[3] There are also plenty of birds and beasts.

[1] This passage, it must be confessed, is wholly unintelligible as it now stands, and we are to presume that the words of our author have been misunderstood and perverted, although it may be found impracticable to restore them to a consistent sense. His object apparently was to explain the distinction between the two races of which the subjects of Ungkhan consisted, viz. Mungals and Turkis or Turks, to whom, in latter times, the general name of Tartars or Tatars is exclusively applied: a distinction which, notwithstanding the marked diversity of language, is rendered obscure from the mixture of tribes under the same government; for, in consequence of the splendid reputation acquired by the immediate dependants of Jengiz-khan, the various auxiliary tribes affected to consider themselves as Mungals; whilst, on the other hand, it is evident that the Chinese applied to them indiscriminately the appellation of Tata or Tartars. It may be observed with respect to the scriptural names of Gog and Magog, that they are here spoken of as being improperly given to these people by Europeans, and not as appellations known in the country. By the generality of Arabians and Persians, who pronounce the names Yajuj and Majuj, they are understood to belong to the inhabitants of the mountainous region on the north-western side of the Caspian Sea, or ancient Scythians, against whose predatory incursions the strong rampart of Derbend, together with the line of works extending from it, and regarded as supernatural, were constructed at a very remote period. Other situations, however, have been assigned to this wandering and terrific description of people, by the oriental writers of the middle ages, some of whom place them in the northern part of Tartary.

[2] During the successive reigns of the Mungal emperors of China, many considerable towns were built in that part of Tartary which lies between the river Kerlon and the Chinese province of Pe-che-li; but they were afterwards destroyed, upon the expulsion of that dynasty by those of the Ming, whose object it was to deface every vestige of the power of their late masters.

[3] The name of Sindicin or Sindichin, which in the Basle edition is Sindacui, in the Italian epitomes Sindatoy, in the early Latin Sindatus, and which should perhaps be Sindi or Sinda-cheu, (the last syllable denoting the word "town,") is not to be traced in the Jesuits' map, but may have belonged to one of the places destroyed by the Ming, as mentioned in the preceding note. Idifa, Idifu, or Idica, has equally eluded my research, although the circumstance of a silver mine in its neighbour-

CHAPTER LVI

OF THE CITY OF CHANGANOR—OF DIFFERENT SPECIES OF CRANES—AND OF PARTRIDGES AND QUAILS BRED IN THAT PART BY THE ORDERS OF THE GRAND KHAN

LEAVING the city and province last mentioned, and travelling three days, you arrive at a city named Changa-nor, which signifies, the "white lake."[1] At this place the grand khan has a great palace, which he is fond of visiting, because it is surrounded with pieces of water and streams, the resort of many swans; and there is a fine plain, where are found in great numbers cranes, pheasants, partridges, and other birds. He derives the highest degree of amusement from sporting with gerfalcons and hawks, the game being here in vast abundance. Of the cranes they reckon five species.[2] The first sort are entirely black as coals, and have long wings. The

hood might have helped to point out its situation. Upon the whole, indeed, and particularly from the description of the manufactures said to flourish there, I am inclined to think that a transposition of matter (of which some indubitable examples will be hereafter observed) has taken place in this instance, and that the passage beginning with the words, "Travelling seven days through this province," to the conclusion of the chapter, has no proper connexion either with what precedes it, respecting the country of the Mungals, or what follows respecting Changanor, but must have applied to a more civilized country, nearer to the borders of China.

[1] The Cianganor or Changanor of Ramusio, Cianiganiorum of the Basle edition, Cyagamorum of the older Latin, Cyangamor of the B.M. and Berlin manuscripts, and Cyagnuorum of the Italian epitomes, are obviously intended for the Tsahan-nor, Chahan-nor, or White lake of the maps; and it is probable that the Changai mountains of Strahlenberg, or Hangai-alin of the Jesuits, derive their appellation from the same quality, real or imaginary, of whiteness. In the Kalmuk-Mungalian vocabulary of the former, the word for "white" is *zagan*, (probably a soft pronunciation of *chagan*,) and in the Mancheu dictionary of Langles it is *changuien*.

[2] These birds being termed *gru* in the Italian versions, and *grus* in the Latin, I have called them cranes in the English translation; but it may be doubted whether the heron (*ardea*), or the stork (*ciconia*), be not rather meant by our author's description of them. "On trouve," says the translator, or the commentator of Abu'lghazi, "une grande quantité d'oiseaux d'une beauté particulière dans les vastes plaines de la Grande Tartarie, et l'oiseau dont il est parlé en cet endroit pourroit bien estre une espèce de *heron*, qu'on trouve dans le pays des Moungales vers les frontières de la Chine, et qui est tout blanc, excepté le bec, les ailes, et la queue, qu'il a d'un fort beau rouge. . . . Peut estre aussi que c'est d'une cicogne dont nostre auteur veut parler."—Hist. généal. des Tatares, p. 205. This is the *Crus Leucogeranus* or Siberian crane of Pennant.

second sort have wings still longer than the first, but are white, and the feathers of the wings are full of eyes, round like those of the peacock, but of a gold colour and very bright; the head is red and black, and well formed; the neck is black and white, and the general appearance of the bird is extremely handsome. The third sort are of the size of ours [in Italy]. The fourth are small cranes, having the feathers prettily streaked with red and azure. The fifth are of a grey colour, with the head red and black, and are of a large size.[1] Nigh to this city is a valley frequented by great numbers of partridges and quails, for whose food the grand khan causes millet, panicum, and other grains suitable to such birds, to be sown along the sides of it every season, and gives strict command that no person shall dare to reap the seed; in order that they may not be in want of nourishment. Many keepers, likewise, are stationed there for the preservation of the game, that it may not be taken or destroyed, as well as for the purpose of throwing the millet to the birds during the winter. So accustomed are they to be thus fed, that upon the grain being scattered and the man's whistling, they immediately assemble from every quarter. The grand khan also directs that a number of small buildings be prepared for their shelter during the night; and, in consequence of these attentions, he always finds abundant sport when he visits this country; and even in the winter, at which season, on account of the severity of the cold, he does not reside there, he has camel-loads of the birds sent to him, wherever his court may happen to be at the time.[2] Leaving this place, we shall now direct our course three days' journey towards the north-east.

[1] [The early Latin text has, "Quarta generatio sunt parvæ et habent ad aures pennas nigras. Quinta generatio est quia sunt omnes grigiæ et maxime, et habent caput nigrum et album."]

[2] Game in large quantities is brought from Tartary to Peking during the winter in a frozen state.—Lettres édif. tom. xxii. p. 177. ed. 1781.

CHAPTER LVII

OF THE GRAND KHAN'S BEAUTIFUL PALACE IN THE CITY OF SHANDU—OF HIS STUD OF WHITE BROOD-MARES, WITH WHOSE MILK HE PERFORMS AN ANNUAL SACRIFICE—OF THE WONDERFUL OPERATIONS OF THE ASTROLOGERS ON OCCASIONS OF BAD WEATHER—OF THE CEREMONIES PRACTISED BY THEM IN THE HALL OF THE ROYAL PALACE—AND OF TWO DESCRIPTIONS OF RELIGIOUS MENDICANTS, WITH THEIR MODES OF LIVING

DEPARTING from the city last mentioned, and proceeding three days' journey in a north-easterly direction, you arrive at a city called Shandu, built by the grand khan Kublai, now reigning.[1] In this he caused a palace to be erected, of marble and other handsome stones, admirable as well for the elegance of its design as for the skill displayed in its execution. The halls and chambers are all gilt, and very handsome. It presents one front towards the interior of the city, and the other towards the wall; and from each extremity of the building runs another wall to such an extent as to enclose sixteen miles in circuit of the adjoining plain, to which there is no access but through the palace.[2] Within the bounds of this royal park there are rich and beautiful meadows, watered by many rivulets, where a variety of animals of the deer and goat kind are pastured, to serve as food for the hawks and other birds employed in the chase, whose mews are also in the grounds. The number of these birds is upwards of two hundred; and the

[1] Shandu is the Chang-tou (Shangtu) of the Jesuits' map, and by P. Couplet, in his Notes to the " Observations Chronologiques " of P. Gaubil, is spoken of as " Ville détruite; elle étoit dans le païs de Kartchin en Tartarie." Lat. 40° 22′ NN.E. of Peking. (P. 197.) In the year 1691 it was thus spoken of by P. Gerbillon: " Nous fîmes encore quarante *lys* dans une plaine qui s'appelle Cabaye, sur le bord d'une petite rivière nommée Chantou, le long de laquelle étoit autrefois bâtie la ville de Chantou, où les empereurs de la famille des Yuen tenoient leur cour durant l'été. On en voit encore les restes." (Du Halde, tom. iv. p. 258.) If the distance between Changa-nor and this place was only three days' journey, the former could not have been on the northern side of the desert; but the numbers, from inattention in transcribing, are extremely incorrect, and the decimals may, in this instance, have been omitted.

[2] " This forest," says Bell, speaking of the hunting-seat of the emperor Kang-hi, " is really a most delightful place; it is well stored with a great variety of game, and is of great extent, as will easily be conceived from the account I have given of our two days' hunting. It is all enclosed with a high wall of brick."—Travels, vol. ii. p. 84.

grand khan goes in person, at least once in the week, to inspect them. Frequently, when he rides about this enclosed forest, he has one or more small leopards carried on horseback, behind their keepers;[1] and when he pleases to give direction for their being slipped, they instantly seize a stag, or goat, or fallow deer, which he gives to his hawks, and in this manner he amuses himself. In the centre of these grounds, where there is a beautiful grove of trees, he has built a royal pavilion, supported upon a colonnade of handsome pillars, gilt and varnished. Round each pillar a dragon, likewise gilt, entwines its tail, whilst its head sustains the projection of the roof, and its talons or claws are extended to the right and left along the entablature.[2] The roof is of bamboo cane, likewise gilt, and so well varnished that no wet can injure it. The bamboos used for this purpose are three palms in circumference and ten fathoms in length, and being cut at the joints, are split into two equal parts, so as to form gutters, and with these (laid concave and convex) the pavilion is covered; but to secure the roof against the effect of wind, each of the bamboos is tied at the ends to the frame.[3] The building is supported on every side (like a tent) by more than two hundred very strong silken cords, and otherwise, from the lightness of the materials, it would be liable to oversetting by the force of high winds. The whole is constructed with so much ingenuity of contrivance that all the parts may be taken asunder, removed, and again set up, at his majesty's pleasure. This spot he has selected

[1] This animal, if it be not the ounce, is the *felis jubata* or hunting leopard, much smaller in size than the common species. In Hindustan it is named the *chita*, and is employed by the native princes in the chase of the antelope. See an account of "the Manner of Hunting amongst the Princes of Hindostan," in the Asiatic Miscellany, vol. ii. p. 68, where this animal is called the *cheetar* or panther.

[2] It is well known that the dragon with five claws (instead of four, as in the ordinary representations) is the imperial symbol, and forms a conspicuous part of every article of dress, piece of furniture, or ornament connected with the court of China.

[3] The mode of covering here described is well known in the eastern islands, and is mentioned in the following passage of the History of Sumatra: "There is another kind of house, erected mostly for a temporary purpose, the roof of which is flat, and is covered in a very uncommon, simple, and ingenious manner. Large straight bamboos are cut of a length sufficient to lie across the house, and being split exactly in two, and the joints knocked out, a first layer of them is disposed in close order, with the inner or hollow sides up; after which a second layer, with the outer or convex sides up, is placed upon the others in such manner that each of the convex falls into the two contiguous concave pieces, covering their edges; the latter serving as gutters to carry off the water that falls upon the upper or convex layer."—P. 58, third edition.

for his recreation on account of the mild temperature and salubrity of the air, and he accordingly makes it his residence during three months of the year, namely, June, July, and August; and every year, on the twenty-eighth day of the moon, in the last of these months, it is his established custom to depart from thence, and proceed to an appointed place, in order to perform certain sacrifices, in the following manner. It is to be understood that his majesty keeps up a stud of about ten thousand horses and mares, which are white as snow;[1] and of the milk of these mares no person can presume to drink who is not of the family descended from Jengiz-khan, with the exception only of one other family, named Boriat, to whom that monarch gave the honourable privilege, in reward of valorous achievements in battle, performed in his own presence.[2] So great, indeed, is the respect shown to these horses that, even when they are at pasture in the royal meadows or forests, no one dares to place himself before them, or otherwise to impede their movements. The astrologers whom he entertains in his service, and who are deeply versed in the diabolical art of magic, having pronounced it to be his duty, annually, on the twenty-eighth day of the moon in August, to scatter in the wind the milk taken from these mares, as a libation to all the spirits and idols whom they adore, for the purpose of propitiating them and ensuring their protection of the people, male and female, of the cattle, the fowls, the grain and other fruits of the earth; on this account it is that his majesty adheres to the rule that has been mentioned, and on that particular day proceeds to the spot where, with his own hands, he is to make the offering of milk. On such occasions these astrologers, or magicians as they may be termed, sometimes display their skill in a wonderful manner; for if it should happen that the sky becomes cloudy and threatens rain, they ascend the roof of the palace where the grand khan resides at the time, and by the force of their incantations they prevent the rain from falling and stay the

[1] Establishments ot brood mares and stallions, on as great a scale, have been kept up by later emperors. The white colour does not now appear to be thought so essential as it was by the Mungal-Tartar emperors.

[2] This family name is variously written Boriat, Horiach, Horiath, Orati, and Orari. It was no doubt the eminent Tartar family of which Malcolm speaks in his History of Persia, where he says: "The powerful tribe of Byât came originally from Tartary with Chinghiz-khan. They were long settled in Asia Minor, and a number of them fought in the army of Bajazet against Timour."—Vol. ii. p. 218, note.

tempest; so that whilst, in the surrounding country, storms of rain, wind, and thunder are experienced, the palace itself remains unaffected by the elements.[1] Those who operate miracles of this nature are persons of Tebeth and Kesmir, two classes of idolaters more profoundly skilled in the art of magic than the natives of any other country. They persuaded the vulgar that these works are effected through the sanctity of their own lives and the merits of their penances; and presuming upon the reputation thus acquired, they exhibit themselves in a filthy and indecent state, regardless as well of what they owe to their character as of the respect due to those in whose presence they appear. They suffer their faces to continue always uncleansed by washing and their hair uncombed, living altogether in a squalid style.[2] They are addicted, moreover, to this beastly and horrible practice, that when any culprit is condemned to death, they carry off the body, dress it on the fire, and devour it; but of persons who die a natural death they do not eat the bodies.[3] Besides the appellations before mentioned, by which they are distinguished from each other, they are likewise termed *baksi*, which applies to their religious sect or order,—as we should say, friars, preachers, or minors.[4] So expert are they in their infernal art, they may be said to perform whatever they will; and one instance shall be given, although it may be thought

[1] That magical arts were commonly resorted to by the princes of the family of Jengiz-khan appears from other accounts.

[2] These appear to have been Indian yogis or goseins, who are known to travel by the way of Kashmir into Tibet, and from thence, frequently, to the northern parts of Tartary. Their naked and squalid appearance has been the subject of description at all periods, as well as their extraordinary penances or mortifications.

[3] The agreement between the account here given of this barbarous practice, and what is known of the Batta people of Sumatra, who devour the bodies of condemned criminals, is so striking, that a doubt can scarcely be entertained of a transposition having taken place in the order of our author's notes, by which a remark upon the peculiar manners of the latter, amongst whom he resided several months, has been detached from its proper place, and introduced into this chapter, where savages of a different description, and to whom cannibalism has not been imputed by any traveller since his time, are the subject.

[4] We find in the Ayin Akbari of Abu'lfazel, a confirmation of what is here asserted to be the meaning of the term *baksi*, *bakshi*, or, according to the Bengal pronunciation of Persian, *bukshi*, which is not furnished by the dictionaries. Under the head of the "Doctrine of Boodh," he says: "The learned among the Persians and Arabians call the priests of this religion Bukshee, and in Tibbet they are stiled Lama." (Vol. iii. p. 157.) Klaproth, in his "Abhandlung über die Sprache und Schrift der Uiguren," observes that the word Bakschi is of Mongol origin, and is the usual appellation of the sages (gelehrten) of that country, who are by the Chinese named Schu (Shu).—P. 77, note.

to exceed the bounds of credibility. When the grand khan sits at meals, in his hall of state (as shall be more particularly described in the following book), the table which is placed in the centre is elevated to the height of about eight cubits, and at a distance from it stands a large buffet, where all the drinking vessels are arranged. Now, by means of their supernatural art, they cause the flagons of wine, milk, or any other beverage, to fill the cups spontaneously, without being touched by the attendants, and the cups to move through the air the distance of ten spaces until they reach the hand of the grand khan. As he empties them, they return to the place from whence they came; and this is done in the presence of such persons as are invited by his majesty to witness the performance.[1] These *baksis*, when the festival days of their idols draw near, go to the palace of the grand khan, and thus address him:—"Sire, be it known to your majesty, that if the honours of a holocaust are not paid to our deities, they will in their anger afflict us with bad seasons, with blight to our grain, pestilence to our cattle, and with other plagues. On this account we supplicate your majesty to grant us a certain number of sheep with black heads,[2] together with so many pounds of incense and of lignum aloes, in order that we may be enabled to perform the customary rites with due solemnity." Their words, however, are not spoken immediately to the grand khan, but to certain great officers, by whom the communication is made to him. Upon receiving it he never fails to comply with the whole of

[1] What is here ascribed to sorcery appears to have been nothing more than a pantomimical trick, and capable of being effected by no extraordinary artifice. The emperor, we may presume, and perhaps also such of his confidential servants as had the honour of sitting near his elevated table, might be aware of the machinery employed; but the guests in general, and even the courtiers or mandarins of inferior rank, amongst whom was probably our author's place, might be deceived; their distance being such as to render imperceptible the wires by which the vessels were made to move, as if spontaneously, from one part of the hall of entertainment to the other. The peculiar fancy of these Tartar princes for having their liquor (an object always of the first importance) served in a manner calculated to raise surprise, is well exemplified in the travels of Rubruquis, who describes a curious piece of machinery constructed by a French artist, for conveying into the hall a variety of liquors, which issued from the mouths of silver lions.

[2] "A peculiar species of sheep," says Turner, "seems indigenous to this climate, marked almost invariably by black heads and legs. They are of a small size, their wool is soft, and their flesh, almost the only animal food eaten in Tibet, is, in my opinion, the finest mutton in the world." (P. 302.) A similar breed is noticed by Hamilton on the coast of Yemen. "Their sheep," he says, "are all white, with jet black heads, and small ears, their bodies large, and their flesh delicate."—Vol. i. p. 15.

their request; and accordingly, when the day arrives, they sacrifice the sheep, and by pouring out the liquor in which the meat has been seethed, in the presence of their idols, perform the ceremony of worship. In this country there are great monasteries and abbeys, so extensive indeed that they might pass for small cities, some of them containing as many as two thousand monks, who are devoted to the service of their divinities, according to the established religious customs of the people.[1] These are clad in a better style of dress than the other inhabitants; they shave their heads and their beards,[2] and celebrate the festivals of their idols with the utmost possible solemnity, having bands of vocal music and burning tapers. Some of this class are allowed to take wives.[3] There is likewise another religious order, the members of which are named *sensim*, who observe strict abstinence and lead very austere lives, having no other food than a kind of pollard, which they steep in warm water until the farinaceous part is separated from the bran, and in that state they eat it. This sect pay adoration to fire, and are considered by the others as

[1] The extensive monasteries in the province of Tangut have been spoken of before. A particular description of them will be found in the Alphabetum Tibetanum, and an enumeration in the Mémoires concern. les Chinois, tom. xiv. p. 219, under the head of "Miao ou temples qui sont dans le pays des Si-fan," and commencing with that of Pou-ta-la, near the city of La-sa. There were many likewise in more northern parts of Tartary; but these have been mostly destroyed in the wars that took place upon the extinction of the Mongal dynasty of China, not only between the new dynasty and the adherents of their predecessors, but amongst the independent tribes themselves, under the denomination of Eluths and Kalkas. With respect to the number of persons here said to be contained in these monastic establishments, it is entirely consistent with the accounts given by our modern travellers. Turner informs us that there were two thousand five hundred gylongs (or monks) in one of the monasteries which he visited.

[2] All accounts we have of these people speak of the attention paid to uniformity of dress amongst the persons devoted to the offices of religion and the monastic life, according to their several classes and ranks; as well as of the colours (yellow and red) affected by the two great sects into which the lamas are divided. The tonsure also is mentioned by different authorities. "The priests of this religion," says the Ayin Akbari, "shave their heads, and wear dresses of leather [evidently a mistake for the word yellow] and red cloth." (Vol. iii. p. 158.) Rubruquis also, describing the Tartars of Kara-korum, observes that, "All their priests had their heads and beards shaven quite over, and they are clad in saffron-coloured garments."—Purchas, vol. iii. p. 21.

[3] Although celibacy appears to be usually enjoined to the priests of Buddha, Shakia-muni, or Fo, it is not universal. "Ce mandarin," says P. Magalhanes, "après s'en estre informé avec soin, me dit que dans la seule ville et cour de Pe-kim il y avoit 10,668 bonzes non mariez, et que nous appellons ho-xam (ho-shang), et 5,022 mariez."—Nouv. Relat. de la Chine, p. 57.

schismatics, not worshipping idols as they do.[1] There is a material difference between them in regard to the rules of their orders, and these last described never marry in any instance. They shave their heads and beards like the others, and wear hempen garments of a black or dull colour; but even if the material were silk, the colour would be the same.[2] They sleep upon coarse mats, and suffer greater hardships in their mode of living than any people in the world.[3] We shall now quit this subject, and proceed to speak of the great and wonderful acts of the supreme lord and emperor, Kublaï-kaan.

[1] The word *sensim or sensin* seems to be intended for the Two Chinese monosyllables *seng-sin*, the former of which (according to De Guignes) signifies bonzes or priests of Fo. In Morrison's dictionary, under the word *sang*, we read: "Priests of the sect of Fuh, who are otherwise called *sha-mun* : also denominated *shang-jin*. There are several other names by which they are designated; *ho-shang* is that most commonly given to them." From the account of their diet we are led to conclude them Hindu devotees, and perhaps Sannyasîs, who amongst a people where the religion of Buddha prevailed would be regarded as schismatics.

[2] The circumstance of the dark-coloured dresses (nere e biave) worn by this class, seems to have been mentioned in order to distinguish them from the ho-shang and lamas, who are always clad in yellow or red, according to their sect, and adds to the probability that they were not Buddists.

[3] The austerities to which, under the name of penances, the Indian yogîs, sannyasîs, goseins, and other denominations of ascetics, expose themselves, have been already adverted to. Their pilgrimages often lead them to the borders of China and to the remote provinces of Tartary.

BOOK II

CHAPTER I

OF THE ADMIRABLE DEEDS OF KUBLAI-KAAN, THE EMPEROR NOW REIGNING—OF THE BATTLE HE FOUGHT WITH NAYAN, HIS UNCLE, AND OF THE VICTORY HE OBTAINED

§ 1. In this Book it is our design to treat of all the great and admirable achievements of the grand khan now reigning, who is styled Kublaï-kaan; the latter word implying in our language lord of lords,[1] and with much propriety added to his name; for in respect to number of subjects, extent of territory, and amount of revenue, he surpasses every sovereign that has heretofore been or that now is in the world; nor has any other been served with such implicit obedience by those whom he governs. This will so evidently appear in the course of our work, as to satisfy every one of the truth of our assertion.

Kublaï-kaan, it is to be understood, is the lineal and legitimate descendant of Jengiz-khan the first emperor, and the rightful sovereign of the Tartars. He is the sixth grand khan,[2] and began his reign in the year 1256.[3] He obtained the sovereignty by his consummate valour, his virtues, and his prudence, in opposition to the designs of his brothers, supported by many of the great officers and members of his own family. But the succession appertained to him of right.[4]

[1] Kaan was the title which Jengiz directed his son and successor Oktaï to assume, and which is explained in dictionaries, as it is in our text, by the terms khan of khans, or lord of lords.

[2] He was properly the fifth, not the sixth emperor. Our author seems to have included Batu in his enumeration, who was the eldest of the grandsons of Jengiz, but waived his right to the sovereignty in favour of Mangu his nephew.

[3] As emperor of China the reign of Kublaï is not understood to have commenced till 1280, when the conquest of the southern provinces was completed, and the ancient dynasty destroyed.

[4] The right of succession, according to our ideas, would have been in one of the sons of Mangu, of whom the eldest was named Asutaï; but amongst the Mungals this hereditary claim was modified by circum-

It is forty-two years since he began to reign to the present year, 1288, and he is fully eighty-five years of age. Previously to his ascending the throne he had served as a volunteer in the army, and endeavoured to take a share in every enterprise. Not only was he brave and daring in action, but in point of judgment and military skill he was considered to be the most able and successful commander that ever led the Tartars to battle. From that period, however, he ceased to take the field in person,[1] and entrusted the conduct of expeditions to his sons and his captains; excepting in one instance, the occasion of which was as follows. A certain chief named Nayan, who, although only thirty years of age, was kinsman to Kublaï,[2] had succeeded to the dominion of many cities and provinces, which enabled him to bring into the field an army of four hundred thousand horse. His predecessors, however, had been vassals of the grand khan.[3] Actuated by youthful vanity upon finding himself at the head of so great a force, he formed, in the year 1286, the design of throwing off his allegiance, and usurping the sovereignty. With this view he

stances, and the dying sovereign generally nominated that person of the family who was best qualified, from his age and talents, to hold the reins of government, or rather to command the armies; an appointment which was, however, to be subject to the approval or rejection of the chiefs of tribes, in a grand assembly or diet, termed Kurultai. Accordingly we find that whilst the succession was for a time disputed between Kublaï and his younger brother, the sons of Mangu, instead of asserting their own rights, took part with him who eventually proved to be the weaker of their uncles.

[1] That is, from the period of his becoming emperor of China, in 1280, or, what is more to the point, subsequently to our author's arrival at his court; for in 1262 he proceeded in person against his brother Artigbuga.

[2] In the Latin version the relationship of Nayan to Kublaï is expressed by the word *patruus*, in the Italian epitomes by *avo*, and in Ramusio's text by *barba*, which the dictionaries inform us is the Lombard term for *zio*, or uncle; but as he was the younger person by thirty or forty years (according to what is here stated), it is nearly impossible that he could have stood in that degree of consanguinity, and it is reasonable to suppose that the original phrase must have been misunderstood by the translators. With more plausibility he might have been called his nephew; but the actual relationship was much more distant, their common ancestor being the father of Jengiz-khan. Kublaï was the grandson of that monarch, and Nayan the great-grandson of Belgatai his brother. Consequently they were second cousins once removed, according to the English mode of expression.

[3] The dominions which this prince inherited from his ancestor, the fourth brother of Jengiz-khan, lay in eastern Tartary; as those of Kaidu comprehended generally the country westward from the great desert and Altai mountains, towards Kashgar. These chiefs were bound, of course, to do homage to the person who was considered as the head of the family, and are therefore said to have been the vassals of Kublaï.

privately despatched messengers to Kaidu, another powerful chief, whose territories lay towards the greater Turkey,[1] and who, although a nephew of the grand khan, was in rebellion against him, and bore him determined ill-will, proceeding from the apprehension of punishment for former offences. To Kaidu, therefore, the propositions made by Nayan were highly satisfactory, and he accordingly promised to bring to his assistance an army of a hundred thousand horse. Both princes immediately began to assemble their forces, but it could not be effected so secretly as not to come to the knowledge of Kublaï, who upon hearing of their preparations lost no time in occupying all the passes leading to the countries of Nayan and of Kaidu, in order to prevent them from having any information respecting the measures he was himself taking. He then gave orders for collecting, with the utmost celerity, the whole of the troops stationed within ten days' march of the city of Kambalù. These amounted to three hundred and sixty thousand horse, to which was added a body of a hundred thousand foot, consisting of those who were usually about his person, and principally his falconers and domestic servants.[2] In the course of twenty days they were all in readiness. Had he assembled the armies kept up for the constant protection of the different provinces of Cathay, it must necessarily have required thirty or forty days; in which time the enemy would have gained information of his arrangements, and been enabled to effect their junction, and to occupy such strong positions as would best suit with their designs. His object was, by promptitude, which is ever the companion of victory, to anticipate the preparations of Nayan, and by falling upon him whilst single, destroy his power with more certainty and effect than after he should have been joined by Kaidu.

It may be proper here to observe, whilst on the subject of the armies of the grand khan, that in every province of Cathay and of Manji,[3] as well as in other parts of his dominions, there were

[1] Turkistan, or the country possessed by the Turkî tribes, to whom the name of Tartars or Tatars has of late been exclusively applied.

[2] The employment of troops of this description (corresponding to the bostangis, or gardeners of the Turkish seraglio), marks the already perceptible decline of that vigorous system which enabled the Tartars to subdue their civilized and luxurious neighbours, but which inevitably became relaxed from inactivity and indulgence in the manners of the conquered.

[3] By these we are to understand Northern and Southern China, separated by the great river Hoang-ho on the eastern, and by the southern limits of Shen-si on the western side.

many disloyal and seditious persons, who at all times were disposed to break out in rebellion against their sovereign,[1] and on this account it became necessary to keep armies in such of the provinces as contained large cities and an extensive population, which are stationed at the distance of four or five miles from those cities, and can enter them at their pleasure. These armies the grand khan makes it a practice to change every second year, and the same with respect to the officers who command them. By means of such precautions the people are kept in quiet subjection, and no movement nor innovation of any kind can be attempted. The troops are maintained not only from the pay they receive out of the imperial revenues of the province, but also from the cattle and their milk, which belong to them individually, and which they send into the cities for sale, furnishing themselves from thence, in return, with those articles of which they stand in need.[2] In this manner they are distributed over the country, in various places, to the distance of thirty, forty, and even sixty days' journey. If even the half of these corps were to be collected in one place, the statement of their number would appear marvellous and scarcely entitled to belief.

§ 2. Having formed his army in the manner above described, the grand khan proceeded towards the territory of Nayan, and by forced marches, continued day and night, he reached it at the expiration of twenty-five days. So prudently, at the same time, was the expedition managed, that neither that prince himself nor any of his dependents were aware of it, all the roads being guarded in such a manner that no persons who attempted to pass could escape being made prisoners. Upon arriving at a certain range of hills, on the other side of which was the plain where Nayan's army lay encamped, Kublaï halted his troops, and allowed them two days of rest. During this interval he called upon his astrologers to ascertain by virtue of their art, and to declare in presence of the whole army,

[1] Not only a great part of the population, especially of Southern China, must have been loyally attached to the ancient race of their kings, but also there were in all the western provinces numerous partisans of the rival branches of Kublaï's own family, who were eager to seize all opportunities of fomenting disturbance.

[2] These details, so probable in themselves, are not, I believe, to be found in any other original writer. It must have been the policy of Kublaï to keep his Tartarian troops as distinct as possible from the Chinese, and therefore, instead of quartering them in the great towns, they were encamped at the distance of some miles from them, and the semblance at least of their former pastoral life was preserved, whilst they were surrounded with their herds and flocks.

to which side the victory would incline. They pronounced that it would fall to the lot of Kublaï. It has ever been the practice of the grand khans to have recourse to divination for the purpose of inspiriting their men. Confident therefore of success, they ascended the hill with alacrity the next morning, and presented themselves before the army of Nayan, which they found negligently posted, without advanced parties or scouts, whilst the chief himself was asleep in his tent, accompanied by one of his wives. Upon awaking, he hastened to form his troops in the best manner that circumstances would allow, lamenting that his junction with Kaidu had not been sooner effected. Kublaï took his station in a large wooden castle, borne on the backs of four elephants,[1] whose bodies were protected with coverings of thick leather hardened by fire, over which were housings of cloth of gold. The castle contained many cross-bow-men and archers, and on the top of it was hoisted the imperial standard, adorned with representations of the sun and moon. His army, which consisted of thirty battalions of horse, each battalion containing ten thousand men, armed with bows, he disposed in three grand divisions; and those which formed the left and right wings he extended in such a manner as to out-flank the army of Nayan. In front of each battalion of horse were placed five hundred infantry, armed with short lances and swords, who, whenever the cavalry made a show of flight, were practised to mount behind the riders and accompany them, alighting again when they returned to the charge, and killing with their lances the horses of the enemy. As soon as the order of battle was arranged, an infinite number of wind instruments of various kinds were sounded, and these were succeeded by songs, according to the custom of the Tartars before they engage in fight, which commences upon the signal given by the cymbals and drums, and there was such a beating of the cymbals and drums, and such singing, that it was wonderful to hear. This signal, by the orders of the grand khan, was first given to the

[1] Elephants have never been commonly used in China, either for war or parade; but during the operations carried on by Kublaï (whilst acting as his brother's lieutenant) in the province of Yunnan, bordering on Ava and other countries where these noble animals abound, he must have become well acquainted with the uses to which they might be rendered subservient; and it appears in a subsequent chapter, that only three years before the period of which we are speaking, he had taken a number of elephants from the king of Mien or Ava (whom his generals defeated in 1283), and employed them in his armies. This consistency of circumstances is not unworthy of observation.

right and left wings; and then a fierce and bloody conflict began. The air was instantly filled with a cloud of arrows that poured down on every side, and vast numbers of men and horses were seen to fall to the ground. The loud cries and shouts of the men, together with the noise of the horses and the weapons, were such as to inspire terror into those who heard them. When their arrows had been discharged, the hostile parties engaged in close combat with their lances, swords, and maces shod with iron; and such was the slaughter, and so large were the heaps of the carcases of men, and more especially of horses, on the field, that it became impossible for the one party to advance upon the other. Thus the fortune of the day remained for a long time undecided, and victory wavered between the contending parties from morning until noon; for so zealous was the devotion of Nayan's people to the cause of their master, who was most liberal and indulgent towards them, that they were all ready to meet death rather than turn their backs to the enemy. At length, however, Nayan, perceiving that he was nearly surrounded, attempted to save himself by flight, but was presently made prisoner, and conducted to the presence of Kublaï, who gave orders for his being put to death.[1] This was carried into execution by enclosing him between two carpets, which were violently shaken until the spirit had departed from the body; the motive for this peculiar sentence being, that the sun and the air should not witness the shedding of the blood of one who belonged to the imperial family.[2] Those of his troops which survived the battle came to make their submission, and swear allegiance to Kublaï. They were inhabitants of the four noble provinces of Chorza, Karli, Barskol, and Sitingui.[3]

Nayan, who had privately undergone the ceremony of baptism, but never made open profession of Christianity, thought proper, on this occasion, to bear the sign of the cross

[1] The particulars of the combat, as given in the text, do not well agree with the account furnished by De Guignes; but this is not surprising when we consider how rarely two descriptions of any great battle are found to correspond. It may be remarked that Marco Polo seems to have been present.

[2] This affectation of avoiding to shed blood in the act of depriving of life a person of high rank, is observable in many instances, and may perhaps have given occasion to the use of the bow-string in the Turkish seraglio.

[3] It is not possible to identify in any modern map or account of Northern Tartary the names of these tribes, which may have long ceased to exist under the same denominations. The difficulty is further increased by the extraordinary corruption of the words in different versions and editions.

in his banners, and he had in his army a vast number of Christians, who were left amongst the slain. When the Jews[1] and the Saracens perceived that the banner of the cross was overthrown, they taunted the Christian inhabitants with it, saying, "Behold the state to which your (vaunted) banners, and those who followed them, are reduced!" On account of these derisions the Christians were compelled to lay their complaints before the grand khan, who ordered the former to appear before him, and sharply rebuked them. "If the Cross of Christ," he said, "has not proved advantageous to the party of Nayan, the effect has been consistent with reason and justice, inasmuch as he was a rebel and a traitor to his lord, and to such wretches it could not afford its protection. Let none therefore presume to charge with injustice the God of the Christians, who is Himself the perfection of goodness and of justice."

CHAPTER II

OF THE RETURN OF THE GRAND KHAN TO THE CITY OF KANBALU AFTER HIS VICTORY—OF THE HONOUR HE CONFERS ON THE CHRISTIANS, THE JEWS, THE MAHOMETANS, AND THE IDOLATERS, AT THEIR RESPECTIVE FESTIVALS—AND THE REASON HE ASSIGNS FOR HIS NOT BECOMING A CHRISTIAN

THE grand khan, having obtained this signal victory, returned with great pomp and triumph to the capital city of Kanbalu. This took place in the month of November, and he continued to reside there during the months of February and March, in which latter was our festival of Easter. Being aware that this was one of our principal solemnities, he commanded all the Christians to attend him, and to bring with them their Book, which contains the four Gospels of the Evangelists. After causing it to be repeatedly perfumed with incense, in a ceremonious manner, he devoutly kissed it, and directed that the same should be done by all his nobles who were present. This was his usual practice upon each of the principal Christian

[1] This is the first occasion on which our author speaks of Jews in Tartary or China. Of their existence in the latter country, at an early period, there is no room to doubt. In the relations of the Mahometan travellers of the ninth century, we are told that in the massacre which took place at the city of Canfu, when taken by a rebel leader after an obstinate siege, many of that race perished.

festivals, such as Easter and Christmas; and he observed the same at the festivals of the Saracens, Jews, and idolaters.[1] Upon being asked his motive for this conduct, he said: "There are four great Prophets who are reverenced and worshipped by the different classes of mankind. The Christians regard Jesus Christ as their divinity; the Saracens, Mahomet; the Jews, Moses;[2] and the idolaters, Sogomombar-kan,[3] the most eminent amongst their idols. I do honour and show respect to all the four, and invoke to my aid whichever amongst them is in truth supreme in heaven." But from the manner in which his majesty acted towards them, it is evident that he regarded the faith of the Christians as the truest and the best; nothing, as he observed, being enjoined to its professors that was not replete with virtue and holiness. By no means, however, would he permit them to bear the cross before them in their processions, because upon it so exalted a personage as Christ had been scourged and (ignominiously) put to death. It may perhaps be asked by some, why, if he showed such a preference to the faith of Christ, he did not conform to it, and become a Christian? His reason for not so doing, he assigned to Nicolo and Maffio Polo, when, upon the occasion of his sending them as his ambassadors to the Pope, they ventured to address a few words to him on the subject of Christianity. "Wherefore," he said, "should I become a Christian? You yourselves must perceive that the Christians of these countries are ignorant, inefficient persons, who do not possess the faculty of performing anything (miraculous); whereas you see that the idolaters can do whatever they will. When I sit at table the cups that were in the middle of the hall come to me filled with wine and other beverage, spontaneously and without being touched by human hand, and I drink from them. They have

[1] This conduct towards the professors of the several systems of faith is perfectly consistent with the character of Kublaï, in which policy was the leading feature. It was his object to keep in good humour all classes of his subjects, and especially those of the capital or about the court, by indulging them in the liberty of following unmolested their own religious tenets, and by flattering each with the idea of possessing his special protection. Many of the highest offices, both civil and military, were held by Mahometans.

[2] Neither do those who profess the Mussulman faith regard Mahomet as a divinity, nor do the Jews so regard Moses; but it is not to be expected that a Tartar emperor should make very accurate theological distinctions.

[3] This word, probably much corrupted by transcribers, must be intended for one of the numerous titles of Buddha or Fo, who, amongst the Mungals, as in India also, is commonly termed Shakia-muni, and in Siam, Sommona-kodom.

the power of controlling bad weather and obliging it to retire to any quarter of the heavens, with many other wonderful gifts of that nature. You are witnesses that their idols have the faculty of speech, and predict to them whatever is required. Should I become a convert to the faith of Christ, and profess myself a Christian, the nobles of my court and other persons who do not incline to that religion will ask me what sufficient motives have caused me to receive baptism, and to embrace Christianity. 'What extraordinary powers,' they will say, 'what miracles have been displayed by its ministers? Whereas the idolaters declare that what they exhibit is performed through their own sanctity, and the influence of their idols.' To this I shall not know what answer to make, and I shall be considered by them as labouring under a grievous error; whilst the idolaters, who by means of their profound art can effect such wonders, may without difficulty compass my death. But return you to your pontiff, and request of him, in my name, to send hither a hundred persons well skilled in your law, who being confronted with the idolaters shall have power to coerce them, and showing that they themselves are endowed with similar art, but which they refrain from exercising, because it is derived from the agency of evil spirits, shall compel them to desist from practices of such a nature in their presence. When I am witness of this, I shall place them and their religion under an interdict, and shall allow myself to be baptized. Following my example, all my nobility will then in like manner receive baptism, and this will be imitated by my subjects in general; so that the Christians of these parts will exceed in number those who inhabit your own country." From this discourse it must be evident that if the Pope had sent out persons duly qualified to preach the gospel, the grand khan would have embraced Christianity, for which, it is certainly known, he had a strong predilection. But, to return to our subject, we shall now speak of the rewards and honours he bestows on such as distinguish themselves by their valour in battle.

CHAPTER III

OF THE KIND OF REWARDS GRANTED TO THOSE WHO CONDUCT THEMSELVES WELL IN FIGHT, AND OF THE GOLDEN TABLETS WHICH THEY RECEIVE

THE grand khan appoints twelve of the most intelligent amongst his nobles, whose duty it is to make themselves acquainted with the conduct of the officers and men of his army, particularly upon expeditions and in battles, and to present their reports to him,[1] and he, upon being apprised of their respective merits, advances them in his service, raising those who commanded an hundred men to the command of a thousand, and presenting many with vessels of silver, as well as the customary tablets or warrants of command and of government.[2] The tablets given to those commanding a hundred men are of silver; to those commanding a thousand, of gold or of silver gilt; and those who command ten thousand receive tablets of gold, bearing the head of a lion;[3] the former being of the weight of a hundred and twenty *saggi*,[4] and these with the lion's head, two hundred and twenty. At the top of the inscription on the tablet is a sentence to this effect: "By the power and might of the great God, and through the grace

[1] In the establishment of a board of this nature it is probable that Kublaï only conformed to the system of the former or ancient Chinese government, which placed the various concerns of the state under the management of distinct tribunals named *pû*, to each of which another word, expressive of the particular nature of the department, is prefixed. "La quatrième cour souveraine," says Du Halde, "se nomme *ping-pou*, c'est-à-dire, le tribunal des armes. La milice de tout l'empire est de son ressort. C'est de ce tribunal que dépendent les officiers de guerre généraux et particuliers," etc. (Tom. ii. p. 24.) Under a warlike monarch, who owed the empire of China to his sword, it might well have been considered as the first in consequence, although now inferior in rank to three others.

[2] See note [1], p. 16, where some account is given of these tablets or letters patent, called *tchi-kouei*, according to the French orthography.

[3] The Chinese representation of a lion, like the *singa* of the Hindu mythology, from whence it seems to have been borrowed, is a grotesque figure, extremely unlike the real animal. An engraving of it will be found in Staunton's Account of Lord Macartney's Embassy, (vol. ii. p. 311;) and the figure is not uncommon in our porcelain collections. Occasion will be taken hereafter to show that where the lion is spoken of by our author as a living animal, and an object of hunting sport, the tiger must be understood.

[4] The saggio of Venice being equal to the sixth part of an ounce, these consequently weighed twenty ounces, and the others in proportion up to fifty ounces.

which he vouchsafes to our empire, be the name of the kaan blessed; and let all such as disobey (what is herein directed) suffer death and be utterly destroyed." The officers who hold these tablets have privileges attached to them, and in the inscription is specified what are the duties and the powers of their respective commands. He who is at the head of a hundred thousand men, or the commander in chief of a grand army, has a golden tablet weighing three hundred *saggi*, with the sentence above mentioned, and at the bottom is engraved the figure of a lion, together with representations of the sun and moon. He exercises also the privileges of his high command, as set forth in this magnificent tablet. Whenever he rides in public, an umbrella is carried over his head, denoting the rank and authority he holds;[1] and when he is seated, it is always upon a silver chair. The grand khan confers likewise upon certain of his nobles tablets on which are represented figures of the gerfalcon,[2] in virtue of which they are authorized to take with them as their guard of honour the whole army of any great prince. They can also make use of the horses of the imperial stud at their pleasure, and can appropriate the horses of any officers inferior to themselves in rank.

CHAPTER IV

OF THE FIGURE AND STATURE OF THE GRAND KHAN—OF HIS FOUR PRINCIPAL WIVES—AND OF THE ANNUAL SELECTION OF YOUNG WOMEN FOR HIM IN THE PROVINCE OF UNGUT

KUBLAI, who is styled grand khan, or lord of lords, is of the middle stature, that is, neither tall nor short; his limbs are well formed, and in his whole figure there is a just proportion. His complexion is fair, and occasionally suffused with red, like the bright tint of the rose, which adds much grace to his countenance. His eyes are black and handsome, his nose is well shaped and prominent. He has four wives of the first

[1] In many parts of the East, the parasol or umbrella with a long handle, borne by an attendant, is a mark of high distinction, and even denotes sovereignty when of a particular colour. Du Halde, in describing the parade of a *tsong-tû* or viceroy of a province, enumerates amongst the insignia "un parasol de soye jaune à triple étage."

[2] Amongst the emblematical ornaments worn by great officers, the eagle is mentioned by Du Halde, but it may probably have been intended for the gerfalcon, a bird more prized as the instrument of royal sport.

rank, who are esteemed legitimate,[1] and the eldest born son of any one of these succeeds to the empire, upon the decease of the grand khan.[2] They bear equally the title of empress, and have their separate courts. None of them have fewer than three hundred young female attendants of great beauty, together with a multitude of youths as pages, and other eunuchs, as well as ladies of the bedchamber; so that the number of persons belonging to each of their respective courts amounts to ten thousand.[3] When his majesty is desirous of the company of one of his empresses, he either sends for her, or goes himself to her palace. Besides these, he has many concubines provided for his use, from a province of Tartary named Ungut, having a city of the same name, the inhabitants of which are distinguished for beauty of features and fairness of complexion.[4] Thither the grand khan sends his officers every second year, or oftener, as it may happen to be his pleasure,

[1] "Il avoit épousé plusieurs femmes," says De Guignes, "dont cinq portoient le titre d'impératrices;" but it is probable that not more than four of these (if so many) were contemporaneous; and the legitimacy of the latter number, which does not appear to be sanctioned by the ancient Chinese institutions, may have been suggested by the Mahometan usage. Three queens are mentioned by P. Magalhanes as belonging to the emperor Kang-hi, and the establishment of the late emperor Kien Lông consisted, in like manner, of one female with the rank of empress, two queens of the second order, and six of the third.

[2] According to the laws of China, as we are told by Du Halde, the eldest son (or son of the superior wife), though he may have a preferable claim, has not an indefeasible right to the succession. Amongst the predecessors of Kublaï, also, in the Moghul empire, we have instances of the hereditary claim being set aside, and Oktaï himself was named grand khan by his father, in preference to Jagataï, the eldest son. Our author must therefore be understood to say, that the son first born to any one of the four empresses was considered as the presumptive heir; and this in fact having been the case with respect to the eldest son of Kublaï, whose succession, had he outlived his father, was undoubted, the prevailing sentiment of the court might naturally be mistaken for the established custom of the empire.

[3] This number appears excessive, but we are not to measure the extravagancies of enormous and uncontrolled power by any standard of our own ideas. Perhaps besides the establishment of female attendants and of eunuchs, old and young, a numerous military guard of honour might be attached to the court of each of the empresses. The early Venice edition, however, states the number much lower: "Ciascuna de queste quatro regine hanno in sua corte piu de quatro millia persone infra homini e donne." P. Martini speaks of numerous females, below the rank of concubines, for the service of the palace.

[4] The country here named Ungut is in other versions called Origiach, Origiathe, and Ungrac. There is little doubt of its being intended for that of the Ighurs, Eighurs, or Uighurs, who in the time of Jengiz-khan possessed the countries of Turfan and Hami or Kamil, and were always considered as superior, in respect both of person and acquirements, to the other nations of Tartary.

who collect for him, to the number of four or five hundred, or more, of the handsomest of the young women, according to the estimation of beauty communicated to them in their instructions. The mode of their appreciation is as follows. Upon the arrival of these commissioners, they give orders for assembling all the young women of the province, and appoint qualified persons to examine them, who, upon careful inspection of each of them separately, that is to say, of the hair, the countenance, the eyebrows, the mouth, the lips, and other features, as well as the symmetry of these with each other, estimate their value at sixteen, seventeen, eighteen, or twenty, or more carats, according to the greater or less degree of beauty.[1] The number required by the grand khan, at the rates, perhaps, of twenty or twenty-one carats, to which their commission was limited, is then selected from the rest, and they are conveyed to his court. Upon their arrival in his presence, he causes a new examination to be made by a different set of inspectors, and from amongst them a further selection takes place, when thirty or forty are retained for his own chamber at a higher valuation. These, in the first instance, are committed separately to the care of the wives of certain of the nobles, whose duty it is to observe them attentively during the course of the night, in order to ascertain that they have not any concealed imperfections, that they sleep tranquilly, do not snore, have sweet breath, and are free from unpleasant scent in any part of the body. Having undergone this rigorous scrutiny, they are divided into parties of five, one of which parties attends during three days and three nights, in his majesty's interior apartment, where they are to perform every service that is required of them, and he does with them as he likes. When this term is completed, they are relieved by another party, and in this manner successively, until the whole number have taken their turn; when the first five recommence their attendance. But whilst the one party officiates in the inner chamber, another is stationed in the outer apartment adjoining; in order that if his majesty should have occa-

[1] If by this gold weight is meant the carat consisting of four grains, the estimated value of beauty must have been very low in that age and country, as twenty carats or eighty grains of gold, at four pounds sterling the ounce, amount to no more than thirteen shillings and fourpence. But the probability is that our author's words expressed some Chinese weight (the *täel*, perhaps, or the *mace*, which latter would bring it to about eight or nine pounds sterling), and the foreign term he employed may have been inaccurately rendered by *carato*.

sion for anything, such as drink or victuals, the former may signify his commands to the latter, by whom the article required is immediately procured: and thus the duty of waiting upon his majesty's person is exclusively performed by these young females.[1] The remainder of them, whose value had been estimated at an inferior rate, are assigned to the different lords of the household; under whom they are instructed in cookery, in dressmaking, and other suitable works; and upon any person belonging to the court expressing an inclination to take a wife, the grand khan bestows upon him one of these damsels, with a handsome portion. In this manner he provides for them all amongst his nobility. It may be asked whether the people of the province do not feel themselves aggrieved in having their daughters thus forcibly taken from them by the sovereign? Certainly not; but, on the contrary, they regard it as a favour and an honour done to them; and those who are the fathers of handsome children feel highly gratified by his condescending to make choice of their daughters. "If," say they, "my daughter is born under an auspicious planet and to good fortune, his majesty can best fulfil her destinies, by matching her nobly; which it would not be in my power to do." If, on the other hand, the daughter misconducts herself, or any mischance befalls her (by which she becomes disqualified), the father attributes the disappointment to the malign influence of her stars.

CHAPTER V

OF THE NUMBER OF THE GRAND KHAN'S SONS BY HIS FOUR WIVES, WHOM HE MAKES KINGS OF DIFFERENT PROVINCES —AND OF CHINGIS HIS FIRST-BORN—ALSO OF THE SONS BY HIS CONCUBINES, WHOM HE CREATES LORDS

THE grand khan has had twenty-two sons by his four legitimate wives, the eldest of whom, named Chingis,[2] was designed

[1] It would appear from hence that Kublaï, although he adopted the Chinese custom of employing eunuchs as the attendants or guards of his females, did not so far forget his original manly habits as to admit them near his own person.

[2] Gaubil and De Guignes name this prince Tchingkin and Tchenkin, and such may perhaps have been the manner in which it was pronounced by the Chinese, who terminate all their monosyllables either with a vowel or a nasal; but the name as found in most of the versions of our author is apparently more correct, being that of the great ancestor of the family;

to inherit the dignity of grand khan, with the government of the empire; and this nomination was confirmed to him during the life-time of his father. It was not, however, his fate to survive him; but leaving a son, whose name is Themur, he, as the representative of his father, is to succeed to the dominion.[1] The disposition of this prince is good, and he is endowed with wisdom and valour; of the latter he has given proofs in several successful battles. Besides these, his majesty has twenty-five sons by his concubines, all of them brave soldiers, having been continually employed in the military profession. These he has placed in the rank of nobles. Of his legitimate sons, seven are at the head of extensive provinces and kingdoms,[2] which they govern with wisdom and prudence, as might be expected of the children of one whose great qualities have not been surpassed, in the general estimation, by any person of the Tartar race.

CHAPTER VI

OF THE GREAT AND ADMIRABLE PALACE OF THE GRAND KHAN, NEAR TO THE CITY OF KANBALU

THE grand khan usually resides during three months of the year, namely, December, January, and February, in the great city of Kanbalu, situated towards the north-eastern extremity of the province of Cathay;[3] and here, on the southern side of the new city, is the site of his vast palace, the form and dimensions of which are as follows. In the first place is a square enclosed with a wall and deep ditch; each side of the square being eight miles in length,[4] and having at an equal distance

and in the early Venice epitome it is expressly said: " So primo hebbe nome Chinchis chan per amor de Chinchis."

[1] The name here written Themur, and in other versions Temur, is evidently the well-known Tartar name of Timur, although the great conqueror so called did not acquire his celebrity until a century after.

[2] De Guignes enumerates ten of his sons, born of five empresses, and mentions the provinces of Shensi, Sechuen, and Tibet as being governed by Mangkola, the third son. P. Magalhanes notices the custom of sending the princes of the royal family into the provinces with the title of kings; but in the reign of Kang-hi their authority was merely nominal.

[3] Relatively to the vast extent of the whole empire at that period, Cathay, or Northern China, is termed by our author a province, although it contained the capital of that empire, and the seat of government.

[4] These dimensions, as applicable to a palace, even for an emperor of China, appear at first view to be extravagant; but the seeming difficulty arises from the misapplication of a term, in calling that a palace which was, in fact, the enclosure of a royal park and encampment.

from each extremity an entrance-gate, for the concourse of people resorting thither from all quarters. Within this enclosure there is, on the four sides, an open space one mile in breadth, where the troops are stationed;[1] and this is bounded by a second wall, enclosing a square of six miles,[2] having three gates on the south side, and three on the north, the middle portal of each being larger than the other two, and always kept shut, excepting on the occasions of the emperor's entrance or departure. Those on each side always remain open for the use of common passengers.[3] In the middle of each division of these walls is a handsome and spacious building, and consequently within the enclosure there are eight such buildings, in which are deposited the royal military stores; one building being appropriated to the reception of each class of stores. Thus, for instance, the bridles, saddles, stirrups, and other furniture serving for the equipment of cavalry, occupy one storehouse; the bows, strings, quivers, arrows, and other articles belonging to archery, occupy another; cuirasses, corselets, and other armour formed of leather, a third storehouse; and so of the rest. Within this walled enclosure there is still another, of great thickness, and its height is full twenty-five feet. The battlements or crenated parapets are all white. This also forms a square four miles in extent, each side being one mile, and it has six gates, disposed like those of the former enclosure.[4] It contains in like manner eight large buildings,

[1] The area allotted to the troops upon this plain would be twenty-eight square miles. Their number was, of course, very great, and being chiefly cavalry, the barracks or sheds for their accommodation would necessarily occupy a vast range. In the early part of the last century, the cavalry stationed in and about Peking was reckoned at 80,000. Supposing it to have been about 112,000 in the days of Kublaï, this would allow only a square mile for 4,000 horse.

[2] As this second enclosure not only contained the royal arsenals, eight in number, for every description of military store, but formed also a park for deer, there is nothing remarkable in its extent. It is not easy, however, to reconcile its position in respect to the city with some of the circumstances here mentioned; but we must suppose that the interior enclosure (afterwards described), which contained the palace properly so called, was situated towards the northern side of this park, and was at the same time contiguous to the southern wall of the city.

[3] The custom of reserving particular gates for the exclusive use of the emperor is still observed.

[4] To this last enclosure it is that the appellation of the Palace should be restricted; and when we read the description of the Meidan of Ispahan, or of the Escurial with its twenty-two courts, we shall not deem the area of a square mile any extraordinary space to be occupied by the various buildings required for such an establishment as that of Kublaï. It is at the same time to be remarked that there is a striking agreement between the measure here stated and that assigned to the modern palace in the descriptions we have from the Jesuits.

similarly arranged, which are appropriated to the wardrobe of the emperor.[1] The spaces between the one wall and the other are ornamented with many handsome trees, and contain meadows in which are kept various kinds of beasts, such as stags, the animals that yield the musk, roe-bucks, fallow-deer, and others of the same class. Every interval between the walls, not occupied by buildings, is stocked in this manner. The pastures have abundant herbage. The roads across them being raised three feet above their level, and paved, no mud collects upon them, nor rain-water settles, but on the contrary runs off, and contributes to improve the vegetation. Within these walls, which constitute the boundary of four miles, stands the palace of the grand khan, the most extensive that has ever yet been known. It reaches from the northern to the southern wall, leaving only a vacant space (or court), where persons of rank and the military guards pass and repass. It has no upper floor, but the roof is very lofty.[2] The paved foundation or platform on which it stands is raised ten spans above the level of the ground, and a wall of marble, two paces wide, is built on all sides, to the level of this pavement, within the line of which the palace is erected; so that the wall, extending beyond the ground plan of the building, and encompassing the whole, serves as a terrace, where those who walk on it are visible from without. Along the exterior edge of the wall is a handsome balustrade, with pillars, which the people are allowed to approach.[3] The sides of the great halls and the

[1] It is well known to have been the practice of Eastern monarchs, from the earliest ages, to deliver changes of raiment to those whom they meant to distinguish by their favour. The Persian term *khilât* is generally applied to these vestments, which consist of pelisses in the northern parts of Asia, and of dresses of cloth, silk, or muslin, in the temperate and warmer climates. We read of vast numbers of them being distributed on the occasion of great victories, or the dismissal of important embassies; and this may account for the bulk of the wardrobes or buildings for what are here termed the *paramenti* of the emperor, which may also include the regalia carried in their splendid processions.

[2] It will be seen in the plates accompanying the accounts of various embassies to Peking, that although the flooring of the palaces is elevated from the ground, they consist of but a single story. The height of the ornamented roofs is a striking feature in the architecture of these people.

[3] The height of the terrace is said, in Ramusio's text, to be *dieci palmi*, or about seven feet; but in the epitomes it is *doi brazza e mezo*, or about twice that elevation; and this accords best with modern descriptions. All the accounts of missionaries and travellers serve to show that, in point of structure, materials, and style of embellishment, there has existed a perfect resemblance between the buildings of Kublaï, as described by our author, and those of Kang-hi and Kien-long, in the seventeenth and eighteenth centuries.

apartments are ornamented with dragons in carved work and gilt, figures of warriors, of birds, and of beasts, with representations of battles. The inside of the roof is contrived in such a manner that nothing besides gilding and painting presents itself to the eye.[1] On each of the four sides of the palace there is a grand flight of marble steps, by which you ascend from the level of the ground to the wall of marble which surrounds the building, and which constitute the approach to the palace itself. The grand hall is extremely long and wide, and admits of dinners being there served to great multitudes of people. The palace contains a number of separate chambers, all highly beautiful, and so admirably disposed that it seems impossible to suggest any improvement to the system of their arrangement. The exterior of the roof is adorned with a variety of colours, red, green, azure, and violet, and the sort of covering is so strong as to last for many years.[2] The glazing of the windows is so well wrought and so delicate as to have the transparency of crystal.[3] In the rear of the body of the palace there are large buildings containing several apartments, where is deposited the private property of the monarch, or his treasure in gold and silver bullion, precious stones, and pearls, and also his vessels of gold and silver plate.[4]

[1] "Cette salle," adds Du Halde, "a environ cent trente pieds de longueur, et est presque quarrée. Le lambris est tout en sculpture vernissé de verd, et chargé de dragons dorez: les colonnes qui soutiennent le toit en dedans sont de six à sept pieds de circonférence par le bas: elles sont incrustées d'une espèce de pâte enduite d'un vernis rouge."—Tom. i. p. 117.

[2] The roofs are invariably covered with baked tiles, which, for the principal buildings, have a vitrified glazing of a bright colour. Such as are used for the palaces at the present day are exclusively yellow; but this etiquette may not have been so strictly adhered to under the dynasty of the Yuen. "Le tout est couvert de tuiles vernissées d'un si beau jaune, que de loin elles ne paroissent guères moins éclatantes, que si elles étoient dorées."—Du Halde, tom. i. p. 116.

[3] Ramusio employs the word *vitreate,* which I have translated *glazing,* although there is no reason to suppose that glass was used for windows in China at that period. The meaning may be, that the pellucid substance employed for glazing (perhaps talc or laminæ of shells) was so delicately wrought (*così ben fatte e così soltilmente*) as to have nearly the transparency of crystal. "Les fenêtres des maisons," says De Guignes, "sont garnies avec des coquilles minces et assez transparentes, ou avec du papier." (Tom. ii. p. 178.) Staunton mentions that the windows of some of the yachts or barges had glass panes, but the manufacture was probably European.

[4] In the modern palace, the buildings for this purpose are described as being (less appropriately) round the court, in *front* of the great hall of audience; but we ought not to be surprised at any variation with respect to the arrangement of these buildings, when we learn that the whole of the palace has been repeatedly destroyed by fire

Here are likewise the apartments of his wives and concubines; and in this retired situation he despatches business with convenience, being free from every kind of interruption. On the other side of the grand palace, and opposite to that in which the emperor resides, is another palace, in every respect similar, appropriated to the residence of Chingis, his eldest son, at whose court are observed all the ceremonials belonging to that of his father, as the prince who is to succeed to the government of the empire.[1] Not far from the palace, on the northern side, and about a bow-shot distance from the surrounding wall, is an artificial mount of earth, the height of which is full a hundred paces, and the circuit at the base about a mile. It is clothed with the most beautiful evergreen trees; for whenever his majesty receives information of a handsome tree growing in any place, he causes it to be dug up, with all its roots and the earth about them, and however large and heavy it may be, he has it transported by means of elephants to this mount, and adds it to the verdant collection. From this perpetual verdure it has acquired the appellation of the Green Mount. On its summit is erected an ornamental pavilion, which is likewise entirely green. The view of this altogether,—the mount itself, the trees, and the building, form a delightful and at the same time a wonderful scene. In the northern quarter also, and equally within the precincts of the city, there is a large and deep excavation, judiciously formed, the earth from which supplied the material for raising the mount.[2] It is furnished with water by a small rivulet, and has the appearance of a fish-pond, but its use is for watering the cattle. The stream passing from thence along an aqueduct, at the foot of the Green Mount, proceeds to fill another great and very deep excavation formed between the private palace of the emperor and that of his son Chingis; and the earth from hence equally

[1] "A l'est de la même cour est un autre palais, habité par le prince héritier, lorsqu'il y en a un de déclaré." (De L'isle, Descr. de la Ville de Peking, p. 16.) It will not escape the observation of the reader that, in a previous page, our author noticed the untimely death of this prince, (see pp. 165, 166,) who, notwithstanding, is here mentioned as a living person. This is obviously to be accounted for from the circumstance of the work being composed, not from recollection merely, but from notes made at different periods, amongst which a description of the palaces might have been one of the earliest. Kublaï also, the event of whose death is related in the course of the returning journey, is spoken of throughout the work as the emperor actually reigning.

[2] This artificial hill exists at the present day, and retains its original name of King-shan, or the Green Mountain; but it would seem, from modern relations, that four others of inferior size have since been added.

served to increase the elevation of the mount. In this latter basin there is great store and variety of fish, from which the table of his majesty is supplied with any quantity that may be wanted. The stream discharges itself at the opposite extremity of the piece of water, and precautions are taken to prevent the escape of the fish by placing gratings of copper or iron at the places of its entrance and exit. It is stocked also with swans and other aquatic birds. From the one palace to the other there is a communication by means of a bridge thrown across the water. Such is the description of this great palace. We shall now speak of the situation and circumstances of the city of Taidu.

CHAPTER VII

OF THE NEW CITY OF TAI-DU, BUILT NEAR TO THAT OF KANBALU —OF A RULE OBSERVED RESPECTING THE ENTERTAINMENT OF AMBASSADORS—AND OF THE NIGHTLY POLICE OF THE CITY

THE city of Kanbalu is situated near a large river in the province of Cathay, and was in ancient times eminently magnificent and royal. The name itself implies "the city of the sovereign;"[1] but his majesty having imbibed an opinion from the astrologers, that it was destined to become rebellious

[1] The name of this celebrated city, which our author writes Cambalu (for Canbalu, the *m* being substituted for *n* at the end of a syllable, in the old Italian, as well as in the Portuguese orthography), is by the Arabians and Persians written Khan-balik and Khan-baligh, signifying, in one of the dialects of Tartary, the "city of the khan or sovereign." This terminating appellative is not uncommon, as we find it in Kabaligh and Bish-baligh, cities of Turkistan; in Ordu-baligh, one of the names of Kara-korum; and in Mu-baligh, or the "city of desolation," a name given to Bamian, in the territory of Balkh, upon the occasion of its destruction by Jengiz-khan. With respect to the particular situation of the city, it is said, in the words of Ramusio, to have been "*sopra* un gran fiume," but in the Latin version, "*juxta* magnum fluvium," which affords more latitude. By this river must be understood the Pe-ho, which is navigable for loaded vessels up to Tong-cheu, within twelve miles of the capital; but in the higher part of its course it seems to approximate nearer. Our knowledge of the country that surrounds Pe-king is, however, extremely imperfect; nor do the different maps accord with respect to the number or course of the streams that, coming from the neighbouring mountains of Tartary, appear to unite at or above Tong-cheu. It should be observed, also, that the old city of Yen-king, or Khan-balig, might have stood some miles nearer to the Pe-ho than the site of the more modern city of Peking.

to his authority, resolved upon the measure of building another capital, upon the opposite side of the river, where stand the palaces just described: so that the new and the old cities are separated from each other only by the stream that runs between them.[1] The new-built city received the name of Tai-du,[2] and all the Cathaians, that is, all those of the inhabitants who were natives of the province of Cathay, were compelled to evacuate the ancient city, and to take up their abode in the new. Some of the inhabitants, however, of whose loyalty he did not entertain suspicion, were suffered to remain, especially because the latter, although of the dimensions that shall presently be described, was not capable of containing the same number as the former, which was of vast extent.[3]

This new city is of a form perfectly square, and twenty-

[1] This would seem to imply a removal of the capital to a different side of the Pe-ho, or larger river just mentioned; but it may be thought more probable that our author here speaks only of the rivulet which at the present day passes between what are denominated the Chinese and the Tartar cities, over which (however insignificant the stream) there is a handsome bridge of communication. Martini, in his "Atlas Sinensis," distinguishes two streams as contributing to supply the city with water.

[2] The name of Tai-du (more correctly written Ta-tû) signifies the "great court," and was the Chinese appellation for the new city, which the Tartars, and the western people in general, continued to name Khan-baligh. A doubt may be entertained whether the city of Yen-king, which Kublaï, from motives of superstition or of policy, abandoned, occupied the site of that now called the ancient or Chinese city, which is separated from the other only by a rivulet, and by the wall of the latter. But there is evidence of a positive kind of their being the same; for Yong-lo, the rebuilder of Peking, after it had been nearly destroyed in the preceding wars, erected within the bounds of what was equally in his time denominated the old city, and which could be no other than that depopulated by Kublaï a century and a half before, two remarkable temples, one of them dedicated to the Heavens and the other to the Earth, which temples are to be found in Du Halde's and De Lisle's plates, and exist in the Chinese city at the present day. All the works of this great monarch, the third of the dynasty by which the Mungals were driven out, and who sat on the throne at the period of Shah Rokh's embassy, were begun about the year 1406, and completed about 1421.

[3] In the "Mémoires concernant les Chinois," we find the following account of the extent of its walls at different periods: "Sous le Kin (the dynasty overturned by Jengiz-khan) dont il fut aussi la capitale, il eut soixante-quinze *li* de tour, ou sept lieues et demie. Les Yuen qui le nommèrent d'abord la *capitale du milieu*, puis la grande capitale, ne lui donnèrent que six lieues de tour et onze portes, lorsqu'ils en réparèrent les ruines en 1274. Le fondateur de la dynastie des Ming rasa deux de ces portes du côté du Midi pour le dégrader; et Yong-lo, qui en rebâtit les murailles en 1409, ne leur donna que quatre lieues de tour: c'est leur mesure d'aujourd'hui, étant restées les mêmes. Quant à la ville Chinoise, ce fut Chin-tsong, de la dynastie précédente, qui en fit faire l'enceinte en murs de terre l'an 1524. . . . Ce ne fut qu'en 1564 qu'elle obtint l'honneur d'être incorporée à l'ancienne ville, avec celui d'avoir des murailles et des portes en briques."—Tom. ii. p. 553.

four miles in extent, each of its sides being neither more nor less than six miles.[1] It is enclosed with walls of earth, that at the base are about ten paces thick, but gradually diminish to the top, where the thickness is not more than three paces.[2] In all parts the battlements are white.[3] The whole plan of the city was regularly laid out by line, and the streets in general are consequently so straight, that when a person ascends the wall over one of the gates, and looks right forward, he can see the gate opposite to him on the other side of the city.[4] In the public streets there are, on each side, booths and shops of every description.[5] All the allotments of ground upon which the habitations throughout the city were constructed are square, and exactly on a line with each other; each allotment being sufficiently spacious for handsome buildings, with corresponding courts and gardens. One of these was assigned to each head of a family; that is to say, such a person of such a tribe had one square allotted to him, and so of the rest. Afterwards the property passed from hand to hand.

[1] The square form prevails much amongst the cities and towns of China, wherever the nature of the ground and the course of the waters admit of it. This probably had its origin in the principles of castrametation. The dimensions of the present Tartar city, according to De Lisle, are eleven *li* in the length from north to south, by nine in width from east to west, making forty *li* or fifteen miles in the whole extent. He adds, that in the time of Kublaï the extent was sixty *li*, or twenty-two miles and a half, which does not differ materially from the measurement in the text. It appears, therefore, that when Yong-lo rebuilt the walls of the ruined city, he contracted its limits, as it was natural for him to do.

[2] When it is said that the walls of the capital were of earth (*di terra*), I am inclined to think that *terra cotta* or bricks should be understood; as they were in general use amongst the Chinese from the earliest ages, and employed in the construction of the great wall. It may be proper to observe, that the distinguishing appellations of Tartar and Chinese cities did not take place under the Yuen, or Mungal dynasty, nor until the subjugation of the empire by the Tsing or present race of Manchu Tartars, who succeeded to the Ming or Chinese dynasty, and drove the native inhabitants from what is commonly termed the new or northern city into the old or southern, to make room for their Tartar followers.

[3] These battlements or *merli* must have been of solid materials (whether of white bricks or stone); which seems to be inconsistent with the supposition of a mud or turf rampart, unless there was at least a *revêtement* of masonry. "The parapet," says Staunton, "was deeply crenated, but had no regular embrazures."—Vol. ii. p. 116.

[4] The straightness of the streets of Peking is apparent from De Lisle's plan, and corroborated by the accounts of all who have visited that city.

[5] "In front of most of the houses in this main street," says Staunton, "were shops painted, gilt, and decorated like those of Tong-choo-foo, but in a grander style. Over some of them were broad terraces covered with shrubs and flowers. . . . Outside the shops, as well as within them, was displayed a variety of goods for sale."—Vol. ii. p. 118.

In this manner the whole interior of the city is disposed in squares, so as to resemble a chess-board, and planned out with a degree of precision and beauty impossible to describe. The wall of the city has twelve gates, three on each side of the square, and over each gate and compartment of the wall there is a handsome building; so that on each side of the square there are five such buildings, containing large rooms, in which are disposed the arms of those who form the garrison of the city,[1] every gate being guarded by a thousand men.[2] It is not to be understood that such a force is stationed there in consequence of the apprehension of danger from any hostile power whatever, but as a guard suitable to the honour and dignity of the sovereign. Yet it must be allowed that the declaration of the astrologers has excited in his mind a degree of suspicion with regard to the Cathaians. In the centre of the city there is a great bell suspended in a lofty building, which is sounded every night, and after the third stroke no person dares to be found in the streets,[3] unless upon some urgent occasion, such as to call assistance to a woman in labour, or a man attacked with sickness; and even in such necessary cases the person is required to carry a light.[4]

Withoutside of each of the gates is a suburb so wide that it reaches to and unites with those of the other nearest gates on both sides, and in length extends to the distance of three or

[1] The practice of erecting places of arms over gates subsists at the present day.

[2] This would seem to be the number that usually constitutes the guard of important gates in that country. "Having travelled about six or eight miles," says John Bell, "we arrived at the famous wall of China. We entered at a great gate, which is shut every night, and always guarded by a thousand men."—Tom. i. p. 336.

[3] "Il y a dans chaque ville," says Du Halde, "de grosses cloches, ou un tambour d'une grandeur extraordinaire, qui servent à marquer les veilles de la nuit. Chaque veille est de deux heures: la première commence vers les huit heures du soir. Pendant les deux heures que dure cette première veille, on frappe de tems en tems un coup, ou sur la cloche, ou sur le tambour. Quand elle est finie, et que la seconde veille commence, on frappe deux coups tant qu'elle dure: on en frappe trois à la troisième, et ainsi de toutes les autres." (Tom. ii. p. 50.) To this third or midnight watch it is that our author alludes, when a treble stroke is given. Staunton also speaks of "the great fabric, of considerable height, which includes a bell of prodigious size and cylindric form, that, struck on the outside with a wooden mallet, emits a sound distinctly heard throughout the capital."—Tom. ii. p. 122.

[4] "Les petites rues qui aboutissent aux grandes, ont des portes faites de treillis de bois, qui n'empêchent pas de voir ceux qui y marchent. . . . Les portes à treillis sont fermées la nuit par le corps de garde, et il ne la fait ouvrir que rarement, à gens connus, qui ont une lanterne à la main, et qui sortent pour une bonne raison, comme seroit celle d'appeller un médecin."—Du Halde, tom. i. p. 115.

four miles, so that the number of inhabitants in these suburbs exceeds that of the city itself. Within each suburb there are, at intervals, as far perhaps as a mile from the city, many hotels, or caravanserais, in which the merchants arriving from various parts take up their abode;[1] and to each description of people a separate building is assigned, as we should say, one to the Lombards, another to the Germans, and a third to the French. The number of public women who prostitute themselves for money, reckoning those in the new city as well as those in the suburbs of the old, is twenty-five thousand.[2] To each hundred and to each thousand of these there are superintending officers appointed, who are under the orders of a captain-general. The motive for placing them under such command is this: when ambassadors arrive charged with any business in which the interests of the grand khan are concerned, it is customary to maintain them at his majesty's expense, and in order that they may be treated in the most honourable manner, the captain is ordered to furnish nightly to each individual of the embassy one of these courtezans, who is likewise to be changed every night, for which service, as it is considered in the light of a tribute they owe to the sovereign, they do not receive any remuneration. Guards, in parties of thirty or forty, continually patrol the streets during the course of the night, and make diligent search for

[1] These establishments for the accommodation of persons arriving from distant countries are incidentally noticed by Trigault (Histoire du Royaume de la Chine), who speaks of "le palais des estrangers" at Peking. It would seem, however, that they are now situated within the walls of the Chinese town, rather than in the suburbs.

[2] It is evident that there is here a mistake in Ramusio's text, as not only all the modern authorities agree in the fact of the public women being excluded from the city and confined to the suburbs, but it is expressly so stated in the other versions of our author. This regulation of police appears to have been equally enforced under later dynasties. "Il y a," says Du Halde, "des femmes publiques et prostituées à la Chine comme ailleurs, mais comme ces sortes de personnes sont ordinairement la cause de quelques désordres, il ne leur est pas permis de demeurer dans l'enceinte des villes: leur logement doit être hors des murs; encore ne peuvent-elles pas avoir des maisons particulières; elles logent plusieurs ensemble et souvent sous la conduite d'un homme, qui est responsable du désordre, s'il en arrivoit; au reste ces femmes libertines ne sont que tolérées, et on les regarde comme infâmes." (Tom. ii. p. 51.) Respecting their numbers, under the reign of Kang-hi, the missionaries do not furnish us with any information. [In the early Latin text of Marco Polo, printed by the Paris Geographical Society, we here read: "Et istæ mulieres quæ fallunt pro pecuniâ sunt bene viginti millia; et omnes habent satisfacere, propter multam gentem quæ illuc concurrit de mercatoribus et aliis forensibus. Et sic potestis videre si in ista civitate est maxima gens, si malæ mulieres sunt tot."]

persons who may be from their homes at an unseasonable hour, that is, after the third stroke of the great bell. When any are met with under such circumstances, they immediately apprehend and confine them, and take them in the morning for examination before officers appointed for that purpose,[1] who, upon the proof of any delinquency, sentence them, according to the nature of the offence, to a severer or lighter infliction of the bastinade, which sometimes, however, occasions their death. It is in this manner that crimes are usually punished amongst these people, from a disinclination to the shedding of blood, which their *baksis* or learned astrologers instruct them to avoid.[2] Having thus described the interior of the city of Tai-du, we shall now speak of the disposition to rebellion shown by its Cathaian inhabitants.

CHAPTER VIII

OF THE TREASONABLE PRACTICES EMPLOYED TO CAUSE THE CITY OF KANBALU TO REBEL, AND OF THE APPREHENSION AND PUNISHMENT OF THOSE CONCERNED

PARTICULAR mention will hereafter be made of the establishment of a council of twelve persons, who had the power of disposing, at their pleasure, of the lands, the governments, and everything belonging to the state. Amongst these was a Saracen, named Achmac,[3] a crafty and bold man, whose influence with the grand khan surpassed that of the other members. To such a degree was his master infatuated with him that he indulged him in every liberty. It was discovered, indeed, after his death, that he had by means of spells so fascinated his majesty as to oblige him to give ear and credit

[1] "Ils ne permettent à personne de marcher la nuit, et ils interrogent même ceux que l'empereur auroit envoyé pour quelques affaires. Si leur réponse donne lieu au moindre soupçon, on les met en arrêt au corps de garde. . . . C'est par ce bel ordre, qui s'observe avec la dernière exactitude, que la paix, le silence, et la sûreté règnent dans toute la ville." —Du Halde, tom. i. p. 115.

[2] It has been already observed, that the priests of Buddha, who in Tibet are called *lamas*, are by the Arabians and Persians named *bakshi*; and it is well known, that to abstain from shedding of blood, and particularly from bloody sacrifices, is the characteristic precept of that sect, in which, say the Brahmans, his disciples make virtue and religion to consist.

[3] The name of this powerful and corrupt Arabian minister, whom the Chinese call Ahama, was doubtless Ahmed. the Achmet of our Turkish historians.

to whatever he represented, and by these means was enabled to act in all matters according to his own arbitrary will. He gave away all the governments and public offices, pronounced judgment upon all offenders, and when he was disposed to sacrifice any man to whom he bore ill-will, he had only to go to the emperor and say to him, "Such a person has committed an offence against your majesty, and is deserving of death," when the emperor was accustomed to reply, "Do as you judge best;" upon which he caused him to be immediately executed. So evident were the proofs of the authority he possessed, and of his majesty's implicit faith in his representations, that none had the hardiness to contradict him in any matter; nor was there a person, however high in rank or office, who did not stand in awe of him. If any one was accused by him of capital crime, however anxious he might be to exculpate himself, he had not the means of refuting the charge, because he could not procure an advocate, none daring to oppose the will of Achmac. By these means he occasioned many to die unjustly. Besides this, there was no handsome female who became an object of his sensuality that he did not contrive to possess, taking her as a wife if she was unmarried, or otherwise compelling her to yield to his desires. When he obtained information of any man having a beautiful daughter, he despatched his emissaries to the father of the girl, with instructions to say to him: "What are your views with regard to this handsome daughter of yours? You cannot do better than give her in marriage to the Lord Deputy or Vicegerent"[1] (that is, to Achmac, for so they termed him, as implying that he was his majesty's representative). "We shall prevail upon him to appoint you to such a government or to such an office for three years." Thus tempted, he is prevailed upon to part with his child; and the matter being so far arranged, Achmac repairs to the emperor and informs his majesty that a certain government is vacant, or that the period for which it is held will expire on such a day, and recommends the father as a person well qualified to perform the duties. To this his

[1] The term employed by Ramusio is Bailo, which particularly belonged to the person who represented, at Constantinople, the republic of Venice; not as ambassador (when the appointment first took place), but as joint sovereign with the Latin emperor. It is not easy to find an equivalent term in our language; nor does the Chinese title of Colao convey the idea intended to be given, of his inordinate power. The Arabs indeed might have styled him Khalifah, which signifies a substitute, deputy, or vicegerent.

majesty gives his consent, and the appointment is immediately carried into effect. By such means as these, either from the ambition of holding high offices or the apprehension of his power, he obtained the sacrifice of all the most beautiful young women, either under the denomination of wives, or as the slaves of his pleasure. He had sons to the number of twenty-five, who held the highest offices of the state, and some of them, availing themselves of the authority of their father, formed adulterous connexions, and committed many other unlawful and atrocious acts. Achmac had likewise accumulated great wealth, for every person who obtained an appointment found it necessary to make him a considerable present.

During a period of twenty-two years he exercised this uncontrolled sway.[1] At length the natives of the country, that is, the Cathaians, no longer able to endure his multiplied acts of injustice or the flagrant wickedness committed against their families, held meetings in order to devise means of putting him to death and raising a rebellion against the government. Amongst the persons principally concerned in this plot was a Cathaian, named Chen-ku, a chief of six thousand men, who, burning with resentment on account of the violation of his mother, his wife, and his daughter, proposed the measure to one of his countrymen, named Van-ku, who was at the head of ten thousand men,[2] and recommended its being carried into execution at the time when the grand khan, having completed his three months' residence in Kanbalu, had departed for his palace of Shan-du,[3] and when his son Chingis also had retired to the place he was accustomed to visit at that season; because the charge of the city was then entrusted to Achmac, who communicated to his master whatever matters occurred during his absence, and received in return the signification of his pleasure. Van-ku and Chen-ku, having held

[1] His death took place in 1281, and his functions of Minister of Finance are first noticed by De Guignes (Histoire des Mogols de la Chine) in 1262; which includes a space of nineteen years: but he might have been in office some time before his extortions gave notoriety to his name.

[2] I apprehend that these were not military commands, but that the civil jurisdiction of the country was established on a footing analogous to that of the army. At the present day every tenth Chinese inhabitant is responsible for the conduct (so far as the public peace is concerned) of nine of his neighbours. Such was also the principle of our English tithings and hundreds. These conspirators were evidently citizens, not soldiers.

[3] It will appear that, according to the Chinese authorities, this opportunity of the emperor's periodical absence was actually seized by the conspirators.

this consultation together, imparted their designs to some of the leading persons of the Cathaians, and through them to their friends in many other cities. It was accordingly determined amongst them that, on a certâin day, immediately upon their perceiving the signal of a fire, they should rise and put to death all those who wore beards; and should extend the signal to other places, in order that the same might be carried into effect throughout the country. The meaning of the distinction with regard to beards was this; that whereas the Cathaians themselves are naturally beardless, the Tartars, the Saracens, and the Christians wear beards.[1] It should be understood that the grand khan not having obtained the sovereignty of Cathay by any legal right, but only by force of arms, had no confidence in the inhabitants, and therefore bestowed all the provincial governments and magistracies upon Tartars, Saracens, Christians, and other foreigners, who belonged to his household, and in whom he could trust. In consequence of this, his government was universally hated by the natives, who found themselves treated as slaves by these Tartars, and still worse by the Saracens.[2]

Their plans being thus arranged, Van-ku and Chen-ku contrived to enter the palace at night, where the former, taking his place on one of the royal seats, caused the apartment to be lighted up, and sent a messenger to Achmac, who resided in the old city, requiring his immediate attendance upon Chingis, the emperor's son, who (he should say) had unexpectedly arrived that night. Achmac was much astonished at the intelligence, but, being greatly in awe of the prince, instantly obeyed.[3] Upon passing the gate of the (new) city, he met a Tartar officer named Kogatai, the commandant of the guard of twelve thousand men, who asked him whither he was going at that late hour. He replied that he was proceeding to wait upon Chingis, of whose arrival he had just heard. "How is it possible," said the officer, "that he can have arrived in so secret a manner, that I should not have been aware of his

[1] It is not in strictness a fact that the Chinese are naturally beardless; but, like the Malays, their beards are slight, and the growth of them is discouraged, excepting in particular cases.

[2] "Les historiens Chinois," says P. Gaubil, "exagèrent les défauts de Houpilié (Kublaï), et ne parlent guères de ses vertus. Ils lui reprochent beaucoup d'entêtement pour les superstitions et les enchantemens des lamas, et ils se plaignent qu'il a donné trop d'autorité aux gens d'Occident."—Observ. Chronol. p. 201.

[3] The jealousy with which this prince regarded the conduct of the minister is repeatedly noticed.

approach in time to order a party of his guards to attend him?"[1] In the meanwhile the two Cathaians felt assured that if they could but succeed in despatching Achmac they had nothing further to apprehend. Upon his entering the palace and seeing so many lights burning, he made his prostrations before Van-ku, supposing him to be the prince, when Chen-ku, who stood there provided with a sword, severed his head from his body. Kogatai had stopped at the door, but upon observing what had taken place, exclaimed that there was treason going forward, and instantly let fly an arrow at Van-ku as he sat upon the throne, which slew him. He then called to his men, who seized Chen-ku, and despatched an order into the city, that every person found out of doors should be put to death. The Cathaians perceiving, however, that the Tartars had discovered the conspiracy, and being deprived of their leaders, one of whom was killed and the other a prisoner, kept within their houses, and were unable to make the signals to the other towns, as had been concerted. Kogatai immediately sent messengers to the grand khan, with a circumstantial relation of all that had passed, who, in return, directed him to make a diligent investigation of the treason, and to punish, according to the degree of their guilt, those whom he should find to have been concerned. On the following day, Kogatai examined all the Cathaians, and upon such as were principals in the conspiracy he inflicted capital punishment. The same was done with respect to the other cities that were known to have participated in the guilt.

When the grand khan returned to Kanbalu, he was desirous of knowing the causes of what had happened, and then learned that the infamous Achmac and seven of his sons (for all were not equally culpable) had committed those enormities which have been described. He gave orders for removing the treasure which had been accumulated by the deceased to an incredible amount, from the place of his residence in the old city to the new, where it was deposited in his own treasury.

[1] It must have been at the southern gate that the minister, on his way from the old city, was challenged by the officer commanding the guard, whilst the prince, had he arrived as was pretended, would have entered by the northern or the western gates, being those which opened towards the country palaces. The words of the latter must therefore be understood as expressive only of surprise that he should not have had an immediate report from the proper officer, and not as implying a direct contradiction of the fact. From the sequel it appears that this officer as well as Ahama proceeded on the supposition of the prince being actually in the palace.

He likewise directed that his body should be taken from the tomb, and thrown into the street to be torn in pieces by the dogs.[1] The sons who had followed the steps of their father in his iniquities he caused to be flayed alive. Reflecting also upon the principles of the accursed sect of the Saracens, which indulge them in the commission of every crime, and allow them to murder those who differ from them on points of faith, so that even the nefarious Achmac and his sons might have supposed themselves guiltless, he held them in contempt and abomination. Summoning, therefore, these people to his presence, he forbade them to continue many practices enjoined to them by their law,[2] commanding that in future their marriages should be regulated by the custom of the Tartars, and that instead of the mode of killing animals for food, by cutting their throats, they should be obliged to open the belly. At the time that these events took place Marco Polo was on the spot. We shall now proceed to what relates to the establishment of the court kept by the grand khan.

CHAPTER IX

OF THE PERSONAL GUARD OF THE GRAND KHAN

THE body-guard of the grand khan consists, as is well known to every one, of twelve thousand horseman, who are termed *kasitan*, which signifies "soldiers devoted to their master."[3] It is not, however, from any apprehensions entertained by him that he is surrounded by this guard, but as matter of state. These twelve thousand men are commanded by four superior officers, each of whom is at the head of three thousand; and each three thousand does constant duty in the palace during

[1] "Kublai n'ouvrit les yeux sur sa conduite d'Ahama qu après l'exécution; il fit déterrer, mettre en pièces le corps du ministre Ahama, et livra tous ses biens au pillage." (P. 174.) The manner in which our author states the wealth to have been disposed of, is more consistent both with the particular character of Kublaï and with the general practice of the country than the giving it up to plunder.

[2] Interdicts of this nature, regarding only foreigners, the Chinese annals were not likely to notice, and we have no other authority than that of our author for this humiliation of the Mahometans. Many of them were subsequently employed in the higher ranks of the army.

[3] I cannot trace this word (probably much corrupted) in any Mungal vocabulary, and dare not trust myself in the dubious paths of Chinese etymology, where the sound only is to be the guide. [In the early Latin text it is *quiesitani*.]

three successive days and nights, at the expiration of which they are relieved by another division. When all the four have completed their period of duty, it comes again to the turn of the first. During the day-time, the nine thousand who are off guard do not, however, quit the palace, unless when employed upon the service of his majesty, or when the individuals are called away for their domestic concerns, in which case they must obtain leave of absence through their commanding officer; and if, in consequence of any serious occurrence, such as that of a father, a brother, or any near relation being at the point of death, their immediate return should be prevented, they must apply to his majesty for an extension of their leave. But in the night-time these nine thousand retire to their quarters.

CHAPTER X

OF THE STYLE IN WHICH THE GRAND KHAN HOLDS HIS PUBLIC COURTS, AND SITS AT TABLE WITH ALL HIS NOBLES—OF THE MANNER IN WHICH THE DRINKING VESSELS OF GOLD AND SILVER, FILLED WITH THE MILK OF MARES AND CAMELS, ARE DISPOSED IN THE HALL—AND OF THE CEREMONY THAT TAKES PLACE WHEN HE DRINKS

WHEN his majesty holds a grand and public court, those who attend it are seated in the following order. The table of the sovereign is placed before his elevated throne, and he takes his seat on the northern side, with his face turned towards the south; and next to him, on his left hand, sits the empress. On his right hand, upon seats somewhat lower, are placed his sons, grandsons, and other persons connected with him by blood, that is to say, who are descended from the imperial stock. The seat, however, of Chingis, his eldest son, is raised a little above those of his other sons, whose heads are nearly on a level with the feet of the grand khan. The other princes and the nobility have their places at still lower tables; and the same rules are observed with respect to the females, the wives of the sons, grandsons, and other relatives of the grand khan being seated on the left hand, at tables in like manner gradually lower;[1] then follow the wives of the nobility and military

[1] At the modern Chinese festivals no women, of any class whatever, make their appearance; but during the reign of Kublaï, the Tartar customs were blended with the Chinese at the imperial court; and ac-

officers: so that all are seated according to their respective ranks and dignities, in the places assigned to them, and to which they are entitled. The tables are arranged in such a manner that the grand khan, sitting on his elevated throne, can overlook the whole. It is not, however, to be understood that all who assemble on such occasions can be accommodated at tables. The greater part of the officers, and even of the nobles, on the contrary, eat, sitting upon carpets, in the hall; and on the outside stand a great multitude of persons who come from different countries, and bring with them many rare and curious articles. Some of these are feudatories, who desire to be reinstated in possessions that have been taken from them, and who always make their appearance upon the appointed days of public festivity, or occasions of royal marriages.[1]

In the middle of the hall, where the grand khan sits at table, there is a magnificent piece of furniture, made in the form of a square coffer, each side of which is three paces in length, exquisitely carved in figures of animals, and gilt. It is hollow within, for the purpose of receiving a capacious vase, shaped like a jar, and of precious materials, calculated to hold about a tun, and filled with wine.[2] On each of its four sides stands

cording to those, the females were regarded as efficient members of society. Even at the present day the Tartar women (who are distinguished as such, although descended of families who have been settled in China for many generations) enjoy a degree of liberty to which the Chinese women are strangers. Under the dynasty which succeeded that of the Yuen or Mungals, the females of rank were spectators of the festival, although themselves unseen.

[1] It seems to have always been the policy of the Chinese court to defer the reception of ambassadors and their presents, until the occasion of some public festival; by which the double purpose is answered, of giving additional splendour to the business of the day, and at the same time of impressing the strangers with the magnificence of the ceremony attending the delivery of their credentials. It may likewise be observed in the accounts of all European embassies, that their presentations are accompanied by those of the envoys or deputies of the neighbouring or dependent states.

[2] Although the juice of the grape is expressed in some parts of China, what is usually termed Chinese wine is a fermented liquor from grain. "This conversation being finished," says John Bell, "the emperor gave the ambassador, with his own hand, a gold cup, full of warm *tarassun* (written *dirasoun* in the journal of Shah Rokh's embassy), a sweet, fermented liquor, made of various sorts of grain, as pure and strong as canary wine, of a disagreeable smell, although not unpleasant to the taste." (Vol. ii. p. 8.) "During the repast," says Staunton, "he sent them (the English) several dishes from his own table; and, when it was over, he sent for them, and presented with his own hands to them a goblet of warm Chinese wine, not unlike Madeira of an inferior quality." (Vol. ii. p. 237.) Pallas says that the tarassun may be compared to a

a smaller vessel, containing about a hogshead, one of which is filled with mare's milk, another with that of the camel, and so of the others, according to the kinds of beverage in use.[1] Within this buffet are also the cups or flagons belonging to his majesty, for serving the liquors. Some of them are of beautiful gilt plate.[2] Their size is such that, when filled with wine or other liquor, the quantity would be sufficient for eight or ten men. Before every two persons who have seats at the tables, one of these flagons is placed,[3] together with a kind of ladle, in the form of a cup with a handle, also of plate; to be used not only for taking the wine out of the flagon, but for lifting it to the head. This is observed as well with respect to the women as the men. The quantity and richness of the plate belonging to his majesty is quite incredible.[4] Officers of rank are likewise appointed, whose duty it is to see that all strangers who happen to arrive at the time of the festival, and are unacquainted with the etiquette of the court, are suitably accommodated with places; and these stewards are continually visiting every part of the hall, inquiring of the guests if there is anything with which they are unprovided, or whether any of them wish for wine, milk, meat, or other articles, in

mixture of brandy with English beer. (Reise, dritter Theil, p. 131.) " Ils ne laissent pas de boire souvent du vin," says Du Halde: " ils le font d'une espèce particulière de ris, différent de celui dont ils se nourrissent."—Tom. ii. p. 118.

[1] That milk is the favourite beverage of the Tartars is well known; and as the court and the army were, at the period in question, almost exclusively of that nation, we must not be surprised to find it introduced at a festival in the capital of China. With respect to the probability of camels' milk being found there, Staunton notices the employment of camels or dromedaries in great numbers, for the conveyance of goods, in the parts of Tartary bordering on the northern provinces of that country, and Du Halde enumerates " les chameaux à deux bosses " amongst the Chinese animals.

[2] Ramusio's expression is, " Sonvi alcuni d'oro bellissimi, che si chiamano vernique," and he again uses *verniqua* as the name of the vessel. I suspect, however, some confusion. *Vernicato d'oro* (from *vernice*, varnish,) signifies gilt or washed with gold, and *verniqua* seems to be connected with this meaning. Besides, it is obvious that vessels capable of containing liquor for eight or ten persons, would, if formed of massive gold, be much too ponderous for use.

[3] The tables at Chinese feasts are small, and generally calculated for two persons only.

[4] After plundering a great part of the world, it is not surprising that the family of Jengiz-khan should be possessed of a quantity of the precious metals enormously large in proportion to what circulated in Europe or Asia before the discovery of the Mexican and Peruvian mines. Frequent mention is made of golden cups or goblets, and Bell speaks of large dishes of massive gold sent by the emperor to their lodgings.

which case it is immediately brought to them by the attendants.[1]

At each door of the grand hall, or of whatever part the grand khan happens to be in, stand two officers, of a gigantic figure, one on each side, with staves in their hands, for the purpose of preventing persons from touching the threshold with their feet, and obliging them to step beyond it. If by chance any one is guilty of this offence, these janitors take from him his garment, which he must redeem for money; or, when they do not take the garment, they inflict on him such number of blows as they have authority for doing. But, as strangers may be unacquainted with the prohibition, officers are appointed to introduce them, by whom they are warned of it; and this precaution is used because touching the threshold is there regarded as a bad omen.[2] In departing from the hall, as some of the company may be affected by the liquor, it is impossible to guard against the accident, and the order is not then strictly enforced.[3] The numerous persons who attend at the sideboard of his majesty, and who serve him with victuals and drink, are all obliged to cover their noses and mouths with handsome veils or cloths of worked silk, in order that his victuals or his wine may not be affected by their breath. When drink is called for by him, and the page in waiting has presented it, he retires three paces and kneels down, upon which the courtiers, and all who are present, in like manner make their prostration. At the same moment all the musical instruments, of which there is a numerous band, begin to play, and continue to do so until he has ceased drinking, when all the company recover their posture; and this reverential salutation is made so often as his majesty drinks.[4] It is unnecessary to say anything of the victuals, because it

[1] For the degree of civilization which these attentions imply, we should give credit to the long-established usages of the conquered people, rather than to any regulations introduced by the family then on the throne. All our travellers concur in their description of the order and propriety observed at these entertainments, where a silence reigns approaching to solemnity.

[2] This superstition is noticed both by Plan de Carpin and Rubruquis as existing amongst the Tartars.

[3] This is one of the innumerable instances of *naïveté* or honest simplicity in our author's relations and remarks. Inebriety was the favourite vice of the Tartars, and at this period it had been but partially corrected by the more sober example of the Chinese.

[4] Music invariably accompanies these festivities. "The music," says John Bell, "played all the time of dinner. The chief instruments were flutes, harps, and lutes, all tuned to the Chinese taste."—Vol. ii. p. 12.

may well be imagined that their abundance is excessive. When the repast is finished, and the tables have been removed, persons of various descriptions enter the hall, and amongst these a troop of comedians and performers on different instruments, as also tumblers and jugglers, who exhibit their skill in the presence of the grand khan, to the high amusement and gratification of all the spectators.[1] When these sports are concluded, the people separate, and each returns to his own house.

CHAPTER XI

OF THE FESTIVAL THAT IS KEPT THROUGHOUT THE DOMINIONS OF THE GRAND KHAN ON THE TWENTY-EIGHTH OF SEPTEMBER, BEING THE ANNIVERSARY OF HIS NATIVITY

ALL the Tartar and other subjects of the grand khan celebrate as a festival the day of his majesty's birth, which took place on the twenty-eighth day of the month of September;[2] and this is their greatest festival, excepting only that kept on the first day of the year, which shall be hereafter described. Upon this anniversary the grand khan appears in a superb dress of cloth of gold, and on the same occasion full twenty thousand nobles and military officers are clad by him in dresses similar to his own in point of colour and form; but the materials are not equally rich. They are, however, of silk, and of the colour of gold;[3] and along with the vest they likewise receive a girdle

[1] These histrionic, athletic, and juggling exhibitions, which at all periods have very much resembled each other, will be found circumstantially described in the accounts of the several embassies to Pekin, from that of Shah Rokh, in the beginning of the fifteenth century, to those of the English and Dutch, in the latter part of the eighteenth.

[2] According to the "Histoire générale de la Chine" (p. 282), Kublaï or Hupilaï (as the Chinese pronounce the name), was born in the eighth moon of the year corresponding to 1216; which, as will be seen in a subsequent note respecting the commencement of the Kataian year, answers satisfactorily to the month of September, as stated by our author.

[3] Although yellow has long been the imperial colour in China, it is said not to have been such at all periods, some of the early dynasties having affected red and other colours. It may be conjectured that the attachment to it has proceeded from its being worn by the predominant sect of lamas in Tibet, to whose superstitions the emperors of China have been zealously addicted; although, on the other hand, it is possible that this sect of lamas may have adopted the imperial colour. To Kublaï, indeed, the establishment of the lama hierarchy, on its present footing, is by some attributed, and the first Dalaï lama is said to have been nominated by him. Others, however, suppose that the titles of Dalaï lama and Panchan lama were not conferred before the reign of

of chamois leather, curiously worked with gold and silver thread, and also a pair of boots.[1] Some of the dresses are ornamented with precious stones and pearls to the value of a thousand bezants of gold, and are given to those nobles who, from their confidential employments, are nearest to his majesty's person, and are termed *quiècitari*.[2] These dresses are appointed to be worn on the thirteen solemn festivals celebrated in the thirteen (lunar) months of the year,[3] when those who are clad in them make an appearance that is truly royal. When his majesty assumes any particular dress, the nobles of his court wear corresponding, but less costly, dresses, which are always in readiness.[4] They are not annually renewed, but on the contrary are made to last about ten years. From this parade an idea may be formed of the magnificence of the grand khan, which is unequalled by that of any monarch in the world.

On the occasion of this festival of the grand khan's nativity, all his Tartar subjects, and likewise the people of every kingdom and province throughout his dominions, send him valuable presents, according to established usage. Many persons who repair to court in order to solicit principalities to which they have pretensions, also bring presents, and his majesty accordingly gives direction to the tribunal of twelve, who have cognisance of such matters, to assign to them such territories and governments as may be proper.[5] Upon this day likewise all the Christians, idolaters, and Saracens, together with every

Hiuen-te, fifth emperor of the Ming. Both dynasties appear to have been assiduous in their encouragement of these ecclesiastics, through whose influence they were enabled to govern the western provinces with more facility.

[1] "People of condition," says the Abbé Grosier, "never go abroad but in boots, which are generally of satin." This article of dress is again mentioned in chap. xxvi.

[2] This word appears to be bastard Italian, a noun of agency formed from the verb "quiescere," and may be thought to denote those persons who, throughout the East, are employed, in various modes, to lull great personages to rest.

[3] "Le calendrier ordinaire," observes the younger De Guignes, "divise l'année par mois lunaires."—Voy. à Peking, tom. ii. p. 418.

[4] This uniformity of court-dress is not the practice in modern times; on the contrary, the imperial colour is confined to the family of the sovereign.

[5] It may be inferred from hence that all the feudal principalities, governments, and public offices, were bestowed upon those who brought the richest presents, or, in other words, were sold to the highest bidders. The boundless expenditure of this monarch, on the one hand, and the avaricious propensity with which he is reproached, appear to have produced a system of general rapacity. It is probable, however, that the avarice may have been only inferred from the extortion.

other description of people, offer up devout prayers to their respective gods and idols, that they may bless and preserve the sovereign, and bestow upon him long life, health, and prosperity. Such, and so extensive, are the rejoicings on the return of his majesty's birth-day. We shall now speak of another festival, termed the White Feast, celebrated at the commencement of the year.

CHAPTER XII

OF THE WHITE FEAST, HELD ON THE FIRST DAY OF THE MONTH OF FEBRUARY, BEING THE COMMENCEMENT OF THEIR YEAR —OF THE NUMBER OF PRESENTS THEN BROUGHT—AND OF THE CEREMONIES THAT TAKE PLACE AT A TABLE WHEREON IS INSCRIBED THE NAME OF THE GRAND KHAN

It is well ascertained that the Tartars date the commencement of their year from the month of February,[1] and on that occasion it is customary for the grand khan, as well as all who are subject to him, in their several countries, to clothe themselves in white garments, which, according to their ideas, are the emblem of good fortune;[2] and they assume this dress at

[1] In this assertion our author presents a most unexceptionable test of his authenticity. It must be observed that, in stating the commencement of the year to be reckoned from the month of February (*del mese di Febraio*), he does not fix it to any precise day of our calendar; which, in fact, he could not have done with correctness; and although Ramusio, in his title to the chapter, mentions the first day of the month, and the Latin version implies the same by the phrase of "in die calendarum Februarii," it is otherwise in the Italian epitomes, and their reading is justified by the actual circumstances. In the "Epochæ celebriores" of Ulugh Beig (the son of Shah Rokh), translated by the learned Greaves, we are informed that the solar year of the Kataians and Igurians commences on that day in which the sun attains the middle point of the constellation of Aquarius; and this we find from the Ephemeris fluctuates between the third and the fifth of February, according to our bissextile. With respect to their civil year, which must be that of which our author speaks, we have a satisfactory account of it in the "Voyage de la Chine" of P. Trigault, compiled from the writings of the eminent Matt. Ricci, who says: "A chasque nouvelle an, qui commence à la nouvelle lune qui précède ou suit prochainement le cinquiesme de Février, duquel les Chinois content le commencement du printemps, on envoye de chasque province un ambassadeur pour visiter officieusement le roy" (p. 60): by which we should understand, the new moon that falls the nearest to (either before or after) the time of the sun's reaching the middle point of Aquarius; and consequently the festival cannot be assigned to any particular day of the European calendar.

[2] The superstition of considering white, which is naturally the emblem of purity, as having an influence in producing good fortune, has been

the beginning of the year, in the hope that, during the whole course of it, nothing but what is fortunate may happen to them, and that they may enjoy pleasure and comfort. Upon this day the inhabitants of all the provinces and kingdoms who hold lands or rights of jurisdiction under the grand khan, send him valuable presents of gold, silver, and precious stones, together with many pieces of white cloth, which they add, with the intent that his majesty may experience throughout the year uninterrupted felicity, and possess treasures adequate to all his expenses. With the same view the nobles, princes, and all ranks of the community, make reciprocal presents, at their respective houses, of white articles; embracing each other with demonstrations of joy and festivity, and saying (as we ourselves are accustomed to do), "May good fortune attend you through the coming year, and may everything you undertake succeed to your wish."[1] On this occasion great numbers of beautiful white horses are presented to the grand khan; or if not perfectly white, it is at least the prevailing colour. In this country white horses are not uncommon.

It is moreover the custom in making presents to the grand khan, for those who have it in their power to furnish nine times nine of the article of which the present consists. Thus,

very prevalent throughout the world; as black, on the contrary, from its connexion with impurity, darkness, and the grave, has been thought the foreboder of ill-luck, and become the type of sadness. The Chinese, however, whose customs, in many respects, run counter to those of other nations, have judged proper to establish the former, instead of the latter, as their mourning dress; but Kublaï, although he adopted most of the civil institutions of his new and more civilized subjects, did not, and possibly could not, even if he had wished it, oblige his own people to change their ancient superstitions. It accordingly appears that, during his reign at least, and probably so long as his dynasty held the throne, the festival of the new year was celebrated in white dresses, and white horses were amongst the most acceptable presents to the emperor. When the dynasty of the Ming, which was native Chinese, succeeded to that of the Mungals, the use of white on this occasion was again proscribed.

[1] "The first day of the new year, and a few succeeding days," Barrow observes, "are the only holidays, properly speaking, that are observed by the working part of the community. On these days the poorest peasant makes a point of procuring new clothing for himself and his family; they pay their visits to friends and relations, interchange civilities and compliments, make and receive presents; and the officers of government, and the higher ranks, give feasts and entertainments." (Trav. in China, p. 155.) "Their whole time," says L'Abbé Grosier, "is employed in plays, diversions, and feasting. The shops are everywhere shut; and all the people, dressed out in their richest attire, go to visit their parents, friends, and patrons. Nothing in this respect can have a greater resemblance to our visits on the first day of the new year."—Vol. ii. p. 323.

for instance, if a province sends a present of horses, there are nine times nine, or eighty-one head in the drove; so also of gold, or of cloth, nine times nine pieces.[1] By such means his majesty receives at this festival no fewer than a hundred thousand horses. On this day it is that all his elephants, amounting to five thousand, are exhibited in procession, covered with housings of cloth, fancifully and richly worked with gold and silk, in figures of birds and beasts.[2] Each of these supports upon its shoulders two coffers filled with vessels of plate and other apparatus for the use of the court. Then follows a train of camels, in like manner laden with various necessary articles of furniture.[3] When the whole are properly arranged, they pass in review before his majesty, and form a pleasing spectacle.

On the morning of the festival, before the tables are spread, all the princes, the nobility of various ranks,[4] the cavaliers,

[1] The superstitious ideas prevailing amongst the nations of Tartary respecting the properties of this number are circumstantially detailed by Strahlenberg, from whose well-known work the following passage, which will be found abundantly sufficient to justify our author's assertion, is extracted: "I shall therefore proceed to relate," says this observing traveller and laborious investigator, "what I myself have observed in those North-eastern parts, as also what I have remarked in other writers, who have treated of this part of the world, concerning this subject, and particularly with regard to the number Nine, what yet remains among the inhabitants of these parts. L'Histoire du grand Ghenghizcan, par M. Pétis de la Croix, p. 79, informs us, that when Temugin was elected Great Chan, and named Ghenghiz-can, all the people bowed their knees to him nine times, to wish him a prosperous continuation of his reign: and this is yet a custom with the Chinese-Tartarian emperors, before whom ambassadors, when they are admitted to audience, are obliged to make their obeisances kneeling, *nine* times at their entrance, and just as often at their departure. The same ceremony is yet in use with the Usbeck Tartars; for when a person has anything of importance to ask of, or to treat with, their chan, he must not only offer a present, consisting of *nine* particular things or curiosities, but when he approaches him to deliver it, must bow nine times; which ceremony these Tartars call the Zagataian audience."—Introduction, p. 86.

[2] As Kublaï had subdued Ava, and other southern provinces, where elephants are found in great number, and where they had been opposed to his armies in battle, it is natural that he should be inclined to add these powerful animals to his establishment, if not for military purposes, at least for parade or as beasts of burden; and they were accordingly delivered to him in tribute from the conquered princes. A few are kept by the emperors of the dynasty now reigning, but, as it would seem, merely for state.

[3] It has already been mentioned that camels or dromedaries, especially those with two bunches, are common in China.

[4] Amongst the Chinese or Tartars there is no hereditary nobility, and the term is here, and elsewhere, employed, in default of a better, to express that class or rank of persons who hold the [illegible] offices of state, and are in Persia and Hindustan styled Amîrs. The reader must be well aware that in the modern intercourse of Europeans with China,

astrologers, physicians, and falconers, with many others holding public offices, the prefects of the people and of the lands,[1] together with the officers of the army, make their entry into the grand hall, in front of the emperor. Those who cannot find room within, stand on the outside of the building, in such a situation as to be within sight of their sovereign. The assemblage is marshalled in the following order. The first places are assigned to the sons and grandsons of his majesty and all the imperial family. Next to these are the provincial kings [2] and the nobility of the empire, according to their several degrees, in regular succession. When all have been disposed in the places appointed for them, a person of high dignity, or as we should express it, a great prelate,[3] rises and says with a loud voice: "Bow down and do reverence;" when instantly all bend their bodies until their foreheads touch the floor. Again the prelate cries: "God bless our lord, and long preserve him in the enjoyment of felicity." To which the people answer: "God grant it." Once more the prelate says: "May God increase the grandeur and prosperity of his empire; may he preserve all those who are his subjects in the blessings of peace and contentment; and in all their lands may abundance prevail." The people again reply: "God grant it." They then make their prostrations four times.[4] This being

officers of all degrees, civil and military, from those who manage the great concerns of the empire down to the persons stationed in boats to prevent (or connive at) smuggling, are indiscriminately called mandarins; but of this title, although it might often be convenient in translating, I do not avail myself, not only on account of the vagueness of its application, but because, as it was not known in our author's time, its introduction into his text would be a species of anachronism.

[1] With a view not only to political security, but to the more ready collection of the capitation and other taxes, the people were numbered, and divided into classes, on a progressive decimal scale, from ten to ten thousand, over each of which a responsible officer presided; and as the revenue from the lands was collected in kind, officers, not unlike the *zemindars* of the Moghul government in Hindustan, were appointed by the emperor to watch over and transmit the produce to the royal granaries near Pekin.

[2] The Chinese title of *vang*, which the Portuguese render by the word *regulo*, and the French Jesuits by *roitelet* and *roi*, was usually conferred on the tributary princes throughout Tartary.

[3] The term *prelato*, which has nothing corresponding to it in the other versions, seems to be gratuitous on the part of Ramusio. In the Basle edition the words are, "surgit unus in medio," and in the epitomes, "el se leva uno huomo in mezo." [In the best Italian text, that published by Boni, the words are, "si leva un grande parlato."]

[4] "Le maître des cérémonies," says the younger De Guignes, "qui est un des premiers mandarins du Ly-pou, ou tribunal des rites, s'étant placé près de la porte Ou-men, crie d'une voix haute et perçante: 'Mettez-vous en ordre· tournez-vous; mettez-vous à genoux; frappez la tête

done, the prelate advances to an altar, richly adorned, upon which is placed a red tablet inscribed with the name of the grand khan. Near to this stands a censer of burning incense, with which the prelate, on the behalf of all who are assembled, perfumes the tablet and the altar, in a reverential manner; when every one present humbly prostrates himself before the tablet.[1] This ceremony being concluded, they return to their places, and then make the presentation of their respective gifts; such as have been mentioned. When a display has been made of these, and the grand khan has cast his eyes upon them, the tables are prepared for the feast, and the company, as well women as men, arrange themselves there in the manner and order described in a former chapter. Upon the removal of the victuals, the musicians and theatrical performers exhibit for the amusement of the court, as has been already related. But on this occasion a lion is conducted into the presence of his majesty, so tame, that it is taught to lay itself down at his feet.[2] The sports being finished, every one returns to his own home.

contre terre; frappez encore; frappez de nouveau; levez-vous.' On se remet encore à genoux, et l'on recommence deux fois le salut; ainsi l'hommage consiste à faire trois fois trois saluts. Après le dernier, le mandarin crie: 'Levez-vous; tournez-vous; mettez-vous en ordre:' puis il se met à genoux lui-même devant la porte, et dit: 'Seigneur, les cérémonies sont terminées.'" (Voy. à Peking, etc. tom. iii. p. 44.) An account agreeing precisely in substance with the above, but more circumstantial in the detail, will be found in the Nouv. Relat. of P. Magalhanes, p. 304. "The master of the ceremonies," says John Bell, "brought back the ambassador, and then ordered all the company to kneel, and make obeisance nine times to the emperor. At every third time we stood up and kneeled again. Great pains were taken to avoid this piece of homage, but without success. The master of the ceremonies stood by, and delivered his orders in the Tartar language, by pronouncing the words *morgu* and *boss*; the first meaning to bow, and the other to stand; two words which *I cannot soon forget*." (Vol. ii. p. 7.) All the editions of our author's work agree in stating that this ceremony was repeated four times; whereas it is well known that the repetitions are *three* and *nine*. Either his memory must have failed him, or, which is more probable, the numeral figures of an early manuscript may have been mistaken by the copyists.

[1] The ceremony of making prostrations before the empty throne, or before a tablet on which is written the name of the emperor, appears to belong rather to the festival of his nativity, than to that of the new year.

[2] Frequent mention is made of lions (which are not found either in China or Chinese Tartary) being sent as presents from the western potentates

CHAPTER XIII

OF THE QUANTITY OF GAME TAKEN AND SENT TO THE COURT, DURING THE WINTER MONTHS

At the season when the grand khan resides in the capital of Cathay, or during the months of December, January, and February, at which time the cold is excessive, he gives orders for general hunting parties to take place in all the countries within forty stages of the court; and the governors of districts are required to send thither all sorts of game of the larger kind, such as wild boars, stags, fallow deer, roebucks, and bears, which are taken in the following manner:—All persons possessed of land in the province repair to the places where these animals are to be found, and proceed to enclose them within a circle, when they are killed, partly with dogs, but chiefly by shooting them with arrows.[1] Such of them as are intended for his majesty's use are first paunched for that purpose, and then forwarded on carriages, in large quantities, by those who reside within thirty stages of the capital. Those, in fact, who are at the distance of forty stages, do not, on account of the length of the journey, send the carcases, but only the skins, some dressed and others raw, to be made use of for the service of the army as his majesty may judge proper.

CHAPTER XIV

OF LEOPARDS AND LYNXES USED FOR HUNTING DEER—OF LIONS HABITUATED TO THE CHASE OF VARIOUS ANIMALS—AND OF EAGLES TAUGHT TO SEIZE WOLVES

The grand khan has many leopards and lynxes kept for the purpose of chasing deer, and also many lions, which are larger than the Babylonian lions, have good skins and of a handsome colour—being streaked lengthways, with white, black, and red stripes. They are active in seizing boars, wild oxen and asses, bears, stags, roebucks, and other beasts that are the objects of sport. It is an admirable sight, when the lion is let loose in pursuit of the animal, to observe the savage eagerness and

[1] This mode of hunting by surrounding the game within extensive lines, gradually contracted, has been often described by travellers.

speed with which he overtakes it. His majesty has them conveyed for this purpose, in cages placed upon cars,[1] and along with them is confined a little dog, with which they become familiarised. The reason for thus shutting them up is, that they would otherwise be so keen and furious at the sight of the game that it would be impossible to keep them under the necessary constraint. It is proper that they should be led in a direction opposite to the wind, in order that they may not be scented by the game, which would immediately run off, and afford no chance of sport. His majesty has eagles also, which are trained to stoop at wolves, and such is their size and strength that none, however large, can escape from their talons.

CHAPTER XV

OF TWO BROTHERS WHO ARE PRINCIPAL OFFICERS OF THE CHASE TO THE GRAND KHAN

HIS majesty has in his service two persons, brothers both by the father and mother, one of them named Bayan[2] and the other Mingan, who are, what in the language of the Tartars are called, *chivichi*,[3] that is to say, "masters of the chase,"

[1] It has already been observed that the Moghuls of Hindustan keep small leopards, to be employed in hunting. It would seem, however, that the largest animals of this genus were also tamed for the imperial sport. The former are described as being carried on horseback, behind their keepers; but these in cages on a sort of car. By some other of the old Italian writers they are termed "*leonze* domestice da cacciare." It is evident from this description, as well as from the whole context, that the beast here spoken of as the lion is in fact no other than the tiger, and ought to have been so named; but whether the mistake is to be attributed to our author himself, who might have forgotten some of the terms of his native language, or to his first translators, we have not the means of determining. The lion is known to be of a tawny colour, nearly uniform, whereas the tiger is marked with the colours mentioned above, if only for red we substitute a reddish yellow. It will not be thought an improbable supposition that the confounding of these appellations may have proceeded from our author's intercourse with Persians and other Mahometans, in his journey from China to Europe, as it is well known to oriental scholars that with these people the same terms are almost indiscriminately applied to both species of animal.

[2] This may have been the person of the same name who so eminently distinguished himself as commander-in-chief of Kublaï's armies, and who is mentioned in a subsequent chapter as the conqueror of Southern China. In the early Italian epitomes the names of the two brothers are written Baxam and Mitigam.

[3] Our vocabularies of the Mungal language are so imperfect, that even if the words occurring in the text had been correctly written and preserved, we might fail in our endeavours to identify them; but cor-

having charge of the hounds fleet and slow, and of the mastiffs. Each of these has under his orders a body of ten thousand chasseurs; those under the one brother wearing a red uniform, and those under the other, a sky-blue, whenever they are upon duty. The dogs of different descriptions which accompany them to the field are not fewer than five thousand.[1] The one brother, with his division, takes the ground to the right hand of the emperor, and the other to the left, with his division, and each advances in regular order, until they have enclosed a tract of country to the extent of a day's march. By this means no beast can escape them. It is a beautiful and an exhilarating sight to watch the exertions of the huntsmen and the sagacity of the dogs, when the emperor is within the circle, engaged in the sport, and they are seen pursuing the stags, bears, and other animals, in every direction. The two brothers are under an engagement to furnish the court daily, from the commencement of October to the end of March, with a thousand pieces of game, quails being excepted; and also with fish, of which as large a quantity as possible is to be supplied, estimating the fish that three men can eat at a meal as equivalent to one piece of game.

CHAPTER XVI

OF THE GRAND KHAN'S PROCEEDING TO THE CHASE, WITH HIS GERFALCONS AND HAWKS—OF HIS FALCONERS—AND OF HIS TENTS

When his majesty has resided the usual time in the metropolis, and leaves it in the month of March, he proceeds in a

rupted as they are by transcription, the attempt is vain. This, which in Ramusio's version is *civici*, (or *chivichi* according to our orthography,) is, in the Italian epitome of 1496, written *civitri*, in the earliest Latin edition *cynici*, and in the B.M. and Berlin manuscripts *canici;* from which latter, if the spelling has not been perverted by the fancy of copyists, we might be led to suppose the word a derivative from the Italian *cane*, a dog. [In the Latin text published by the French Geographical Society, it is *cinuchi*.]

[1] It is not common to find any mention of sporting dogs amongst the Chinese or Chinese Tartars; but of their existence Bell furnishes us with direct proof. "After this entertainment," he says, "the Aleggada (colao) carried us first to see his dogs, of which he had great variety. I formerly observed that this gentleman was a great sportsman. He took greater pleasure in talking of hounds than of politics; though at the same time he had the character of a very able minister and an honest man."—Vol. ii. p. 22.

north-easterly direction, to within two days' journey of the ocean,[1] attended by full ten thousand falconers, who carry with them a vast number of gerfalcons, peregrine falcons, and sakers, as well as many vultures, in order to pursue the game along the banks of the river.[2] It must be understood that he does not keep all this body of men together in one place, but divides them into several parties of one or two hundred or more, who follow the sport in various directions, and the greater part of what they take is brought to his majesty. He has likewise with him ten thousand men of those who are termed *taskaol*,[3] implying that their business is to be upon the watch, and, who, for this purpose, are detached in small parties of two or three to stations not far distant from each other, in such a manner as to encompass a considerable tract of country. Each of them is provided with a call and a hood, by which they are enabled, when necessary, to call in and to secure the birds. Upon the command being given for flying the hawks, those who let them loose are not under the necessity of following them, because the others, whose duty it is, look out so attentively that the birds cannot direct their flight to any quarter where they are not secured, or promptly assisted if there should be occasion. Every bird belonging to his majesty, or to any of his nobles, has a small silver label fastened to its leg, on which is engraved the name of the owner and also the name of the keeper. In consequence of this precaution, as soon as the hawk is secured, it is immediately known to whom it belongs,

[1] The simple construction of the words in Ramusio's text, " indi partendosi il mese di Marzo, va verso Greco al mare oceano, il quale da li è discosta per due giornate," would imply that he proceeded from the capital to the ocean, which was distant from thence two days' journey: but either the author's sense must have been misunderstood, when he meant to say that the route was to a country situated within two days' journey of the ocean, or there must be a gross error in the number of days, which should rather be read, months; for the whole context shows that he is speaking of one of the emperor's distant progresses, through the Manchu country, into the wilds of Eastern Tartary, and by no means of a petty excursion to the shore of the Yellow Sea, which is only a few stages from Pekin.

[2] The river here spoken of may be either the Songari, which was the limit of Kang-hi's expedition, or it may be the Usuri, to which latter I incline, as it is the most eastern, and consequently the nearest to the ocean, of the great streams that unite with the Sagalien ûla, and contribute to form the Amûr, the boundary between the Russian and Chinese dominions in that quarter.

[3] The word, which in different versions takes the forms of *toscaol*, *toscaor*, *roscanor*, *roschaor*, *restaor*, and, in the early Italian epitome, *tastori*, I am unable to refer to any known language. In the Basle edition it is translated " custodes; " by Ramusio, " huomini che stanno alla custodia."

and restored accordingly. If it happens that, although the name appears, the owner, not being personally known to the finder, cannot be ascertained in the first instance, the bird is, in that case, carried to an officer termed *bulangazi*,[1] whose title imports that he is the "guardian of unclaimed property." If a horse, therefore, a sword, a bird, or any other article is found, and it does not appear to whom it belongs, the finder carries it directly to this officer, by whom it is received in charge and carefully preserved. If, on the other hand, a person finds any article that has been lost, and fails to carry it to the proper depositary, he is accounted a thief. Those by whom any property has been lost make their application to this officer, by whom it is restored to them. His situation is always in the most elevated part of the camp, and distinguished by a particular flag, in order that he may be the more readily found by such as have occasion to apply to him. The effect of this regulation is, that no articles are ultimately lost.

When his majesty makes his progress in this manner, towards the shores of the ocean, many interesting occurrences attend the sport, and it may truly be said that it is unrivalled by any other amusement in the world.[2] On account of the narrowness of the passes in some parts of the country where the grand khan follows the chase, he is borne upon two elephants only, or sometimes a single one, being more convenient than a greater number; but under other circumstances he makes use of four, upon the backs of which is placed a pavilion of wood, handsomely carved,[3] the inside being lined

[1] All endeavours to ascertain by any probable etymology the true orthography of this word, also, have been unsuccessful. It is written in the different versions, *bulangazi balangugi*, *bularguci*, *bugiami*, and *bugrim*. The first two may be presumed the more nearly correct, because all the nouns in the Kalmuk-Mungalian language that denote employments terminate in *izchi*, according to the German of Strahlenberg, which is equivalent to the Italian *zi* or *ci*. The establishment of such an office does credit to the police of a Tartar camp.

[2] Our author, who, from this and many other expressions in the course of his work, appears to have been passionately fond of the sports of the field, must have recommended himself to the favour of his master by this congenial taste.

[3] It does not appear that any of the modern emperors of China have made use of these grand animals for their personal conveyance. "He" (the emperor Kang-hi), says Bell, "was seated, cross-legged, in an open machine, carried by four men, with long poles rested on their shoulders. Before him lay a fowling-piece, a bow, and sheaf of arrows. This has been his hunting equipage for some years, since he left off riding; but in his youth he went usually, every summer, several days' journey without the long wall, and carried with him all the princes his sons, and many persons of distinction, to the number frequently of some

with cloth of gold, and the outside covered with the skins of lions,[1] a mode of conveyance which is rendered necessary to him during his hunting excursions, in consequence of the gout, with which he is troubled. In the pavilion he always carries with him twelve of his best gerfalcons, with twelve officers, from amongst his favourites, to bear him company and amuse him. Those who are on horseback by his side give him notice of the approach of cranes or other birds, upon which he raises the curtain of the pavilion, and when he espies the game, gives direction for letting fly the gerfalcons, which seize the cranes and overpower them after a long struggle. The view of this sport, as he lies upon his couch, affords extreme satisfaction to his majesty, as well as to the officers who attend him, and to the horsemen by whom he is surrounded. After having thus enjoyed the amusement for some hours, he repairs to a place named Kakzarmodin,[2] where are pitched the pavilions and tents of his sons, and also of the nobles, the life-guards,[3] and the falconers; exceeding ten thousand in number, and making a handsome appearance. The tent of his majesty, in which he gives his audiences, is so long and wide that under it ten thousand soldiers might be drawn up, leaving room for the superior officers and other persons of rank.[4] Its entrance fronts the south, and on the eastern side it has another tent

thousands, in order to hunt in the woods and deserts, where he continued for the space of two or three months."—Travels, vol. ii. p. 76.

[1] That is, of tigers or leopards, the skins of which are known to be in common use for covering seats, and other similar purposes, amongst persons of rank in China; as the animal itself abounds in Tartary, and is the subject of royal sport; whereas all travellers agree in assuring us that the lion is not a native of that region. See p. 194, note [1].

[2] This name of Kakzar-modin, which in the Latin manuscript of the British Museum, and early Italian epitome, is written Cacia-mordin, has some resemblance to Chakiri-mondou, situated, according to the Jesuits' map, at the head of the Usuri river (which falls into the Amûr), and about midway between a considerable lake amongst the mountains and the sea. [In the Latin text of the Société de Géographie, it is written Cacchiatriodum, and in the Italian of Boni, Tarcarmodu.]

[3] The *cavalieri* here mentioned appear to be that military class which Van Braam describes under the name of *chiouais*, and especially those of the third order. The *chiaoux* of the Turkish or Ottoman court perform duties analogous to those of the *huissiers* in France.

[4] This number appears large, but it is no more than a body of one hundred men in rank, and as many in file, who might also, by narrowing their front, be drawn up under an awning of fifty yards by two hundred in depth. The armies of the Tartars, as well as of the Persians, are commonly reckoned by *tomans*, or brigades of ten thousand. It is recorded of Timur, that he was accustomed to estimate the strength of his armies, not by individual numeration, but by the *quantity* of men who could stand within a given space, which was occupied in succession, until the whole were measured.

connected with it, forming a capacious saloon, which the emperor usually occupies, with a few of his nobility, and when he thinks proper to speak to any other persons, they are introduced to him in that apartment. In the rear of this there is a large and handsome chamber, where he sleeps; and there are many other tents and apartments (for the different branches of the household), but which are not immediately connected with the great tent. These halls and chambers are all constructed and fitted up in the following manner. Each of them is supported by three pillars of wood, richly carved and gilt. The tents are covered on the outside with the skins of lions, streaked white, black, and red, and so well joined together that neither wind nor rain can penetrate. Withinside they are lined with the skins of ermines and sables, which are the most costly of all furs; for the latter, if of a size to trim a dress, is valued at two thousands besants of gold, provided it be perfect; but if otherwise, only one thousand. It is esteemed by Tartars the queen of furs.[1] The animal, which in their language is named *rondes*,[2] is about the size of a polecat. With these two kinds of skin, the halls as well as the sleeping-rooms are handsomely fitted up in compartments, arranged with much taste and skill. The tent-ropes, or cords by which they stretch the tents, are all of silk. Near to the grand tent of his majesty are situated those of his ladies, also very handsome and splendid. They have in like manner their gerfalcons, their hawks, and other birds and beasts, with which they partake in the amusement.[3] The number of persons collected in these encampments is quite incredible, and a spectator might conceive himself to be in the midst of a populous city, so great is the assemblage from every part of the empire. The grand khan is attended on the occasion by the whole of his family and

[1] The northern Chinese are curious and expensive in furs, and the first of the sea-otter skins brought from the north-west coast of America were purchased at extravagant prices, although not so high as the sum mentioned in the text. The besant is supposed to have been equivalent to the sequin, the ducat, and the Arabian dinar, or about nine shillings of our money.

[2] The word *rondes* (probably corrupted) is not to be traced in Strahlenberg's or other Mungalian vocabularies, but it evidently means the sable. The animal is more particularly mentioned in book iii. chap. xliv. [The early Italian text reads *leroide*, and the Latin, *lenoidæ pellonæ*.]

[3] It has been before observed that the Tartar customs impose no particular restraint upon the women, who, on the contrary, in their camps, are said to be the principal dealers in cattle and other articles.

household; that is to say, his physicians, astronomers, falconers, and every other description of officer.[1]

In these parts of the country he remains until the first vigil of our Easter,[2] during which period he never ceases to frequent the lakes and rivers, where he takes storks, swans, herons, and a variety of other birds. His people also being detached to several different places, procure for him a large quantity of game. In this manner, during the season of his diversion, he enjoys himself to a degree that no person who is not an eye-witness can conceive; the excellence and the extent of the sport being greater than it is possible to express. It is strictly forbidden to every tradesman, mechanic, or husbandman throughout his majesty's dominions, to keep a vulture, hawk, or any other bird used for the pursuit of game, or any sporting dog; nor is a nobleman or cavalier to presume to chase beast or bird in the neighbourhood of the place where his majesty takes up his residence, (the distance being limited to five miles, for example, on one side, ten on another, and perhaps fifteen in a third direction,) unless his name be inscribed in a list kept by the grand falconer, or he has a special privilege to that effect. Beyond those limits it is permitted. There is an order, however, which prohibits every person throughout all the countries subject to the grand khan, whether prince, nobleman, or peasant, from daring to kill hares, roebucks, fallow deer, stags, or other animals of that kind, or any large birds, between the months of March and October; to the intent that they may increase and multiply; and as the breach of this order is attended with punishment, game of every description increases prodigiously. When the usual time is elapsed, his majesty returns to the capital by the road he went; continuing his sport during the whole of the journey.

[1] This was rather an extraordinary assemblage for a hunting expedition; but, on similar occasions, Kang-hi was accustomed to have in his suite some of the European missionaries who were astronomers and mathematicians, and amused himself in observing with them the culmination of the stars, and in taking with a quadrant the altitude of mountains, buildings, and even of a gigantic statue of the idol Fo. It may be suspected, however, that Kublaï's astronomers were no other than astrologers, or *shamans*.

[2] The Kataian festivals being regulated, as ours are, by the new and full moons before or after the sun's reaching certain fixed points of the heavens, it is not surprising that the emperor's movements should seem to be regulated by our calendar. In the diaries of Plan de Carpin and Rubruquis, all the events of their journeys are noted according to the feasts, fasts, or Saints' days of their rubric, instead of the days of the month.

CHAPTER XVII

OF THE MULTITUDE OF PERSONS WHO CONTINUALLY RESORT TO AND DEPART FROM THE CITY OF KANBALU—AND OF THE COMMERCE OF THE PLACE

UPON the return of the grand khan to his capital, he holds a great and splendid court, which lasts three days, in the course of which he gives feasts and otherwise entertains those by whom he is surrounded. The amusements of these three days are indeed admirable. The multitude of inhabitants, and the number of houses in the city, as also in the suburbs without the city (of which there are twelve, corresponding to the twelve gates), is greater than the mind can comprehend. The suburbs are even more populous than the city, and it is there that the merchants and others whose business leads them to the capital, and who, on account of its being the residence of the court, resort thither in great numbers, take up their abode. Wherever, indeed, his majesty holds his court, thither these people flock from all quarters, in pursuit of their several objects. In the suburbs there are also as handsome houses and stately buildings as in the city, with the exception only of the palace of the grand khan. No corpse is suffered to be interred within the precincts of the city; [1] and those of the idolaters, with whom it is customary to burn their dead, are carried to the usual spot beyond the suburbs.[2] There likewise all public executions take place. Women who live by prostituting themselves for money dare not, unless it be secretly, to exercise their profession in the city, but must confine themselves to the suburbs, where, as has already been stated, there reside above five-and-twenty thousand; nor is this number greater than is necessary for the vast concourse of merchants and other strangers, who, drawn thither by the court, are continually arriving and departing. To this city everything that is most rare and valuable in all parts of the world finds its way; and more especially does this apply to India, which furnishes precious stones, pearls, and various drugs and spices. From

[1] "Il est défendu aux Chinois," says Du Halde, "d'enterrer leurs morts dans l'enceinte des villes, et dans les qu'on habite."—Tom. ii. p. 125.

[2] The general practice of the Chinese is to bury, and not to burn their dead; but it was otherwise with the Tartars, so long as they preserved their original habits.

the provinces of Cathay itself, as well as from the other provinces of the empire, whatever there is of value is carried thither, to supply the demands of those multitudes who are induced to establish their residence in the vicinity of the court. The quantity of merchandise sold there exceeds also the traffic of any other place; for no fewer than a thousand carriages and pack-horses, loaded with raw silk, make their daily entry; and gold tissues and silks of various kinds are manufactured to an immense extent.[1] In the vicinity of the capital are many walled and other towns, whose inhabitants live chiefly by the court, selling the articles which they produce in the markets of the former, and procuring from thence in return such as their own occasions require.

CHAPTER XVIII

OF THE KIND OF PAPER MONEY ISSUED BY THE GRAND KHAN, AND MADE TO PASS CURRENT THROUGHOUT HIS DOMINIONS

In this city of Kanbalu is the mint of the grand khan, who may truly be said to possess the secret of the alchemists, as he has the art of producing money by the following process.[2] He causes the bark to be stripped from those mulberry-trees the leaves of which are used for feeding silk-worms, and takes from it that thin inner rind which lies between the coarser bark and the wood of the tree. This being steeped, and afterwards pounded in a mortar, until reduced to a pulp, is made into paper,[3] resembling (in substance) that which is manufactured from cotton, but quite black. When ready for use, he has it cut into pieces of money of different sizes, nearly square, but

[1] The prodigious quantity of silk produced in China is matter of notoriety.

[2] This is, perhaps, the only instance in which our author relaxes from the general gravity of his style, and condescends to be witty. It is not in the earlier texts.

[3] The accounts given by travellers of the vegetable and other substances from which paper is manufactured in China vary considerably, and it would appear that in different provinces different materials are employed. The most common, and at the same time the least probable assertion is, that it is made from the soft inner bark of the bamboo cane (*arundo bambos*); but Du Halde informs us that it is not from the bark, but from the substance, that paper is made. Du Halde quotes the authority of a Chinese book, which relates that a certain ancient emperor "fit faire un excellent papier du chanvre . . . que dans la province de Fokien il se fait de tendres bambous; (et) que dans les provinces du nord, on y emploie *l'écorce des muriers*."—P. 240.

somewhat longer than they are wide. Of these, the smallest pass for a denier tournois; the next size for a Venetian silver groat; others for two, five, and ten groats; others for one, two, three, and as far as ten besants of gold.[1] The coinage of this paper money is authenticated with as much form and ceremony as if it were actually of pure gold or silver; for to each note a number of officers, specially appointed, not only subscribe their names, but affix their signets also; and when this has been regularly done by the whole of them, the principal officer, deputed by his majesty, having dipped into vermilion the royal seal committed to his custody, stamps with it the piece of paper, so that the form of the seal tinged with the vermilion remains impressed upon it,[2] by which it receives full authenticity as current money, and the act of counterfeiting it is punished as a capital offence.[3] When thus coined in large quantities, this paper currency is circulated in every part of the grand khan's dominions; nor dares any person, at the peril of his life, refuse to accept it in payment. All his subjects receive it without hesitation, because, wherever their business may call them, they can dispose of it again in the purchase of merchandise they may have occasion for; such as pearls, jewels, gold, or silver. With it, in short, every article may be procured.[4]

[1] The *grosso* or *gros* is the *drachma* or *dram*, being the eighth part of an ounce of silver, and the coin should, if of full weight, be equivalent to about eightpence of our money. The *picciolo tornese* is the denier or tenth part of the dram of silver, and consequently equal to four-fifths of our penny. As the former is the *tsien* or *mas*, so the latter is the *fen* or *candorin*, of the Chinese reckoning. Upon the same principle, ten grossi or tsien constitute the *leang* or *taël*, which is valued at six shillings and eightpence. It may be necessary to observe, that the French missionaries apply the term of *denier* to the small Chinese coin of base metal, named *caxa* by the Portuguese and *cash* by the English, of which a thousand are equal to the taël. The besant, a gold coin of the Greek empire, is equivalent, as has already been observed, to the Venetian sequin.

[2] "La matière dont on se sert," says De Guignes fils, "pour imprimer avec les cachets, est composée de couleur rouge, mêlée avec de l'huile; on la tient renfermée dans un vase de porcelaine destiné à cet usage, et couvert avec soin de peur qu'elle ne se dessèche."—Voy. à Peking, etc. tom. ii. p. 230.

[3] "Ceux qui en feront de fausse," (says the inscription on paper money issued by the Ming,) "auront la teste coupée."—Du Halde, tom. ii. p. 168, planche.

[4] According to P. Gaubil, paper money had already been current at Pekin, under the grand khan Oktaï, who himself only imitated what had been practised by the dynasty that preceded the Yuen or family of Jengiz-khan. "C'est cette année (1234) qu'on fit la monnoie de papier; les billets s'appelloient *tchao*. Le sceau du *pou-tchin-se*, ou trésorier-général de la province, étoit empreint dessus, et il y en avoit de tout valeur. Cette monnoie avoit déjà couru sous les princes de Kin."

Several times in the course of the year, large caravans of merchants arrive with such articles as have just been mentioned, together with gold tissues, which they lay before the grand khan. He thereupon calls together twelve experienced and skilful persons, selected for this purpose, whom he commands to examine the articles with great care, and to fix the value at which they should be purchased. Upon the sum at which they have been thus conscientiously appraised he allows a reasonable profit, and immediately pays for them with this paper; to which the owners can have no objection, because, as has been observed, it answers the purpose of their own disbursements; and even though they should be inhabitants of a country where this kind of money is not current, they invest the amount in other articles of merchandise suited to their own markets.[1] When any persons happen to be possessed of paper money which from long use has become damaged, they carry it to the mint, where, upon the payment of only three per cent., they may receive fresh notes in exchange.[2] Should

(Observ. Chronol. p. 192.) By Du Halde we are informed that its establishment was attempted also by the first prince of the dynasty that succeeded the Mungals; and he has given an engraving of the billets, from specimens still preserved by the Chinese with superstitious care, as relics of a monarch who relieved them from a foreign yoke. When he adds, "On l'avoit employé avec aussi peu de succès sous la dynastie de Yuen," the assertion may be doubted; because the success of Kublaï's financial measures, oppressive as they were, would not, if at all noticed in the Chinese records, be impartially stated. It will be seen, on reference to note [4], p. 29, that an attempt was made by a Moghul ruler of Persia, the grand-nephew of Kublaï, to introduce a system of paper currency in his dominions, at the period when the Polo family, returning from China, resided at his court; and that, upon a revolution which deprived him of the throne, this measure constituted one of the criminal charges against him. In Malcolm's History of Persia (vol. i. p. 430), the reader will find several curious facts and judicious observations connected with this subject, which strongly tend to confirm the statements of our author; and it there appears indubitably, from the native historians, that a minister on the part of the emperor of China and Tartary had arrived at the court of Persia about this period, and been consulted respecting the currency.

[1] In most states the issue of government paper is the resource of an exhausted treasury; but Kublaï's plan seems not to have been confined to the substitution of paper for cash in the public disbursements, but to have gone the length of endeavouring, by the operation of a forced currency, to draw all the specie and bullion of the country into his exchequer; for, although it is not expressly asserted, it is not improbable that the merchandise which he monopolized in the manner described, and paid for with his notes, was by him disposed of for gold and silver. In Siam, and many other countries of the further East, the king is the principal merchant of his dominions; and no individual can purchase a cargo, until his majesty's agent has exercised the right of pre-emption.

[2] Our author seems to consider this charge of three per cent. for renewing the decayed notes as no more than what was reasonable, and to

any be desirous of procuring gold or silver for the purposes of manufacture, such as of drinking-cups, girdles, or other articles wrought of these metals, they in like manner apply at the mint, and for their paper obtain the bullion they require.[1] All his majesty's armies are paid with this currency, which is to them of the same value as if it were gold or silver. Upon these grounds, it may certainly be affirmed that the grand khan has a more extensive command of treasure than any other sovereign in the universe.

CHAPTER XIX

OF THE COUNCIL OF TWELVE GREAT OFFICERS APPOINTED FOR THE AFFAIRS OF THE ARMY, AND OF TWELVE OTHERS, FOR THE GENERAL CONCERNS OF THE EMPIRE

The grand khan selects twelve noblemen of high rank and consequence (as has been mentioned), whose duty it is to decide upon every point respecting the army; such as the removal of troops from one station to another; the change of officers commanding them; the employment of a force where it may be judged necessary; and the numbers which it may be proper to detach upon any particular service, according to the degree of its importance. Besides these objects, it is their business to distinguish between officers who have given proofs of valour in combat, and those who have shown themselves base and cowardly, in order to advance the former and to degrade the latter. Thus, if the commander of a thousand has been found to conduct himself in an unbecoming manner, this tribunal, considering him to be unworthy of the rank he held,

explain the whole system of extortion with complacency, as affording a proof of the consummate policy and grand resources of his master. It appears that the dynasty of the Ming was less exorbitant, and demanded only two per cent. Josaphat Barbaro, when he was at Asof in the Crimea, about the year 1450, was informed by an intelligent Tartar, who had been on an embassy to Cataio or China, that, "in quel luogo si spende moneta di carta; laquale ogni anno è mutata con nuova stampa et la moneta vecchia in capo dell' anno si porta alla zecca, ove à chi laporta è data altrettanta della nuova e bella; pagando tutta via due per cento di moneta d'argento buona, et la moneta vecchia si butta nel fuoco."—Viaggio alla Persia, etc. p. 44, 12mo.

[1] This scheme of finance having the tendency of depriving the manufactures in gold and silver of the materials of their trade, which were drawn out of the market by its vortex, a remedy became necessary for so serious an inconvenience, and the demands were accordingly supplied from the treasury.

reduce him to the command of an hundred men; or, on the contrary, if he has displayed such qualities as give claim to promotion, they appoint him commander of ten thousand. All this, however, is done with the knowledge and subject to the approval of his majesty, to whom they report their opinion of the officer's merit or demerit, and who, upon confirming their decision, grants to him who is promoted to the command of ten thousand men (for example) the tablet or warrant belonging to his rank, as before described; and also confers on him large presents, in order to excite others to merit the same rewards.

The tribunal composed of these twelve nobles is named Thai, denoting a supreme court, as being responsible to no other than the sovereign.[1] Besides this, there is another tribunal, likewise of twelve nobles, appointed for the superintendence of everything that respects the government of the thirty-four provinces of the empire. These have in Kanbalu a large and handsome palace or court, containing many chambers and halls. For the business of each province there is a presiding law-officer, together with several clerks, who have their respective apartments in the court, and there transact whatever business is necessary to be done for the province to which they belong, according to the directions they receive from the tribunal of twelve. These have authority to make choice of persons for the governments of the several provinces, whose names are presented to the grand khan for confirmation of their appointments and delivery of the tablets of gold or of silver appropriated to their ranks. They have also the superintendence of every matter that regards the collection of the revenue, both from land and customs, together with its disposal, and have the control of every other department of the state; with the exception only of what relates to the army.[2]

[1] *Thai* is evidently the *tay* (No. 1121) of De Guignes' Chinese Dictionary, which he renders by "eminens, altus." The usual Chinese term for this tribunal denotes its military functions, but the name in the text is expressly said to refer to its supremacy as a court, which the word *thai* or *tay* directly implies.

[2] This grand tribunal for the civil administration of the empire appears to have united in Kublai's time the objects of two of those six which now constitute the official government. "La fonction de la première de ces cours souveraines qui s'appellent *Lij pou*, est de fournir des mandarins pour toutes les provinces de l'empire, de veiller sur leur conduite, d'examiner leurs bonnes ou mauvaises qualitez, d'en rendre compte à l'empereur, etc." "La seconde cour souveraine, appellée *hou pou*, c'est-à-dire, grand trésorier du roy, a la surintendance des finances, et a le soin du domaine, des trésors, de la dépense, et des revenus de l'empereur, etc.

This tribunal is named Sing, implying that it is a second high court,[1] and, like the other, responsible only to the grand khan. But the former tribunal, named Thai, which has the administration of military affairs, is regarded as superior in rank and dignity to the latter.[2]

CHAPTER XX

OF THE PLACES ESTABLISHED ON ALL THE GREAT ROADS FOR SUPPLYING POST-HORSES—OF THE COURIERS ON FOOT—AND OF THE MODE IN WHICH THE EXPENSE IS DEFRAYED

FROM the city of Kanbalu there are many roads leading to the different provinces, and upon each of these, that is to say, upon every great high road, at the distance of twenty-five or thirty miles, accordingly as the towns happen to be situated, there are stations, with houses of accommodation for travellers, called *yamb* or post-houses.[3] These are large and handsome

Pour l'aider dans ce prodigieux détail, elle a quatorze tribunaux subalternes pour les affaires des quatorze provinces dont est composé l'empire; car la province de Pe-tche-li étant la province de la cour, . . . jouit en beaucoup de choses des prérogatives de la cour et de la maison de l'empereur." (Du Halde, tom. ii. p. 23.) Besides these fifteen provinces of the modern empire (or sixteen including the island of Hainan), Kublaı had under his government all the kingdoms possessed by his family before their conquest of China. In this sense it is that our author speaks of thirty-four provinces as under the jurisdiction of this tribunal.

[1] The Chinese terms that present themselves as corresponding in sound to this of *singh*, and having at the same time an appropriate signification, are *sing* (No. 2938 of the Dictionary), which is rendered by "advertere, cognoscere," and *sing* (6606), by "examinare, considerare;" both of which, if they can be said to differ in sense, are completely applicable to the nature of a high court of justice; more so, perhaps, than *tsing* (3947), "claritas, splendor," or *tsing* (7698), "rectum, bonum, perfectum." That it should have received its appellation, according to the phrase in Ramusio's text, from the circumstance of its being second to any other tribunal, is not probable in itself, nor justified by any analogy of sound.

[2] In modern times, on the contrary, precedence is given to the civil departments, and the Ping-pû or war tribunal ranks only as fourth of the six high courts. That it should have been otherwise under the government of a monarch who held the empire of China by the sword, and that in his estimation the department of the army should be paramount to all others, is what might be expected.

[3] This word, which in Ramusio's text is printed *lamb*, we find to be *ianli* in the Basle edition, *ianbi* in the older Latin, and *iamb*, or, as we should write it, *yamb*, in the B.M. manuscript; and there explained by the term of "mansiones equorum." It is evident therefore that the *l* for *i*, in the Italian, is a mistake of transcription, and we may conclude the word to be the Persian *yâm* or *ïâm* which Meninski translates, "stationarius, veredus seu veredarius equus," but which, in the journal of

buildings, having several well-furnished apartments, hung with silk, and provided with everything suitable to persons of rank. Even kings may be lodged at these stations in a becoming manner,[1] as every article required may be obtained from the towns and strong places in the vicinity; and for some of them the court makes regular provision. At each station four hundred good horses are kept in constant readiness, in order that all messengers going and coming upon the business of the grand khan, and all ambassadors, may have relays, and, leaving their jaded horses, be supplied with fresh ones.[2] Even in mountainous districts, remote from the great roads, where there were no villages, and the towns are far distant from each other, his majesty has equally caused buildings of the same kind to be erected, furnished with everything necessary, and provided with the usual establishment of horses. He sends people to dwell upon the spot, in order to cultivate the land, and attend to the service of the post; by which means large villages are formed. In consequence of these regulations, ambassadors to the court, and the royal messengers, go and return through every province and kingdom of the empire with the greatest convenience and facility;[3]

Shah Rokh's ambassadors, is made to denote the inn or post-house (agreeably to our author's use of it), and not the post-horses. Meninski remarks that it belongs to the dialect spoken in Korasmia, which at the period of its conquest by Jengiz-khan and his sons was amongst the most civilized countries of Asia, and the most likely to have had establishments of that nature. By the Chinese their post-houses are termed *tchan* or *chan*, and twenty-five or thirty miles is said to be their distance from each other. The Persian *marhileh* and *manzil* equally signify, "a stage or halting-place, after a day's journey (of about thirty miles)." The *σταθμὸς*, *statio*, *mansio*, of the Greeks, was of the same nature.

[1] By *kings* are here meant persons of that rank which the Chinese term Vang, and the Portuguese Regulo. They may be compared to the Princes of the German empire, or to the Hindu Rajas under the Moghul government.

[2] To those who form their judgment of the ancient establishments of the Chinese empire from modern descriptions, this number of horses at each station, or the end of each day's ordinary journey, may appear improbable; but the assertion is justified by the authority of the same journal that has so often served to throw light upon our author's relations, although written subsequently to his time by about a century and a half.

[3] By ambassadors, in Chinese history and accounts of China, we are to understand not only the representatives of foreign princes, to whom we confine the term, but every petty vassal of the empire, or deputy of such vassal, who repairs to the court, invested with a public character. Those of the first mentioned class were in the practice of taking under their protection, as a part of their suite, large bodies of traders, who by that means had an opportunity of introducing their goods into the country, in contravention of the established regulations, but obviously with the connivance of the governors of frontier towns, and perhaps of the court

in all which the grand khan exhibits a superiority over every other emperor, king, or human being. In his dominions no fewer than two hundred thousand horses are thus employed in the department of the post, and ten thousand buildings, with suitable furniture, are kept up.[1] It is indeed so wonderful a system, and so effective in its operation, as it is scarcely possible to describe. If it be questioned how the population of the country can supply sufficient numbers for these duties, and by what means they can be victualled, we may answer, that all the idolaters, and likewise the Saracens, keep six, eight, or ten women, according to their circumstances, by whom they have a prodigious number of children;[2] some of them as many as thirty sons capable of following their fathers in arms; whereas with us a man has only one wife, and even although she should prove barren, he is obliged to pass his life with her, and is by that means deprived of the chance of raising a family. Hence it is that our population is so much inferior to theirs. With regard to food, there is no deficiency of it, for these people, especially the Tartars, Cathaians, and inhabitants of the province of Manji (or Southern China), subsist, for the most part, upon rice, panicum, and millet; which three grains yield, in their soil, an hundred measures for one.[3] Wheat, indeed, does not yield a similar increase, and bread not being in use with them, it is eaten only in the form of vermicelli or of pastry. The former grains they boil in milk or stew with their meat. With them no spot of earth is suffered to lie idle, that can possibly be cultivated; and their cattle of different kinds multiply exceedingly, insomuch that when they take the field, there is scarcely an individual that does

itself. This is avowed by Shah Rokh's ambassadors, and particularly described by Benedict Goez, who himself travelled in the capacity of a merchant.

[1] An inconsistency in the numbers, not easy to reconcile, presents itself in this place; for if by ten thousand buildings are meant so many post-houses, the total number of horses, instead of being two hundred thousand, should amount to four millions. It is probable that a cipher should be cut off from the former, and that, for *ten*, we should read *one* thousand, which would bring the error within moderate bounds; or, it may be intended to include in that number the stations, at short intervals, for couriers on foot.

[2] The modern accounts of Chinese polygamy or concubinage lead us to suppose that it is not common amongst the lower classes of society.

[3] In Sumatra the rate of produce of up-land rice is reckoned at eighty, and of low-land, at an hundred and twenty for one. This increase, so disproportionate to what is known in Europe, I have ventured to attribute rather to the saving of grain in the mode of sowing, than to any superior fertility of soil.—See Hist. of Sumatra, third edit. p. 77. See also Voy. à Peking, etc. par De Guignes fils, tom. iii. p. 332.

not carry with him six, eight, or more horses, for his own personal use. From all this may be seen the causes of so large a population, and the circumstances that enable them to provide so abundantly for their subsistence.

In the intermediate space between the post-houses, there are small villages settled at the distance of every three miles, which may contain, one with another, about forty cottages. In these are stationed the foot messengers, likewise employed in the service of his majesty.[1] They wear girdles round their waists, to which several small bells are attached, in order that their coming may be perceived at a distance; and as they run only three miles, that is, from one of these foot-stations to another next adjoining, the noise serves to give notice of their approach, and preparation is accordingly made by a fresh courier to proceed with the packet instantly upon the arrival of the former.[2] Thus it is so expeditiously conveyed from station to station, that in the course of two days and two nights his majesty receives distant intelligence that in the ordinary mode could not be obtained in less than ten days;[3] and it often happens that in the fruit season, what is gathered in the morning at Kanbalu is conveyed to the grand khan, at Shan-du, by the evening of the following day; although the distance is generally considered as ten days' journey. At each of these three-mile stations there is a clerk, whose business it is to note the day and hour at which the one courier arrives and the other departs; which is likewise done at all the post-houses. Besides this, officers are directed to pay monthly visits to every station, in order to examine into the management of them, and to punish those couriers

[1] "Upon the road," says Bell, "we met with many turrets, called post-houses, erected at certain distances from one another. . . . These places are guarded by a few soldiers, who run a-foot, from one post to another, with great speed, carrying letters or despatches that concern the emperor. . . . The distance of one post-house from another is usually five Chinese li or miles. . . . I compute five of their miles to be about two and a half English."—Vol. i. p. 340.

[2] The use of bells for this purpose would seem, from what is stated by De Guignes, to be now confined to the messengers on horseback. (Tom. ii. p. 223.) It is likely, however, that the foot-messengers have some similar mode of making known their approach.

[3] An active man may, with perfect ease, run three miles at the rate of eight miles in the hour, and consequently one hundred and ninety-two miles might be performed by successive couriers in twenty-four hours, or nearly four hundred miles in two days and nights: but if by the "ordinary mode" is to be understood ten stages of thirty miles, it is only necessary that three hundred miles should be performed in that time, which is at the rate of six miles in the hour.

who have neglected to use proper diligence. All these couriers are not only exempt from the (capitation) tax, but also receive from his majesty good allowances. The horses employed in this service are not attended with any (direct) expense; the cities, towns, and villages in the neighbourhood being obliged to furnish, and also to maintain them. By his majesty's command the governors of the cities cause examination to be made by well informed persons, as to the number of horses the inhabitants, individually, are capable of supplying. The same is done with respect to the towns and villages; and according to their means the requisition is enforced; those on each side of the station contributing their due proportion. The charge of the maintenance of the horses is afterwards deducted by the cities out of the revenue payable to the grand khan; inasmuch as the sum for which each inhabitant would be liable is commuted for an equivalent of horses or share of horses, which he maintains at the nearest adjoining station.[1]

It must be understood, however, that of the four hundred horses the whole are not constantly on service at the station, but only two hundred, which are kept there for the space of a month, during which period the other half are at pasture; and at the beginning of the month, these in their turn take the duty, whilst the former have time to recover their flesh; each alternately relieving the other. Where it happens that there is a river or a lake which the couriers on foot, or the horsemen, are under the necessity of passing, the neighbouring cities are obliged to keep three or four boats in continual readiness for that purpose; and where there is a desert of several days' journey, that does not admit of any habitation, the city on its borders is obliged to furnish horses to such persons as ambassadors to and from the court, that they may be enabled to pass the desert, and also to supply provisions to them and their suite; but cities so circumstanced have a remuneration from his majesty. Where the post stations lie at a distance from the great road, the horses are partly those of his majesty, and are only in part furnished by the cities and towns of the district.

When it is necessary that the messengers should proceed

[1] It is not easy to comprehend to whom it is meant that this establishment was not attended with expense. If deducted from the amount of taxes to which the inhabitants were otherwise liable, it was ultimately a charge upon the revenue of the monarch. The whole is far from being clear, but the probable meaning is, that it was without expense, ultimately, to the individuals who performed the duty.

with extraordinary despatch, as in the cases of giving information of disturbance in any part of the country, the rebellion of a chief, or other important matter, they ride two hundred, or sometimes two hundred and fifty miles in the course of a day. On such occasions they carry with them the tablet of the gerfalcon as a signal of the urgency of their business and the necessity for despatch. And when there are two messengers, they take their departure together from the same place, mounted upon good fleet horses; and they gird their bodies tight, bind a cloth round their heads, and push their horses to the greatest speed. They continue thus till they come to the next post-house, at twenty-five miles distant,[1] where they find two other horses, fresh and in a state for work; they spring upon them without taking any repose, and changing in the same manner at every stage, until the day closes, they perform a journey of two hundred and fifty miles. In cases of great emergency they continue their course during the night, and if there should be no moon, they are accompanied to the next station by persons on foot, who run before them with lights; when of course they do not make the same expedition as in the day-time, the light-bearers not being able to exceed a certain pace. Messengers qualified to undergo this extraordinary degree of fatigue are held in high estimation. Now we will leave this subject, and I will tell you of a great act of benevolence which the grand khan performs twice a-year.

CHAPTER XXI

OF THE RELIEF AFFORDED BY THE GRAND KHAN TO ALL THE PROVINCES OF HIS EMPIRE, IN TIMES OF DEARTH OR MORTALITY OF CATTLE

THE grand khan sends every year his commissioners to ascertain whether any of his subjects have suffered in their crops of corn from unfavourable weather, from storms of wind or violent rains, or by locusts, worms, or any other plague; and in such cases he not only refrains from exacting the usual tribute of that year, but furnishes them from his granaries with so much corn as is necessary for their subsistence, as well as for sowing their land. With this view, in times of great

[1] [In other MSS. it is thirty-five miles.]

plenty, he causes large purchases to be made of such kinds of grain as are most serviceable to them, which is stored in granaries provided for the purpose in the several provinces, and managed with such care as to ensure its keeping for three or four years without damage.[1] It is his command, that these granaries be always kept full, in order to provide against times of scarcity; and when, in such seasons, he disposes of the grain for money, he requires for four measures no more than the purchaser would pay for one measure in the market. In like manner where there has been a mortality of cattle in any district, he makes good the loss to the sufferers from those belonging to himself, which he has received as his tenth of produce in other provinces. All his thoughts, indeed, are directed to the important object of assisting the people whom he governs, that they may be enabled to live by their labour and improve their substance.[2] We must not omit to notice a peculiarity of the grand khan, that where an accident has happened by lightning to any herd of cattle, flock of sheep, or other domestic animals, whether the property of one or more persons, and however large the herd may be, he does not demand the tenth of the increase of such cattle during three years; and so also if a ship laden with merchandise has been struck by lightning, he does not collect from her any custom or share of her cargo, considering the accident as an ill omen. God, he says, has shown himself to be displeased with the owner of the goods, and he is unwilling that property bearing the mark of divine wrath should enter his treasury.[3]

[1] "In such times (of scarcity) the emperor of China," says Staunton, . . . "orders the granaries to be opened; he remits the taxes to those who are visited by misfortunes; he affords assistance to enable them to retrieve their affairs." (Vol. ii. p. 89.) "In China," says Barrow, "there are no great farmers who store their grain to throw into the market in seasons of scarcity. In such seasons the only resource is that of the government opening its magazines, and restoring to the people that portion of their crop which it had demanded from them as the price of its protection." The same circumstance is noticed by other travellers.

[2] The edicts of the Chinese emperors, even of such as were kept by their eunuchs and other favourites in profound ignorance of the affairs of their empire, are filled with sentiments expressive of the most tender and anxious concern for the welfare of their people, whom they term their children. In Kublaï's actions there was probably no affectation of philanthropy; but from his general character it may be suspected that a regard for his own interest was the motive that actuated his benevolence to his Chinese subjects, of whose loyalty he always showed himself suspicious.

[3] No direct proof of the existence of this superstition in China has presented itself. That thunder and lightning are regarded with feelings of extraordinary terror, is evident from the frightful representations of the deity who presides over, and is supposed to wield this engine of divine wrath.

CHAPTER XXII

OF THE TREES WHICH HE CAUSES TO BE PLANTED AT THE SIDES OF THE ROADS, AND OF THE ORDER IN WHICH THEY ARE KEPT

There is another regulation adopted by the grand khan, equally ornamental and useful. At both sides of the public roads he causes trees to be planted, of a kind that become large and tall, and being only two paces asunder, they serve (besides the advantage of their shade in summer) to point out the road (when the ground is covered with snow); which is of great assistance and affords much comfort to travellers.[1] This is done along all the high roads, where the nature of the soil admits of plantation; but when the way lies through sandy deserts or over rocky mountains, where it is impossible to have trees, he orders stones to be placed and columns to be erected, as marks for guidance. He also appoints officers of rank, whose duty it is to see that all these are properly arranged and the roads constantly kept in good order. Besides the motives that have been assigned for these plantations, it may be added that the grand khan is the more disposed to make them, from the circumstance of his diviners and astrologers having declared that those who plant trees are rewarded with long life.

CHAPTER XXIII

OF THE KIND OF WINE MADE IN THE PROVINCE OF CATHAY—AND OF THE STONES USED THERE FOR BURNING IN THE MANNER OF CHARCOAL

The greater part of the inhabitants of the province of Cathay drink a sort of wine made from rice mixed with a variety of

[1] "Il y a de certaines provinces," says Du Halde, "où les grandes chemins sont comme autant de grandes allées, bordées d'arbres fort hauts." (Tom. ii. p. 52.) De Guignes describes the high roads of the provinces through which he travelled, as generally planted with trees. (Tom. ii. pp. 215, 216.) The paces by which the distance of the trees is estimated by our author, must be understood as geometric or Roman paces of five feet; and even on that scale the interval is too small. It is not improbable that he may in this instance, as well as in other parts of the work, have expressed himself in the measures of the country, which are rendered by Italian terms not strictly corresponding; or the passage may have been corrupted. The explanatory words between brackets are added in the translation.

spices and drugs. This beverage, or wine as it may be termed, is so good and well flavoured that they do not wish for better. It is clear, bright, and pleasant to the taste, and being (made) very hot, has the quality of inebriating sooner than any other.

Throughout this province there is found a sort of black stone, which they dig out of the mountains, where it runs in veins. When lighted, it burns like charcoal, and retains the fire much better than wood; insomuch that it may be preserved during the night, and in the morning be found still burning. These stones do not flame, excepting a little when first lighted, but during their ignition give out a considerable heat. It is true there is no scarcity of wood in the country, but the multitude of inhabitants is so immense, and their stoves and baths, which they are continually heating, so numerous, that the quantity could not supply the demand; for there is no person who does not frequent the warm bath at least three times in the week, and during the winter daily, if it is in their power. Every man of rank or wealth has one in his house for his own use; and the stock of wood must soon prove inadequate to such consumption; whereas these stones may be had in the greatest abundance, and at a cheap rate.[1]

CHAPTER XXIV

OF THE GREAT AND ADMIRABLE LIBERALITY EXERCISED BY THE GRAND KHAN TOWARDS THE POOR OF KANBALU, AND OTHER PERSONS WHO APPLY FOR RELIEF AT HIS COURT

IT has been already stated that the grand khan distributes large quantities of grain to his subjects (in the provinces). We

[1] This circumstantial account of the use made by the Chinese of pit or fossil coal, at a period when its properties were so little known in Europe, will deservedly be thought an interesting record of the fact, as well as a proof of undoubted genuineness and originality on the part of our author. " Les mines de charbon de pierre sont en si grande quantité dans les provinces," says Du Halde, " qu'il n'y a apparemment aucun royaume au monde, où il y en ait tant, et de si abondantes. Il s'en trouve sans nombre dans les montagnes des provinces de Chen-si, de Chan-si, et de Pe-che-li: aussi s'en sert-on pour tous les fourneaux des ouvriers, dans les cuisines de toutes les maisons, et dans les hypocaustes des chambres qu'on allume tout l'hyver. Sans un pareil secours, ces peuples auroient peine à vivre dans des pays si froids, où le bois de chauffage est rare, et par conséquent très-cher." (Tom. i. p. 29.) " Stoves," says Staunton, " are common in large buildings. They are fed from without with fossil coal, found plentifully in the neighbourhood." —Vol. ii. p. 338.

shall now speak of his great charity to and provident care of the poor in the city of Kanbalu. Upon his being apprised of any respectable family, that had lived in easy circumstances, being by misfortunes reduced to poverty, or who, in consequence of infirmities, are unable to work for their living or to raise a supply of any kind of grain: to a family in that situation he gives what is necessary for their year's consumption, and at the customary period they present themselves before the officers who manage the department of his majesty's expenses and who reside in a palace where that business is transacted, to whom they deliver a statement in writing of the quantity furnished to them in the preceding year, according to which they receive also for the present. He provides in like manner for their clothing, which he has the means of doing from his tenths of wool, silk, and hemp. These materials he has woven into the different sorts of cloth, in a house erected for that purpose, where every artisan is obliged to work one day in the week for his majesty's service. Garments made of stuffs thus manufactured he orders to be given to the poor families above described, as they are wanted for their winter and their summer dresses. He also has clothing prepared for his armies, and in every city has a quantity of woollen cloth woven, which is paid for from the amount of the tenths levied at the place.[1]

It should be known that the Tartars, when they followed their original customs, and had not yet adopted the religion of the idolaters, were not in the practice of bestowing alms, and when a necessitous man applied to them, they drove him away with injurious expressions, saying, "Begone with your complaint of a bad season which God has sent you; had he loved you, as it appears he loves me, you would have prospered as I do." But since the wise men of the idolaters, and especially the baksis, already mentioned, have represented to his majesty that providing for the poor is a good work and highly acceptable to their deities, he has relieved their wants in the manner stated, and at his court none are denied food who come to ask it. Not a day passes in which there are not distributed, by the regular officers, twenty thousand vessels of rice, millet, and

[1] At the present day the manufacture of woollen cloth or stuffs in China is very inconsiderable, but it may have been affected in the course of several centuries by the importations from Europe, which are known to have progressively increased. For its existence in the seventeenth century we have the authority of the missionaries.

panicum.[1] By reason of this admirable and astonishing liberality which the grand khan exercises towards the poor, the people all adore him as a divinity.[2]

CHAPTER XXV

OF THE ASTROLOGERS OF THE CITY OF KANBALU

THERE are in the city of Kanbalu, amongst Christians, Saracens, and Cathaians, about five thousand astrologers and prognosticators,[3] for whose food and clothing the grand khan provides in the same manner as he does for the poor families above mentioned, and who are in the constant exercise of their art. They have their astrolabes, upon which are described the planetary signs, the hours (at which they pass the meridian), and their several aspects for the whole year. The astrologers (or almanac-makers) of each distinct sect annually proceed to the examination of their respective tables, in order to ascertain from thence the course of the heavenly bodies, and their relative positions for every lunation. They discover therein what the state of the weather shall be, from the paths and configurations of the planets in the different signs, and thence foretell the peculiar phenomena of each month: that in such a month, for instance, there shall be thunder and storms; in such another, earthquakes; in another, strokes of lightning and violent rains; in another, diseases, mortality, wars, discords, conspiracies. As they find the matter in their astrolabes, so they declare it will come to pass; adding, however, that God, according to his good pleasure, may do more or less than they have set down. They write their predictions for the year upon certain small squares, which are called *takuini*, and these they sell, for a groat apiece, to all persons who are desirous of peeping into futurity. Those whose pre-

[1] Purchas translates *scudelle* by "crowns" (écus), and supposes that grain to the amount of twenty thousand of that coin was distributed daily; but the dictionaries tell us that the Italian *scudella* is the French *écuelle*, a pipkin or porringer; and this meaning is the more simple and natural of the two. [Instead of this, the early Latin and French texts published by the French Geographical Society, say simply that thirty thousand *people* were thus fed at court, and the Italian text of Boni makes the number of persons to be three hundred thousand.]

[2] "He appears to his subjects," says Staunton, "as standing almost in the place of Providence in their favour."—Vol. ii. p. 90.

[3] To account for this extraordinary number of astrologers, we must suppose that the priests of every description were adepts in the occult art.

dictions are found to be the more generally correct are esteemed the most perfect masters of their art, and are consequently the most honoured.[1] When any person forms the design of executing some great work, of performing a distant journey in the way of commerce, or of commencing any other undertaking, and is desirous of knowing what success may be likely to attend it, he has recourse to one of these astrologers, and, informing him that he is about to proceed on such an expedition, inquires in what disposition the heavens appear to be at the time. The latter thereupon tells him, that before he can answer, it is necessary he should be informed of the year, the month, and the hour in which he was born; and that, having learned these particulars, he will then proceed to ascertain in what respects the constellation that was in the ascendant at his nativity corresponds with the aspect of the celestial bodies at the time of making the inquiry. Upon this comparison he grounds his prediction of the favourable or unfavourable termination of the adventure.[2]

It should be observed that the Tartars compute their time by a cycle of twelve years; to the first of which they give the name of the lion; to the second year, that of the ox; to the third, the dragon; to the fourth, the dog; and so of the rest, until the whole of the twelve have elapsed. When a person, therefore, is asked in what year he was born, he replies, In the course of the year of the lion, upon such a day, at such an hour and minute; all of which has been carefully noted by his parents in a book. Upon the completion of the twelve years of the cycle, they return to the first, and continually repeat the same series.[3]

[1] In later times the publication of the Chinese almanac has been an affair of government, and none is circulated but under the sanction of the emperor; the astronomical part being computed by Europeans, and the astrological part invented by the Chinese.

[2] It appears that the astrologers of Pekin were not exempt from the suspicion of sometimes using flagitious means to make the events tally with their prophecies, of which the journal of Shah Rokh's ambassadors affords a remarkable instance. "Les astrologues du Khataï," they observe, "avoient pronostiqué que cette année le palais de l'empereur seroit endommagé du feu, et cette prédiction fut le sujet de cette illumination. Les émirs (mandarins) s'étant assemblés, l'empereur leur fit un festin, et les régala." Three months afterwards we find the following passage: "La nuit suivante, par un décret de Dieu, le feu prit au nouveau palais de l'empereur, non sans quelque soupçon de quelque fourberie des astrologues. L'appartement principal qui avoit quatre-vingt coudées de long et trente de large. . . . fut entièrement brûlé." —Pp. 9—12.

[3] "Les Tartares," says De Guignes, père, "ont aussi un cycle de douze ans. Les dénominations de chaque année sont prises des noms de

CHAPTER XXVI

OF THE RELIGION OF THE TARTARS—OF THE OPINIONS THEY HOLD RESPECTING THE SOUL—AND OF SOME OF THEIR CUSTOMS

As has already been observed, these people are idolaters, and for deities, each person has a tablet fixed up against a high part of the wall of his chamber, upon which is written a name, that serves to denote the high, celestial, and sublime God; and to this they pay daily adoration, with incense burning.[1] Lifting up their hands and then striking their faces against the floor three times,[2] they implore from him the blessings of sound intellect and health of body; without any further petition. Below this, on the floor, they have a statue which they name *Natigai*, which they consider as the God of all terrestrial things or whatever is produced from the earth. They give him a wife and children,[3] and worship him in a similar manner, burning incense, raising their hands, and bending to the floor. To him

différens animaux; ainsi l'on disoit l'année de la souris, du bœuf, etc., pour dire la première ou la seconde année; et à la fin des douze années on recommençoit de la même façon. Les Chinois ont quelquefois fait usage de ce cycle." (Hist. des Huns, tom. i. p. xlvii.) In the names of the years, as furnished by different writers, there is some variation, but according to the most modern of the authorities they are as follows: "the rat, ox, tiger, hare, dragon, serpent, horse, sheep, monkey, cock, dog, and hog;" from whence it appears that our author's account of the cycle is not merely imperfect, but incorrect, if he really placed the names in the order in which they are given in the text. By the lion (as has already been shown in note [1], p. 194) is meant the tiger; but this animal, instead of being the first of the series, is only the third, and should follow, instead of preceding the ox; nor does the dragon or the dog belong to those numerical years to which they are assigned. What he has said is fully sufficient to evince a general acquaintance with the Tartar calendar, and probably what he wrote or dictated amounted to this,—that each of the twelve years bore the name of an animal, such as the lion, ox, dog, etc., without any intention of furnishing an exact list.

[1] The custom of paying adoration to a written tablet instead of the image or representation of a deity was properly Kataian rather than Tartar, but it might have been adopted by the latter people along with other Chinese practices, and especially by the emperor. The words inscribed are *tien*, heaven, *hoang-tien*, supreme heaven, *shang-ti*, sovereign lord.

[2] *Sbattere i denti* is literally to gnash the teeth or strike them against each other; but this is obviously a misapprehension of what was meant to express the act of prostration and striking the ground with the forehead. The prostrations before the throne or tablet of the emperor are three times three.

[3] Staunton speaks of the worship of Fo's wife and child in the Putala or temple of Zhehol (Jehol) in Tartary, vol. ii. p. 258.

they pray for seasonable weather, abundant crops, increase of family, and the like. They believe the soul to be immortal, in this sense, that immediately upon the death of a man, it enters into another body, and that accordingly as he has acted virtuously or wickedly during his life, his future state will become, progressively, better or worse.[1] If he be a poor man, and has conducted himself worthily and decently, he will be re-born, in the first instance, from the womb of a gentlewoman, and become, himself, a gentleman; next, from the womb of a lady of rank, and become a nobleman; thus continually ascending in the scale of existence until he be united to the divinity. But if, on the contrary, being the son of a gentleman, he has behaved unworthily, he will, in his next state, be a clown, and at length a dog, continually descending to a condition more vile than the preceding.[2]

Their style of conversation is courteous; they salute each other politely, with countenances expressive of satisfaction,[3] have an air of good breeding, and eat their victuals with particular cleanliness. To their parents they show the utmost reverence; but should it happen that a child acts disrespectfully to or neglects to assist his parents in their necessity, there is a public tribunal, whose especial duty it is to punish with severity the crime of filial ingratitude, when the circumstance is known.[4] Malefactors guilty of various crimes, who are apprehended and thrown into prison, are executed by strangling; but such as remain till the expiration of three years, being the time appointed by his majesty for a general gaol delivery, and are then liberated, have a mark imprinted upon one of their cheeks, that they may be recognised.[5]

[1] This is the Hindu doctrine of the metempsychosis, which, along with the schismatic religion of Buddha, was introduced into China (as the annals of that country inform us) about the year 65 of our era. It had not, however, (according to the elder De Guignes,) made any considerable progress until the year 335, when the emperor then reigning took it under his protection.

[2] According to the Hindu belief the souls of men reanimate new bodies, "until by repeated regenerations all their sins are done away, and they attain such a degree of perfection as will entitle them to what is called *mukti*, eternal salvation, by which is understood a release from future transmigration, and an absorption in the nature of the Godhead." Wilkins, Notes to Bhagvat Gita, p. 140.

[3] It is evidently of the Kataians, and not of the rude Tartars, that our author here speaks.

[4] "Un fils," says De Guignes, "qui accuse son père ou sa mère, même avec raison, est puni par l'exil."—Tom. iii. p. 117.

[5] The distinction in the degree of punishment between executing a criminal soon after condemnation, or at the regulated period, is frequently adverted to in the Lettres édifiantes.

The present grand khan has prohibited all species of gambling and other modes of cheating, to which the people of this country are addicted more than any others upon earth; and as an argument for deterring them from the practice, he says to them (in his edict), "I subdued you by the power of my sword, and consequently whatever you possess belongs of right to me: if you gamble, therefore, you are sporting with my property." He does not, however, take anything arbitrarily in virtue of this right. The order and regularity observed by all ranks of people, when they present themselves before his majesty, ought not to pass unnoticed. When they approach within half a mile of the place where he happens to be, they show their respect for his exalted character by assuming a humble, placid, and quiet demeanour, insomuch that not the least noise, nor the voice of any person calling out, or even speaking aloud, is heard.[1] Every man of rank carries with him a small vessel, into which he spits, so long as he continues in the hall of audience, no one daring to spit on the floor;[2] and this being done, he replaces the cover, and makes a salutation. They are accustomed likewise to take with them handsome buskins made of white leather, and when they reach the court, but before they enter the hall (for which they wait a summons from the grand khan), they put on these white buskins, and give those in which they had walked to the care of the servants. This practice is observed that they may not soil the beautiful carpets, which are curiously wrought with silk and gold, and exhibit a variety of colours.[3]

[1] This perfect silence at the court of Pekin is particularly noticed by Bell, who says: "As we advanced we found all the ministers of state, and officers belonging to the court, seated upon fur-cushions, cross-legged, before the hall in the open air; among these, places were appointed for the ambassador and his retinue, and in this situation we remained . . . till the emperor came into the hall. During this interval . . . not the least noise was heard from any quarter." (Vol. ii. p. 5.) Again he observes: "By this time the hall was pretty full, and, what is surprising, there was not the least noise, hurry, or confusion. . . . In short, the characteristic of the court of Pekin is order and decency, rather than grandeur and magnificence."—P. 9.

[2] This kind of utensil is common in many parts of the East Indies, where it is commonly termed, from the Portuguese, a *cuspidór*. It might be inferred from hence that the practice then prevailed of masticating something of the nature of betel.

[3] In the modern descriptions of Chinese furniture we do not find any notice taken of carpets, for which mats appear to be substituted; but it does not follow that they were equally disused in the palaces of Kublaï, whose family were the conquerors of Persia and other countries of Asia, where the manufacture of this article of luxury was in perfection. Du Halde, however, in describing the capital city of the province of Shan-si,

CHAPTER XXVII

OF THE RIVER NAMED PULISANGAN, AND OF THE BRIDGE OVER IT

Having thus completed the account of the government and police of the province of Cathay and city of Kanbalu, as well as of the magnificence of the grand khan, we shall now proceed to speak of other parts of the empire. You must know then that the grand khan sent Marco as his ambassador to the west; and leaving Kanbalu, he travelled westward during full four months; we shall now tell you all he saw going and coming.

Upon leaving the capital and travelling ten miles,[1] you come to a river named Pulisangan, which discharges itself into the ocean, and is navigated by many vessels entering from thence, with considerable quantities of merchandise.[2] Over this river there is a very handsome bridge of stone, perhaps unequalled by another in the world. Its length is three hundred paces, and its width eight paces; so that ten men can, without inconvenience, ride abreast.[3] It has twenty-four arches, supported by twenty-five piers erected in

says: " Outre différentes étoffes qui se fabriquent en cette ville, comme ailleurs, on y fait en particulier des tapis façon de Turquie, de quelque grandeur qu'on les commande."—Tom. i. p. 204.

[1] In the epitome of 1496 and subsequent Venice editions the words are, *mesi* x., ten months, instead of *dieci miglia*, ten miles; in which latter consistent sense the Basle edition agrees with Ramusio. The period also of our author's journey is extended from four to fourteen months, the one error having evidently given birth to the other.

[2] This river, the name of which is variously written Pulisangan, Pulisangium, Pulisachniz, Pulsanchimz, and Paluisanguis, appears from the circumstances stated to be the Hoen-ho of the Jesuits' map, which, uniting with another stream from the north-west, forms the Pe-ho or White River. This, in the lower part of its course, and to the distance of many miles from the Yellow Sea, into which it disembogues, is navigable for vessels of considerable burthen, although too rapid for that purpose at the part where it crossed our author's route to the south-west. It may be remarked that in the Persian language the words *puli-sangi* signify the " stone bridge," and it is not improbable that the western people in the service of the emperor may have given this appellation to the place where a bridge of great celebrity was thrown over the river, which is here applied to the river itself. It will be found to occur in Elphinstone's Account of Caubul, p. 429, and in Ouseley's Ibn Haukul, p. 277.

[3] Ten horsemen could not draw up abreast in a less space than thirty feet, and might probably require forty when in motion. The paces here spoken of must therefore be geometric; and upon this calculation the bridge would be five hundred yards in length.

the water, all of serpentine stone,[1] and built with great skill. On each side, and from one extremity to the other, there is a handsome parapet, formed of marble slabs and pillars arranged in a masterly style. At the commencement of the ascent the bridge is something wider than at the summit, but from the part where the ascent terminates, the sides run in straight lines and parallel to each other.[2] Upon the upper level there is a massive and lofty column, resting upon a tortoise of marble, and having near its base a large figure of a lion, with a lion also on the top.[3] Towards the slope of the bridge there is another handsome column or pillar, with its lion, at the distance of a pace and a half from the former; and all the spaces between one pillar and another, throughout the whole length of the bridge, are filled up with slabs of marble, curiously sculptured, and mortised into the next adjoining pillars, which are, in like manner, a pace and a half asunder, and equally surmounted with lions,[4] forming altogether a beautiful spectacle. These parapets serve to prevent accidents

[1] The serpent-stone, or *serpentinstein* of the Germans, is a well-known species, and considered as an inferior kind of jade.

[2] By P. Magalhanes, who particularly notices this description, our author is understood to speak here of the perfect level of the surface, and not of the straightness of the sides: "Aux deux extremités," he translates, "il est plus large qu'au haut de la montée: mais quand on a achevé de monter, on le trouve plat et de niveau comme s'il avoit esté tiré à la ligne." (Nouv. Relat. p. 14.) But the words, "uguale per longo come se fosse tirato per linea," seem rather to refer to the general parallelism of the sides, although at the ends they diverged, as is the case with almost all bridges.

[3] It has been observed before, that when our author speaks of lions in China, as living animals, he undoubtedly means tigers; but it is otherwise with respect to the imaginary and grotesque representations of the lion, in marble, bronze, and porcelain, employed as ornaments in the public buildings and gardens of these people. The ideas of the symbolic lion and of the tortoise are borrowed from the *singa* and the *kûrma* of Hindu mythology.

[4] It is difficult to understand from the words of the text (the obscurity of which is likely to have been increased by successive transcripts) the position of these larger columns with regard to the other parts of the bridge; but it seems to be meant, that in the line of the parapet or balustrade, which was formed of alternate slabs of marble and pillars, there was in the middle (or over the centre arch or pier) a column of a size much larger than the rest, having a tortoise for its base or pedestal; and it may be presumed, although not so expressed, that there was a similar column in the balustrade on the opposite side. Our author seems, indeed, to have been sensible of this kind of deficiency in his description, when he says at the conclusion of the chapter, "Et nelle discesa del ponte è come nell' ascesa." One of the Jesuit missionaries who mentions a bridge which he had crossed in this part of the province says, "Les gardefous en sont de marbre; on conte de chaque côté cent quarante-huit poteaux avec des lionceaux au-dessus . . . et aux deux bouts du pont quatre éléphans accroupis."—Lett. édif. tom. xvii. p. 263.

that might otherwise happen to passengers. What has been said applies to the descent as well as to the ascent of the bridge.[1]

CHAPTER XXVIII

OF THE CITY OF GOUZA

AFTER having passed this bridge, proceeding thirty miles in a westerly direction, through a country abounding with fine buildings, amongst vineyards and much cultivated and fertile grounds, you arrive at a handsome and considerable city, named Gouza,[2] where there are many convents of the idolaters. The inhabitants in general live by commerce and manual arts. They have manufactures of gold tissues and the finest kind of gauze. The inns for accommodating travellers are there numerous.[3] At the distance of a mile beyond this place, the roads divide; the one going in a westerly, and the other in a south-easterly direction, the former through the province of Cathay, and the latter towards the province of Manji.[4] From

[1] Notwithstanding any partial difficulties in the description, or seeming objections to the credibility of the account given of this magnificent bridge, there is unquestionable authority for the existence of one similar to it in all the essential circumstances, and as nearly about the situation mentioned as can be ascertained from the conciseness of the itinerary, so lately as the seventeenth century. It may well, however, be supposed that in the lapse of four hundred years material changes must have taken place, in consequence of accidents, repairs, and perhaps renewals.

[2] From the relative situation and other circumstances mentioned of this place, I do not hestitate to consider it as intended for Tso-cheu, a city of the second class, spoken of in the preceding note; and this will appear the more probable when it is understood, that, although corruptly written Gou-za in Ramusio's text, it is Gio-gu in the early Venice epitomes, [Gio-guy in the Paris Latin text,] Geo-gui in that of Basle, and Cyongium in the B.M. and Berlin manuscripts, in all of which the first letter is meant to be soft, and evidently to represent the Chinese sound which we more aptly express by *Ts*. It has already been observed, and the instances will again frequently occur, of the Chinese appellative term *cheu* or *tcheou* (for a city of the second order) being corrupted to *gui*, apparently an orthographical mistake for *giu*, which nearly approaches to the true sound. Tso-cheu, according to the journals both of Van Braam and De Guignes, is twelve French leagues distant from Pekin, but as the former adds that it was a hundred and twenty Chinese li, and as this is more likely to be the true distance (for certainly those gentlemen did not measure it), we are justified in considering it as upwards of *forty* Italian miles, [the earliest and best MSS. have *thirty*, as given in our text,] at which number our author states it.

[3] Van Braam observes, that at Tso-cheu they found an excellent *conquan* (*kong-kuan*), or inn.

[4] The road by which the persons who composed the Dutch embassy

the city of Gouza it is a journey of ten days through Cathay to the kingdom of Ta-in-fu;[1] in the course of which you pass many fine cities and strong places, in which manufactures and commerce flourish, and where you see many vineyards and much cultivated land. From hence grapes are carried into the interior of Cathay, where the vine does not grow. Mulberry-trees also abound, the leaves of which enable the inhabitants to produce large quantities of silk. A degree of civilization prevails amongst all the people of this country, in consequence of their frequent intercourse with the towns, which are numerous and but little distant from each other. To these the merchants continually resort, carrying their goods from one city to another, as the fairs are successively held at each. At the end of five days' journey beyond the ten that have been mentioned, it is said there is another city still larger and more handsome (than Ta-in-fu), named Achbaluch,[2] to which the limits of his majesty's hunting grounds extend, and within which no persons dare to sport, excepting the princes of his own family, and those whose names are inscribed on the grand falconer's list; but beyond these limits, all persons qualified by their rank are at liberty to pursue game. It happens, however, that the grand khan scarcely ever takes the amusement of the chase on this side of the country;[3] and the consequence is, that the wild animals, especially hares, multiply to such a degree as to occasion the destruction of all the growing corn of the province. When this came to the

of 1795 travelled from Canton to Pekin was this latter, which is here described as leading through Tso-cheu to Manji or Southern China. The western road diverges at this point, and is that which was taken, in 1668, by P. Fontaney, who particularly describes it in his journal, published by Du Halde.

[1] Ta-in-fu, or Tainfu, is obviously Tai-yuen-fu, the capital of the modern province of Shan-si, which was frequently, in ancient times, the seat of an independent government. Its direction is about west-south-west from Tso-cheu, and the distance appears to be about ten easy stages.

[2] The circumstances stated do not supply the means of identifying this place, which was known to our author only by report. Its situation was probably to the north-west, as he afterwards proceeds to speak of places more remote, in a south-western direction; and it may have been intended for the city of Tai-tong-fu, which lies in that direction. The name of Ach-baluch is evidently Tartar, and serves to show that the want of the final guttural in Kanbalu, which the Persians give to it, is an accidental omission. No mention of this city is found in the Latin editions.

[3] We have seen that the usual hunting expeditions of the grand khan took place either at Shang-tu, which lies northward of Pekin, or in the direction of Eastern Tartary and the river Amûr.

knowledge of the grand khan, he repaired thither, with the whole of his court, and innumerable multitudes of these animals were taken.

CHAPTER XXIX

OF THE KINGDOM OF TA-IN-FU

At the end of ten days' journey from the city of Gouza, you arrive (as has been said) at the kingdom of Ta-in-fu, whose chief city, the capital of the province, bears the same name. It is of the largest size, and very beautiful.[1] A considerable trade is carried on here, and a variety of articles are manufactured, particularly arms and other military stores, which are at this place conveniently situated for the use of the grand khan's armies. Vineyards are numerous, from which grapes in vast abundance are gathered; and although within all the jurisdiction of Ta-in-fu no other vines are found than those produced in the district immediately surrounding the capital, there is yet a sufficient supply for the whole of the province.[2]

[1] "La ville capitale de Tai-yuen," says P. Martini, whom Du Halde copies, "a toujours esté mise au rang des plus considérables, ancienne, magnifique, et bien bastie: elle a de très-fortes murailles, environ de trois lieues de circuit, fort peuplée; au reste, est située dans un lieu fort agréable et fort sain. . . . Il ne faut pas s'estonner s'il s'y trouve si grande quantité de bastimens et si magnifiques, puis que ç'a esté la demeure de tant de roys." (Thevenot, tom. ii. p. 48.) It may be necessary here to remark, that what appears to be the concluding syllable in the names of Chinese towns (but which is a distinct monosyllable), serves to indicate their size or rank, and municipal jurisdiction or dependence: thus *fû* or *fou* denotes a city of the first class, having under its superintendence a certain number of those belonging to the inferior classes; *cheu* or *tcheu* denotes a city of the second class, subject to the jurisdiction of its *fû*; and *hien* a city or town of the third class, subject to its *cheu*. It also appears that each greater city contains these subordinate jurisdictions within itself.

[2] In this instance I have ventured to correct the text of Ramusio, by substituting "grapes" for "wine," although it is in conformity with the Venice epitome and the Latin version; because I am persuaded that, from ignorance of the facts, the expression of the original has been misunderstood, and our author is made to assert of the liquor what was only intended to apply to the fruit. "La Chine," says De Guignes, "produit du raisin, mais le pays n'est pas vignoble: le raisin même paroît peu propre à faire du vin, et ce n'est qu'avec peine que les missionnaires à Peking réussissent à en faire." (Tom. iii. p. 348.) That these dried grapes, or raisins, as they are termed in English, were the article of trade that our author meant to describe, will, I trust, be considered as at least highly probable, inasmuch as the correction renders him consistent with himself, and his information, with the knowledge we have since acquired.

Other fruits also grow here in plenty, as does the mulberry-tree, together with the worms that yield the silk.

CHAPTER XXX

OF THE CITY OF PI-AN-FU

LEAVING Ta-in-fu, and travelling westward, seven days' journey, through a fine country in which there are many cities and strong places, where commerce and manufactures prevail, and whose merchants, travelling over various parts of the country, obtain considerable profits, you reach a city named Pi-an-fu, which is of a large size and much celebrated.[1] It likewise contains numerous merchants and artisans. Silk is produced here also in great quantity. We shall not say anything further of these places, but proceed to speak of the distinguished city of Ka-chan-fu; first noticing, however, a noble fortress named Thai-gin.

CHAPTER XXXI

OF THE FORTRESS OF THAIGIN OR TAI-GIN

IN a western direction from Pi-an-fu there is a large and handsome fortress named Thai-gin,[2] which is said to have been

[1] This is the city of Pin-yang-fu, situated in the direction of south-south-west from the former, upon the same river; the banks of which, in its whole course, appear to be covered with towns. From its situation with respect to the Hoang-ho, or Yellow River, we are enabled to ascertain it to be the city visited by Shah Rokh's ambassadors, when they had crossed the famous bridge of boats, and of which, after describing the magnificence of its great temple, it is said: "Ils y remarquèrent trois bordels publics, où il y avoit des filles de joye d'une grande beauté. Quoique les filles du Khataï soient belles communément, néanmoins elles sont là plus belles qu'ailleurs, et la ville pour ce sujet s'appelle la ville de la beauté." (Thevenot, iv. partie, p. 5.) This we may conjecture to be the kind of celebrity to which our author so modestly alludes.

[2] The place here called Thai-gin and Tai-gin is in the Latin versions Chin-cui and Cay-cui, and in the Italian epitomes Chai-cui, [in the Paris Latin Cay-tui]: names so unlike that it may well be thought difficult to identify it from the orthography; but its situation between Pin-yang and the great Yellow River points it out with some probability, as the Kiai-tcheou of the Jesuits' map; nor will the sound of the word Kiai, which is the essential part of the name, be found to differ materially from the Cay and Chaï of the Latin and early Italian versions. With

built, at a remote period, by a king who was called Dor.[1] Within the walls of the fort stands a spacious and highly-ornamented palace, the hall of which contains paintings of all the renowned princes who, from ancient times, have reigned at this place, forming together a superb exhibition. A remarkable circumstance in the history of this king Dor shall now be related. He was a powerful prince, assumed much state, and was always waited upon by young women of extraordinary beauty, a vast number of whom he entertained at his court. When, for recreation, he went about the fortress, he was drawn in his carriage by these damsels, which they could do with facility, as it was of a small size. They were devoted to his service, and performed every office that administered to his convenience or amusement. In his government he was not wanting in vigour, and he ruled with dignity and justice. The works of his castle, according to the report of the people of the country, were beyond example strong. He was, however, a vassal of Un-khan, who, as we have already stated, was known by the appellation of Prester John; but, influenced by pride, he rebelled against him. When this came to the knowledge of Prester John, he was exceedingly grieved,

respect to the latter monosyllable, whether it be corruptly written *gin* (for *giu*) or *cui* (for *ciu*), it is indubitably meant for the term *cheu*, *tcheou*, *giu*, or *ciu* (according to the mode of writing it with the different European alphabets), which denotes (as already observed) a city of the second order.

[1] The name of this prince, which in Ramusio's text, as well as in the Italian epitome, is written Dor, is in some Latin editions absurdly transformed to Darius. The former, it must be confessed, bears no resemblance to a Chinese, and but little to a Tartar word; yet, even on the supposition of the story being merely a popular legend with which our author was amused in the course of his travels through the country, the names of the actors ought not to be the less in harmony with the language of its inhabitants. I am therefore disposed to hazard a conjecture respecting it, that by some may be thought too bold, but which I am persuaded will appear most probable to those readers who are best acquainted with the histories of these people. It is known that, previously to the invasion of Jengiz-khan, the northern provinces of China were held in subjection by a race from Eastern Tartary, called Niuche, but whose dynasty received the appellation of Kin, from a term signifying "gold" in the Chinese language. "L'an 1118," says the historian of the Huns, "O-ko-ta fut proclamé empereur, et donna à sa dynastie le nom de Kin en Chinois, et d'Altoun dans la langue de ces peuples, c'est-à-dire, Or; c'est de-là que les Arabes les ont appellés Altoun-khans." (Tom. i. p. 208.) May not the prince here spoken of have belonged to this family of the Kin, who were the contemporaries of Un-khan; and may not the D'Or, or Doro, of our author be intended for a translation of the Chinese term? The word enters into the composition of many proper names, and is often rendered by its equivalent in European languages; as in the instance of "Kin-chan ou Montagne d'or."

being sensible that, from the strong situation of the castle, it would be in vain to march against it, or even to proceed to any act of hostility. Matters had remained some time in this state, when seven cavaliers belonging to his retinue presented themselves before him, and declared their resolution to attempt the seizure of king Dor's person, and to bring him alive to his majesty. To this they were encouraged by the promise of a large reward. They accordingly took their departure for the place of his residence, and feigning to have arrived from a distant country, made him an offer of their services. In his employment they so ably and diligently performed their duties that they gained the esteem of their new master, who showed them distinguished favour, insomuch that when he took the diversion of hunting, he always had them near his person. One day when the king was engaged in the chase, and had crossed a river which separated him from the rest of his party, who remained on the opposite side, these cavaliers perceived that the opportunity now presented itself of executing their design. They drew their swords, surrounded the king, and led him away by force towards the territory of Prester John, without its being possible for him to receive assistance from his own people. When they reached the court of that monarch, he gave orders for clothing his prisoner in the meanest apparel, and, with the view of humiliating him by the indignity, committed to him the charge of his herds. In this wretched condition he remained for two years, strict care being taken that he should not effect his escape. At the expiration of that period, Prester John caused him to be again brought before him, trembling from apprehension that they were going to put him to death. But on the contrary, Prester John, after a sharp and severe admonition, in which he warned him against suffering pride and arrogance to make him swerve from his allegiance in future, granted him a pardon, directed that he should be dressed in royal apparel, and sent him back to his principality with an honourable escort. From that time forward he always preserved his loyalty, and lived on amicable terms with Prester John. The foregoing is what was related to me on the subject of king Dor.[1]

[1] It will be observed that our author does not express himself with any degree of confidence as to the authenticity of this romantic adventure. If it was only an idle tale imposed upon him for an historical fact, it must have been the invention of Tartars rather than of Chinese, who would not have made a prince of Shan-si the vassal of a Tartar sovereign. On the contrary, it is asserted by Gaubil that their annals describe Un-

CHAPTER XXXII

OF THE VERY LARGE AND NOBLE RIVER CALLED THE KARA-MORAN

UPON leaving the fortress of Thai-gin, and travelling about twenty miles, you come to a river called the Kara-moran,[1] which is of such magnitude, both in respect to width and depth, that no solid bridge can be erected upon it. Its waters are discharged into the ocean, as shall hereafter be more particularly mentioned.[2] On its banks are many cities and castles, in which a number of trading people reside, who carry on an extensive commerce. The country bordering upon it produces ginger, and silk also in large quantities. Of birds the multitude is incredible, especially of pheasants,[3] which are sold at the rate of three for the value of a Venetian groat. Here likewise grows a species of large cane, in infinite abundance, some of a foot, and others a foot and a half (in circumference), which are employed by the inhabitants for a variety of useful purposes.[4]

khan himself as tributary to the sovereigns of the dynasty of Kin; and that the Chinese title of *vang*, or prince, was prefixed to his original title of *khan*, forming together Vang-khan, of which the Arabs made Ung-khan or Un-khan. [The account of his reception by Prester John is told with rather more detail in the Latin text published by the Paris Geographical Society.]

[1] This name (written Caromoran in the Latin, Carmoro in the early epitomes, and Cathametam in the Paris Latin), which signifies the Black River, is well known to be the Tartar appellation of that vast stream which, with a very winding course, traverses the whole of China, under the name of the Hoang-ho, or Yellow River; so called from the colour of its waters, impregnated as they are with yellow clay. It is at the same time not improbable that in the upper part of its course, through a different and perhaps mossy soil, its hue may equally justify the epithet of Black.

[2] Some of the rivers of Tartary discharge themselves into lakes, whilst others are lost in the sandy deserts.

[3] Frequent mention is made of these birds, at places in the vicinity of the Yellow River.

[4] The bamboo cane (*arundo bambos*), one of the most useful materials with which nature has furnished the inhabitants of warm climates, is known to be common in China. In the Mém. concern. les Chinois, tom. ii. p. 532, it is observed that the greater part of the houses in the province of Se-chuen are constructed of bamboos. The latitude of the part of the Kara-muran or Hoang-ho here spoken of is about 35°. Further northward the bamboo is not likely to flourish.

CHAPTER XXXIII

OF THE CITY OF KA-CHAN-FU

HAVING crossed this river and travelled three days' journey, you arrive at a city named Ka-chan-fu,[1] whose inhabitants are idolaters. They carry on a considerable traffic, and work at a variety of manufactures. The country produces in great abundance, silk, ginger, galangal,[2] spikenard, and many drugs that are nearly unknown in our part of the world. Here they weave gold tissues, as well as every other kind of silken cloth. We shall speak in the next place of the noble and celebrated city of Ken-zan-fu, in the kingdom of the same name.

CHAPTER XXXIV

OF THE CITY OF KEN-ZAN-FU

DEPARTING from Ka-chan-fu, and proceeding eight days' journey in a westerly direction, you continually meet with cities and commercial towns, and pass many gardens and cultivated grounds, with abundance of the mulberry or tree that contributes to the production of silk. The inhabitants in general worship idols, but there are also found here Nestorian Christians,[3] Turkomans,[4] and Saracens. The wild beasts of the country afford excellent sport, and a variety of birds also

[1] The name of Cacianfu, or Ka-chan-fu, which in the early Venice epitome is Cancianfu, and in the Basle, Cianfu (but which does not occur in the B.M. manuscript, nor in the early Latin edition), cannot be traced in Du Halde's map; nor does there appear any city of the first class (implied by the adjunct *fu*) between that part of the Hoang-ho and the capital of the province of Shen-si, towards which our author's route is here directed.

[2] Galanga, or galangal, well known in the *materia medica*, is the root of the Kæmpferia. By the Italian *spico* I suppose is meant spikenard (*Nardus Indica*).

[3] The province of Shen-si is understood to have been the principal seat of Christianity, when preached in this country, at an early period, by the Nestorians. Being the most western of the provinces that compose the empire of China, it was the easiest of access to those who travelled by land from Syria, and other countries bordering on the Mediterranean.

[4] By Turkomans we are not to understand the Tartars of the Desert, but merchants either from Turkomania of Asia Minor (the kingdom of the Seljuks of Rûm), or from Bokhâra, formerly the capital of Turkistạn, a place of considerable traffic and civilization.

are taken. At the end of those eight stages you arrive at the city of Ken-zan-fu,[1] which was anciently the capital of an extensive, noble, and powerful kingdom, the seat of many kings, highly descended and distinguished in arms.[2] At the present day it is governed by a son of the grand khan, named Mangalu, upon whom his father has conferred the sovereignty.[3] It is a country of great commerce, and eminent for its manufactures. Raw silk is produced in large quantities, and tissues of gold and every other kind of silk are woven there. At this place likewise they prepare every article necessary for the equipment of an army. All species of provisions are in abundance, and to be procured at a moderate price. The inhabitants in general worship idols, but there are some Christians, Turkomans, and Saracens.[4] In a plain, about five miles from the city, stands a beautiful palace belonging to king Mangalu, embellished with many fountains and rivulets, both within and on the outside of the buildings. There is also a fine park, surrounded by a high wall, with battlements, enclosing an extent of five miles, where all kinds of wild animals, both beasts and birds, are kept for sport. In its centre is this spacious palace, which, for symmetry and beauty, cannot be surpassed. It contains many halls and chambers, ornamented with paintings in gold and the finest azure, as well as with great profusion of marble. Mangalu, pursuing the footsteps of his father, governs his principality with strict equity, and is beloved by his people. He also takes much delight in hunting and hawking.

[1] However different the name of Ken-zan-fu may be from Si-ngan-fu, or Si-gan-fu (as it is more commonly written), circumstances show that the eminent city described in the text is meant for the capital of the province of Shen-si, which appears to be distant about nine stages from the passage of the Hoang-ho. The practice of changing the appellations (always significant) of important places, upon the accession of a new family, is matter of notoriety; and accordingly the several names of Kan-chug, Yun-ghing, Chang-gan, and Ngan-si, which under the dynasty of the Ming (1370) was reversed and made Si-ngan, are recorded as having at different periods belonged to this city.

[2] See Appendix II.

[3] In a list of the sons of Kublaï, given by De Guignes (Hist. gén. des Huns, liv. xvi. p. 189), we find the third, there named Mangkola, to have been governor of Shen-si, Se-chuen, and Tibet.

[4] " Les Mogols ou Yuen," says the younger De Guignes, " qui s'emparèrent du trône en 1279 et chassèrent les Song, amenèrent un grand nombre de Mussulmans. Ceux-ci furent très-nombreux jusqu'à la dynastie des Ming, qui commença à régner en 1368, après avoir détruit les Tartares."

CHAPTER XXXV

OF THE BOUNDARIES OF CATHAY AND MANJI

TRAVELLING westward three days from the residence of Mangalu, you still find towns and castles, whose inhabitants subsist by commerce and manufactures, and where there is an abundance of silk; but at the end of these three stages you enter upon a region of mountains and valleys, which lie within the province of Kun-kin.[1] This tract, however, has no want of inhabitants, who are worshippers of idols, and cultivate the earth. They live also by the chase, the land being much covered with woods. In these are found many wild beasts, such as lions (tigers), bears, lynxes, fallow deer, antelopes, stags, and many other animals, which are made to turn to good account. This region extends to the distance of twenty days' journey, during which the way lies entirely over mountains and through valleys and woods, but still interspersed with towns where travellers may find convenient accommodation. This journey of twenty days towards the west being performed, you arrive at a place called Ach-baluch Manji, which signifies, the white city [2] on the confines of Manji, where the country becomes level, and is very populous. The inhabitants live by trade and manual arts. Large quantities of ginger are produced here, which is conveyed through all the province of Cathay, with great advantage to the merchants.[3] The country yields wheat, rice, and other grain plentifully, and at a reasonable rate. This plain, thickly covered with

[1] The country to which our author's description here applies is evidently the province of Se-chuen, which lies south-westward from Si-nganfu, and is a mountainous region.

[2] It has been already noticed that *baligh* is a term used in Tartary for "city," and *ak*, in the dialects of Turkistan, is known to signify "white," which justifies our author's interpretation of the name; but why he should express it in the Tartar language, unless on the supposition of his having forgotten the Chinese appellation, does not appear. I confess, also, that with such imperfect lights I am unable to make any satisfactory conjecture with regard to its position; and this is the more to be regretted, as it would have enabled us to ascertain the north-western limits of Manji, or Southern China.

[3] It may be doubted whether the root here called ginger was not rather intended for that which we call China-root, and the Chinese *fu-lin* (smilax), produced in its greatest perfection in this province, and for which, as it was at that period little if at all known in European pharmacy, it might be found necessary to substitute a familiar term. "La vraye racine de Sina," says P. Martini, "se trouve seulement dans cette province; pour la sauvage, on la trouve par tout."—P. 79.

habitations, continues for two stages, after which you again come to high mountains, valleys, and forests. Travelling twenty days still further to the west, you continue to find the country inhabited, by people who worship idols, and subsist upon the produce of their soil, as well as that of the chase. Here also, besides the wild animals above enumerated, there are great numbers of that species which produces the musk.

CHAPTER XXXVI

OF THE PROVINCE OF SIN-DIN-FU, AND OF THE GREAT RIVER KIAN

HAVING travelled those twenty stages through a mountainous country, you reach a plain on the confines of Manji, where there is a district named Sin-din-fu, by which name also the large and noble city, its capital, formerly the seat of many rich and powerful kings, is called.[1] The circumference of the city is twenty miles; but at the present day it is divided in consequence of the following circumstances. The late old king had three sons; and it being his wish that each of them should reign after his death, he made a partition of the city amongst them, separating one part from the other by walls, although the whole continued to be surrounded by one general enclosure. These three brothers accordingly became kings, and each had for his portion a considerable tract of country, the territory of their father having been extensive and rich. But, upon its conquest by the grand khan, he destroyed these three princes, and possessed himself of their inheritance.[2]

The city is watered by many considerable streams, which, descending from the distant mountains, surround and pass

[1] This city, which in the Basle edition as well as in that of Ramusio is named Sin-din-fu, in the older Latin Syn-dy-fu, and in the early epitomes, Sindirifa, appears from the circumstances mentioned to be that now called Ching-tu-fu, situated on the western side of the province of Se-chuen, of which it is the capital. The western boundary of Manji, as has been observed, is not well known, but it is evident from the military operations of 1236 and 1238, that the Song, who then ruled it, were masters of this city of Ching-tu. When taken by the Mungals it is said (with no little exaggeration) that one million four hundred thousand persons were put to the sword.—Hist. gén. de la Chine, tom. ix. p. 219.

[2] The king here spoken of must have been a tributary either of the Song or of the Mungals, and might be one of those who received the Chinese title of Vang, and were more or less independent, according to the energy of the general government.

through it in a variety of directions. Some of these rivers are half a mile in width, others are two hundred paces, and very deep, over which are built several large and handsome stone bridges, eight paces in breadth, their length being greater or less according to the size of the stream. From one extremity to the other there is a row of marble pillars on each side, which support the roof; for here the bridges have very handsome roofs, constructed of wood, ornamented with paintings of a red colour, and covered with tiles. Throughout the whole length also there are neat apartments and shops, where all sorts of trades are carried on.[1] One of the buildings, larger than the rest, is occupied by the officers who collect the duties upon provisions and merchandise, and a toll from persons who pass the bridge. In this way, it is said, his majesty receives daily the sum of a hundred besants of gold.[2] These rivers, uniting their streams below the city, contribute to form the mighty river called the Kian,[3] whose course, before it discharges itself into the ocean, is equal to a hundred days' journey;[4] but of its properties occasion will be taken to speak in a subsequent part of this book.

On these rivers and in the parts adjacent are many towns and fortified places, and the vessels are numerous, in which large quantities of merchandise are transported to and from the city. The people of the province are idolaters. Departing from thence you travel five stages, partly along a plain, and partly through valleys, where you see many respectable

[1] This peculiarity of the bridges in Se-chuen is not noticed in the meagre accounts we have of that province, which all resolve themselves into the original information given by P. Martini, in his Atlas Sinensis (1655). The Latin edition of our author states, that the shops or booths were set up in the morning, and removed from the bridge at night.

[2] In the other versions, instead of a hundred, it is stated at a thousand besants (or sequins).

[3] The numerous streams by which the city of Ching-tu is surrounded, form their junction successively, and discharge their united waters into the great river Kiang, as is here described, but its distance from the latter is more considerable than the words of the text would lead us to suppose. In the Basle edition, indeed, the Kiang is said to pass through the city; " per medium hujus civitatis transit fluvius qui dicitur Quian-fu (Kiang-su); " [in the Paris Latin text the name of the river is Quingia-fu;] but besides that the nature of the river disproves the fact, the mistake is explained by the Italian reading of the same passage, in the early epitomes, where the expression is, " *per mezo* questa terra passa uno grande fiume," by which is to be understood, as *terra* is here distinguished from *città*, that it flowed through the *district*.

[4] In the Latin it is said to be ninety, and in the early Italian, seventy stages or days' journey. The distance from the city of Su-cheu-fu, which stands at the junction of the river that runs from Ching-tu, with the Kiang, is equal to about four-fifths of the breadth of China.

mansions, castles, and small towns. The inhabitants subsist by agriculture. In the city there are manufactures, particularly of very fine cloths and of crapes or gauzes.[1] This country, like the districts already mentioned, is infested with lions (tigers), bears, and other wild animals. At the end of these five days' journey you reach the desolated country of Thebeth.

CHAPTER XXXVII

OF THE PROVINCE OF THEBETH

THE province named Thebeth[2] was laid entirely waste at the time that Mangu-khan carried his arms into that country. To the distance of twenty days' journey you see numberless towns and castles in a state of ruin; and in consequence of the want of inhabitants, wild beasts, and especially tigers, have multiplied to such a degree that merchants and other travellers are exposed there to great danger during the night. They are not only under the necessity of carrying their provisions along with them, but are obliged, upon arriving at their halting places, to employ the utmost circumspection, and to take the following precautions, that their horses may not be devoured. In this region, and particularly in the neighbourhood of rivers, are found canes (bamboos) of the length of ten paces, three palms in circumference, and three palms also in the space between each knot or joint. Several of these, in their green state, the travellers tie together, and place them, when evening approaches, at a certain distance from their quarters, with a fire lighted around them, when, by the action of the heat, they burst with a tremendous explosion.[3] The noise is so loud as to be heard at the dis-

[1] This sentence is a continuation of the account of Sin-din-fu, and ought to have had place in an earlier part of the chapter. It shows the inartificial manner in which the work was composed.

[2] The name of Thebeth, Thibet, or Tibet, is sometimes confined to that country, on the northern side of the Himalaya mountains, which is under the immediate government of the Dalai lama and Panchin lama, and sometimes is made to embrace the whole of what is otherwise called Tangut, including the nations bordering on the provinces of Se-chuen and Shen-si, whom the Chinese term the Si-fan or Tu-fan. It appears to be of this eastern part, commencing at about five days' journey from the city of Ching-tu, that our author proceeds to speak.

[3] The very loud explosion of burning bamboos is well known to those who have witnessed the conflagration of a village or a bazaar, in countries where the buildings are of that material. What most resembles it is the irregular but incessant firing of arms of all descriptions during a night of public rejoicing, in England.

tance of two miles, which has the effect of terrifying the wild beasts and making them fly from the neighbourhood. The merchants also provide themselves with iron shackles, in order to fasten the legs of their horses, which would otherwise, when alarmed by the noise, break their halters and run away; and, from the neglect of this precaution, it has happened that many owners have lost their cattle. Thus you travel for twenty days through a desolated country, finding neither inns nor provisions, unless perhaps once in three or four days, when you take the opportunity of replenishing your stock of necessaries. At the end of that period you begin to discover a few castles and strong towns, built upon rocky heights, or upon the summits of mountains, and gradually enter an inhabited and cultivated district, where there is no longer any danger from beasts of prey.

A scandalous custom, which could only proceed from the blindness of idolatry, prevails amongst the people of these parts, who are disinclined to marry young women so long as they are in their virgin state, but require, on the contrary, that they should have had previous commerce with many of the other sex; and this, they assert, is pleasing to their deities, and that a woman who has not had the company of men is worthless.[1] Accordingly, upon the arrival of a caravan[2] of merchants, and as soon as they have set up their tents for the night, those mothers who have marriageable daughters conduct them to the place, and each, contending for a preference, entreats the strangers to accept of her daughter and enjoy her society so long as they remain in the neighbourhood.[3] Such as have most beauty to recommend them are of course chosen, and the others return home disappointed and chagrined, whilst the former continue with the travellers until the period of their

[1] P. Martini, speaking of the province of Yun-nan, which adjoins to that of Tibet, says of its inhabitants: "Personne n'epousoit de fille parmi eux, qu'un autre n'eust eu premièrement sa compagnie: ce sont les paroles de nostre auteur Chinois."—P. 196.

[2] This is the second instance in the course of the work of the employment of the word "caravan," taken from the Persian *karwân*, and adopted into most European languages. (See book ii. chap. xviii.) The Arabic term, which we might have thought more likely to have been introduced by the Crusaders, is *kâfilah*.

[3] Such is the depravity of human nature, that not only the moral but the instinctive principle may be subdued by the thirst of gain or the cravings of appetite. In his journey through Cooch Bahar on the road to Tibet, Turner observes that "nothing is more common than to see a mother dress up her child, and bring it to market, with no other hope, no other view than to enhance the price she may procure for it."—Embassy to Tibet, p. 11.

departure. They then restore them to their mothers, and never attempt to carry them away. It is expected, however, that the merchants should make them presents of trinkets, rings, or other complimentary tokens of regard, which the young women take home with them. When, afterwards, they are designed for marriage, they wear all these ornaments about the neck or other part of the body, and she who exhibits the greatest number of them is considered to have attracted the attention of the greatest number of men, and is on that account in the higher estimation with the young men who are looking out for wives; nor can she bring to her husband a more acceptable portion than a quantity of such gifts. At the solemnization of her nuptials, she accordingly makes a display of them to the assembly, and he regards them as a proof that their idols have rendered her lovely in the eyes of men. From thenceforward no person can dare to meddle with her who has become the wife of another, and this rule is never infringed. These idolatrous people are treacherous and cruel, and holding it no crime or turpitude to rob, are the greatest thieves in the world.[1] They subsist by the chase and by fowling, as well as upon the fruits of the earth.

Here are found the animals that produce the musk, and such is the quantity, that the scent of it is diffused over the whole country. Once in every month the secretion takes place, and it forms itself, as has already been said, into a sort of imposthume, or boil full of blood, near the navel; and the blood thus issuing, in consequence of excessive repletion, becomes the musk.[2] Throughout every part of this region the animal abounds, and the odour generally prevails. They are called *gudderi* in the language of the natives,[3] and are taken

[1] This thievish character may have belonged to the Si-fan, who border on the Chinese provinces (as it has belonged to most borderers), but travellers describe the manners of the people of Tibet Proper as particularly ingenuous and honest.

[2] With respect to the supposed lunar influence on the secretion of musk, Strahlenberg informs us that it is not at all times of the same strength, but "is best in summer, in rutting time, and at the full of the moon."—P. 340.

[3] The word *gudderi*, or any other approaching to it, is not to be found in the vocabularies we have of the languages of Tartary. In the northern parts, according to Bell, the animal is named *kaberda*, or *kabardyn* according to Strahlenberg; and Kirkpatrick, in his account of Nepaul, names it *kastoora*. It is not indeed improbable that *gudderi* or *gadderi* (as it is written in the Latin text) may be a corruption of the Persian word *kastûri*, which is the common term for the drug in every part of the East, and would be used by the Mahometan merchants even on the borders of China.

with dogs. These people use no coined money, nor even the paper money of the grand khan, but for their currency employ coral.[1] Their dress is homely, being of leather, undressed skins, or of canvas. They have a language peculiar to the province of Thebeth, which borders on Manji. This was formerly a country of so much importance as to be divided into eight kingdoms, containing many cities and castles. Its rivers, lakes, and mountains are numerous. In the rivers gold-dust is found in very large quantities.[2] Not only is the coral, before mentioned, used for money, but the women also wear it about their necks, and with it ornament their idols.[3] There are manufactures of camlet and of gold cloth, and many drugs are produced in the country that have not been brought to ours. These people are necromancers, and by their infernal art perform the most extraordinary and delusive enchantments that were ever seen or heard of. They cause tempests to arise, accompanied with flashes of lightning and thunderbolts, and produce many other miraculous effects. They are altogether an ill-conditioned race. They have dogs of the size of asses,[4] strong enough to hunt all sorts of wild beasts, par-

[1] It may not appear likely that the valuable red coral produced in the Mediterranean should have been carried to the borders of China in sufficient quantity to be there made use of as currency; nor is it a substance so readily divisible as to be convenient for the purpose; but of its general use in the way of ornament ample proof is furnished by Tavernier. It is remarkable that to the present day the people of Tibet have no coinage of their own, but are supplied with a currency by their neighbours of Nepâl.

[2] Several of the streams which take their rise in the eastern parts of Tibet, and by their junctions form the great rivers of China, yield much gold, which is collected from their beds in grains or small lumps. This is principally remarked of the Kin-sha-kiang. "De tant de rivières qu'on voit sur la carte," says Du Halde, "on ne peut dire quelles sont celles qui fournissent tout l'or qui se transporte à la Chine. . . . Il faut qu'on en trouve dans les sables de plusieurs de ces rivières: il est certain que la grande rivière Kin-cha-kiang qui entre dans la province d'Yunnan, en charie beaucoup dans son sable, car son nom signifie, fleuve à sable d'or." (Tom. iv. p. 470.) "Les Tou-fan, appellés Nan-mo, ont une rivière qui porte le nom de Ly-nieou, dans laquelle il se trouve beaucoup d'or."—Mém. conc. les Chinois, tom. xiv. p. 183.

[3] In describing the manners of a certain people in the Ava or Birmah country, Dr. F. Buchanan observes that "some of the women wore rich strings of coral round their necks."—Syme's Embassy, p. 465.

[4] This may appear to be an exaggeration, but other travellers describe the dogs of Tibet as of an uncommon size. "On the left," says Turner, "was a row of wooden cages, containing a number of huge dogs, tremendously fierce, strong, and noisy. They were natives of Tibet; and whether savage by nature, or soured by confinement, they were so impetuously furious, that it was unsafe, unless the keepers were near, even to approach their dens." And in another place, "The instant I entered the gate, to my astonishment, up started a huge dog, big enough, if his

ticularly the wild oxen, which are called *beyamini*,[1] and are extremely large and fierce. Some of the best laner falcons are bred here, and also sakers, very swift of flight, and the natives have good sport with them. This province of Thebeth is subject to the grand khan, as well as all the other kingdoms and provinces that have been mentioned. Next to this is the province of Kaindu.

CHAPTER XXXVIII

OF THE PROVINCE OF KAIN-DU

KAIN-DU is a western province, which was formerly subject to its own princes; but, since it has been brought under the dominion of the grand khan, it is ruled by the governors whom he appoints. We are not to understand, however, that it is situated in the western part (of Asia), but only that it lies westward with respect to our course from the north-eastern quarter. Its inhabitants are idolaters. It contains many cities and castles, and the capital city, standing at the commencement of the province, is likewise named Kain-du.[2] Near to it there is a large lake of salt water, in which are found abundance of pearls, of a white colour, but not round.[3]

courage had been equal to his size, to fight a lion." (Embassy to Tibet, pp. 155—215.) Under this sanction our author must stand excused of hyperbole, although some other accounts do not convey an idea of the same magnitude. "One of them," says Captain Raper, "was a remarkably fine animal, as large as a good-sized Newfoundland dog, with very long hair and a head resembling a mastiff's. His tail was of an amazing length, like the brush of a fox, and curled half-way over his back. He was however so fierce that he would allow no stranger to approach him."—Asiat. Res. vol. xi. p. 529.

[1] For an account of this animal, the *bos grunniens*, see before, p. 136, note [2], p. 137, note [1]. Of the word *beyamini* (which does not occur either in the Latin or the Italian epitomes) I can discover no trace. It may be a corruption of *brahmini*. The animal is said to be called *yak* in Tartary, *chowri* in Tibet, and *suragâi* in Hindustan.

[2] The city that in point of situation and other circumstances appears to answer best to this description of Kain-du, is Yung-ning-tu, which stands on the western side of the Ya-long-kiang, in about latitude 28°; although from some resemblance of sound we might rather suppose it to be Li-kiang-tu, a city at no great distance from the former, but standing on the western side of the Kin-sha-kiang, above its junction with the former river.

[3] I do not find it elsewhere asserted that the lake near Yung-ning-tu yields pearls, but they are enumerated by Martini amongst the valuable productions of that part of China: "On tire encore de cette province des rubis, des saphirs, des agathes . . . avec plusieurs pierres précieuses, et des perles." (P. 194.) The fishery of pearls in a river of Eastern Tartary is noticed by many writers.

So great indeed is the quantity, that, if his majesty permitted every individual to search for them, their value would become trifling; but the fishery is prohibited to all who do not obtain his licence. A mountain in the neighbourhood yields the turquoise stone, the mines of which cannot be worked without the same permission.

The inhabitants of this district are in the shameful and odious habit of considering it no mark of disgrace that those who travel through the country should have connexion with their wives, daughters, or sisters; but, on the contrary, when strangers arrive, each householder endeavours to conduct one of them home with him, and, giving up all the females of the family to him, leaves him in the situation of master of the house, and takes his departure. And while the stranger is in the house, he places a signal at the window, as his hat or some other thing; and as long as this signal is seen in the house, the husband remains absent. And this custom prevails throughout that province. This they do in honour of their idols, believing that by such acts of kindness and hospitality to travellers a blessing is obtained, and that they shall be rewarded with a plentiful supply of the fruits of the earth.

The money or currency they make use of is thus prepared. Their gold is formed into small rods, and (being cut into certain lengths) passes according to its weight, without any stamp.[1] This is their greater money: the smaller is of the following description. In this country there are salt-springs, from which they manufacture salt by boiling it in small pans.[2] When the water has boiled for an hour, it becomes a kind of paste, which is formed into cakes of the value of twopence each. These, which are flat on the lower, and convex on the upper side, are placed upon hot tiles, near a fire, in order to dry and harden. On this latter species of money the stamp of the grand khan is impressed, and it cannot be prepared by

[1] This substitute for coin resembles the *larin* of the Gulf of Persia, but with the difference, that the latter bears an imperfect stamp. In those districts of Sumatra where gold-dust is procured, commodities of all kinds, even so low as the value of a single grain, are purchased with it. The forming the metal into rods, and cutting off pieces as they are wanted for currency, may be considered as one step towards a coinage. The Chinese of Canton cut the Spanish dollar in the same manner to make up their fractional payments.

[2] P. Martini, in describing the town of Yao-gan, in the same province, says: "Près de la ville il y a un puits d'eau salée; on en puise pour faire du sel, qui est très-blanc, dont on se sert dans tout le pays, et s'appelle Pe-yen-cing, c'est-à-dire le puits du sel blanc." (P. 204.) The name of Pe-yen-cing appears in Du Halde's map of Yun-nan.

any other than his own officers. Eighty of the cakes are made to pass for a saggio of gold.[1] But when these are carried by the traders amongst the inhabitants of the mountains and other parts little frequented, they obtain a saggio of gold for sixty, fifty, or even forty of the salt cakes, in proportion as they find the natives less civilized, further removed from the towns, and more accustomed to remain on the same spot; inasmuch as people so circumstanced cannot always have a market for their gold, musk, and other commodities. And yet even at this rate it answers well to them who collect the gold-dust from the beds of the rivers, as has been mentioned. The same merchants travel in like manner through the mountainous and other parts of the province of Thebeth, last spoken of, where the money of salt has equal currency. Their profits are considerable, because these country people consume the salt with their food, and regard it as an indispensable necessary; whereas the inhabitants of the cities use for the same purpose only the broken fragments of the cakes, putting the whole cakes into circulation as money. Here also the animals called *gudderi*, which yield the musk, are taken in great numbers, and the article is proportionably abundant.[2] Many fish, of good kinds, are caught in the lake. In the country are found tigers, bears, deer, stags, and antelopes. There are numerous birds also, of various sorts. The wine is not made from grapes, but from wheat and rice, with a mixture of spices, which is an excellent beverage.

This province likewise produces cloves. The tree is small; the branches and leaves resemble those of the laurel, but are somewhat longer and narrower. Its flowers are white and small, as are the cloves themselves, but as they ripen they become dark-coloured. Ginger grows there and also cassia in abundance, besides many other drugs, of which no quantity is ever brought to Europe.[3] Upon leaving the city of Kain-du,

[1] The saggio of Venice was the sixth part of an ounce, and consequently the cake of salt was in value the four hundred and eightieth part of an ounce of gold, which, at the price of four pounds sterling, is exactly twopence for the value of each cake: a coincidence that could hardly have been expected. Its precision, however, must depend on a comparison between the English pence and Venetian denari of that day.

[2] The western parts of China and eastern of Tibet, or the country of the Si-fan, are those in which the best musk is found. Martini, in his Atlas Sinensis, speaks of it as the production of various places in Yunnan.

[3] This appears to be the most unqualified error that has hitherto occurred in the course of the work, as cloves (*garofali*) and cassia or cinnamon (*canella*) certainly do not grow in that part of the world, nor

the journey is fifteen[1] days to the opposite boundary of the province; in the course of which you meet with respectable habitations, many fortified posts, and also places adapted to hunting and fowling. The inhabitants follow the customs and manners that have already been described. At the end of these fifteen days, you come to the great river Brius, which bounds the province, and in which are found large quantities of gold-dust.[2] It discharges itself into the ocean. We shall now leave this river, as nothing further that is worthy of observation presents itself, and shall proceed to speak of the province of Karaian.

CHAPTER XXXIX

OF THE GREAT PROVINCE OF KARAIAN, AND OF YACHI ITS PRINCIPAL CITY

HAVING passed the river above mentioned, you enter the province of Karaian, which is of such extent as to be divided into seven governments.[3] It is situated towards the west; the

anywhere beyond the tropics. The only manner in which it is possible to account for an assertion so contrary to fact, is by supposing that a detached memorandum of what our author had observed in the spice islands (which there is great probability of his having visited whilst in the service of the emperor) has been introduced in a description where it is entirely irrelevant.

[1] [Some of the early texts have ten instead of fifteen.]

[2] However unlike a Chinese or Tartar word, most of the editions agree in the orthography of the name of Brius given to this river, which seems to be intended for the Kin-sha-kiang, or "river with the golden sands." But if, on the other hand, Li-kiang-tu, which is situated on its south-western side, should be considered as the Kain-du of the text, it will follow that the Brius is either the Lan-tsan-kiang, or the Nû-kiang, presumed to be the Irabatty of the kingdom of Ava. "The river Nou-kian," says Major Rennell, "little if at all inferior to the Ganges, runs to the south, through that angle of Yunan which approaches nearest to Bengal." (Memoir, 3d edit. p. 295.) [In the Paris Latin text it is Ligays; and in the early Italian, Brunis.]

[3] Karaian is generally understood to be the province of Yun-nan, or rather its north-western part, which is bounded, in great measure, by the Kin-sha-kiang. In the "Account of an Embassy to Ava," we find mention made of a race of people whose name corresponds with that of Karaian, and who may have been prisoners of war brought from the neighbouring country of Yun-nan, with which the people of Ava were often in hostility, and distributed in the latter as colonists. "He told me," says Colonel Symes, speaking of a respectable Italian missionary, "of a singular description of people called Carayners, or Carianers, that inhabit different parts of the country. . . . He represented them as a simple, innocent race, speaking a language distinct from that of the

inhabitants are idolaters; and it is subject to the dominion of the grand khan, who has constituted as its king his son named Cen-Temur, a rich, magnificent, and powerful prince, endowed with consummate wisdom and virtue, and by whom the kingdom is ruled with great justice.[1] In travelling from this river five days' journey, in a westerly direction, you pass through a country fully inhabited, and see many castles. The inhabitants live upon flesh meat and upon the fruits of the earth. Their language is peculiar to themselves, and is difficult to be acquired. The best horses are bred in this province.[2] At the end of these five days you arrive at its capital city, which is named Yachi, and is large and noble.[3] In it are found merchants and artisans, with a mixed population, consisting of (the native) idolaters, Nestorian Christians, and Saracens or Mahometans; but the first is the most numerous class. The land is fertile in rice and wheat. The people, however, do not use wheaten bread, which they esteem unwholesome, but eat rice; and of the other grain, with the addition of spices, they make wine, which is clear, light-coloured, and most pleasant to the taste.[4] For money they employ the white porcelain

Birmans, and entertaining rude notions of religion. They lead quite a pastoral life, and are the most industrious subjects of the state. . . . Agriculture, the care of cattle, and rearing poultry is almost their only occupation. A great part of the provisions used in the country is raised by the Carianers, and they particularly excel in gardening." (Pp. 207—467.) By Dr. F. Buchanan the name is written Karayn; and he speaks also of the Ka-kiayn, "a wild people on the frontiers of China."—Asiat. Res. vol. vi. p. 228.

[1] This prince is named in the B.M. and Berlin manuscripts, Gusen-temur; in the Basle edition, Esen-temur; and in the Italian epitomes, Hensen-temur. In the Tables Chronologiques of De Guignes he is simply called Timour-khan; but one of his successors (a nephew) appears in the same list by the name of Yeson-timour, which, whether more or less correct in its orthography than any of the preceding, is evidently intended for the same appellation. He was, however, the grandson, not the son of Kublaï, whom he succeeded in consequence of the premature death of his father Chingis.

[2] "Ce pays," says P. Martini, "produit de très-bons chevaux, de basse taille pour la pluspart, mais forts et hardis." (P. 196.) This is probably the same breed as the *tangun* or *tanyan* horses of Lower Tibet, carried from thence for sale to Hindustan. The people of Bûtan informed Major Rennell that they brought their *tanyans* thirty-five days' journey to the frontier.

[3] The present capital of the province of Yun-nan is a city of the same name; but there appears reason to conclude that, although the Karaian of our author be a part of that province, its city of Jaci, or Yachi, was not Yun-nan-fu, but Tali-fu, now considered as the second in rank. This, as we are informed by P. Martini, was named Ye-chu by the prince who founded it, and Yao-cheu by a subsequent dynasty; whilst the name of Tali was given to it by one of the Yuen or family of Kublaï.

[4] Our author, who seems to have been of a sociable disposition, misses

shell, found in the sea, and these they also wear as ornaments about their necks.[1] Eighty of the shells are equal in value to a saggio of silver or two Venetian groats, and eight saggi of good silver, to one of pure gold.[2] In this country also there are salt-springs, from which all the salt used by the inhabitants is procured. The duty levied on this salt produces a large revenue to the king.

The natives do not consider it as an injury done to them, when others have connexion with their wives, provided the act be voluntary on the woman's part. Here there is a lake nearly a hundred miles in circuit, in which great quantities of various kinds of fish are caught; some of them being of a large size. The people are accustomed to eat the undressed flesh of fowls, sheep, oxen, and buffaloes, but cured in the following manner. They cut the meat into very small particles, and then put it into a pickle of salt, with the addition of

no opportunity of praising the good qualities of this liquor; but modern travellers, from prejudices perhaps, do not speak of it in such advantageous terms. It is a kind of beer rather than of wine.

[1] These are the well-known cowries (*kari*) of Bengal, called by our naturalists *Cypræa monetæ*, which in former times may have found their way, through the province of Silhet, to the countries bordering on China, and were probably current in Yun-nan before its mountaineers were brought under regular subjection, and incorporated with the empire, which was a difficult and tedious measure of policy, chiefly effected by transplanting colonies of Chinese from the interior. "In 1764," says Major Rennell, "I was told that Silhet (an inland province to the north-east of Bengal) produced cowries, and that they were dug up. This, of course, I disbelieved; but when I was there in 1767 and 1768, I found no other currency of any kind in the country; and upon an occasion when an increase in the revenue of the province was enforced, several boat-loads (not less than fifty tons each) were collected and sent down the Burrampooter, to Dacca. Their accumulation was probably the consequence of Silhet being, at that period, the most remote district in which they passed current, and from whence they could not find a way out but by returning to Bengal." It is not uncommon to suppose that this genus of shells, called *porcellana*, derives its appellation from the variegated appearance of its polished coat, resembling the glazed earthenware or porcelain of China; but the early use of the word by our author renders it more likely that the shell having already obtained the name of *porcellana* (a diminutive of *porco*), on account of the gibbous form of its back, the foreign ware was subsequently called porcelain in Europe, from its possessing some of the most beautiful qualities of the shell.

[2] According to this estimation, if the numbers be correct, the value of the cowries must have been enormously increased by their carriage from Bengal to the frontiers of China. Their average price in the bazaar of Calcutta is said to be about five thousand for a rupee, which may be considered as equal to three saggi of silver; and if sold at eighty for the saggio, the profit would consequently be at the rate of five thousand for two hundred and forty, or more than twenty for one. Perhaps, therefore, instead of eighty, we should read eight hundred cowries to the saggio, which would still leave a profit of cent. per cent.

several of their spices. It is thus prepared for persons of the higher class, but the poorer sort only steep it, after mincing, in a sauce of garlic, and then eat it as if it were dressed.

CHAPTER XL

OF THE PROVINCE NAMED KARAZAN

LEAVING the city of Yachi, and travelling ten days in a westerly direction, you reach the province of Karazan, which is also the name of its chief city.[1] The inhabitants are idolaters. The country belongs to the dominion of the grand khan, and the royal functions are exercised by his son, named Kogatin.[2] Gold is found in the rivers, both in small particles and in lumps; and there are also veins of it in the mountains. In consequence of the large quantity obtained, they give a saggio of gold for six saggi of silver. They likewise use the before-mentioned porcelain shells in currency; which, however, are not found in this part of the world, but are brought from India. As I have said before, these people never take virgins for their wives.

Here are seen huge serpents, ten paces in length, and ten spans in the girt of the body. At the fore part, near the head, they have two short legs, having three claws like those of a tiger, with eyes larger than a fourpenny loaf (*pane da quattro denari*) and very glaring. The jaws are wide enough to swallow a man, the teeth are large and sharp, and their whole appearance is so formidable, that neither man, nor any kind of animal, can approach them without terror.[3] Others are met with of a

[1] This name of Karazan, which a Chinese might be supposed to pronounce Ka-la-shan, seems to be only that of another portion of the province of Yun-nan; as the places mentioned in the subsequent chapter unquestionably are: but so imperfect is our information respecting this part of the country, that the means are wanting by which its particular situation might be ascertained. It should be remarked, at the same time, that the name of Karazan, as distinct from that of Karaian, does not occur either in the Latin or in the early epitomes; all the circumstances related in this chapter being there considered as applying to the last-mentioned province or district.

[2] The name of Kogatin does not appear in the list of the legitimate sons of Kublaï; but he had many others. The orthography, however, is more than usually uncertain. In the B.M. and Berlin manuscripts the name is written Cogaam; in the old Latin edition it is Cogatuy; in the Basle, Cogracam (Cogra-khan); and in the early Italian epitomes, Cocagio.

[3] This distorted account of the alligator or crocodile is less creditable to our author's fidelity than any other of his natural history descriptions, although generally more or less defective.

smaller size, being eight, six, or five paces long; and the following method is used for taking them. In the day-time, by reason of the great heat, they lurk in caverns, from whence, at night, they issue to seek their food, and whatever beast they meet with and can lay hold of, whether tiger, wolf, or any other, they devour; after which they drag themselves towards some lake, spring of water, or river, in order to drink. By their motion in this way along the shore, and their vast weight, they make a deep impression, as if a heavy beam had been drawn along the sands. Those whose employment it is to hunt them observe the track by which they are most frequently accustomed to go, and fix into the ground several pieces of wood, armed with sharp iron spikes, which they cover with the sand in such a manner as not to be perceptible. When therefore the animals make their way towards the places they usually haunt, they are wounded by these instruments, and speedily killed.[1] The crows, as soon as they perceive them to be dead, set up their scream; and this serves as a signal to the hunters, who advance to the spot, and proceed to separate the skin from the flesh, taking care immediately to secure the gall, which is most highly esteemed in medicine. In cases of the bite of a mad dog, a pennyweight of it, dissolved in wine, is administered. It is also useful in accelerating parturition, when the labour pains of women have come on. A small quantity of it being applied to carbuncles, pustules, or other eruptions on the body, they are presently dispersed; and it is efficacious in many other complaints. The flesh also of the animal is sold at a dear rate, being thought to have a higher flavour than other kinds of meat, and by all persons it is esteemed a delicacy.[2] In this province the horses are of a large size, and whilst young, are carried for sale to India. It is the practice to deprive them of one joint of the tail, in order to prevent them from lashing it from side to side, and to occasion its remaining pendent; as the whisking it about, in riding,

[1] The natives of India are particularly ingenious in their contrivances for destroying beasts of prey, particularly the tiger, which is sometimes made to fall upon sharp-pointed stakes, after walking up an inclined plane; but the alligator is most commonly taken in the water, with a large hook.

[2] The flesh of the guana or inguana, an animal intermediate in size between the lizard and the alligator, I have known to be eaten both by Chinese and Europeans, and by the former at least to be considered as a delicacy. I cannot assert the same of the alligator, but in a book of Natural History I read that "the Africans and Indians eat its flesh, which is white, and of a kind of perfumed (musky) flavour."

appears to them a vile habit.[1] These people ride with long stirrups, as the French do in our part of the world; whereas the Tartars, and almost all other people, wear them short, for the more conveniently using the bow; as they rise in their stirrups above the horse, when they shoot their arrows. They have complete armour of buffalo-leather, and carry lances, shields, and cross-bows. All their arrows are poisoned. I was assured, as a certain fact, that many persons, and especially those who harbour bad designs, always carry poison about them, with the intention of swallowing it, in the event of their being apprehended for any delinquency, and exposed to the torture, that, rather than suffer it, they may effect their own destruction. But their rulers, who are aware of this practice, are always provided with the dung of dogs, which they oblige the accused to swallow immediately after, as it occasions their vomiting up the poison,[2] and thus an antidote is ready against the arts of these wretches. Before the time of their becoming subject to the dominion of the grand khan, these people were addicted to the following brutal custom. When any stranger of superior quality, who united personal beauty with distinguished valour, happened to take up his abode at the house of one of them, he was murdered during the night; not for the sake of his money, but in order that the spirit of the deceased, endowed with his accomplishments and intelligence, might remain with the family, and that through the efficacy of such an acquisition, all their concerns might prosper. Accordingly the individual was accounted fortunate who possessed in this manner the soul of any noble personage; and many lost their lives in consequence. But from the time of his majesty's beginning to rule the country, he has taken measures for suppressing the horrid practice, and from the effect of severe punishments that have been inflicted, it has ceased to exist.

[1] It appears from hence that the practice of docking the tails of horses, by separating one or more of the vertebræ, which has become so common in England, existed many hundred years ago amongst the people of Yunnan, in the remotest part of China.

[2] Such might have been the vulgar belief respecting the substance employed as an emetic on these occasions, although perhaps with as little foundation as the idea entertained by the common people in England that ipecacuanha is the powder of human bones.

CHAPTER XLI

OF THE PROVINCE OF KARDANDAN AND THE CITY OF VOCHANG

PROCEEDING five days' journey in a westerly direction from Karazan, you enter the province of Kardandan, belonging to the dominion of the grand khan, and of which the principal city is named Vochang.[1] The currency of this country is gold by weight, and also the porcelain shells. An ounce of gold is exchanged for five ounces of silver, and a saggio of gold for five saggi of silver; there being no silver mines in this country, but much gold; and consequently the merchants who import silver obtain a large profit. Both the men and the women of this province have the custom of covering their teeth with thin plates of gold, which are fitted with great nicety to the shape of the teeth, and remain on them continually. The men also form dark stripes or bands round their arms and legs, by puncturing them in the following manner. They have five needles joined together, which they press into the flesh until blood is drawn; and they then rub the punctures with a black colouring matter, which leaves an indelible mark. To bear these dark stripes is considered as an ornamental and honourable distinction.[2] They pay little attention to anything but horsemanship, the sports of the chase, and whatever belongs to

[1] What is here named the province of Kardandan, is in the B.M. and Berlin manuscripts, and old Latin edition, written Ardandam, in the Basle, Arcladam, and in the epitomes Caridi; none of which can be discovered in Du Halde's map; but from the name of the chief city, which immediately follows, it is evident that the places spoken of are still within the limits of the modern province of Yun-nan. The name, indeed, of Vochang (or Vociam in the old Italian orthography), would have been equally unascertainable with that of the province, but that we are assisted in this instance by the readings of some of the other versions. In the early Latin edition the word in Uncian, in the Basle, Unchiam, and in the early edition of Venice, Nocian, which point out the place to be the city of Yung-chang, in the western part of Yun-nan.

[2] " D'autres se marquent diverses figures sur leur visage," says Martini, speaking of the inhabitants of Yung-chang, " le perçant avec une aiguille, et appliquant du noir, comme plusieurs Indiens ont accoustumé de faire." Accounts of this practice of tatooing have been rendered familiar to us by the voyages to the South Sea islands; but it prevails also amongst the Birmah people of the kingdom of Ava, immediately contiguous to Yun-nan. The custom is noticed by the old writers, and confirmed by the testimony of Colonel Symes, who says: " They (the Birmans) tatoo their thighs and arms into various fantastic shapes and figures, which they believe operate as a charm against the weapons of their enemies."—Embassy to Ava, p. 312.

the use of arms and a military life; leaving the entire management of their domestic concerns to their wives, who are assisted in their duties by slaves, either purchased or made prisoners in war.

These people have the following singular usage. As soon as a woman has been delivered of a child, and, rising from her bed, has washed and swathed the infant, her husband immediately takes the place she has left, has the child laid beside him, and nurses it for forty days. In the meantime, the friends and relations of the family pay to him their visits of congratulation; whilst the woman attends to the business of the house, carries victuals and drink to the husband in his bed, and suckles the infant at his side. These people eat their meat raw, or prepared in the manner that has been described, and along with it eat rice. Their wine is manufactured from rice, with a mixture of spices, and is a good beverage.

In this district they have neither temples nor idols, but pay their worship to the elder or ancestor of the family, from whom, they say, as they derive their existence, so to him they are indebted for all that they possess.[1] They have no knowledge of any kind of writing, nor is this to be wondered at, considering the rude nature of the country, which is a mountainous tract, covered with the thickest forests. During the summer season, the atmosphere is so gloomy and unwholesome, that merchants and other strangers are obliged to leave the district, in order to escape from death.[2] When the natives have

[1] This appears to have reference to the extraordinary respect known to be paid by the Chinese to their parents, or to the veneration, approaching to an idolatrous worship, in which they hold the manes of their ancestors—a superstition not only unconnected with the doctrines of the two prevailing sects, but religiously observed by those who hold the adoration of images in abhorrence. It seems probable that instead of "il piu vecchio di casa," or according to the epitome, "lo mazor de la casa," "the eldest person of the family," our author meant "the common ancestor;" for although the several descendants might subsist upon the patriarchal bounty of the former, they cannot be understood to have derived their possessions from him during his lifetime.

[2] Districts lying near the base of great ranges of mountains, and especially within the tropical latitudes, are always found to be unhealthy. "At the foot of the Bootan mountains," says Turner, "a plain extends for about thirty miles in breadth, choked, rather than clothed, with the most luxuriant vegetation. The exhalations necessarily arising from the multitude of springs which the vicinity of the mountains produces, are collected and confined by these almost impervious woods, and generate an atmosphere through which no traveller ever passed with impunity." (Embassy, p. 21.) This pestilential quality of the air extends westward, through what is called the Morung country, and by analogy may be supposed to prevail on the eastern side also, the Yun-nan moun-

transactions of business with each other, which require them to execute any obligation for the amount of a debt or credit, their chief takes a square piece of wood, and divides it in two. Notches are then cut on it, denoting the sum in question, and each party receives one of the corresponding pieces, as is practised in respect to our tallies. Upon the expiration of the term, and payment made by the debtor, the creditor delivers up his counterpart, and both remain satisfied.

Neither in this province, nor in the cities of Kaindu, Vochang, or Yachi, are to be found persons professing the art of physic. When a person of consequence is attacked with a disorder, his family send for those sorcerers who offer sacrifices to the idols, to whom the sick person gives an account of the nature of his complaint. The sorcerers thereupon give directions for the attendance of persons who perform on a variety of loud instruments, in order that they may dance and sing hymns in honour and praise of their idols; and which they continue to do, until the evil spirit has taken possession of one of them, when their musical exertions cease. They then inquire of the person so possessed the cause of the man's indisposition, and the means that should be used for effecting his cure. The evil spirit answers by the mouth of him into whose body he has entered, that the sickness has been occasioned by an offence given to a certain deity. Upon which the sorcerers address their prayers to that deity, beseeching him to pardon the sinner, on the condition that when cured he shall offer a sacrifice of his own blood. But if the demon perceives that there is no prospect of a recovery, he pronounces the deity to be so grievously offended that no sacrifice can appease him. If, on the contrary, he judges that a cure is likely to take place, he requires that an offering be made of so many sheep with black heads; that so many sorcerers, with their wives, be assembled, and that the sacrifice be performed by their hands; by which means, he says, the favour of the deity may be conciliated. The relations comply immediately with all that has been demanded, the sheep are slain, their blood is sprinkled towards the heavens, the sorcerers (male and female) light up and perfume with incense the whole house of the sick person, making a smoke with wood of aloes. They cast into the air the water in which the flesh has been seethed, together with some

tains being of great height, whilst the great Nu-kiang, said to be navigable between that province and Ava, must flow chiefly through a plain and comparatively low country.

of the liquor brewed with spices; and then laugh, sing, and dance about, with the idea of doing honour to their idol or divinity. They next inquire of the demoniac whether, by the sacrifice that has been made, the idol is satisfied, or if it is his command that another be yet performed. When the answer is, that the propitiation has been satisfactory, the sorcerers of both sexes, who had not ceased their songs, thereupon seat themselves at the table, and proceed to feast on the meat that had been offered in sacrifice, and to drink the spiced liquor, of which a libation had been made, with signs of great hilarity. Having finished their meal, and received their fees, they return to their homes; and if, through God's providence, the patient recovers, they attribute his cure to the idol for whom the sacrifice was performed; but if he happens to die, they then declare that the rites had been rendered ineffective by those who dressed the victuals having presumed to taste them before the deity's portion had been presented to him. It must be understood that ceremonies of this kind are not practised upon the illness of every individual, but only perhaps once or twice in the course of a month, for noble or wealthy personages. They are common, however, to all the idolatrous inhabitants of the whole provinces of Cathay and Manji, amongst whom a physician is a rare character. And thus do the demons sport with the blindness of these deluded and wretched people.[1]

CHAPTER XLII

OF THE MANNER IN WHICH THE GRAND KHAN EFFECTED THE CONQUEST OF THE KINGDOM OF MIEN AND BANGALA

BEFORE we proceed further (in describing the country), we shall speak of a memorable battle that was fought in this kingdom of Vochang (Unchang, or Yun-chang). It happened that in the year 1272 the grand khan sent an army into the countries of Vochang and Karazan, for their protection and defence against any attack that foreigners might attempt to make;[2] for at this period he had not as yet appointed his own

[1] The sorcerers or wizards here spoken of are evidently the *shamans* or juggling priests of Fo, who are met with chiefly in the less civilized regions of Tartary, but who probably find their way into all parts of the Chinese empire.

[2] This date of 1272 appears not only in Ramusio's text, but in that of the Berlin manuscript and of the older Latin edition; whilst in the Basle copy (followed by Müller) it is 1282. Some countenance is given to the latter date by a passage in L'Histoire gén. de la Chine, tom. ix. p. 411.

sons to the governments, which it was afterwards his policy to do; as in the instance of Cen-temur, for whom those places were erected into a principality. When the king of Mien[1] and Bangala,[2] in India, who was powerful in the number of his subjects, in extent of territory, and in wealth, heard that an army of Tartars had arrived at Vochang, he took the resolution of advancing immediately to attack it, in order that by its destruction the grand khan should be deterred from again attempting to station a force upon the borders of his dominions. For this purpose he assembled a very large army, including a multitude of elephants (an animal with which his country abounds), upon whose backs were placed battlements or castles, of wood, capable of containing to the number of twelve or sixteen in each. With these, and a numerous army of horse and foot, he took the road to Vochang, where the grand khan's army lay, and encamping at no great distance from it, intended to give his troops a few days of rest. As soon as the approach of the king of Mien, with so great a force, was known to Nestardín,[3] who commanded the troops of the grand khan, although a brave and able officer, he felt much alarmed, not having under his orders more than twelve thousand men (veterans, indeed, and valiant soldiers); whereas the enemy had sixty thousand, besides the elephants armed as has been described. He did not, however, betray any sign of apprehension, but descending into the plain of Vochang,[4] took a position in which his flank was covered by a thick wood of large trees, whither, in case of a furious charge by the elephants, which his troops might not be able to sustain, they could retire,

[1] By P. Gaubil (or his commentator, P. Souciet), De Guignes, Grosier and D'Anville, Mien has been considered as the name of the country of Pegu, but it is plainly meant for the Birmah country, or, as we usually term it, the kingdom of Ava, which nearly borders on the province of Yun-nan, whilst the other lies far to the southward, and is unconnected with any part of the Chinese territory. The name by which the Birmahs call their own country is *Myam-ma ;* by the Chinese writers it is named *Mien-tien.*

[2] In the Basle edition the words are, "rex Mien et rex Bangala," implying two confederated sovereigns, but the whole context shows that only one personage is intended, who might at that period have styled himself king of Bangala as well as of Mien, from the circumstance of his having conquered some eastern district belonging to Bengal, from which the country of Ava is separated only by forests.

[3] This name, which in Ramusio's version is Nestardin, is elsewhere written Neschardyn, Noscardyn, and Nastardyn; which are all corruptions of the common Mahometan name of Nasr-eddîn.

[4] This we may presume to be the plain through which the Irabatty, (otherwise written Irawaddy,) or great river of Ava runs, in the upper part of its course.

and from thence, in security, annoy them with their arrows. Calling together the principal officers of his army, he exhorted them not to display less valour on the present occasion than they had done in all their preceding engagements, reminding them that victory did not depend upon the number of men, but upon courage and discipline. He represented to them that the troops of the king of Mien and Bangala were raw and unpractised in the art of war, not having had the opportunities of acquiring experience that had fallen to their lot; that instead of being discouraged by the superior number of their foes, they ought to feel confidence in their own valour so often put to the test; that their very name was a subject of terror, not merely to the enemy before them, but to the whole world; and he concluded by promising to lead them to certain victory. Upon the king of Mien's learning that the Tartars had descended into the plain, he immediately put his army in motion, took up his ground at the distance of about a mile from the enemy, and made a disposition of his force, placing the elephants in the front, and the cavalry and infantry, in two extended wings, in their rear, but leaving between them a considerable interval. Here he took his own station, and proceeded to animate his men and encourage them to fight valiantly, assuring them of victory, as well from the superiority of their numbers, being four to one, as from their formidable body of armed elephants, whose shock the enemy, who had never before been engaged with such combatants, could by no means resist. Then giving orders for sounding a prodigious number of warlike instruments, he advanced boldly with his whole army towards that of the Tartars, which remained firm, making no movement, but suffering them to approach their entrenchments. They then rushed out with great spirit and the utmost eagerness to engage; but it was soon found that the Tartar horses, unused to the sight of such huge animals, with their castles, were terrified, and wheeling about endeavoured to fly; nor could their riders by any exertions restrain them, whilst the king, with the whole of his forces, was every moment gaining ground. As soon as the prudent commander perceived this unexpected disorder, without losing his presence of mind, he instantly adopted the measure of ordering his men to dismount and their horses to be taken into the wood, where they were fastened to the trees. When dismounted, the men, without loss of time, advanced on foot towards the line of elephants, and commenced a brisk discharge of arrows; whilst, on the other side, those who were stationed in the castles, and the rest of the king's army, shot volleys in return with great activity; but their arrows did not make the same impression as those of the Tartars, whose bows were drawn with a stronger arm. So incessant were the discharges of the latter, and all their weapons (according to the instructions of their commander) being directed against the elephants, these were soon covered with arrows, and, suddenly giving way, fell back upon their own people in the rear, who were thereby thrown into confusion. It soon became impossible for their drivers to manage them, either by force or address. Smarting under the pain of their wounds, and terrified by the shouting of the assailants, they were no longer governable, but without guidance or control ran about in all directions, until at length, impelled by rage and fear, they rushed into a part of the wood not occupied by the Tartars. The consequence of this was, that from the closeness of the branches of large trees, they broke, with loud crashes, the battlements or castles that were upon their backs, and involved in the destruction those who sat upon them. Upon seeing the rout of the elephants the Tartars acquired fresh courage, and filing off by detachments, with perfect order and regularity, they remounted their horses, and joined their several divisions, when a sanguinary and dreadful combat was renewed. On the part of the king's troops there was no want of valour, and he himself went amongst the ranks entreating them to stand firm, and not to be alarmed by the accident that had befallen the elephants. But the Tartars, by their consummate skill in archery, were too powerful for them, and galled them the more exceedingly, from their not being provided with such armour as was worn by the former. The arrows having been expended on both sides, the men grasped their swords and iron maces, and violently encountered each other. Then in an instant were to be seen many horrible wounds, limbs dismembered, and multitudes falling to the ground, mained and dying; with such effusion of blood as was dreadful to behold. So great also was the clangour of arms, and such the shoutings and the shrieks, that the noise seemed to ascend to the skies. The king of Mien, acting as became a valiant chief, was present wherever the greatest danger appeared, animating his soldiers, and beseeching them to maintain their ground with resolution. He ordered fresh squadrons from the reserve to advance to the support of those that were exhausted; but perceiving at length that it was impossible any longer to sustain the conflict or to withstand the impetuosity of the Tartars, the greater part of his troops being either killed or wounded, and all the field covered with the carcases of men and horses, whilst those who survived were beginning to give way, he also found himself compelled to take to flight with the wreck of his army, numbers of whom were afterwards slain in the pursuit.

The losses in this battle, which lasted from the morning till noon, were severely felt on both sides; but the Tartars were finally victorious; a result that was materially to be attributed to the troops of the king of Mien and Bangala not wearing armour as the Tartars did, and to their elephants, especially those of the foremost line, being equally without that kind of defence, which, by enabling them to sustain the first discharges of the enemy's arrows, would have allowed them to break his ranks and throw him into disorder. A point perhaps of still greater importance is, that the king ought not to have made his attack on the Tartars in a position where their flank was supported by a wood, but should have endeavoured to draw them into the open country, where they could not have resisted the first impetuous onset of the armed elephants, and where, by extending the cavalry of his two wings, he might have surrounded them. The Tartars having collected their force after the slaughter of the enemy, returned towards the wood into which the elephants had fled for shelter, in order to take possession of them, where they found that the men who had escaped from the overthrow were employed in cutting down trees and barricading the passages, with the intent of defending themselves. But their ramparts were soon demolished by the Tartars, who slew many of them, and with the assistance of the persons accustomed to the management of the elephants, they possessed themselves of these to the number of two hundred or more. From the period of this battle the grand khan has always chosen to employ elephants in his armies, which before that time he had not done. The consequences of the victory were, that he acquired possession of the whole of the territories of the king of Bangala and Mien, and annexed them to his dominions.

CHAPTER XLIII

OF AN UNINHABITED REGION, AND OF THE KINGDOM OF MIEN

LEAVING the province of Kardandan, you enter upon a vast descent, which you travel without variation for two days and a half, in the course of which no habitations are to be found. You then reach a spacious plain,[1] whereon, three days in every week, a number of trading people assemble, many of whom come down from the neighbouring mountains, bringing their gold to be exchanged for silver, which the merchants who repair thither from distant countries carry with them for this purpose;[2] and one saggio of gold is given for five of silver. The inhabitants are not allowed to be the exporters of their own gold, but must dispose of it to the merchants, who furnish them with such articles as they require; and as none but the natives themselves can gain access to the places of their residence, so high and strong are the situations, and so difficult of approach, it is on this account that the transactions of business are conducted in the plain. Beyond this, in a southerly direction, towards the confines of India, lies the city of Mien.[3]

[1] This must be understood of the plain at the foot of the Yun-nan mountains, already spoken of, from whence the river is said to be navigable to Ava.

[2] In consequence of the strict regulations of the Chinese with respect to the admission of strangers within the bounds of the empire, it becomes necessary for the purposes of trade or exchange of commodities, that fairs or markets should be held on the frontiers, where the merchants arrive at stated times with their goods. "The principal article of export from Ava," says Symes, "is cotton. This commodity is transported up the Irrawaddy in large boats, as far as Bamoo, where it is bartered at the common jee or mart, with Chinese merchants, and conveyed by the latter, partly by land and partly by water, into the Chinese dominions." (P. 325.) Thus also at the village of Topa, near Sining, on the borders of Shen-si; "On y trouve," says Du Halde, "presque tout ce qu'on peu souhaiter de marchandises étrangères et de la Chine, diverses drogues, du saffran, des dattes, du caffé, etc."—Tom. i. p. 40.

[3] In this place there is a remarkable variation in the early Italian epitome from all the other versions, and being of some importance in a geographical point of view, I shall give the passage in its own words: "Quando l'huomo se parti de la provincia de Caraian ello trova una grande desmontada par laquale ello va doe zornade pur descendendo, in laqual non è habitatione alchuna ma sige (gliè) uno logo in loqual se fa festa tre di a la setemena. Ivi se da uno sazo doro per v. dargento. E quando l'homo è andado quelle v. zornade ello trova la provincia de Michai laquale confina con l'India et è verso lo mezo di. L'homo va ben xv. zornade per salvazi paesi. Ivi se trova molti elephanti e unicorni e molte bestie salvaze e non ge (gliè) niuna habitation. Quando

The journey occupies fifteen days, through a country much depopulated, and forests abounding with elephants, rhinoceroses, and other wild beasts, where there is not the appearance of any habitation.

CHAPTER XLIV

OF THE CITY OF MIEN, AND OF A GRAND SEPULCHRE OF ITS KING

AFTER the journey of fifteen days that has been mentioned, you reach the city of Mien, which is large, magnificent, and the capital of the kingdom.[1] The inhabitants are idolaters, and have a language peculiar to themselves. It is related that there formerly reigned in this country a rich and powerful monarch, who, when his death was drawing near, gave orders for erecting on the place of his interment, at the head and foot of the sepulchre, two pyramidal towers, entirely of marble, ten paces in height, of a proportionate bulk, and each terminating with a ball.[2] One of these pyramids was covered with a plate of gold an inch in thickness, so that nothing

l'homo e andado xv. zornade ello trova una cita la qual ha nome Mien." (Capitoli xc. et xci.) From hence it is to be understood that upon descending from the heights of Karaian or Yun-nan, you do not immediately enter the country of Mien or Ava Proper, but after a journey of five days reach the province of Michai, which we may reasonably suppose to be the Meckley of our maps; and from thence, after travelling fifteen days through forests, arrive at the capital. "The space between Bengal and China," says Major Rennell, "is occupied by the province of Meckley, and other districts, subject to the king of Burmah or Ava:" and again; "The king of Burmah, whose reputed capital is Ava, and from whence the whole kingdom, though erroneously, is often denominated, is said to possess not only the country of Meckley, in addition to those of Pegu and Burmah, but also the whole tract which lies on the north of it, between China, Thibet, and Assam."—Mem. 3d edit. pp. 295—297. The mention of this intermediate province adds much to the consistency of the narrative.

[1] The present capital, called Ummerapoora or Amrapura, is a city of modern date. This of Mien must therefore either have been the old city of Ava, now in ruins, or some one of earlier times, the seat of government having been often changed. "Pagahm," says Symes, "is said to have been the residence of forty-five successive monarchs, and was abandoned 500 years ago, in consequence of a divine admonition: whatever may be its true history, it certainly was once a place of no ordinary splendour." (P. 269.) The coincidence of dates is here remarkable, as the elapsed period of five centuries would place the ruin of Pagahm in 1295, or just about the time of the Mungal conquest.

[2] Temples of a pyramidal form, both with square and circular bases, are found wherever the religion of Buddha prevails. Many of these, on a magnificent scale, are described by Colonel Symes, in the course of his journey to Ava.

besides the gold was visible; and the other with a plate of silver, of the same thickness. Around the balls were suspended small bells of gold and of silver, which sounded when put in motion by the wind.[1] The whole formed a splendid object. The tomb was in like manner covered with a plate, partly of gold and partly of silver. This the king commanded to be prepared for the honour of his soul, and in order that his memory might not perish. The grand khan, having resolved upon taking possession of this city, sent thither a valiant officer to effect it, and the army, at its own desire, was accompanied by some of the jugglers or sorcerers, of whom there were always a great number about the court.[2] When these entered the city, they observed the two pyramids so richly ornamented, but would not meddle with them until his majesty's pleasure respecting them should be known. The grand khan, upon being informed that they had been erected in pious memory of a former king, would not suffer them to be violated nor injured in the smallest degree; the Tartars being accustomed to consider as a heinous sin the removal of any article appertaining to the dead.[3] In this country were found many elephants, large and handsome wild oxen,[4] with stags, fallow deer, and other animals in great abundance.

[1] "Round the lower limb of the *tee*," says Symes, "are appended a number of bells, which, agitated by the wind, make a continual jingling." —P. 189.

[2] In Ramusio's text these persons who accompanied the army are styled "*giocolari* overo *buffoni*," but in that of the early epitome, "*zugolari e incantadori*," which gives an intelligible sense; as we know, both from preceding passages of the work, and from general information of the manners of these countries, that diviners or religious jugglers have always formed a part of the staff of a military chief, who is either influenced by their prognostications, or makes them subservient to his designs. Purchas in his version calls them "jesters," but in Harris's collection of voyages, edited by Campbell, and in some modern publications, the word "cavalry" is discreetly substituted, as being more appropriate. There appears, however, to be something defective in the story, and that a sentence has been omitted, which should follow that in which the appointment of a valiant officer is mentioned. [In the Paris Latin text they are called *histriones* and *joculatores*.]

[3] This laudable respect shown by the Tartar tribes to the sanctity of the grave, has been the occasion of the Russians discovering in the burial places of these people a great number and variety of undisturbed articles, as well as large deposits of the precious metals, which former conquerors had not presumed to violate.

[4] This is not the chowry-tailed ox, *yak*, or *bos grunniens*, described by Turner, and mentioned by our author in a former chapter, which is the native of a colder region, but the *gayal*, or *bos gavæus*, an animal found wild in the provinces on the eastern side of Bengal, and fully described in vol. viii. of the Asiat. Researches.

CHAPTER XLV

OF THE PROVINCE OF BANGALA

THE province of Bangala is situated on the southern confines of India,[1] and was (not yet) brought under the dominion of the grand khan at the time of Marco Polo's residence at his court; (although) the operations against it occupied his army for a considerable period, the country being strong and its king powerful, as has been related. It has its peculiar language. The people are worshippers of idols, and amongst them there are teachers, at the head of schools for instruction in the principles of their idolatrous religion and of necromancy, whose doctrine prevails amongst all ranks, including the nobles and chiefs of the country.[2] Oxen are found here almost as tall as elephants, but not equal to them in bulk.[3] The inhabitants live upon flesh, milk, and rice, of which they have abundance.[4]

[1] The name of Bangala, as applied in this place to the kingdom of Bengal, approaches nearer to the genuine pronunciation and orthography (Bangâlah) than that in which we are accustomed to write the word.

[2] This passage has an obvious reference to the Hindu schools of philosophy, where the doctrine of the Vedas and Sastras is explained by learned panditas and gurus, in all the principal cities of Bengal and Hindustan. The *ch'handas, tantra sastra,* or art of necromancy, is considered by these people as one of the six great "*angas* or bodies of learning."

[3] If it were fair to justify one exaggeration by another, the authority of a "British officer," quoted by Kerr and Turton in their translation of the Systema Naturæ of Linnæus, might be adduced in support of our author's account of the oxen of Bengal; the former of whom was led to describe and figure, under the name of *bos arnee,* an animal fourteen feet in height, (but reduced by the latter to eight feet,) said to have been met in the country above Bengal; but which proves to be only the wild buffalo, there called *arna.* The buffalo, however, or *bos bubalus,* "a very large and formidable animal," is afterwards distinctly mentioned by our author; and what is here said can apply to no other than the *gayal,* or *bos gavæus,* which abounds in some of the eastern districts, and can only in a figurative sense be compared to the elephant.

[4] Rice and milk are chief articles of sustenance with the natives of Bengal; but, although many of their castes are free from scruples about eating any kind of meat excepting beef, the assertion is too strong that flesh is their ordinary food. It is evident, indeed, that our author's ideas of the country are formed upon what he had seen or learned of the people inhabiting the mountainous districts by which Bengal is bounded on the eastern side, where the manners are widely different from those which prevail on the banks of the Ganges, and where the gayal-ox, as well as deer, wild hogs, and wild animals in general, are commonly eaten as food. The nature and extent of the scruples of those amongst the mountaineers who profess Hinduism, may be judged of from the following passages in a paper by Mr. Colebrooke, in the Asiatic Researches: "The Hindus in this province (Chatgoan

Much cotton is grown in the country, and trade flourishes. Spikenard, galangal, ginger, sugar, and many sorts of drugs are amongst the productions of the soil;[1] to purchase which the merchants from various parts of India resort thither. They likewise make purchases of eunuchs, of whom there are numbers in the country, as slaves; for all the prisoners taken in war are presently emasculated; and as every prince and person of rank is desirous of having them for the custody of their women, the merchants obtain a large profit by carrying them to other kingdoms, and there disposing of them.[2] This province is thirty days' journey in extent, and at the eastern extremity of it lies a country named Kangigu.

CHAPTER XLVI

OF THE PROVINCE OF KANGIGU

KANGIGU is a province situated towards the east,[3] and is governed by a king. The people are idolaters, have a peculiar language, and made a voluntary submission to the grand khan, to whom they pay an annual tribute. The king is so devoted

or Chittagong) will not kill the *gabay*, which they hold in equal veneration with the cow; but the *asl-gáyal*, or *seloï*, they hunt and kill, as they do the wild buffalo. The animal here alluded to is another species of *gayál* found wild in the hills."

[1] These are well known productions of Bengal and the adjoining provinces; particularly the article of sugar, which is extensively cultivated, and exported to many parts of Asia, as well as to Europe.

[2] That the courts and harems of India abounded with eunuchs, who often attained to the highest offices of the state, appears from all the histories of that country; but it is not generally understood that any number of them were supplied from Bengal. It must be observed, indeed, that, with the exception of a few meagre notices in Ferishta's history, we are ignorant of the affairs, and more especially of the manners, of the people of that country in the thirteenth century; and even the dates of inscriptions on some of the principal buildings in Gaur, or Luknauti, considered as its ancient capital, are no earlier than the fifteenth. From the writings of Barbosa, however, which were finished in 1516, and of the genuineness of which no well-informed reader can doubt, we learn that in his time the practice of emasculation prevailed there, although not amongst the Hindu natives, to whose ideas it would be abhorrent.

[3] The country here named Kangigu, in the older Latin version Kanziga, and in the early Italian epitome Cargingu, [in the Latin, Talugigla,] appearing to lie in the route from the eastern part of Bengal towards the northern part of the Birmah country, may be either the Cach'har situated between Silhet and Meckley, or else Kassay, between the latter and Ava. The terminating syllable *gu* may probably be the Chinese word *koue*, or *kue*, "kingdom," which will be seen in the Jesuits' map to prevail in that quarter.

to sensual pleasures, that he has about four hundred wives; and when he hears of any handsome woman, he sends for her, and adds her to the number.[1] Gold is found here in large quantities, and also many kinds of drugs; but, being an inland country, distant from the sea, there is little opportunity of vending them. There are elephants in abundance, and other beasts. The inhabitants live upon flesh, rice, and milk. They have no wine made from grapes, but prepare it from rice and a mixture of drugs. Both men and women have their bodies punctured all over, in figures of beasts and birds; and there are among them practitioners whose sole employment it is to trace out these ornaments with the point of a needle, upon the hands, the legs, and the breast. When a black colouring stuff has been rubbed over these punctures, it is impossible, either by water or otherwise, to efface the marks. The man or woman who exhibits the greatest profusion of these figures, is esteemed the most handsome.

CHAPTER XLVII

OF THE PROVINCE OF AMU

AMU, also, is situated towards the east,[2] and its inhabitants are subjects of the grand khan. They are idolaters, and live upon the flesh of their cattle and the fruits of the earth. They have a peculiar language. The country produces many horses and oxen, which are sold to the itinerant merchants, and conveyed to India. Buffaloes also, as well as oxen, are numerous,[3] in consequence of the extent and excellence of the pastures. Both men and women wear rings, of gold and silver, upon their wrists, arms, and legs; but those of the females are the more costly. The distance between this province and that of Kangigu is twenty-five[4] days' journey, and thence to Bangala

[1] In Mr. Colebrooke's paper (referred to in note [4], p. 260) the raja of Cach'har is spoken of as a Cshatriya of the Suryabansi race. In former times his territory may have been more extensive, and his revenue more adequate to the maintenance of a harem of such magnitude, than they are at the present day. The epitome reduces the number to one hundred: "Lo re ha ben cento moiere."

[2] Amu appears to correspond in situation with Bamu, which is described by Symes as a frontier province between the kingdom of the Birmahs and Yun-nan in China.

[3] These are the *bos bubalus* and *bos gavæus*. See note [8], p. 260.

[4] [The Paris Latin text reads fifteen.]

is twenty days' journey. We shall now speak of a province named Tholoman, situated eight days' journey from the former.

CHAPTER XLVIII

OF THOLOMAN

THE province of Tholoman lies towards the east,[1] and its inhabitants are idolaters. They have a peculiar language, and are subjects of the grand khan. The people are tall and good-looking; their complexions inclining rather to brown than fair. They are just in their dealings, and brave in war. Many of their towns and castles are situated upon lofty mountains. They burn the bodies of their dead; and the bones that are not reduced to ashes, they put into wooden boxes, and carry them to the mountains, where they conceal them in caverns of the rocks, in order that no wild animal may disturb them.[2] Abundance of gold is found here. For the ordinary small currency they use the porcelain shells that come from India; and this sort of money prevails also in the two before-mentioned provinces of Kangigu and Amu. Their food and drink are the same that has been already mentioned.

[1] No name resembling Tholoman, Toloman, or Coloman, as the word appears in different versions, is to be found in any map or description of these parts; but as the circumstances stated render it probable that the country spoken of is that of the people variously called Birmahs, Burmahs, Bomans, and Burmans, we may conjecture that the word was intended for Po-lo-man, which is known to be the mode in which the Chinese pronounce Burman and Brahman, and by which they often designate the people of India in general.

[2] The ceremonies practised by certain mountaineers of Ava or the Burmah country, named Kayn, bear a strong resemblance to what is here described: "They burn their dead," says Symes, "and afterwards collect their ashes in an urn, which they convey to a house, where, if the urn contains the relics of a man, they keep it six days, if of a woman, five; after which it is carried to the place of interment and deposited in a grave, and on the sod that covers it is laid a wooden image of the deceased to pray to the *mounzing* (deity) and protect the bones and ashes." He added, "that the *mounzing* resided on the great mountain Gnowa, where the images of the dead are deposited."—Embassy to Ava, p. 447.

CHAPTER XLIX

OF THE CITIES OF CHINTIGUI, SIDIN-FU, GIN-GUI, AND PAZAN-FU

LEAVING the province of Tholoman, and pursuing a course towards the east,[1] you travel for twelve days by a river, on each side of which lie many towns and castles; when at length you reach the large and handsome city of Chintigui,[2] the inhabitants of which are idolaters, and are the subjects of the grand khan. They are traders and artisans. They make cloth of the bark of certain trees, which looks well, and is the ordinary summer clothing of both sexes. The men are brave warriors. They have no other kind of money than the stamped paper of the grand khan.[3]

In this province the tigers are so numerous, that the inhabitants, from apprehension of their ravages, cannot venture to sleep at night out of their towns; and those who navigate the river dare not go to rest with their boats moored near the banks; for these animals have been known to plunge into the water, swim to the vessel, and drag the men from thence; but find it

[1] The countries last spoken of appear indubitably to have belonged to that region which geographers term "India extra Gangem." These our author's route now leaves behind, and what follows in the remaining chapters of this book applies only to China or its immediate dependencies.

[2] We cannot discover in the southern part of Yun-nan (towards which he might be supposed to have returned) any city resembling Chinti-gui or Chinti-giu in name; but a material difference between the text of Ramusio and those of the other versions occurs here, which might be hoped to afford a clue for tracing the progress of the route. According to the former our author prosecutes his journey from Tholoman by the course of a river (whether wholly or in part only, is not clearly expressed) to the city above mentioned. In the Basle edition, on the contrary, it is said: "A provincia Tholoman ducit iter versus orientem ad provinciam Gingui, iturque duodecim diebus juxta fluvium quendam, donec perveniatur ad civitatem grandem Sinuglu:" and in the early Italian epitome, "Cuigui sie una provincia verso oriente laqual ello trovo l'homo quando se parti da Toloman tu vai su per uno fiume per xii. zornade trovando cita e castelli: e trovi la cita de Similgu grande e nobile;" to which city of Sinulgu or Similgu are attributed all the circumstances above related of Cintigui. [The name in the Paris Latin text is Funilgul.] If the reading of Cui-gui or Kui-giu be more correct than the others, we might conjecture it to be intended for the Chinese province of Koei-cheu or Quei-cheu, which, adjoining to that of Yun-nan on the eastern side, would be in point of direction no unlikely road to the capital.

[3] The circumstance of the emperor's paper money being current, shows that the country here spoken of was an integral part of the empire, and not one of its remote dependencies, where the sovereignty was more nominal than real.

necessary to anchor in the middle of the stream, where, in consequence of its great width, they are in safety.[1] In this country are likewise found the largest and fiercest dogs that can be met with: so courageous and powerful are they, that a man, with a couple of them, may be an over-match for a tiger. Armed with a bow and arrows, and thus attended, should he meet a tiger, he sets on his intrepid dogs, who instantly advance to the attack. The animal instinctively seeks a tree, against which to place himself, in order that the dogs may not be able to get behind him, and that he may have his enemies in front. With this intent, as soon as he perceives the dogs, he makes towards the tree, but with a slow pace, and by no means running, that he may not show any signs of fear, which his pride would not allow. During this deliberate movement, the dogs fasten upon him, and the man plies him with his arrows. He, in his turn, endeavours to seize the dogs, but they are too nimble for him, and draw back, when he resumes his slow march; but before he can gain his position, he has been wounded by so many arrows, and so often bitten by the dogs, that he falls through weakness and from loss of blood. By these means it is that he is at length taken.[2]

There is here an extensive manufacture of silks, which are exported in large quantities to other parts [3] by the navigation of the river, which continues to pass amongst towns and castles; and the people subsist entirely by trade. At the end of twelve days, you arrive at the city of Sidin-fu, of which an account has been already given.[4] From thence, in twenty

[1] Numerous instances are recorded of boats being attacked at night by tigers, amongst the alluvial islands at the mouth of the Ganges, called the Sunderbunds, and sometimes it happens that whole crews are destroyed whilst sleeping on board.

[2] If the beast here spoken of be actually the tiger and not the lion (of which latter none are found in China), it must be confessed that the manners ascribed to him in this story are very different from those which usually mark his feline character. In the old English version of 1579 (from the Spanish), it is not the lion or tiger, but the elephant that is said to be the subject of this mode of baiting with "mastie-dogges." I am assured, however, that dogs do attack both tigers and leopards.

[3] The trade in wrought silks denotes this to be a place in China, and to the south of the Yellow River, beyond which the silkworm is not reared for the purposes of manufacture.

[4] From the context we might be led to infer that the Si-din-fu here spoken of should be the same place as the Chinti-gui mentioned at the commencement of this chapter, inasmuch as the journey of twelve days from Tholoman is here again referred to; but on the other hand we are much more clearly given to understand that it is the city before described (in chap. xxxvi.) by the name of Sin-din-fu, and which was shown (in

days, you reach Gin-gui, in which we were, and in four days more the city of Pazan-fu,[1] which belongs to Cathay, and lies towards the south, in returning by the other side of the province.[2] The inhabitants worship idols, and burn the bodies of

note [1], p. 234) to be intended for Ching-tu-fu, the capital of the province of Se-chuen. This would lie in the route from Ava and the province of Yun-nan towards the city of Pekin.

[1] In this part of the work, indeed, we perceive a more than usual degree of perplexity in the geographical matter, which is increased by a want of agreement in the several versions, not merely in orthography, but in the entire names of places as well as in circumstances. The journey of twenty days stated in Ramusio's text is not mentioned either in the Latin version or early Italian epitome, and it appears in the first instance uncertain whether by Gin-gui is here meant that southern province which in the latter is named Cui-gui, and has been conjectured to be Koci-cheu, or whether it may have been intended for Kin-cheu on the Kiang, or (admitting a large hiatus in the journal) for another Kin-cheu in the province of Pe-che-li. For the city, likewise, which Ramusio names Pazan-fu, the other versions speak of Caucasu or Cancasu. But in addition to the confusion of names, we have, at this point, a new difficulty to contend with; for as the general course of the journey has latterly been to the east, as expressed in the text, or to the north-east, as inferred from positions, so at this place, and from henceforward, we find it described as tending to the south; although from the preceding chapters it might seem that the southern provinces of China had been but just entered from the side of Mien or Ava. Our author's want of accuracy in bearings, as they respect the intermediate points of the compass, has often required the exercise of indulgence: but this cannot be extended to the mistaking north for south; nor would even a correction of this nature in one or two instances avail us; for we shall presently find him approaching the Yellow River from the northern side, crossing that river, and, in the continuance of his southerly course, describing well-known places between it and the Kiang, which he likewise crosses in his way to the province of Fo-kien. It is consequently in one or other of the most *northern* provinces that we should make our search for Pazan-fu, and we shall be fully justified in drawing the conclusion, that a fresh itinerary, hitherto unnoticed, as it would seem, by any editor or commentator, has commenced from some place in the vicinity of the capital; and that the fruitless attempt to connect this with the former route, as constituting one journey, has chiefly given rise to the confusion of which every reader who has endeavoured to follow the course of the travels must have found reason to complain.

[2] It has been shown that about a mile from the town of Tso-cheu, in the province of Pe-che-li, the roads are said to divide, the one leading to the south-western, and the other to the south-eastern provinces. The first was that which our author pursued in his former route, and has described to a certain point, where either his original memoranda left it incomplete, or his early transcribers, to avoid the monotonous repetition of unknown and to them uninteresting names, were induced to terminate it abruptly. The latter road, to the south-east, is that upon which he is now about to enter. Under the conviction, therefore, of a new intinerary having commenced about this part of the narrative from some place near Tso-cheu, where the roads divide, we are naturally led to consider the city now called Ho-kien-fu (the first in the southern route) as the Pa-zan-fu of Ramusio's text, or Ca-cau-su (for *fu*) of the Basle edition; the probability of which, however discordant the sound of the names, we shall find to be strengthened as we proceed to the account of places subsequently visited. Ho-kien-fu (the first syllable of

their dead. There are here also certain Christians, who have a church.[1] They are subjects of the grand khan, and his paper money is current among them. They gain their living by trade and manufacture, having silk in abundance, of which they weave tissues mixed with gold, and also very fine scarfs. This city has many towns and castles under its jurisdiction: a great river flows beside it, by means of which large quantities of merchandise are conveyed to the city of Kanbalu; for by the digging of many canals it is made to communicate with the capital. But we shall take our leave of this, and, proceeding three days' journey, speak of another city named Chan-glu.

CHAPTER L

OF THE CITY OF CHAN-GLU

CHAN-GLU is a large city situated towards the south,[2] and is in the province of Cathay. It is under the dominion of the grand khan. The inhabitants worship idols, and burn the bodies of their dead. The stamped paper of the emperor is current amongst them. In this city and the district surrounding it they make great quantities of salt, by the following process: in the country is found a salsuginous earth; upon this, when laid in large heaps, they pour water, which in its passage through the mass imbibes the particles of salt, and is then collected in channels, from whence it is conveyed to very wide pans, not more than four inches in depth. In these it is well boiled, and then left to crystallize. The salt thus made is white and good, and is exported to various parts.[3] Great

which a Tartar would pronounce Ko) is the third city of the province in rank, and derives its name from its position " between the rivers."

[1] The expression of *certi Christiani* may either mean a sect of Christians distinct from the Nestorians, already so often mentioned, or may refer to the Nestorians themselves, as a sort of Christians, not Catholic.

[2] To the eastward of Ho-kien, but inclining to the south, we find a city of the second order, dependent on the jurisdiction of the former, which in Du Halde's map is properly named Tsan-tcheu, but in Martini's Atlas, Cang-cheu, incorrectly for Cang-cheu. This is evidently Cianglu or Chang-lu here mentioned.

[3] From this detail of the process it may be thought that nitre or saltpetre, rather than common salt, is the article so procured. The following passage, from the translation of Abbé Grosier's Description générale de la Chine, will leave no doubt on this point: " The earth which forms the soil of Petcheli abounds with nitre; whole fields may be seen in the neighbourhood of Pe-king which are covered with it. Every morning

profits are made by those who manufacture it, and the grand khan derives from it a considerable revenue. This district produces abundance of well-flavoured peaches, of such a size that one of them will weigh two pounds troy-weight.[1] We shall now speak of another city, named Chan-gli.

CHAPTER LI

OF THE CITY OF CHAN-GLI

CHAN-GLI also is a city of Cathay,[2] situated towards the south, and belonging to the grand khan, the inhabitants of which are idolaters, and in like manner make use of the khan's paper currency. Its distance from Chan-glu is five days' journey, in the course of which you pass many cities and castles likewise in the dominions of the grand khan. They are places of great commerce, and the customs levied at them amount to a large sum.[3] Through this city passes a wide and deep river, which affords conveyance to vast quantities of merchandise, consisting of silk, drugs, and other valuable articles. We shall now take leave of this place, and give an account of another city named Tudin-fu.

CHAPTER LII

OF THE CITY OF TUDIN-FU

WHEN you depart from Chan-gli, and travel southwards six days' journey, you pass many towns and castles of great im-

at sunrise the country in certain cantons appears as white as if sprinkled by a gentle fall of snow. If a quantity of this substance be swept together, a great deal of *kien*, nitre, and salt may be extracted from it. The Chinese pretend that this salt may be substituted for common salt; however this may be, it is certain that in the (mountainous) extremity of the province, poor people and the greater part of the peasants make use of no other. With regard to the *kien* procured from the earth, they use it for washing linen, as we do soap."—Vol. i. p. 27.

[1] "Peso alla sottile" is explained in the dictionaries by "poids de marchandises fines, plus léger que l'autre," which corresponds to the difference of fourteen and seventeen, between our troy and avoirdupois weights.

[2] The city of Ciangli or Changli appears to be that of Te-cheu, situated at the entrance of the province of Shan-tung, on the river called Oei-ho in Du Halde's map, and Eu-ho, in the account of Lord Macartney's Embassy.

[3] A transit duty (Staunton observes) is laid on goods passing from one

portance and grandeur, whose inhabitants worship idols, and burn the bodies of their dead. They are the subjects of the grand khan, and receive his paper money as currency. They subsist by trade and manufactures, and have provisions in abundance. At the end of these six days you arrive at a city named Tudin-fu,[1] which was formerly a magnificent capital, but the grand khan reduced it to his subjection by force of arms. It is rendered a delightful residence by the gardens which surround it, stored as they are with handsome shrubs and excellent fruits.[2] Silk is produced here in wonderfully large quantities. It has under its jurisdiction eleven cities and considerable towns of the empire, all places of great trade, and having abundance of silk. It was the seat of government of its own king, before the period of its reduction by the grand khan. In 1272 [3] the latter appointed one of his officers of the highest rank, named Lucansor, to the government of this city, with a command of seventy thousand horse, for the protection of that part of the country. This man upon finding himself master of a rich and highly productive district, and at the head of so powerful a force, became intoxicated with pride, and formed schemes of rebellion against his sovereign. With this view he tampered with the principal persons of the city, persuaded them to become partakers in his evil designs, and by their means succeeded in producing a revolt throughout all the towns and fortified places of the province. As soon as the grand khan became acquainted with these traitorous proceedings, he despatched to that quarter an army of a hundred thousand men, under the orders of two others of his nobles, one of whom was named Angul and the other Mongatai. When the approach of this force was known to Lucansor, he lost no time

province of China to another; each province being noted, chiefly, for the production of some particular article, the conveyance of which, to supply the demand for it in the others, raises this duty to a considerable sum, and forms the great internal commerce and revenue of the empire.

[1] We have historical evidence that Tudin-fu is Tsi-nan-fu (by Martini written Cinan-fu), the capital of the province of Shan-tung.

[2] The routes of our modern travellers have not led them to visit this city, but that of the Dutch embassy of 1795, in its return, passed through several of the towns under its jurisdiction. Upon the approach to one of these named Ping-yuen-shen, Van Braam describes the scenery in terms similar to, but more luxuriant than those employed by our author. and the orchards of fruit are particularly noticed.

[3] The circumstance of which our author proceeds to speak, is, by L'Histoire générale de la Chine, assigned to a period ten years earlier. The Roman numerals, in which dates are expressed in the old manuscripts, are more liable to errors than the Arabic, or rather Indian figures, now in use.

in assembling an army no less numerous than that of his opponents, and brought them as speedily as possible to action. There was much slaughter on both sides, when at length, Lucansor being killed, his troops betook themselves to flight. Many were slain in the pursuit, and many were made prisoners. These were conducted to the presence of the grand khan, who caused the principals to be put to death, and pardoning the others took them into his own service, to which they ever afterwards continued faithful.

CHAPTER LIII

OF THE CITY OF SINGUI-MATU

TRAVELLING from Tudin-fu three days, in a southerly direction, you pass many considerable towns and strong places, where commerce and manufactures flourish. The inhabitants are idolaters, and are subjects of the grand khan. The country abounds with game, both beasts and birds, and produces an ample supply of the necessaries of life. At the end of three days you arrive at the city of Singui-matu,[1] which is noble, large, and handsome, and rich in merchandise and manufactures; all the inhabitants of this city are idolaters, and are subjects of the grand khan and use paper money; within it, but on the southern side, passes a large and deep river, which the inhabitants divided into two branches, one of which, taking its course to the east, runs through Cathay, whilst the other, taking a westerly course, passes towards the province of Manji.[2] This river is navigated by so many vessels that the

[1] The circumstances here mentioned of Sin-gui-matu seem to point to the large commercial town of Lin-tsin-cheu, situated at the northern extremity, or commencement, of the Yun-ho or grand canal. The term *matu* or *mateou*, subjoined to names, signifies, as we are told by Du Halde (tom. i. p. 137), " lieux de commerce établis sur les rivières, pour la commodité des négocians et la levée des droits de l'empereur; " and by P. Magalhanes, *mà-teû* is defined to be, " lieu fréquenté pour le commerce; parceque les barques s'y assemblent et y jettent l'ancre pour y passer la nuit."—Nouv. Relat. de la Chine, p. 9.

[2] These expressions might be considered as intended to describe the formation of the canal itself, which must, of course, have been supplied with water by diverting so much of the stream of the river as was necessary for that purpose; and the operation might consequently be said to divide it into two branches; but they may be thought rather to refer to the following curious circumstance noticed in the Account of Lord Macartney's Embassy: " On the 25th of October (the third day after its departure from Lin-tsing) the yachts arrived at the highest part of the

number might seem incredible, and serves to convey from both provinces, that is, from the one province to the other, every requisite article of consumption. It is indeed surprising to observe the multitude and the size of the vessels that are continually passing and repassing, laden with merchandise of the greatest value.[1] On leaving Singui-matu and travelling towards the south for sixteen days, you unceasingly meet with commercial towns and with castles. The people throughout the country are idolaters, and subjects of the grand khan. They burn the bodies of their dead and use paper money. At the end of eight days' journey you find a city named Lingui. It is a very noble and great city; the men are warlike; and it has manufactures and commerce. There are plenty of animals, and abundance of everything for eating and drinking. After leaving Lingui you proceed three days' journey to the south, passing plenty of cities and castles, all under the grand khan. All the inhabitants are idolaters, and burn their dead. At the end of these three days you find a good city called Pingui, where there are all the necessaries of life, and this city furnishes a great revenue to the grand khan. You go thence two days' journey to the south, through fair and rich countries, to a city called Cingui, which is very large, and abounding in commerce and manufactures. All its inhabitants are idolaters and burn their dead; they use paper money, and are subjects of the grand khan. They have much grain and wheat. In the country through which you pass subsequently, you find cities, towns, and castles, and very handsome and useful dogs, and abundance of wheat. The people resemble those just described.

canal, being about two-fifths of its entire length. Here the river Luen, the largest by which the canal is fed, falls into it with a rapid stream, in a line which is perpendicular to the course of the canal. A strong bulwark of stone supports the opposite western bank; and the waters of the Luen striking with force against it, part of them follow the northern, and part the southern course of the canal—a circumstance which, not being generally explained or understood, gave the appearance of wonder to an assertion, that if a bundle of sticks be thrown into that part of the river, they would soon separate and take opposite directions." (Vol. ii. p. 387.) The name of this place is Tci-ngin-tcheou in Du Halde's map, and Tsin-jin-tchoo in that of the Embassy; which bears an evident resemblance to the Sin-gui of our text.

[1] "I should say, that next to the exuberance of population," says Mr. Ellis, "the amount of vessels employed on the rivers is the most striking circumstance hitherto observed, belonging to the Chinese empire."—Journal of an Embassy, etc. p. 109.

CHAPTER LIV

OF THE GREAT RIVER CALLED THE KARA-MORAN, AND OF THE CITIES OF KOI-GAN-ZU AND KUAN-ZU

At the end of two days' journey you reach, once more, the great river Kara-moran,[1] which has its source in the territories that belonged to Prester John. It is a mile wide and of vast depth, and upon its waters great ships freely sail with their full loading. Large fish in considerable quantities are caught there. At a place in this river, about a mile distant from the sea, there is a station for fifteen thousand vessels, each of them capable of carrying fifteen horses and twenty men, besides the crews to navigate them, and the necessary stores and provisions.[2] These the grand khan causes to be kept in a constant state of readiness for the conveyance of an army to any of the islands in the (neighbouring) ocean that may happen to be in rebellion, or for expeditions to any more distant region. These vessels are moored close to the bank of the river, not far from a city named Koi-gan-zu,[3] on the opposite side to which is another named Kuan-zu, but the former is a large place, and the latter a small one.[4] Upon crossing this river you enter the noble province of Manji; but it must not be understood that a complete account has been given of the province of Cathay. Not the twentieth part have I described. Marco Polo, in

[1] This is the Tartar name for the great river by the Chinese called the Hoang-ho, and by us the Yellow River, which has its source in the country between the western borders of China and the great desert.

[2] The number of fifteen thousand must be a prodigious exaggeration, if we should not rather suppose it to be an error in transcribing. The early Italian epitome says fifteen vessels; but this is an absurdity in the opposite extreme, and it is probable that fifteen hundred was the number intended. The station of these transports, instead of being one mile, is said in other versions to be one day's journey from the sea.

[3] Both from its situation and the resemblance of name, we cannot hesitate to consider this as the city of Hoai-gnan-fu, which stands near the south-eastern bank of the Hoang-ho, at the part where it is crossed by the line of the grand canal, and is itself connected, by means of a small cut, with that river. All Chinese words commencing with the aspirate are pronounced by the Western Tartars with a hard guttural sound; as, on the other hand, the guttural articulation of these people is softened by the Chinese to the aspirate: thus for Khan they pronounce Han; for Ko-ko-nor (a certain great lake), Ho-ho-nor; and for Kutukh-tu (the second rank of lamas), Hu-tu-tu.

[4] The place here named Kuan-zu or Quan-zu, in the Basle edition Cai-gui, and in the early epitomes Cai-cui, does not appear in the maps, but seems to be the place which De Guignes mentions by the name of Yang-kia-yn.

travelling through the province, has only noted such cities as lay in his route, omitting those situated on the one side and the other, as well as many intermediate places, because a relation of them all would be a work of too great length, and prove fatiguing to the reader. Leaving these parts we shall therefore proceed to speak, in the first instance, of the manner in which the province of Manji was acquired, and then of its cities, the magnificence and riches of which shall be set forth in the subsequent part of our discourse.

CHAPTER LV

OF THE MOST NOBLE PROVINCE OF MANJI, AND OF THE MANNER IN WHICH IT WAS SUBDUED BY THE GRAND KHAN

THE province of Manji is the most magnificent and the richest that is known in the eastern world.[1] About the year 1269 it was subject to a prince who was styled Facfur,[2] and who surpassed in power and wealth any other that for a century had reigned in that country. His disposition was pacific, and his actions benevolent. So much was he beloved by his people, and such the strength of his kingdom, enclosed by rivers of the largest size, that his being molested by any power upon earth was regarded as an impossible event. The effect of this opinion was, that he neither paid any attention himself to military affairs, nor encouraged his people to become acquainted with military exercises. The cities of his dominions were remarkably well fortified, being surrounded by deep ditches, a bow-shot in width, and full of water. He did not keep up any force in cavalry, because he was not apprehensive of attack. The means of increasing his enjoyments and multi-

[1] We have not materials for assigning precise boundaries either to Manji or to Khataï; but it is evident that our author considered, generally, that part of China which lies southward of the Hoang-ho, or Yellow River, as belonging to what he terms the province of Manji, or, with some few limitations, to the empire of the Song; and the part that lies northward of that river, which was conquered by the Mungals, not from the Chinese, but from the dynasty of the Kin or Niuche Tartars, by whom it had been previously subdued, as Khataï or Cathay.

[2] This word Facfur was not the name of the individual prince, but the title of Faghfûr, applied by the Arabs and other Eastern people to the emperors of China, as distinguished from the Tartar sovereigns. It also denotes (according to the dictionaries) the porcelain of China-ware, and probably, in general. what the French term " magots de la Chine." The name of the emperor who reigned at that period was Tu-tsong.

plying his pleasures were the chief employment of his thoughts. He maintained at his court, and kept near his person, about a thousand beautiful women, in whose society he took delight. He was a friend to peace and to justice, which he administered strictly. The smallest act of oppression, or injury of any kind, committed by one man against another, was punished in an exemplary manner, without respect of persons. Such indeed was the impression of his justice, that when shops, filled with goods, happened, through the negligence of the owners, to be left open, no person dared to enter them, or to rob them of the smallest article. Travellers of all descriptions might pass through every part of the kingdom, by night as well as by day, freely and without apprehension of danger. He was religious, and charitable to the poor and needy.[1] Children whom their wretched mothers exposed in consequence of their inability to rear them, he caused to be saved and taken care of, to the number of twenty thousand annually.[2] When the boys attained a sufficient age, he had them instructed in some handicraft, and afterwards married them to young women who were brought up in the same manner.[3]

Very different from the temper and habits of Facfur were those of Kublaï-khan, emperor of the Tartars, whose whole delight consisted in thoughts of a warlike nature, of the conquest of countries, and of extending his renown. After having

[1] His character is painted in more favourable colours by our author than by the Chinese historians, who do not relieve its dark shades with the light of any virtue.

[2] The practice in China of exposing infants, and especially females, has become matter of notoriety since this first and unequivocal notice of it by our author. "The number of children," says Barrow, "thus unnaturally and inhumanly slaughtered, or interred alive, in the course of a year, is differently stated by different authors, some making it about ten, and others thirty thousand in the whole empire. The truth, as generally happens, may probably lie about the middle. The missionaries, who alone possess the means of ascertaining nearly the number that is thus sacrificed in the capital, differ very materially in their statements: taking the mean, as given by those with whom we conversed on the subject, I should conclude that about twenty-four infants were on an average, in Pekin, daily carried to the pit of death. . . . This calculation gives about nine thousand yearly for the capital alone, where it is supposed about an equal number are exposed to that of all the other parts of the empire."—Travels in China, p. 169.

[3] The Latin edition describes the manner in which the emperor provided for a part of these children, in the following terms: "Rex tamen infantes, quos sic colligi jubet, tradit divitibus quibusque, quos in regno suo habet; præsertim illis qui liberis carent, et ut in adoptionis suscipiant filios mandat. Eos verò quos ipse nutrit, matrimonio tradit puellis ejusdem conditionis." It appears that in the reign of Kang-hi, also, (who died in 1722,) there was a public establishment at Pekin for the recovery of infants so exposed.

annexed to his dominions a number of provinces and kingdoms, he now directed his views to the subduing that of Manji, and for this purpose assembled a numerous army of horse and foot, the command of which he gave to a general named Chin-san Bay-an, which signifies in our language, the "Hundred-eyed."[1] This occurred in the year 1273. A number of vessels were put under his orders, with which he proceeded to the invasion of Manji. Upon landing there, he immediately summoned the inhabitants of the city of Koi-gan-zu to surrender to the authority of his sovereign.[2] Upon their refusal to comply, instead of giving orders for an assault, he advanced to the next city, and when he there received a similar answer, proceeded to a third and a fourth, with the same result. Deeming it no longer prudent to leave so many cities in his rear, whilst not only his army was strong, but he expected to be soon joined by another of equal force, which the grand khan was to send to him from the interior,[3] he resolved upon the attack of one of these cities; and having, by great exertions and consummate skill, succeeded in carrying the place, he put every individual found in it to the sword. As soon as the intelligence of this event reached the other cities, it struck their inhabitants with such consternation and terror, that of their own accord they hastened to declare their submission. This being effected, he advanced, with the united force of his two armies, against the royal city of Kinsai, the residence of king Facfur, who felt all the agitation and dread of a person who had never seen a battle, nor been engaged in any sort of warfare. Alarmed for the safety of his person, he made his escape to a fleet of vessels that lay in readiness for the purpose, and embarking all his treasure and valuable effects, left the charge of the city to his queen, with directions for its being defended to the utmost; feeling assured that her sex would be a protection to her, in the event of her falling into the hands of the enemy. He from thence proceeded to sea, and reaching certain islands, where were some strongly fortified posts, he continued there

[1] Ba-yan, or, as the Chinese pronounce the name, Pe-yen, literally signifies, in that language, "a hundred eyes," and may be considered as the *agnomen* or epithet of this distinguished warrior, derived from his vigilance, circumspection, and quickness in improving an advantage.

[2] The earliest operation of the war against the Song, or dynasty who reigned in Manji, took place (according to L'Hist. gén.) to the westward, at Siang-yang, which was invested in 1269 (before our author's arrival in China), although not captured till 1273.

[3] This was perhaps the army that had been employed in the reduction of Siang yang.

till his death.[1] After the queen had been left in the manner related, it is said to have come to her knowledge that the king had been told by his astrologers that he could never be deprived of his sovereignty by any other than a chief who should have a hundred eyes. On the strength of this declaration she felt confident, notwithstanding that the city became daily more and more straitened, that it could not be lost, because it seemed a thing impossible that any mortal could have that number of eyes. Inquiring, however, the name of the general who commanded the enemy's troops, and being told it was Chin-san Bay-an, which means a hundred eyes, she was seized with horror at hearing it pronounced, as she felt a conviction that this must be the person who, according to the saying of the astrologers, might drive her husband from his throne. Overcome by womanish fear, she no longer attempted to make resistance, but immediately surrendered.[2] Being thus in possession of the capital, the Tartars soon brought the remainder of the province under their subjection.[3] The queen was sent to the presence of Kublaï-khan, where she was honourably received by him, and an allowance was by his orders assigned, that enabled her to support the dignity of her rank. Having stated the manner in which the conquest of Manji was effected, we shall now speak of the different cities of that province, and first of Koi-gan-zu.

[1] Our author appears in this place to have crowded under one reign events that belong to two or more, which followed each other in rapid succession. The emperor Tu-tsong, whose unwarlike and depraved character was said to have been the occasion of the misfortunes that befel his country, died in 1274; when the minister by whose evil counsels he had been implicitly governed placed his second son, an infant, on the throne, and caused the empress, his mother, to be declared regent during the minority. This prince, who was named Kong-tsong, afterwards fell into the hands of the Tartars; but the Chinese, who still adhered to the fortunes of the expiring dynasty, conferred the imperial title upon his elder brother, named Tuan-tsong; and to *his* fate it is that the passage in the text applies.

[2] Such we may suppose to have been the popular story, which our author repeats as he heard it, but which, probably, had no better foundation than a Chinese *équivoque* upon the name of this great captain, to whose talents his master was indebted for the conquest of Southern China, and of whom it is said by the Chinese historians that "he conducted a large army as if it had been a single man."

[3] The surrender of the capital took place in 1276, but it was not until the end of the year 1279 that the conquest of China was completed by the issue of a great naval engagement.

CHAPTER LVI

OF THE CITY OF KOI-GAN-ZU

KOI-GAN-ZU is a very handsome and wealthy city, lying in a direction between south-east and east, at the entrance of the province of Manji, where a prodigious number of vessels are continually passing, its situation (as we have already observed) being near the bank of the river Kara-moran.[1] Large consignments of merchandise are forwarded to this city, in order that the goods may be transported, by means of this river, to various other places. Salt is manufactured here in great quantities, not only for the consumption of the city itself, but for exportation to other parts; and from this salt the grand khan derives an ample revenue.[2]

CHAPTER LVII

OF THE TOWN OF PAU-GHIN

UPON leaving Koi-gan-zu, you travel one day's journey towards the south-east, by a handsome stone causeway, leading into the province of Manji. On both sides of the causeway there are very extensive marshy lakes, the waters of which are deep, and may be navigated;[3] nor is there besides this any other road by which the province can be entered. It is, however, accessible by means of shipping; and in this manner it was that the officer who commanded the grand khan's armies invaded it, by effecting a landing with his whole force.[4] At the

[1] The city is about five miles distant from the Yellow River, with which it communicates by means of the grand canal.

[2] "Proche de là," says P. Martini, "il y a des marais salans, où il se fait du sel en abondance."—Thevenot, iii. partie, p. 321.

[3] These causeways form the embankments of the canal, and separate it, on a higher level, from the waters of the lake. It would seem that in our author's time there was only a single embankment at this part, by means of which the waters of the lake, on that side which was fed by the rivulets, were kept up to an artificial level. Much of the country, Staunton observes, that was formerly under water, has been drained and brought into cultivation.

[4] From this it must be understood that the fleet of transports entered the canal, or the portion of the lake that served the purpose of a canal, and conveyed the troops to the neighbourhood of the city of Hoai-gnan, which stands on its bank in the midst of a swamp.

end of the day's journey, you reach a considerable town named Pau-ghin.[1] The inhabitants worship idols, burn their dead, use paper money, and are the subjects of the grand khan. They gain their living by trade and manufacture: they have much silk, and weave gold tissues. The necessaries of life are there in abundance.

CHAPTER LVIII

OF THE CITY OF KAIN

At the distance of a day's journey from Pau-ghin, towards the south-east, stands the large and well-built city of Kain.[2] Its inhabitants are idolaters, use the paper money as their currency, and are the subjects of the grand khan. Trade and manufactures flourish amongst them. They have fish in abundance, and game also, both beasts and birds. Pheasants, in particular, are in such plenty, that for a bit of silver equal in value to a Venetian groat you may purchase three of these birds, of the size of pea-fowls.

CHAPTER LIX

OF THE CITIES OF TIN-GUI AND CHIN-GUI

At the end of a day's journey from the last-mentioned place, in the course of which many villages and much tilled land are met with, you reach a city named Tin-gui, not of any great size, but plentifully furnished with all the necessaries of life. The people are idolaters, the subjects of the grand khan, and use his paper money. They are merchants, and have many trading vessels. Both beasts and birds are here found in plenty. The situation of this city is towards the south-east, and on the left-hand—that is, on the eastern side of it, at the distance of three days' journey—you find the sea. In the intermediate

[1] This is the Pau-in-cheu of Van Braam's journal, the Pao-yn-hien of Du Halde's map, and the Pao-yng-shien of Staunton's.

[2] However different the names may appear, this is evidently the town of Kao-yu, on the banks of the lake and canal; and it is not improbable that Ka-in is a typographical mistake of Ka-iu, or Ka-yu, as in almost every name we have observed the final *u* to be changed for some other letter resembling it in form.

space there are many salt-works, where large quantities of salt are manufactured.[1] You next come to the large and well-built town of Chin-gui, from whence salt is exported sufficient for the supply of all the neighbouring provinces.[2] On this article the grand khan raises a revenue, the amount of which would scarcely be credited. Here also the inhabitants worship idols, use paper money, and are the subjects of his majesty.

CHAPTER LX

OF THE CITY OF YAN-GUI, OF WHICH MARCO POLO HELD THE GOVERNMENT

PROCEEDING in a south-easterly direction from Chin-gui, you come to the important city of Yan-gui, which, having twenty-four towns under its jurisdiction, must be considered as a place of great consequence.[3] It belongs to the dominion of the grand khan. The people are idolaters, and subsist by trade and manual arts. They manufacture arms and all sorts of warlike accoutrements; in consequence of which many troops are stationed in this part of the country. The city is the place of residence of one of the twelve nobles before

[1] Tingui, or Tingiu, appears to be the Tai-cheu of the maps, a city of the second order, dependent upon Yang-cheu-fu; but of which, as it lies out of the route of travellers, we have little information. The situation, however, with respect to the sea, and in the midst of salt-works, serves to establish their identity. "Il y a beaucoup de salines," observes Martini, "vers l'orient de la ville (de Yang-cheu) où le sel se fait de l'eau de la mer."—P. 129.

[2] This place, as a mart for exporting the salt to different provinces, we may presume to lie near the great river, and Tsing-kiang-hien presents itself as favourably circumstanced for that traffic. It must, however, be observed that Chin-gui, or Cin-gui, as distinct from Tin-gui, is not to be found in the Basle edition or Venice epitome.

[3] The points of the compass must here be greatly perverted; but whatever may be the situations assigned to the inconsiderable places just mentioned, no doubts can be entertained of Yan-gui, or Yan-giu, being the city of Yang-cheu-fu; although the jurisdiction of the latter comprehended, in the seventeenth century, according to Martini, only ten, instead of twenty-four towns. "C'est une ville forte marchande," says Du Halde, "et il s'y fait un grand commerce de toutes sortes d'ouvrages Chinois. . . Le reste du canal jusqu'à Pe-king, n'a aucune ville qui lui soit comparable. . . Yang-tcheou a deux lieues de circuit, et l'on y compte, tant dans la ville, que dans les fauxbourgs, deux millions d'ames." (Tom. i. p. 134.) Staunton speaks of it as a city of the first order, bearing the marks of great antiquity. "It still," he says, "had the appearance of carrying on a considerable trade; and there were not fewer than a thousand vessels of different sizes lying at anchor close to it."—P. 420.

spoken of, who are appointed by his majesty to the government of the provinces;[1] and in the room of one of these, Marco Polo, by special order of the grand khan, acted as governor of this city during the space of three years.

CHAPTER LXI

OF THE PROVINCE OF NAN-GHIN

NAN-GHIN is the name of a large and distinguished province of Manji, situated towards the west.[2] The people are idolaters, use paper money in currency, are subjects of the grand khan, and are largely engaged in commerce. They have raw silk, and weave tissues of silver and gold in great quantities, and of various patterns. The country produces abundance of corn, and is stored as well with domestic cattle as with beasts and birds that are the objects of the chase, and plenty of tigers. It supplies the sovereign with an ample revenue, and chiefly from the imposts levied upon the rich articles in which the merchants trade. We shall now speak of the noble city of Sa-yan-fu.

CHAPTER LXII

OF THE CITY OF SA-YAN-FU, THAT WAS TAKEN BY THE MEANS OF NICOLO AND MAFFEO POLO

SA-YAN-FU is a considerable city of the province of Manji, having under its jurisdiction twelve wealthy and large towns.[3]

[1] From the account of the Civil Tribunal of Twelve, given in chap. xix. of this book, and note [2], p. 206, it did not appear, as this passage implies, that the governors of the provinces, or viceroys, as they are termed (*tsong-tu*), were chosen from their own body. Such a selection may have taken place occasionally, without being the established practice.

[2] By Nan-ghin (in the Basle edition Nauigui, and in the manuscripts as well as the epitome Naingui) must unquestionably be meant Nankin, formerly the name of the province to which the reigning dynasty has given that of Kiang-nan.

[3] In proceeding to the description of this remarkable city, our author departs from the forms of an itinerary, and makes no mention of its distance or its bearings from any of the places already noticed. Siang-yang is situated in the northern part of the province of Hu-kuang, adjoining to that of Kiang-nan, upon the river Han, which discharges itself into the Kiang. The number of towns under its jurisdiction at the time Martini wrote, was seven, exclusive of some fortresses.

It is a place of great commerce and extensive manufactures. The inhabitants burn the bodies of their dead, and are idolaters.[1] They are the subjects of the grand khan, and use his paper currency. Raw silk is there produced in great quantity, and the finest silks, intermixed with gold, are woven. Game of all kinds abounds. The place is amply furnished with everything that belongs to a great city, and by its uncommon strength it was enabled to stand a siege of three years; refusing to surrender to the grand khan, even after he had obtained possession of the province of Manji.[2] The difficulties experienced in the reduction of it were chiefly occasioned by the army's not being able to approach it, excepting on the northern side; the others being surrounded with water,[3] by means of which the place continually received supplies, which it was not in the power of the besiegers to prevent. When the operations were reported to his majesty, he felt extremely hurt that this place alone should obstinately hold out, after all the rest of the country had been reduced to obedience. The circumstance having come to the knowledge of the brothers Nicolo and Maffeo, who were then resident at the imperial court,[4] they immediately presented themselves to the grand khan, and proposed to him that they should be allowed to construct machines, such as were made use of in the West, capable of throwing stones of three hundred pounds weight, by which the buildings of the city might be destroyed and the inhabitants killed. Their memorial was attended to

[1] We are naturally surprised at these repeated assertions, that, even in the central parts of the empire, the inhabitants were accustomed to burn the bodies of their dead. It appears, however, from the observations made by the gentlemen of the Dutch embassy, in passing through the province of Kiang-nan, that regular inhumation is not, even now, so general as had been supposed; and it may be fair to conjecture that, as many of the Chinese superstitions, and along with them the doctrine of the metempsychosis, were borrowed from their Indian neighbours, the rites of the funeral pile may formerly have been still more prevalent.

[2] According to those who have written on the authority of the Chinese annals, Siang-yang was invested in 1269, and taken in 1273; whereas Hang cheu, the capital of the Song, was not summoned until 1276. Our author, therefore, instead of saying that the whole of Manji had been conquered during the continuance of the siege, should have confined his assertion to a considerable part.

[3] The operations were directed, in the first instance, against Fan-ching, on the northern side of the Han, opposite to, and a kind of suburb of, Siang-yang, which appears from the plan in Du Halde to be in part encompassed by a bend of that river.

[4] In the Basle edition the author ascribes to himself a share of the merit; the words being: "Illo enim tempore ego et pater meus atque patruus fuimus in imperatoris aula;" and in the Italian epitome: "Certamente la fo presa per industria de miser Nicolo e Mafio e Marco."

by the grand khan, who, warmly approving of the scheme, gave orders that the ablest smiths and carpenters should be placed under their direction; amongst whom were some Nestorian Christians, who proved to be most able mechanics.[1] In a few days they completed their mangonels, according to the instructions furnished by the two brothers; and a trial being made of them in the presence of the grand khan, and of his whole court, an opportunity was afforded of seeing them cast stones, each of which weighed three hundred pounds. They were then put on board of vessels, and conveyed to the army. When set up in front of the city of Sa-yan-fu, the first stone projected by one of them fell with such weight and violence upon a building, that a great part of it was crushed, and fell to the ground. So terrified were the inhabitants by this mischief, which to them seemed to be the effect of a thunderbolt from heaven,[2] that they immediately deliberated upon the expediency of surrendering. Persons authorized to treat were accordingly sent from the place, and their submission was accepted on the same terms and conditions as had been granted to the rest of the province. This prompt result of their ingenuity increased the reputation and credit of these two Venetian brothers in the opinion of the grand khan and of all his courtiers.[3]

[1] These people we might understand from the text of Ramusio to be Asiatic Christians, and possibly Ighurs or Rumîs, who were then accounted the most ingenious and best instructed people employed at the courts or in the armies of the Tartar and other Eastern princes. In the Basle edition, on the contrary, they are spoken of as "fabros lignarios Christianos quos nobiscum habuimus;" and in the epitome, as "maestri Venetiani che era (erano) in quelle parte."

[2] Frequent notice is taken in the Chinese annals of the fall of meteoric stones. See. Voy à Peking par De Guignes, tom. i. pp. 195—250.

[3] It must not here be passed unnoticed, that the consistency of our author is put to a severe test by the date commonly assigned to the reduction of Siang-yang, which, if it actually took place at the close of the year 1273, allows no more than two years for the journey of the Polo family from Acre, in Palestine, which they certainly left about the end of 1271 (as shown in note [1], p. 19), until their arrival at Pekin; whilst in Ramusio's text, although not in the Basle edition, it is said to have occupied three years and a half. It becomes necessary therefore to adopt the opinion, either that the time they were on the road did not in fact exceed the first-mentioned period, or that the siege was not terminated so early as P. Gaubil and P. Mailla have stated; to which latter supposition some degree of probability is given by the repeated assertion of our author that this was amongst the last places of Manji that held out against the Tartars.

CHAPTER LXIII

OF THE CITY OF SIN-GUI, AND OF THE VERY GREAT RIVER KIANG

LEAVING the city of Sa-yan-fu, and proceeding fifteen days' journey towards the south-east, you reach the city of Sin-gui, which, although not large, is a place of great commerce.[1] The number of vessels that belong to it is prodigious, in consequence of its being situated near the Kiang, which is the largest river in the world, its width being in some places ten, in others eight, and in others six miles.[2] Its length, to the place where it discharges itself into the sea, is upwards of one hundred days' journey.[3] It is indebted for its great size to the vast number of other navigable rivers that empty their waters into it, which have their sources in distant countries. A great number of cities and large towns are situated upon its banks, and more than two hundred, with sixteen provinces,[4] partake of the advantages of its navigation, by which the transport of merchandise is to an extent that might appear incredible to those who have not had an opportunity of witnessing it. When we consider, indeed, the length of its course, and the multitude of rivers

[1] Our author had stepped out of what might be regarded as the line of his route to speak of a place so remarkable as Siang-yang, and here again, by a large stride, returns to the eastern provinces. There is no town that appears to answer so well to the description he has given of Sin-gui, as that of Kiu-kiang, at the northern extremity of the province of Kiang-si, and which, as we are informed by Martini, was named Tin-kiang under the dynasty of the Song.

[2] At the place where the Kiang is crossed by the line of the canal the width is stated by Sir G. Staunton at about two English miles, and by M. De Guignes at a French league; but nearer to the sea it is, of course, much greater. As our author should, however, be supposed to speak of its width near the city he is describing, we ought perhaps to understand not Italian but Chinese miles, or li, which are to the former in the proportion of three to eight, and consequently his estimation would agree with that of the modern travellers. It is to the city of Kiu-kiang that the tides of the sea, at the full and change, are perceived to extend; and here, on this account, it is said to change its appellation of Ta-kiang, or the great river, for that of Yâng-tsè-kiang, or the son of the sea.

[3] The length of its course is computed by Barrow at two thousand two hundred miles, which would give an average of twenty-two miles for each day's passage, or perhaps thirty, when the unavoidable stoppages in so long a tract are considered. By a day's journey must not in general be understood what a person could travel in a given number of hours, but the interval between two accustomed resting places.

[4] The division of the provinces was not the same at that period as it exists at present; the whole number being now fifteen, exclusively of the island of Hai-nan.

that communicate with it (as has been observed), it is not surprising that the quantity and value of articles for the supply of so many places, lying in all directions, should be incalculable. The principal commodity, however, is salt, which is not only conveyed by means of the Kiang, and the rivers connected with it, to the towns upon their banks, but afterwards from thence to all places in the interior of the country.[1] On one occasion, when Marco Polo was at the city of Sin-gui, he saw there not fewer than fifteen thousand vessels; and yet there are other towns along the river where the number is still more considerable.[2] All these vessels are covered with a kind of deck, and have a mast with one sail.[3] Their burthen is in general about four thousand *cantari*, or quintals, of Venice, and from that upwards to twelve thousand cantari, which some of them are capable of loading.[4] They do not employ hempen cordage, excepting for the masts and sails (standing and running rigging). They have canes of the length of fifteen paces, such as have been already described, which they split, in their whole length, into very thin pieces, and these, by twisting them together, they form into ropes three hundred paces long.[5] So skilfully are they manufactured, that they are equal in strength to cordage made of hemp. With these ropes the vessels are tracked along the rivers, by means of ten or twelve horses to

[1] Salt appears to be principally manufactured in that part of Kiang-nan which lies between the sea, on the east, the Kao-yeu lake on the west, and the Kiang on the south. Being shipped on the latter, it is conveyed to the most distant parts of China, but a considerable portion goes to the metropolis.

[2] The city of Kiu-kiang, which answers best to the circumstances related of Sin-gui, is thus spoken of by P. Martini: "Kiu-kiang est une grande ville et fort marchande sur le bord méridional de la rivière de Kiang où elle se joint avec le grand lac de Poyang: on auroit de la peine à croire le grand nombre de vaisseaux qu'il y a, à moins que de l'avoir vue; car ils viennent de tous les endroits les plus éloignés de la Chine dans cette rivière, qui est comme leur rendez-vous, où ils s'assemblent pour se mettre en mer."—P. 111.

[3] Representations of these vessels may be seen in the plates accompanying the accounts of all the Embassies to China.

[4] The *cantaro* is commonly translated by quintal or hundredweight, which would make the burthen of these vessels two hundred, and up to six hundred tons: but the cantaro of some parts of Italy is smaller than that of others.

[5] Persons who have seen the cables belonging to praws of the Eastern Islands might suppose that this account of twisting the bamboo into cordage, was a mistake for the manufacture of cables by twisting or platting the rattan, so commonly applied to that purpose; but our author's correctness as to the material is fully proved by the testimony of modern travellers. "Even the ropes," says Mr. Ellis, "by which the buckets were attached to the wheel, were of bamboo."—Journal, etc. p. 383.

each,[1] as well upwards, against the current, as in the opposite direction. At many places near the banks of this river there are hills and small rocky eminences, upon which are erected idol temples and other edifices, and you find a continual succession of villages and inhabited places.

CHAPTER LXIV

OF THE CITY OF KAYN-GUI

KAYN-GUI is a small town on the southern bank of the before-mentioned river,[2] where annually is collected a very large quantity of corn and rice, the greatest part of which is conveyed from thence to the city of Kanbalu, for the supply of the establishment of the grand khan;[3] for through this place is the line of communication with the province of Cathay, by means of rivers, lakes, and a wide and deep canal which the grand khan has caused to be dug, in order that vessels may pass from one great river to the other, and from the province of Manji, by water, as far as Kanbalu, without making any part of the voyage by sea.[4] This magnificent work is deserving of admiration; and not so much from the manner in which it is conducted through the country, or its vast extent, as from its utility and the benefit it produces to those cities which lie in its course. On its banks, likewise, are constructed strong and wide terraces, or *chaussées*, upon which the travelling by land also is rendered perfectly convenient. In the midst of the

[1] At the present day it would seem that vessels of every description are tracked by men only, and not by horses, which, as well as other cattle, are to a certain degree scarce in China; but there is reason to believe that under the Mungal princes, great numbers were brought from Tartary, and much encouragement given to breeding them. It may be observed at the same time that very little is known of the inland navigation of the country, excepting what is immediately connected with the grand canal.

[2] There is reason to conclude that by Kayn-gui must be meant a town situated at the entrance of the canal, on the southern side of the Kiang, named by P. Magalhanes Chin-kiang-keù, signifying the mouth or port of Chin-kiang (the Tsin-kiang of De Guignes), a city standing on the same canal, and which is the subject of the succeeding chapter.

[3] The journals of Van Braam and of De Guignes make frequent mention of the interruption their yachts experienced from the vast number of vessels laden with rice for Pekin, that were collected at this part of the canal.

[4] In every account of China the description of this grand canal forms a prominent feature: " an inland navigation of such extent and magnitude," says Barrow, " as to stand unrivalled in the history of the world." Its completion, as it now exists, is said to have been effected in the reign of Yong-lo, third emperor of the Ming, about the year 1409.

river, opposite to the city of Kayn-gui, there is an island entirely of rock, upon which are built a grand temple and monastery, where two hundred monks, as they may be termed, reside, and perform service to the idols; and this is the supreme head of many other temples and monasteries.[1] We shall now speak of the city of Chan-ghian-fu.

CHAPTER LXV

OF THE CITY OF CHAN-GHIAN-FU

CHAN-GHIAN-FU is a city of the province of Manji,[2] the inhabitants of which are idolaters, subjects of the grand khan, and use his paper money. They gain their living by trade and manufacture, and are wealthy. They weave tissues of silk and gold. The field sports are there most excellent in every species of game, and provisions are abundant. There are in this city three churches of Nestorian Christians, which were built in the year 1278, when his majesty appointed a Nestorian, named Mar-Sachis, to the government of it for three years. By him these churches were established, where there had not been any before; and they still subsist.[3] Leaving this place, we shall now speak of Tin-gui-gui.

[1] Our author's notice of this island, so peculiarly circumstanced, at the same time that it presents an unquestionable proof of the genuineness of his observations, serves to mark with certainty the place at which he crossed the Kiang. "In crossing the river," says Staunton, "the attention was particularly attracted by an island situated in the middle, called Chin-shan, or the golden mountain, which rose almost perpendicularly out of the river. . . . It belonged to the emperor, who had built upon it a large and handsome palace, and on the highest eminence several temples and pagodas. The island also contained a large monastery of priests, by whom it is chiefly inhabited."—Vol. ii. p. 424.

[2] "Ceux qui liront les escrits de Marco Polo de Venise," says P. Martini, "verront clairement par la situation de cette ville et le nom qu'elle a (Chin-kiang-fu) que c'est celle qu'il nomme Cingiam (Chin-gian). Elle est bastie sur le bord de la rivière de Kiang, et à l'orient d'un canal fait par artifice, qu'on a conduit jusques dans la rivière de Kiang; de l'autre costé du canal, sur le bord qui regarde l'occident, est son fauxbourg, qui n'est pas moins peuplé, et où l'abord est aussi grand que celuy de la ville mesme." It is evident that this *fauxbourg* is the town that has been described under the corrupted name of Kayn-gui, and what has been said of the resort of shipping might have been reserved for this place.

[3] The existence of these churches, of which no reasonable doubt can be entertained, is a curious fact in the history of the progress made by the Christian religion in the eastern or remoter parts of China. The name of the individual is, in the Basle edition, Mar-Sarcis, and in the Berlin manuscript, Mar-Iarchis. The title or appellation of Mar, equivalent, in Syriac, to Dominus in Latin, is well known to have been commonly

CHAPTER LXVI

OF THE CITY OF TIN-GUI-GUI

DEPARTING from Chan-ghian-fu, and travelling four days towards the south-east, you pass many towns and fortified places, the inhabitants of which are idolaters, live by arts and commerce, are the subjects of the grand khan, and use his paper money. At the end of these four days, you reach the city of Tin-gui-gui, which is large and handsome,[1] and produces much raw silk, of which tissues of various qualities and patterns are woven. The necessaries of life are here in plenty, and the variety of game affords excellent sport. The inhabitants were a vile, inhuman race. At the time that Chinsan Ba-yan, or the hundred-eyed, subdued the country of Manji, he despatched certain Alanian Christians,[2] along with a party of his own people, to possess themselves of this city; who, as soon as they appeared before it, were suffered to enter without resistance. The place being surrounded by a double wall, one of them within the other, the Alanians occupied the first enclosure, where they found a large quantity of wine; and having previously suffered much from fatigue and privation, they were eager to quench their thirst, and, without any consideration, proceeded to drink to such excess, that, becoming intoxicated, they fell asleep. The people of the city, who were within the second enclosure, as soon as they perceived that their enemies lay slumbering on the ground, took the opportunity of murdering them, not suffering one to escape. When Chinsan Ba-yan learned the fate of his detachment, his indignation and anger were raised to the highest

affixed to the names of Nestorian bishops, as well as of other persons of rank, and as that of Mar-Sergius often occurs in the annals of their church, it seems likely to have been the name of which Sachis and Sarcis are corruptions.

[1] The distance of four days' journey, in the line of the canal, from the last-mentioned place, shows that this city, which in the early Venice epitome is named Tin-gin-gui, and in the Berlin manuscript Chin-chin-gui, must be the Tchang-tcheou-fou of Du Halde's map, or Chang-cheu-fû according to our orthography: " ville célèbre et d'un grand commerce qui est située proche du canal."

[2] Without entering upon the ancient and obscure history of the Alani or Alanians of Scythia or Turkistan, it will be sufficient to observe that after their defeat and dispersion by the Huns, a considerable portion of them settled on the northern slope of the range of Caucasus, on the western side of the Caspian, and, if not actually the same people, are now confounded with the Abkhas and Cherkess or Circassians.

pitch, and he sent another army to attack the place. When it was carried, he gave orders for putting to the sword all the inhabitants, great and small, without distinction of sex, as an act of retaliation.

CHAPTER LXVII

OF THE CITIES OF SIN-GUI AND VA-GIU

SIN-GUI is a large and magnificent city, the circumference of which is twenty miles.[1] The inhabitants are idolaters, subjects of the grand khan, and use his paper money. They have vast quantities of raw silk, and manufacture it, not only for their own consumption, all of them being clothed in dresses of silk, but also for other markets. There are amongst them some very rich merchants, and the number of inhabitants is so great as to be a subject of astonishment. They are, however, a pusillanimous race, and solely occupied with their trade and manufactures. In these indeed they display considerable ability, and if they were as enterprising, manly, and warlike, as they are ingenious, so prodigious is their number, that they might not only subdue the whole of the province (Manji), but might carry their views still further. They have amongst them many physicians of eminent skill, who can ascertain the nature of the disorder, and know how to apply the proper remedies.[2] There are also persons distinguished as professors of learning, or, as we should term them, philosophers, and

[1] By Sin-gui is to be understood the eminent city of Su-cheu, situated in the line of the canal, and much celebrated by travellers, who compare it in some respects, to Venice. "The streets of the city of Sou-choo-foo," says Staunton, "through the suburbs of which the yachts now passed, were divided, like Venice, by branches from the principal canal. Over each of those branches was erected an elegant stone bridge. The fleet of the embassy was nearly three hours in passing the suburbs of Sou-choo-foo, before they arrived at the city walls." (Vol. ii. p. 427.) "Les murailles de la ville de Sucheu," says Martini, "ont quarante stades Chinoises de circuit; mais si vous y comprenez les fauxbourgs, vous en trouverez sans doute plus de cent." (P. 124.) Forty Chinese *li* are equal to fifteen Italian miles.

[2] Su-cheu-fu being a place of great wealth and luxury, it is natural that the medical art should there be liberally encouraged, and its practitioners skilful. By some writers the Chinese physicians are said to "have made a proficiency that would astonish the ablest of ours in Europe;" whilst others consider their elaborate process of feeling the pulse, and their pretensions of being from thence enabled to ascertain the seat of the disorder, as nothing better than solemn mummery. See General Description of China, by the Abbé Grosier, vol. ii. p. 480; and Barrow's Travels in China, p. 343.

others who may be called magicians or enchanters.[1] On the mountains near the city, rhubarb grows in the highest perfection, and is from thence distributed throughout the province.[2] Ginger is likewise produced in large quantities, and is sold at so cheap a rate, that forty pounds weight of the fresh root may be had for the value, in their money, of a Venetian silver groat. Under the jurisdiction of Sin-gui there are sixteen respectable and wealthy cities and towns, where trade and arts flourish. By the name of Sin-gui is to be understood "the city of the earth," as by that of Kin-sai, "the city of heaven."[3] Leaving Sin-gui, we shall now speak of another

[1] By philosophers and magicians, he evidently alludes to the disciples of Confucius (commonly termed *literati*), and to those of Lao-kiun, or the sect of the *tao-tse;* as in other places, by the appellation of idolaters, he means the worshippers of Fo, or Buddha, who constitute the most numerous class. The first of these study the moral and metaphysical works of their great master, and take regular degrees in philosophy, which qualify them, according to their attainments, for holding the several offices of government, and becoming what Europeans term "mandarins of letters." The *tao-tse*, or "sons of immortality," as they style themselves, hold doctrines which some writers describe as resembling those of the Hindu *yogis* or quietists (from whom they seem, in fact, to be derived); whilst others, judging from their worldly habits, attribute to them those of the Epicurean school; but whatever their dogmas may be, they devote themselves to the practice of magic, and delude their followers by the visions and reveries of the *illuminati*.

[2] "Le *tai-hoam* (more correctly, according to De Guignes, *ta-hoang*, grand jaune) ou la rhubarbe," says P. Perennin, "croît en plusieurs endroits de la Chine. La meilleure est celle de Sse-tchouen; celle qui vient dans la province de Xensi et dans le royaume de Thibet, lui est fort inférieure." (Lett. édif. tom. xix. p. 307.) The mountains of the province of Kiang-nan, being in the same latitude as the former, may likewise produce a good kind, although not noticed by our modern travellers, who in general have had little opportunity of making botanical researches beyond the borders of the canals and high roads. It is evident that a mistake has here been made, probably in the arrangement of our author's original notes. What is said of the growth of rhubarb in the neighbourhood of this Sin-gui or Su-cheu, in the eastern province of Kiang-nan, was undoubtedly meant to apply to another Singui, or Si-ning, a well-known place of trade in the western province of Shen-si, and on the road to Tibet. The commerce in that article particularly belongs to the latter place, and the Russians, as Pallas informs us, make their contracts for it with Bucharian merchants settled there. It is not only in itself improbable that two places of the same name, in opposite extremes of China, should boast of this production, but the fact of its being found in any one of the eastern provinces is entirely unsupported. With respect to ginger, the quantity that might be purchased for a Venetian groat is said in the Italian epitome to be five only, not forty pounds weight. [The best texts agree in reading *forty*.]

[3] Although our author may be mistaken in his etymology and in his distinctive epithets of celestial and terrestrial paradise, it is plain that his observation refers to a well-known Chinese saying, that, "what the heavens are, above, Su-cheu and Hang-cheu are upon earth." P. Martini gives the proverb in the original words. Thevenot, iii. partie, p. 124.

city, distant from it only a day's journey, named Va-giu, where, likewise, there is a vast abundance of raw silk, and where there are many merchants as well as artificers. Silks of the finest quality are woven here, and are afterwards carried to every part of the province.[1] No other circumstances presenting themselves as worthy of remark, we shall now proceed to the description of the principal city and metropolis of the province of Manji, named Kin-sai.

CHAPTER LXVIII

OF THE NOBLE AND MAGNIFICENT CITY OF KIN-SAI

§ 1. UPON leaving Va-giu you pass, in the course of three days' journey, many towns, castles, and villages, all of them well inhabited and opulent. The people are idolaters, and the subjects of the grand khan, and they use paper money and have abundance of provisions. At the end of three days you reach the noble and magnificent city of Kin-sai, a name that signifies " the celestial city," and which it merits from its pre-eminence to all others in the world, in point of grandeur and beauty, as well as from its abundant delights, which might lead an inhabitant to imagine himself in paradise.[2] This city was frequently visited by Marco Polo,[3] who carefully and diligently observed and inquired into every circumstance respecting it, all of which he entered in his notes, from whence the following particulars are briefly stated. According to

[1] The city of Va-gie, of which no mention is made in the other versions, must be either Ho-cheu, situated on the side of Lake Tai, opposite to that on which Su-cheu stands, or else (and more probably) the city called Kia-hing in modern times, and formerly Siu-cheu, which is in the direct line of the canal, and midway between Su-cheu and Hang-cheu. Both of them are celebrated for the richness of their commerce, particuarly in silk, both raw and manufactured.

[2] At the time when this city, the capital of Southern China under the dynasty of the Song, was surrendered to the arms of Kublaï, the Chinese annals call it by the name of Lin-gnan. This was changed by the Ming for that of Hang-cheu, which it had borne at an earlier period, and which it still retains. Quinsai, Kin-sai, or, according to De Guignes, Kin-tsay, must therefore be considered only as a descriptive appellation, grounded, perhaps, upon the proverbial saying already noticed, which terms it a celestial abode, although the meaning of the component words may not be precisely that which our author has assigned to them.

[3] The city of Yang-cheu-fu, of which he was the provisional governor for three years, being distant only about a week's journey, by the canal, from Hang-cheu-fu, he had consequently the opportunity of occasional intercourse with that capital.

common estimation, this city is an hundred miles in circuit.[1] Its streets and canals are extensive, and there are squares, or market-places, which, being necessarily proportioned in size to the prodigious concourse of people by whom they are frequented, are exceedingly spacious. It is situated between a lake of fresh and very clear water on the one side,[2] and a river of great magnitude on the other, the waters of which, by a number of canals, large and small, are made to run through every quarter of the city, carrying with them all the filth into the lake, and ultimately to the sea.[3] This, whilst it contributes much to the purity of the air, furnishes a communication by water, in addition to that by land, to all parts of the town; the canals and the streets being of sufficient width to allow of boats on the one, and carriages in the other, conveniently

[1] These dimensions, taken in their literal sense, must be regarded as extravagant, even although they should be understood to include the suburbs; but there has already been frequent occasion to remark, that when, in describing the size of places, our author speaks of miles, he must be supposed to mean Chinese miles, or li, which are to the Italian in the proportion of three to eight. Even such an extent might seem excessive, were it not that the walls even of the modern city are estimated by travellers at sixty li, and that, if in the course of five centuries they have undergone alterations, it is to be presumed their limits may have been considerably contracted. It is rarely indeed that strangers can have the opportunity of measuring the works of fortified places: they must derive their information from the natives, who, from ignorance or vanity, are likely to deceive them.

[2] The lake here spoken of is the Si-hu, or "western lake," so called from its being situated on the western side of the city. Although inconsiderable in point of extent, it is highly celebrated by all travellers on account of the beauty of its surrounding scenery, and the peculiar transparency of its waters. "The lake," says Staunton, "formed a beautiful sheet of water, about three or four miles in diameter, and surrounded to the north, east, and south by an amphitheatre of picturesque mountains. . . . It was in most places shallow, the water perfectly pellucid, and the bottom gravelly." (P. 444.) "The water," says Barrow, who made an excursion on it, "was as clear as crystal."—P. 524.

[3] The river upon which this ancient capital of southern China stands is the Tsien-tang-kiang. "The tide," says Staunton, "increases the width of this river to about four miles opposite the city. At low water there is a fine level strand near two miles broad, which extends towards the sea as far as the eye can reach." (P. 438.) According to the words of our author there appears to have been, in his time, a passage of water from the river, through the numerous canals of the city, into the lake. This would take place at the flood tide; and at the ebb, through the same channels, there would be a reflux from the lake into the river, necessary for the purpose of cleansing them. But in the modern accounts of Hang-cheu-fu no mention is made of any such communication between the river and the city or the lake, and to account for the disagreement we might be led to conclude that from the receding of the sea, or other natural causes, a change of circumstances may have been produced in so long a course of time.

passing, with articles necessary for the consumption of the inhabitants.[1] It is commonly said that the number of bridges, of all sizes, amounts to twelve thousand.[2] Those which are thrown over the principal canals and are connected with the main streets, have arches so high, and built with so much skill, that vessels with their masts can pass under them,[3] whilst, at the same time, carts and horses are passing over their heads,—so well is the slope from the street adapted to the height of the arch. If they were not in fact so numerous, there would be no convenience of crossing from one place to another.

§ 2. Beyond the city, and enclosing it on that side, there is a fosse about forty miles in length, very wide, and full of water that comes from the river before mentioned. This was excavated by the ancient kings of the province, in order that when the river should overflow its banks, the superfluous water might be diverted into this channel; and to serve at the same time as a measure of defence.[4] The earth dug out from

[1] All the modern accounts of this city concur in describing its numerous canals, but they likewise insist upon the narrowness of its paved streets. Our author, it is true, in a subsequent part of his description, speaks of the principal street as being forty paces in width (about equal to that of Pekin); but it must be considered that at the period when he wrote, Hang-cheu still retained the magnificence of a great capital and imperial residence, and that in a country repeatedly ravaged by foreign and domestic conquerors, it cannot be supposed to have escaped repeated destruction, nor, when renewed, to have assumed, in the new arrangement of its streets, any other character than that of a provincial city, although of the first class.

[2] Amongst the exaggerations imputed to our author, in his account of China, none has been more commonly pointed out by those who take a part against him, than this assertion, that a city, whatever its extent and magnificence might be, should have contained twelve thousand bridges. It cannot be denied that the truth is here outstepped; but it must be recollected that he does not state the fact upon the authority of any enumeration of his own, but merely as the popular story (*è fama* is the expression) related by the inhabitants of the place, whose vanity, in this and other instances, led them to impose upon admiring credulity.

[3] "Outre ces digues," says P. Le Comte, speaking of the grand canal, "on a basti une infinité de ponts pour la communication des terres: ils sont de trois, de cinq, et de sept arches; celle du milieu est extraordinairement haute, afin que les barques en passant, ne soient pas obligées d'abaisser leurs masts." (Nouv. Mém. de la Chine, tom. i. p. 161.) "De tous les environs," says Du Halde, in his description of a neighbouring city, "on peut venir, entrer, et aller dans toute la ville en bateau. Il n'y a point de rue où il n'y ait un canal; c'est pourquoi il y a quantité de ponts qui sont fort élevés, et presque tous d'une seule arche." (Tom. i. p. 179.) But most directly to our purpose is Barrow's observation, that "over this main trunk and most of the other canals and rivers, are a great variety of bridges. . . . Some have the piers of such an extraordinary height, that the largest vessels, of two hundred tons, sail under them without striking their masts."—P. 337.

[4] The existence of this fosse, commencing at the lake, and terminating at the river, may be traced in Du Halde's plan of the city. Its length

thence was thrown to the inner side, and has the appearance of many hillocks surrounding the place. There are within the city ten principal squares or market-places, besides innumerable shops along the streets. Each side of these squares is half a mile in length,[1] and in front of them is the main street, forty paces in width, and running in a direct line from one extremity of the city to the other. It is crossed by many low and convenient bridges. These market-squares (two miles in their whole dimension) are at the distance of four miles from each other. In a direction parallel to that of the main street, but on the opposite side of the squares, runs a very large canal, on the nearer bank of which capacious warehouses are built of stone, for the accommodation of the merchants who arrive from India and other parts, together with their goods and effects, in order that they may be conveniently situated with respect to the market-places.[2] In each of these, upon three days in every week, there is an assemblage of from forty to fifty thousand persons, who attend the markets and supply them with every article of provision that can be desired. There is an abundant quantity of game of all kinds, such as roebucks, stags, fallow deer, hares, and rabbits, together with partridges, pheasants, francolins, quails, common fowls, capons, and such numbers of ducks and geese as can scarcely be expressed; for so easily are they bred and reared on the lake, that, for the value of a Venetian silver groat, you may purchase a couple of geese and two couple of ducks.[3] There, also, are the shambles,

there appears to exceed the proportion here assigned of four-tenths of the whole extent of the walls, but all the plans in that collection are without scale, and seem to have been drawn by Chinese artists, from memory rather than from actual survey. With regard to the object of this excavation, it may rather be thought intended to carry off the overflowings of the lake, than to receive those of the river, and Staunton accordingly speaks of the stream that flows through it at ordinary times, as being supplied from the former.

[1] The interior of this and of every other Chinese city must have undergone an entire change since the days of our author, and the bazars or market-places here mentioned are unnoticed by modern travellers. According to the length of the Chinese li, as established by the most accurate writers, at 296 French toises, each side of these squares would be about 320 English yards, and their distance from each other about 2,560.

[2] The regulations of the Chinese government with regard to foreign commerce appear to have been nearly the same, at a remote period, as those to which the European concerns at the port of Canton are subjected at the present day.

[3] Perhaps instead of the conjunction copulative "and," we should here read the disjunctive "or," and consider two of the smaller of these aquatic birds as an equivalent for one of the larger.

where they slaughter cattle for food, such as oxen, calves, kids, and lambs, to furnish the tables of rich persons and of the great magistrates. As to people of the lower classes, they do not scruple to eat every other kind of flesh, however unclean, without any discrimination.[1] At all seasons there is in the markets a great variety of herbs and fruits, and especially pears of an extraordinary size, weighing ten pounds each, that are white in the inside, like paste, and have a very fragrant smell.[2] There are peaches also, in their season, both of the yellow and the white kind,[3] and of a delicious flavour. Grapes are not produced there, but are brought in a dried state, and very good, from other parts. This applies also to wine, which the natives do not hold in estimation, being accustomed to their own liquor prepared from rice and spices. From the sea, which is fifteen miles distant, there is daily brought up the river, to the city, a vast quantity of fish; and in the lake also there is abundance, which gives employment at all times to persons whose sole occupation it is to catch them. The sorts

[1] Staunton observes, that "of the larger kind (of quadrupeds) the common people have little opportunity of ever tasting, unless of such as die by accident or disease. In such cases the appetite of a Chinese surmounts all scruple; whether it be an ox or camel, a sheep or ass, it is equally acceptable. This people know no distinction of clean and unclean meat. . . . Quadrupeds that can find some resources for subsistence about dwelling-houses, such as hogs and dogs, are the most common animal food, and are sold at the public markets." (P. 399.) The Arabian travellers of the ninth century notice in like manner the indiscriminate style of feeding to which the Chinese were addicted in their days.

[2] Pears of the weight of ten pounds are, it must be confessed, an extraordinary production of nature, and must have been of a kind still unknown in Europe, where, I believe, the largest are not found to exceed two pounds; nor have I been able to ascertain the weight of any pear grown in England, exceeding twenty-six ounces. It is well known, indeed, that the varieties of the pyrus, as well as of other fruits, not only degenerate in size and quality, but in a long course of years actually become extinct. But the credibility of our author's assertion does not rest for support upon the mere presumption of what might have been the state of Chinese horticulture in the thirteenth century; for we learn from the accounts of modern travellers that pears of uncommon magnitude are still produced in the eastern provinces of China. Mr. Henry Browne, who for many years filled the situation of Chief of the Company's factory at Canton, assured Mr. Marsden that he had seen pears, supposed to have been produced in the province of Fo-kien, the bulk of which equalled that of a moderate sized wine decanter. What is said of their inner substance resembling paste, is meant to describe that quality which Van Braam terms *fondante* or melting, and which De Guignes, speaking of the same fruit, expresses by *beurrée*. The latter pronounces them to be "fort grosses et excellentes."—Tom. iii. p. 355.

[3] By peaches of the yellow kind it may be conjectured that our author means apricots, which, as well as peaches, are the produce of that part of China. No mention is made of oranges.

are various according to the season of the year, and, in consequence of the offal carried thither from the town, they become large and rich. At the sight of such an importation of fish, you would think it impossible that it could be sold; and yet, in the course of a few hours, it is all taken off, so great is the number of inhabitants, even of those classes which can afford to indulge in such luxuries, for fish and flesh are eaten at the same meal. Each of the ten market-squares is surrounded with high dwelling-houses,[1] in the lower part of which are shops, where every kind of manufacture is carried on, and every article of trade is sold; such, amongst others, as spices, drugs, trinkets, and pearls. In certain shops nothing is vended but the wine of the country, which they are continually brewing, and serve out fresh to their customers at a moderate price. The streets connected with the market-squares are numerous, and in some of them are many cold baths, attended by servants of both sexes, to perform the offices of ablution for the men and women who frequent them, and who from their childhood have been accustomed at all times to wash in cold water, which they reckon highly conducive to health. At these bathing places, however, they have apartments provided with warm water, for the use of strangers, who, from not being habituated to it, cannot bear the shock of the cold. All are in the daily practice of washing their persons, and especially before their meals.

§ 3. In other streets are the habitations of the courtesans, who are here in such numbers as I dare not venture to report: and not only near the squares, which is the situation usually appropriated for their residence, but in every part of the city they are to be found, adorned with much finery, highly perfumed, occupying well-furnished houses, and attended by many female domestics.[2] These women are accomplished,

[1] The generality of Chinese houses having only one floor, those which are raised to a second story may, comparatively, be termed *case alte*.

[2] At Kanbalu, or Pekin, it was the custom in our author's time, as it is at the present day, to restrict the residence of the public women to the suburbs of the city, where the numerous strangers who resort to the capital were likewise quartered. Here, on the other hand, they are described as inhabiting the most frequented parts of the town, and especially the vicinity of the squares or bazars, as if the accommodation of the foreign merchants, in this respect also, was particularly consulted. "Ces femmes" (says the second of the Arabian travellers, after explaining the manner in which they were registered and licensed by the officers of government) "marchent les soirs habillées d'estoffes (silks) de diverses couleurs, et elles ne portent point de voiles. Elles s'abandonnent à tous les estrangers nouvellement arrivés dans le païs, lors qu'ils

and are perfect in the arts of blandishment and dalliance, which they accompany with expressions adapted to every description of person, insomuch that strangers who have once tasted of their charms, remain in a state of fascination, and become so enchanted by their meretricious arts, that they can never divest themselves of the impression. Thus intoxicated with sensual pleasures, when they return to their homes they report that they have been in Kin-sai, or the celestial city, and pant for the time when they may be enabled to revisit paradise. In other streets are the dwellings of the physicians and the astrologers, who also give instructions in reading and writing, as well as in many other arts. They have apartments also amongst those which surround the market-squares. On opposite sides of each of these squares there are two large edifices, where officers appointed by the grand khan are stationed, to take immediate cognisance of any differences that may happen to arise between the foreign merchants, or amongst the inhabitants of the place. It is their duty likewise to see that the guards upon the several bridges in their respective vicinities (of whom mention shall be made hereafter) are duly placed, and in cases of neglect, to punish the delinquents at their discretion.[1]

On each side of the principal street, already mentioned as extending from one end of the city to the other, there are houses and mansions of great size, with their gardens, and near to these, the dwellings of the artisans, who work in shops, at their several trades; and at all hours you see such multitudes of people passing and repassing, on their various avocations, that the providing food in sufficiency for their maintenance might be deemed an impossibility;[2] but other ideas will be formed when it is observed that, on every market-day, the squares are crowded with tradespeople, who cover the whole space with the articles brought by carts and boats, for all of which they find a sale. By instancing the single article of

aiment la desbauche. Les Chinois les font venir chez eux, et elles n'en sortent que le matin. Louons Dieu, de ce qu'il nous a exemptez de semblables infamies."—Anc. Relat. p. 57.

[1] In the account given by De Guignes of the several ranks of civil mandarins or magistrates (*kouan*), he mentions "le nan-hay, chef de police, et ses assesseurs ou lieutenants de quartiers." The officers spoken of in the text were probably of this latter class.

[2] "It was difficult," says Staunton, "to pass along the streets, on account of the vast concourse of people not assembled merely to see the strangers, or on any other public occasion, but each individual going about his own concerns."—P. 439.

pepper, some notion may be formed of the whole quantity of provisions, meat, wine, groceries, and the like, required for the consumption of the inhabitants of Kin-sai; and of this, Marco Polo learned from an officer employed in the grand khan's customs, the daily amount was forty-three loads, each load being two hundred and forty-three pounds.[1]

§ 4. The inhabitants of the city are idolaters, and they use paper money as currency. The men as well as the women have fair complexions, and are handsome. The greater part of them are always clothed in silk, in consequence of the vast quantity of that material produced in the territory of Kin-sai, exclusively of what the merchants import from other provinces.[2] Amongst the handicraft trades exercised in the place, there are twelve considered to be superior to the rest, as being more generally useful; for each of which there are a thousand workshops, and each shop furnishes employment for ten, fifteen, or twenty workmen, and in a few instances as many as forty, under their respective masters. The opulent principals in these manufactories do not labour with their own hands, but, on the contrary, assume airs of gentility and affect parade. Their wives equally abstain from work. They have much beauty, as has been remarked, and are brought up with delicate and languid habits.[3] The costliness of their dresses,

[1] As our author professes to have obtained his information on this head from an officer of the customs, it follows that the quantity of pepper stated in the text was that of the importation (which alone could come under his cognisance), and not the quantity consumed in the city; with which, however, it was not unlikely to be confounded in the mind of the former. The daily entry being stated at 10,449 lbs., the annual quantity would be 3,813,885 lbs., or (at the customary rate of 16 cwt. to the ton, in this article) about 2,130 tons. This may be thought large, but in a paper drawn up by Mr. F. Pigou, and published in Dalrymple's Oriental Repertory (vol. ii. p. 305), it is asserted that "the usual import, at all the trading ports of China, is about 40,000 peculs, or, at 133 lbs. to the pecul, about 3,000 tons. "Les Hollandois et les Anglois," says De Guignes, speaking of the modern commerce of the Chinese, "ont vendu 1,465,053 livres pesant de poivre, 46,371 livres de girofle, et 8,979 livres de muscade. Cette quantité d'épiceries, si l'on considère la population de la Chine, est plus qu'insuffisante, et n'est rien en raison de ce que l'empire devroit consummer." (Tom. iii. p. 304.) In regard to the inadequacy of this importation it should be observed, that it is not upon the European trade alone the Chinese depend for their supplies of pepper. Their junks frequent many of the eastern islands, and at the port of Borneo Proper, in particular, annually take on board large cargoes of that article.

[2] "The flowered and embroidered satins, and other branches in the manufacture of silk, every part of which is done by women, occupy," says Staunton, "vast numbers of them in Han-choo-foo. Most of the men were gaily dressed; and appeared to be in comfortable circumstances."—Embassy, vol. ii. p. 439.

[3] The softness of feature, delicacy of shape, and languid habits of the

in silks and jewellery, can scarcely be imagined. Although the laws of their ancient kings ordained that each citizen should exercise the profession of his father, yet they were allowed, when they acquired wealth, to discontinue the manual labour, provided they kept up the establishment, and employed persons to work at their paternal trades.[1] Their houses are well built and richly adorned with carved work. So much do they delight in ornaments of this kind, in paintings, and fancy buildings, that the sums they lavish on such objects are enormous. The natural disposition of the native inhabitants of Kin-sai is pacific, and by the example of their former kings, who were themselves unwarlike, they have been accustomed to habits of tranquillity. The management of arms is unknown to them, nor do they keep any in their houses.[2] Contentious broils are never heard among them.[3] They conduct their mercantile and manufacturing concerns with perfect candour and probity.[4] They are friendly towards each other,

Chinese women of superior rank, may be observed in their paintings. "Though the ladies," says Staunton, "reckon corpulence a beauty in a man, they consider it as a palpable blemish in their own sex, and aim at preserving a slimness and delicacy of shape." (P. 440.) The practice of reducing the size and impeding the use of their feet, by early bandaging, is not adverted to by our author, unless he may be thought to have had it in view when he employed the phrase "allevate morbidamente." In respect to this and some other instances of extraordinary peculiarities, (such as the growth of the finger-nails to the length of two or three inches, and the preserving them in cases,) he may have been doubtful of gaining credit, or apprehensive of being exposed to ridicule, should he relate them as facts. It may also admit of question whether such fashions did actually prevail at that period.

[1] If this hereditary exercise of professions was anciently a custom amongst the Chinese, as it is with the people of India, it must be allowed that the traces of it are not apparent in modern times.

[2] The unwarlike disposition and habits of the Chinese are generally known; yet in the defence of their towns they have on many occasions shown the highest degree of patriotic and desperate resolution; nor would the Mungals have effected the subjugation of the country, if the people had not been betrayed by their superior officers.

[3] The exterior deportment of these people is grave and placid, but their temper is naturally irascible and vindictive, and the infrequency of broils is chiefly to be attributed to a rigorous police.

[4] To this character for probity it may be thought that the Chinese traders of the present day have little claim, as all our accounts of their manners abound with stories of the ingenious frauds practised at Canton upon the less cunning Europeans; but these apply chiefly to the lower class of dealers, who, perhaps, if they could be heard in their own defence, might justify their knavery upon the principle of retaliation. In the long-continued intercourse that has subsisted between the agents of the European companies and the more eminent of the Chinese merchants, whatever injustice the former may have experienced from the effects of court intrigue, complaints on the ground of commercial unfairness have been extremely rare, and on the contrary their transactions have been marked with the most perfect good faith and mutual confidence.

and persons who inhabit the same street, both men and women, from the mere circumstance of neighbourhood, appear like one family. In their domestic manners they are free from jealousy or suspicion of their wives, to whom great respect is shown, and any man would be accounted infamous who should presume to use indecent expressions to a married woman. To strangers also, who visit their city in the way of commerce, they give proofs of cordiality, inviting them freely to their houses, showing them hospitable attention, and furnishing them with the best advice and assistance in their mercantile transactions. On the other hand, they dislike the sight of soldiery, not excepting the guards of the grand khan, as they preserve the recollection that by them they were deprived of the government of their native kings and rulers.

§ 5. On the borders of the lake are many handsome and spacious edifices belonging to men of rank and great magistrates. There are likewise many idol temples, with their monasteries, occupied by a number of monks, who perform the service of the idols.[1] Near the central part are two islands, upon each of which stands a superb building, with an incredible number of apartments and separate pavilions. When the inhabitants of the city have occasion to celebrate a wedding, or to give a sumptuous entertainment, they resort to one of these islands, where they find ready for their purpose every article that can be required, such as vessels, napkins, table-linen, and the like, which are provided and kept there at the common expense of the citizens, by whom also the buildings were erected. It may happen that at one time there are a hundred parties assembled there, at wedding or other feasts, all of whom, notwithstanding, are accommodated with separate rooms or pavilions, so judiciously arranged that they do not interfere with or incommode each other. In addition to this, there are upon the lake a great number of pleasure vessels or barges, calculated for holding ten, fifteen, to twenty persons, being from fifteen to twenty paces in length, with a wide and

[1] "The lake," says Staunton, "formed a beautiful sheet of water, about three or four miles in diameter, and surrounded, to the north, east, and south, by an amphitheatre of mountains, between the base of which and the margin of the lake, the narrow slip of level ground was laid out in a pleasing style suitable to the situation. It was ornamented with houses and gardens of mandarins, as well as a palace belonging to the emperor, together with temples, monasteries for the *hoshaung* or priests of Fo, and a number of light and fanciful stone bridges that are thrown across the arms of the lake. . . . Upon the summit also were erected pagodas, one of which attracted particular attention."—P. 444.

flat flooring, and not liable to heel to either side in passing through the water. Such persons as take delight in the amusement, and mean to enjoy it, either in the company of their women or that of their male companions, engage one of these barges, which are always kept in the nicest order, with proper seats and tables, together with every other kind of furniture necessary for giving an entertainment. The cabins have a flat roof or upper deck, where the boatmen take their place, and by means of long poles, which they thrust to the bottom of the lake (not more than one or two fathoms in depth), they shove the barges along, until they reach the intended spot. These cabins are painted within-side of various colours and with a variety of figures; all parts of the vessel are likewise adorned with painting.[1] There are windows on each side, which may either be kept shut, or opened, to give an opportunity to the company, as they sit at table, of looking out in every direction and feasting their eyes on the variety and beauty of the scenes as they pass them. And truly the gratification afforded in this manner, upon the water, exceeds any that can be derived from the amusements on the land; for as the lake extends the whole length of the city, on one side, you have a view, as you stand in the boat, at a certain distance from the shore, of all its grandeur and beauty, its palaces, temples, convents, and gardens, with trees of the largest size growing down to the water's edge, whilst at the same time you enjoy the sight of other boats of the same description, continually passing you, filled in like manner with parties in pursuit of amusement. In fact, the inhabitants of this place, as soon as the labours of the day have ceased, or their mercantile transactions are closed, think of nothing else than of passing the remaining hours in parties of pleasure, with their wives or their mistresses, either in these barges, or about the city in carriages, of which it will here be proper to give some account, as constituting one of the amusements of these people.

It must be observed, in the first place, that the streets of

[1] "Navires," says P. Martini, "qu'on pourroit appeller avec raison des palais dorés, parce qu'ils sont peints de diverses couleurs, et que tout y brille du plus fin et du meilleur or: de sorte que c'est là où la magnificence et la pompe des festins, des spectacles, et des jeux éclatent tous les jours. Ces Chinois de Hang-cheu, qui sont autant d'esclaves de la volupté, y trouvent en abondance tout ce qu'ils peuvent souhaiter." (P. 141.) "Vast numbers of barges," says Barrow, speaking of the same lake, "were sailing to and fro, all gaily decorated with paint and gilding and streaming colours; the parties within them apparently all in pursuit of pleasure."—P. 524.

Kin-sai are all paved with stones and bricks, and so likewise are all the principal roads extending from thence through the province of Manji, by means of which passengers can travel to every part without soiling their feet; but as the couriers of his majesty, who go on horseback with great speed, cannot make use of the pavement, a part of the road, on one side, is on their account left unpaved. The main street of the city, of which we have before spoken, as leading from one extremity to the other, is paved with stone and brick to the width of ten paces on each side, the intermediate part being filled up with small gravel, and provided with arched drains for carrying off the rain-water that falls, into the neighbouring canals, so that it remains always dry. On this gravel it is that the carriages are continually passing and repassing. They are of a long shape, covered at top, have curtains and cushions of silk, and are capable of holding six persons. Both men and women who feel disposed to take their pleasure, are in the daily practice of hiring them for that purpose, and accordingly at every hour you may see vast numbers of them driven along the middle part of the street.[1] Some of them proceed to visit certain gardens, where the company are introduced, by those who have the management of the place, to shady recesses contrived by the gardeners for that purpose; and here the men indulge themselves all day in the society of their women, returning home, when it becomes late, in the manner they came.

§ 6. It is the custom of the people of Kin-sai, upon the birth of a child, for the parents to make a note, immediately, of the day, hour, and minute at which the delivery took place. They then inquire of an astrologer under what sign or aspect of the heavens the child was born; and his answer is likewise committed carefully to writing. When therefore he is grown up, and is about to engage in any mercantile adventure, voyage, or treaty of marriage, this document is carried to the astrologer, who, having examined it, and weighed all the circumstances,

[1] The carriages which stand for hire in the streets of Pekin are of a smaller size than these described by our author, but in other respects the construction is the same. See plate 41, of those annexed to M. De Guignes' work, where it will be observed that the carriages nearly resemble what we term in England a tilted cart. As the habits of the ancient Chinese capital were much more luxurious than those of Pekin under the Tartar dominion, at any period, we may conclude that the vehicles of the former were fitted up with more attention to ease and convenience, as well as with more splendour, than the clumsy machines above described. Staunton, indeed, speaks of "cushions stuffed with cotton, and covered with silk, to sit upon," in the waggons of Hang-cheu-fu.—P. 447.

pronounces certain oracular words, in which these people, who sometimes find them justified by the event, place great confidence. Of these astrologers, or rather magicians, great numbers are to be met with in every market-place, and no marriage is ever celebrated until an opinion has been pronounced upon it by one of that profession.

It is also their custom, upon the death of any great and rich personage, to observe the following ceremonies. The relations, male and female, clothe themselves in coarse dresses, and accompany the body to the place appointed for burning it. The procession is likewise attended by performers on various musical instruments, which are sounded as it moves along, and prayers to their idols are chanted in a loud voice. When arrived at the spot, they throw into the flame many pieces of cotton-paper, upon which are painted representations of male and female servants, horses, camels, silk wrought with gold, as well as of gold and silver money. This is done, in consequence of their belief that the deceased will possess in the other world all these conveniences, the former in their natural state of flesh and bones, together with the money and the silks. As soon as the pile has been consumed, they sound all the instruments of music at the same time, producing a loud and long-continued noise; and they imagine that by these ceremonies their idols are induced to receive the soul of the man whose corpse has been reduced to ashes, in order to its being regenerated in the other world, and entering again into life.

§ 7. In every street of this city there are stone buildings or towers, to which, in case of a fire breaking out in any quarter (an accident by no means unusual, as the houses are mostly constructed of wood), the inhabitants may remove their effects for security. By a regulation which his majesty has established, there is a guard of ten watchmen stationed, under cover, upon all the principal bridges, of whom five do duty by day and five by night. Each of these guard-rooms is provided with a sonorous wooden instrument as well as one of metal, together with a *clepsydra* (*horiuolo*), by means of which latter the hours of the day and night are ascertained.[1] As soon as the first hour of the night is expired, one of the watchmen gives a single stroke upon the wooden instrument, and also upon the metal *gong* (*bacino*), which announces to the people of the neighbouring streets that it is the first hour. At the expiration of the second, two strokes are given; and so on progres-

[1] This clepsydra, or water-clock, is noticed by more modern travellers.

sively, increasing the number of strokes as the hours advance.[1] The guard is not allowed to sleep, and must be always on the alert. In the morning, as soon as the sun begins to appear, a single stroke is again struck, as in the evening, and so onwards from hour to hour. Some of these watchmen patrol the streets, to observe whether any person has a light or fire burning after the hour appointed for extinguishing them. Upon making the discovery, they affix a mark to the door, and in the morning the owner of the house is taken before the magistrates, by whom, if he cannot assign a legitimate excuse for his offence, he is condemned to punishment. Should they find any person abroad at an unseasonable hour, they arrest and confine him, and in the morning he is carried before the same tribunal. If, in the course of the day, they notice any person who from lameness or other infirmity is unable to work, they place him in one of the hospitals, of which there are several in every part of the city, founded by the ancient kings, and liberally endowed. When cured, he is obliged to work at some trade. Immediately upon the appearance of fire breaking out in a house, they give the alarm by beating on the wooden machine, when the watchmen from all the bridges within a certain distance assemble to extinguish it, as well as to save the effects of the merchants and others, by removing them to the stone towers that have been mentioned. The goods are also sometimes put into boats, and conveyed to the islands in the lake. Even on such occasions the inhabitants dare not stir out of their houses, when the fire happens in the night-time, and only

[1] "On distingue ordinairement," says Le Comte, "cinq (veilles de la nuit) qui commencent à sept ou huit heures du soir. Au commencement de la première on frappe un seul coup, un moment après on redouble encore, ce qu'on répète continuellement durant deux heures, jusqu'à la seconde veille. Car alors on frappe deux coups, et on continue toujours à frapper jusqu'à la troisième veille, etc. . . . augmentant le nombre des coups, à mesure qu'on passe d'une veille à l'autre, de sorte que ce sont autant d'horloges à répétition, qui font connoistre à tout moment quelle heure il est. On sert encore pour marquer les mesmes veilles d'un tambour, d'une grandeur extraordinaire, sur lequel on frappe toute la nuit selon les mesmes proportions." (Tom. i. p. 127.) This continued repetition of the strokes, during the intervals of the several watches (similar to calling the hours in the streets of our own metropolis), is not stated in the text. The practice may have undergone a change; but it seems more likely that our author's words may have been misunderstood by those who, being accustomed to the mechanical striking of a town-clock, have brought his meaning to that standard. It is remarkable at the same time, that what P. Le Comte has so distinctly explained is not adverted to in the journals of the late embassies. "La première veille," says De Guignes, "s'annonce par un coup de tambour; la troisième, par trois coups, et ainsi de suite."—Tom. ii. p. 426.

those can be present whose goods are actually removing, together with the guard collected to assist, which seldom amounts to a smaller number than from one to two thousand men. In cases also of tumult or insurrection amongst the citizens, the services of this police guard are necessary; but, independently of them, his majesty always keeps on foot a large body of troops, both infantry and cavalry, in the city and its vicinity, the command of which he gives to his ablest officers, and those in whom he can place the greatest confidence, on account of the extreme importance of this province, and especially its noble capital, which surpasses in grandeur and wealth every other city in the world. For the purposes of nightly watch, there are mounds of earth thrown up, at the distance of above a mile from each other, on the top of which a wooden frame is constructed, with a sounding board, which being struck with a mallet by the guard stationed there, the noise is heard to a great distance. If precautions of this nature were not taken upon occasions of fire, there would be danger of half the city being consumed; and their use is obvious also in the event of popular commotion, as, upon the signal being given, the guards at the several bridges arm themselves, and repair to the spot where their presence is required.

§ 8. When the grand khan reduced to his obedience the province of Manji, which until that time had been one kingdom, he thought proper to divide it into nine parts,[1] over each of which he appointed a king or viceroy, who should act as supreme governor of that division, and administer justice to the people.[2] These make a yearly report to commissioners acting for his majesty, of the amount of the revenue, as well as of every other matter pertaining to their jurisdiction. Upon

[1] There is reason to believe that the boundaries of the several provinces were not, in former times, exactly the same as we find them at present. Generally, however, these nine parts into which Manji, or Southern China, was divided, may be considered as the provinces of Kiang-nan, Kiang-si, Che-kiang, Fo-kien, Kuan-tong, Kuang-si, Koei-cheu, Hu-kuang, and Ho-nan. Cathay or Khataï appears to have consisted of Pe-che-li, Shan-tung, Shan-si, and the eastern part of Shen-si. The remaining provinces of the fifteen, namely Se-chuen and Yun-nan, as well as the western portion of Shen-si, had been but imperfectly subdued by the Chinese emperors, and seem not to have belonged, in our author's time, to either of the two grand divisions.

[2] The great officer or mandarin, here styled a king (*re*), or, more properly, viceroy, is by the Chinese termed *tsong-tu;* of whom there are eleven throughout the empire; some of them having jurisdiction over more than one province. The proper governor of each province is named *fu-yuen*, whom the missionaries frequently style the viceroy, although avowedly subordinate to the former.

the third year they are changed, as are all other public officers. One of these nine viceroys resides and holds his court in the city of Kin-sai, and has authority over more than a hundred and forty cities and towns, all large and rich.[1] Nor is this number to be wondered at, considering that in the whole of the province of Manji there are no fewer than twelve hundred, containing a large population of industrious and wealthy inhabitants.[2] In each of these, according to its size and other circumstances, his majesty keeps a garrison, consisting, in some places, of a thousand, in others of ten or twenty thousand men, accordingly as he judges the city to be, in its own population, more or less powerful. It is not to be understood that all these troops are Tartars. On the contrary, they are chiefly natives of the province of Cathay. The Tartars are universally horsemen, and cavalry cannot be quartered about those cities which stand in the low, marshy parts of the province, but only in firm, dry situations, where such troops can be properly exercised. To the former, he sends Cathaians, and such men of the province of Manji as appear to have a military turn; for it is his practice to make an annual selection amongst all his subjects of such as are best qualified to bear arms; and these he enrolls to serve in his numerous garrisons, that may be considered as so many armies. But the soldiers drawn from the province of Manji he does not employ in the duty of their native cities; on

[1] This number much exceeds what is allotted to the jurisdiction of any of the great cities at the present day; but it must be considered that Hang-cheu-fu had then recently been the capital of the proper Chinese empire, and its municipal influence might not have been brought down to the level of other provincial cities.

[2] According to Du Halde's list, the nine provinces of the south-eastern part of China contain 101 cities of the first class, 84 of the second, and 625 of the third, making together 810 cities; independently of any portions of Yun-nan or Se-chuen that might then have belonged to the kingdom of Manji. This, it will be seen, does not fall very far short of our author's statement, who might, besides, have intended to include some populous towns of the fourth order. With respect to those of the third, Du Halde observes: "Quand on parle de *hien* ou ville du troisième ordre, il ne faut pas s'imaginer que ce soit un district de peu d'étendue: il y a tel *hien* qui a 60, 70, et même 80 lieues de circuit, et que paye à l'empereur plusieurs millions de tribut." (Tom. i. p. 2.) P. Le Comte makes the number of cities more considerable than Du Halde: "On les divise ordinairement," he observes, "en trois ordres. Dans le premier, il y en a plus de 160; dans le second 270, et dans le troisième, pres de 1200; sans compter 300 autres villes murées qu'on met hors de rang, quoy qu'elles soient presque toutes fort peuplées et qu'on y fasse un grand commerce." (Tom. i. p. 118.) This seems to exceed also the enumeration of our author; but it must be recollected that the latter speaks of Manji only, which excludes the three northern provinces of China.

the contrary, he marches them to others at the distance of perhaps twenty days' journey, where they are continued for four or five years, at the expiration of which they are allowed to return to their homes, and others are sent to replace them. This regulation applies equally to the Cathaians. The greater part of the revenues of the cities, paid into the treasury of the grand khan, is appropriated to the maintenance of these garrisons. When it happens that a city is in a state of rebellion (and it is not an uncommon occurrence for these people, actuated by some sudden exasperation, or when intoxicated, to murder their governors), a part of the garrison of a neighbouring city is immediately despatched with orders to destroy the place where such guilty excesses have been committed; whereas it would be a tedious operation to send an army from another province, that might be two months on its march. For such purposes, the city of Kin-sai constantly supports a garrison of thirty thousand soldiers; and the smallest number stationed at any place is one thousand.[1]

§ 9. It now remains to speak of a very fine palace that was formerly the residence of king Facfur, whose ancestors enclosed with high walls an extent of ground ten miles in compass, and divided it into three parts. That in the centre was entered by a lofty portal, on each side of which was a magnificent colonnade, on a flat terrace, the roofs of which were supported by rows of pillars, highly ornamented with the most beautiful azure and gold. The colonnade opposite to the entrance, at the further side of the court, was still grander than the others, its roof being richly adorned, the pillars gilt, and the walls on the inner side ornamented with exquisite paintings, representing the histories of former kings.[2] Here,

[1] That it should be found necessary to station an army of that number of men in or near the populous capital of a newly-conquered empire is by no means improbable; nor that a thousand men should at that period have constituted the ordinary garrison of cities of the first or second class; however deficient of troops they may be found (according to some travellers) at the present time. In the seventeenth century, as we are told by P. Le Comte, the garrison of Hang-cheu consisted of 10,000 men, of whom 3,000 were Chinese. (Tom. i. p. 129.)

[2] The plans of Chinese palaces seem nearly to resemble each other, and particularly in respect to this kind of court on a raised terrace, in front of the principal part of the building, where those persons assemble whose rank entitles them to the privilege of paying their compliments to the sovereign. In the "Gezandtschaft" of Nieuhof (p. 172) will be found a representation of the anterior court of the palace of Pekin, which Van Braam commends for its fidelity. The hotel or palace of a great officer of state, or wealthy individual, seems to be built upon the same plan, and decorated in the same manner.

annually, upon certain days consecrated to the service of their idols, king Facfur was accustomed to hold his court, and to entertain at a feast his principal nobles, the chief magistrates, and the opulent citizens of Kin-sai. Under these colonnades might be seen, at one time, ten thousand persons suitably accommodated at table. This festival lasted ten or twelve days, and the magnificence displayed on the occasion, in silks, gold, and precious stones, exceeded all imagination; for every guest, with a spirit of emulation, endeavoured to exhibit as much finery as his circumstances would possibly allow. Behind the colonnade last mentioned, or that which fronted the grand portal, there was a wall, with a passage, that divided this exterior court of the palace from an interior court, which formed a kind of large cloister, with its rows of pillars sustaining a portico that surrounded it, and led to various apartments for the use of the king and queen. These pillars were ornamented in a similar manner, as were also the walls. From this cloister you entered a covered passage or corridor, six paces in width, and of such a length as to reach to the margin of the lake. On each side of this there were corresponding entrances to ten courts, in the form of long cloisters, surrounded by their porticoes, and each cloister or court had fifty apartments, with their respective gardens, the residence of a thousand young women, whom the king retained in his service.[1] Accompanied sometimes by his queen, and on other occasions by a party of these females, it was his custom to take amusement on the lake, in barges covered with silk, and to visit the idol temples on its borders. The other two divisions of this seraglio were laid out in groves, pieces of water, beautiful gardens stored with fruit-trees, and also enclosures for all sorts of animals that are the objects of sport, such as antelopes, deer, stags, hares, and rabbits. Here likewise the king amused himself, in company with his damsels, some in carriages and some on horseback. No male person was allowed to be of these parties, but on the other hand, the females were practised in the art of coursing with dogs, and pursuing the animals that have been mentioned. When fatigued with these exercises, they retired into the groves on the banks of the lake, and there quitting their dresses, rushed into the water in a state of nudity, sportively swimming about, some in one direction and

[1] "Avant que les Tartares se fussent emparés de l'empire," says De Guignes, "certains empereurs Chinois ont eu jusqu'à *dix* mille femmes." —Tom. ii. p. 284.

some in another, whilst the king remained a spectator of the exhibition. After this they returned to the palace. Sometimes he ordered his repast to be provided in one of these groves, where the foliage of lofty trees afforded a thick shade, and was there waited upon by the same damsels. Thus was his time consumed amidst the enervating charms of his women, and in profound ignorance of whatever related to martial concerns, the consequence of which was, that his depraved habits and his pusillanimity enabled the grand khan to deprive him of his splendid possessions, and to expel him with ignominy from his throne as has been already stated. All these particulars were communicated to me, when I was in that city, by a rich merchant of Kin-sai, then very old, who had been a confidential servant of king Facfur, and was acquainted with every circumstance of his life.[1] Having known the palace in its original state, he was desirous of conducting me to view it. Being at present the residence of the grand khan's viceroy, the colonnades are preserved in the style in which they had formerly subsisted, but the chambers of the females had been suffered to go to ruin, and the foundations only were visible. The wall likewise that enclosed the park and gardens was fallen to decay, and neither animals nor trees were any longer to be found there.

§ 10. At the distance of twenty-five miles from this city, in a direction to the northward of east, lies the sea, near to which is a town named Gan-pu, where there is an extremely fine port, frequented by all the ships that bring merchandise from India.[2] The river that flows past the city of Kin-sai forms this port, at the place where it falls into the sea. Boats are continually employed in the conveyance of goods up and down the river, and those intended for exportation are there put on board of ships bound to various parts of India and of Cathay.

Marco Polo, happening to be in the city of Kin-sai at the time of making the annual report to his majesty's commissioners

[1] Tu-tsong, the *faghfur* or emperor of the Song, here alluded to, having ceased to reign in 1274, and the Polo family having quitted China in or about the year 1291, our author might well have conversed with the domestics of that prince, and particularly whilst he held the government of Yang-cheu, in the adjoining province.

[2] Gan-pu, here described as the seaport of Kin-sai or Hang-cheu, answers to the port of Ning-po, situated on a river the entrance of which is sheltered by the islands of Chu-san, where H.M. ship Lion and the East India Company's ship Hindostan lay, in the year 1793. To those islands Captain Macintosh, who had accompanied Lord Macartney, proceeded from Hang-cheu-fu, to rejoin his ship, passing through Ning-po in his route.

of the amount of revenue and the number of inhabitants, had an opportunity of observing that the latter were registered at one hundred and sixty *tomans* of fire-places, that is to say, of families dwelling under the same roof; and as a *toman* is ten thousand, it follows that the whole city must have contained one million six hundred thousand families,[1] amongst which multitude of people there was only one church of Nestorian Christians. Every father of a family, or housekeeper, is required to affix a writing to the door of his house, specifying the name of each individual of his family, whether male or female, as well as the number of his horses. When any person dies, or leaves the dwelling, the name is struck out, and upon the occasion of a birth, it is added to the list. By these means the great officers of the province and governors of the cities are at all times acquainted with the exact number of the inhabitants. The same regulation is observed throughout the province of Cathay as well as of Manji.[2] In like manner, all the keepers of inns and public hotels inscribe in a book the names of those who take up their occasional abode with them, particularising the day and the hour of their arrival and departure; a copy of which is transmitted daily to those magistrates who have been spoken of as stationed in the market-squares. It is a custom in the province of Manji, with the indigent class of the people, who are unable to support their

[1] This statement of the number of families in Hang-cheu, even admitting that the suburbs are meant to be included, appears excessive; but it is unfair to measure the population of an ancient capital of China, by the standard of a modern city. Yet Staunton observes that " its population is indeed immense; and is supposed to be not very much inferior to that of Pekin," which he computes at about three millions; remarking, at the same time, that few of the circumstances take place in the metropolis of China, which contribute to the aggrandisement of other capitals; Pekin being merely the seat of government of the empire. It is neither a port nor a place of inland trade or manufacture, and forms no rendezvous for pleasure and dissipation. (Pp. 149, 439.) The former, on the other hand, possessed these advantages in an eminent degree.

[2] It does not appear in the writings either of the missionaries or of modern travellers, that mention is made of such lists of the inhabitants being affixed (at stated periods we may presume) on the outside of houses; but I have the verbal assurance of Mr. Reeves, who resided many years in China, and is lately returned to that country, that the regulation exists at the present day: to which he added his opinion that it was established not merely on account of the facility it gives to the officers of revenue and police, but from a regard to delicacy, that there might be no pretence for intrusion into the apartments of the females. The practice is adverted to by Mr. Ellis, who says: " The municipal regulation existing throughout China, which requires that every householder should affix on the outside of his house a list of the number and description of persons dwelling under his roof, ought to afford most accurate data in forming a census of the population."—P. 432.

families, to sell their children to the rich, in order that they may be fed and brought up in a better manner than their own poverty would admit.

CHAPTER LXIX

OF THE REVENUES OF THE GRAND KHAN

We shall now speak of the revenue which the grand khan draws from the city of Kin-sai and the places within its jurisdiction, constituting the ninth division or kingdom of Manji. In the first place, upon salt, the most productive article, he levies a yearly duty of eighty tomans of gold, each toman being eighty thousand saggi, and each saggio fully equal to a gold florin, and consequently amounting to six millions four hundred thousand ducats.[1] This vast produce is occasioned by the vicinity of the province to the sea, and the number of salt lakes or marshes, in which, during the heat of summer, the water becomes crystallized, and from whence a quantity of salt is taken, sufficient for the supply of five of the other divisions of the province.[2] There is here cultivated and manufactured a large quantity of sugar,[3] which pays, as do all other groceries, three and one-third per cent. The same is also levied upon the wine, or fermented liquor, made of rice. The twelve classes of artisans, of whom we have already spoken, as having each a thousand shops, and also the merchants, as well those who import the goods into the city, in the first instance, as those

[1] Estimating the gold ducat of Venice at ten shillings English, (for the sake of round numbers,) this revenue derived from the article of salt would amount to the sum of £3,200,000, which may be thought excessive, as applying, not to the empire at large, but to that portion of China of which Hang-cheu-fu was the capital. It must, however, be considered that all the northern provinces, as well as those of the interior, are supplied from the south-eastern parts of the coast, and that the quantity exported from the places of manufacture must consequently be enormous. One half of the duties upon articles of produce is understood to be paid in kind, and we are informed that the stock of salt collected upon government account at Tien-sing on the Pe-ho, was calculated by the gentlemen of Lord Macartney's embassy, at three millions of bags, or six hundred millions of pounds weight. (Vol. ii. p. 21.) The gabelle or revenue from salt, in France, about the year 1780, is stated by M. Necker to have been 54,000,000 livres, or £2,250,000.

[2] Sea salt is produced by a similar process of solar evaporation, in many of the southern parts of Europe, as well as on the coasts of India.

[3] "The valleys along the river," says Staunton, speaking of that which flows by Hang-cheu-fu, "were cultivated chiefly in sugar-canes, then almost ripe, and about eight feet high."—Tom. ii. p. 460.

who carry them from thence to the interior, or who export them by sea, pay, in like manner, a duty of three and one-third per cent.; but goods coming by sea from distant countries and regions, such as from India, pay ten per cent. So likewise all native articles of the country, as cattle, the vegetable produce of the soil, and silk, pay a tithe to the king. The account being made up in the presence of Marco Polo, he had an opportunity of seeing that the revenue of his majesty, exclusively of that arising from salt, already stated, amounted in the year to the sum of two hundred and ten tomans (each toman being eighty thousand saggi of gold), or sixteen million eight hundred thousand ducats.[1]

CHAPTER LXX

OF THE CITY OF TA-PIN-ZU

LEAVING the city of Kin-sai, and travelling one day's journey towards the south-east, continually passing houses, villas, and delightful gardens, where every kind of vegetable is produced in abundance, you arrive at the city of Ta-pin-zu, which is very handsome and large, and belongs to the jurisdiction of Kin-sai.[2] The inhabitants worship idols, use paper money, burn the bodies of their dead, are subjects of the grand khan, and gain their subsistence by trade and manual arts. This place not demanding any more particular notice, we shall proceed to speak of the city of Uguiu.

[1] This sum is equal to £8,400,000 of our money, and the aggregate to £11,600,000, an amount which the revenues and expenses of our own country, in recent times, have taught us to consider as almost insignificant.

[2] No name resembling the Ta-pin-zu of our text or the Tam-pin-gui of the Latin versions presents itself, at the distance of one day's journey, in a southerly direction, from Hang-cheu-fu, nor could it under those circumstances be a place of more importance than the second rank of cities. P. Magalhanes (p. 10) asserts without hesitation that it is intended for Tai-ping-fu in the province of Nan-king or Kiang-nan; but however unexceptionable the agreement in sound may be, the situation of the latter, to the north-west of Hang-cheu, presents a formidable difficulty, which cannot otherwise be resolved than by supposing that liberties have been taken with our author's words, and that places which he has thought proper to notice, although lying out of the direct road, have been forced by his translators into the line of an itinerary, to which he never professes to adhere. This remark will be found to apply equally to the city spoken of in the next chapter.

CHAPTER LXXI

OF THE CITY OF UGUIU

FROM Ta-pin-zu, travelling three days towards the south-east, you come to the city of Uguiu,[1] and still further, in the same direction, two days' journey, you pass in continual succession so many towns, castles, and other inhabited places, and such is their vicinity to each other, that to a stranger they have the appearance of one extended city. All of them are dependent upon Kin-sai. The people are idolaters, and the country supplies the necessaries of life in great abundance. Here are found canes of greater bulk and length than those already noticed, being four spans in girth and fifteen paces long.[2]

CHAPTER LXXII

OF THE CITIES OF GEN-GUI, ZEN-GIAN, AND GIE-ZA

PROCEEDING further, three days' journey in the same direction, you reach the town of Gen-gui,[3] and still advancing to the south-east, you never cease to meet with towns full of inhabitants, who are employed at their trades, and cultivate the soil. In this part of the province of Manji there are not any sheep to be seen, but many oxen, cows, buffaloes, and goats, and of swine a vast number.[4] At the end of the fourth day you arrive at the city of Zen-gian, built upon a hill that stands insulated in the river, which, by dividing itself into two

[1] The name of U-guiu or U-giu, which is U-gui in the Italian epitomes, but is omitted in the Basle edition, has an obvious affinity to that of Hu-cheu on the bank of the lake Tai, not far from Hang-cheu, but like Tai-ping is situated in a direction opposite to that of south-east, as expressed in the text. [The Paris Latin text calls the town Un-gui.]

[2] Hu-cheu and the places subsequently mentioned being surrounded by a low country, and situated in a warm climate, it is reasonable to suppose that the bamboo cane should there be found in abundance and perfection, and accordingly Du Halde says: "Le Tche-kiang en est plus fourni qu'aucune autre province. Il y en a des forêts entières."—Tom. i. p. 174.

[3] Gen-gui, which in the B.M. and Berlin manuscripts is written Cheu-gui, appears to be the Tchu-ki of Du Halde's map, a town of the third order. [In the Paris Latin text it is Ciansiam.]

[4] In the journals of our modern travellers, as well as in the writings of the missionaries, we find repeated remarks on the paucity of sheep and abundance of pork in this part of China.

branches, appears to embrace it. These streams take opposite directions, one of them pursuing its course to the south-east, and the other to the north-west.[1] The cities last mentioned are likewise under the dominion of the grand khan, and depen dent upon Kin-sai. The people worship idols, and subsist by trade. There is in the country abundance of game, both beasts and birds. Proceeding further, three days' journey, you reach the large and noble city of Gie-za, which is the last within the jurisdiction of Kin-sai.[2] Having passed this city, you enter upon another kingdom or viceroyalty of Manji, named Kon-cha.

CHAPTER LXXIII

OF THE KINGDOM OR VICEROYALTY OF KON-CHA, AND ITS CAPITAL CITY NAMED FU-GIU

UPON leaving the last city of the kingdom or viceroyalty of Kin-sai, named Gie-za, you enter that of Kon-cha,[3] the principal city of which is named Fu-giu.[4] In the course of six days' journey through this country, in a south-east direction, over hills and along valleys,[5] you continually pass towns and

[1] That Zen-gian, which in the early Italian epitome is Eian-giari, and in the early Latin, Cyangy, was intended for the city of Yen-cheu (called also Nian-cheu), will hardly admit of a doubt; the names approaching as near as the usual corruptions of the syllable *cheu* or *giu* can be expected to allow. With respect to local circumstances it must be admitted, that the modern city is not built upon a hill, but at the foot of high mountains, and just at the meeting (which in ascending rivers is often termed the branching) of two streams that contribute to form the Tsien-tang-kiang.

[2] This name of Gie-za, or, as it appears in the other versions, En-giu and Cu-gui, belongs evidently to the city of Kiu-cheu, situated as it is, at the south-western extremity of the province of Che-kiang, on the border of a distinct viceroyalty, and in the usual, perhaps the only route to the provinces of Fo-kien and Kuang-tong.

[3] Kon-cha, or Kon-ka, as an Italian would pronounce the word, which is Kon-chay in the early Latin version, and Tonza in the Italian epitome, seems to have been the name of a viceroyalty that included the provinces of Fo-kien, Kiang-si, and Kuang-tong; but at the present day, Che-kiang and Fo-kien are governed by one viceroy, or *tsong-tu*, as Kuang-tong and Kiang-si are by another.

[4] The Fu-giu of our author [Fuchiu of the Paris Latin text] is the city of Fu-cheu-fu, the capital of the province of Fo-kien. It is here mentioned incidentally, and not as lying in the direction of his route; but it appears to be the city afterwards described in chap. lxxvi.

[5] These hills or, more properly, mountains, constitute the chain which separates the province of Che-kiang from those of Kiang-si and Fo-kien. The distance from Kiu-cheu to the first considerable town on the south-western side of the mountains may be considered as a journey of six days.

villages, where the necessaries of life are in abundance, and there is much field sport, particularly of birds. The people are idolaters, the subjects of the grand khan, and are engaged in commerce and manufactures. In these parts there are tigers of great size and strength. Ginger and also galangal[1] are produced in large quantities, as well as other drugs.[2] For money equal in value to a Venetian silver groat you may have eighty pounds weight of fresh ginger, so common is its growth. There is also a vegetable which has all the properties of the true saffron, as well the smell as the colour, and yet it is not really saffron. It is held in great estimation, and being an ingredient in all their dishes, it bears, on that account, a high price.[3]

The people in this part of the country are addicted to eating human flesh, esteeming it more delicate than any other, provided the death of the person has not been occasioned by disease. When they advance to combat they throw loose their hair about their ears, and they paint their faces of a bright blue colour. They arm themselves with lances and swords, and all march on foot excepting their chief, who rides on horseback. They are a most savage race of men, insomuch that when they slay their enemies in battle, they are anxious to drink their blood, and afterwards they devour their flesh. Leaving this subject, we shall now speak of the city of Kue-lin-fu.

CHAPTER LXXIV

OF THE CITY OF KUE-LIN-FU

THE journey of six days (mentioned in the preceding chapter) being accomplished, you arrive at the city of Kue-lin-fu,

[1] De Guignes, in his account of the articles exported from China, speaking of the galanga, says: " C'est la racine noueuse d'une plante qui croît à près de deux pieds de hauteur, et dont les feuilles ressemblent à celles du myrte."—Tom. iii. p. 254.

[2] If I am warranted in the conjecture (which will be found to gain strength as we advance) that our author's original notes have been transposed in this place, it will account for the circumstance of the article tea, the production of this part of China, and distinctly mentioned by the Arabian travellers of the ninth century, being here omitted in the enumeration of drugs.

[3] By this yellow dye is indubitably meant the *curcuma longa*. " Le turmerick, ou terra merita, ou curcuma," says De Guignes, " est appelé en Chinois, *cha-kiang;* il vient du Quang-tong: cette racine est bonne

which is of considerable size, and contains three very handsome bridges, upwards of a hundred paces in length, and eight paces in width.[1] The women of the place are very handsome, and live in a state of luxurious ease. There is much raw silk produced here, and it is manufactured into silk pieces of various sorts. Cottons are also woven, of coloured threads,[2] which are carried for sale to every part of the province of Manji. The people employ themselves extensively in commerce, and export quantities of ginger and galangal. I have been told, but did not myself see the animal, that there are found at this place a species of domestic fowls which have no feathers, their skins being clothed with black hair, resembling the fur of cats.[3] Such a sight must be extraordinary. They lay eggs like other fowls, and they are good to eat. The multitude of tigers renders travelling through the country dangerous, unless a number of persons go in company.

CHAPTER LXXV

OF THE CITY OF UN-GUEN

UPON leaving the city of Kue-lin-fu, and travelling three days, during which you are continually passing towns and castles, of which the inhabitants are idolaters, have silk in abundance, and export it in considerable quantities, you reach the city of

pour la teinture: la plus longue est la meilleure." (Tom. iii. p. 264.) But in China it is not commonly, if it is at all, employed in cookery; whereas amongst the Malays, and other people of the Eastern islands, it enters into the composition of every dish, whilst it is by them equally applied to the purposes of a dye-stuff.

[1] From its position with respect to the road across the mountains, and other circumstances, there appears to be reason for agreeing in opinion with P. Martini, that this is the city of Kien-ning-fu, in the province of Fo-kien. It must at the same time be observed that the name of Queiling-fu belongs to the capital of the province of Kuang-si; but this lies at so great a distance from the places already mentioned, and is so entirely unconnected with them, that it cannot be considered as the city here meant, unless on the supposition that the accounts of intermediate parts have been omitted.

[2] The words of the text express no more than that the cotton received its colour in the yarn, and not in the piece, which would scarcely deserve notice as a peculiarity; but the Nankin cotton, which is known to be, in its raw state, of the colour it bears in the manufacture, may perhaps be that which is meant to be described.

[3] The account of this uncommon species of fowl appears to have been thought too incredible by some early translators; yet the same breed, or one equally singular, is described by Du Halde.

Uu-guen.[1] This place is remarkable for a great manufacture of sugar, which is sent from thence to the city of Kanbalu for the supply of the court. Previously to its being brought under the dominion of the grand khan, the natives were unacquainted with the art of manufacturing sugar of a fine quality, and boiled it in such an imperfect manner, that when left to cool it remained in the state of a dark-brown paste.[2] But at the time this city became subject to his majesty's government, there happened to be at the court some persons from Babylon[3] who were skilled in the process, and who, being sent thither, instructed the inhabitants in the mode of refining the sugar by means of the ashes of certain woods.[4]

CHAPTER LXXVI

OF THE CITY OF KAN-GIU

TRAVELLING fifteen miles further in the same direction, you come to the city of Kan-giu, which belongs to the kingdom or viceroyalty of Kon-cha, one of the nine divisions of Manji.[5] In this place is stationed a large army for the protection of the country, and to be always in readiness to act, in the event of any city manifesting a disposition to rebel. Through the midst of it passes a river, a mile in breadth, upon the banks of which, on either side, are extensive and handsome buildings. In front of these, great numbers of ships are seen lying, having merchandise on board, and especially sugar, of which large quantities are manufactured here also. Many

[1] With whatever modern name that of Un-guen, or U-gueu (as it appears in the early Venice epitome), may be thought to accord, it is evident from the circumstances that it must be one of the cities of the second or third class, within the jurisdiction of Fu-gui, or Fu-cheu-fu, and in the neighbourhood of that capital.

[2] Sugar in that moist and imperfect state is termed *jaggri* in most parts of the East Indies.

[3] [Babylon was in the middle ages the name for Cairo in Egypt.]

[4] It is well known that alkaline substances are used in the process of granulating sugars. "Towards the end of this boiling," says the Dictionary of Arts and Sciences, "they throw into the juice a strong lixivium of wood-ashes, with some quick-lime."

[5] It cannot be doubted that the word Kan-giu is here intended for Kuang-cheu or Quang-cheu, the name of the city improperly termed by Europeans, Canton, being a corruption of Kuang-tong, which belongs to the province of which it is the capital. It is evident that the Kan-giu of our author is the Can-su described by the Arabian travellers; and this latter is proved by the historical events to have been Kuang-cheu, or Canton.

vessels arrive at this port from India, freighted by merchants who bring with them rich assortments of jewels and pearls, upon the sale of which they obtain a considerable profit. This river discharges itself into the sea, at no great distance from the port named Zai-tun. The ships coming from India ascend the river as high up as the city, which abounds with every sort of provision, and has delightful gardens, producing exquisite fruits.

CHAPTER LXXVII

OF THE CITY AND PORT OF ZAI-TUN, AND THE CITY OF TIN-GUI

UPON leaving the city of Kan-giu and crossing the river to proceed in a south-easterly direction, you travel during five days through a well-inhabited country, passing towns, castles, and substantial dwellings, plentifully supplied with all kinds of provisions. The road lies over hills, across plains, and through woods, in which are found many of those shrubs from whence the camphor is procured.[1] The country abounds also with game. The inhabitants are idolaters. They are the subjects of the grand khan, and within the jurisdiction of Kan-giu. At the end of five days' journey, you arrive at the noble and handsome city of Zai-tun, which has a port on the sea-coast celebrated for the resort of shipping, loaded with merchandise, that is afterwards distributed through every part of the province of Manji.[2] The quantity of pepper imported there is so considerable, that what is carried to Alexandria, to supply the demand of the western parts of the world, is trifling in comparison, perhaps not more than the hundredth part. It is

[1] This tree, the *laurus camphora* of China and Japan, grows to a large size, and is improperly termed by Ramusio an *arboscello*, or shrub. Staunton speaks of "the shining leaves of the thick and spreading camphor-tree,"—the only species of the laurel genus growing in China, and there a large and valuable timber tree. It is not to be confounded with the camphor-tree of Borneo and Sumatra, which is also remarkable for its great size, but is of a genus entirely distinct from the *laurus*.

[2] This famous port of Zai-tun, named Zarten in the Basle edition, Zaizen in the older Latin, and Jaitoni in the epitome, is generally supposed to be the place named Tsuen-cheu by the Chinese (the Suen-tcheou of Du Halde's map). Yet it may be thought that the description applies with equal justness to the nearly adjoining port of Hia-muen, called Emoui by the French and Amoy by the English navigators, which, until the last century, participated largely with Canton in the foreign commerce of the empire.

indeed impossible to convey an idea of the concourse of merchants and the accumulation of goods, in this which is held to be one of the largest and most commodious ports in the world. The grand khan derives a vast revenue from this place, as every merchant is obliged to pay ten per cent. upon the amount of his investment. The ships are freighted by them at the rate of thirty per cent. for fine goods, forty-four for pepper, and for lignum aloes, sandalwood, and other drugs, as well as articles of trade in general, forty per cent.; so that it is computed by the merchants, that their charges, including customs and freight, amount to half the value of the cargo; and yet upon the half that remains to them their profit is so considerable, that they are always disposed to return to the same market with a further stock of merchandise. The country is delightful. The people are idolaters, and have all the necessaries of life in plenty: their disposition is peaceable, and they are fond of ease and indulgence. Many persons arrive in this city from the interior parts of India for the purpose of having their persons ornamented by puncturing with needles (in the manner before described), as it is celebrated for the number of its artists skilled in that practice.[1]

The river that flows by the port of Zai-tun is large and rapid, and is a branch of that which passes the city of Kin-sai.[2] At

[1] This assertion may well appear strange and improbable, and must have been occasioned by some mistake either of arrangement of the matter or translation of the passage; for it cannot be supposed that the inhabitants of this most frequented and civilized part of China were then, or at any historical period, in the habit of puncturing or tattooing their skins. It may be, that a memorandum on the subject (as in other instances we have had strong grounds to suspect) belonging to a description either of the Malayan islands or of Ava, where the practice prevails, has been introduced in the wrong place; or, as I am more inclined to think, that what has been here misunderstood for puncturing the face, was meant by our author for the art of portrait-painting, in which the Chinese are such adepts, that few strangers visit Canton without employing a native to take their likeness, or, as it is expressed in the jargon of the factories, "make handsome face."

[2] Into this geographical error our author must have been led by the report of the natives. In all parts of the East there seems to be a disposition to believe, and to persuade others, that several rivers proceed from one common source (generally a lake), and afterwards diverge, in their progress towards the sea; however contrary this may be to the known operations of nature. That there is no such community of origin between the river Tsien-tang, upon which Hang-cheu or Kin-sai stands, and the river Chang, which empties itself at Amoy, is obvious from inspection of the maps of China; but at the same time it will be seen that the sources of the Chang, and those of the great river that passes by Fu-cheu, the capital of the province, are in the same mountains, and may be said to be intermingled. It may also be observed that the northern branch of the latter river, which passes the city of Kien-ning, is separated

the place where it separates from the principal channel stands the city of Tin-gui. Of this place there is nothing further to be observed, than that cups or bowls and dishes of porcelain-ware are there manufactured.[1] The process was explained to be as follows. They collect a certain kind of earth, as it were, from a mine, and laying it in a great heap, suffer it to be exposed to the wind, the rain, and the sun, for thirty or forty years, during which time it is never disturbed. By this it becomes refined and fit for being wrought into the vessels above mentioned. Such colours as may be thought proper are then laid on, and the ware is afterwards baked in ovens or furnaces. Those persons, therefore, who cause the earth to be dug, collect it for their children and grandchildren. Great quantities of the manufacture are sold in the city, and for a Venetian groat you may purchase eight porcelain cups.

We have now described the viceroyalty of Kon-cha, one of the nine divisions of Manji, from whence the grand khan draws as ample a revenue as even from that of Kin-sai. Of the others we shall not attempt to speak, because Marco Polo did not himself visit any of their cities, as he has done those of Kin-sai and Kon-cha. It should be observed that throughout the province of Manji one general language prevails, and one uniform manner of writing, yet in the different parts of the country there is a diversity of dialect, similar to what is found between the Genoese, the Milanese, the Florentine, and the dialects of other Italian states, whose inhabitants, although they have each their peculiar speech, can make themselves reciprocally understood.

Not having yet completed the subjects upon which Marco Polo purposed to write, he will now bring this Second Book to a close, and will commence another with a description of the countries and provinces of India, distinguishing it into the Greater, the Lesser, and the Middle India, parts of which he visited whilst employed in the service of the grand khan,

only by another ridge from the sources of the Tsien-tang, or river of Hang-cheu; and this sort of connexion of the extremes, by the intervention of a middle term, may have given rise to the mistaken idea adopted by our author, upon a subject of which he was not likely to have any practical knowledge.

[1] The city of Ting-cheu, answering to the name of Tin-gui or Tin-giu, stands near the western border of the province of Fo-kien, amongst the mountains that give source to the Chang, mentioned in the preceding note, but upon a river that empties itself near the city of Chao-cheu, in the province of Kuang-tong. It is not, however, at the present day the seat of porcelain works, which are principally carried on at the town of King-te-ching, in the neighbouring province of Kiang-si.

who ordered him thither upon different occasions of business, and afterwards when, accompanied by his father and uncle, in their returning journey they escorted the queen destined for king Argon. He will have the opportunity of relating many extraordinary circumstances observed by himself personally in those countries, but at the same time will not omit to notice others of which he was informed by persons worthy of credit, or which were pointed out to him in the sea-chart of the coasts of India.[1]

[1] It may be presumed that the sea-charts here spoken of were chiefly in the hands of Arabian pilots, who navigated from the Persian Gulf to India and China, and who might have added the results of their experience to the information derived from the geographical work of Ptolemy.

BOOK III

CHAPTER I

OF INDIA, DISTINGUISHED INTO THE GREATER, LESSER, AND MIDDLE—OF THE MANNERS AND CUSTOMS OF ITS INHABITANTS—OF MANY REMARKABLE AND EXTRAORDINARY THINGS TO BE OBSERVED THERE; AND, IN THE FIRST PLACE, OF THE KIND OF VESSELS EMPLOYED IN NAVIGATION

HAVING treated, in the preceding parts of our work, of various provinces and regions, we shall now take leave of them, and proceed to the account of India, the admirable circumstances of which shall be related. We shall commence with a description of the ships employed by the merchants, which are built of fir-timber.[1] They have a single deck, and below this the space is divided into about sixty small cabins, fewer or more, according to the size of the vessels, each of them affording accommodation for one merchant.[2] They are provided with a good helm. They have four masts, with as many sails, and some of them have two masts which can be set up and lowered again, as may be found necessary.[3] Some ships of the larger class have, besides (the cabins), to the number of thirteen bulk-heads or divisions in the hold, formed

[1] The vegetable productions, and especially the timber, of southern or maritime India, being different from the kinds known in Europe, it is improperly (if our author is actually speaking of Indian ships) that the ship-timber is said in the text to be the *abete* and *zapino*, as neither the abies nor pinus are found (in any accessible situation) between the tropics. But, irregular as it may seem, there will in the sequel be found reason to conclude that he is describing ships built in China, although for the Indian trade.

[2] In the Latin of the Basle edition the number of these cabins is stated at forty, and they are said to be upon, not beneath, the upper deck. We know little of the interior of Indian vessels before the period of European intercourse, but in modern times their cabins are usually upon the after part of the quarter deck.

[3] No mention is made of topmasts in any modern description of Chinese junks; nor is it clear that such are here meant. The expressions may rather be understood of masts capable of being raised or lowered in the manner of those belonging to our lighters, and the sense of the passage may be—"They have four masts (with as many sails); two of which may be set up or lowered, as occasion may require."

of thick planks let into each other (*incastrati*, mortised or rabbeted). The object of these is to guard against accidents which may occasion the vessel to spring a leak, such as striking on a rock or receiving a stroke from a whale, a circumstance that not unfrequently occurs; for, when sailing at night, the motion through the waves causes a white foam that attracts the notice of the hungry animal. In expectation of meeting with food, it rushes violently to the spot, strikes the ship, and often forces in some part of the bottom. The water, running in at the place where the injury has been sustained, makes its way to the well, which is always kept clear. The crew, upon discovering the situation of the leak, immediately remove the goods from the division affected by the water, which, in consequence of the boards being so well fitted, cannot pass from one division to another. They then repair the damage, and return the goods to that place in the hold from whence they had been taken. The ships are all double-planked; that is, they have a course of sheathing-boards laid over the planking in every part. These are caulked with oakum both withinside and without, and are fastened with iron nails. They are not coated with pitch, as the country does not produce that article, but the bottoms are smeared over with the following preparation. The people take quick-lime and hemp, which latter they cut small, and with these, when pounded together, they mix oil procured from a certain tree, making of the whole a kind of unguent, which retains its viscous properties more firmly, and is a better material than pitch.[1]

Ships of the largest size require a crew of three hundred men; others, two hundred; and some, one hundred and fifty only, according to their greater or less bulk. They carry from five to six thousand baskets (or mat bags) of pepper.

[1] This mode of preserving the bottoms of their vessels is common to the Chinese and the Indians. "At Surat," says Grose, "they excel in the art of ship-building. Their bottoms and sides are composed of planks let into one another, in the nature, as I apprehend, of what is called rabbet-work, so that the seams are impenetrable. They have also a peculiar way of preserving their ships' bottoms, by occasionally rubbing into them an oil they call wood-oil, which the planks imbibe." (Voyage to the East Indies, vol. i. p. 107.) The mixture of *chunam* or lime with a resinous oil, or with melted *dammar*, is commonly known in the dockyards of India by the name of *gul-gul*. "There would be no exaggeration," adds Grose, "in averring that they (the natives) build incomparably the best ships in the world for duration, and that of any size, even to a thousand tons and upwards. . . . It is not uncommon for one of them to last a century."—P. 108.

In former times they were of greater burthen than they are at present; but the violence of the sea having in many places broken up the islands, and especially in some of the principal ports, there is a want of depth of water for vessels of such draught, and they have on that account been built, in latter times, of a smaller size. The vessels are likewise moved with oars or sweeps, each of which requires four men to work it. Those of the larger class are accompanied by two or three large barks, capable of containing about one thousand baskets of pepper, and are manned with sixty, eighty, or one hundred sailors. These small craft are often employed to tow the larger, when working their oars, or even under sail, provided the wind be on the quarter, but not when right aft, because, in that case, the sails of the larger vessel must becalm those of the smaller, which would, in consequence, be run down. The ships also carry with them as many as ten small boats, for the purpose of carrying out anchors, for fishing, and a variety of other services. They are slung over the sides, and lowered into the water when there is occasion to use them. The barks are in like manner provided with their small boats. When a ship, having been on a voyage for a year or more, stands in need of repair, the practice is to give her a course of sheathing over the original boarding, forming a third course, which is caulked and paid in the same manner as the others; and this, when she needs further repairs, is repeated, even to the number of six layers, after which she is condemned as unserviceable and not seaworthy. Having thus described the shipping, we shall proceed to the account of India; but in the first instance we shall speak of certain islands in the part of the ocean where we are at present, and shall commence with the island named Zipangu.

CHAPTER II

OF THE ISLAND OF ZIPANGU[1]

ZIPANGU is an island in the eastern ocean, situated at the distance of about fifteen hundred miles from the main-land, or

[1] The name which is here, as well as in the B.M. and Berlin manuscripts, written Zipangu, in the Basle edition Zipangri, in the older Latin Cyampagu, and in the early Italian epitomes Cimpagu, is evidently intended for those islands which we, in a collective sense, term Japan. By the Chinese they are named Ge-pen (Jy-pèn according to the orthography of De Guignes, or Jih-pun according to that of Morrison), and

coast of Manji.[1] It is of considerable size; its inhabitants have fair complexions, are well made, and are civilized in their manners. Their religion is the worship of idols. They are independent of every foreign power, and governed only by their own kings.[2] They have gold in the greatest abundance, its sources being inexhaustible,[3] but as the king does not allow of its being exported, few merchants visit the country, nor is it frequented by much shipping from other parts. To this circumstance we are to attribute the extraordinary richness of the sovereign's palace, according to what we are told by those who have access to the place. The entire roof is covered with a plating of gold, in the same manner as we cover houses, or more properly churches, with lead. The ceilings of the halls are of the same precious metal; many of the apartments have small tables of pure gold, of considerable thickness; and the windows also have golden ornaments.[4] So vast, indeed, are the riches of the palace, that it is impossible to convey an idea of them. In this island there are pearls also, in large quantities, of a red (pink) colour, round in shape, and of great size, equal in value to, or even exceeding that of the white pearls.[5] It is customary with one part of the inhabitants to

from thence all the other names are more or less obviously derived. The terminating syllable *gu* appears to be the Chinese word *kue*, signifying "kingdom," which is commonly annexed to the names of foreign countries.

[1] The distance of the nearest part of the southern island from the coast of China, near Ning-po, not being more than 500 Italian miles, we may suppose that our author, in stating it at 1,500, speaks of Chinese miles, or li, which are in the proportion of something more than one-third of the former.

[2] Political independence is a characteristic of the Japanese nation, which does not appear, at any period of its history, to have been brought permanently under a foreign yoke.

[3] "Gold, the richest of all metals," says Kæmpfer, "is dug up in several provinces of the Japanese empire." "The emperor claims the supreme jurisdiction over all the gold mines, and indeed all other mines in the empire. . . . Of the produce of all the mines that are worked, he claims two-thirds." (Hist. of Japan, vol. i. p. 107.) "But of late, as I was informed," he adds, "the veins . . . not only run scarcer, but yield not near the quantity of gold they did formerly."—Ibid.

[4] Kæmpfer, speaking of one of the ancient kings of Japan, says, "He caused a stately palace, named Kojatu, to be built for his residence, the floors whereof were paved with gold and silver." (Vol. i. p. 82.) This account, though perhaps fabulous, shows the idea entertained by the natives of the magnificence of their former sovereigns.

[5] "Pearls, by the Japanese called *kainotamma*," says Kæmpfer, "which is as much as to say, shell-jewels, are found almost everywhere about Saikokf, in oysters and several other shells. Everybody is at liberty to fish them."—Vol. i. p. 110.

bury their dead, and with another part to burn them.[1] The former have a practice of putting one of these pearls into the mouth of the corpse. There are also found there a number of precious stones.

Of so great celebrity was the wealth of this island, that a desire was excited in the breast of the grand khan Kublaï, now reigning, to make the conquest of it, and to annex it to his dominions. In order to effect this, he fitted out a numerous fleet, and embarked a large body of troops, under the command of two of his principal officers, one of whom was named Abbacatan, and the other Vonsancin.[2] The expedition sailed from the ports of Zai-tun and Kin-sai,[3] and, crossing the intermediate sea, reached the island in safety; but in consequence of a jealousy that arose between the two commanders, one of whom treated the plans of the other with contempt and resisted the execution of his orders, they were unable to gain possession of any city or fortified place, with the exception of one only, which was carried by assault, the garrison having refused to surrender. Directions were given for putting the whole to the sword, and in obedience thereto the heads of all were cut off, excepting of eight persons, who, by the efficacy of a diabolical charm, consisting of a jewel or amulet introduced into the right arm, between the skin and the flesh, were rendered secure from the effects of iron, either to kill or

[1] It is necessary to mention that two religions prevail amongst the people of Japan: the ancient, or that of the Sintos, who worship spirits, called by them *sin* and *kami;* and the modern (being subsequent to the date of the Christian era), or that of the Budsdos, worshippers of the Indian Buddha, under the names of Fo-to-ke and Budsd. Of these, the latter only, but who constitute by far the more numerous class, are in the practice of burning the bodies of their dead. "One thing," says Kæmpfer, "remains worthy of observing, which is, that many, and perhaps the greatest part, of those who in their lifetime constantly professed the Sintos religion, and even some of the Siutosjus or moralists, recommend their souls, on their death-bed, to the care of the Budsdo clergy, desiring that the *namanda* might be sung for them, and their bodies burnt and buried, after the manner of the Budsdoists. The adherents of the Sintos religion do not believe the Pythagorean doctrine of the transmigration of souls, although most universally received by the Eastern nations."—History of Japan, vol. i. p. 213.

[2] These names appear to be intended for Abaka-khan, a Mungal or Moghul, and Vang-san-chin, a Chinese. Many of the latter nation were employed by Kublaï, both in civil and military capacities, and rendered him good service. [In the Paris Latin, the names are Abatar and Vonsanchi.]

[3] By the port of Zai-tun is probably meant Amoy, and by Kin-sai the port of Ning-po or of Chu-san, which are at the entrance of the river which flows by Hang-cheu-fu, the Kin-sai of our author.

wound. Upon this discovery being made, they were beaten with a heavy wooden club, and presently died.[1]

It happened, after some time, that a north wind began to blow with great force, and the ships of the Tartars, which lay near the shore of the island, were driven foul of each other. It was determined thereupon, in a council of the officers on board, that they ought to disengage themselves from the land; and accordingly, as soon as the troops were re-embarked, they stood out to sea. The gale, however, increased to so violent a degree that a number of the vessels foundered. The people belonging to them, by floating upon pieces of the wreck, saved themselves upon an island lying about four miles from the coast of Zipangu. The other ships, which, not being so near to the land, did not suffer from the storm, and in which the two chiefs were embarked, together with the principal officers, or those whose rank entitled them to command a hundred thousand or ten thousand men, directed their course homewards, and returned to the grand khan. Those of the Tartars who remained upon the island where they were wrecked, and who amounted to about thirty thousand men, finding themselves left without shipping, abandoned by their leaders, and having neither arms nor provisions, expected nothing less than to become captives or to perish; especially as the island afforded no habitations where they could take shelter and refresh themselves. As soon as the gale ceased and the sea became smooth and calm, the people from the main island of Zipangu came over with a large force, in numerous boats, in order to make prisoners of these shipwrecked Tartars, and having landed, proceeded in search of them, but in a straggling, disorderly manner. The Tartars, on their part, acted with prudent circumspection, and, being concealed from view by some high land in the centre of the island, whilst the enemy were hurrying in pursuit of them by one road, made a circuit of the coast by another, which brought them to the place where the fleet of boats was at anchor. Finding these all abandoned, but with their colours flying, they instantly seized them, and pushing off from the island, stood for the principal city of Zipangu, into which, from the appearance of the colours, they were suffered to enter unmolested.[2]

[1] The idea of being rendered invulnerable by the use of amulets is common amongst the natives of the Eastern islands.

[2] If the original operations were directed, as might be presumed, against the ancient capital, we should infer that the city here spoken of was Osakka, situated at the mouth of the river upon which, at some distance from the coast, Mia-ko stands, and which is known to have

Here they found few of the inhabitants besides women, whom they retained for their own use, and drove out all others. When the king was apprised of what had taken place, he was much afflicted, and immediately gave directions for a strict blockade of the city, which was so effectual that not any person was suffered to enter or to escape from it, during six months that the siege continued. At the expiration of this time, the Tartars, despairing of succour, surrendered upon the condition of their lives being spared. These events took place in the course of the year 1264.[1] The grand khan having learned some years after that the unfortunate issue of the expedition was to be attributed to the dissension between the two commanders, caused the head of one of them to be cut off; the other he sent to the savage island of Zorza,[2] where it is the custom to execute criminals in the following manner. They are wrapped round both arms, in the hide of a buffalo fresh taken from the beast, which is sewed tight. As this dries, it compresses the body to such a degree that the sufferer is incapable of moving or in any manner helping himself, and thus miserably perishes.[3]

CHAPTER III

OF THE NATURE OF THE IDOLS WORSHIPPED IN ZIPANGU, AND OF THE PEOPLE BEING ADDICTED TO EATING HUMAN FLESH

In this island of Zipangu and the others in its vicinity, their idols are fashioned in a variety of shapes, some of them having

been formerly much frequented by Chinese shipping. But, according to P. Gaubil, the island was that of Ping-hou or Firando, near the city of Nangasaki; not then a place of so much importance as it has since become.

[1] There is here a manifest error in the date, which, instead of 1264, should rather be 1284. In the early Venice epitome it is 1269, [as well as in the early texts printed by the Paris Geographical Society;] and in the Basle edition, 1289. Our author cannot be made accountable for these contradictions amongst his transcribers.

[2] No clue presents itself by which to discover the island meant by the name of Zorza, or (allowing for the Venetian pronunciation) Jorja. We should be induced to look for it in some one of the lakes of Tartary.

[3] This must have been a Tartar, not a Chinese mode of punishment. In the History of Sinde we are told of its having been inflicted by Abd-al-malik, khalif of Baghdad, upon one of his generals, who was accused by certain princesses, his captives, of a heinous offence. "That monarch," says Pottinger, "was highly enraged at this supposed insult, and sent an order to the general who was second in command, to sew

the heads of oxen, some of swine, of dogs, goats, and many other animals. Some exhibit the appearance of a single head, with two countenances; others of three heads, one of them in its proper place, and one upon each shoulder. Some have four arms, others ten, and some an hundred; those which have the greatest number being regarded as the most powerful, and therefore entitled to the most particular worship.[1] When they are asked by Christians wherefore they give to their deities these diversified forms, they answer that their fathers did so before them. "Those who preceded us," they say, "left them such, and such shall we transmit them to our posterity." The various ceremonies practised before these idols are so wicked and diabolical that it would be nothing less than impiety and an abomination to give an account of them in this our book. The reader should, however, be informed that the idolatrous inhabitants of these islands, when they seize the person of an enemy who has not the means of effecting his ransom for money, invite to their house all their relations and friends, and putting their prisoner to death, dress and eat the body, in a convivial manner, asserting that human flesh surpasses every other in the excellence of its flavour.

Mohummud bin Kasim into a raw hide, and thus forward him to the presence. . . . Though consciously innocent, he allowed the unjust and cruel punishment of his sovereign to be inflicted on himself. He died the third day after."—Travels in Beloochistan and Sinde, p. 389.

[1] The idols here described belong to the Budsdo, or what Kæmpfer terms the foreign pagan worship, and not to that of the Sintos, whose objects of veneration, the Sin and Kami, seem to have been the personification of deceased heroes. It is true that Buddha, whom the Japanese named Buds or Budz, and Siaka, is commonly represented of the natural human shape, although often of a monstrous size; but, either along with his religion (said to have been introduced in Japan about the first century of the Christian era), or, probably, at an antecedent period, these people, as well as the Chinese, appear to have adopted the multiform divinities of the Hindu mythology. Many of these, it is well known, have the heads of various animals, as that of the boar, in the third incarnation of Vishnu, and of the elephant, in the figures of Ganesa; to which may be added the bull of Siva, and Hanumân, the prince of monkeys. Of many-headed deities the instances, in that system, are frequent, as the four heads of Brahma, the five of Mahadeva-panchamukhi, and the *trimurti* or Hindu triad. Those which exhibit numerous arms are at least equally common. Such appear to be at this day the idols of the Japanese; although with some modifications peculiar to themselves.

CHAPTER IV

OF THE SEA OF CHIN, BETWEEN THIS ISLAND AND THE PROVINCE OF MANJI

It is to be understood that the sea in which the island of Zipangu is situated is called the Sea of Chin,[1] and so extensive is this eastern sea, that according to the report of experienced pilots and mariners who frequent it, and to whom the truth must be known, it contains no fewer than seven thousand four hundred and forty islands, mostly inhabited.[2] It is said that of the trees which grow in them, there are none that do not yield a fragrant smell.[3] They produce many spices and drugs, particularly lignum-aloes and pepper, in great abundance, both white and black.[4] It is impossible to estimate the value of the gold and other articles found in the islands; but their distance from the continent is so great, and the navigation attended with so much trouble and inconvenience, that the vessels engaged in the trade, from the ports of Zai-tun and Kin-sai, do not reap large profits, being obliged to consume a whole year in their voyage, sailing in the winter and returning in the summer. For in these regions only two winds prevail; one of them during the winter, and the other during the summer season; so that they must avail themselves of the one for the

[1] Whatever uncertainty may prevail respecting the name which the Chinese themselves give to their country, it is well known that by all the other people of the East it is denominated Chîn and Chîna; the former being the manner in which the word is pronounced by the Persians and natives of Hindustan, and the latter, by the Malays and other islanders. That which our navigators term the China Sea, is in the Malayan language invariably called Laut Chîna.

[2] The limits of the China Sea, not being accurately defined, it is impossible to verify this pretended enumeration of its islands, which is evidently meant to include the Moluccas or those from whence the spices are chiefly procured.

[3] " Les campagnes," says M. Poivre, " sont couvertes be bois odoriférens. . . . On y respire un air embaumé par une multitude de fleurs agréables qui se succédent toute l'année, et dont l'odeur suave pénétre jusqu'à l'âme, et inspire la volupté la plus séduisante." (Voy. d'un Philosophe, p. 56.) This picture of the Malayan countries, though certainly overcharged, is a complete justification of our author's report of their productions.

[4] It is remarkable that this distinction of white and black pepper, which is effected by the process of blanching the grains in their ripest state, should have been noticed at so early a period. Until within the last half century they were generally supposed in Europe to be the productions of different plants.

outward, and of the other for the homeward-bound voyage.[1] These countries are far remote from the continent of India. In terming this sea the Sea of Chin, we must understand it, nevertheless, to be a part of the ocean; for as we speak of the English Sea, or of the Egean Sea, do so the eastern people of the Sea of Chin and of the Indian Sea; whilst all of them are comprehended under the general term of the ocean. We shall here cease to treat further of these countries and islands, as well on account of their lying so far out of the way, as of my not having visited them personally, and of their not being under the dominion of the grand khan.[2] We return now to Zai-tun.

CHAPTER V

OF THE GULF OF KEINAN, AND OF ITS RIVERS

DEPARTING from the port of Zai-tun, and steering a westerly course, but inclining to the south, for fifteen hundred miles, you pass the gulf named Keinan,[3] which extends to the distance of two months' navigation, along its northern shore, where it bounds the southern part of the province of Manji, and from thence to where it approaches the countries of Ania,

[1] Such also at the present day is the state of navigation amongst the Chinese, whose junks are employed in trading to Java and other islands of the archipelago, but not being adapted, either by their construction or mode of rigging, to work against a contrary wind, require two monsoons for the performance of their outward and homeward-bound voyages. The account here given of these periodical winds is substantially correct. In the China seas the north-east or winter monsoon, being that which is favourable for sailing from the southern ports of China to the straits of Malacca or Java, commences about the month of October or November, and lasts till about February or March: the south-west monsoon sets in about April or May, and blows till August or September, during which latter season the junks return homewards.

[2] There is much reason to believe that, whilst employed in the service of the emperor, Marco Polo had visited some of the eastern islands, lying the nearest to the coast of China; such, perhaps, as the Philippines. A voyage of this nature is directly mentioned in book i. chap. i. sect. 5. By those "lying far out of the way," may be understood the Moluccas, whose valuable productions must always have made their existence known.

[3] Keinan, or, according to the Italian orthography, Cheinan, is indisputably Hai-nan, the name of a large and important island, lying off the southern coast of China, and by some enumerated as a sixteenth province of that empire. It may naturally be supposed to have communicated its appellation to the bight or gulf in which it is situated, although by our seamen the latter is commonly termed the gulf of Tung-king.

Toloman, and many others already mentioned.[1] Within this gulf there are a multitude of islands, for the most part well inhabited,[2] about the coasts of which much gold-dust is collected from the sea, at those places where the rivers discharge themselves. Copper also and many other articles are found there,[3] and with these a trade is carried on, the one island supplying what another does not produce. They traffic also with the people of the continent, exchanging their gold and copper for such necessaries as they may require. In the most of these islands grain is raised in abundance. This gulf is so extensive and the inhabitants so numerous, that it appears like another world.

CHAPTER VI

OF THE COUNTRY OF ZIAMBA, OF THE KING OF THAT COUNTRY, AND OF HIS BECOMING TRIBUTARY TO THE GRAND KHAN

We now resume our former subject. Upon leaving Zai-tun and navigating fifteen hundred miles across this gulf, as has been mentioned, you arrive at a country named Ziamba, which is of great extent, and rich.[4] It is governed by its own kings, and has its peculiar language. The inhabitants are

[1] By Ania must be understood the country of Anan or Tung-king, by the Portuguese written Anam or Annam, from whence the language of that country, as well as of Kochinchina, is termed in the dictionary of Alexander de Rhodes, "lingua Annamitica." The Chinese, who never commence a word with the sound of A, pronounce it Ngan-nan; as it stands in the Jesuits' and D'Anville's maps. With respect to the name of Toloman, some conjectures have been offered in a note on a former page. From the context we might be led to suppose it was here meant for Kochinchina, the Kiao-chi of the Chinese; but neither is this warranted by any resemblance of sound, nor does it appear from the former part of the itinerary (b. i. c. xlviii.) that Toloman or Tholoman was situated upon the coast. Our author may not, however, have intended by this passage to assert its maritime situation, but only to say that as the gulf was bounded on the one side by China, so it was, on the other, by the land which contains Anan or Tung-king, Toloman (which may be Po-lo-man, the country of the Burmans, according to Chinese pronunciation), and other provinces of which he had before spoken.

[2] The account given of these islands may be supposed to apply, not to the small ones lying close to the main land, at the bottom of the gulf, but rather to the Philippines, together with Palawan or Paragua, situated opposite to it, although at a considerable distance. This appears to be justified by the subsequent mention of its vast extent.

[3] Copper, as well as gold, is found in the Philippines and several of the eastern islands; but the greatest quantity, and that of the finest quality, is procured from Japan.

[4] No doubt can be entertained of the Ziamba of Ramusio's text, which in the early Latin version also is Ziamba, in the Basle, Ciamba, and in

worshippers of idols.[1] An annual tribute, in elephants and lignum-aloes, is paid to the grand khan,[2] the occasion and circumstances of which shall be related.[3] About the year 1268, Kublaï, having received accounts of the great wealth of this kingdom, resolved upon the measure of sending a large force, both of infantry and cavalry, to effect the conquest of it,[4] and the country was accordingly invaded by a powerful army, placed under the command of one of his generals, named Sogatu. The king, whose name was Accambale,[5] and who was far advanced in years, feeling himself incapable of making resistance in the field to the forces of the grand khan, retired to his strongholds, which afforded him security, and he there defended himself valiantly. The open towns, however, and habitations on the plains, were in the meantime overrun and laid waste, and the king, perceiving that his whole territory would be ruined by the enemy, sent ambassadors to the grand khan for the purpose of representing that, being himself an old man, who had always preserved his dominions in a state of tranquillity and peace, he was anxious to save them from the destruction with which they were threatened, and, upon the condition of the invading army being withdrawn, he was willing to pay yearly an honorary tribute of elephants and sweet-scented wood. Upon receiving this proposal, the grand khan, from motives of compassion, immediately sent orders to Sogatu for his retreat from thence with the force under his

the early Italian epitome Cianban, being the Tsiampa, Siampa, Ciampa, or Champa, of our maps; situated to the southward of Kochinchina, in the south-eastern part of what may be termed the peninsula of Kamboja.

[1] "La religion de Fo," say the Mémoires, speaking of Tchen-la, "est la seule qui ait cours dans le pays." (P. 119.) "Leur religion," says P. A. de Rhodes, speaking of the Kochinchinese, "est la mesme que celle de la Chine, à laquelle autrefois ils estoient attachez, aussi bien que le Tunquin."—Voyages et Missions, p. 64.

[2] In the year 1373 we find the king of Tchen-la sending tribute (that is, complimentary presents by an ambassador) to the emperor Hong-ou, one of the descendants of Kublaï.

[3] The Chinese historians place the operations of the campaign in a different, and probably a juster light.

[4] Marco Polo's dates are often erroneous, probably owing to mistakes of the transcribers, and they vary much in the different texts. This expedition took place in 1281 or 1282.

[5] The name of Accambale is not to be traced in the histories of these countries, and as it does not occur in the other versions of our author, we are deprived of that chance of obtaining a more correct orthography. According to the historian of the Huns, the name of the king who reigned in "Gan-nan or Tun-kin," from 1262 to 1290, was Tchin-goei-hoang, otherwise called Kuang-ping; and in "Tchen-tching," or Kochinchina, Po-yeou-pou-la-tche-ou, who in 1282, he adds, was engaged in war with Kublaï-khan.—Liv. iii. pp. 171—173.

command, and directed him to proceed to the conquest of other countries, which was executed without delay.[1] From that time the king has annually presented to the grand khan, in the form of tribute, a very large quantity of lignum-aloes,[2] together with twenty of the largest and handsomest elephants to be found in his districts.[3] Thus it was that the king of Ziamba became the subject of the grand khan.

Having related the foregoing, we shall now mention some circumstances respecting this king and his country. In the first place it should be noticed that in his dominions no young woman can be given in marriage, until she has been first proved by the king. Those who prove agreeable to him he retains for some time, and when they are dismissed, he furnishes them with a sum of money, in order that they may be able to obtain, according to their rank in life, advantageous matches. Marco Polo, in the year 1280, visited this place,[4] at which period the king had three hundred and twenty-six children, male and female. Most of the former had distinguished themselves as valiant soldiers. The country abounds with elephants and with lignum-aloes. There are also many forests of ebony of a fine black, which is worked into various handsome articles of furniture.[5] No other circumstance requires particular mention. Leaving this place, we shall now speak of the island called Java Major.

[1] By the contemporary annalists of China, the events are described in a manner much less creditable to the arms of their sovereign. It is possible, however, that, as the Chinese reprobated these attempts at foreign conquest, they may have been led to exaggerate their disastrous consequences.

[2] It may be necessary to inform some readers that lignum-aloes, agallochum, or agila wood, called by the Malays and other eastern people *kalambak*, is an unctuous, and, apparently, decayed wood, that melts away in burning, like a resin, emitting a fragrant smoke that is highly esteemed as a perfume.

[3] It would seem that until the period of these invasions, rather than conquests, of Mien or Ava, and Ngan-nan or Tung-king, the Mungal emperors had not been in the practice of employing elephants, either as a military arm or as beasts of burthen. In later times a few only are kept for parade, or for transporting the baggage of the court from one palace to another.

[4] If this was actually in 1280, he must have been then employed on a special mission, in the service of the emperor. The early Italian epitome, with less appearance of being correct, assigns the date of 1275. It seems probable that the fleet in which he took his final departure from China, also touched there about the year 1291.

[5] In Loureiro's Flora, speaking of the "Ebenoxylum verum," or true ebony, it is said: "Habitat vastas sylvas Cochinchinæ, maximè prope confinia Cambodiæ ad 11 gradum lat. bor. ubi has arbores iteratò vidi. Usus. Nigredine et nitore (polish) excellit in scriniis et minoribus operibus, præsertim quando ebure vel margaritarum conchis discernitur."

CHAPTER VII

OF THE ISLAND OF JAVA

DEPARTING from Ziamba, and steering between south and south-east, fifteen hundred miles, you reach an island of very great size, named Java,[1] which, according to the reports of some well-informed navigators, is the largest in the world, being in circuit above three thousand miles. It is under the dominion of one king only, nor do the inhabitants pay tribute to any other power. They are worshippers of idols. The country abounds with rich commodities. Pepper, nutmegs, spikenard, galengal, cubebs, cloves, and all the other valuable spices and drugs, are the produce of the island;[2] which occasion it to be visited by many ships laden with merchandise, that yields to the owners considerable profit. The quantity of gold collected there exceeds all calculation and belief. From thence it is that the merchants of Zai-tun and of Manji in general have imported, and to this day import, that metal to a great amount, and from thence also is obtained the greatest part of the spices that are distributed throughout the world.[3] That the grand khan has not brought the island under subjection to him, must be attributed to the length of the voyage and the dangers of the navigation.[4]

[1] In this chapter Marco Polo seems to have mixed together information which he had collected relating to two islands, Java and Borneo, some of it applying to one, and some to the other.

[2] Pepper is produced both in Borneo and Java; cloves or nutmegs are not the growth of either; but Batavia has been in modern times the great mart for the sale of them, in consequence of the Moluccas being under the dominion of those who govern Java. Such may likewise have been the case at the period when the country was ruled by the sovereigns of Majapahit; a subject upon which we have much curious information from the pen of Sir T. Stamford Raffles, in his excellent history of that interesting island. Speaking of the political occurrences about this period, he observes that "All the provinces (after a rebellion) again fell under the authority of Majapáhit. According to some accounts Dámar Wúlan had also been successful in repelling an invasion from Kambója." (Vol. ii. p. 112.) The intercourse between Java and Tsiampa or Chámpa is also repeatedly noticed.

[3] Java is not celebrated for the production of gold; in Borneo, on the contrary, much is collected.

[4] This observation is much more applicable to Java than to Borneo, as the navigation to the latter, from the southern ports of China, is neither distant nor attended with any particular difficulty. It may be proper to notice in this place, that the Chinese historians speak of a kingdom named Koua-oua against which an expedition was sent by Kublaï, about the year 1287, according to P. Amiot, or in 1292, according to the elder De Guignes.

CHAPTER VIII

OF THE ISLANDS OF SONDUR AND KONDUR, AND OF THE COUNTRY OF LOCHAC

UPON leaving the island of Java, and steering a course between south and south-west, seven hundred miles, you fall in with two islands, the larger of which is named Sondur, and the other Kondur.[1] Both being uninhabited, it is unnecessary to say more respecting them. Having run the distance of fifty miles from these islands, in a south-easterly direction, you reach an extensive and rich province, that forms a part of the main land, and is named Lochac.[2] Its inhabitants are idolaters. They have a language peculiar to themselves, and are governed by their own king, who pays no tribute to any other, the situation of the country being such as to protect it from any hostile attack. Were it assailable, the grand khan would not have delayed to bring it under his dominion. In

[1] If, as there is reason to presume, the Kondur here mentioned be the Condore of our maps (by the Malays named Kondûr, signifying a species of gourd), it is evident that the bearings and distance assigned must be erroneous, as a south-south-west course from Java, instead of leading to an island on the coast of Kamboja, would carry the navigator into the southern ocean. Such errors appear to have arisen from a misconception of the itinerary, into which our author, avowedly, introduces places of which he had only hearsay information, along with those which he actually visited. That his voyage did not lead him to the island of Java (as distinguished from that which he afterwards terms Java Minor) is apparent from his own words; but upon leaving China and reaching Tsiampa, which he either touched at, or saw in passing, he digresses in his narrative, in order to mention the distance and some particulars of that celebrated island, and having so done, returns to the point he had left; from whence he proceeds (in his desultory manner) with the sequel of his proper route, which naturally leads him to the small island of Condore. The early transcribers of his manuscript, not adverting to so material a distinction, have attempted to render the journal more regular, according to their idea, by forcing these excursive notices, however inconsistent with geography, into one uniform track, and for that purpose assigning imaginary bearings. The name of Sondur cannot be identified. If in fact a distinct place, and not another reading of Kondur (which itself consists of a greater and a smaller island), it may be meant for Pulo Sapata, which lies in the route, but at a considerable distance from the former.

[2] The Lochac of Ramusio's text, and Lochach of the epitome, is Laach in one early Latin, and Boeach in the Basle edition. In one version it is said to lie in a south-east, and in another, in a south-south-west direction from Kondur: both equally inconsistent with the geographical fact. It appears from the circumstances to be intended for some part of the country of Kamboja, the capital of which was named Loech, according to the authority of Gaspar de Cruz, who visited it during the reign of Sebastian, king of Portugal. (See Purchas, vol. iii. p. 169.) In D'Anville's map the name is written Levek.

this country sappan, or brezil wood, is produced in large quan tities. Gold is abundant to a degree scarcely credible; elephants are found there; and the objects of the chase, either with dogs or birds, are in plenty. From hence are exported all those porcelain shells, which, being carried to other countries, are there circulated for money, as has been already noticed.[1] Here they cultivate a species of fruit called *berchi,* in size about that of a lemon, and having a delicious flavour.[2] Besides these circumstances there is nothing further that requires mention, unless it be that the country is wild and mountainous, and is little frequented by strangers, whose visits the king discourages, in order that his treasures and other secret matters of his realm may be as little known to the rest of the world as possible.[3]

CHAPTER IX

OF THE ISLAND OF PENTAN, AND OF THE KINGDOM OF MALAIUR

DEPARTING from Lochac, and keeping a southerly course for five hundred miles, you reach an island named Pentan,[4] the

[1] Excepting at Sulu, near the north-eastern coast of Borneo, I am not aware of the production of cowries in any part of the eastern or China seas, and suspect that there may have been here a transposition or mistake of some other kind, as the words of the text are applicable to the Maldives alone. In the Latin version it is said: " Utuntur incolæ pro moneta glebis quibusdam aureis; " by which may be understood small lumps of gold, such in form as those pieces of silver resembling flattened bullets, which are current in Siam: but these could not be exported for circulation in other countries.

[2] Without a more particular description, it is impossible, even with the assistance of Loureiro's Flora Cochinchinensis, to ascertain the kind of fruit here named *berci* or *berchi.* In a country where the mangustin (*garcinia mangostana*) should be found, it might be thought to merit this special notice; but we are not informed of that exquisite fruit being a native of Kamboja.

[3] Very different reasons are assigned in the several versions for this seclusive state of the country. Here we find it attributed to motives of jealous policy; in the Basle edition the occasion is said to be, " adeò inhumani sunt habitatores ejus; " and in the early epitome, " perche elli si e fora de via; " which last, as it is the simplest, may be the most genuine cause.

[4] Pentan, which in the Basle edition is Petan, but in the older Latin, Pentayn, appears to be the island of Bintan, or, as it is more commonly written, Bintang, near the eastern mouth of the straits of Malacca, whose port, called Riyu or Rhio, is a place of considerable trade. The course to it from Kamboja is nearly south, as stated both in the Italian and the Latin texts, and the distance does not materially differ from five hundred miles.

coast of which is wild and uncultivated, but the woods abound with sweet-scented trees. Between the province of Lochac and this island of Pentan, the sea, for the space of sixty miles, is not more than four fathoms in depth, which obliges those who navigate it to lift the rudders of their ships (in order that they may not touch the bottom).[1] After sailing these sixty miles, in a south-easterly direction, and then proceeding thirty miles further, you arrive at an island, in itself a kingdom, named Malaiur, which is likewise the name of its chief city.[2] The people are governed by a king, and have their own peculiar language. The town is large and well-built. A considerable trade is there carried on in spices and drugs, with which the place abounds. Nothing else that requires notice presents itself. Proceeding onwards from thence, we shall now speak of Java Minor.

CHAPTER X

OF THE ISLAND OF JAVA MINOR

Upon leaving the island of Pentan, and steering in the direction of south-east for about one hundred miles, you reach the island of Java the Lesser.[3] Small, however, as it may be termed by comparison, it is not less than two thousand miles in circuit. In this island there are eight kingdoms, governed by so many kings, and each kingdom has its own proper language, distinct from those of all the others. The people are idolaters.

[1] In the navigation from the coast of Kamboja to the island of Bintan and straits of Malacca, there are numerous shoals and coral reefs, but the particular tract of shallow water to which the passage in the text refers cannot be precisely ascertained.

[2] By the island and kingdom of Malaiur (in the Basle edition Maletur, but in the older Latin, Maleyur) it will scarcely to doubted that our author means to speak of the kingdom of the Malays (*orang malâyu*), founded about a century before, at the south-eastern extremity of the peninsula that bears their name; for although about the year 1252 the seat of government was transferred to Malacca, the appellation of Tanah malâyu, "the Malayan land," seems to have been always applied emphatically to that part of the country where the original establishment was formed, which is now included in the kingdom of Johor. From the name of their first city, the straits, formed by an island which lies close to the extreme point of the land, obtained the appellation of the straits of Singa-pura, or, vulgarly, Sincapore.

[3] Every circumstance tends to confirm the opinion that by the Giaua Minor of Ramusio's text, and the Jaua Minor of the Latin, is meant the island of Sumatra, a name very little known to the natives, and probably of Hindu origin.

It contains abundance of riches, and all sorts of spices, lignum-aloes, sappan-wood for dyeing, and various other kinds of drugs,[1] which, on account of the length of the voyage and the danger of the navigation, are not imported into our country, but which find their way to the provinces of Manji and Cathay.

We shall now treat separately of what relates to the inhabitants of each of these kingdoms; but in the first place it is proper to observe that the island lies so far to the southward as to render the north star invisible.[2] Six of the eight kingdoms were visited by Marco Polo; and these he will describe, omitting the other two, which he had not an opportunity of seeing.

CHAPTER XI

OF THE KINGDOM OF FELECH, IN THE ISLAND OF JAVA MINOR

We shall begin with the kingdom of Felech, which is one of the eight.[3] Its inhabitants are for the most part idolaters, but many of those who dwell in the seaport towns have been converted to the religion of Mahomet, by the Saracen merchants who constantly frequent them.[4] Those who inhabit the

[1] The other drugs here alluded to are probably the gum benzoin and the native camphor (as distinguished from the factitious camphor of the shops, imported from China and Japan); both of them staple articles of trade in Sumatra.

[2] The island being intersected by the equinoctial line, the north star must be invisible to the inhabitants of all the southern portion; and even by those of the northern it can be seen but rarely, and only under particular circumstances.

[3] The name here written Felech is in the Latin edition Ferlech, and in the Italian epitomes Ferlach, equivalent to Ferlak. It appears therefore to be intended for a place named Perlak, situated at the eastern extremity of the northern coast; and as we find in the sequel that the detention of the fleet in a port of this island was occasioned by the unfavourable circumstances of the weather, it may be conjectured that after leaving the island of Bintan, and having nearly cleared the straits, they were encountered by westerly gales, as they made the high land of Tanjong Perlak, or the Diamond Point of our charts, and they would be forced to seek for shelter in a neighbouring bay.

[4] The assertion of our author's finding Mahometans amongst these people, about the year 1291, is fully justified by the authority of the annals of the princes of Malacca, which state that in the peninsula the establishment of that religion took place during the reign of a king who ascended the throne in 1276 and died in 1333; whilst at the same time it is obvious that the conversion of individuals, even in great numbers, may have preceded by many years the adoption of Islamism as the religion of the government.—See Hist. of Sumatra, 3d edit. p. 343.

mountains live in a beastly manner; they eat human flesh,[1] and indiscriminately all other sorts of flesh, clean and unclean.[2] Their worship is directed to a variety of objects, for each individual adores throughout the day the first thing that presents itself to his sight when he rises in the morning.[3]

CHAPTER XII

OF THE SECOND KINGDOM, NAMED BASMAN

UPON leaving the last-mentioned kingdom, you enter that of Basman,[4] which is independent of the others, and has its peculiar language. The people profess obedience to the grand khan, but pay him no tribute, and their distance is so great, that his troops cannot be sent to these parts. The whole island, indeed, is nominally subject to him, and when ships pass that way the opportunity is taken of sending him rare and curious articles, and especially a particular sort of falcon.[5]

In the country are many wild elephants and rhinoceroses, which latter are much inferior in size to the elephant, but

[1] This character plainly refers to the people named Battas, who inhabit a considerable part of the interior of Sumatra, towards its northern extremity, and whose cannibalism has been noticed by travellers and writers of all periods since the island was first known to Europeans.

[2] "It is only on public occasions that they (the Battas) kill cattle for food; but not being delicate in their appetites, they do not scruple to eat part of a dead buffalo, hog, rat, alligator, or any wild animal with which they happen to meet."—Hist. of Sumatra, 3d edition, p. 380.

[3] A similar assertion is made by Ludovico Barthema respecting the people of Java: "La fede loro è questa," says this extraordinary, but genuine traveller: "alcuni adorano gli idoli come fanno in Calicut (that is, they worship those of the Hindûs), e alcuni sono che adorano il sole; altri la luna, molti adorano il bue; gran parte la prima cosa che scontrano la mattina."—Ramusio, tom. i. p. 168.

[4] The Basma of Ramusio's and of the older Italian text, or Basman of the Basle edition, has been supposed, from a fair analogy of sound, to refer to Pasaman, on the western coast, immediately under the equinoctial line; but there is no probability of our author's having visited any place on that side of the island, and especially one so far to the southward. All the circumstances, on the contrary, lead us to conclude that it is intended for Pasé (by the old travellers written Paçem), on the northern coast, not far from Diamond Point. "Pedir," says J. de Barros, "was the principal city of these parts before the founding of Malacca; but subsequently to that period, and particularly after the arrival of the Portuguese, it began to decline, and Paçem, in its vicinity, to rise in importance."—Decad. iii. fol. 115.

[5] This account is rendered probable by the known ambition of Kublai to extend the fame of his empire to places situated beyond the reach of his arms, and particularly to establish a vassalage, though merely nominal, amongst the princes of the Eastern islands.

their feet are similar. Their hide resembles that of the buffalo. In the middle of the forehead they have a single horn; but with this weapon they do not injure those whom they attack, employing only for this purpose their tongue, which is armed with long, sharp spines, and their knees or feet; their mode of assault being to trample upon the person, and then to lacerate him with the tongue.[1] Their head is like that of a wild boar, and they carry it low towards the ground. They take delight in muddy pools, and are filthy in their habits.[2] They are not of that description of animals which suffer themselves to be taken by maidens, as our people suppose, but are quite of a contrary nature.[3] There are found in this district monkeys of various sorts, and vultures as black as crows, which are of a large size, and pursue the quarry in a good style.

It should be known that what is reported respecting the dried bodies of diminutive human creatures, or pigmies, brought from India, is an idle tale, such pretended men being manufactured in this island in the following manner. The country produces a species of monkey, of a tolerable size, and having a countenance resembling that of a man. Those persons who make it their business to catch them, shave off the hair, leaving it only about the chin, and those other parts where it naturally grows on the human body. They then dry and preserve them with camphor and other drugs; and having prepared then in such a mode that they have exactly the appearance of little men, they put them into wooden boxes, and sell them to trading people, who carry them to all parts of the world. But this is merely an imposition, the practice being

[1] Both the elephant and rhinoceros are well known to be natives of Sumatra. With respect to the uses of its horn as a weapon of offence, and the spiny structure of the tongue, our author was deceived by what he was told or had read. The belief of its tearing the flesh by licking was general throughout the world, from the days of Pliny to a very modern period. Bontius, a Dutch physician, who wrote at Batavia in 1629, tells us that "if it be exasperated, it will toss up a man and horse like a fly, whom it will kill with licking, while by the roughness of its tongue it lays bare the bones."—An Account of the Diseases, etc., p. 183.

[2] What is said of its delighting in muddy pools is conformable to the known habits of the animal. "Like the hog," say the Hist. of Quadrupeds, "the rhinoceros is fond of wallowing in the mire."—P. 177.

[3] [It was a common superstition of the middle ages, set forth in all the treatises on Natural History (or Bestiaries, as they were called), that there was only one way of taking the unicorn, which was by placing a pure virgin near his haunts. It was believed that the animal immediately became so tame, that he went and laid his head in the maiden's bosom, while the hunter seized the opportunity of killing him.]

such as we have described; and neither in India, nor in any other country, however wild (and little known), have pigmies been found of a form so diminutive as these exhibit.[1] Sufficient having been said of this kingdom, which presents nothing else remarkable, we shall now speak of another, named Samara.

CHAPTER XIII

OF THE THIRD KINGDOM, NAMED SAMARA

LEAVING Basman, you enter the kingdom of Samara,[2] being another of those into which the island is divided. In this Marco Polo resided five months, during which, exceedingly against his inclination, he was detained by contrary winds.[3] The north star is not visible here, nor even the stars that are in the wain.[4] The people are idolaters; they are governed by a powerful prince, who professes himself the vassal of the grand khan.

As it was necessary to continue for so long a time at this island Marco Polo established himself on shore, with a party of about 2,000 men; and in order to guard against mischief

[1] At a period when the eastern part of the world was little known to the people of Europe, who were credulous in proportion to their ignorance, it is by no means improbable that such impositions were practised by the travelling Mahometan and Armenian traders who visited the islands where the orang utan or pongo (*simia satyrus*) was found, and might have been in the practice of selling their stuffed carcases to the virtuosi of Italy, for the mummies of a pigmy race of men.

[2] The place that appears to answer best to Samara is Sama-langa, situated between Pedir and Pasé, on the same northern coast, and described in the writings of the Malays as having the advantage of a well-sheltered anchorage or roadstead.

[3] If the expedition which our author accompanied left China about the beginning of the year 1291 (as inferred in note [1], page 27), and was three months on its passage to Java Minor or Sumatra (as stated by himself in the first chapter of the work, p. 27), it would have met the south-west monsoon at the western opening of the straits of Malacca, about the month of May in that year; and having found it necessary, in consequence to anchor in one of the bays on the northern coast of that island, they might have been detained there till the change of the monsoon, in the month of October following, when, with the return of the north-east wind, they might expect fair and settled weather.

[4] When our author tells us that, at a place distant only about five degrees from the equator, the polar-star was not to be seen, the fact will be readily admitted; but the further assertion, that the stars of the Wain or Great Bear were also invisible, cannot be otherwise accounted for than by imputing to him the mistaken idea that, because the body of the constellation was not above the horizon in the night-time, during the greater part of his stay on the island, it was not to be seen at any other season.

from the savage natives, who seek for opportunities of seizing stragglers, putting them to death, and eating them, he caused a large and deep ditch to be dug around him on the land side, in such manner that each of its extremities terminated in the port, where the shipping lay. This ditch he strengthened by erecting several blockhouses or redoubts of wood, the country affording an abundant supply of that material; and being defended by this kind of fortification, he kept the party in complete security during the five months of their residence. Such was the confidence inspired amongst the natives, that they furnished supplies of victuals and other necessary articles according to an agreement made with them.[1]

No finer fish for the table can be met with in any part of the world than are found here. There is no wheat produced, but the people live upon rice. Wine is not made; but from a species of tree resembling the date-bearing palm they procure an excellent beverage in the following manner. They cut off a branch, and put over the place a vessel to receive the juice as it distils from the wound, which is filled in the course of a day and a night.[2] So wholesome are the qualities of this liquor, that it affords relief in dropsical complaints, as well as in those of the lungs and of the spleen.[3] When these shoots that have been cut are perceived not to yield any more juice, they contrive to water the trees, by bringing from the river, in pipes or channels, so much water as is sufficient for the purpose; and upon this being done, the juice runs again as it did at first.[4] Some trees naturally yield it of a reddish, and others of a pale colour. The Indian nuts also grow here, of the size

[1] It is mentioned that, in the year 1522, the Portuguese garrison of a fort built at Paçem (Pasé), in the vicinity of the place here spoken of, was distressed from the "want of provisions, which the country people withheld from them, discontinuing the fairs that they were used to keep three times a week."—Hist. of Sum. 3d ed. p. 419.

[2] "This palm, named in Sumatra *anau*, and by the eastern Malays *gomuto*, is the *borassus gomutus* of Loureiro, and the *saguerus pinnatus* of the Batavian Transactions. . . . In order to procure the *nira*, or toddy (held in higher estimation than that from the coco-nut-tree), one of the shoots for fructification is cut off a few inches from the stem; the remaining part is tied up and beaten, and an incision is then made, from which the liquor distils into a vessel or bamboo, closely fastened beneath. This is replaced every twenty-four hours."—Hist. of Sum. p. 88.

[3] The sanative qualities of this liquor, like those of many other specifics, are probably imaginary; but our author could speak only of the popular belief as to its virtues. Indulgence in the use of it is generally thought to produce dysentery.

[4] It is natural to suppose that watering the trees during the dry season would have the effect of increasing the quantity of sap, and consequently of the juice or liquor distilled.

of a man's head, containing an edible substance that is sweet and pleasant to the taste, and white as milk. The cavity of this pulp is filled with a liquor clear as water, cool, and better flavoured and more delicate than wine or any other kind of drink whatever.[1] The inhabitants feed upon flesh of every sort, good or bad, without distinction.

CHAPTER XIV

OF THE FOURTH KINGDOM, NAMED DRAGOIAN

DRAGOIAN is a kingdom governed by its own prince, and having its peculiar language.[2] Its inhabitants are uncivilized, worship idols, and acknowledge the authority of the grand khan. They observe this horrible custom, in cases where any member of the family is afflicted with a disease:—The relations of the sick person send for the magicians, whom they require, upon examination of the symptoms, to declare whether he will recover or not. These, according to the opinion suggested to them by the evil spirit, reply, either that he will recover or the contrary. If the decision be that he cannot, the relations then call in certain men, whose peculiar duty it is and who perform their business with dexterity, to close the mouth of the patient until he be suffocated. This being done, they cut the body in pieces, in order to prepare it as victuals; and when it has been so dressed, the relations assemble, and in a convivial manner eat the whole of it, not leaving so much as the marrow in the bones. Should any particle of the body be suffered to remain, it would breed vermin, as they observe; these vermin, for want of further sustenance, would perish, and their death would prove the occasion of grievous punishment

[1] This description of the coco-nut (*cocos nucifera*) is well known, even to those who have only seen the fruit as brought to Europe, to be perfectly just; but the grateful refreshment afforded by its liquor when drunk from the young nut, whilst the outer husk is green and the kernal still gelatinous, can only be judged of by those who have travelled, under a fervid sun, in those countries where it is produced.

[2] Dragoian, which is the same in the Basle and older Latin editions—in the manuscripts Dagoyam, and in the Italian epitomes Deragola—is supposed, by Valentyn and other Dutch writers, to be intended for Indragiri, or, as it is more commonly written, Andragiri, a considerable river on the eastern side of the island; which, although far to the southward, and consequently distant from the place where the fleet anchored, might have been visited by our adventurous traveller during his five months' detention.

to the soul of the deceased. They afterwards proceed to collect the bones, and having deposited them in a small, neat box, carry them to some cavern in the mountains, where they may be safe against the disturbance of wild animals. If they have it in their power to seize any person who does not belong to their own district, and who cannot pay for his ransom, they put him to death, and devour him.

CHAPTER XV

OF THE FIFTH KINGDOM, NAMED LAMBRI

LAMBRI, in like manner, has its own king and its peculiar language:[1] the people also worship idols, and call themselves vassals of the grand khan. The country produces verzino (brezil or sappan wood) in great abundance,[2] and also camphor, with a variety of other drugs.[3] They sow a vegetable which resembles the sappan, and when it springs up and begins to throw out shoots, they transplant it to another spot, where it is suffered to remain for three years. It is then taken up by the roots, and used as a dye-stuff.[4] Marco Polo brought some of the seeds of this plant with him to Venice, and sowed them there; but the climate not being sufficiently warm, none of them came up. In this kingdom are found men with tails,

[1] The name of Lambri appears without any variation in the several editions, excepting that at one place, where it recurs in the early Latin, it is printed Jambri. If the last-mentioned district was Indragiri, this would seem to be Jambi, another large river, lying still more to the southward. In the German (Nürnberg) ed. of 1477, this kingdom or district is named Jambu, which approaches nearly to the name of Jambi.

[2] This is the *cæsalpinia sappan* of Lin., well known as a dye-stuff by the name of Brezil wood, which it is generally supposed to have acquired from the country so called; but the reverse appears to be the fact. The words *verzino* in Italian and *barcino* in Spanish, of which *berzin* and *berzil* are corruptions, existed long before the discovery of the New World, and the name was given to that part of South America in consequence of its abounding with the tree which yields this useful dye.

[3] Our author might have seen camphor at the town of Jambi, but it must have been carried thither, for sale, from the inland country lying far to the north-west of it, as the tree does not grow anywhere to the south of the Line.

[4] What is here said of a second kind of dye-stuff, distinct from the *verzino*, is in the Latin editions confounded with it, and to both the name of *berci* is applied, which is evidently connected with *berzin* and *barcino*. Excepting the Indigo plant (*indigofera tinctoria*), I do not know of any vegetable used for dying, of which the leaves, stalk, and root are indiscriminately employed. The same plant is more particularly described in chap. xx. of this Book, by the name of *endigo*.

a span in length, like those of the dog, but not covered with hair. The greater number of them are formed in this manner, but they dwell in the mountains, and do not inhabit towns.[1] The rhinoceros is a common inhabitant of the woods, and there is abundance of all sorts of game, both beasts and birds.

CHAPTER XVI

OF THE SIXTH KINGDOM, NAMED FANFUR, WHERE MEAL IS PROCURED FROM A CERTAIN TREE

FANFUR is a kingdom of the same island,[2] governed by its own prince, where the people likewise worship idols, and profess obedience to the grand khan. In this part of the country a species of camphor, much superior in quality to any other, is produced. It is named the camphor of Fanfur, and is sold for its weight in gold.[3] There is not any wheat nor other corn, but the food of the inhabitants is rice, with milk, and the wine extracted from trees in the manner that has been described in the chapter respecting Samara. They have also a tree from which, by a singular process, they obtain a kind of meal.[4] The stem is lofty, and as thick as can be grasped by two men. When from this the outer bark is stripped, the ligneous substance is found to be about three inches in thickness, and the central part is filled with pith, which yields a meal or flour, resembling that procured from the acorn.[5] The

[1] The notion of the mountaineers with tails seems to have its origin in the name of orang utan, or "wild men," given to certain apes that more particularly resemble the human species.

[2] Fanfur has been supposed to mean the island of Panchor, separated from the eastern coast of Sumatra by a narrow strait; but although not warranted by analogy of sound, I incline to think it intended for Kampar (which the Arabian pilots would pronounce Kanfar) on a river opening into the same strait, which, at the period when Pasé flourished, was likewise a place of some consequence, and is frequently mentioned by J. de Barros and other early writers.

[3] The superiority of the native camphor, in the opinion of the Chinese (who are the principal purchasers), over that prepared in their own country and in Japan, has already been noticed. Its price, in modern times, although by no means equal to its weight in gold, is more than double its weight in silver. According to a price-current of goods at Batavia, for the year 1814, the finest sort of Camphor-barus is stated at 50 rupees, or £6 5s. per lb., whilst in the market the China or Japan camphor is less than one rupee, or about 2s. per lb.

[4] By this is meant the sago-tree, called *rumbiya* and *puhn sagu* by the Malays.

[5] The expression in the text is, "come quella del *carvolo*," a word not

pith is put into vessels filled with water, and is stirred about with a stick, in order that the fibres and other impurities may rise to the top, and the pure farinaceous part subside to the bottom. When this has been done, the water is poured off, and the flour which remains, divested of all extraneous matter, is applied to use, by making it into cakes and various kinds of pastry.[1] Of this, which resembles barley bread in appearance and taste, Marco Polo has frequently eaten, and some of it he brought home with him to Venice.[2] The wood of the tree, in thickness about three inches (as has been mentioned), may be compared to iron in this respect, that when thrown into water it immediately sinks. It admits of being split in an even direction from one end to the other, like the bamboo cane. Of this the natives make short lances: were they to be of any considerable length, their weight would render it impossible to carry or to use them. They are sharpened at one end, and rendered so hard by fire that they are capable of penetrating any sort of armour, and in many respects are preferable to iron.[3] What we have said on the subject of this kingdom (one of the divisions of the island) is

to be found in the Italian dictionaries, as applied to any vegetable. In Portuguese *carvalho* is the oak.

[1] The method of preparing the sago from the farinaceous and glutinous pith of the tree, has been fully described by Rumphius, Poivre, and others, but more succinctly in the Asiat. Researches. "The principal article of their food," says my late estimable friend, Mr. John Crisp, speaking of the inhabitants of the Poggy islands, lying off the coast of Sumatra, "is sago, which is found in plenty on these islands. The tree, when ripe, is cut down, and the pith, which forms the sago, taken out, and the mealy part separated from the fibrous by maceration and treading it in a large trough, continually supplied with fresh water; the mealy part subsides, and is kept in bags made of a kind of rush, and in this state it may be preserved for a considerable time. When they take it from their store for immediate use some further preparation of washing is necessary, but they do not granulate it. One tree will sometimes yield two hundred pounds of sago: when they cook it, it is put into the hollow joints of a thin bamboo, and roasted over the fire."—Vol. vi. p. 83.

[2] Captain Thomas Forrest brought to England in 1778, and exhibited at Sir Joseph Banks's, cakes of sago-bread, prepared by the natives of New Guinea, as well as the earthen oven used for baking them, of which there is an engraving in the account of his voyage to that country, p. 388.

[3] It is evident that our author has fallen into an error, in supposing that this hard and heavy wood, which admits of being split longitudinally into laths, like the bamboo cane, is the ligneous part of the sago-tree, the texture of which is very different. What he describes as fit for making lances is the stem of another palm growing in the same parts of the country, called by the natives of Sumatra and Java *nibong*, and by naturalists *caryota urens*, which he has confounded with its neighbouring tree. Botanists of great celebrity, however, have not shown more discrimination with regard to some of the *genera* of which the order of palms is composed.

sufficient. Of the other kingdoms composing the remaining part we shall not speak, because Marco Polo did not visit them. Proceeding further, we shall next describe a small island named Nocueran.

CHAPTER XVII

OF THE ISLAND OF NOCUERAN

UPON leaving Java (minor) and the kingdom of Lambri, and sailing about one hundred and fifty miles, you fall in with two islands, one of which is named Nocueran,[1] and the other Angaman. Nocueran is not under the government of a king, and the people are little removed from the conditions of beasts; all of them, both males and females, going naked, without a covering to any part of the body. They are idolaters. Their woods abound with the noblest and most valuable trees, such as the white and the red sandal, those which bear the Indian (coco) nuts, cloves, and sappan; besides which they have a variety of drugs.[2] Proceeding further, we shall speak of Angaman.

CHAPTER XVIII

OF THE ISLAND OF ANGAMAN

ANGAMAN is a very large island, not governed by a king.[3] The inhabitants are idolaters, and are a most brutish and

[1] The island here called Nocueran, in the Basle edition Necuram, in the older Latin Necuran, and in the Italian epitome Necunera, is evidently one of the Nicobar islands, named in our maps Noncoury, Nancowrie, Noncavery, and in that of D'Anville Nicavery; which, although not the largest of them, is, on account of its harbour, the best known. Its distance from the extreme point of Sumatra is about two degrees and a half, or one hundred and fifty nautical miles.

[2] "Trees of great height and size," says a writer in the Asiatic Researches, vol. iii. p. 160, "are to be seen in their woods of a compact texture, well calculated for naval construction." Note. "One of these our people cut down, that measured nine fathoms in circumference, or fifty-four feet." Noble trees indeed! "But the productions of which they are more particularly careful are the coco and areca (betel-nut) trees. . . . Wild cinnamon and sassafras grow there also."

[3] No doubts will be entertained of the Angaman of Ramusio's and the older Latin texts, the Angania of the Basle, and the Nangama of the Italian epitomes, being intended for those islands on the eastern side of the bay of Bengal, which we term the Greater and Lesser Andaman.

savage race, having heads, eyes, and teeth resembling those of the canine species.[1] Their dispositions are cruel, and every person, not being of their own nation, whom they can lay their hands upon, they kill and eat. They have abundance and variety of drugs. Their food is rice and milk, and flesh of every description. They have Indian nuts, apples of paradise,[2] and many other fruits different from those which grow in our country.

CHAPTER XIX

OF THE ISLAND OF ZEILAN

TAKING a departure from the island of Angaman, and steering a course something to the southward of west, for a thousand miles, the island of Zeilan presents itself.[3] This, for its actual size, is better circumstanced than any other island in the world. It is in circuit two thousand four hundred miles, but in ancient times it was still larger, its circumference then measuring full three thousand six hundred miles, as the Mappa-Mundi says.[4]

[1] "The Andaman islands," says Mr. R. H. Colebrooke, "are inhabited by a race of men the least civilized perhaps in the world, being nearer to a state of nature than any other we read of. Their colour is of the darkest hue, their stature in general small, and their aspect uncouth. Their limbs are ill-formed and slender, their bellies prominent, and like the Africans they have woolly heads, thick lips, and flat noses. They go quite naked." (Asiat. Res. vol. iv. p. 389.) "Ils sont noirs," says the Arabian travellers, "ils ont les cheveux crespus, le visage et les yeux affreux, les pieds fort grands et presque longs d'une coudée, et ils vont tout nuds." (Anciennes Relat. p. 5.) This early description sufficiently confutes the ill-founded tale of the islands having been originally peopled by a cargo of African slaves preserved from the wreck of a Portuguese ship, invented and credited by persons who were ignorant of the circumstance of many of the eastern islands being equally peopled with a race of negroes.

[2] By the *pomi paradisi* are meant plantains, the *pisang* of the Malays, and *musa paradisiaca* of Linnæus.

[3] The name of this important island, which is pronounced Selan by the Persians and people of Hindustan (who also call it Serendib), has been preserved, through the several versions, more free from corruption than almost any other in the work. In Ramusio's text it is written Zeilan, in that of the Bâsle edition, Seilam, in the older Latin, Seylam, and in the Italian epitomes, Silan; all of which are preferable to the orthography of Ceylon, as we (from the Dutch I presume) are accustomed to write the word. The course to the southernmost part of it, from the Andamans, is nearly west-south-west, and the distance, by measurement on the map, something more than nine hundred geographical miles.

[4] [*Sicut dicit Mappa-mundi.* I have given the literal translation of the Latin words, rather than Marsden's version of the text of Ramusio. *Mappa-mundi*, or *Mappemonde*, was the name given in the Middle Ages

But the northern gales, which blow with prodigious violence, have in a manner corroded the mountains, so that they have in some parts fallen and sunk in the sea, and the island, from that cause, no longer retains its original size. It is governed by a king whose name is Sender-naz.[1] The people worship idols, and are independent of every other state. Both men and women go nearly in a state of nudity, only wrapping a cloth round the middle part of their bodies.[2] They have no grain besides rice and sesamé, of which latter they make oil. Their food is milk, rice, and flesh, and they drink the wine drawn from trees, which has already been described.[3] There is here the best sappan-wood that can anywhere be met with. The island produces more beautiful and valuable rubies than are found in any other part of the world, and likewise sapphires, topazes, amethysts, garnets, and many other precious and costly stones.[4] The king is reported to possess the grandest

to the sort of map of the world then in use, and it was also sometimes used as the title of a treatise on geography. In fact, a map of the world was in some measure a treatise on geography, as a written description was commonly added to each place on the map, which explains the word *dicit*.] The mappe-monde used by Marco Polo was, no doubt, an eastern one—Chinese, or Arabian. Mr. Cordiner, in his Description of Ceylon, published in 1807, states it to be "a tradition of the natives (supported, as it is said, by astronomical observations) that the island is much diminished in size from what it was formerly; which tradition is particularly mentioned by Marco Paolo, a Venetian, who visited the east in the thirteenth century."—Vol. i. p. 2.

[1] Indian proper names are always significant. That of Sender-naz appears to be intended for Chandra-nas, implying the wane or disappearance of the moon. Although not perhaps the king of Candy, or of the whole island, he may have reigned over a district on the western coast, and probably that which is inhabited by a race of people from the opposite continent.

[2] "The dress of the common people," says Mr. Cordiner, "is nothing more than a piece of calico or muslin wrapped round the waist, the size and quality of which correspond to the circumstances of the wearer. The more indigent are very sparingly covered."—Vol. i. p. 94.

[3] "Fruit," says the same writer, "is the principal article of their food. Rice is a luxury of which many of them seldom partake:] fish and flesh come nearly under the same description." "They occasionally drink the sweet limpid water which is found within the coco-nut, and sometimes palm-wine, or liquor drawn from the top of the tree, before it attains an inebriating quality." (P. 104.) "Of rice," says Knox, "they have several sorts." "Tolla is a seed used to make oil." (P. 7—12.) This is the *til*, or sesamé seed, of Gladwin's Materia Medica.

[4] "In this island," says Knox, "are several sorts of precious stones, which the king, for his part, has enough of, and so careth not to have more discovery made. . . . Also there are certain rivers out of which it is generally reported they do take rubies and sapphires, for the king's use, and cats'-eyes." (P. 31.) Mr. Cordiner enumerates, as the production of Ceylon, the ruby, emerald, topaz, amethyst, sapphire, cats' eye or opal, cinnamon stone or garnet, agate, sardonix, and some others. —Vol. i. p. 14

ruby that ever was seen, being a span in length, and the thickness of a man's arm, brilliant beyond description, and without a single flaw. It has the appearance of a glowing fire,[1] and upon the whole is so valuable that no estimation can be made of its worth in money. The grand khan, Kublaï, sent ambassadors to this monarch, with a request that he would yield to him the possession of this ruby; in return for which he should receive the value of a city. The answer he made was to this effect: that he would not sell it for all the treasure of the universe; nor could he on any terms suffer it to go out of his dominions, being a jewel handed down to him by his predecessors on the throne.[2] The grand khan failed therefore to acquire it. The people of this island are by no means of a military habit, but, on the contrary, are abject and timid;[3] and when there is occasion to employ soldiers, they are procured from other countries, in the vicinity of the Mahometans. Nothing else of a remarkable nature presenting itself, we shall proceed to speak of Maabar.

CHAPTER XX

OF THE PROVINCE OF MAABAR

§ 1. LEAVING the island of Zeilan, and sailing in a westerly direction sixty miles,[4] you reach the great province of Maabar,[5]

[1] This description seems to be intended for what is vaguely termed the carbuncle, which Woodward defines to be "a stone of the ruby kind, of a rich blood-red colour," and is believed to have the quality of shining in the dark.

[2] If this extraordinary stone had any real existence, it may have been a lump of coloured crystal; but it is not uncommon with eastern princes, in the preambles of their letters and warrants, to boast the possession of imaginary and improbable curiosities; and, in this instance, the fallacy of the pretension will account for the king's rejecting the magnificent terms held out for the purchase of it by the emperor of China.

[3] "The Cingalese," says Mr. Cordiner, "are indigent, harmless, indolent, and unwarlike, remarkable for equanimity, mildness, bashfulness, and timidity." "An attempt was made some years ago to train a body of them as soldiers, but, after great perseverance, it completely failed of success." (P. 92.) [Other accounts, ancient and modern, agree in this character.]

[4] The distance between Aripo on Ceylon and the nearest part of the continent is exactly sixty geographical miles, but such precision not being uniform in our author's work, is not here to be insisted on; and it is probable that the port in which the fleet lay was Columbo rather than Aripo.

[5] The name of this country, which both in the Bâsle edition and the older Latin is Maabar, and Moabar in the epitomes, is Malabar in the text

which is not an island, but a part of the continent of the greater India, as it is termed, being the noblest and richest country in the world. It is governed by four kings, of whom the principal is named Sender-bandi.[1] Within his dominions is a fishery for pearls, in the gulf of a bay that lies between Maabar and the island of Zeilan,[2] where the water is not more than from ten to twelve fathoms in depth, and in some places not more than two fathoms.[3] The business of the fishery is conducted in the following manner. A number of merchants form themselves into separate companies, and employ many vessels and boats of different sizes, well provided with ground-tackle, by which to ride safely at anchor.[4] They engage and carry with them persons who are skilled in the art of diving for the oysters in which the pearls are enclosed. These they bring up in bags made of netting that are fastened about their bodies, and then repeat the operation, rising to the surface when they can no longer keep their breath, and after a short

of Ramusio, of which the former has been supposed a corruption; but the reverse is the case, for circumstances unequivocally point to the southern part of the coast of Coromandel as the place where the fleet arrived after leaving Ceylon; and what puts the matter beyond all doubt is, that the province of Malabar is afterwards distinctly mentioned in its proper place. Maàbar, signifying a "passage, ferry, ford, trajectus" (see the dictionaries of Meninski and Richardson), was an appellation given by the Mahometans to what we call the Tinevelly, Madura, and, perhaps, Tanjore countries—from their vicinity, as it would seem, to the celebrated chain of sand-banks and coral reefs named Rama's or Adam's bridge. It has now fallen into disuse, but is to be found in the works of all the oriental geographers and historians who have treated of this portion of India.

[1] The princes of India were supposed to belong to the *kshetri* or military tribe, and to be descended from one or other of two illustrious races, termed the *surya vangsa*, or race of the sun, and *chandra vangsa*, or race of the moon. The king here spoken of appears to have belonged to the latter, and his name of Chandra Bandi may be understood to signify the "slave or servant of the moon." [The Paris Latin text reads Sanderba rex de Var.]

[2] The banks on which the fishery for pearls takes place appear to occupy, to a considerable extent, the coast on both sides of the gulf that separates the island of Ceylon from the continent of India, or, more strictly, of that portion of the gulf which lies to the southward of Adam's bridge. On the eastern side, the banks most commonly fished are near the small island of Manár, and on the western or continental side, near the bay of Tutakorîn. This latter, or some place in its vicinity, may be presumed to have been the scene of our author's observations.

[3] "The depth of water over the different banks," says Cordiner, "varies from three to fifteen fathoms; but the best fishing is found in from six to eight fathoms." (Description of Ceylon, vol. ii. p. 41.) A paper in the Asiatic Res., vol. v. p. 401, states the depth at from five to ten fathoms. At Sooloo, the pearl-oysters are taken from the depth of from three to four fathoms only.

[4] It is probable that the privilege of fishing for the pearl-oysters was then farmed, as at the present day, to one or more merchant adventurers.

interval diving again.[1] In this operation they persevere during the whole of the day, and by their exertions accumulate (in the course of the season) a quantity of oysters sufficient to supply the demands of all countries.[2] The greater proportion of the pearls obtained from the fisheries in this gulf, are round, and of a good lustre. The spot where the oysters are taken in the greatest number is called Betala, on the shore of the mainland; and from thence the fishery extends sixty miles to the southward.[3]

In consequence of the gulf being infested with a kind of large fish, which often prove destructive to the divers, the merchants take the precaution of being accompanied by certain enchanters belonging to a class of Brahmans, who, by means of their diabolical art, have the power of constraining and stupefying these fish, so as to prevent them from doing mischief;[4] and as the fishing takes place in the daytime only,

[1] "The crew consists of twenty-three persons, ten of whom are divers." "Each boat is supplied with five diving stones, and five netted baskets." (Descr. of Ceylon, p. 41.) "These Indians, accustomed to dive from their earliest infancy, fearlessly descend to the bottom in a depth of from five to ten fathoms, in search of treasures. By two cords a diving stone and a net are connected with the boat. The diver, putting the toes of his right foot on the hair rope of the diving stone, and those of his left on the net, seizes the two cords with one hand, and shutting his nostrils with the other, plunges into the water. On reaching the bottom, he hangs the net round his neck, and collects into it the pearl shells as fast as possible during the time he finds himself able to remain under water, which usually is about two minutes. He then resumes his former posture and, making a signal by pulling the cords, he is immediately lifted into the boat." "When the first five divers come up, and are respiring, the other five are going down with the same stones. Each brings up about one hundred oysters in his net, and, if not interrupted by any accident, may make fifty trips in a forenoon." (Asiat. Res. vol. v. p. 401.) The account of these operations, as given by Mr. Cordiner, is still more circumstantial; but what has been stated is sufficient to show the correctness of our author's relation.

[2] "One boat has been known to bring to land, in one day, thirty-three thousand oysters, and in another not more than three hundred." "At many fisheries, upwards of two millions of oysters have been brought on shore at one time."—Descript. of Ceylon, p. 57.

[3] In the map of the peninsula of India, given by Valentyn in his fifth volume, we find a place named Wedale, or Vedale, situated at the northern extremity of the bay of Tutakorin, and immediately within the island of Ramiseram. This may be the Betala of Ramusio's text, which is not mentioned in any other version.

[4] "The superstition of the divers renders the shark-charmers a necessary part of the establishment of the pearl fishery. All these imposters belong to one family, and no person who does not form a branch of it can aspire to that office. The natives have firm confidence in their power over the monsters of the sea; nor would they descend to the bottom of the deep without knowing that one of those enchanters were present in the fleet. Two of them are constantly employed. One of them goes out regularly in the head pilot's boat; the other performs certain cere-

they discontinue the effect of the charm in the evening; in order that dishonest persons who might be inclined to take the opportunity of diving at night and stealing the oysters, may be deterred by the apprehension they feel of the unrestrained ravages of these animals.[1] The enchanters are likewise profound adepts in the art of fascinating all kinds of beasts and birds. The fishery commences in the month of April, and lasts till the middle of May.[2] The privilege of engaging in it is farmed of the king, to whom a tenth part only of the produce is allowed; to the magicians they allow a twentieth part, and consequently they reserve to themselves a considerable profit.[3] By the time the period above-mentioned is completed, the stock of oysters is exhausted; and the vessels are then taken to another place, distant full three hundred miles from this gulf, where they establish themselves in the month of September, and continue till the middle of October.[4] Independently of the tenth of the pearls to which the king is entitled, he requires to have the choice of all such as are large and

monies on shore." "The shark-charmer is called in the Malabar language *Cadal-cutti*, and in the Hindostanee *Hybanda*, each of which signifies a binder of sharks."—Descript. of Ceylon, vol. ii. p. 51.

[1] "Their superstition in this particular is favourable to the interests of government, as, from their terror at diving without the protection of the charms, it prevents any attempt being made to plunder the oyster banks." (P. 53.) It may have been invented or encouraged with that view.

[2] Our author is correct as to the duration of the fishery, being commonly thirty days, although that period is sometimes exceeded when interruptions have taken place; but he has stated the commencement later by at least one month than is the established rule. If, as some suppose, there is a slow progressive variation of seasons, the monsoons might formerly have changed somewhat later than they do at present; or there might, in the year 1292, have been something particular in the weather to retard the commencement, and to favour the protraction of the fishery. It is, however, the most probable that, in his notes, our author wrote April and May by mistake for March and April.

[3] Instead of taking, as the royalty, a proportion of the produce, which is the more equitable, though less convenient mode, modern governments have been in the practice of selling the exclusive privilege for the season to the highest responsible bidder; but the divers and other agents employed in the fishery are remunerated in kind.

[4] It does not appear what place it was, at the distance of three hundred miles, to which the vessels were accustomed to retire upon quitting the fishery on this coast. According to Cordiner, "the boats, with their crews and divers, come from Manaar, Jaffna, Ramisseram, Nagore, Tutakoreen, Travancore, Kilkerry, and other parts on the coast of Coromandel;" but in the Asiatic Researches it is said that "the *donies* (boats) appointed for the fishery are not all procured at Ceylon; many come from the coasts of Coromandel and Malabar." (Vol. v. p. 400.) On the latter, it may be observed, the seasons are the reverse of what they are on the eastern side of the peninsula.

well-shaped; and as he pays liberally for them, the merchants are not disinclined to carry them to him for that purpose.[1]

§ 2. The natives of this part of the country always go naked, excepting that they cover with a piece of cloth those parts of the body which modesty dictates.[2] The king is no more clothed than the rest, except that he has a piece of richer cloth; but is honourably distinguished by various kinds of ornaments, such as a collar set with jewels, sapphires, emeralds, and rubies, of immense value. He also wears, suspended from the neck and reaching to the breast, a fine silken string containing one hundred and four large and handsome pearls and rubies. The reason for this particular number is, that he is required by the rules of his religion to repeat a prayer or invocation so many times, daily, in honour of his gods; and this his ancestors never failed to perform.[3] The daily prayer consists of these words, *pacauca, pacauca, pacauca,* which they repeat one hundred and four times. On each arm he wears three gold bracelets, adorned with pearls and jewels; on three different parts of the leg, golden bands ornamented in the same manner; and on the toes of his feet, as well as on his fingers, rings of inestimable value.[4] To this king it is indeed a matter of facility to display such splendid regalia, as the precious stones and the pearls are all the produce of his own dominions.[5] He

[1] At some periods the kings have required that all pearls exceeding a stated size should be considered as royal property, and reserved for their use.

[2] "Quelquefois leur habillement," says Sonnerat, "est encore plus simple; il n'est pas rare de voir des Indiens dont tout le vêtement n'est qu'un morceau de toile qui sert à cacher les parties naturelles." (Voy. aux Indes, etc., tom. i. p. 29.) "L'habito di queste genti è que vanno tutte nude, salvo que portano un panno intorno alla parte inhoneste."—Itin. di Lodovico Barthema, fol. 158–2.

[3] Rosaries or chaplets, the use of which is to assist the memory in counting the repetition of prayers, are employed for this purpose by the followers of Brahma, Buddha or Fo, and Mahomet, as well as by a part of the Christian Church. The number of beads in the chaplets borne by the natives of Hindustan, as well as by the worshippers of Fo, is said to be one hundred and eight. It is, therefore, probable that the number of one hundred and four, mentioned in the text, is an error, to which the mode of notation in the old manuscripts, by Roman figures, is extremely liable; but at the same time I must avow that I have not been able to ascertain with precision the divisions of the rosary used either by a Hindu or a Mahometan.

[4] The description of the ornaments worn by this prince is conformable to what we read in the voyage of Lodovico Barthema, who says: "Non si potria stimare le gioie e perle che porta il re." "Portava tante gioie nell' orrechie, e nelle mani, nelle bracchia, ne piedi e nelle gambe, che era cosa mirabile a vedere." (Fol. 161.) See also Anciennes Relations, par Renaudot.

[5] It would appear that our author does not speak of the *raja* of a limited

has at the least one thousand wives and concubines; and when he sees a woman whose beauty pleases him, he immediately signifies his desire to possess her. In this manner he appropriated the wife of his brother, who being a discreet and sensible man, was prevailed upon not to make it the subject of a broil, although repeatedly on the point of having recourse to arms. On these occasions their mother remonstrated with them, and exposing her breasts, said: "If you, my children, disgrace yourselves by acts of hostility against each other, I shall instantly sever from my body these breasts from which you drew your nourishment;" and thus the irritation was allowed to subside.

The king retains about his person many knights, who are distinguished by an appellation, signifying "the devoted servants of his majesty, in this world and the next." These attend upon his person at court, ride by his side in processions, and accompany him on all occasions. They exercise considerable authority in every part of the realm. Upon the death of the king, and when the ceremony of burning his body takes place, all these devoted servants throw themselves into the same fire, and are consumed with the royal corpse; intending by this act to bear him company in another life.[1] The following custom likewise prevails. When a king dies, the son who succeeds him does not meddle with the treasure which the former had amassed, under the impression that it would reflect upon his own ability to govern, if being left in full possession of the territory, he did not show himself as capable of enriching the treasury as his father was. In consequence of this prejudice it is supposed that immense wealth is accumulated by successive generations.

No horses being bred in this country, the king and his three royal brothers expend large sums of money annually in the purchase of them from merchants of Ormus, Diufar, Pecher, and Adem,[2] who carry them thither for sale, and become rich

district contiguous to the coast of the fishery, but of a sovereign whose dominions embraced the inland country where diamonds and other precious stones are found. The king of Narsinga, whose capital at a subsequent period was Bijanagar or Golconda, ruled at this period not only the Telinga and Karnata country, but all the coast of Coromandel, as far southward as Cape Komari, or Comorin.

[1] The authorities for the practice of burning the servants, as well as the wives, of Hindoo princes, along with the bodies of their masters, are numerous: from a passage in the narrative of Barbosa, we find also a confirmation of their performing the sacrifice in consequence of a previous voluntary engagement.

[2] The ports enumerated in the Latin version are Curmos, Chisi, Durfar,

by the traffic, as they import to the number of five thousand, and for each of them obtain five hundred saggi of gold, being equal to one hundred marks of silver. At the end of the year, in consequence, as it is supposed, of their not having persons properly qualified to take care of them or to administer the requisite medicines, perhaps not three hundred of these remain alive, and thus the necessity is occasioned for replacing them annually.[1] But it is my opinion that the climate of the province is unfavourable to the race of horses, and that from hence arises the difficulty in breeding or preserving them. For food they give them flesh dressed with rice, and other prepared meats,[2] the country not producing any grain besides rice. A mare, although of a large size, and covered by a handsome horse, produces only a small ill-made colt, with distorted legs, and unfit to be trained for riding.

The following extraordinary custom prevails at this place. When a man who has committed a crime, for which he has been tried and condemned to suffer death, upon being led to execution, declares his willingness to sacrifice himself in honour of some particular idol, his relations and friends immediately place him in a kind of chair, and deliver to him twelve knives of good temper and well sharpened. In this manner they carry him about the city, proclaiming, with a loud voice, that this brave man is about to devote himself to a voluntary death, from motives of zeal for the worship of the idol. Upon reaching the place where the sentence of the law would have been executed, he snatches up two of the knives, and crying out, "I devote myself to death in honour of such an idol," hastily strikes one of them into each thigh, then one into each arm, two into the belly, and two into the breast. Having in this manner thrust all the knives but one into different parts of his body, repeating at every wound the words that have

Ser, and Eden. Of Curmos, Hormuz (or Ormuz), as well as of Adem, Eden, or Aden, it is unnecessary to speak in this place. Chisi is Kîs or Kês, an island in the Persian Gulf, to which the trade of Siraf was removed. Diufar and Pecher, which in the Basle edition are Durfar and Ser, appear to be the same places as Escier and Dulfar of chap. xli. and xlii., and consequently may be supposed the towns of Sheher and Durfâr on the Arabian coast, to the eastward of Aden.

[1] Even at the present day there is no breed of horses in the southern part of the peninsula, and all the cavalry employed there are foreign.

[2] However extraordinary it may be thought, the fact is certain, that on the coast of Coromandel, in addition to gram (*dolichos bifloris*, Lin.) and the roots of grass, the horses are occasionally fed with meat, chiefly of boiled sheeps' heads, made up into balls. Similar expedients are employed in other places. "In questo paese," says Barbosa, speaking of the coast of Sind, "mangiano li peschi secchi et ancho li danno a mangiare alli cavalli e ad altri bestiami."—Fol. 295.

been mentioned, he plunges the last of them into his heart, and immediately expires.[1] As soon as this scene has been acted, his relations proceed, with great triumph and rejoicing, to burn the body; and his wife, from motives of pious regard for her husband, throws herself upon the pile, and is consumed with him. Women who display this resolution are much applauded by the community, as, on the other hand, those who shrink from it are despised and reviled.[2]

§ 3. The greater part of the idolatrous inhabitants of this kingdom show particular reverence to the ox; and none will from any consideration be induced to eat the flesh of oxen.[3] But there is a particular class of men termed gaui, who although they may eat of the flesh, yet dare not to kill the animal; but when they find a carcase, whether it has died a natural death or otherwise, the gaui eat of it;[4] and all descriptions of people daub their houses with cow-dung.[5] Their mode of sitting is upon carpets on the ground; and when asked why they sit in that manner, they reply that a seat on the earth is honourable; that as we are sprung from the earth, so we shall again return to it; that none can do it sufficient honour, and much less should any despise the earth. These gaui and all their tribe are the descendants of those who slew Saint Thomas the

[1] In various modern accounts we have indubitable authority for the practice of self-immolation amongst the people of India, at the feasts of Jagarnat'ha and other idols, where the victims of fanaticism throw themselves before the wheels of ponderous machines, to be crushed to death.

[2] Every account of the Hindu people and their manners furnishes us with a description of the ceremony of wives burning themselves with the bodies of their deceased husbands, of the arts that are employed to stimulate their enthusiasm, and of the disgrace and abandonment that attends their refusal to comply with this horrible custom. Under the Mahometan and European influence, it is supposed to be much less common than it was in former times.

[3] "The people in this part of the country," says Buchanan, in the journal of his route through the southern Carnatic, "consider the ox as a living god, who gives them their bread; and in every village there are one or two bulls, to whom weekly or monthly worship is performed." "On the north side of the Cavery this superstition is not prevalent. The bull is there considered as respectable, on account of Iswara having chosen one of them for his steed."—Vol. ii. p. 174.

[4] From this account of the manners of the gaui, our author may be supposed to speak of the outcast tribe generally named pariah and chandala, but who are known also by other appellations in different parts of India.

[5] "When the dung is recent," says Grose, "they make a compost of it, with which they smear their houses, pavements, and sides of them, in the style of a lustration." (P. 185.) "Il piano della casa," says Barthema, "è tutto imbrattato con sterco di vacche per honoroficentia." —Ramusio, fol. 161*

Apostle, and on this account no individual of them can possibly enter the building where the body of the blessed apostle rests, even were the strength of ten men employed to convey him to the spot, being repelled by the supernatural power of the holy corpse.[1]

The country produces no other grain than rice and sesamé.[2] The people go to battle with lances and shields, but without clothing, and are a despicable unwarlike race.[3] They do not kill cattle nor any kind of animals for food, but when desirous of eating the flesh of sheep or other beasts, or of birds, they procure the Saracens, who are not under the influence of the same laws and customs, to perform the office.[4] Both men and women wash their whole bodies in water twice every day, that is, in the morning and the evening. Until this ablution has taken place they neither eat nor drink; and the person who should neglect this observance, would be regarded as a heretic.[5] It ought to be noticed, that in eating they make use of the right hand only, nor do they ever touch their food with the left. For every cleanly and delicate work they employ the former, and reserve the latter for the base uses of personal abstersion, and other offices connected with the animal functions. They drink out of a particular kind of vessel, and each individual from his own, never making use of the drinking pot of another person. When they drink they do not apply the vessel to the mouth, but hold it above the head, and pour the liquor into the mouth, not suffering the vessel on any account to touch the

[1] "About this mount," says Fryer, "live a cast of people, one of whose legs is as big as an elephant's, which gives occasion for the divulging of it to be a judgment on them, as the generation of the assassins and murtherers of the blessed apostle St. Thomas, one of whom I saw at Fort St. George."—New Account of East India and Persia, p. 43.

[2] The *sesamum indicum*, called *til* in the Hindustani language, is extensively cultivated in most parts of India, for the sake of the oil obtained from its seeds. "Nell' paese di Calicut si trova gran quantità di zerzelino del quale ne fanno oglio perfetissimo."—Barthema, p. 162.

[3] The effeminacy of the natives of India, and particularly of the southern provinces, has been in all ages a subject of observation.

[4] In Dalrymple's Oriental Repertory, vol. i. p. 49, we find a list of the Hindu castes which are restricted from eating animal food of any kind, and also of those which are permitted to eat certain kinds. Amongst the latter are enumerated "Woriar Brahmineys," who may eat fish, mutton, and game, but not fowls; and also "Rajahs." None, however, of any caste (as is generally believed) are allowed to eat beef, and to kill a cow is an offence inferior only to the murder of a Brahman.

[5] "According to the rules of their religion they ought to pray thrice a day. . . . They should at the same time perform their ablutions, and when they have an opportunity, should prefer a running stream to standing water. But it is an indispensable duty to wash themselves before meals."—Hindoo Sketches, vol. i. p. 221.

lips.[1] In giving drink to a stranger, they do not hand their vessel to him, but, if he is not provided with one of his own, pour the wine or other liquor into his hands, from which he drinks it, as from a cup.[2]

Offences in this country are punished with strict and exemplary justice, and with regard to debtors the following customs prevail. If application for payment shall have been repeatedly made by a creditor, and the debtor puts him off from time to time with fallacious promises, the former may attach his person by drawing a circle round him, from whence he dare not depart until he has satisfied his creditor, either by payment, or by giving adequate security. Should he attempt to make his escape, he renders himself liable to the punishment of death, as a violator of the rules of justice.[3] Messer Marco, when he was in this country on his return homeward, happened to be an eye-witness of a remarkable transaction of this nature. The king was indebted in a sum of money to a certain foreign merchant, and although frequently importuned for payment, amused him for a long time with vain assurances. One day when the king was riding on horseback, the merchant took the opportunity of describing a circle round him and his horse. As soon as the king perceived what had been done, he immediately ceased to proceed, nor did he move from the spot until the demand of the merchant was fully satisfied. The bystanders beheld what passed with admiration, and pronounced that king to merit the title of most just, who himself submitted to the laws of justice.

[1] This mode of pouring water into the mouth is represented in a plate, p. 87, of Knox's Account of Ceylon. "When they drink," he says, almost in the words of our author, "they touch not the pot with their mouths, but hold it at a distance and pour it in." This practice is common, likewise, in other parts of the east. "In drinking," says the History of Sumatra, "they generally hold the vessel (a labu or calabash) at a distance above their mouths, and catch the stream as it falls, the liquid descending to the stomach without the action of swallowing."—Third edit. p. 61.

[2] Sonnerat (tom. i. p. 257) mentions the circumstance of boiled rice being put into the hands of a mendicant who has no vessel to receive it; but it is also no uncommon practice to pour liquor into the hands of such a person, who for his purpose holds them close to his mouth.

[3] This legal process is circumstantially described by Lodovico Barthema. "They have a good way," says Hamilton, "of arresting people for debt, viz.:—there is a proper person sent with a small stick from the judge, who is generally a Brahman, and when that person finds the debtor, he draws a circle round him with that stick, and charges him, in the king's and judge's name, not to stir out of it till the creditor is satisfied either by payment or surety; and it is no less than death for the debtor to break prison by going out of the circle."—Vol. i. p. 316.

These people abstain from drinking wine made from grapes; and should a person be detected in the practice, so disreputable would it be held, that his evidence would not be received in court.[1] A similar prejudice exists against persons frequenting the sea, who, they observe, can only be people of desperate fortunes, and whose testimony, as such, ought not to be admitted.[2] They do not hold fornication to be a crime. The heat of the country is excessive, and the inhabitants on that account go naked. There is no rain excepting in the months of June, July, and August, and if it was not for the coolness imparted to the air during these three months by the rain, it would be impossible to support life.[3]

In this country there are many adepts in the science denominated physiognomy, which teaches the knowledge of the nature and qualities of men, and whether they tend to good or evil. These qualities are immediately discerned upon the appearance of the man or woman. They also know what events are portended by meeting certain beasts or birds. More attention is paid by these people to the flight of birds than by any others in the world, and from thence they predict good or bad fortune. In every day of the week there is one hour which they regard as unlucky, and this they name *choiach*;[4] thus, for example, on Monday the (canonical) hour

[1] In the Latin text the words are: "Vini usus apud eos interdictus est;" nor is it by any means probable that our author should have spoken of *grape* wine, specifically, as being prohibited, in a country where it could scarcely have been known. What he meant in this and several other places where the term "wine" is used, is any intoxicating liquor, but more especially that made by fermentation from the juice of the palm, and by distillation from that juice together with rice. "No Hindoo of any of the four castes," says Craufurd, "is allowed by his religion to taste any intoxicating liquor; it is only drunk by strangers, dancers, players, and chandalahs or outcasts."—Sketches, vol. i. p. 140.

[2] Although there are navigators amongst the Hindus, and particularly in vessels from the coast of Coromandel to Achin and the straits of Malacca, yet the natural disposition of the people is abhorrent of the sea; nor can persons of any respectable caste embark on it without the risk of pollution, both in respect to contact and food, whatever precautions may be taken to avoid it. Our author, however, attributes their dislike of seafaring people to an opinion that none but those of desperate fortunes and relaxed morals would devote themselves to a profession where domestic comfort is sacrificed and life exposed, in the pursuit of precarious advantage.

[3] The rainy season here described is that which prevails on the Malabar coast.

[4] The word Choiach or Koiach (probably much corrupted) is not to be recognised amongst the barbarous astrological terms of the south of India. "Parmi les natchétrons. les yogons, les tidis, les laquenons, les carenons, et les jours de la semaine," as we are informed by Sonnerat, "il y en a de bons et de mauvais." "Je n'ai jamais pu savoir d'aucun. Brame ce

of *mi-tierce,* on Tuesday the hour of *tierce,* on Wednesday the hour of *none;* [1] and on these hours they do not make purchases, nor transact any kind of business, being persuaded that it would not be attended with success. In like manner they ascertain the qualities of every day throughout the year, which are described and noted in their books.[2] They judge of the hour of the day by the length of a man's shadow when he stands erect.[3] When an infant is born, be it a boy or a girl, the father or the mother makes a memorandum in writing of the day of the week on which the birth took place; also of the age of the moon, the name of the month, and the hour. This is done because every future act of their lives is regulated by astrology. As soon as a son attains the age of thirteen years, they set him at liberty, and no longer suffer him to be an inmate in his father's house; giving him to the amount, in their money, of twenty to twenty-four groats. Thus provided, they consider him as capable of gaining his own livelihood, by engaging in some kind of trade and thence deriving a profit. These boys never cease to run about in all directions during the whole course of the day, buying an article in one place, and selling it in another.[4] At the season when the pearl fishery is going on, they frequent the beach, and make purchases from the fishermen or others, of five, six, or more (small) pearls, according to their means, carrying them afterwards to the merchants, who, on account of the heat of the sun, remain sitting in their houses, and to whom they say: "These pearls have cost us so much;

que c'étoit qu'un yogon et un carenon." "Les jours bons ou mauvais, les heures funestes ou heureuses, le retour d'un voyage, la guerison d'un malade, la perte de quelques effets, enfin, tout donne matière à recourir aux devins."—Pp. 305—313.

[1] [The canonical division of the day, called *tierce* (*hora tertia,*) began at nine o'clock, A.M., and lasted till twelve. . *None* began at three o'clock, P.M. *Mi-tierce* (*mezza-terza,* or, in Latin, *media tertia*) is not fixed in the regular lists of the canonical hours, but it may be supposed to have been half way between *tierce,* or nine o'clock, and *sext,* or twelve.]

[2] The books here spoken of are almanacs, called *panjangan* in the language of the Tamuls.

[3] The original Indian method of ascertaining the altitude of the sun and latitude of a place, is by measuring the length of the shadow thrown by a perpendicular gnomon of a determined height, or by the absence of that shadow when the sun is in the zenith. Upon this principle, in places situated within the tropics, and especially near the equator, a man may form a tolerably correct judgment of the hour of the day, by observing his own shadow, which, for example, when equal to the height of his person, would show the altitude to be forty-five degrees, and the hour, consequently, about nine in the morning or three in the afternoon.

[4] "Li lor figluioli," says Barbosa, "come passano dieci anni, vanno facendo il medesimo come li padri, di andar comprando monete piccole, et imparare il mestiere."—Fol. 310—2.

pray allow such a profit on them as you may judge reasonable." The merchants then give something beyond the price at which they had been obtained. In this way likewise they deal in many other articles, and become excellent and most acute traders. When business is over for the day, they carry to their mothers the provisions necessary for their dinners, which they prepare and dress for them; but these never eat anything at their fathers' expense.

§ 4. Not only in this kingdom, but throughout India in general, all the beasts and birds are unlike those of our own country, excepting the quails, which perfectly resemble ours; the others are all different.[1] There are bats as large as vultures, and vultures as black as crows, and much larger than ours. Their flight is rapid, and they do not fail to seize their bird.[2]

In their temples there are many idols, the forms of which represent them of the male and the female sex; and to these, fathers and mothers dedicate their daughters. Having been so dedicated, they are expected to attend whenever the priests of the convent require them to contribute to the gratification of the idol; and on such occasions they repair thither, singing and playing on instruments, and adding by their presence to the festivity. These young women are very numerous, and form large bands.[3] Several times in the week they carry an offering of victuals to the idol to whose service they are devoted, and of this food they say the idol partakes. A table for the purpose is placed before it, and upon this the victuals are suffered to remain for the space of a full hour; during which damsels never cease to sing, and play, and exhibit wanton gestures. This lasts as long as a person of condition would require for making a convenient meal. They then declare that the spirit of the idol is content with its share of the entertainment provided, and, ranging themselves around it,

[1] This assertion may appear too general, but is in a great measure justified by the observations of Dr. F. Buchanan, who informs us that neither horses, asses, swine, sheep, nor goats are bred in the southern part of the peninsula, or at least that their number is perfectly inconsiderable, and that the original natives had no poultry, even the common fowls, as well as geese, ducks, and turkeys, having been introduced by Europeans.—Vol. ii. p. 383.

[2] The former of these is the *vespertilio vampyrus* of Lin., the wings of which are four feet in extent; the latter, " le vautour royal de Pondicheri, dont le dos, le ventre, les ailes, et la queue, sont noirs."—Sonnerat, tom. ii. p. 182.

[3] This account of females attached to the service of the temples, and contributing by the prostitution of their persons to the support of the establishment, might be amply corroborated by numerous authorities.

they proceed to eat in their turn; after which they repair to their respective homes. The reason given for assembling the young women, and performing the ceremonies that have been described, is this:—The priests declare that the male divinity is out of humour with and incensed against the female, refusing to have connexion or even to converse with her; and that if some measure were not adopted to restore peace and harmony between them, all the concerns of the monastery would go to ruin, as the grace and blessing of the divinities would be withheld from them. For this purpose it is, they expect the votaries to appear in a state of nudity, with only a cloth round their waists, and in that state to chaunt hymns to the god and goddess. These people believe that the former often solaces himself with the latter.

The natives make use of a kind of bedstead, or cot, of very light cane-work, so ingeniously contrived that when they repose on them, and are inclined to sleep, they can draw close the curtains about them by pulling a string. This they do in order to exclude the tarantulas, which bite grievously, as well as to prevent their being annoyed by fleas and other small vermin; whilst at the same time the air, so necessary for mitigating the excessive heat, is not excluded.[1] Indulgences of this nature, however, are enjoyed only by persons of rank and fortune; others of the inferior class lie in the open streets.[2]

In this province of Maabar[3] is the body of the glorious martyr, Saint Thomas the Apostle, who there suffered martyrdom. It rests in a small city, not frequented by many merchants, because unsuited to the purposes of their commerce; but, from devout motives, a vast number both of Christians

[1] What is here described is the musquito curtain, formed of a kind of gauze, and so contrived as effectually to exclude gnats and other flying insects. The tarantulas and fleas mentioned in Ramusio's (but not in the Latin) text, must have been imagined by some of our author's ingenious translators.

[2] In Benares and other ancient cities, where the thoroughfares are narrow and the circulation of air confined, it is common for the inhabitants, during the hot weather, to bring their beds to the outside of the houses, and to sleep with their families in the public streets.

[3] It appears from this passage that our author considered the kingdom of Maabar as extending from the southern extremity of the peninsula, along the Coromandel coast, as far as the Tamul language prevails, which is to some distance northward of Madras: a tract which the Hindu geographers term Drávida-desa. The Latin versions speak here of a kingdom of Var or Vaar as forming a portion of Maabar. If this is a genuine distinction, it may refer to the small territory of Maravar or Marawar, near the southern extremity of the peninsula.

and Saracens resort thither.[1] The latter regard him as a great prophet, and name him Ananias, signifying a holy personage.[2] The Christians who perform this pilgrimage collect earth from the spot where he was slain, which is of a red colour, and reverentially carry it away with them; often employing it afterwards in the performance of miracles, and giving it, when diluted with water, to the sick, by which many disorders are cured.[3] In the year of our Lord 1288, a powerful prince of the country,[4] who at the time of gathering the harvest had accumulated (as his proportion) a very great quantity of rice, and had not granaries sufficient wherein to deposit it all, thought proper to make use of the religious house belonging to the church of Saint Thomas for that purpose. This being against the will of those who had the guardianship of it, they beseeched him not to occupy in this manner a building appropriated to the accommodation of pilgrims who came to visit the body of this glorious saint. He, notwithstanding, obstinately persisted. On the following night the holy apostle appeared to him in a

[1] The place here spoken of is the small town of San Thomé, situated a few miles to the southward of Madras, where, on a mount, as it is termed, or elevated rock (the more remarkable from the general flatness of the neighbouring country), stands an ancient Christian church. It was formerly a city of some consequence, called by the natives Maliapur, or, perhaps more correctly, Mailapur. By the Arabians it is denominated Beit-tuma or temple of Thomas.

[2] Admitting the reading of this passage in Ramusio's text to be correct, it must be observed that the name of Ananias has not in Hebrew nor Arabic the meaning here given to it; but the internal evidence is strongly in favour of a very different reading presented by the Latin of the Basle edition, where it is said: "Incolæ regionis illius dicunt Apostolum prophetam magnum fuisse, vocantque eum Avarijam, hoc est, sanctum virum." Here the native Hindus, and not the Mahometans, are stated to be those who bestowed upon St. Thomas the appellation of a holy personage, and in their writings we find the word Avyar to have been the appellation of a celebrated Tamul philosopher.

[3] This pilgrimage is noticed by all who have written on the subject of the Malabar or San Thomé Christians.

[4] It is commonly understood that the eastern side of the peninsula was at this period ruled by the kings of Narsinga, whose capital was Vijayanagara, or, in the vulgar dialect, Bija-nagar; but we learn from the researches of Dr. F. Buchanan, that the celebrated city so named was not founded until the year 1335-6, and that the southern part of the coast (called Drávada by Hindu geographers) was subject to princes whose seat of government was Woragulla (Warancul of the Mussulmans and Warangole of our maps) the chief place in Andray or Telingana. The king who reigned from 1268 to 1322, which includes the year mentioned in the text, was named Pratápa Rudra, and it is remarkable, that in 1309, or about sixteen years after our author's visit to this part of India, Telingana was invaded by the arms of Ala-ed-din, the Mahometan emperor of Delhi, and the raja of Woragulla obliged to become his tributary. It may be, however, that the prince here spoken of was only a raja, who governed the country under a superior lord.

vision, holding in his hand a small lance, which he pointed at the throat of the king, saying to him: "If thou dost not immediately evacuate my house which thou hast occupied, I shall put thee to a miserable death." Awaking in a violent alarm, the prince instantly gave orders for doing what was required of him, declaring publicly that he had seen the apostle in a vision. A variety of miracles are daily performed there, through the interposition of the blessed saint. The Christians who have the care of the church possess groves of those trees which produce the Indian nuts, and from thence derive their means of subsistence, paying, as a tax to one of the royal brothers, a groat monthly for each tree.[1] It is related that the death of this most holy apostle took place in the following manner. Having retired to a hermitage, where he was engaged in prayer, and being surrounded by a number of pea-fowls, with which bird the country abounds, an idolater of the tribe of the Gaui, before described, who happened to be passing that way, and did not perceive the holy man, shot an arrow at a peacock, which struck the apostle in the side. Finding himself wounded, he had time only to thank the Lord for all his mercies, and into His hands he resigned his spirit.[2]

In this province the natives, although black, are not born of so deep a dye as they afterwards attain by artificial means, esteeming blackness the perfection of beauty. For this purpose, three times every day, they rub the children over with oil of sesamé.[3] The images of their deities they represent black, but the devil they paint white, and assert that all the demons are of that colour.[4] Those amongst them who pay

[1] For "groat" it is probable we should read fanam, the common currency of the place, in value about twopence halfpenny. This would make the yearly tax half-a-crown. In Sumatra the produce of a coconut tree is commonly estimated at a Spanish dollar, or about five shillings.

[2] In giving the etymology of the names of places in this part of the Indian peninsula, Paolino writes: "Mallapuri o Mallaparum, città de pavoni, Meliapur o St. Tomè degli Europæi." Admitting this explanation to be correct, it may be questioned whether the legend, of which the peacocks are so conspicuous a feature, may not have been suggested by the name of the place. The bird itself is very common in India.

[3] The original inhabitants of the southern part of the peninsula are in general extremely dark, and it is probable that our author was mistaken in his supposition that there was anything artificial in their degree of blackness. The practice of rubbing their children with oil may have been for a different purpose. It is customary indeed in most parts of India, for persons of all ages to anoint their bodies frequently.

[4] The Hindu idols are most commonly either of copper, or, when large, of a kind of black granite; but be the material what it may, they all acquire a sooty colour from the smoke of lamps or of incense burnt within the temples, as well as from the practice of smearing them with oil. The

adoration to the ox, take with them, when they go to battle, some of the hair of a wild bull, which they attach to the manes of their horses, believing its virtue and efficacy to be such, that every one who carries it about with him is secure from all kind of danger. On this account the hair of the wild bull sells for a high price in these countries.

CHAPTER XXI

OF THE KINGDOM OF MURPHILI OR MONSUL

THE kingdom of Murphili is that which you enter upon leaving the kingdom of Maabar, after proceeding five hundred miles in a northerly direction.[1] Its inhabitants worship idols, and are independent of any other state. They subsist upon rice, flesh, fish, and fruits. In the mountains of this kingdom it is that diamonds are found.[2] During the rainy season the water descend in violent torrents amongst the rocks and caverns, and when these have subsided the people go to search

notion of the devil being painted white by those of the human race who are themselves black, has been very prevalent, and may be justified by particular instances of asûrs or demons of the Hindu mythology being represented of that complexion; but there is no personage in that mythology answering to the description of Satan or Eblis. In Persian romances we read of the Dîv Sefêd or white demon, a celebrated antagonist of Rustam.

[1] The kingdom here called Murphili or Monsul (perhaps for Mousul), in the Basle edition Murfili, and in the B.M. and Berlin manuscripts, Muthfili, (in the Paris Latin Molfuli, for Molsuli,) but omitted entirely in the epitomes, is no other than Muchli-patan, or, as it is more commonly named, Masuli-patam; the name of a principal town, by a mistake not unusual, being substituted for that of the country. "This," says Rennell, "is a city and port of trade, near the mouth of the Kistna river; and appears to be situated within the district named Mesolia by Ptolemy." (Memoir, 1793, p. 210.) It belongs to what was at one period termed the kingdom of Golconda, more anciently named Telingana. With respect of Maabar, our author is consistent with himself (whatever may be thought of his geographical correctness), as he had already told us that it included the place where St. Thomas was buried, not far from the modern city of Madras. It is evident that he considered it to extend as far to the northward as the Tamul language is spoken, or, in other words, to the line where the Telinga commences (near the Pennar river), which we shall find to be little less than five hundred miles from cape Komorin. It seems, indeed, not very improbable that the application of the name of Maabar to that part of the coast of Coromandel, may have given rise to the practice amongst Europeans (who confounded the two words) of denominating the natives on the eastern side of the peninsula so improperly, Malabars.

[2] Golconda, of which Masulipatam is the principal seaport, is celebrated for the production of diamonds.

for diamonds in the beds of the rivers, where they find many.[1] Messer Marco was told that in the summer, when the heat is excessive and there is no rain, they ascend the mountains with great fatigue, as well as with considerable danger from the number of snakes with which they are infested. Near the summit, it is said, there are deep valleys, full of caverns and surrounded by precipices, amongst which the diamonds are found; and here many eagles and white storks, attracted by the snakes on which they feed, are accustomed to make their nests. The persons who are in quest of the diamonds take their stand near the mouths of the caverns, and from thence cast down several pieces of flesh, which the eagles and storks pursue into the valley, and carry off with them to the tops of the rocks. Thither the men immediately ascend, drive the birds away, and recovering the pieces of meat, frequently find diamonds sticking to them. Should the eagles have had time to devour the flesh, they watch the place of their roosting at night, and in the morning find the stones amongst the dung and filth that drops from them.[2] But you must not suppose that

[1] Tavernier, speaking of the mines of Sumbhulpur, in another part of the country, says, "Voicy de quelle manière on cherche les diamans dans cette rivière. Après que les grandes pluyes sont passées, ce qui est d'ordinaire au mois de Décembre, on attend encore tout le mois de Janvier que la rivière s'éclaircisse, parce qu'en ce temps-là en plusieurs endroits elle n'a pas plus de deux pieds. . . . On commence à chercher dans la rivière au bourg de Soumelpour, et on va toujours en remontant jusques aux montagnes d'où elle sort." (Voy. des Indes, liv. ii. p. 346.) Mr. Thomas Motte, who visited this place in 1766, learned from a person on the spot, that "it was his business to search in the river, after the rains, for red earth washed down from the mountains, in which earth diamonds were always found."—Asiat. Miscellany, vol. ii. p. 58.

[2] This relation of the mode of obtaining precious stones from an inaccessible valley is identical with the story in one of the adventures of Sinbad the sailor in the Arabian Nights. It is probable that the story of the valley of diamonds was current in India and other parts of the eastern world, and its antiquity is satisfactorily proved by the following extract from Epiphanius "de duodecim lapidibus rationali sacerdotis infixis," a work written in the fourth century of our era:—"Ibi igitur in eremo magnæ Scythiæ penitiori vallis est quæ hinc atque inde montibus lapideis veluti muris cincta, hominibus est invia, longèque profundissima ita ut e sublimi vertice montium tanquam ex mœnibus despectanti non liceat vallis solum intueri, sed ob loci profunditatem densæ adeo sunt tenebræ, ut chaos ibi quoddam esse videatur. A regibus qui illuc aliquando sunt profecti, quidam rei ad illa loca damnantur, qui mactatos agnos in vallem, detractâ pelle, projiciunt. Adhærescunt lapilli, seque ad eas carnes agglutinant. Aquilæ vero, quæ in illorum montium vertice degunt, nidorem carnium secutæ devolant, agnosque quibus lapilli adhæserunt exportant. Dum autem carnibus vescuntur, lapilli in cacumine montium remanent. At ii qui ad ea loca sunt damnati, observantes ubi carnes aquilæ depaverint, accurrunt feruntque lapillos." In a note he adds: "Epiphanius was bishop of Salamis, and died in the year 403. He is spoken of in terms of great respect by many ecclesiastical writers;

the good diamonds come among Christians, for they are carried to the grand khan, and to the kings and chiefs of that country. In this country they manufacture the finest cottons that are to be met with in any part of India.[1] They have cattle enough, and the largest sheep in the world, and plenty of all kinds of food.

CHAPTER XXII

OF THE PROVINCE OF LAC, LOAC, OR LAR

LEAVING the place where rests the body of the glorious apostle Saint Thomas, and proceeding westward, you enter the province of Lar, from whence the Bramins, who are spread over India, derive their origin.[2] These are the best and most honourable merchants that can be found.[3] No consideration

and St. Jerom styles the little treatise from which I have quoted, 'egregium volumen, quod si legere volueris plenissimam scientiam consequeris.'"

[1] At all periods the coast of Coromandel has been celebrated for the finest and most perfect manufacture of cotton cloths, to which the name of "calico" has been given by Europeans; and Masulipatam, in particular, for chintzes. [The Paris Latin text says here: "Item, in ista contracta de Molfili fit melior vochosame et magis subtile quod sit in mundo, et magis carum, et videtur tela aranei."]

[2] Amongst the places on the continent of India noticed by our author, there is none so little capable of being identified from any resemblance of orthography as that which is the subject of the present chapter; nor does it appear that it was actually visited by him. Lac, Loac, or Lar, as it is variously written in Ramusio's text, Lahe in the early Italian epitomes, Laē in the Basle, and Lach in the older Latin, is said to be a province or district lying westward from the burial-place of St. Thomas, and consequently should be that part in which stands the city of Arcot (Arrukati) and also the celebrated temples or pagodas of Conjeveram (Kanjipuram), where there is, at the present day, a considerable establishment of Brahmans. (See Buchanan's Journey from Madras, etc. vol. i. p. 12.) Whether any tradition or record exists of this being the spot from whence the sacred tribe dispersed themselves throughout the peninsula, is a point for others to determine; but in the map annexed to D'Anville's "Antiquité de l'Inde," we find the word Brachmé (on the authority of Ptolemy) placed near Arcatis and in the situation of Conjeveram, which is about forty miles westward, inclining to the south, from St. Thomé. In the text also of that learned geographer we meet with the following passage: "Les Brachmani Magi, et leur ville appelée Brachmé, entre Arcate et la mer dans Ptolémée, fixent notre vue sur Canjé-varam, distante à-peu-près également et d'environ dix lieues d'Arcate comme de la mer; et dans laquelle les Brahmènes conservent une des plus fameuses écoles de leur doctrine."—P. 129.

[3] Such occupations may seem inconsistent with the sacred character supposed to belong to this caste; but we have abundant authority to show, not only that Brahmans are not necessarily devoted to the offices of the priesthood, but that many of them employ themselves in worldly pursuits.

whatever can induce them to speak an untruth, even though their lives should depend upon it. They have also an abhorrence of robbery or of purloining the goods of other persons.[1] They are likewise remarkable for the virtue of continence, being satisfied with the possession of one wife.[2] When any foreign merchant, unacquainted with the usages of the country, introduces himself to one of these, and commits to his hands the care of his adventure, this Bramin undertakes the management of it, disposes of the goods, and renders a faithful account of the proceeds, attending scrupulously to the interests of the stranger, and not demanding any recompense for his trouble, should the owner uncourteously omit to make him the gratuitous offer.[3] They eat meat, and drink the wine of the country. They do not, however, kill any animal themselves, but get it done by the Mahometans.[4] The Bramins are distinguished by a certain badge, consisting of a thick cotton thread, which passes over the shoulder and is tied under the arm, in such a manner that the thread appears upon the breast and behind the back.[5] The king is extremely rich and powerful, and has

[1] Many, perhaps, will not be disposed to subscribe to this favourable character of the Brahmanical order, yet our author is not singular in his opinion of their virtues. "On the whole," says Moor, "the Brahmans are, I think, the most moral and best behaved race of men that I ever met with." (Hindu Pantheon, p. 359.) "Summarily," observes the liberal author of the Ayin Akbari, "the Hindoos are religious, affable, courteous to strangers, cheerful, enamoured of knowledge, fond of inflicting austerities upon themselves, lovers of justice, given to retirement, able in business, grateful, admirers of truth, and of unbounded fidelity in all their dealings." (Vol. iii. p. 2.) "Impartiality must allow," adds the same Mahometan writer, "that those among them who dedicate their lives to the worship of the Deity exceed men of every other religion (he knew little of Christians) in piety and devotion."—P. 81..

[2] "Questi bramini," says Barbosa, "e cosi parimente brancani (*baniani*), tolgano moglie all' usanza nostra, et ciascuno piglia una sola, et una volta solamente." (Fol. 295-2.) Amongst our modern writings on the subject of the order of Brahmans, or translations from the Hindu ordinances, I have not been successful in discovering any direct assertion that polygamy is forbidden to them, and that a Brahman should be "the husband of one wife," although it is everywhere implied, and particularly in the Institutes of Menu, where the propriety of abstaining from a second marriage, upon the loss of a first wife, is likewise inculcated.

[3] Some parts of this description seem to apply to a class of people wholly engaged in commerce; and there is much reason to believe that in this chapter our author treated, not of Brahmans only, but also of the class of traders called banyans, or in the Italian, baniani, which his translators, mistaking them for the same word, have confounded.

[4] Mr. Wilkins, in a note to his translation of the Hitopadesa, observes that "although the Brahmans are by no means confined to a vegetable diet, as is generally supposed, still, like the Jews and Mussulmans, they are forbidden to taste of many kinds of flesh and fish." (P. 318.) This, of course, must apply more extensively to the inferior castes.

[5] "The *zennar*, or sacred string," says Craufurd, "is hung round the body from the left shoulder."—Sketches, vol. ii. p. 41.

much delight in the possession of pearls and valuable stones.[1] When the traders from Maabar present to him such as are of superior beauty, he trusts to their word with respect to the estimation of their value, and gives them double the sum that each is declared to have cost them. Under these circumstances, he has the offer of many fine jewels. The people are gross idolaters, and much addicted to sorcery and divination. When they are about to make a purchase of goods, they immediately observe the shadow cast by their own bodies in the sunshine; and if the shadow be as large as it should be, they make the purchase that day.[2] Moreover, when they are in any shop for the purpose of buying anything, if they see a tarantula, of which there are many there, they take notice from which side it comes, and regulate their business accordingly. Again, when they are going out of their houses, if they hear any one sneeze, they return into the house, and stay at home. They are very abstemious in regard to eating, and live to an advanced age. Their teeth are preserved sound by the use of a certain vegetable which they are in the habit of masticating. It also promotes digestion, and conduces generally to the health of the body.[3]

Amongst the natives of this region there is a class peculiarly devoted to a religious life, who are named *tingui*, and who in honour of their divinities lead most austere lives.[4] They go perfectly naked, not concealing any part of their bodies, and say there can be no shame in that state of nudity in which they came into the world; and with respect to what are called the parts of shame, they observe that, not being with them the organs of sin, they have no reason to blush at their exposure.[5]

[1] If this was in fact a separate kingdom, it must still have been dependent upon the king of Telingana, mentioned in a former note, whose dominions, after being overrun by the Patan emperor of Delhi, appear to have subsequently merged in those of the Hindu king of Narsinga, as he is commonly styled, whose capital was Bijanagar or Vijaya-nagara.

[2] By observing their shadows, when about to conclude a bargain or do any other act, no more is meant than that they ascertain the hour of the day, from the altitude of the sun, in order to judge whether it be propitious or otherwise.

[3] The composition called betel is here meant, consisting of the leaf of the betel plant, the areca nut, and lime of calcined shells, which is too generally known to require any further description.

[4] This name of *tingui*, which is the early Venice epitome is *cuigni*, but does not appear in the Latin versions, is certainly intended for those ascetic philosophers, or, as others would term them, religious mendicants, one class of whom are called *jogi* or *yogi*, and another *sannyasi*. They are often termed also *fakirs*, but improperly, as that word should apply only to mendicants of the Mahometan religion.

[5] From this state of absolute nudity they were by the ancients

They pay adoration to the ox, and carry a small figure of one, of gilt brass or other metal, attached to their foreheads.[1] They also burn the bones of oxen, reduce them to powder, and with this make an unguent for the purpose of marking various parts of the body, which they do in a reverential manner. If they meet a person with whom they are upon cordial terms, they smear the centre of his forehead with some of these prepared ashes.[2] They do not deprive any creature of life, not even a fly, a flea, or a louse, believing them to be animated with souls; and to feed upon any animal they would consider as a heinous sin. They even abstain from eating vegetables, herbs, or roots, until they have become dry; holding the opinion that these also have souls. They make no use of spoons nor of platters, but spread their victuals upon the dried leaves of the Adam's apple, called likewise apples of paradise.[3] When they have occasion to ease nature, they go to the sea-beach, and having dropped their burden in the sand, immediately scatter it in all directions, to prevent its giving birth to vermin, whose consequent death by hunger would load their consciences

denominated gymnosophists. "Calanus," as Craufurd observes, "who burnt himself in the presence of Alexander, has by some been called a Brahman; but it is evident that he was one of those devotees who travel about the country. He is said to have gone naked; but the Brahmans never go naked, nor commit any acts of extravagance."—Vol. i. p. 247.

[1] The ox is held in veneration chiefly by the Saivas, or sect who are worshippers of Siva and Bhawáni, whose vahana, monture, or vehicle that animal is; but what they most generally wear appended to their necks, is not the figure of the ox, but of the linga and yoni, which, from delicacy, our author, or his translators, may have been unwilling to describe. (Asiat. Res. vol. vii. p. 281.) "Lingam o fallo del dio Shiva," says Paolino, "simbolo della virtù generativa del Sole. Alcuni lo portano al collo, alteri al braccio, altri dipinto sulla fronte."—P. 300.

[2] All the different sects of Hindus are distinguished by peculiar marks worn on the forehead and breast. The ashes used in the composition employed for making or painting these marks are most commonly of cow-dung, or of whatever is burnt upon the sacrificial hearth, which they mix or vary with the dust of sandal-wood and other ingredients. "As well as the forehead," says Moor, "it will have been observed that Hindus paint their arms and breasts also, and sometimes their throats: sandal-powder, turmeric, chuna or lime, ashes from a consecrated fire, cow-dung, and other holy combustibles, made adhesive by a size of rice-water, or sometimes rubbed on dry, are the ingredients and usages on this occasion. Several lines of white, ashen, or yellow hue, are commonly seen drawn across the arms and breasts; and I understand that *yogis* and *sannyasis*, and other pious persons, frequently carry about them a little packet of these holy pigments, with which they mark those who show them respect, in repayment of their attentions."—Hindu Pantheon, p. 409.

[3] The plantain (*musa paradisiaca* of Lin., formerly named *pomum paradisiacum*) is remarkable for the size of its leaf, a part of which is commonly used by the natives as a dish for holding their boiled rice.

with a grievous offence.[1] They live to a great age, some of them even to a hundred and fifty years, enjoying health and vigour, although they sleep upon the bare earth. This must be attributed to their temperance and chastity.[2] When they die, their bodies are burned, in order for the same reason that they might not breed worms.

CHAPTER XXIII

OF THE ISLAND OF ZEILAN

I AM unwilling to pass over certain particulars which I omitted when before speaking of the island of Zeilan, and which I learned when I visited that country in my homeward voyage. In this island there is a very high mountain, so rocky and precipitous that the ascent to the top is impracticable, as it is said, excepting by the assistance of iron chains employed for that purpose. By means of these some persons attain the summit, where the tomb of Adam, our first parent, is reported to be found. Such is the account given by the Saracens.[3]

[1] The sandy shores of the great rivers are much frequented for the same purpose by those who live at a distance from the sea, and in such numbers, at the same hour, as to render it remarkable.

[2] Strong proofs are mentioned by various writers, as well of the general austerity of their lives, as of their chastity in particular, or of the degree to which the sensual feelings of these *yogis* or *sannyasis* are subdued. (See Thevenot, Voyages des Indes, liv. iii. chap. vi.; Grose, Voy. to the East Indies, vol. i. p. 196.) With respect to their longevity, it is difficult to find any direct evidence; but it is strongly implied in the Ayin Akbari, where, in describing the *char asherum*, or four Hindu degrees, and the severities of ascetic discipline, generally confined to the fourth or last stage, it is said: "Some perform all these austerities in the first and second degrees; some allow twenty-five years for each of these states."—Vol. iii. pp. 222—225. [The Latin text of Marco Polo adds here: "Dormiunt nudi in terra, nullum habentes vestitum infra nec supra, et hoc est mirabile quomodo sani evadunt, et toto anno jejunant, nec comedunt aliquid aliud nec bibunt quam panem et equam, et habent suos regulares qui custodiunt idola. Et quando volunt probare quod isti sunt boni et honesti, mittunt pro puellis quæ sunt oblatæ idolis, et faciunt quod illæ tangunt eos huc et illuc et in pluribus locis corporis, et stant in magno solatio cum eis; et si membrum erigitur vel mutatur, emittunt eum et dicunt quod non est honestus; sin autem, faciunt eum servire idolis suis in monasterio illo."]

[3] It is not uncommon to suppose that the lofty and remarkable mountain in Ceylon, known by the name of Adam's Peak, acquired that appellation from the Portuguese or other European navigators; but we have indubitable evidence that however designated by the Singalese, or their Hindu neighbours, the Mahometans, from an early period, connected it with the name and legend of the prophet Adam. According to Sale, "the Mahometans say, that when they were cast down from Paradise, Adam fell on the island of Ceylon or Serendib, and Eve near Joddah in Arabia."—The Koran, p. 5, note.

But the idolaters assert that it contains the body of Sogomonbarchan, the founder of their religious system, and whom they revere as a holy personage.[1] He was the son of a king of the island, who devoted himself to an ascetic life, refusing to accept of kingdoms or any other worldly possessions, although his father endeavoured, by the allurements of women, and every other imaginable gratification, to divert him from the resolution he had adopted.[2] Every attempt to dissuade him was in vain, and the young man fled privately to this lofty mountain, where, in the observance of celibacy and strict abstinence, he at length terminated his mortal career.[3] By the idolaters he

[1] By the holy personage here described is meant Buddha, the founder of the religious system of the Singalese, who amongst a number of appellations given to him, from his supposed attributes, is most commonly known by what of Saka or Sakya-muni, signifying the "astute sage." To this our author has annexed the word barchan, for burchan, signifying the "deity," in the language of the Mungal Tartars; and there seems little reason to doubt that by the emperor Kublaï and his court, who, equally with the people of Ceylon, acknowledged the divinity of Buddha, he was styled Saka-muni-burchan, here corrupted to Sogo-mon-barchan. Of his worship in this island we have ample testimony. "There is another great god," says Knox, after speaking of the Creator of heaven and earth, "whom they call Buddou, unto whom the salvation of souls belongs. Him they believe once to have come upon the earth. . . . He departed from the earth from the top of the highest mountain on the island, called Pico Adam: where there is an impression like a foot, which they say is his." (Relation of Ceylon, p. 72.) "It is generally believed," says Cordiner, "that there exists upon the top of it (Adam's Peak) a carved stone, called an impression of the foot of Buddha, in some respects similar to those in the kingdoms of Ava and Siam." (Description of Ceylon, vol. i. p. 8.) Hence it appears that what the Mahometans believe respecting Adam is, by the Indians, attributed to Buddha.

[2] According to some accounts, and those entitled to the most consideration, his birthplace was Gaya in the province of Bahár; according to others, Kashmir; but authorities (if such they can be termed) are not wanting for his being a native of Ceylon. "Le père de Sommonocodom," says M. La Loubere, speaking of the object of worship in Siam, who is unquestionably the Buddha or Sakya-muni of other parts of the East, "étoit, selon ce même livre, Bali, un roy de Teve Lancà, c'est à dire un roy de la célèbre Ceylan." (Du Royaume de Siam, tom. i. p. 525.) "Pour ce qui concerne la personne de Xaca," says la Croze, "dont l'idole a été nommée Foë après son apothéose, il est originaire des Indes, et, selon le sentiment le mieux établi, il est né dans l'île de Ceylan."—Hist. du Christianisme des Indes, p. 505.

[3] There is a degree of minute correctness in this account of the father's endeavours to allure his son from the life of retirement to which he had devoted himself, that will not a little surprise the reader, when he compares it with a passage in the "Account of the Incarnation of Boodhu," translated from the Burman language by Mr. F. Carey, and given to the world, at Serampore in Bengal, by Mr. W. Ward, of the Baptist Mission, in his "View of the history, literature, and religion of the Hindoos." "The king, reflecting, etc., said, 'O Son! I will bestow upon thee the elephant-drivers, the charioteers, the horsemen, and arrayed footmen, with delightful horses: I will also give thee the maidens adorned with all sorts of ornaments; raise up progeny by them, and thou shalt

is regarded as a saint. The father, distracted with the most poignant grief, caused an image to be formed of gold and precious stones, bearing the resemblance of his son, and required that all the inhabitants of the island should honour and worship it as a deity. Such was the origin of the worship of idols in that country; but Sogomon-barchan is still regarded as superior to every other. In consequence of this belief, people flock from various distant parts in pilgrimage to the mountain on which he was buried. Some of his hair, his teeth, and the basin he made use of, are still preserved, and shown with much ceremony. The Saracens, on the other hand, maintain that these belonged to the prophet Adam, and are in like manner led by devotion to visit the mountain.[1]

It happened that, in the year 1281, the grand khan heard from certain Saracens who had been upon the spot, the fame of these relics belonging to our first parent, and felt so strong a desire to possess them, that he was induced to send an embassy to demand them of the king of Zeilan. After a long and tedious journey, his ambassadors at length reached the place of their destination, and obtained from the king two large back-teeth, together with some of the hair, and a handsome vessel of porphyry.[2] When the grand khan received

become our sovereign. Virgins well versed in dancing and singing, and perfected in the four accomplishments, shall delight thee with their attractions. What dost thou in this wilderness?'" "To show his disregard of the kingdom, Muhasutwu (Maha-satwa, the great saint) replied, 'O Sire! why temptest thou me with perishing wealth, dying (mortal) beauty, and youthful bloom? O king! what is love, the pleasant look, present delight, anxiety in pursuit of wealth, sons, and daughters, and wives, to me who am released from the bonds of iniquity? I know that death will not forget me; therefore of what use are pleasures and riches?. . . Return, return, O king! I have no desire for the kingdom.'" (Pp. 407—409.) "In the manner and precisely at the time predicted by the astrologers," says the Ayin Akbari, "it came to pass that he turned his mind from the affairs of the world, and made choice of a life of retirement." "He died at the age of one hundred and twenty years."—Vol. iii. p. 157.

[1] These pilgrimages have been noticed by many travellers. Mr. Duncan, in his historical remarks on the coast of Malabar, speaking of the conversion of a king of that country (during the lifetime of Mahomet) says, on the authority of a native historian, "that it was effected by a company of dervises from Arabia, who touched at Crungloor of Cranganore (then the seat of government in Malabar) on their voyage to visit the Footstep of Adam, on that mountain in Ceylon which mariners distinguish by the name of Adam's Peak." In a note he adds: "This Footstep of Adam is, under the name of Sreepud or the 'holy foot,' equally reverenced and resorted to by the Hindus."—Asiatic Res. vol. v. p. 9.

[2] It is not stated that this extraordinary embassy proceeded to India by sea. Its route must therefore have been either through the province of Yun-nan to Bengal, or by the way of Tibet, to Hindustan and the

intelligence of the approach of the messengers, on their return with such valuable curiosities, he ordered all the people of Kanbalu to march out of the city to meet them, and they were conducted to his presence with great pomp and solemnity.[1] Having mentioned these particulars respecting the mountain of Zeilan, we shall return to the kingdom of Maabar, and speak of the city of Kael.

CHAPTER XXIV

OF THE CITY OF KAEL

KAEL is a considerable city,[2] governed by Astiar, one of the four brothers, kings of the country of Maabar, who is rich in gold and jewels, and preserves his country in a state of profound peace.[3] On this account it is a favourite place of resort for foreign merchants, who are well received and treated by the king. Accordingly all the ships coming from the west—as from Ormus, Chisti, Adem, and various parts of Arabia—laden

peninsula. So extensive at that time were the dominions of the Moghul Tartar family, that even in the ordinary transaction of political business, their people were accustomed to the performance of journeys of great distance and duration. In regard to its object it is not without its parallel in the histories of other countries.

[1] This ceremonious introduction of a relic to the palace of the emperor, is likewise not a new circumstance in the Chinese annals. "L'année quatorzième de son regne (says Du Halde, speaking of the seventeenth prince of the dynasty of the Tang,) il fit porter avec pompe dans son palais, un os de l'idole Foĕ."—Tom. i. p. 456.

[2] In the Tamul language the word Kael or Koil signifies a temple, and forms the terminating syllable in the names of several places in the southern part of the peninsula. It was also, pre-eminently, the name of a considerable town and port of trade, in what we now term the Tinevelly country, not many miles from Tutacorin. Its situation may be seen in the map prefixed to Valentyn's Beschryving van Choromandel (vol. v.), where its ancient consequence is denoted by the addition of the word patnam; but having disappeared in modern maps, we may conclude that Kael-patnam no longer exists, even as a town; yet in Dalrymple's collection of Plans of Ports we find one (from Van Keulen) which lays down the situation not only of Cayl-patnam, but also of Porto Cayl, and of a place termed old Cayl.

[3] It would seem that the king of Narsinga or Telingana placed the southern provinces of his extensive dominions under the immediate rule of his several brothers, who exercised the full authority of kings within their respective territories. The name of Astiar is probably a corruption, but the imperfect remains of Hindu annals that have come to our knowledge, afford little chance of ascertaining the genuine orthography. It will appear that, at a subsequent period, this part of the country was wrested from the kings of Narsinga by those of Koulam or Kolam, on the Malabar coast.

with merchandise and horses, make this port, which is besides well situated for commerce. The prince maintains in the most splendid manner not fewer than three hundred women.

All the people of this city, as well as the natives of India in general, are addicted to the custom of having continually in their mouths the leaf called *tembul;* which they do, partly from habit, and partly from the gratification it affords.[1] Upon chewing it, they spit out the saliva to which it gives occasion. Persons of rank have the leaf prepared with camphor and other aromatic drugs, and also with a mixture of quick-lime.[2] I have been told that it is extremely conducive to health. If it is an object with any man to affront another in the grossest and most contemptuous manner, he spits the juice of this masticated leaf in his face. Thus insulted, the injured party hastens to the presence of the king, states the circumstances of his grievance, and declares his willingness to decide the quarrel by combat. The king thereupon furnishes them with arms, consisting of a sword and small shield; and all the people assemble to be spectators of the conflict, which lasts till one of them remains dead on the field. They are, however, forbidden to wound with the point of the sword.[3]

CHAPTER XXV

OF THE KINGDOM OF KOULAM

UPON leaving Maabar and proceeding five hundred miles towards the south-west, you arrive at the kingdom of Koulam.[4]

[1] We here find the leaf of the betel called by its true Persian name, *tembul*.

[2] Besides the ordinary ingredients, it is not unusual to mix in the composition cardamoms, gutta gambir, and other articles of a pungent and aromatic flavour; but I am not aware, nor is it probable from the qualities of the drug, that camphor is ever employed in this manner. It may therefore be suspected that there has been a substitution of the name of one article of the composition for another, and it is to be observed that in the Malayan language (which was more familiar to the traders of the coast of Coromandel, in early times, than it is at present) the word *kapûr* (the *kafur* of the Arabs) is applied not only to camphor, but also to lime (*calx viva*), which is an essential ingredient in the preparation of betel.

[3] The circumstances of this juridical practice of duelling are particularly detailed by Barbosa, in speaking of Batacala, a place on the opposite coast of Malabar, near Onore.

[4] Koulam or Kolam, the Coulan of our maps, was a place of much celebrity when India was first visited by the Portuguese, who received

It is the residence of many Christians and Jews, who retain their proper language. The king is not tributary to any other. Much good sappan-wood grows there,[1] and pepper in great abundance, being found both in the woody and the open parts of the country. It is gathered in the months of May, June, and July; and the vines which produce it are cultivated in plantations.[2] Indigo also, of excellent quality and in large quantities, is made here. They procure it from an herbaceous plant, which is taken up by the roots and put into tubs of water, where it is suffered to remain till it rots; when they press out the juice. This, upon being exposed to the sun, and evaporated, leaves a kind of paste, which is cut into small pieces of the form in which we see it brought to us.[3]

The heat during some months is so violent as to be scarcely supportable; yet the merchants resort thither from various parts of the world, such, for instance, as the kingdom of Manji and Arabia,[4] attracted by the great profits they obtain both

assistance from its princes against the king of Calicut, or the Samorin, as he was styled. In modern times its importance, as a place of trade, seems to be lost in that of Anjengo, in its neighbourhood. The name signifies a tank, pool, or basin, in the Tamul language. The distance from Kael, however, is more nearly two hundred than five hundred miles.

[1] " Narravit mihi aliquis qui eo suscepit iter. . . ibi esse arborem ol Bakkami (seu Brasillam) cujus lignum simile sit ligno granati mali." (Abilfedæ Geographia, p. 274.) Sandal-wood is more frequently mentioned as the produce of the mountains in the interior of the country.

[2] " Nasce in questo luogo," says Barbosa, speaking of Koulam, " molto pepe, del quale se ne caricano molte navi." (Fol. 312—2.) It would be superfluous to multiply authorities for the purpose of showing that pepper is cultivated in the Travancore country, within which Koulam is situated. Our author is mistaken, however, in regard to the seasons, as on the Malabar coast the pepper-vine flowers about the month of June, and the berries ripen in December.

[3] A tolerably correct account is here given of the rude progress of manufacturing indigo. The plant itself grows, and is made use of as a dye-stuff in almost every part of India. The word is endigo in Ramusio and the epitomes, and eudici (for endici) in the Basle edition.

[4] There are strong grounds for believing that in early times the Chinese did (reciprocally with the Arabians) trade, not only to the peninsula of India, but also to the Persian gulf. This was the deliberate opinion of Dr. Robertson, who had studied the subject: see Historical Disquisitions, etc. p. 95. The Arabian travellers of the ninth century leave it in some measure doubtful whether the ships employed in the trade between Siraf and Canton might not have been wholly Arabian, although called in Renaudot's translation, " vaisseaux Chinois," as we term those employed in the same trade, China ships: but the authority of Edrisi, who wrote in the twelfth century, is direct to the point. " Ex ipsa," he says of a port in Yemen, " solvuntur navigia Sindæ, Indiæ, et Sinarum, et ad ipsam deferuntur vasa Sinica." (Geographia, p. 25.) Of the fact we have a corroboration on the part of the Chinese themselves, as related by De Guignes,

upon the merchandise they import, and upon their returning cargoes. Many of the animals found here are different from those of other parts. There are tigers entirely black;[1] and various birds of the parrot kind, some of them as white as snow, with the feet and the beak red; others whose colours are a mixture of red and azure, and others of a diminutive size. The peacocks also are handsomer and larger than ours, as well as of a different form, and even the domestic fowls have a peculiar appearance.[2] The same observation will apply to the fruits. The cause of such diversity, it is said, is the intense heat that prevails in these regions. Wine is made from the sugar yielded by a species of palm. It is extremely good, and inebriates faster than the wine made from grapes.[3] The inhabitants possess abundance of everything necessary for the food of man excepting grain, of which there is no other kind than rice; but of this the quantity is very great. Among them are many astrologers and physicians, well versed in their art. All the people, both male and female, are black, and, with the exception of a small piece of cloth attached to the front of their bodies, they go quite naked.[4] Their manners are extremely sensual, and they take as wives their relations by blood, their mothers-in-law, upon the death of their fathers, and the widows of their deceased brothers.[5] But this, as I have been informed, is the state of morals in every part of India.

[1] It has already been noticed that our author on all occasions applies the name of lion to the tiger or the leopard; and of such, although the word is leoni in the text, he means to speak on this occasion. Of the existence of black tigers or leopards, there is no doubt.

[2] The birds here described may perhaps be intended for the kokatua, lury, and paroquet; although the former are not natives of the place at which he saw them. Peacocks have been already mentioned as a common bird in India. Of domestic fowls there are some species of a much larger size than those bred in Europe.—See Hist. of Sumatra, 3d edit. p. 125.

[3] What our author terms wine in this place is properly an ardent spirit, distilled from the coarse, imperfectly granulated sugar, called jaggri or jagory, which is itself an inspissation of the juice (tari or toddy) drawn from the *borassus flabelliformis*, vulgarly called the brab palm in the peninsula of India.

[4] "Il popolo minuto," says Lodovico Barthema, speaking of the subjects of the king of Narsinga, "vanno tutti nudi, salvo che intorno le parti inhoneste portano un panno." (Fol. 159–2.) "These higher ranks of people in Malayala (Malabar) use very little clothing, but they are remarkably clean in their persons."—Buchanan, vol. ii. p. 353.

[5] However sensual the manners in general of these people may be, I find no direct proof of incestuous marriages amongst them; but it is probable that some confusion and mistake on this subject may have arisen from certain extraordinary customs peculiar to them, and especially to the class of Nairs, who follow, for the most part, the profession of arms. According to these, it is the nephew by the eldest sister, and not the son, who suceeds to the property of the father, or, in the royal family, to the

CHAPTER XXVI

OF KOMARI

KOMARI [1] is a province where a part of our northern constellation, invisible at Java, and to within about thirty miles of this place, may be just seen, and where it appears to be the height of a cubit above the horizon.[2] The country is not much culti-

crown: a practice connected with another of a licentious character, that will be best explained in the words of Dr. F. Buchanan: "Having assembled the most respectable of the Nairs in this neighbourhood," says this intelligent observer, "they gave me the following account of their customs. The Nair, or in the plural the Naimar, are the pure Súdras of Malayala, and all pretend to be born soldiers; but they are of various ranks and professions." "The Nairs marry before they are ten years of age . . .; but the husband never afterwards cohabits with his wife. Such a circumstance indeed would be considered as very indecent. He allows her oil, clothing, ornaments, and food; but she lives in her mother's house, or, after her parents' death, with her brothers, and cohabits with any person that she chooses of an equal or higher rank than her own. If detected in bestowing her favours on any low man, she becomes an outcast. It is no kind of reflection on a woman's character to say that she has formed the closest intimacy with many persons; on the contrary, the Nair women are proud of reckoning among their favoured lovers many Bráhmans, Rájás, and other persons of high birth." "In consequence of this strange manner of propagating the species, no Nair knows his father; and every man looks upon his sisters' children as his heirs. He, indeed, looks upon them with the same fondness that fathers in other parts of the world have for their own children." "A man's mother manages his family; and after her death his eldest sister assumes the direction. Brothers almost always live under the same roof; but, if one of the family separates from the rest, he is always accompanied by his favourite sister."—Journey from Madras, etc. vol. ii. pp. 408—412. In such a domestic arrangement it is not surprising that a traveller, who had not the means of close investigation, should suspect an incestuous intercourse.

[1] Komari, or, as it appears in the Latin version, Comari, is the correct name of the extreme southern promontory of India, mentioned by Ptolemy as the Κομάρια ἄκρον, *promontarium Kamariæ*, and called by modern Europeans Cape Comorin. In the course of our author's route from the eastern to the western coast of the peninsula, this place ought to have been noticed before the city of Koulam, an inaccuracy that may have arisen from the transposition of detached materials.

[2] In some parts of the work *la tramontana*, or *nostra tramontana*, appears to denote, as it properly should, the north polar star, but in others, the constellation of the Grear Bear. Being here described as *partly* visible, the latter must of course be understood, and our author's unscientific remark can be explained only on the supposition that *Ursa Major* was below the horizon, at night, during most part of the time employed in his navigation of these seas; which is the case in low latitudes, for about six months of the year. This solution may be equally applied to a passage in Pliny (lib. vi. cap. 24,) where it is said that a navigator who had been driven into the Indian ocean, and landed at Hippuri in the island of Taprobane, reported, on his return to Rome, that the septemtrio or Great

vated, being chiefly covered with forests, which are the abode of a variety of beasts, especially apes, so formed, and of such a size, as to have the appearance of men.[1] There are also long-tailed monkeys, very different from the former in respect to magnitude. Tigers, leopards, and lynxes, abound.

CHAPTER XXVII

OF THE KINGDOM OF DELY

LEAVING the province of Komari, and proceeding westward three hundred miles, you reach the kingdom of Dely, which has its proper king and peculiar language.[2] It does not pay tribute to any other state. The people worship idols. There is no harbour for shipping, but a large river with a safe entrance.[3] The strength of the country does not consist in the

Bear was not visible on the island. But if, on the other hand, his observation was meant to apply to the polar star itself, the expression might be taken in this sense: that although invisible from Java Minor, yet when within a few miles of Cape Comorin (in latitude 8°), it was occasionally distinguishable at a small height above the horizon; where a star of the third magnitude is not readily seen, unless the atmosphere in that part be more clear than it is in common. The mode of estimating its altitude by cubits or fathoms, instead of degrees, however rude, appears, from the travels of Cada Mosto in the fifteenth century, to have been then still in use.

[1] The worship of Hanuman, a rational and very amusing ape, of the Hindu mythology—who, with an army of his own species, assisted Rama in the conquest of Ceylon, after having rescued his wife Sita from the power of Ravana, its tyrant, by whom she had been carried off—has produced a feeling of veneration for the whole race, but particularly for those of the larger class, whose form approaches nearest to the human. The consequence of this superstition is, that the breed, being unmolested, multiply exceedingly, to the great annoyance of the inhabitants of villages. It has been conjectured, with much plausibility, that the monkeys of Rama's army were in fact the half-savage mountaineers of the country near Cape Comorin.

[2] The Dely of Ramusio's text, which in the Basle edition is Eli, in the older Latin Hely, and in the early Venice epitome Elli, is the Mount Dilla of the English, and Delli of the Dutch maps, in the latitude of about 12° N., where, according to Paolino, who names it Monte D'Illi, the country of Malabar or Malayala terminates, and that of Kanara commences. Buchanan, however, extends the boundary of the former to the Chandragiri river, about half a degree further north than Mount Dilla, which he describes as "a hill separated from the continent by salt water creeks, and forming on the coast a remarkable promontory, the native name of which," he observes, "is extremely harsh, and can hardly be pronounced by an European, or expressed in our characters. It is somewhat like Yesay Malay."—Vol. ii. p. 559.

[3] The river here noticed is one that discharges itself immediately to the southward of Mount Dilla, not far from Cananore, after running

multitude of its inhabitants, nor in their bravery, but in the difficulty of the passes by which it must be approached, and which render its invasion by an enemy nearly impossible.[1] It produces large quantities of pepper and ginger, with many other articles of spicery.[2] Should a vessel be accidentally driven within the mouth of its river, not having intended to make that port, they seize and confiscate all the goods she may have on board, saying: " It was your intentions to have gone elsewhere, but our gods have conducted you to us, in order that we may possess your property." The ships from Manji arrive here before the expiration of the fine-weather season, and endeavour to get their cargoes shipped in the course of a week, or a shorter time if possible; the roadstead being unsafe, in consequence of sand-banks along the coast, which often prove dangerous, however well provided they may be with large wooden anchors, calculated for riding out hard gales of wind.[3] The country is infested with tigers, and many other ferocious animals.

CHAPTER XXVIII

OF MALABAR

MALABAR is an extensive kingdom of the Greater India, situated towards the west; concerning which I must not omit to relate

through the country of the Cherical or Colastry rajas, whose kingdom flourished at the period of which our author speaks. " It derives its name," says Buchanan, " from a town called Valya-pattanam." " At the mouth it is very wide, and immediately within the bar divides into two branches, both navigable in boats to a considerable distance."

[1] The opinion of our author is confirmed by Paolino, who says: " Questo paese . . . è quasi inespugnabile, essendo coperto da alte montagne, e tutto tagliato da' fiumi, che impediscono la cavalleria, il passo delle truppe, il tragitto veloce d'un esercito, e la permanenza sicura, d'un inimico che non è pratico del paese. Questo è il vero motivo per cui giammai fu conquistato." (P. 71.) " The rájás of Malabar," observes Buchanan, " do not seem to have ever trusted to fortifications for the defence of their country."—P. 462.

[2] After a circumstantial account of the mode of cultivating pepper in these districts, Dr. Buchanan proceeds to say: " In the gardens of this neighbourhood much ginger and turmeric are cultivated." " The ginger intended for sale is scraped with a knife to remove the outer skin; and having been sprinkled with the ashes of cow-dung, is spread out on mats, and dried eight or ten days; when it is fit for sale." (P. 469.) Cardamoms are also an article of produce.

[3] The circumstances of the anchorage here described are the same at Tellicherry, Mahé, and Anjengo, from whence the pepper for Europe is put on board the East India Company's ships, in the open road, where they not unfrequently part their cables.

some particulars.[1] The people are governed by their own king, who is independent of every other state, and they have their proper language. In this country the north star is seen about two fathoms above the horizon. As well here as in the kingdom of Guzzerat, which is not far distant, there are numerous pirates, who yearly scour these seas with more than one hundred small vessels, seizing and plundering all the merchant ships that pass that way.[2] They take with them to sea their wives and children of all ages, who continue to accompany them during the whole of the summer's cruise. In order that no ships may escape them, they anchor their vessels at the distance of five miles from each other; twenty ships thereby occupying a space of a hundred miles. Upon a trader's appearing in sight of one of them, a signal is made by fire or by smoke; when they all draw closer together, and capture the vessel as she attempts to pass. No injury is done to the persons of the crew; but as soon as they have made prize of the ship, they turn them on shore, recommending to them to provide themselves with another cargo, which, in case of their passing that way again, may be the means of enriching their captors a second time.

In this kingdom there is vast abundance of pepper, ginger, cubebs, and Indian nuts; and the finest and most beautiful cottons are manufactured that can be found in any part of the world.[3] The ships from Manji bring copper as ballast;

[1] The name of Malabar (in the other versions Melibar,) though commonly applied to the whole western coast of the peninsula, properly belongs only to that part of it which lies to the southward of Mount Della, called by the natives Malayala and Malayalam. Our author is guilty, therefore, of inaccuracy, in giving the name, on the contrary, to the portion of the coast that extends northward from that promontory, which is in fact what we term the province of Canara and the Concan, instead of the tract extending northward from Cape Comorin, estimated by him, correctly, at about three hundred miles.

[2] "This multitude of small ports, uninterrupted view along shore, and elevated coast, favourable to distant vision, have fitted this coast," says Rennell, "for the seat of piracy; and the alternate land and sea-breezes that prevail during a great part of the year oblige vessels to navigate very near the shore. No wonder, then, that Pliny should notice the depredations committed on the Roman East India trade in his time; and although a temporary check has been given to them by the destruction of Angria's fleets, etc., yet we may expect the practice will be continued while commerce lasts. The pirates are protected by the shallowness of their ports, and the strength of the country within." (Memoir, ed. 1793, p. 30.) "It appears from the earliest antiquity," says Grose, "that the inhabitants had the strongest propensity to piracy; and at this day all the different principalities on the coast employ vessels to cruise upon those of all other nations which they can overpower."—Vol. ii. p. 211.

[3] In speaking of Rajapore, a place near Gheriah, and consequently on

and besides this, gold brocades, silks, gauzes, gold and silver bullion, together with many kinds of drugs not produced in Malabar; and these they barter for the commodities of the province.[1] There are merchants on the spot who ship the former for Aden, from whence they are transported to Alexandria.[2]

Having now spoken of the kingdom of Malabar, we shall proceed to describe that of Guzzerat, which borders on it. Should we attempt to treat of all the cities of India, the account would be prolix, and prove tiresome. We shall, therefore, touch only upon those respecting which we have particular information.

CHAPTER XXIX

OF THE KINGDOM OF GUZZERAT

THE kingdom of Guzzerat, which is bounded on the western side by the Indian Sea, is governed by its own king, and has its peculiar language.[3] The north-star appears from hence to have six fathoms of altitude. This country affords harbour to pirates of the most desperate character,[4] who, when in their cruises they seize upon a travelling merchant, immedi-

what is termed the pirate-coast, Hamilton observes that the country thereabouts produced the finest muslins and betillas in India.—P. 243.

[1] This was probably Japan copper, which has always been in high request. The other articles enumerated are well known to be the produce of the respective countries.

[2] It appears from a passage in Barbosa's travels that in his time these merchants were partly at least, if not chiefly, Parsis, as we have been accustomed to call those natives of Persia and their descendants, who, on account of their adherence to the religion of their ancestors—which was that of Zerdusht or Zoroaster, and termed fire-worship—were driven from their own country by the Mahometans. He, however, ignorantly calls them Moors, and seems to confound them with Arabian and other traders whose commercial operations he describes.

[3] The name of Guzzerat, as it appears in Ramusio's text, as well as in our modern maps, has suffered less by transcription than most others, being Gozurath in the Basle, and also the older Latin editions, Guzurach in the B.M. and Berlin manuscripts, and Gesurach in the early epitomes. In the Persian and Arabic writings it is Gujrât, or Gujurât. It seems doubtful whether what is now termed the peninsula of Guzerat was anciently an integral part of the kingdom so named, of which Nehrwaleh or Puttan was the capital.

[4] The territory of Guzerat having fallen under the dominion of the Moghul emperors of Delhi, who adopted active measures for restraining the inhabitants of that part of the coast from their piratical habits, the navigators of the fifteenth and sixteenth centuries do not speak of depredations further to the north than Tanah, on the island of Salsette.

ately oblige him to drink a dose of sea-water, which by its operation on his bowels discovers whether he may not have swallowed pearls or jewels, upon the approach of an enemy, in order to conceal them.

Here there is great abundance of ginger, pepper, and indigo. Cotton is produced in large quantities from a tree that is about six yards in height, and bears during twenty years; but the cotton taken from trees of that age is not adapted for spinning, but only for quilting. Such, on the contrary, as is taken from trees of twelve years old, is suitable for muslins and other manufactures of extraordinary fineness.[1] Great numbers of skins of goats, buffaloes, wild oxen, rhinoceroses, and other beasts are dressed here; and vessels are loaded with them, and bound to different parts of Arabia. Coverlets for beds are made of red and blue leather, extremely delicate and soft, and stitched with gold and silver thread;[2] upon these the Mahometans are accustomed to repose. Cushions also, ornamented with gold wire in the form of birds and beasts, are the manufacture of this place; and in some instances their value is so high as six marks of silver. Embroidery is here performed

[1] According to the words of the text, our author may be thought to have mistaken the bombax, or silk-cotton-tree, which grows commonly to the height of from fifteen to twenty feet, for the *gossypium arboreum*, a shrub, or the *gossypium herbaceum*, an annual plant; but with these latter, being the produce of the Levant, and probably cultivated in some parts of Italy, both he and his countrymen must have been well acquainted, and his object could only have been to describe a species of cotton-bearing tree that was new to them. Such was probably the case with respect to the bombax. He proceeds, however, to inform them that its cotton is not adapted to the purposes of the loom, and is only used for quilting, or, he might have added, for stuffing pillows. When, in the sequel, he is made to say, that if taken from the tree at the age of only twelve years, it was fit to be employed in the manufacture of fine muslins, which is contrary to the fact, there is the strongest reason to believe that his sense has been perverted. No expression to that purport is found in any other version of the work; and it is evident that he here means to speak of the common annual or shrub cotton, as contrasted with the beautiful but almost useless sort he had just been describing.

[2] This may be thought an extraordinary traffic for an Indian port, but Linschoten (whose voyages commenced in the year 1583), speaking of the country between Guzerat and the Indus, notices the manufacture of leathern articles in the following terms: "Ex corio item peritè quædam facta, floribusque ex bysso (silk, in the Dutch copy) variis coloribus ornata. Hisque utuntur in tapetorum vicem, et lectis mensisque imponunt." (Navig. ac Itiner. cap. vii. p. 12.) No mention is made of the preparation of the skins; but Dr. F. Buchanan, in the course of his journey through the central parts of the peninsula, describes minutely the process used by the natives in dressing, tanning, and dyeing, not only the skins of goats and sheep, but also the hides of oxen and buffaloes. —Vol. i. p. 227.

with more delicacy than in any other part of the world.[1] Proceeding further, we shall now speak of the kingdom named Kanan.

CHAPTER XXX

OF THE KINGDOM OF KANAN

Kanan is a large and noble kingdom, situated towards the west.[2] We say towards the west, because Messer Marco's journey being from the eastern side, he speaks of the countries in the direction in which he found them. It is governed by a prince, who does not pay tribute to any other. The people are idolaters and have a peculiar language. Neither pepper nor ginger grows here, but the country produces a sort of incense, in large quantities, which is not white, but on the contrary of a dark colour. Many ships frequent the place in order to load this drug, as well as a variety of other articles.[3] They likewise take on board a number of horses, to be carried for sale to different parts of India.[4]

[1] "Eadem arte," Linschoten adds, "stragula faciunt serico filo exornata, et acu picta . . . lectica Indica, mulierum sellas, aliaque minuta." —Cap. ix. p. 13.

[2] A more than ordinary want of conformity appears in the modes of writing the name of this place, which in Ramusio's text is Canam or Kanan, in the Basle edition Tana, in the older Latin Thana, Chane, and Chana, in the B.M. and Berlin manuscripts, Caria, and in the early epitomes Toma. [It may be observed that *t* and *c* are constantly interchanged in Medieval manuscripts.] It is probable that among these, Tana is the true reading, and such it is considered by D'Anville, who, after noticing that a place of that name appears in the Tables of Nasreddîn and Ulugh-beg, observes that "Marc-Pol en parle comme d'un royaume, qu'il joint à ceux de Cambaeth et de Semenat." (P. 101.) It may be doubted whether the place which is the subject of this note, called Tana in the Basle edition, and Toma in the epitomes, was not meant for Tatta, a celebrated commercial city at the head of the delta of the Indus, rather than for Tanah of Salsette, so much to the south of Guzerat.

[3] Pepper is not produced so far to the northward as Bombay, nor is there any considerable cultivation of it beyond the province of Kanara. The incense here spoken of is evidently gum benzoin; which indeed is not the growth of any part of the continent of India, but would be seen in large quantities in the warehouses of the merchants, by whom it is imported from Sumatra, in order to supply the markets of Arabia, Persia, Syria, and Asia Minor. It is generally of a dark brown colour, the finest sort only being mixed with veins of white.

[4] Horses were carried from the Red Sea, Persian Gulf, and places in their vicinity, to the northern ports of India, from whence their breed was exported to the southern provinces. Such at least appears to have been the course of the traffic before it was disturbed by European influence.

CHAPTER XXXI

OF THE KINGDOM OF KAMBAIA

This also is an extensive kingdom, situated towards the west, governed by its own king, who pays no tribute to any other, and having its proper language.[1] The people are idolaters. In this country the north-star is seen still higher than in any of the preceding, in consequence of its lying further to the north-west. The trade carried on is very considerable, and a great quantity of indigo is manufactured.[2] There is abundance of cotton cloth, as well as of cotton in the wool.[3] Many skins well dressed are exported from hence, and the returns are received in gold, silver, copper, and tutty.[4] There not being anything else deserving of notice, I shall proceed to speak of the kingdom of Servenath.

CHAPTER XXXII

OF THE KINGDOM OF SERVENATH

Servenath, likewise, is a kingdom lying towards the west,[5] the inhabitants of which are idolaters, are governed by a king

[1] It has been observed that where mention was made of Guzerat, the account seemed to apply not to the peninsula of that name, but to the more southern part of the kingdom, which includes the city of Surat, and extended along the coast as far as Tanah or Bombay. Consistently with this idea, and with our author's progress towards the north, he now treats, in order, of Kambaia, a celebrated port of trade, situated at the bottom of the gulf to which it gives name. This place is enumerated in the Ayin Akbari, by the name of Kambayet, amongst the principal cities of Gujerat, of which Nehrwaleh, commonly termed Puttan (as shown by Rennell), was anciently the capital.

[2] "Annil sive indigo," says Linschoten, "in Cambaia præparatur, ac per universas orbis partes distrahitur." (Navig. ac Itiner. p. 13.) The Ayin Akbari, describing a place in the neighbourhood of Ahmedabad, the modern capital, which stands not far from the port of Kambaia, says: "Here grows very fine indigo, which is exported to Room, and other distant places."—Vol. ii. p. 77.

[3] Cotton-wool is exported in large quantities at the present day from Surat and Bombay to China.

[4] Tutty has been already mentioned, in Book I. chap. xx., as a preparation from a mineral (zinc or antimony) found in the eastern part of Persia. It is carried to India chiefly for the purpose of making the collyrium, named *surmeh* and *anjan*, much used by the women of Hindustan.

[5] Servenath, which in the Basle edition is more correctly named Semenath, and in the older Latin, Semenach, but is omitted in the early

who pays no tribute, have their peculiar language, and are a well-disposed people. They gain their living by commerce and manufactures, and the place is frequented by a number of merchants, who carry thither their articles of merchandise, and take away those of the country in return. I was informed, however, that the priests who serve in the temples of the idols are the most perfidious and cruel that the world contains.[1] We shall now proceed to speak of the kingdom named Kesmacoran.

CHAPTER XXXIII

OF THE KINGDOM OF KESMACORAN

THIS is an extensive country, having its proper king and its peculiar language.[2] Some of the inhabitants are idolaters,

epitomes (unless Sebelech be intended for it, and not for Cambaeth), is obviously the place called Sumenât, celebrated for the ravages committed there (in the year 1025) by Mahmud of Ghizni, a Mahometan bigot, who destroyed a famous Hindu temple, broke in pieces its gigantic idol, and carried away the precious stones with which it was adorned.

[1] The cruelties exercised by the Mussulmans upon the Hindu inhabitants of this place, who, according to Abulfeda, were slaughtered in great numbers "(Ea in urbe, Sumenat, ingentem Indorum numerum necabat Mahmud, omnes auferebat divitias, et super idolo rogum accendebat)," might have produced a violent spirit of retaliation, especially amongst the priests, and occasioned their seizing opportunities of revenging the injuries they had sustained; and it is not improbable that our author may have received his information respecting their character from his Mahometan shipmates.

[2] The name of this place, which is Chesmacoran or Kesmacoran in Ramusio's text, Resmacoram in the Basle edition, Resmacoron in the older Latin, and Resmaceran in the early epitomes, seemed to present great difficulties. Major Rennell identifies it with Kidg-Makran, "which might have been classed at that time as belonging to India, as Kandahar and other Persian provinces have in latter times. It happens that I had previously exercised my judgment on this place, and I now find, by a note in Astley, that the editor thought the same. In India they always join Kidg and Makran together, as is very commonly done with regard to other places. Kidg, or Kedge, may have been the former capital. It is, I doubt not, the Gedrosia of the ancients." Kedge is spoken of by Pottinger as the modern capital of Makran, an extensive province, near the sea, on the western side of the Indus. The places in the vicinity of this river had been the bounds of our author's previous description; on which occasion he says (Book I. chap. xxvii.): "If I were to proceed in the same direction, it would lead me to India; but I have judged it proper to reserve the description of that country for a Third Book:" and he is therefore consistent in terminating his account of the coast of India, upon his reaching, in an opposite course, the province which connects it with Persia, and which has been considered, at different periods, as politically dependent on the one or the other. According to the system of the ancient geographers, Makran belonged to Sind, as distinguished from Hind, but both were included in their definition of India, in its extensive acceptation.

but the greater part are Saracens.[1] They subsist by trade and manufactures. Their food is rice and wheat, together with flesh and milk, which they have in abundance. Many merchants resort thither, both by sea and land. This is the last province of the Greater India, as you proceed to the north-west; for, as it begins at Maabar, so it terminates here.[2] In describing it, we have noticed only the provinces and cities that lie upon the sea-coast; for were we to particularise those situated in the interior of the land, it would render our work too prolix. We shall now speak of certain islands, one of which is termed the Island of Males, and the other, the Island of Females.

CHAPTER XXXIV

OF THE ISLANDS OF MALES AND OF FEMALES

DISTANT from Kesmacoran about five hundred miles towards the south, in the ocean, there are two islands within about thirty miles from each other, one of which is inhabited by men, without the company of women, and is called the island of males; and the other by women, without men, which is called the island of females.[3] The inhabitants of both are of the same race, and are baptized Christians, but hold the law of the Old Testament. The men visit the island of females, and remain with them for three successive months, namely, March, April, and May, each man occupying a separate habitation along with his wife. They then return to the island of males,

[1] "Many of the inhabitants of Makran," says Ebn Haukal, "resemble the Arabs; they eat fowl and fish: others of them are like the Curds. Here is the extreme boundary of the land of Islam in this direction. Now we shall turn back, and begin to describe Armenia, etc." (P. 155.) It is remarkable that our author should have adopted nearly the same grand line of division as this Arabian geographer, who preceded him by about three centuries; but it may be accounted for by his intercourse with Arabian pilots.

[2] By Maabar (as distinguished from Malabar) is meant the eastern coast of the peninsula, from near the Kistnah, or, perhaps more strictly, from the Pennar River to Cape Comorin, or that tract in which the Tamul language prevails.

[3] Of what particular islands this tale of wonder was related to our author would be difficult to ascertain with any degree of precision; but notwithstanding the objections that present themselves with regard to distances, there is reason to believe them intended for those which lie near the island of Socotra, called Abd-al-curia and "Les deux sœurs" in some maps, or "Les deux frères" in others. In Fra. Mauro's map, these islands are named Mangla and Nebila.

where they continue all the rest of the year, without the society of any female. The wives retain their sons with them until they are of the age of twelve years, when they are sent to join their fathers. The daughters they keep at home until they become marriageable, and then they bestow them upon some of the men of the other island. This mode of living is occasioned by the peculiar nature of the climate, which does not allow of their remaining all the year with their wives, unless at the risk of falling a sacrifice. They have their bishop, who is subordinate to the see of the island of Soccotera.[1] The men provide for the subsistence of their wives by sowing the grain, but the latter prepare the soil and gather in the harvest. The island likewise produces a variety of fruits. The men live upon milk, flesh, rice, and fish. Of these they catch an immense quantity, being expert fishermen. Both when fresh taken and when salted, the fish are sold to the traders resorting to the island,[2] but whose principal object is to purchase ambergris, of which a quantity is collected there.

CHAPTER XXXV

OF THE ISLAND OF SOCCOTERA

UPON leaving these islands, and proceeding five hundred miles in a southerly direction, you reach the island of Soccotera, which is very large, and abounds with the necessaries of life.[3] The inhabitants find much ambergris upon their coasts, which is voided from the entrails of whales.[4] Being an article of

[1] It will be seen, in the notes to the following chapter, that Christianity was established in this quarter (as well as in Abyssinia) at a very early period. The ecclesiastical subordination to Socotra argues a contiguity, although it does not amount to proof.

[2] Salt-fish is well known to be an important article of trade in these regions, where, from the excessive heat and arid quality of the soil, vegetation is rare, and the food of men and cattle procured with difficulty. On this account it was that the natives of the coast were termed by the Greeks *Ichthyophagi*, or persons whose chief sustenance was fish.

[3] This considerable island, the Socotora of D'Anville and Socotra of English geographers, is situated near Cape Guardafui, the north-eastern point of the continent of Africa. In Ramusio's text it is correctly named Soccotera, but in the Basle edition Scoira, in the older Latin Scoyran, and in the early Italian epitomes Scorsia: so inattentive have the copyists been in transcribing proper names even of well-known places.

[4] Frequent mention is made of ambergris being found in the neighbouring coast of Africa.

merchandise in great demand, they make it a business to take these fish; and this they do by means of a barbed iron, which they strike into the whale so firmly that it cannot be drawn out. To the iron (harpoon) a long line is fastened, with a buoy at the end, for the purpose of discovering the place where the fish, when dead, is to be found. They then drag it to the shore, and proceed to extract the ambergris from its belly, whilst from its head they procure several casks of (spermaceti) oil.[1]

All the people, both male and female, go nearly naked, having only a scanty covering before and behind, like the idolaters who have been described. They have no other grain than rice, upon which, with flesh and milk, they subsist. Their religion is Christianity, and they are duly baptized,[2] and are under the government, as well temporal as spiritual, of an archbishop, who is not in subjection to the pope of Rome, but to a patriarch who resides in the city of Baghdad, by whom he is appointed, or, if elected by the people themselves, by whom their choice is confirmed.[3] Many pirates resort to this island with the goods they have captured, and which the natives purchase of them without any scruple, justifying themselves on the ground of their being plundered from idolaters and

[1] This mention of oil taken from the head of the fish shows it to be the spermaceti whale, and is a proof of accuracy on the part of our author. The mode of harpooning also is correctly described.

[2] The existence of Christianity, at an early period, in the island of Socotra, is proved by ample testimony. "Dans cette mer," says the latter of the two Arabian travellers of the ninth century, "on trouve l'isle de Socotra, où croist l'aloës socotrin. Elle est situeé près du païs des Zinge et du païs des Arabes, et la pluspart des habitans de cette isle sont Chrestiens, dont on rapporte cette raison." Edrisi, who compiled his work about the middle of the twelfth century, adopts the authority and employs nearly the terms of the Mahometan traveller, Barbosa, whose voyages were performed about the end of the fifteenth, speaks contemptuously of the species of Christianity found there by his countrymen, the Portuguese, upon their first visits to the island; but as the inhabitants were schismatics at best, some allowance should be made for a feeling of intolerance. J. de Barros gives a circumstantial account of Soccotora, and says of the natives, "Todos sao Christiaos Jacobitas da casta dos Abexijs (Habeshis or Abyssinians), però que muitas cousas nao guardao de seus costumes." "Sua adoraçao he a Cruz, e sao tao devotos della, que per habito todos trazem hua ao pescoço."—Dec. ii. l. i. cap. iii.

[3] It is evident that our author supposed the inhabitants to be Nestorians, Zatolia being a typographical mistake for Zatolic, which is itself a Venetian corruption of Katholicos, the title given to the head of the Nestorian church, whose seat was at Baghdad. More probably, however, they were Jacobites (as asserted by the Portuguese), and subject to the spiritual jurisdiction of a Patriarch who resided, in early times, at Antioch and at Alexandria, and afterwards at Maredin in Mesopotamia.

Saracens.[1] All ships bound to the province of Aden touch here, and make large purchases of fish and of ambergris, as well as of various kinds of cotton goods manufactured on the spot.

The inhabitants deal more in sorcery and witchcraft than any other people, although forbidden by their archbishop, who excommunicates and anathematises them for the sin. Of this, however, they make little account; and if any vessel belonging to a pirate should injure one of theirs, they do not fail to lay him under a spell, so that he cannot proceed on his cruise until he has made satisfaction for the damage; and even although he should have had a fair and leading wind, they have the power of causing it to change, and thereby of obliging him, in spite of himself, to return to the island. They can, in like manner, cause the sea to become calm, and at their will can raise tempests, occasion shipwrecks, and produce many other extraordinary effects, that need not be particularised.[2] We shall now speak of the island of Madagascar.

CHAPTER XXXVI

OF THE GREAT ISLAND OF MADAGASCAR

Leaving the island of Soccotera, and steering a course between south and south-west for a thousand miles, you arrive at the great island of Madagascar, which is one of the largest and most fertile in the world. In circuit it is three thousand miles.[3] The inhabitants are Saracens, or followers of the law of

[1] That this island, before the period of its occupation by the Portuguese, should have been made a dépôt for goods plundered by piratical vessels, is highly probable, and the conscientious salvo of the native Christians much in character; but Abulfeda appears to have considered the latter as principals in the depredations, when he says, "Incolæ eius sunt Christiani, piratæ."—Geographia, tab. xvi. p. 278.

[2] The belief in witchcraft and the efficacy of spells to disturb the ordinary course of nature, and particularly to control the winds, was prevalent at this time, and to a much later period, even in the most civilized parts of the world. We are not, therefore, to be surprised at finding the art imputed by navigators to the inhabitants of a remote island, which, like the "still-vext Bermudas," is described as being subject to violent tempests. De Barros, a grave historian of the sixteenth century, speaks of the sorcery practised by the females of Socotora, of whom he says: "Por hoje serem ainda tao grandes feiticeiras, que fazem cousas maravilhosas." (Dec. ii. liv. i. cap. iii.) The compiler of Astley's Voyages gives some curious instances of the extreme credulity of the Portuguese with respect to this supposed præternatural agency.—Vol. i. p. 63, note.

[3] Its actual circuit is about two, not three, thousand miles.

Mahomet.[1] They have four sheikhs, which in our language may be expressed by "elders," who divide the government amongst them.[2] The people subsist by trade and manufacture, and sell a vast number of elephants' teeth, as those animals abound in the country, as they do also in that of Zenzibar, from whence the exportation is equally great.[3] The principal food eaten at all seasons of the year is the flesh of camels. That of the other cattle serves them also for food, but the former is preferred, as being both the most wholesome and the most palatable of any to be found in this part of the world.[4] The woods contain many trees of red sandal, and, in proportion to the plenty in which it is found, the price of it is low. There is also much ambergris from the whales; and as the tide throws it on the coast, it is collected for sale. The natives catch lynxes, tigers, and a variety of other animals,[5] such as stags, antelopes, and fallow deer, which afford much sport; as do also birds, which are different from those of our climates.

The island is visited by many ships from various parts of the world, bringing assortments of goods consisting of brocades and silks of various patterns, which are sold to the merchants of the island, or bartered for goods in return; upon all of which they make large profits. There is no resort of ships to the other numerous islands lying further south, this and the island of Zenzibar alone being frequented. This is the consequence

[1] The natives in general are not Mahometans; but it will appear not only that the Arabs had established themselves and spread their religion in many districts along the coast, but that, by mixture with the aborigines, there are several races of people who make profession of that faith, however imperfectly they may observe its ordinances.

[2] The Arabic word *sheikh* has the double signification of an elder (as noticed in the text) and a chief or head of a tribe. In this latter sense it is that we commonly find it used, and it is probable that the tribes mentioned in the preceding note were governed by chiefs with the title of *sheikh*, as those on the opposite coast of Africa, where the Arabs established themselves, are known to have been.

[3] Elephants and ivory, which abound on the African shore (as noticed in the succeeding chapter), but certainly not upon the island of Madagascar; so that Marco Polo must have been misinformed, or he has confused his information.

[4] Some have supposed that by the camel should here be understood the Madagascar ox, or bison, which is remarkable for the protuberance or hump on its shoulder. It is certain, however, that the Arabs, and probably the Mahometans in general, prefer the flesh of camels, where they can procure it, to every other meat.

[5] It is here again apparent that the circumstances mentioned apply to the opposite coast of Africa, and not to the island, where no lions, nor animals of the tiger kind, are known to exist. In fact, nearly the whole of what is said of Madagascar seems to be information given to our author by Arabian navigators respecting the southern coast of Africa, and introduced, from his notes, in the wrong place.

of the sea running with such prodigious velocity in that direction, as to render their return impossible. The vessels that sail from the coast of Malabar for this island, perform the voyage in twenty or twenty-five days, but in their returning voyage are obliged to struggle for three months; so strong is the current of water, which constantly runs to the southward.[1]

The people of the island report that at a certain season of the year, an extraordinary kind of bird, which they call a rukh, makes its appearance from the southern region. In form it is said to resemble the eagle, but it is incomparably greater in size; being so large and strong as to seize an elephant with its talons, and to lift it into the air, from whence it lets it fall to the ground, in order that when dead it may prey upon the carcase. Persons who have seen this bird assert that when the wings are spread they measure sixteen paces in extent, from point to point; and that the feathers are eight paces in length, and thick in proportion. Messer Marco Polo, conceiving that these creatures might be griffins, such as are represented in paintings, half birds and half lions, particularly questioned those who reported their having seen them as to this point; but they maintained that their shape was altogether that of birds, or, as it might be said, of the eagle. The grand khan having heard this extraordinary relation, sent messengers to the island, on the pretext of demanding the release of one of his servants who had been detained there, but in reality to examine into the circumstances of the country, and the truth of the wonderful things told of it. When they returned to the presence of his majesty, they brought with them (as I have heard) a feather of the rukh, positively affirmed to have measured ninety spans, and the quill part to have been two palms in circumference. This surprising exhibition afforded his majesty extreme pleasure, and upon those by whom it was presented he bestowed valuable gifts.[2] They were also the bearers of the

[1] The currents which set to the southward through the Mozambique Channel, and then taking a westerly direction, sweep round the Cape of Good Hope, are matter of notoriety to all our East Indian navigators. From hence it was that a point of the main land of Africa, situated opposite to St. Augustin's Bay, in Madagascar, and nearly under the tropic, was named by the Portuguese discoverers, Cabo das Correntes. Our author's notice of this remarkable circumstance, in a part of the globe which at that period had not been visited by Europeans, is worthy of particular note.

[2] All who have read the stories of the "Thousand and One Nights" must be acquainted with the size and powers of this extraordinary bird, there called the *roc;* but its celebrity is not confined to that work. "*Rukh,*" says the Arabic and Persian Dictionary, "is the name of a

tusk of a wild boar, an animal that grows there to the size of a buffalo, and it was found to weigh fourteen pounds.[1] The island contains likewise camelopards, asses, and other wild animals, very different from these of our country. Having said what was necessary on this subject, we shall now proceed to speak of Zenzibar.

monstrous bird, which is said to have powers sufficient to carry off a live rhinoceros." Its existence seems, indeed, to have been universally credited in the East; and those Arabian navigators with whom our author conversed would not hestitate to attest a fact of such notoriety; but they might find it convenient, at the same time, to lay the scene of its appearance at a place so little frequented as the southern extremity of Madagascar, because the chances were small of any contradiction from local knowledge. The circumstance, however, of its resorting thither from the southern ocean, gives room to a conjecture that the tale, although exaggerated, may not be altogether imaginary, and that it may have taken its rise from the occasional sight of a real bird of vast, although not miraculous dimensions. This may be either the albatross (*diomedea exulans*), which, although the inhabitant of more southern latitudes, may accidentally visit the shores of Madagascar, or the condor of southern Africa. Some of the former are known to measure no less than fifteen feet between the extremities of the wings, and must appear to those who see them for the first time an extraordinary phenomenon. Of the bulk and powers of the latter bird we are enabled to form an idea from the account given of it by Barrow, in his Travels in South Africa. "Crows, kites, and vultures," he says, "are almost the only kinds of birds that are met with (in the Roggeveld). Of the last, I broke the wing of one of that species called by ornithologists the condor, of an amazingly large size. The spread of its wings was ten feet and one inch. It kept three dogs for some time completely at bay, and having at length seized one of them with its claws, and torn away a large piece of flesh from its thigh, they all immediately retreated." (Vol. i. p. 358, 2d edit.) If the *passi* of the text are intended for the ordinary steps of two feet and a half, the measure given to the wings of the *roc* would be forty feet. In the description of the quill-feathers, the exaggeration is still greater, and those of the albatross or the condor would be diminutive in comparison; but it must be observed that with respect to the specimen said to have been produced by the messengers whom the grand khan had sent to examine into the natural curiosities, as well as the political state of the country, our author expresses himself with caution, and employs the qualifying terms, "si come intesi," and "la qual li fu affermato;" as wishing to it be understood that he did not pretend to have seen the thing himself; but that he believed in the existence of the bird cannot be doubted.

1 "The African wild boar, or *sus Æthiopicus*," says the History of Quadrupeds, "has four tusks: two very large ones proceed from the upper jaw, and turn upwards like a horn; they are nine inches long, and full five inches round at the base; the two other tusks, which come from the lower jaw, project but three inches from the mouth. These tusks the animal makes use of as the dreadful instruments of his vengeance." The tusks of boars, as well as of elephants, must differ considerably in size, according to age and other circumstances: that which was carried to China, and said to weigh fourteen pounds, may have belonged to an uncommon animal of the species.

CHAPTER XXXVII

OF THE ISLAND OF ZENZIBAR

BEYOND the island of Madagascar lies that of Zenzibar, which is reported to be in circuit two thousand miles.[1] The inhabitants worship idols, have their own peculiar language, and do not pay tribute to any foreign power. In their persons they are large, but their height is not proportioned to the bulk of their bodies. Were it otherwise, they would appear gigantic. They are, however, strongly made, and one of them is capable of carrying what would be a load for four of our people. At the same time, he would require as much food as five. They are black, and go naked; covering only the private parts of the body with a cloth.[2] Their hair is so crisp, that even when dipped in water it can with difficulty be drawn out. They have large mouths, their noses turn up towards the forehead, their ears are long, and their eyes so large and frightful, that they have the aspect of demons. The women are equally ill-favoured, having wide mouths, thick noses, and large eyes. Their hands, and also their heads, are out of proportion large.[3] There are in this

[1] The name which in Ramusio's text is Zenzibar, in both of the Latin versions Zanzibar, and in the early epitomes Tangibar, is the Zanguebar of modern geography. This name is applied particularly to a small island near the African shore, and also to a tract of coast within that island, bounded by Melinda on the north, and Cape Dalgada on the south; but it seems probable that those persons from whom our author acquired his information were in the habit of using the term in a more vague sense (like that of Ethiopia), and perhaps of applying it to the whole of the southern coast of Africa, inhabited, generally, by the people whom the Arabs denominate Zengi, and we, Negroes or Caffrees. It may be further conjectured that as the Arabic word *jezireh* signifies equally an island and a peninsula, they may have intended, by what our author has termed the island of Zenzibar, to denote the whole southern extremity, or peninsula, of Africa, the extent of which, from the northern part of what may be called Zanguebar Proper, is just thirty degrees of latitude, or about two thousand miles. In the two Arabians, and other oriental writers, we read the same name given to this tract, with the title of Zingis or Zingues applied generally to all the inhabitants of the eastern coast of Africa. "Le païs des Zinges ou Negres," says the travellers above referred to, "est d'une grande estenduë." (Anc. Relat. p. III.) De Barros also gives the name of Zanguebar an extensive application; nor is it likely, from its import (" the country of the Ethiopians "), to have been originally confined to a small spot.

[2] [The early Latin text adds here a further remark, which we leave in the original language: "Sed cooperiunt suam naturam; et faciunt magnum sensum quando eam cooperiunt, eo quod habent eam multum magnam et turpem, et horribilem ad videndum."]

[3] The reader will judge for himself how far this description of the negro race, which seems to be distorted in passing through the medium of

island the most ill-favoured women in the world; with large mouths and thick noses, and ill-favoured breasts, four times as large as those of other women. They feed on flesh, milk, rice, and dates.[1] They have no grape vines, but make a sort of wine from rice and sugar, with the addition of some spicy drugs, very pleasant to the taste, and having the intoxicating quality of the other. In this island elephants are found in vast numbers, and their teeth form an important article of trade. With respect to these quadrupeds it should be observed, that their mode of copulating is the reverse of that of the brute creation in general, in consequence of the position of the female organ, and follows that of the human species.[2]

In this country is found also the giraffe or camelopard, which is a handsome beast. The body is well-proportioned, the fore-legs long and high, the hind-legs short, the neck very long, the head small, and in its manners it is gentle. Its prevailing colour is light, with circular reddish spots. Its height (or length of the neck), including the head, is three paces.[3] The sheep of the country are different from ours, being all white excepting their heads, which are black;[4] and this also is the colour of the dogs. The animals in general have a different appearance from ours. Many trading ships visit the place, which barter the goods they bring for elephants' teeth and ambergris, of which much is found on the coasts of the island, in consequence of the sea abounding with whales.

Mahometan prejudice, is conformable to his own observation. He must bear in mind, at the same time, that although with respect to the breadth and flatness of the nose, the thickness of the lips, and the woolly texture of the hair, there is a general uniformity, yet in size, figure, intensity of colour, and ferocity of aspect, the natives of one part of Africa differ materially from those of another.

[1] The dates here spoken of were, probably, not those of the genuine kind, produced by the phœnix or *palma dactylifera,* unless imported as an article of food. De Barros, it is true, speaking of the country about Quiloa, says, "Ella he mui fertil de palmeiras;" but this, although the word *palmeira* is translated in the dictionaries, "the date or palm-tree," seems to mean only the *palma sylvestris* of Kæmpfer. This species being named by the Portuguese *palmeira brava,* the wild palm,—or, as pronounced in the corrupt dialect of their eastern colonies, *braba*—has acquired amongst other Europeans the vulgar appellation of the *brab* tree.

[2] All that can be urged in excuse for this unfounded story respecting the mode of copulating amongst these animals is, that the error was ancient and very general, and remained uncontroverted in consequence of the opportunities for disproving it being rare.

[3] The giraffe, or *cervus camelopardalis* of Linnæus, is now well known in England.

[4] "Their sheep," says Hamilton, speaking of the coast of Zeyla, near Cape Guardafui, "are all white, with jet-black heads and small ears, their bodies large, and their flesh delicate, their tails as broad as their buttocks."—Vol. i. p. 15.

The chiefs of the island are sometimes engaged in warfare with each other, and their people display much bravery in battle and contempt of death.[1] They have no horses, but fight upon elephants and camels. Upon the backs of the former they place castles, capable of containing from fifteen to twenty men, armed with swords, lances, and stones, with which weapons they fight.[2] Previously to the combat they give draughts of wine to their elephants, supposing that it renders them more spirited and more furious in the assault.[3]

CHAPTER XXXVIII

OF THE MULTITUDE OF ISLANDS IN THE INDIAN SEA

In treating of the provinces of India, I have described only the principal and most celebrated; and the same has been done with respect to the islands, the number of which is quite incredible. I have heard, indeed, from mariners and eminent pilots of these countries, and have seen in the writings of those who have navigated the Indian seas, that they amount to no fewer than twelve thousand seven hundred, including the

[1] "They have large strong bodies and limbs," says Hamilton, "and are very bold in war."—Vol. i. p. 8.

[2] It is correctly stated that the coast of Africa does not furnish any breed of horses; but although wild elephants abound in the country, there is no reason to believe that the natives are anywhere accustomed, at the present day, to domesticate or employ them in their wars; but that it must formerly have been the case is argued with much ingenuity in the travels of the meritorious and unfortunate Park. "It has been said," he observes, "that the African elephant is of a less docile nature than the Asiatic, and incapable of being tamed. The Negroes certainly do not at present tame them; but when we consider that the Carthaginians had always tame elephants in their armies, and actually transported some of them to Italy in the course of the Punic wars, it seems more likely that they should have possessed the art of taming their own elephants, than have submitted to the expense of bringing such vast animals from Asia." (P. 307.) Notwithstanding this, I am disposed to think that either our author was misinformed as to the fact, or that his remark on the employment of elephants may have been intended to apply to some other country than Zanzibar; Abyssinia, perhaps, or Ceylon.

[3] Bang, an intoxicating juice, expressed from the leaves of hemp, is said to be sometimes given to Indian elephants, for the purpose of rendering them furious and insensible to danger—an expedient that must be attended with no small risk to the party employing it. The Syro-Macedonians appear to have used a different stimulus to produce the same effect: "To the end they might provoke the elephants to fight, they showed them the blood of grapes and mulberries."—1 Macc. vi. 34.

uninhabited with the inhabited islands.[1] The division termed the Greater India extends from Maabar to Kesmacoran, and comprehends thirteen large kingdoms, of which we have enumerated ten. The Lesser India commences at Ziampa, and extends to Murfili, comprehending eight kingdoms, exclusive of those in the islands, which are very numerous. We shall now speak of the Second or Middle India, which is called Abascia.[2]

CHAPTER XXXIX

OF THE SECOND OR MIDDLE INDIA, NAMED ABASCIA (OR ABYSSINIA)

ABASCIA is an extensive country, termed the Middle or Second India. Its principal king is a Christian. Of the others, who are six in number, and tributary to the first, three are Christians and three are Saracens.[3] I was informed that

[1] By this "multitude of islands" in the Indian Sea, is plainly meant the extensive cluster called the Maldives, with the addition of the less numerous cluster called the Laccadives. Should there be an exaggeration in stating their total number at twelve thousand six hundred, not only our author, but also those experienced pilots to whose authority he refers, must stand excused, as it will be shown to have been the general belief throughout India, and in the islands themselves, that the former alone consisted of eleven or twelve thousand, of all descriptions. "Quidam harum insularum numerum," says Linschoten, "and 11,000 ferunt; sed non est certa ratio. Innumerabiles enim sunt."—Cap. xiii. p. 16. [Other old authorities might be cited to the same effect.] In chap. viii. of this book, on the subject of Lochac, supposed to be Kamboja, the following sentence appeared:—"From hence are exported all those porcelain shells, which, being carried to other countries, are there circulated for money." This assertion is strictly and almost exclusively applicable to the Maldive islands, and was intended by our author (as I am fully persuaded) to be introduced at this place.

[2] This division of India into the Greater, the Lesser, and the Middle, does not appear to have reference either to geographical position or relative importance. By the Lesser is here understood what was termed India extra Gangem, or, more strictly, the space included between the eastern coast of the peninsula of India, and that of Kochinchina or Tsiampa. The Greater is made to comprehend the whole of Hindustan Proper and the peninsula, as far westward as the province of Makran, or the country extending from the Ganges to the Indus inclusive. The appellation of Middle or Second India our author applies expressly to Abyssinia, but seems to intend that the coast of Arabia also, as far as the Persian Gulf, should be comprised in this division.

[3] "Uni tamen regi," says Ludolfus, "Habessinia paret: qui ob subjectos quosdam regulos, regem regum Æthiopiæ semet vocat." (Hist. Æthiop. Procem.) "Christianity," says Gibbon, "had raised that nation above the level of African barbarism. Their intercourse with Egypt and the successors of Constantine had communicated the rudiments of the

the Christians of these parts, in order to be distinguished as such, make three signs or marks (on the face), namely, one on the forehead, and one on each cheek, which latter are imprinted with a hot iron—and this may be considered as a second baptism with fire, after the baptism with water. The Saracens have only one mark, which is on the forehead, and reaches to the middle of the nose. The Jews, who are likewise numerous here, have two marks, and these upon the cheeks.

The capital of the principal Christian king is in the interior of the country.[1] The dominions of the Saracen princes lie towards the province of Aden.[2] The conversion of these people to the Christian faith was the work of the glorious apostle, St. Thomas, who having preached the gospel in the kingdom of Nubia, and converted its inhabitants, afterwards visited Abascia, and there, by the influence of his discourses and the performance of miracles, produced the same effect. He subsequently went to abide in the province of Maabar; where, after converting an infinite number of persons, he received, as we have already mentioned, the crown of martyrdom, and was buried on the spot. These people of Abascia are brave and good warriors, being constantly engaged in hostility with the soldan of Aden, the people of Nubia, and many others whose countries border upon theirs. In consequence of this unceasing practice in arms, they are accounted the best soldiers in this part of the world.[3]

arts and sciences; their vessels traded to the island of Ceylon; and seven kingdoms obeyed the Negus or supreme prince of Abyssinia." (Vol. iv. p. 267.) This number must have fluctuated at different periods, and accordingly we find in B. Tellez, Ludolfus, and other writers, enumerations of from fourteen to thirty provinces; which the latter, however, in his History, reduces to nine principal. Dapper gives the names of seven kingdoms, which he considers as forming the dominions of the Abyssinian monarch of his day.—P. 320.

[1] The central situation here alluded to is that of Axuma, or Akshuma, the ancient capital of Abyssinia, and seat of the prince who, by Alvarez, Barbosa, and other early Portuguese writers, is styled Prete Joao, or Prester John, of Ethiopia.

[2] It will appear hereafter more probable that the country here spoken of is intended for Adel, a kingdom adjoining to Abyssinia on the southern side, than for Adem, or Aden, which is divided from it by the Red Sea, or Arabian Gulf. The Basle edition says, more precisely: "Contingit hanc regionem (Abasiam) alia quædam provincia Aden dicta."

[3] For the existence of inveterate enmity and perpetual warfare between the sovereigns of Abyssinia and of Adel (whose principal port is Zeila, on the south-western coast of the Red Sea), we have ample authority; and particularly in the writings of Andrea Corsali, a Florentine, and Francisco Alvarez, a Portuguese, which are to be found in Ramusio, vol. i. fol. 176—260. The reader will apply these historical facts to the conjecture offered in the preceding note, that Adel, not Aden, was meant as the neighbouring state of Abyssinia.

In the year 1288, as I was informed, this great Abyssinian prince adopted the resolution of visiting in person the holy sepulchre of Christ in Jerusalem, a pilgrimage that is every year performed by vast numbers of his subjects; but he was dissuaded from it by the officers of his government, who represented to him the dangers to which he would be exposed in passing through so many places belonging to the Saracens, his enemies. He then determined upon sending thither a bishop as his representative, a man of high reputation for sanctity, who, upon his arrival at Jerusalem, recited the prayers and made the offerings which the king had directed. Returning, however, from that city, through the dominions of the soldan of Aden, the latter caused him to be brought into his presence, and endeavoured to persuade him to become a Mahometan. Upon his refusing with becoming firmness to abandon the Christian faith, the soldan, making light of the resentment of the Abyssinian monarch, caused him to be circumcised, and then suffered him to depart. Upon his arrival, and making a report of the indignity and violence to which he had been subjected, the king immediately gave orders for assembling an army, at the head of which he marched, for the purpose of exterminating the soldan; who on his part called to his assistance two Mahometan princes, his neighbours, by whom he was joined with a very large force. In the conflict that ensued, the Abyssinian king was victorious, and having taken the city of Aden, he gave it up to pillage, in revenge for the insult he had sustained in the person of his bishop.[1]

The inhabitants of this kingdom live upon wheat, rice, flesh, and milk. They extract oil from sesamé, and have abundance of all sorts of provisions. In the country there are elephants, lions, camelopards, and a variety of other animals, such as wild asses, and monkeys that have the figure of men, together with many birds, wild and domestic.[2] It is extremely rich in

[1] Respecting this conquest made by the king of Abyssinia, whether of the capital of the soldan of Adel, on the African shore, or of Aden, on the Arabian side of the Red Sea, there might have been hopes of obtaining some light from Bruce's Annals of that country, and particularly as the second chapter professes to relate transactions from the year 1283 to 1312, embracing the period of which our author speaks; but the information contained in it is of a general nature, and, although it corroborates the accounts of interminable dissensions with Adel, does not record any specific operation.

[2] "The elephant, rhinoceros, giraffa, or camelopardalis, are inhabitants of the low flat country; nor is the lion or leopard, *faadh*, which is the panther, seen in the high and cultivated country. There are no tigers in Abyssinia, nor, as far as I know, in Africa. . . . Innumerable flocks

gold,[1] and much frequented by merchants, who obtain large profits. We shall now speak of the province of Aden.

CHAPTER XL

OF THE PROVINCE OF ADEN[2]

The province of Aden is governed by a king, who bears the title of soldan.[3] The inhabitants are all Saracens, and utterly detest the Christians. In this kingdom there are many towns and castles, and it has the advantage of an excellent port, frequented by ships arriving from India with spices and drugs. The merchants who purchase them with the intention of conveying them to Alexandria, unlade them from the ships in which they were imported, and distribute the cargoes on board of other smaller vessels or barks, with which they navigate a gulf of the sea for twenty days, more or less, according to the weather they experience. Having reached their port, they then load their goods upon the backs of camels, and transport

of apes and baboons, of different kinds, destroy the fields of millet everywhere." (Bruce, vol. v. Appendix, p. 84.) "The number of birds in Abyssinia exceeds that of other animals beyond proportion."—P. 149.

[1] Although gold is enumerated amongst the articles of export from Abyssinia, and is said to be found in its rivers, it is not spoken of by modern writers as abounding in the country; yet, as the adjoining coasts of Africa have at all periods been celebrated for the production of gold, it is reasonable to suppose that, during the flourishing days of the empire, it may have been collected there from the southward, in large quantities, and at a price to afford considerable profit when disposed of to the merchants of Arabia. "On trouve," says Niebuhr, in his description of the latter country, "beaucoup d'or de Habbesch dans les villes bien commerçantes."—P. 124.

[2] Whatever place it may have been, against which the hostility of the king of Abyssinia was directed (as mentioned in the preceding chapter), there can be no doubt of the Aden here described being the famous city and port of Aden, in the south-eastern extremity of Yemen or Arabia Felix, and not far from the entrance of the Red Sea. It is not, indeed, surprising that two places so nearly resembling each other in name (as Adel and Aden), and spoken of in successive chapters, should have been confounded by the translators of the work, and mistaken for the same; nor is it impossible that our author himself might have misapprehended the information he received from the Arabian pilots.

[3] De Guignes, speaking of the princes of the family of Saladin, who reigned at Aden from the year 1180, says: "Après la mort de ce prince, qui a dû arriver vers l'an 637 de l'Hegire, de J. C. 1239, un Turkoman, appellé Noureddin Omar, qui s'étoit emparé de ce pays, envoya demander au khalif Mostanser une patente et l'investiture en qualité de sulthan de l'Yemen, ce qui lui fut accordé." "Cette famille a possédé l'Yemen jusqu'après l'an 800 de l'Hégire, de J. C. 1397." (Tab. Chronol. liv. vii. p. 426.) Consequently, it was one of these sultans or soldans who reigned at the period of which our author treats.

them overland (thirty days' journey) to the river Nile, where they are again put into small vessels, called *jerms*, in which they are conveyed by the stream of that river to Kairo, and from thence, by an artificial canal, named Kalizene, at length to Alexandria.[1] This is the least difficult, and the shortest route the merchants can take with their goods, the produce of India, from Aden to that city. In this port of Aden, likewise, the merchants ship a great number of Arabian horses, which they carry for sale to all the kingdoms and islands of India, obtaining high prices for them, and making large profits.[2]

The soldan of Aden possesses immense treasures, arising from the imposts he lays, as well upon the merchandise that comes from India, as upon that which is shipped in his port as the returning cargo; this being the most considerable mart in all that quarter for the exchange of commodities, and the place to which all trading vessels resort. I was informed that when the soldan of Babylon led his army the first time against the city of Acre, and took it, this city of Aden furnished him with thirty thousand horses and forty thousand camels, stimulated by the rancour borne against the Christians.[3] We shall now speak of the city of Escier.

CHAPTER XLI

OF THE CITY OF ESCIER

The ruler of this city is a Mahometan, who governs it with exemplary justice, under the superior authority of the sultan

[1] A correct account is here given of the progress of what we term the overland trade from India. The merchandise collected at the port of Aden, just without the Red Sea, (as, in modern times, at Mokha, just within it,) was from thence transported in vessels of an easy draft of water (on account of the numerous shoals) to Koseir, a place on the western coast of that sea, to the northward of the ancient station of Berenice. Here it was laden on the backs of camels, and in that manner conveyed across the desert to Kûs, and latterly to Kené, on the Nile, within the territory of Egypt, where it was put into boats correctly called *jerms*, in order to its being carried down the stream of the river to Cairo, and thence by means of the khalij or grand canal, to Alexandria, the emporium of eastern commodities for supplying the markets of Europe.

[2] The exportation of horses from Arabia and the gulf of Persia to India, and particularly the southern provinces, has been already spoken of in former notes.

[3] [It has been already stated that Babylon was the mediæval name of Cairo, in Egypt.]

of Aden. Its distance from thence is about forty miles to the south-east.[1] Subordinate to it there are many towns and castles. Its port is good, and it is visited by many trading ships from India, which carry back a number of excellent horses, highly esteemed in that country, and sold there at considerable prices.

This district produces a large quantity of white frankincense of the first quality,[2] which distils, drop by drop, from a certain small tree that resembles the fir. The people occasionally tap the tree, or pare away the bark, and from the incision the frankincense gradually exudes, which afterwards becomes hard. Even when an incision is not made, an exudation is perceived to take place, in consequence of the excessive heat of the climate. There are also many palm-trees, which produce good dates in abundance. No grain excepting rice and millet is cultivated in this country, and it becomes necessary to obtain supplies from other parts. There is no wine made from grapes; but they prepare a liquor from rice, sugar, and dates, that is a delicious beverage.[3] They have a small breed of sheep, the ears of which are not situated like those in others of the species; two small horns growing in the place of them, and lower down, towards the nose, there are two orifices that serve the purpose of ears.

These people are great fishermen, and catch the tunny in such numbers, that two may be purchased for a Venetian groat. They dry them in the sun;[4] and as, by reason of the extreme heat, the country is in a manner burnt up, and no sort

[1] Although with respect to the bearings of this place from Aden, we must necessarily read north-east for south-east, and the distance is considerably more than forty miles, there is little room for doubt that Escier must be the Schähhr of Niebuhr (or Sheher in our orthography), the Sahar of D'Anville, and the Seer of Ovington's voyage. If pronounced with the Arabic article, Al-sheher, or, more correctly, As-sheher, it would approach still more nearly to the Italian pronunciation of Escier.

[2] "The product of the country," says Hamilton, "is myrrh and olibanum or frankincense, which they barter for coarse calicoes from India; but they have no great commerce with strangers." (Vol. i. p. 55.) The native trade of that part of the world had much declined in his day, from what it was at the period when Barbosa wrote, soon after the Portuguese discovery.

[3] The mode of obtaining a fermented and inebriating liquor from the infusion of dates in warm water, as practised by people inhabiting the coast of the Persian gulf, has been spoken of before. A spirit is also distilled from them.

[4] This part of the coast of Arabia not having been visited by Niebuhr, our information respecting it is not so direct or circumstantial as it would otherwise have been; but the practice of drying fish in the sun (by no means an uncommon one), although unnoticed by him under the head of "Nourriture des Arabes," is sufficiently proved from other authorities.

of vegetable is to be seen, they accustom their cattle, cows, sheep, camels, and horses, to feed upon dried fish, which being regularly served to them, they eat without any signs of dislike. The fish used for this purpose are of a small kind, which they take in vast quantities during the months of March, April, and May; and when dried, they lay up in their houses for the food of their cattle. These will also feed upon the fresh fish, but are more accustomed to eat them in the dried state. In consequence also of the scarcity of grain, the natives make a kind of biscuit of the substance of the larger fish, in the following manner: they chop it into very small particles, and moisten the preparation with a liquor rendered thick and adhesive by a mixture of flour, which gives to the whole the consistence of paste. This they form into a kind of bread, which they dry and harden by exposure to a burning sun. A stock of this biscuit is laid up to serve them for the year's consumption. The frankincense before mentioned is so cheap in the country as to be purchased by the governor at the rate of ten besants (gold ducats) the quintal, who sells it again to the merchants at forty besants. This he does under the direction of the soldan of Aden,[1] who monopolises all that is produced in the district at the above price, and derives a large profit from the re-sale. Nothing further presenting itself at this place, we shall now speak of the city of Dulfar.

CHAPTER XLII

OF THE CITY OF DULFAR

DULFAR is a large and respectable city or town, at the distance of twenty miles from Escier, in a south-easterly direction.[2] Its inhabitants are Mahometans, and its ruler also is a subject

[1] The importance of Aden with respect to the neighbouring countries has changed considerably at different periods. In our author's time, and afterwards under the Turkish government, its influence extended to Sheher, Keschîn, and other places on the southern coast of Yemen and that of Hadramaut. In the seventeenth century, Aden was subordinate to the Imâm of Yemen or of Mokha. In later times it has been independent and insignificant.

[2] The Dulfar of our text is the Dafâr of Niebuhr and of our charts. Its direction from the last-mentioned place, conformably to that of the coast in general, is about north-east, and its distance considerably greater than what is here stated.

of the soldan of Aden.[1] This place lies near the sea, and has a good port, frequented by many ships. Numbers of Arabian horses are collected here from the inland country, which the merchants buy up and carry to India, where they gain considerably by disposing of them. Frankincense is likewise produced here, and purchased by the merchants. Dulfar has other towns and castles under its jurisdiction. We shall now speak of the gulf at Kalayati.

CHAPTER XLIII

OF THE CITY OF KALAYATI

KALAYATI is a large town situated near a gulf which has the name of Kalatu, distant from Dulfar about fifty miles towards the south-east.[2] The people are followers of the law of Mahomet, and are subjects to the melik of Ormus,[3] who, when he is attacked and hard pressed by another power, has recourse to the protection afforded by this city, which is so strong in itself, and so advantageously situated, that it has never yet been taken by an enemy.[4] The country around it not yielding any kind of grain, it is imported from other districts. Its harbour is good, and many trading ships arrive there from India, which sell their piece-goods and spiceries to great advantage, the demand being considerable for the supply of towns and castles lying at a distance from the coast.[5] These likewise

[1] This town has in like manner shaken off the yoke of successive masters. "Dafâr," says the former writer, "a son Schech indépendant." (P. 248.) "The king of this place," Ovington adds, "engages now and then in skirmishes and martial disputes with his neighbouring princes, the kings of Seer (Escier or Sheher) and Casseen (Keschîn)."—P. 452.

[2] Kalayati is obviously Kalhât, on the coast of Omân, not far to the southward of Maskát or Muscat. In D'Anville map, the name is written "Kalhat ou Kalajate." Niebuhr (p. 257) speaks of it as one of the most ancient towns on that coast. The distance and bearings in the text are, as too often happens, quite incorrect.

[3] The title of melik properly signifies "king," but is often applied to tributary princes and governors of provinces. The sultan or melik of Ormuz (noticed in B. i. ch. xv.) acknowledged himself to be tributary to, although he was often at war with, the king of Kirman.

[4] The name of Kalhat has so near an affinity to kalàt, a castle or fortress, especially on the top of a rock, that we may consider this place as having derived its appellation from the circumstance, and to have been called (like many others in different parts) *the* castle, pre-eminently.

[5] From this account of the goodness of the harbour (an advantage that Kalhat itself is not supposed to possess), we may conjecture that the description was meant to include the celebrated port of Muskat, in its neighbourhood, and probably at that time under its dependence; which,

carry away freights of horses, which they sell advantageously in India.

The fortress is so situated at the entrance of the gulf of Kalatu, that no vessel can come in or depart without its permission. Occasionally it happens that the melik of this city, who is under certain engagements with, and is tributary to the king of Kermain, throws off his allegiance in consequence of the latter's imposing some unusual contribution. Upon his refusing to pay the demand, and an army being sent to compel him, he departs from Ormus, and makes his stand at Kalayati, where he has it in his power to prevent any ship from entering or sailing. By this obstruction of the trade the king of Kermain is deprived of his duties, and being thereby much injured in his revenue, is constrained to accommodate the dispute with the melik. The strong castle at this place constitutes, as it were, the key, not only of the gulf, but also of the sea itself, as from thence the ships that pass can at all times be discovered.[1] The inhabitants in general of this country subsist upon dates and upon fish, either fresh or salted, having constantly a large supply of both;[2] but persons of rank, and those who can afford it, obtain corn for their use from other parts. Upon leaving Kalayati, and proceeding three hundred miles towards the north-east, you reach the island of Ormus.

CHAPTER XLIV

OF ORMUS

UPON the island of Ormus there is a handsome and large city, built close to the sea.[3] It is governed by a melik, which is

being situated at the bottom of a bay or cove, our author terms the gulf of Kalatu.

[1] By this must be understood that its prominent situation, affording shelter to vessels equipped for cruising, and enabling its garrison to discern those which approached the coast, whilst it was itself secure from attack, gave the prince who possessed it the command of those seas, as well as of the great commercial port in its vicinity. That it is usual for ships to make this point is evident from Niebuhr's journal of his voyage from Bombay to Maskát. The kind of petty warfare spoken of in the text has always subsisted, and still subsists, in this quarter.

[2] "The staple commodity of the country," says Ovington, "is dates, of which there are whole orchards for some miles together." "The dates are so plentiful, so pleasant and admired, that they mix them with all their other food, and eat them instead of bread, through all these parts of Arabia, both with their fish and flesh."—Voyage to Surat, Pp. 423—427.

[3] The city of Ormuz having been already described in B. i. ch. xv.,

a title equivalent to that of lord of the marches with us, and he has many towns and castles under his authority. The inhabitants are Saracens, all of them professing the faith of Mahomet. The heat that reigns here is extreme; but in every house they are provided with ventilators, by means of which they introduce air to the different floors, and into every apartment, at pleasure. Without this resource it would be impossible to live in the place.[1] We shall not now say more of this city, as in a former book we have given an account of it, together with Kisi and Kerman.[2]

Having thus treated sufficiently at length of those provinces and cities of the Greater India which are situated near the sea-coast, as well as of some of the countries of Ethiopia, termed the Middle India, I shall now, before I bring the work to a conclusion, step back, in order to notice some regions lying towards the north, which I omitted to speak of in the preceding books.

It should be known, therefore, that in the northern parts of the world there dwell many Tartars, under a chief of the name of Kaidu, who is of the race of Jengiz-khan, and nearly related to Kublaï, the grand khan.[3] He is not the subject of any other

what is here said of it is little more than a repetition: but although this may be regarded as exposing a want of method or a confusion in the plan of the work, it is on the other hand a proof of its genuineness, and even of its consistency; for it may be perceived that this distinguished city, at which our author seems to have made some stay, constitutes a sort of resting-place in his description, from whence he had proceeded to trace the several inland countries and principal towns, intermediate between the shores of the Persian gulf and the empire of China, and to which, in a circuit through the Chinese, Indian, Ethiopic, and Arabian seas, he finally conducts his readers.

[1] "Comme pendant le solstice d'Eté, le soleil est presque perpendiculairement au dessus de l'Arabie, il y fait en général si chaud en Juillet et en Août, que sans un cas de nécessité pressante, personne ne se met en route depuis les 11 heures du matin jusques à 3 heures de l'après-midi. Les Arabes travaillent rarement pendant ce temps-là; pour l'ordinaire ils l'employent à dormir dans un souterrain où le vent vient d'enhaut par un tuyau pour faire circuler l'air: ce que se pratique à Bagdad, dans l'isle de Charedsj, et peut-être en d'autres villes de ce pays." (Descript. de l'Arabie. p. 6.) "Mr. Callander," says Major Rennell, "described to me the ventilators used at Tatta in Sindi, which were pipes or tubes fixed in the walls, and open to somewhat cooler air, answering the same purpose as wind-sails in ships." The notice of this peculiar mode of introducing fresh air to the lower apartments of the houses, will be deemed no common proof of our author's fidelity of observation. On the subject of these ventilators, see also Relation de l'Egypte par Abd-allatif, traduit par Silvestre de Sacy, pp. 295, 301.

[2] Respecting Kisi or Kîs, an island of the Persian gulf, to which the commerce of Sîraf was transferred, see note [2], p. 43; and on the subject of the kingdom or province of Kerman or Kirmân, note [1], p. 56.

[3] In the first chapter of book ii. we were furnished with a detailed

prince.[1] The people observe the usages and manners of their ancestors, and are regarded as genuine Tartars. These Tartars are idolaters, and worship a god whom they call Naagai, that is, the god of earth, because they think and believe that this their god has dominion over the earth, and over all things that are born of it; and to this their false god they make idols and images of felt, as is described in a former book. Their king and his armies do not shut themselves up in castles or strong places, nor even in towns; but at all times remain in the open plains, the valleys, or the woods, with which this region abounds. They have no corn of any kind, but subsist upon flesh and milk, and live amongst each other in perfect harmony; their king, to whom they all pay implicit obedience, having no object dearer to him than that of preserving peace and union amongst his subjects, which is the essential duty of a sovereign. They possess vast herds of horses, cows, sheep, and other domestic animals. In these northern districts are found bears of a white colour, and of prodigious size, being for the most part about twenty spans in length.[2] There are foxes also whose

account of the formidable rebellion which Nayan, in concert with Kaidu, another powerful Tartar prince, raised against Kublaï, their kinsman as well as their paramount lord, and of its suppression by the defeat of the combined princes and the death of the former. To that chapter the reader is referred. It appears, however, from the Chinese historians, that Kaidu (by them named Haitu, consistently with the usual change of literal sounds) was not driven to submission by this failure, but continued in a state of hostility, more or less active, during the remainder of Kublaï's reign, and a part of that of his grandson and successor Timur-khan, when his (Kaidu's) army being entirely routed on the banks of the Irtish, he relinquished the struggle, and died soon after of vexation and despair.

[1] When our author left the court of Pekin, about the year 1291, Kaidu, however nominally the vassal of Kublaï, was actually independent, and, notwithstanding some checks, was still a powerful prince. It would seem that, from the period of the latter's effecting the entire conquest of China—and instead of holding it as a province, placing himself on the throne, and identifying himself with its line of monarchs—the other princes of the family of Jengiz-khan considered him as having virtually abandoned the Mungal-Tartar empire, founded by their common ancestor, and assumed, or attempted to assume, as sovereignties, those vast dominions which they held only as fiefs. Such will appear to have been the state of things in Persia, and in Western as well as in Northern Tartary.

[2] "The polar or great white bear, *ursus albus*, Lin., differs greatly," says the History of Quadrupeds, "from the common bear, in the length of the head and neck, and grows to above twice the size. Some of them are thirteen feet long." The Italian dictionaries leave us in an uncertainty with regard to the measure expressed by the word "palmo," some of them rendering it by the French "empan," a span, and others by "pied," a foot. According to the former acceptation (which is more consistent with propriety), and reckoning the span of a middle-sized man

furs are entirely black,[1] wild asses in great numbers, and certain small animals named rondes, which have most delicate furs, and by our people are called zibelines or sables.[2] Besides these there are various small beasts of the marten or weasel kind, and those which bear the name of Pharaoh's mice. The swarms of the latter are incredible; but the Tartars employ such ingenious contrivances for catching them, that none can escape their hands.

In order to reach the country inhabited by these people, it is necessary to perform a journey of fourteen days across a wide plain, entirely uninhabited and desert—a state that is occasioned by innumerable collections of water and springs, that render it an entire marsh.[3] This, in consequence of the long duration of the cold season, is frozen over, excepting for a few months of the year, when the sun dissolves the ice, and turns the soil to mud, over which it is more difficult and fatiguing to travel than when the whole is frozen. For the purpose, however, of enabling the merchants to frequent their country, and purchase their furs, in which all their trade consists, these people have exerted themselves to render the marshy desert passable for travellers, by erecting at the end of each day's stage a wooden house, raised some height above the ground, where persons are stationed, whose business it is to receive and accommodate the merchants, and on the following day to conduct them to the next station of this kind; and thus they pro-

at eight inches, the two measurements would coincide within a trifle, twenty spans being equal to thirteen feet and four inches.

[1] "The black fox," says the same work, "is most valuable for its fur, which is esteemed in Russia superior to that of the finest sable. A single skin will sell for four hundred roubles." "Their fur," says Bell, "is reckoned the most beautiful of any kind; it is even preferred to the sable, with respect to lightness and warmness."—Vol. i. p. 222.

[2] "The sable, *mustela zibellina*, Lin., so highly esteemed for its skin, is a native of the snowy regions of the North; it is found chiefly in Siberia. . . . The darkest furs are the most valuable. A single skin, though not above four inches broad, is sometimes valued as high as fifteen pounds. The sable differs from all other furs in this, that the hair turns with equal ease to either side." (Hist. of Quadrupeds.) The name of *rondes*, supposed to be a Mungal word, had already occurred in B. ii. chap. xvi., but was not there explained to mean the sable. (See note [2], p. 199.)

[3] It will be seen, by inspection of the map, that a number of great rivers, which discharge themselves towards the north and the east, have their sources in the high plains between the latitudes of 45° and 55°, the original haunts of these wandering hordes; and where, consequently, we may look for a country of waters such as our text describes. "Baraba (between the Irtish and the Oby) is really what its name signifies, an extensive marshy plain. It is generally full of lakes and marshy grounds, overgrown with tall woods of aspen, alder, willows, and other aquatics." —Bell's Travels, vol. i. p. 205.

ceed from stage to stage, until they have effected the passage of the desert.[1] In order to travel over the frozen surface of the ground, they construct a sort of vehicle, not unlike that made use of by the natives of the steep and almost inaccessible mountains in the vicinity of our own country, and which is termed a *tragula* or sledge. It is without wheels, is flat at bottom, but rises with a semicircular curve in front, by which construction it is fitted for running easily upon the ice.[2] For drawing these small carriages they keep in readiness certain animals resembling dogs, and which may be called such, although they approach to the size of asses. They are very strong and inured to the draught.[3] Six of them, in couples, are harnessed to each carriage, which contains only the driver who manages the dogs, and one merchant, with his package of goods.[4] When the day's journey has been performed he quits it, together with that set of dogs, and thus changing both, from day to day, he at length accomplishes his journey across the desert, and afterwards carries with him (in his return) the furs that find their way, for sale, to our part of the world.

[1] These halting places, however insignificant in respect to buildings or inhabitants, are such as in the language of the Russians, whose empire embraces the country here described, would be termed *ostrogs* or villages, and the houses answer to those which travellers to and from Kamchatka name *balagan*, rather than to the *isba* or log-house.

[2] "The body of the sledges," says Captain King, "is about four feet and a half long, and a foot wide, made in the form of a crescent, of light tough wood, strongly bound together with wicker-work. . . . It is supported by four legs, about two feet high, which rest on two long flat pieces of wood, five or six inches broad, extending a foot at each end beyond the body of the sledge. These are turned up before, in the manner of a skate, and shod with the bone of some sea animal."—Cook's third Voyage, Continuation, vol. iii. p. 202.

[3] It is now well known that dogs are employed for the purposes of draught in the north-eastern parts of Tartary. In respect to their size, indeed, there appears to be some exaggeration, although it is possible that in the course of five hundred years the breed may have degenerated. "These dogs," says Captain King, "are in shape somewhat like the Pomeranian breed, but considerably larger." (P. 204.)

[4] "The sledges," says the Captain, "are seldom used to carry more than one person at a time, who sits aside, resting his feet on the lower part of the sledge and carrying his provisions and other necessaries wrapped up in a bundle behind him. The dogs are usually five in number, yoked two and two, with a leader." "As we did not choose to trust to our own skill, we had each of us a man to drive and guide the sledge, which, from the state the roads were now in, proved a very laborious business . . . as the thaw had advanced very considerably." (Pp. 203—205.) "The number of dogs that it is necessary to harness," says Lesseps, "depends upon the load; when it is little more than the weight of the person who mounts the sledge . . . the team consists of four or five dogs. . . . The sledges for baggage are drawn by ten dogs."—P. 118.

CHAPTER XLV

OF THOSE COUNTRIES WHICH ARE TERMED THE REGION OF DARKNESS

BEYOND the most distant part of the territory of those Tartars from whence the skins that have been spoken of are procured, there is another region which extends to the utmost bounds of the north, and is called the Region of Darkness, because during most part of the winter months the sun is invisible, and the atmosphere is obscured to the same degree as that in which we find it just about the dawn of day, when we may be said to see and not to see.[1] The men of this country are well made and tall, but of a very pallid complexion. They are not united under the government of a king or prince, and they live without any established laws or usages, in the manner of the brute creation. Their intellects also are dull, and they have an air of stupidity.[2] The Tartars often proceed on plundering expeditions against these people, to rob them of their cattle and goods. For this purpose they avail themselves of those months in which the darkness prevails, in order that their approach may be unobserved; but, being unable to ascertain

[1] This is a correct description of the phenomena observed about the arctic circle and polar regions, where, during the winter, or season when the sun is below the horizon during the whole of the earth's diurnal revolution, the strength of the twilight prevents, notwithstanding, an entire darkness.

[2] The people here mentioned appear to be the Tongusi, or their neighbours the Samoyeds, on the one side, or, on the other, the Yakûts, who inhabit the country near the river Lena. "The Tongusy," says Bell, "so called from the name of the river (Tonguska), who live along its banks, are the posterity of the ancient inhabitants of Siberia, and differ in language, manners, and dress, and even in their persons and stature, from all the other tribes of these people I have had occasion to see. They have no houses where they remain for any time, but range through the woods or along rivers at pleasure." "The men are tall and able-bodied, brave, and very honest." (Vol. i. p. 225.) "It is to be observed, that, from this river northward to the frozen ocean, there are no inhabitants, except a few Tongusians on the banks of the great rivers; the whole of this most extensive country being overgrown with dark impenetrable woods." (P. 231.) "Before I leave Elimsky," says the same traveller, "I shall give a short account of some of the places adjacent; particularly those to the north-east, towards the river Lena, and Yakutsky, according as I have been informed by travellers, on whose veracity I could entirely depend. The people who travel in winter from hence to these places, generally do it in January or February. It is a very long and difficult journey; and which none but Tongusians, or such hardy people, have abilities to perform." (P. 234.) "The Yakuty differ little from the Tongusians, either in their persons or way of life. Their occupation, like that of the other natives, is fishing and hunting."—P. 240.

the direction in which they should return homeward with their booty, they provide against the chance of going astray by riding mares that have young foals at the time, which latter they suffer to accompany the dams as far as the confines of their own territory, but leave them, under proper care, at the commencement of the gloomy region. When their works of darkness have been accomplished, and they are desirous of revisiting the region of light, they lay the bridles on the necks of their mares, and suffer them freely to take their own course. Guided by maternal instinct, they make their way directly to the spot where they had quitted their foals; and by these means the riders are enabled to regain in safety the places of their residence.

The inhabitants of this (polar) region take advantage of the summer season, when they enjoy continual daylight, to catch vast multitudes of ermines, martens, arcolini,[1] foxes, and other animals of that kind, the furs of which are more delicate, and consequently more valuable, than those found in the districts inhabited by the Tartars, who, on that account, are induced to undertake the plundering expeditions that have been described.[2] During the summer, also, these people carry their furs to the neighbouring countries, where they dispose of them in a manner highly advantageous; and, according to what I have been told, some of them are transported even as far as to the country of Russia;[3] of which we shall proceed to speak in this the concluding part of our work.

[1] The names of the animals which, in Ramusio's text, follow "armellini," or ermines, are, "vari, arcolini." The former of these are the "vares seu varii" of the Latin glossaries, and the French "vairs," denoting a species of marten or weasel, of a whitish grey colour. The latter, which in the Basle edition are "herculini," and "erculini," I am unable to trace either in dictionaries or books of natural history; but in the copious list of furs enumerated by Professor Pallas, as constituting a principal part of the Chinese trade with the Russians on the borders, mention is made of the skin of a small animal named by the Germans, *vielfrass*, by the French, *goulu* or *glouton*, and by the Italians, *arcigoloso*; which later word may perhaps have been corrupted to *arcolino*. Bell notices the same animal in the Mungal country.

[2] It is well known to those who deal in furs, that the richest are procured from the coldest climates; agreeably to the usual economy of nature.

[3] It is probable that at the period when Siberia was independent, the furs intended for the European market were all conveyed to a place named Verchaturia, on the Russian side of Tobolsky, and near the chain of mountains called Verchatursky-gori. "These mountains," says Bell, "divide Russia from Siberia. They run in a ridge from north to south." "What makes Verchaturia considerable, is its being a frontier town, and commanding the only entry from Russia into Siberia."—Vol. i. p. 172.

CHAPTER XLVI

OF THE PROVINCE OF RUSSIA[1]

THE province of Russia is of vast extent, is divided into many parts, and borders upon that northern tract which has been described as the Region of Darkness.[2] Its inhabitants are Christians, and follow the Greek ritual in the offices of their Church. The men are extremely well-favoured, tall, and of fair complexions; the women are also fair and of a good size, with light hair, which they are accustomed to wear long. The country pays tribute to the king of the Western Tartars, with whose dominions it comes in contact on its eastern border.[3] Within it are collected in great abundance the furs of ermines, arcolini, sables, martens, foxes, and other animals of that tribe, together with much wax.[4] It contains several mines, from whence a large quantity of silver is procured.[5] Russia is an exceedingly cold region, and I have been assured that it extends even as far as the Northern Ocean, where, as has been mentioned in a preceding part of the work, jerfalcons and peregrine falcons are taken in vast numbers, and from thence are carried to various parts of the world.

[1] Russia is here termed a province, because it had been overrun and subdued, together with a considerable portion of the kingdoms of Poland and Hungary, by the Tartars, under the command of Batu, the grandson of Jengiz-khan, about the year 1240, and continued till the time when our author wrote, and for many years after, to groan under the yoke of these barbarians.

[2] This applies directly to the country of the Samoyeds, who, as Pinkerton observes, " first appear beyond the river Mezan, about three hundred miles to the east of Archangel, and extend to the Straits of Weygatz, far within the polar circle.

[3] By Western Tartars are here meant the subjects of Batu and his descendants, who inherited as his portion of the dominions of Jengiz-khan, the countries of " Kapchak, Allan, Russ, and Bulgar." As distinguished from these, the denomination of Eastern Tartars is elsewhere applied to the followers of Hulagu and his descendants, who settled in Khorasan and Persia.

[4] The number of wild animals, whose furs constitute articles of trade, was of course much greater in Russia when the country was less populous and cultivated than it is at present. The most numerous, as well as the most valuable of the furs now exported, are the produce of her Siberian territories, and are partly collected as tribute or revenue; but even before the discovery and conquest of that country, they were procured at a moderate price, by barter on the frontier. Wax is exported in large quantities, and chiefly to England.

[5] It does not appear in any modern account of the country, that silver mines are now worked in European Russia; but such may have formerly existed and been exhausted. In the Siberian provinces both gold and silver are found. [Ibn Batuta mentions the silver mines of Russia.]

CHAPTER XLVII[1]

OF GREAT TURKEY

IN Great Turkey there is a king called Kaidu, who is the nephew of the grand khan, for he was son of the son of Ciagatai, who was brother to the grand khan.[2] He possesses many cities and castles, and is a very great lord. He is Tartar, and his men also are Tartar, and they are good warriors, which is no wonder, for they are all men brought up to war; and I tell you that this Kaidu never gave obedience to the grand khan, without first making great war. And you must know that this Great Turkey lies to the north-west when we leave Ormus, by the way already mentioned. Great Turkey is beyond the river Ion,[3] and stretches out northward to the territory of the grand khan. This Kaidu has already fought many battles with the people of the grand khan, and I will relate to you how he came to quarrel with him. You must know for a truth that Kaidu sent word one day to the grand khan that he wanted his part of what they had obtained by conquest, claiming a part of the province of Cathay and of that of Manji. The grand khan told him that he was quite willing to give him his share, as he had done to his other sons, if he, on his part, would repair to his court and attend his council as often as he sent for him; and the grand khan willed further, that he should obey him like the others his sons and his barons; and on this condition the grand khan said that he would give him part of their conquest (of China). Kaidu, who distrusted his uncle the grand khan, rejected this condition, saying that he was willing to yield him obedience in his own country, but that he would not go to his court for any consideration, as he feared lest he should be put to death. Thus originated the quarrel between the grand khan and Kaidu, which led to a great war, and there were many great battles between them. And the grand khan posted an army round the kingdom of Kaidu, to prevent him or his people from committing any injury to his territory or people. But, in spite of all

[1] This, and the following chapters, to chapter 63, come in the original text between the middle of chapter 44 of Marsden's translation and his 45th chapter; but they had been omitted in the texts from which Marsden translated.

[2] In illustration of the historical matters contained in these supplementary chapters, the reader is referred to the text and notes in pages 27 to 30 of the present volume.

[3] The river Gihon; the *Oxus* of the ancients.

these precautions of the grand khan, Kaidu invaded his territory, and fought many times with the forces sent to oppose him. Now king Kaidu, by exerting himself, could bring into the field a hundred thousand horsemen, all good men, and well trained to war and battle. And moreover he has with him many barons of the lineage of the emperor, that is of Jengis-khan, who was the founder of the empire. We will now proceed to narrate certain battles between Kaidu and the grand khan's people; but first we will describe their mode of fighting. When they go to war, each is obliged to carry with him sixty arrows, thirty of which are of a smaller size, intended for shooting at a distance, but the other thirty are larger, and have a broad blade; these they use near at hand, and strike their enemies in the faces and arms, and cut the strings of their bows, and do great damage with them. And when they have discharged all their arrows, they take their swords and maces, and give one another heavy blows with them.

In the year 1266, this king Kaidu, with his cousins, one of whom was called Jesudar, assembled a vast number of people, and attacked two of the grand khan's barons, who also were cousins of king Kaidu, though they held their lands of the grand khan. One of these was named Tabai or Ciban. They were sons of Ciagatai, who had received Christian baptism, and was own brother to the grand khan Kublaï. Well, Kaidu with his people fought with these his two cousins, who also had a great army, for on both sides there were about a hundred thousand horsemen. They fought very hard together, and there were many slain on both sides; but at last king Kaidu gained the victory, and did great damage to the others. But the two brothers, the cousins of king Kaidu, escaped without hurt, for they had good horses, which bore them away with great swiftness. Having thus gained the victory, Kaidu's pride and arrogance increased; and he returned into his own country, where he remained full two years in peace, without any hostilities between him and the grand khan. But at the end of two years Kaidu again assembled a great army. He knew that the grand khan's son, named Nomogan, was at Caracorum, and that with him was George the grandson of Prester John, which two barons had also a very great army of horsemen. King Kaidu, having assembled his host, marched from his own country, and, without any occurrence worth mentioning, arrived in the neighbourhood of Caracorum, where the two barons, the son of the grand khan and the grandson of Prester John, were with their army. The latter, instead of being frightened, prepared to meet them with the utmost ardour and courage; and having assembled their whole army, which consisted of not less than sixty thousand horsemen, they marched out and established their camp very well and orderly at a distance of about ten miles from king Kaidu, who was encamped with his men in the same plain. Each party remained in their camp till the third day, preparing for battle in the best way they could, for their numbers were about equal, neither exceeding sixty thousand horsemen, well armed with bows and arrows, and a sword, mace, and shield to each. Both armies were divided into six squadrons of ten thousand men each, and each having its commander. And when the two armies were drawn up in the field, and waited only for the signal to be given by sounding the nacar,[1] they sang and sounded their instruments of music in such a manner that it was wonderful to hear. For the Tartars are not allowed to commence a battle till they hear the nacars of their lord begin to sound, but the moment it sounds they begin to fight; and it is their custom, while thus waiting the signal of battle, to sing and sound their two-corded instruments very sweetly, and make great solace. As soon as the sound of the nacars was heard, the battle began, and they put their hands to their bows, and placed the arrows to the strings. In an instant the air was filled with arrows like rain, and you might see many a man and many a horse struck down dead, and the shouting and the noise of the battle was so great, that one could hardly have heard God's thunder. In truth, they fought like mortal enemies. And truly, as long as they had any arrows left, those who were able ceased not to shoot; but so many were slain and mortally wounded, that the battle commenced propitiously for neither party. And when they had exhausted their arrows, they placed the bows in their cases, and seized their swords and maces, and, rushing upon each other, began to give terrible blows with them. Thus they began a very fierce and dreadful battle, with such execution upon each other, that the ground was soon covered with corpses. Kaidu especially performed great feats of arms, and but for his personal prowess, which restored courage to his followers, they were several times nearly defeated. And on the other side, the son of the grand khan and the grandson of Prester John also behaved themselves with great bravery. In a word, this

[1] The nacar, or nacaire, was a kind of drum, or a cymbal, used in the east for warlike music, and not unknown in the west.

was one of the most sanguinary battles that had ever taken place among the Tartars; for it lasted till nightfall; and in spite of all their efforts, neither party could drive the other from the field, which was covered with so many corpses that it was pity to see, and many a lady that day was made a widow, and many a child an orphan. And when the sun set, both parties gave over fighting, and returned to their several camps to repose during the night. Next morning, king Kaidu, who had received information that the grand khan had sent a very powerful army against him, put his men under arms at daybreak, and, all having mounted, he ordered them to proceed homewards. Their opponents were so weary with the previous day's battle, that they made no attempt to follow them, but let them go without molestation. Kaidu's men continued their retreat, until they came to Samarcand, in Great Turkey.

CHAPTER XLVIII

WHAT THE GRAND KHAN SAID OF THE INJURIES DONE TO HIM BY KAIDU

Now the grand khan was greatly enraged against Kaidu, who was always doing so much injury to his people and his territory, and he said in himself, that if he had not been his nephew, he should not have escaped an evil death. But his feelings of relationship hindered him from destroying him and his land; and thus Kaidu escaped from the hands of the grand khan. We will now leave this matter, and we will tell you a strange history of king Kaidu's daughter.

CHAPTER XLIX

OF THE DAUGHTER OF KING KAIDU, HOW STRONG AND VALIANT SHE WAS

YOU must know, then, that king Kaidu had a daughter named, in the Tartar language, Aigiarm,[1] which means shining moon. This damsel was so strong, that there was no young man in the

[1] In the Latin text published by the Society of Geography of Paris, the lady's name is written Argialcucor, or Argialchucor. In the Italian it is Aigiarne.

whole kingdom who could overcome her, but she vanquished them all. Her father the king wished to marry her; but she declined, saying, that she would never take a husband till she met with some gentleman who should conquer her by force, upon which the king, her father, gave her a written promise that she might marry at her own will. She now caused it to be proclaimed in different parts of the world, that if any young man would come and try strength with her, and should overcome her by force, she would accept him for her husband. This proclamation was no sooner made, than many came from all parts to try their fortune. The trial was made with great solemnity. The king took his place in the principal hall of the palace, with a large company of men and women; then came the king's daughter, in a dress of cendal, very richly adorned, into the middle of the hall; and next came the young man, also in a dress of cendal. The agreement was, that if the young man overcame her so as to throw her by force to the ground, he was to have her for wife; but if, on the contrary, he should be overcome by the king's daughter, he was to forfeit to her a hundred horses. In this manner the damsel gained more than ten thousand horses, for she could meet with no one able to conquer her, which was no wonder, for she was so well-made in all her limbs, and so tall and strongly built, that she might almost be taken for a giantess. At last, about the year 1280, there came the son of a rich king, who was very beautiful and young; he was accompanied with a very fine retinue, and brought with him a thousand beautiful horses. Immediately on his arrival, he announced that he was come to try his strengh with the lady. King Kaidu received him very gladly, for he was very desirous to have this youth for his son-in-law, knowing him to be the son of the king of Pamar;[1] on which account, Kaidu privately told his daughter that he wished her on this occasion to let herself be vanquished. But she said she would not do so for anything in the world. Thereupon the king and queen took their places in the hall, with a great attendance of both sexes, and the king's daughter presented herself as usual, and also the king's son, who was remarkable no less for his beauty than for his great strength. Now when they were brought into the hall, it was, on account of the superior rank of the claimant, agreed as the conditions of the trial, that if the young prince were conquered, he should forfeit the thousand

[1] This name, omitted in the French, is taken from the Italian text. In one Italian MS. it is Pumar.

horses he had brought with him as his stake. This agreement having been made, the wrestling began; and all who were there, including the king and queen, wished heartily that the prince might be the victor, that he might be the husband of the princess. But, contrary to their hopes, after much pulling and tugging, the king's daughter gained the victory, and the young prince was thrown on the pavement of the palace, and lost his thousand horses. There was not one person in the whole hall who did not lament his defeat. After this the king took his daughter with him into many battles, and not a cavalier in the host displayed so much valour; and at last the damsel rushed into the midst of the enemy, and seizing upon a horseman, carried him off to her own people. We will now quit this episode, and proceed to relate a great battle which fell out between Kaidu and Argon, the son of Abaga the lord of the east.[1]

CHAPTER L

HOW ABAGA SENT ARGON HIS SON WITH AN ARMY

Now Abaga, the lord of the east, held many provinces and many lands, which bordered on the territory of king Kaidu, on the side towards the tree which is called in the book of Alexander,[2] *Arbor Secco*. And Abaga, in consequence of the damages done to his lands by king Kaidu, sent his son Argon with a very great number of horsemen into the country of the Arbor Secco, as far as the river Ion, where they remained to protect the country against king Kaidu's people. In this manner Argon and his men remained in the plain of the Arbor Secco, and garrisoned many cities and castles thereabouts. Thereupon king Kaidu assembled a great number of horsemen, and gave the command of them to his brother Barac, a prudent and brave man, with orders to fight Argon. Barac promised to fulfil his commandment, and to do his best against Argon and his army; and he marched with his army, which was a very numerous one, and proceeded for many days

[1] Of the Eastern Tartars, *i.e.* of Persia and Khorasan. See Note [1], p. 12.

[2] The book of the wonders seen by Alexander in his eastern conquests, pretended to have been written by Aristote, was a very favourite book in the Middle Ages, and was the foundation of many popular notions of geography, as well as of natural history. On the *arbor secco*, see p. 72 of the present volume.

without meeting with any accident worth mentioning, till he reached the river Ion, where he was only ten miles distant from the army of Argon. Both sides immediately prepared for battle, and in a very fierce engagement, which took place three days afterwards, the army of Barac was overpowered, and pursued with great slaughter over the river.

CHAPTER LI

HOW ARGON SUCCEEDED HIS FATHER IN THE SOVEREIGNTY

SOON after this victory, Argon received intelligence that his father Abaga was dead, for which he was very sorrowful, and he set out with all his host on his way to his father's court, a distance of forty days' journey, in order to receive the sovereignty. Now Abaga had a brother named Acomat Soldan, who had become a Saracen, and who no sooner heard of his brother Abaga's death, than he formed the design of seizing the succession for himself, considering that Argon was at too great a distance to prevent him. He therefore collected a powerful army, went direct to the court of his brother Abaga, and seized upon the sovereignty. There he found such an immense quantity of treasure as could hardly be believed, and by distributing this very lavishly among Abaga's barons and knights, he gained so far upon their hearts, that they declared they would have no other lord but him. Moreover, Acomat Soldan showed himself a very good lord, and made himself beloved by everybody. But he had not long enjoyed his usurped power, when news came that Argon was approaching with a very great host. Acomat showed no alarm, but courageously summoned his barons and others, and within a week he had assembled a vast number of cavalry, who all declared that they were ready to march against Argon, and that they desired nothing more than to take him and put him to death.

CHAPTER LII

HOW ACOMAT WENT WITH HIS HOST TO FIGHT ARGON

WHEN Acomat Soldan had collected full sixty thousand horsemen, he set out on his way to encounter Argon and his people, and at the end of ten days' march he halted, having received intelligence that the enemy was only five days' march from him, and equal in number to his own army. Then Acomat established his camp in a very great and fair plain, and announced his intention of awaiting his enemy there, as a favourable place for giving battle. As soon as he arranged his camp, he called together his people, and addressed them as follows: "Lords," said he, "you know well how I ought to be liege lord of all which my brother Abaga held, because I was the son of his father, and I assisted in the conquest of all the lands and territories we possess. It is true that Argon was the son of my brother Abaga, and that some pretend that the succession would go of right to him; but, with all respect to those who hold this opinion, I say that they are in the wrong, for as his father held the whole of so great a lordship, it is but just that I should have it after his death, who ought rightly to have had half of it during his life, though by my generosity he was allowed to retain the whole. But since it is as I tell you, pray, let us defend our right against Argon, that the kingdom and lordship may remain to us all; for I assure you that all I desire for myself is the honour and renown, while you have the profit and the goods and lordships through all our lands and provinces. I will say no more, for I know that you are wise men and love justice, and that you will act for the honour and good of us all." When he had ended, all the barons, and knights, and others who were there, replied with one accord that they would not desert him as long as they had life in their bodies, and that they would aid him against all men whatever, and especially against Argon, adding that they feared not but they should take him and deliver him into his hands. After this, Acomat and his army remained in their camp, waiting the approach of the enemy.

CHAPTER LIII

HOW ARGON HELD COUNCIL WITH HIS BARONS BEFORE ENCOUNTERING ACOMAT

To return to Argon; as soon as he received certain intelligence of the movements of Acomat, and knew that he was encamped with so large an army, he was greatly affected, but he thought it wise to show courage and ardour before his men. Having called all his barons and wise counsellors into his tent, for he was encamped also in a very fair spot, he addressed them as follows: "Fair brothers and friends," said he, "you know well how tenderly my father loved you; while alive he treated you as brothers and sons, and you know in how many battles you were with him, and how you helped him to conquer the land he possessed. You know, too, that I am the son of him who loved you so much, and I myself love you as though you were my own body. It is just and right, therefore, that you aid me against him who comes contrary to justice and right to disherit us of our land. And you know further how he is not of our law, but that he has abandoned it, and has become a Saracen and worships Mahomet, and it would ill become us to let Saracens have lordship over Tartars. Now, fair brethren and friends, all these reasons ought to give you courage and will to do your utmost to prevent such an occurrence; wherefore I implore each of you to show himself a valiant man, and to put forth all his ardour that we may conquer in the battle, and that the sovereignty may belong to you and not to Saracens. And truly every one ought to reckon on victory, since justice is on our side, and our enemies are in the wrong. I will say no more, but again to implore every one of you to do his duty."

CHAPTER LIV

HOW THE BARONS REPLIED TO ARGON

WHEN the barons and knights who were present had heard Argon's address, each resolved that he would prefer death in the battle to defeat; and while they stood silent, reflecting on his words, one of the great barons rose and spoke thus: "Fair sir Argon, fair sir Argon," said he; "we know well that what you have said to us is the truth, and therefore I will be spokesman for all your men who are with you to fight this battle, and tell you openly that we will not fail you as long as we have life in our bodies, and that we would rather all die than not obtain the victory. We feel confident that we shall vanquish your enemies, on account of the justice of our cause, and the wrong which they have done; and therefore I counsel that we proceed at once against them, and I pray all our companions to acquit themselves in such a manner in this battle, that all the world shall talk of them." When this man had ended, all the others declared that they were of his opinion, and the whole army clamoured to be led against the enemy without delay. Accordingly, early next morning, Argon and his people began their march with very resolute hearts, and when they reached the extensive plain in which Acomat was encamped, they established their camp in good order at a distance of about ten miles from him. As soon as he had encamped, Argon sent two trusty messengers on a mission to his uncle.

CHAPTER LV

HOW ARGON SENT HIS MESSENGERS TO ACOMAT

When these two trusty messengers, who were men of very advanced age, arrived at the enemy's camp, they dismounted at Acomat's tent, where he was attended by a great company of his barons, and having entered it, they saluted him courteously. Acomat, who knew them well, received them with the same courtesy, told them they were welcome, and made them sit down before him. After they had remained seated a short space, one of the messengers rose up on his feet and delivered his message as follows: "Fair sir Acomat," said he, "your nephew Argon wonders much at your conduct in taking from him his sovereignty, and now again in coming to engage him in mortal combat; truly this is not well, nor have you acted as a good uncle ought to act towards his nephew. Wherefore he informs you by us that he prays you gently, as that good uncle and father, that you restore him his right, so that there be no battle between you, and he will show you all honour, and you shall be lord of all his land under him. This is the message which your nephew sends you by us."

CHAPTER LVI

ACOMAT'S REPLY TO THE MESSAGE OF ARGON

When Acomat Soldan had heard the message of his nephew Argon, he replied as follows: "Sir Messenger," said he, "what my nephew says amount to nothing, for the land is mine and not his; I conquered it as well as his father; and therefore tell my nephew that if he will, I will make him a great lord, and I will give him land enough, and he shall be as my son, and the highest in rank after me. And if he will not, you may assure him that I will do all in my power to put him to death. Now this is what I will do for my nephew, and no other thing or other arrangement shall you ever have from me." When Acomat had concluded, the messengers asked again, " Is this all the answer which we shall have? " " Yes," said he, " you shall have no other as long as I live." The messengers immediately departed, and riding as fast as they could to Argon's camp, dismounted at his tent and told him all that had passed. When Argon heard his uncle's message, he was so enraged, that he exclaimed in the hearing of all who were near him, " Since I have received such injury and insult from my uncle, I will never live or hold land if I do not take such vengeance that all the world shall talk of it! " After these words, he addressed his barons and knights: " Now we have nothing to do but to go forth as quickly as we can and put these faithless traitors to death; and it is my will that we attack them to-morrow morning, and do our utmost to destroy them." All that night they made preparations for battle; and Acomat Soldan, who knew well by his spies what were Argon's designs, prepared for battle also, and admonished his people to demean themselves with valour.

CHAPTER LVII

THE BATTLE BETWEEN ARGON AND ACOMAT

NEXT morning, Argon, having called his men to arms and drawn them up skilfully in order of battle, addressed to them an encouraging admonition, after which they advanced towards the enemy. Acomat had done the same, and the two armies met on their way and engaged without further parley. The battle began with a shower of arrows so thick that it seemed like rain from heaven, and you might see everywhere the riders cast from the horses, and the cries and groans of those who lay on the earth mortally wounded were dreadful to hear. When they had exhausted their arrows, they took to their swords and clubs, and the battle became so fierce and the noise so great that you could hardly have heard God's thunder. The slaughter was very great on both sides; but at last, though Argon himself displayed extraordinary valour, and set an example to all his men, it was in vain, for fortune turned against him, and his men were compelled to fly, closely pursued by Acomat and his men, who made great havoc of them. And in the flight Argon himself was captured, upon which the pursuit was abandoned, and the victors returned to their camp and tents, glad beyond measure. Acomat caused his nephew, Argon, to be confined and closely guarded, and, being a man given to his pleasures, he returned to his court to enjoy the society of the fair ladies who were there, leaving the command of the army to a great melic, or chief, with strict orders to keep Argon closely guarded, and to follow him to court by short marches, so as not to fatigue his men.

CHAPTER LVIII

HOW ARGON WAS LIBERATED

Now it happened that a great Tartar baron, who was of great age, took pity on Argon, and said in himself that it was a great wickedness and disloyalty thus to hold their lord a prisoner, and that he would do his best to set him free. He began by persuading many other barons to adopt the same sentiments, and his personal influence, on account of his age and known character for justice and wisdom, was so great, that he easily gained them over to the enterprise, and they promised to be directed by him. The name of the leader of this enterprise was Boga, and the chief of his fellow-conspirators were named Elcidai, Togan, Tegana, Taga, Tiar Oulatai, and Samagar. With these, Boga went to the tent where Argon was confined, and told him that they repented of the part they had taken against him, and that in reparation of their error they had come to set him free and take him for their lord.

CHAPTER LIX

HOW ARGON RECOVERED THE SOVEREIGNTY

When Argon heard Boga's words, he thought at first that they came to mock him, and was very angry and cross. "Fair sirs," said he, "you sin greatly in making me an object of mockery, and ought to be satisfied with the wrong you have already done me in imprisoning your rightful lord. You know that you are behaving wrongfully, and therefore I pray go your way and mock me no more." "Fair Sir Argon," said Boga, "be assured that we are not mocking you at all, but what we say is quite true, and we swear to it upon our faith." Then all the barons took an oath that they would hold him for their lord. And Argon on his side swore that he would never trouble them for what was past, but that he would hold them all as dear as his father Abaga had done. And as soon as these mutual oaths had been taken, they took Argon out of prison, and received him as their lord. Then Argon told them to shoot their arrows at the tent in which the melic who had the command of the army was, and they did so, and thus the melic was slain. This melic was named Soldan, and was the greatest lord after Acomat. Thus Argon recovered the sovereignty.

CHAPTER LX

HOW ARGON CAUSED HIS UNCLE ACOMAT TO BE PUT TO DEATH

And when Argon found that he was assured of the sovereignty, he gave orders to the army to commence its march towards the court. It happened one day that Acomat was at court in his principal palace making great festivity, when a messenger came to him and said: "Sir, I bring you news, not such as I would, but very evil. Know that the barons have delivered Argon and raised him to the sovereignty, and have slain Soldan, your dear friend; and I assure you that they are hastening hither to take and slay you; take counsel immediately what is best to be done." When Acomat heard this, he was at first so overcome with astonishment and fear that he knew not what to do or say; but at last, like a brave and prudent man, he told the messenger to mention the news to no one, and hastily ordered his most trusty followers to arm and mount their horses; telling nobody whither he was going, he took the route to go to the Sultan of Babilonia, believing that there his life would be safe. At the end of six days he arrived at a pass which could not be avoided, the keeper of which knew that it was Acomat, and perceived that he was seeking safety by flight. This man determined to take him, which he might easily do, as he was slightly attended. When Acomat was thus arrested, he made great entreaty, and offered great treasure to be allowed to go free; but the keeper of the pass, who was a zealous partizan of Argon, replied that all the treasure in the world should not hinder him from doing his duty towards his rightful lord. He accordingly placed Acomat under a strong guard, and marching with him to the court, arrived there just three days after Argon had taken possession of it, who was greatly mortified that Acomat had escaped. When therefore Acomat was delivered to him a prisoner, he was in the greatest joy imaginable, and commanding the army to be assembled immediately, without consulting with anybody, he ordered one of his men to slay his uncle, and to throw his body into such place as it would never be seen again, which order was immediately executed. Thus ended the affair between Argon and his uncle Acomat.

CHAPTER LXI

THE DEATH OF ARGON

WHEN Argon had done all this, and had taken possession of the principal palace with the sovereignty, all the barons who had been in subjection to his father came to perform their homages as to their lord, and obeyed it as such in everything. And after this, Argon sent Casan, his son, with full thirty thousand horsemen, to the Arbor Secco, which is in that country, to protect his land and people. Argon thus recovered his sovereignty in the year 1286 of the incarnation of Jesus Christ, and Acomat had held the sovereignty two years. Argon reigned six years, at the end of which he died, as was generally said, by poison.

CHAPTER LXII

HOW QUIACATU SEIZED UPON THE SOVEREIGNTY AFTER THE DEATH OF ARGON

WHEN Argon was dead, his uncle, named Quiacatu, seized upon the sovereignty, which he was enabled to do with the more ease in consequence of Casan being so far distant as the Arbor Secco. Casan was greatly angered when he heard of the death of his father and of the usurpation of Quiacatu, but he could not leave his post at that moment for fear of his enemies. He threatened, however, that he would find the occasion to revenge himself as signally as his father had done upon Acomat. Quiacatu held the sovereignty, and all were obedient to him except those who were with Casan; and he took the wife of his nephew Argon and held her as his own, and enjoyed himself much with the ladies, for he was excessively given to his pleasures. Quiacatu held the sovereignty two years, at the end of which he was carried off by poison.

CHAPTER LXIII

HOW BAIDU SEIZED UPON THE SOVEREIGNTY AFTER THE DEATH OF QUIACATU

WHEN Quiacatu was dead, Baidu, who was his uncle, and a Christian, seized upon the sovereignty, and all obeyed him except Casan and the army with him. This occurred in the year 1294. When Casan learnt what had occurred, he was more furious against Baidu than he had been against Quiacatu, and, threatening to take such vengeance on him as should be talked of by everybody, he resolved that he would delay no longer, but march immediately against him. He accordingly provisioned his army, and commenced his march. When Baidu knew for certain that Casan was coming against him, he assembled a vast number of men, and marched forwards full ten days, and then encamped and waited for him to give battle. On the second day Casan appeared, and immediately there began a fierce battle, which ended in the entire defeat of Baidu, who was slain in the combat. Casan now assumed the sovereignty, and began his reign in the year 1294 of the Incarnation. Thus did the kingdom of the Eastern Tartars descend from Abaga to Casan, who now reigns.

CHAPTER LXIV[1]

OF THE LORDS OF THE TARTARS OF THE WEST

THE first lord of the Tartars of the West was Sain, who was a very great and powerful king. He conquered Russia, and Comania, and Alania, and Lac, and Mengiar, and Zic, and

[1] The following chapters follow the last chapter in Marsden's translation.

Gucia, and Gazaria. All these provinces were conquered by king Sain. Before this conquest, they were all Comanians, but they were not under one government; and through their want of union they lost their lands, and were dispersed into different parts of the world; and those who remained were all in a state of serfdom to king Sain. After king Sain reigned king Patu, after him king Berca, next king Mungletemur, then king Totamongur, and lastly Toctai, who now reigns. Having thus given you a list of the kings of the Tartars of the West, we will tell you of a great battle that fell out between Alau, the lord of the East, and Berca, the lord of the West, as well as the cause of the battle, and its result.

CHAPTER LXV

OF THE WAR BETWEEN ALAU AND BERCA, AND THE BATTLE THEY FOUGHT

In the year 1261 there arose a great quarrel between king Alau, lord of the Tartars of the East, and Berca, king of the Tartars of the West, on account of a province which bordered on each of their territories, which both claimed, and each was too proud to yield it to the other. They mutually defied each other, each declaring that he would go and take it, and he would see who dared hinder him. When things had come to this point, each summoned his followers to his banner, and they exerted themselves to such a degree that within six months each had assembled full three hundred thousand horsemen, very well furnished with all things appertaining to war according to their usage. Alau, lord of the East, now began his march with all his forces, and they rode many days without meeting with any adventure worth mentioning. At length they reached an extensive plain, situated between the Iron Gates and the Sea of Sarain, in which they encamped in good order, and there was many a rich pavilion and tent. And there Alau said he would wait to see what course Berca would follow, as this spot was on the borders of the two territories.

CHAPTER LXVI

HOW BERCA AND HIS HOST WENT TO MEET ALAU

Now when king Berca had made all his preparations, and knew that Alau was on his march, he also set out on his way, and in due time reached the same plain where his enemies awaited him, and encamped at about ten miles' distance from him. Berca's camp was quite as richly decked out as that of Alau, and his army was more numerous, for it numbered full three hundred and fifty thousand horsemen. The two armies rested two days, during which Berca called his people together, and addressed them as follows:—"Fair sirs," said he, "you know certainly that since I came into possession of the land I have loved you like brothers and sons, and many of you have been in many great battles with me, and you have assisted me to conquer a great part of the lands we hold. You know that I share everything I have with you, and you ought in return to do your best to support my honour, which hitherto you have done. You know what a great and powerful man Alau is, and how in this quarrel he is in the wrong, and we are in the right, and each of you ought to feel assured that we shall conquer him in battle, especially as our number exceeds his; for we know for certain that he has only three hundred thousand horsemen, while we have three hundred and fifty thousand as good men as his and better. For all these reasons, then, you must see clearly that we shall gain the day, but since we have come so great a distance only to fight this battle, it is my will that we give battle three days hence, and we will proceed so prudently and in such good order that we cannot fail of success, and I pray you all to show yourselves on this occasion men of courage, so that all the world shall talk of your deeds. I say no more than that I expect every one of you to be well prepared for the day appointed."

CHAPTER LXVII

ALAU'S ADDRESS TO HIS MEN

WHEN Alau knew certainly that Berca was come with so great an army, he also assembled his chiefs, and addressed them as follows:—"Fair brothers, and sons, and friends," said he, "you know that all my life I have prized you and assisted you, and hitherto you have assisted me to conquer in many battles, nor ever were you in any battle where we failed to obtain the victory, and for that reason are we come here to fight this great man Berca; and I know well that he has more men than we have, but they are not so good, and I doubt not but we shall put them all to flight and discomfiture. We know by our spy that they intend to give us battle three days hence, of which I am very glad, and I pray you all to be ready on that day, and to demean yourselves as you used to do. One thing only I wish to impress upon you, that it is better to die on the field in maintaining our honour, than to suffer discomfiture; so let each of you fight so that our honour may be safe, and our enemies discomfited and slain."

Thus each of the kings encouraged his men, and waited for the day of the battle, and all prepared for it in the best way they could.

CHAPTER LXVIII

OF THE GREAT BATTLE BETWEEN ALAU AND BERCA

WHEN the day fixed for the battle arrived, Alau rose early in the morning, and called his men to arms, and marshalled his army with the utmost skill. He divided it into thirty squadrons, each squadron consisting of ten thousand horsemen; and to each he gave a good leader and a good captain. And when all this was duly arranged, he ordered his troops to advance, which they did at a slow pace, until they came half way between the two camps, where they halted and waited for the enemy. On the other side, king Berca had drawn up his army, which was arranged in thirty-five squadrons, exactly in the same manner as that of Alau's, and he also ordered his men to advance, which they did within half-a-mile of the others. There they made a short halt, and then they moved forward again till they came to the distance of about two arbalest shots of each other. It was a fair plain, and wonderfully extensive, as it ought to be, when so many thousands of men were marshalled in hostile array, under the two most powerful warriors in the world, who moreover were near kinsmen, for they were both of the imperial lineage of Jengiz-khan. After the two armies had remained a short while in face of each other, the nacars at length sounded, upon which both armies let fly such a shower of arrows at each other that you could hardly see the sky, and many were slain, man and horse. When all their arrows were exhausted, they engaged with swords and maces, and then the battle was so fierce that the noise was louder than the thunder of heaven, and the ground was covered with corpses and reddened with blood. Both the kings distinguished themselves by their valour, and their men were not backward in imitating their example. The battle continued in this manner till dusk, when Berca began to give way, and fled, and Alau's men pursued furiously, cutting down and slaying without mercy. After they had pursued a short distance, Alau recalled them, and they returned to their tents, laid aside their arms, and dressed their wounds; and they were so weary with fighting, that they gladly sought repose. Next morning Alau ordered the bodies of the dead to be buried, enemies as well as friends, and the loss was so great on both sides that it would be impossible to describe it. After this was done, Alau returned to his country with all his men who had survived the battle.

CHAPTER LXIX

HOW TOTAMANGU WAS LORD OF THE TARTARS OF THE WEST

You must know that in the West there was a king of the Tartars named Mongutemur, and the sovereignty descended to Tolobuga, who was a young bachelor,[1] and a very powerful man, named Totamangu, slew Tolobuga, with the assistance of another king of the Tartars, named Nogai. Thus Totamangu obtained the sovereignty by the aid of Nogai, and, after a short reign, he died, and Toctai, a very able and prudent man, was chosen king. Meanwhile the two sons of Tolobuga had grown to be now capable of bearing arms, and they were wise and prudent. The two brothers assembled a very fair company, and went to the court of Toctai, and presented themselves with so much courtesy and humility on their knees that Toctai welcomed them, and told them to stand up. Then the eldest said to the king, "Fair sir Toctai, I will tell you in the best way I can why we are come to court. You know that we are the sons of Tolobuga,[2] who was slain by Totamangu and Nogai. Of Totamangu, I have nothing to say, since he is dead; but we claim justice on Nogai for the slaughter of our father, and we pray you as a righteous lord to grant it us. This is the object of our visit to your court."

[1] *I.e.* A youth not yet arrived at knighthood. Mongutemur and Totamangu are, of course, the same names that are spelt in Chapter lxiv. Mungletemur and Totamongur.

[2] In the printed text from which this is translated, here and during the rest of this and the following chapters, Totamangu is erroneously written for Tolobuga, and *vice versa*, making great confusion in the story: it has been thought advisable to correct this in the translation.

CHAPTER LXX

HOW TOCTAI SENT FOR NOGAI TO COURT

WHEN Toctai had heard the youth, he knew that what he said was true, and he replied, "Fair friend, I will willingly yield to your demand of justice upon Nogai, and for that purpose we will summon him to court, and do everything which justice shall require." Then Toctai sends two messengers to Nogai, and ordered him to come to court to answer to the sons of Tolobuga for the death of their father; but Nogai laughed at the message, and told the messengers he would not go. When Toctai heard Nogai's message, he was greatly enraged, and said in the hearing of all who were about him, "With the aid of God, either Nogai shall come before me to do justice to the sons of Tolobuga, or I will go against him with all my men and destroy him." He then sent two other messengers, who rode in all haste to the court of Nogai, and on their arrival they presented themselves before him and saluted him very courteously, and Nogai told them they were welcome. Then one of the messengers said: "Fair sir, Toctai sends you word that if you do not come to his court to render justice to the sons of Tolobuga, he will come against you with all his host, and do you all the hurt he can both to your property and person; therefore resolve what course you will pursue, and return him an answer by us." When Nogai heard Toctai's message, he was very angry, and replied to the messenger as follows: "Sir messenger," said he, "now return to your lord and tell him from me, that I have small fear of his hostility; and tell him further, that if he should come against me, I will wait for him at the entrance of my territory, for I will meet him half way. This is the message you shall carry back to your lord." The messenger hastened back, and when Toctai received this answer, he immediately sent his messengers to all parts which were under his rule, and summoned his people to be ready to go with him against king Nogai, and he had soon collected a great army. When Nogai knew certainly that Toctai was preparing to come against him with so large a host, he also made great preparation, but not so great as Toctai, because, though a great and powerful king, he was not so great or powerful as the other.

CHAPTER LXXI

HOW TOCTAI PROCEEDED AGAINST NOGAI

When Toctai's army was ready, he commenced his march at the head of two hundred thousand horsemen, and in due time reached the fine and extensive plain of Nerghi, where he encamped to wait for his opponent. With him were the two sons of Tolobuga, who had come with a fair company of horsemen to avenge the death of their father. Nogai also was on his march, with a hundred and fifty thousand horsemen, all young and brave men, and much better soldiers than those of Toctai. He arrived in the plain where Toctai was encamped two days after him, and established his camp at a distance of ten miles from him. Then king Toctai assembled his chiefs, and said to them: " Sirs, we are come here to fight king Nogai and his men, and we have great reason to do so, for you know that all this hatred and rancour has arisen from Nogai's refusal to do justice to the sons of Tolobuga; and since our cause is just, we have every reason to hope for victory. Be therefore of good hope; but at all events I know that you are all brave men, and that you will do your best to destroy our enemies." Nogai also addressed his men in the following terms: " Fair brothers and friends," said he, " you know that we have gained many great and hard fought battles, and that we have overcome better men than these. Therefore be of good cheer. We have right on our side; for you know well that Toctai was not my superior to summon me to his court to do justice to others. I will only further urge you to demean yourselves so in this battle that we shall be talked of everywhere, and that ourselves and our heirs will be the more respected for it." Next day they prepared for battle. Toctai drew up his army in twenty squadrons, each with a good leader and captain; and Nogai's army was formed in fifteen squadrons. After a long and desperate battle, in which the two kings, as well as the two sons of Tolobuga, distinguished themselves by their reckless valour, the army of Toctai was entirely defeated, and pursued from the field with great slaughter by Nogai's men, who, though less numerous, were much better soldiers than their opponents. Full sixty thousand men were slain in this battle, but king Toctai, as well as the two sons of Tolobuga, escaped.

APPENDIX

I.—Note on Book I. Chapter LIV. Page 140

We here find the assertion circumstantially repeated, that not Ung-khan only, but all his descendants, to the days of our author, were Christians; and although it has been common to doubt the fact, no arguments drawn from historical evidence have been employed to disprove it. On the other hand it is supported by the testimony of the travellers Carpini and Rubruquis (with some variations, however, in the circumstances), and sanctioned by the authority of Abu'lfaraj, whose fidelity and discretion as an historian have not been questioned upon other points. By none of these is the existence of such a character in Tartary as that of Prester John spoken of as a new discovery, but as matter of previous notoriety, and especially amongst those who were engaged in the crusades.

It may be asked why there should be so much hesitation to believe, as if it were in itself a thing improbable, that at an early period the Christian faith (according to the ritual of the Greek Church) had spread extensively through Tartary and penetrated to China? The fact does not rest upon the evidence of the Catholic friars alone (who, however, were much more disposed to undervalue than to exaggerate the successes and political consequence of their rivals), but is corroborated by the annals of the Nestorian Church. "Parmy ces peuples, tous compris sous le nom général de Turcs et de Tartares," observes the Abbé Renaudot, "il y avoit un assez grand nombre de Chrestiens, non seulement lorsque Ginghiskhan establit son grand empire, mais longtemps avant cette époque. Car on trouve dans l'histoire des Nestoriens, que Timothée leur Catholique, qui succeda à Hananjechiia, celuy dont il est fait mention dans l'inscription Chinoise et Syriaque, et qui fut ordonné vers l'an 788 de Jesus-Christ, avoit escrit au Cakhan ou empereur des Tartares, et à quelques autres princes du Turkestan pour les exhorter à embrasser la Foy Chrestienne; ce qu'il fit avec deux cens mille de ses sujets. On ne peut pas douter que ce peuple ne fussent de véritables Tartares ou Turcs, puisque le même Catholique fut consulté par l'évêque qu'il envoya dans le païs, touchant la manière dont il devoit leur faire observer la Caresme, et célébrer la liturgie; parce qu'ils estoient accoustumez à vivre de lait et de chair, et qu'ils n'avoient ni bled, ni vin. . . . Depuis ce temps-là, on trouve dans les notices ecclésiastiques de l'Eglise Nestorienne, un Métropolitain de Turkestan, un de Tengat, un de Cambalik ou Cambalu, et un de Caschgar et de Noüakat."—Anciennes Relat. p. 319. See also Dissertatio de Syris Nestorianis, by J. S. Assemanus.

If then it be admitted that at an early period some of the Tartar tribes, with their chiefs, were converted to Christianity, (and why their conversion should be a matter less credible than that of the nations in the North and West of Europe, does not appear,) there can be no special reason for excepting the prince named Ung-khan, whose particular tribe, it may be observed, bore the appellation of Krit, Kera-it or Kerrit, which in the East is a common mode of pronouncing the words Christ and Christian. At his baptism it may be presumed that he received, from his spiritual instructors, a Syrian baptismal name, and none more likely than that of Yuhanna or John the Evangelist. If we further suppose, what is not an unusual circumstance in the history of these people, that their chief was at the same time a lama, he may not have been willing to divest himself of the priestly character, and the Nestorian missionaries in their reports to the Katholicos or metropolitan, at Baghdad or Antioch, might consequently mention him by a title equivalent to that of Johannes Presbuteros.

The belief of an early spreading of the Gospel in these parts derives some additional strength from an opinion entertained by some of the best informed missionaries, that the lama religion itself is no other than a corrupted species of Christianity; and although this may be too hasty an inference from what they had an opportunity of observing in the country, it will not be found upon examination so unlikely as it may at first appear. Our modern acquaintance with the Hindu system of mythology, and particularly with the tenets, rites, and representations of Buddha, whose schism extended itself over the countries lying to the north and east of Hindustan and Bengal, enables us to pronounce with confidence that in its fundamental principles the religion of the country which bears the names of Butan, Tibet, and Tangut, is that of the Bhuddists of India; but at the same time the strong resemblance between many of its ceremonies and those of the Christian churches, both East and West, have been pointed out by every traveller who has visited Tartary, from Carpini and Rubruquis, by whom it was first noticed, to our countrymen and contemporaries, Bogle and Turner, who resided at the court of one of the grand lamas. We find it avowed even by the Jesuit missionaries, whom we cannot suppose to have been influenced in their observation by any undue bias (with which on some occasions they have been charged), as neither their personal vanity could be gratified, nor the interests of their profession advanced, by establishing the invidious comparison.

Under impressions of this kind of resemblance, it is not surprising that some should have adopted an opinion that the prince who acquired amongst the Christians of the East, the appellation of Prester John, was no other than the supreme lama of the Tartars.

II.—Additional Note on page 232, note 2.

776. " Si-gan," says P. Martini, " qui est la ville capitale, cède à fort peu d'autres, si on regarde à sa situation dans un pays fort beau et récréatif, à sa grandeur, à son antiquité, à la force et fer-

meté de ses murailles, à la beauté de son aspect, et à son commerce. . . . Vous pouvez juger de son antiquité, de ce que les trois familles impériales de Cheu, Cin, et Han y ont régné."—Thevenot, partie iii. p. 58.

It was near this capital that an ancient inscription on stone was discovered, which, in Syriac and Chinese characters, recorded the state of Christianity in that province or kingdom, set forth the protection and indulgence it received from different emperors, and contained a list of its bishops. "Cette province," says P. Martini, "est encore celèbre par une pierre fort antique, sur laquelle la loy de Dieu est escrite en caractères Syriaques et Chinois, apporté à ceux de la Chine par les successeurs des Apostres: on y list le nom des évesques et des prestres de ce temps-là, et celui des empereurs Chinois qui leur furent favorables et leur accordèrent des privilèges: elle contient aussi une courte explication de la loy Chrestienne, mais tout-à-fait admirable, composée en langage Chinois très-éloquent. . . . On l'a trouvé l'an 1625 dans la cité de San-yuen, comme on creusoit les fondemens d'une muraille: le gouverneur de la ville, ayant esté informé aussi-tost de ce monument qu'on avoit treuvé, en considéra l'inscription de plus près, et, comme ils sont grands amateurs de l'antiquité, il la fit imprimer, et ensuite un écrit à la louange du monument, et puis après tailler sur une autre pierre de mesme grandeur une copie de celle qu'on avoit treuvée, en observant les mesmes traits et caractères, avec toute la fidélité requise. Les Pères de nostre Société en ont porté à Rome un exemplaire selon l'original, avec l'interprétation: on la garde à présent avec son interprétation, dans la bibliothèque de la Maison professe de Jésus: elle fut imprimée à Rome l'an 1631." Thevenot, p. 57. Some suspicions were naturally excited in Europe, as to the genuineness of a monument of so peculiar a nature, and it has been the subject of much discussion; but those who have been the most forward to pronounce it a forgery, seem actuated rather by a spirit of animosity against the Order of Jesuits, whose members brought it to notice, than by the pure love of truth or a disposition to candid inquiry; and since that hostile feeling has subsided, its authenticity appears to be no longer disputed by those who are best enabled to form a correct judgment. "L'établissement des Nestoriens," says De Guignes, f., "date de 635 ans après J. C. qu'un certain Olopuen vint à la Chine sous Taytsong des Tang: ce fait est prouvé par le monument découvert à Sy-ngan-fou en 1625, sous Hy-tsong des Ming." (Tom. ii. p. 334.) For more particular information respecting this celebrated monument, see the following works: Athanasii Kircheri China illustrata (1667), where will be found a facsimile of the inscription, with a literal translation of each character: Andræ Mülleri Opuscula; De monumento Sinico Commentarius, (1695): Laurentii Moshemii, ad Historiam Ecclesiasticam Tartarorum Appendix, monumenta et epistolas exhibens (1741): and Mémoires de l'Académie des Inscriptions, tom. xxx. p. 802.

INDEX

P